THE MUSIC TRIV[illegible]

OF ROCK 'N' ROLL MUSIC

VOL 1

THE 50'S, THE 60'S & THE 70'S

R&B

POP

COUNTRY

AND EVERYTHING IN BETWEEN

ELVIS / ROCK-A-BILLY / FOLK

BROADWAY HITS / MOVIE HITS / TV HITS / INSTRUMENTALS

THE BEATLES / THE REST OF THE BRITISH INVASION

THE FOREIGN INVASION

THE ONE HIT WONDERS / THE NOVELTIES

WOODSTOCK

FROM JOHNNY ACE THROUGH THE ZOMBIES

TAKE THE CHALLENGE!
TRY OUT THESE QUIZZES, YOU'LL BE AMAZED AT WHAT YOU KNOW, DIDN'T KNOW, OR HAVE FORGOTTEN

YOU'LL LEARN AND HAVE FUN AT THE SAME TIME WITH YOUR FRIENDS AND FAMILY MEMBERS

JIMMY CORREA

VANTAGE PRESS
New York

To my sister, Luisa Burns,
who has spent countless years working on this project with me

FIRST EDITION

Published by Vantage Press, Inc.
419 Park Ave. South, New York, NY 10016

Manufactured in the United States of America
ISBN: 0-533-14962-2

Library of Congress Catalog Card No.: 2004093810

0 9 8 7 6 5 4 3 2 1

CONTENTS

ABOUT THE AUTHOR

MY PERSONAL FAVORITE SONG OF ALL TIME IS PROBABLY "BYE BYE LOVE" BY THE EVERLY BROTHERS, DON AND PHIL. I WAS JUST SEVEN YEARS OLD IN 1957 WHEN THEY CHARTED THIS SONG TO THE NUMBER TWO SPOT ON THE BILLBOARD CHARTS. SOME GUY BY THE NAME OF ELVIS OCCUPIED THE NUMBER ONE SPOT WITH A SONG CALLED "TEDDY BEAR" OR "LET ME BE YOUR TEDDY BEAR". TO ME IT DIDN'T MATTER I THOUGHT THE BROTHERS WERE NUMBER ONE. THEY LOOKED NOT MUCH OLDER THAN MYSELF AND COULD SING IN SWEET HARMONY AND PLAY A MEAN GUITAR. I COULD STILL REMEMBER SEEING THEM ON THE ED SULLIVAN SHOW BELTING OUT THEIR NUMEROUS HIT SONGS.

AS I GREW OLDER AND STARTED TO WORK IN 1968, MY RECORD COLLECTING HOBBY BEGAN. I BOUGHT ALMOST ANYTHING IN SIGHT THAT I LIKED. THE FOUR TOPS, THE TEMPTATIONS, THE SUPREMES, THE FOUR SEASONS, THE DRIFTERS, THE BEACH BOYS AND COUNTLESS OTHERS. OH YEA, EVEN ELVIS, WHO I GREW TO ADMIRE. TODAY I SHOP IN THRIFT STORES LOOKING FOR BARGAINS. YESTERDAY I BOUGHT TWO FRANK SINATRA ALBUMS IN EXCELLENT CONDITION, COVER AND ALL, FOR ONLY TWO DOLLARS. BOY, WHAT A STEAL. TODAY I HAVE CLOSE TO EIGHTEEN HUNDRED TAPES, CD'S, ALBUMS, AND VIDEOS. SOME ARE THE BEST OF OR THE GREATEST HITS OF.

WHEN I'M IN A MELLOW MOOD I PUT ON AL GREEN, LITTLE ANTHONY & THE IMPERIALS, BARRY WHITE, AIR SUPPLY OR MY FAVORITE DIVA OF ALL, CELINE DION. IF I'M IN AN UPTEMPO MOOD I'LL LISTEN TO SOME VAN MORRISON, ELTON JOHN, BOB SEGAR, JOHN COUGAR MELLANCAMP OR TONY ORLANDO & DAWN. THAT'S THE FUN OF OWNING YOUR OWN MUSIC COLLECTION, YOU BECOME YOUR OWN DJ.

ANOTHER HOBBY OF MINE IS GOING TO ROCK 'N ROLL CONCERTS. RADIO CITY MUSIC HALL, MADISON SQUARE GARDEN, THE APOLLO, CENTRAL PARK, CONEY ISLAND, SOUTH STREET SEAPORT, NEW YORK ACADEMY OF MUSIC, THE NORTH DAKOTA STATE FAIR AND SO ON. ONE OF MY GREATEST MOMENTS WAS SEEING HARVEY FUQUA & THE MOONGLOWS. AND TO TOP IT OFF, ONE OF THE MOONGLOWS SAT NEXT TO US AFTER HIS PERFORMANCE WHICH TO ME WAS THE ICING ON THE CAKE. GREAT MEMORIES ALSO COME TO ME WHEN I THINK OF THE OTHER ACTS I'VE SEEN. WHICH INCLUDE

THE LIKES OF: THE STUDENTS, THE DRIFTERS, JOHNNY & JOE, EARL LEWIS AND THE CHANNELS, JOHNNY MAESTRO & THE CRESTS, LITTLE ANTHONY AND THE IMPERIALS, THE DUPREES, THE SPINNERS, THE TEMPTATIONS, CHUBBY CHECKER, THE TYMES, FRED PARRIS & THE FIVE SATINS, THE IMPRESSIONS, JOHNNY MAESTRO AGAIN, THIS TIME WITH THE BROOKLYN BRIDGE, THE ANGELS, BEN E KING, LARRY CHANCE & THE EARLS, WILLIE WINFIELD & THE HARPTONES, ROYAL TEENS, RONNIE SPECTOR, LENNY WELCH, THE STYLISTICS, CHUCK JACKSON, THE RIGHTEOUS BROTHERS, JOHNNY CASH, LLOYD PRICE, SCREAMING JAY HAWKINS, THE COASTERS, DIANA ROSS, LESLEY GORE, THE IMPALAS, JAY BLACK, THE CADILLACS, ARLENE SMITH & THE CHANTELS , LEE ANDREWS AND THE HEARTS, VITO PICONE & THE ELEGANTS, THE MELLO KINGS, SHIRLEY ALSTON REEVES OF THE SHIRELLES, THE MAMAS & THE PAPAS, THE CAPRIS, THE GRASS ROOTS, LENNY COCCO & THE CHIMES, EMIL STUCCIO & THE CLASSICS, RUDY WEST OF THE FIVE KEYS, THE CHIFFONS, THE FLAMINGOS, THE DEL VIKINGS, THE DANLEERS, VITO BALSAMO OF THE SALUTATIONS, THE MYSTICS, ROBERT & JOHNNY, THE SKYLINERS, FELIX CAVALIERE OF THE RASCALS, THE BEACH BOYS, CREEDENCE CLEARWATER REVISITED, BOBBY VEE, EDDIE MONEY & THE CRYSTALS.

WELL THAT'S THE END OF THIS, SO LET'S GET IT ON. HEY, THAT SOUNDS FAMILIAR. ISN'T THAT A NAME OF A SONG. SURE, A TUNE BY THE LATE GREAT MARVIN GAYE. THIS IS HOW IT ALL GOT STARTED FOR ME. WHILE AT HOME OR IN A CAR SOMEONE WOULD ASK ME WHAT'S THE NAME OF THAT SONG OR THE ARTIST. THIS INSPIRED ME TO WRITE THIS TRIVIA BOOK ALONG WITH THE HELP OF MY SISTER. WE MADE IT SO THAT YOU COULD PICK THE DECADE OR ERA YOU GREW UP IN OR LIKED THE BEST. FOR ME IT WAS THE 60'S. REGARDLESS, THIS BOOK WILL HELP TO INCREASE YOUR MUSICAL KNOWLEDGE AND PERHAPS BRING YOU FOND MEMORIES OF ARTISTS AND SONGS YOU ENJOYED LISTENING TO THEN AND NOW. WE'RE CONFIDENT MUSIC FANS ALL OVER AND OF DIFFERENT AGE BRACKETS WILL GET A KICK OUT OF THIS TRIVIA BOOK.

INTRODUCTION

BESIDES BEING AN AVID MUSIC COLLECTOR I ALSO COLLECT MUSIC BOOKS, NEWSPAPER ARTICLES AND MAGAZINE CLIPPINGS. THEY MIGHT BE ABOUT THE AMERICAN MUSIC AWARDS, THE GRAMMIES OR ANYTHING TO DO WITH THE GREAT LEGENDS OF ROCK 'N ROLL. IT STARTED BACK ON AUGUST 16, 1977 WITH THE DEATH OF 'THE KING', ELVIS PRESLEY. ALL THE NEWSPAPERS WERE CARRYING OUT HIS LIFE STORY. FOR ME IT WENT ON TO BE AN OBSESSION. ONE ARTICLE THAT I REALLY TREASURE IS THE ONE ABOUT THE LATE GREAT 'JACKIE WILSON'. HE WAS ORIGINALLY BURIED IN AN UNMARKED PAUPER'S GRAVE. EVENTUALLY HE WAS REBURIED WITH A MARBLE THOMBSTONE BEARING THESE VERY WORDS, "NO MORE LONELY TEARDROPS".

RADIO WAS RESPONSIBLE AT FIRST FOR MOST OF THE TALENT THAT WE WERE EXPOSED TO. DISC JOCKEYS INCLUDING ALAN FREED, JOCKO HENDERSON, MURRAY THE K, COUSIN BRUCIE, SCOTT MUNI, WOLFMAN JACK, CASEY KASEM, RICK DEES AND SO ON, HELPED TO OPEN THE DOORS TO THE MANY FINE TALENTED SINGERS AND MUSICIANS ALL AROUND. TODAY RADIO IS STILL KING. WE MAY BE IN OUR CARS, IN THE PARKS, OR SUNBATHING AT THE BEACHES AND YOU CAN BET THAT THERE IS A RADIO BLASTING SOMEWHERE NEARBY. THEY KEEP US INFORMED OF THE CURRENT BILLBOARD CHART HITS AND BRING BACK FOND MEMORIES OF YESTERYEAR.

WITH THE ADVENT OF THE TELEVISION WE BECAME MORE INSPIRED. WE WATCHED THE ED SULLIVAN SHOW, DICK CLARK'S AMERICAN BANDSTAND, CLAY COLE'S WEEKLY SHOW, AGAIN ALLAN FREED, SHINDIG, HULLABALOO, DON CORNELIUS' 'SOUL TRAIN', CASEY CASEM'S 'AMERICA TOP TEN', AND SOLID GOLD, ONLY TO NAME A FEW. WE WERE FORTUNATE TO LEARN THE CURRENT DANCES AND SONGS JUST BY WATCHING THESE PROGRAMS. WE TWISTED WITH CHUBBY CHECKER OR DANCED TO HIS LIMBO ROCK. WE LOCO-MOTIONED WITH LITTLE EVA. WE OOED AND AAHED TO CONNIE FRANCIS, BRENDA LEE, THE EVERLYS AND LITTLE RICKY NELSON. WE WERE DAZZLED BY THE LIKES OF LITTLE RICHARD, BUDDY HOLLY, CHUCK BERRY, FATS DOMINO AND OF COURSE, ELVIS, THE KING OF THEM ALL. TODAY WE HAVE MTV ON CABLE STATIONS. WE RENT AND PURCHASE VHS AND DVD'S THAT SHOWCASE CONCERTS AND MUSIC VIDEOS OF OUR FAVORITE STARS. MARIAH CAREY, CELINE DION, SHANIA TWAIN, THE EAGLES, HALL & OATES AND SO ON.

WE WATCH MOVIES THAT PORTRAY THE LIVES OF BUDDY HOLLY, RITCHIE VALENS, FRANKIE LYMON, PATSY CLINE, TINA TURNER AND STILL COUNTLESS OTHERS.

DURING THE 50'S WE PURCHASED 78'S AND 33'S ON VINYL. IN THE 60'S THE 45'S EVENTUALLY TOOK OVER AND EIGHT TRACK TAPES, THOUGH BULKY, CAME INTO PLAY DURING THE 70'S ALONG WITH CASSETTES. THE CASSETTES LED THE WAY THROUGH THE 80'S AND 90'S AND STILL VERY POPULAR TODAY. CD'S ARE THE CURRENT TREND ALTHOUGH A LOT MORE EXPENSIVE THAN CASSETTES BUT CAN BE PROGRAMMED TO PLAY AT ANY TRACK PREFERRED DEPENDING ON THE MODEL THAT YOU HAVE.

IT DOESN'T MATTER WHAT YOU BUY JUST AS LONG AS WE THE BUYING PUBLIC CONTINUE TO SUPPORT THESE TALENTED ARTISTS. MUSIC WILL NEVER DIE. THOUGH ARTISTS MAY COME AND GO, THEIR WORKS WILL LIVE ON FOREVER IN THE MEMORIES OF THOSE WHO APPRECIATE FINE MUSIC.

OUR ACKNOWLEDGEMENT

A MAJOR PORTION OF OUR BOOK INFORMATION CAME FROM OUR OWN PERSONAL MUSIC INVENTORY, WHICH COMPRISED WELL OVER TWENTY NINE HUNDRED ALBUMS, TAPES, CD'S AND VIDEOS.

WE WOULD ALSO LIKE TO ACKNOWLEDGE THE TREMENDOUS LEADS OF INFORMATION AND FEEDBACK FROM THE ALL IMPORTANT MEDIAS, RADIO AND TELEVISION. THEY HELPED TO INSPIRE AND TO BROADEN OUR MUSICAL KNOWLEDGE, WHICH IN TURN LED TO SOME MORE INTERESTING TRIVIA. THIS INCLUDES THE FOLLOWING:

THE RICK DEES WEEKLY TOP 40 COUNTDOWN, DICK CLARKS' AMERICAN BANDSTAND, DON CORNELIUS' SOUL TRAIN, CASEY KASEMS' AMERICA TOP TEN, SOLID GOLD, VH1, CMT, BET, THE GRAMMY'S, THE AMERICAN MUSIC AWARDS AND SO FORTH. EACH WERE INSTRUMENTAL IN SHOWCASING THE CURRENT TRENDS IN MUSIC, FROM POP, ROCK, R&B, COUNTRY, HIP HOP, YOU NAME IT. ALSO WE WOULD LIKE TO THANK THE MANY DJ'S IN RADIO LAND THROUGHOUT, FROM THE OLDIES RADIO STATIONS, Z100'S, LIGHT FM'S, CLASSIC ROCKS, THE MIX MUSIC STATIONS, AND SATELLITE RADIO ETC. BUT EQUALLY IMPORTANT, THE BILLBOARD CHARTS, WHICH ENABLED THE ABOVE TO PRESENT ON A DAILY OR WEEKLY BASIS THE MANY HIT SONGS BEING LISTENED TO AND PURCHASED BY THEIR ADORING FANS.

SO WE SAY TO ALL THE TALENTED ARTISTS OUT THERE, SINGERS, SONGWRITERS, MUSICIANS, PRODUCERS, ETC., TO KEEP PLUGGING AWAY AND KEEP THOSE HITS RIGHT ON COMING.

AND LONG LIVE ROCK AND ROLL!

HELP TO SCORE YOUR QUIZ

A SCORE OF	COMMENT ON YOUR SCORE
76% THROUGH 100%	CONGRATULATIONS YOU'RE A MUSIC WIZ.
51% THROUGH 75%	YOU'RE PRETTY GOOD.
26% THROUGH 50%	GETTING THERE, BUT CAN DO BETTER.
0 THROUGH 25%	POORLY - YOU NEED MORE MUSIC IN YOUR LIFE, START BY LISTENING TO THE RADIO AND BUYING SOME MUSIC PREFERABLY BEST OF OR ANTHOLOGIES.

CHART SCORES BASED ON YOUR RIGHT # OF ANSWERS

TEN	TWENTY	TWENTY-FIVE
1=10%	1=5%	1=4%
2=20%	2=10%	2=8%
3=30%	3=15%	3=12%
4=40%	4=20%	4=16%
5=50%	5=25%	5=20%
6=60%	6=30%	6=24%
7=70%	7=35%	7=28%
8=80%	8=40%	8=32%
9=90%	9=45%	9=36%
10=100%	10=50%	10=40%
	11=55%	11=44%
	12=60%	12=48%
	13=65%	13=52%
	14=70%	14=56%
	15=75%	15=60%
	16=80%	16=64%
	17=85%	17=68%
	18=90%	18=72%
	19=95%	19=76%
	20=100%	20=80%
		21=84%
		22=88%
		23=92%
		24=96%
		25=100%

FIFTY

TO FIGURE YOUR SCORE ON A QUIZ OF 50 MULTIPLY, EACH CORRECT ANSWER BY 2. EXAMPLE; 41 OUT OF 50 RIGHT IS 41 X 2 = 82%

ONE HUNDRED

ON A QUIZ OF 100, MULTIPLY EACH CORRECT ANSWER BY 1. EXAMPLE; 79 OUT OF 100 IS 79 X 1 = 79%

THE FIFTIES

THE DECADE OF THE FIFTIES BROUGHT US THE BIRTH OF THIS NEW PHENOMENON IN MUSIC KNOWN AS "ROCK 'N' ROLL". THERE WERE MANY REASONS FOR ITS ORIGIN AND SURVIVAL. ONE SUCH REASON WAS ALAN FREED, THE POPULAR WHITE RADIO DISC JOCKEY OUT OF CLEVELAND, OHIO AND OTHERS LIKE HIM. HE WAS ONE OF THE FIRST TO CATCH ON TO THIS NEW TYPE OF MUSIC THAT HE CALLED "ROCK AND ROLL", OR AT LEAST HELPED TO PUSH ITS TERMINOLOGY THROUGH HIS RADIO SHOWS AND ROCK 'N ROLL CONCERTS THAT HE WAS INSTRUMENTAL IN PROMOTING. PRIOR TO THIS POINT IN TIME, MODERN MUSIC WAS BASICALLY CATEGORIZED INTO THREE MAIN GROUPS, R&B, COUNTRY & WESTERN, AND POP (ALSO KNOWN AS TRADITIONAL POP). DUE TO THE POLITICAL CLIMATE AT THE TIME WITH SEGREGATION, RACE MUSIC, LATER KNOWN AS R&B MUSIC WAS ONLY ALLOWED ON BLACK SPONSORED RADIO STATIONS. AS THIS MUSIC BECAME WIDELY ACCEPTED BY THE WHITE TEENAGE AUDIENCES THROUGHOUT THE COUNTRY RECORD COMPANIES BEGAN TO PROMOTE COVERS. COVERS WERE BLACK SONGS WRITTEN OR SUNG BY BLACK ARTISTS AND NOW RECORDED BY WHITE PERFORMERS WITH SLIGHTLY CHANGED LYRICS AND AT A MUCH TONED DOWN PACE TO AVOID CENSORSHIP. ARTISTS SUCH AS PAT BOONE, THE CREW-CUTS, THE MAGUIRE SISTERS, RICKY NELSON, ETC., RECEIVED A LOT OF ATTENTION FOR DOING JUST THAT, COVER SONGS. WITH THE RISE OF THE CIVIL RIGHTS MOVEMENT MAJOR RECORD COMPANIES AND RADIO STATIONS BEGAN TO ACCEPT THE MORE POPULAR BLACK VERSIONS AS THEY WERE. HAVING THE AIRPLAY, THE MOVERS AND SHAKERS SUCH AS BILL HALEY & HIS COMETS, LITTLE RICHARD, FATS DOMINO, ELVIS, THE PLATTERS, CHUCK BERRY, BUDDY HOLLY AND SO FORTH, HELPED TO FURTHER OPEN THE DOORS TO THIS NEW SOUND. OTHERS CLAIMED THE JAZZY INSTRUMENTATIONS, THE SAXOPHONE, THE DRUMS, THE CONGAS, THE HORNS, THE FLUTES, THE GUITARS, ALL COMING TOGETHER FOR HAVING A MAJOR ROLE IN THE DEVELOPMENT OF ROCK 'N ROLL. STILL OTHERS CREDIT THE MOVIES OF THE DAY, 'BLACKBOARD JUNGLE', 'DON'T KNOCK THE ROCK', AND 'JAILHOUSE ROCK' JUST TO MENTION A FEW, ON BRINGING MORE ATTENTION TO THIS NEW RAW SOUND. ANOTHER MAJOR FACTOR WAS TELEVISION, WHICH WAS A NEW INVENTION JUST A FEW YEARS EARLIER. THROUGH THIS NEW MEDIA, VARIETY SHOWS BY THE DOZENS BROADCASTED MORE AND MORE OF THIS NEW SOUND. THE STEVE ALLEN SHOW, ED SULLIVAN'S 'THE TOAST OF THE TOWN', AND THE COUNTLESS TALENT SHOWS WHICH INCLUDED; 'TED MACK AMATEUR HOUR', ARTHUR GODFREY'S 'TALENT SCOUTS SHOW', JACKIE GLEASON, YOUR HIT PARADE ETC., ALL HELPED TO INTRODUCE NEW TALENT COMPETING FOR RECOGNITION, FORTUNE, AND FAME. 'AMERICAN BANDSTAND' GEARED TO THE YOUNGSTERS AND HOSTED BY DICK CLARK, WHO MANY STILL CONSIDER THE OLDEST LIVING TEENAGER AROUND, ALLOWED THESE NEW YOUNG STARS TO PERFORM

THEIR LATEST HITS AND SHOWCASE THE LATEST DANCES THAT WERE CONSTANTLY POPPING UP. THE STROLL, THE HOP, THE BOP ETC., ALL BECAME HOUSEHOLD DANCES. IN ESSENCE ROCK AND ROLL WAS IN REALITY A MELTING POT OF ALL BLENDS OF MUSIC. COUNTRY NOW BECAME ROCKABILLY OR FOLK, R&B BALLADS WERE NOW CROSSING OVER INTO POP OR ROCK AND NO MATTER WHAT YOU CALLED IT, IT WAS GREAT MUSIC AND HOPEFULLY HERE TO STAY BUT ONLY TIME WOULD TELL.

THE 50'S - QUIZZES IN THIS SECTION

50/1	ELVIS	QUIZ # 1	(20 QUESTIONS = 100)
50/2	ELVIS	2	(25 QUESTIONS = 100)
50/3	R&B ROCKERS	QUIZ # 1	(100 QUESTIONS = 100)
50/4	R&B ROCKERS	2	(50 QUESTIONS = 100)
50/5	R&B ROCKERS	3	(20 QUESTIONS = 100)
50/6	R&B ROCKERS	4	(20 QUESTIONS = 100)
50/7	POP ROCKERS	QUIZ # 1	(100 QUESTIONS = 100)
50/8	POP ROCKERS	2	(20 QUESTIONS = 100)
	POP ROCKERS	BONUS	1
50/9	COUNTRY ROCKERS		(50 QUESTIONS = 100)
	COUNTRY ROCKERS	BONUS	3
50/10	ROCKERS		(10 QUESTIONS = 100)
	ROCKERS	BONUS	2
50/11	MISC (NOVLTY, FOLK, FOREIGN & INSTRMTLS)	# 1	(50 QUESTIONS = 100)
50/12	MISC (NOVLTY, FOLK, FOREIGN & INSTRMTLS)	2	(20 QUESTIONS = 100)
50/13	MATCH THE GROUP WITH THE LEAD SINGER		(25 QUESTIONS = 100)
50/14	MATCH THE GROUP WITH THEIR SONG		(25 QUESTIONS = 100)
50/15	MATCH THE INSTRUMENTAL HIT WITH THE ARTIST		(10 QUESTIONS = 100)
50/16	MATCH THE DUOS AND ALSO THEIR HIT SONG		(20 QUESTIONS = 100)
50/17	MATCH THE ARTIST WITH MOVIE/TV/SHOW SONG		(10 QUESTIONS = 100)
50/18	MATCH THE SONG WITH THE MOVIE/TV SHOW		(10 QUESTIONS = 100)

18 TOTAL QUIZZES

1. 1 x 5

THIS MOVIE STARRING *ELVIS PRESLEY*, RICHARD EGAN, NEVILLE BRAND AND DEBRA PAGET TAKES PLACE DURING THE CIVIL WAR. CHOOSE THE MOVIE TITLED SONG BELOW, RECORDED BY *ELVIS* ABOUT PLEADING WITH HER TO LOVE HIM A CERTAIN WAY AND SO TRUE. THE MOVIE WAS ORIGINALLY CALLED 'THE RENO BROTHERS' BUT CHANGED TO HELP PROMOTE THE MOVIE WITH *ELVIS'* HUGE POPULARITY.

A) LOVE ME WITH ALL YOUR HEART
B) DON'T BE CRUEL
C) MY LOVE WILL NEVER DIE
D) LOVE ME TENDER

2. 1 x 5

ELVIS PORTRAYS A CONVICT IN THIS MOVIE BY THE NAME OF VINCE EDWARDS WHO IS PERSUADED TO PURSUE A SINGING CAREER BY HIS CELLMATE AFTER APPEARING ON A TELEVISED PRISON TALENT SHOW. NAME THIS MOVIE TITLED SONG THAT CO-STARRED DEAN JONES, MICKEY SHAUGHNESSY AND JUDY TYLER.

____

3. 1 x 5

IN THIS PARTICULAR MOVIE *ELVIS* PORTRAYED A TRUCK DRIVER WHO BECOMES A BIG ROCK 'N ROLL SINGER. CHOOSE THE MOVIE TITLED SONG BELOW ABOUT HIS STRONG LOVE FOR YOU AND THAT HE'LL BE TRUE TO YOU, CO-STARRING WENDALL COREY, JAMES GLEASON AND LIZABETH SCOTT.

A) LOVING YOU
B) LOVE ME TENDER
C) JAILHOUSE ROCK
D) DON'T BE CRUEL

4. 1 x 5

ELVIS SECURED A THREE PACKAGE APPEARANCE DEAL WITH THIS TV HOST FOR AN ASTOUNDING FEE OF $50,000 WHICH WAS THE HIGHEST TO DATE IN TV HISTORY. WHOSE SHOW WAS IT THAT *ELVIS* WOULD GUEST STAR, TWICE IN 1956, AND ONCE IN 1957?

A) STEVE ALLEN
B) TED MACK
C) DICK CLARK
D) ED SULLIVAN

5. 1 x 5

NAME *ELVIS'* FIRST RECORD LABEL COMPANY THAT WAS OWNED BY SAM PHILLIPS WHO ONCE QUOTED THAT IF HE COULD FIND A WHITE MAN WITH THE BLACK SOUND HE COULD MAKE A MILLION DOLLARS.

A) DECCA
B) SUN RECORDS
C) RCA
D) CHESS

6. 1 x 5

INITIALLY *ELVIS* USED THESE THREE MUSICIANS BELOW DURING HIS EARLY YEARS. WHO WAS **NOT** FORTUNATE TO BE ONE OF THEM?

A) BILL BLACK
B) SCOTTY MOORE
C) IKE TURNER
D) D J FONTANA

7. **1 x 5**

WHAT SONG WOULD *ELVIS* SING DRESSED IN A TUXEDO AND BLUE SUEDE SHOES TO A SAD BASSET HOUND ON NATIONAL TV.

A) BLUE SUEDE SHOES
B) (LET ME BE YOUR) TEDDY BEAR
C) HOUND DOG
D) DON'T BE CRUEL

8. **1 x 5**

WHAT POPULAR MALE QUARTET GROUP CONSISTING OF *GORDON STOKER, NEAL MATTHEWS, HOYT HAWKINS* AND *HUGH JARRET* WERE *ELVIS'* FAVORITE BACK UP SINGERS AND KNOWN FOR THEIR GOSPEL RENDITIONS? IT IS ESTIMATED THAT THEY HAVE BACKED ON OVER THIRTY THOUSAND SONGS IN THEIR LIFETIME FOR COUNTLESS SINGERS INCLUDING *CONNIE FRANCIS, PATSY CLINE, RICKY NELSON, JIM REEVES* AND SO FORTH, AN ASTOUNDING RECORD UNHEARD OF.

A) THE CRESTS
B) THE JORDANAIRES
C) THE DREAMLOVERS
D) THE IMPERIALS

9. **1 x 5**

CARL PERKINS RECORDED A POPULAR COUNTRY SONG THAT *ELVIS* WOULD ALSO GO ON TO CHART. CHOOSE THIS SONG ABOUT CERTAIN SHOES.

A) BLUE SUEDE SHOES
B) PINK SHOE LACES
C) BOOGIE SHOES
D) THESE BOOTS ARE MADE FOR WALKIN'

10. **1 x 5**

"THAT'S ALL RIGHT" RECORDED ON JULY 5, 1954 WAS THE FIRST SONG TO BE RELEASED BY *ELVIS'* LABEL RECORD COMPANY AND SELL OVER 20,000 COPIES, WITH "GOOD ROCKIN' TONIGHT" TO FOLLOW. NOW NAME THE SONG THAT WOULD BECOME HIS FIRST NATIONAL TOP OF THE CHARTS HIT SONG ABOUT A LONELY STREET.

A) HOTEL HAPPINESS
B) HOTEL CALIFORNIA
C) HEARTBREAK HOTEL
D) LONELY TEARDROPS

11. **3 x 5**

MATCH THE *ELVIS* SONG WITH THE ORIGINAL R&B ARTIST.

	SONG		ORIGINAL R&B ARTIST		
1.	THAT'S ALL RIGHT	A)	WILLIE MAY (BIG MAMA) THORNTON	1.	
2.	GOOD ROCKIN' TONIGHT	B)	ARTHUR CRUDUP	2.	
3.	HOUND DOG	C)	ROY BROWN	3.	

12. **1 x 5**

WHO WAS THE MANAGER FOR *ELVIS* THAT WAS A VERY SHREWD BUSINESSMAN AND ADDED A MILITARY RANK AS PART OF HIS NAME EVEN THOUGH HE HAD NO PROVEN MILITARY SERVICE?

A) BUCK RAM
B) COLONEL TOM PARKER
C) GENERAL PATTON
D) SERGEANT BILKO

13. **1 x 5**

IN 1957 *ELVIS* BOUGHT A MANSION, CONSISTING OF 23 ROOMS, LOCATED IN THE OUTSKIRTS OF MEMPHIS ON HIGHWAY 51 SOUTH WITH OVER THIRTEEN ACRES OF LAND FOR $102,500. THE CURRENT ADDRESS IS 3764 ELVIS PRESLEY BOULEVARD, MEMPHIS TENNESSEE 38116. WHAT WAS IT CALLED?

A) MONTICELLO
B) SUGAR SHACK
C) GRACELAND
D) NEVER NEVER LAND

14. **1 x 5**

WHAT IS *ELVIS'* 'CORRECT' FULL NAME REGARDLESS OF THE MISSPELLING ON HIS GRAVE TOMBSTONE?

____

15. **1 x 5**

ELVIS HAD OVER A DOZEN AND A HALF BACK UP SINGERS DURING HIS CAREER. WHO BELOW WAS NOT FORTUNATE ENOUGH TO BE ONE?

A) THE BLOSSOMS
B) THE SWEET INSPIRATIONS
C) THE DEL SATINS
D) THE JORDANAIRES

16. **1 x 5**

WHAT RECORD LABEL COMPANY BOUGHT OUT *ELVIS'* CONTRACT FROM HIS FIRST RECORD LABEL FOR $35,000 AND ANOTHER $5,000 TO *ELVIS* FOR ANY LOSS OF FUTURE ROYALTIES AT THAT FIRST LABEL? IT WOULD REMAIN HIS LABEL FOR LIFE.

A) CAPIPOL
B) RCA
C) CHESS
D) STAX/VOLT

17. **1 x 5**

ELVIS HIRED THIS ENTOURAGE OF GUYS WHO BECAME HIS INNER CIRCLE THAT WERE ARMED AND BECAME MARTIAL ARTS EXPERTS TO PROTECT AND ACCOMPANY HIM ALL OVER. SOME WERE CHILDHOOD FRIENDS AND SOME FAMILY MEMBERS, COUSINS. WHAT WERE THEY KNOWN AS?

A) THE HELLS ANGELS
B) THE DIXIE BOYS
C) THE MEMPHIS MAFIA
D) THE IMPERIALS

18. **1 x 5**

HOW MANY NUMBER ONES, TOP OF THE CHART HIT SONGS, DID *ELVIS* HAVE DURING HIS LIFETIME OF RECORDING ON THE CHARTS, STARTING WITH "HEARTBREAK HOTEL" AND ENDING WITH "SUSPICIOUS MINDS"?

A) 30
B) 10
C) 17
D) 50

TOTAL POINTS. **20 x 5 = 100**

ELVIS-QUIZ # 2

1. **25 x 4**

ACCORDING TO *ELVIS PRESLEYS'* 'THE COMPLETE 50'S MASTERS' *ELVIS* RECORDED CLOSE TO **140** SONGS IN THE 50'S. COMPLETE THE INITIALS BELOW TO FIGURE OUT THE NAMES OF **25** OF HIS BIGGEST.

1) H--------K H---L

2) B--E S---E S---S

3) I W--T Y--, I N--D Y--, I L--E Y--

4) D--'T B- C---L

5) H---D D--

6) L--E M- T----R

7) L--E M-

8) T-- M--H

9) A-- S---K U-

10) (L-T M- B- Y--R) T---Y B--R

11) L----G Y--

12) J---H---E R--K

13) T---T M- N--E

14) D--'T

15) I B-G O- Y--

16) W--R M- R--G A----D Y--R N--K

17) H--D H----D W---N

18) O-E N---T

19) I G-T S---G

20) (N-W A-D T--N T---E'S) A F--L S--H A- I

21) I N--D Y--R L--E T-----T

22) A B-G H--K O' L--E

23) G--D R-----' T-----T

24) T--T'S A-- R---T

25) M-----Y T---N

TOTAL POINTS. 25 x 4 = 100

50'S

R&B ROCKERS-QUIZ # 1

1. 3 x 1

THE FLAMINGOS, THE POPULAR R&B HARMONY GROUP OUT OF CHICAGO, HAD THESE THREE ROMANTIC BALLADS IN THE 50'S.
ONE, WHAT HE TOLD HER ABOUT THEIR PARTING AND THE WORDS LOVERS SHOULD NEVER SAY.
TWO, HIS EYES ONLY FOR YOU THAT HE CAN'T SEE NO OTHER OR FOR THAT MATTER ANYTHING ELSE.
THREE, THAT HE'S COMING HOME TO BE YOUR SERVANT.
NAME THEM.

1) ______________________________
2) ______________________________
3) ________________

2. 1 x 1

THE HARPTONES HAD A BIG HIT ABOUT A TYPE OF LOVE THAT HE WANTED.

A) TEN COMMANDMENTS OF LOVE
B) THE END
C) APRIL LOVE
D) I WANT A SUNDAY KIND OF LOVE

3. 1 x 1

THE HARPTONES CHARTED ANOTHER DOO WOP SONG ABOUT WHAT LIFE IS.

A) WITHOUT LOVE (THERE IS NOTHING)
B) LIFE IS BUT A DREAM
C) JUST A DREAM
D) THIS MAGIC MOMENT

4. 1 x 1

THE CHANTELS HAD A BIG HIT WITH THE POSSIBILITY IF SHE PRAYED NIGHTLY YOU'D COME BACK, WRITTEN BY THEIR LEAD SINGER *ARLENE SMITH*. WHAT WAS IT CALLED?

A) MAYBE
B) WILL YOU LOVE ME TOMORROW
C) LET IT BE ME
D) DEVOTED TO YOU

5. 1 x 1

THE CHANTELS ALSO CHARTED WHAT OTHER ABOUT WHAT THEY DID EACH NIGHT RELIGIOUSLY?

A) HE'S GOT THE WHOLE WORLD (IN HIS HANDS)
B) EVERY NIGHT (I PRAY)
C) MY PRAYER
D) TONIGHT'S THE NIGHT

6. 1 x 1

THE CADILLACS RECORDED A SONG ABOUT A GUY WHOSE NAME THEY WERE TRYING TO FIGURE OUT. SOME THOUGHT HE WAS MO, OTHERS, JOE, BUT HE'S KNOWN AS WHO ACCORDING TO THE TITLE OF THE SONG?

A) SPEEDY GONZALES
B) MR BLUE
C) SPEEDO
D) MR LEE

7. 1 x 1

IN THE 50'S *THE PLATTERS* CHARTED THIS SONG THAT HAD THE SAME TITLE OF ONE THAT *LITTLE BRENDA LEE* WOULD ALSO CHART IN THE 60'S BUT WITH DIFFERENT LYRICS. NAME THAT APOLOGETIC SONG.

 ____

8. **1 x 1**

THE DRIFTERS WITH *BEN E KING* IN LEAD RECORDED WHAT NUMBER TWO HIT SONG IN THE LATE 50'S ABOUT THEIR BABY WHO HE BROKE HER HEART AND HE NEEDS TO KNOW WHAT TO DO TO WIN HER BACK?
A) BABY IT'S YOU
B) ALL ALONE AM I
C) SECRETLY
D) THERE GOES MY BABY

9. **1 x 1**

THE DRIFTERS HAD ANOTHER ABOUT WANTING TO DANCE WITH HER AND BE HELD TIGHTER AND HOPEFULLY END UP AS A PERMANENT TWOSOME, ALSO WITH BEN E KING IN LEAD ON THIS LATIN INSPIRED HIT.
A) DANCE WITH ME
B) DO YOU WANT TO DANCE
C) LITTLE GIRL OF MINE
D) LET'S DANCE

10. **6 x 1**

NAME THESE SIX HITS BY *LITTLE ANTHONY AND THE IMPERIALS,* THE POPULAR TEEN GROUP OUT OF BROOKLYN, NY.
ONE, WHAT'S ON HIS PILLOW.
TWO, A JUKEBOX THAT HAD THEIR SONG AND DESPERATELY HOPING SHE'LL BE HIS ONCE MORE.
THREE, A CERTAIN CHRONICLE LEDGER BOOK WITH A LOCK AND KEY WRITTEN AND ALSO RECORDED BY *NEIL SEDAKA*.
FOUR, A SONG ABOUT TWO PEOPLE.
FIVE, ABOUT THAT NEW GIRL NEXT DOOR.
SIX, ONE OF THE BEST RENDITIONS OF THE WALT DISNEY MOVIE SONG FEATURED IN "PINOCCHIO" ABOUT A STAR.

1) ______________________________
2) ______________________________
3) _________________
4) __________________________________
5) ______________________________
6) __________________________________

11. **1 x 1**

EARL GRANT RECORDED THIS ROMANTIC BALLAD THAT IF SHE TOLD HIM THAT SHE WOULD ONLY BE HIS AND LOVE ONLY HIM, THEIR LOVE WOULD FLOURISH 'TIL ETERNITY. WHAT WAS THAT RAINBOW HIT SONG?
A) THIS MAGIC MOMENT
B) THE END
C) TILL THEN
D) WHAT A WONDERFUL WORLD

12. **1 x 1**

THE DUO OF *ROBERT & JOHNNY* HAD THIS ONE BIG CLASSIC HIT BACK IN THE LATE 50'S ABOUT THEIR BEING TOGETHER.
A) WE BELONG TOGETHER
B) MR SANDMAN
C) EDDIE MY LOVE
D) MY LOVE WILL NEVER DIE

13. **1 x 1**

BROOK BENTON RECORDED A SONG THAT ONE DAY YOU'RE GOING TO REALIZE WHAT YOU HAD AND HOPE TO HAVE ONCE MORE.
A) FOR THE GOOD TIMES
B) IT'S JUST A MATTER OF TIME
C) JUST A DREAM
D) HE'LL HAVE TO GO

14. **1 x 1**

THE DELLS CHARTED THIS SONG ABOUT THAT SPECIAL NIGHT AND REMARKABLE GIRL THAT HE COULDN'T FORGET AND WHY HE LOVED HER SO. IN THE 60'S THEY WOULD RECORD IT ONCE AGAIN WITH SLIGHTLY DIFFERENT LYRICS AND TITLE SPELLING THAT ALSO INCLUDED A ROMANTIC OPENING MONOLOGUE.

A) MY SPECIAL ANGEL
B) DREAM LOVER
C) OH WHAT A NITE
D) ONLY YOU

15. **1 x 1**

THIS TEEN GROUP, *THE STUDENTS*, CHARTED WHAT SONG ABOUT THEIR DESIRE TO GET MARRIED BUT IMPOSSIBLE BECAUSE OF THEIR TENDER AGES? THOUGH IT DIDN'T CHART WELL AT THE TIME, IT STILL BECAME A POPULAR CLASSIC HIT TO THIS DAY.

A) A PRAYER AND A JUKEBOX
B) I WISH THAT WE WERE MARRIED
C) A MILLION TO ONE
D) SO YOUNG

16. **1 x 1**

THE STUDENTS RECORDED ANOTHER ABOUT TAKING A LOVE, FROM ANY POINT IN TIME OR DAY JUST AS LONG THAT IT WAS REAL AND SO TRUE.

A) WILL YOU LOVE ME TOMORROW
B) EVERYDAY OF THE WEEK
C) BABY IT'S YOU
D) LET THE GOOD TIMES ROLL

17. **1 x 1**

THE HEARTBEATS, A TRIO GROUP, LED BY *JIM SHEPPARD* HAD THIS ROMANTIC BALLAD THAT DADDY WOULD BE ARRIVING HOME SHORTLY.

A) 500 MILES
B) A THOUSAND MILES AWAY
C) TWENTY FIVE MILES
D) 26 MILES (SANTA CATALINA)

18. **1 x 1**

ED TOWNSEND, THE TALENTED SINGER/SONGWRITER, IS BEST REMEMBERED FOR RECORDING THIS LOVE SONG BELOW PROCLAIMING THAT HE WOULD DO ANYTHING OR GO ANYWHERE IN ORDER TO HAVE YOUR LOVE AND YOUR KISS. IT'S A SONG *PEACHES & HERB* WOULD ALSO GO ON TO RECORD IN THE LATE 60'S.

A) MAYBE
B) FOR YOUR LOVE
C) FOR YOUR PRECIOUS LOVE
D) THAT'S MY DESIRE

19. **1 x 1**

THE FIVE SATINS, THE VERY POPULAR GROUP OUT OF CONNECTICUT, RECORDED A ROMANTIC SONG IN 1956 WITH *FRED PARRIS* IN LEAD ABOUT THAT NIGHT IN MAY WHEN HE HELD YOU AND THE VOW TO NEVER GIVE YOU UP. IT'S A SONG THAT SOME CLASSIC OLDIES RADIO STATIONS CONSIDER TO BE ONE OF THE GREATEST ROCK AND ROLL DOO WOP HITS OF ALL TIME.

A) FOR YOUR LOVE
B) THERE'S A MOON OUT TONIGHT
C) IN THE STILL OF THE NIGHT
D) MY GIRL

20. **1 x 1**

THE FIVE SATINS CHARTED ANOTHER, THIS TIME WITH *BILL BAKER* AT THE HELM, ABOUT EVERY STEP PULLING YOU CLOSER DOWN THAT CEREMONIAL PATH AS MAN AND WIFE.
A) WHEN WE GET MARRIED
B) TO THE AISLE
C) THE HAWAIIAN WEDDING SONG (KE KALI NEI AU)
D) DOWN THE AISLE (WEDDING SONG)

21. **1 x 1**

CHOOSE BELOW THE HEARTBREAK HIT SONG BY *JACKIE WILSON*, CO-WRITTEN BY BERRY GORDY THE FUTURE FOUNDER OF THE MOTOWN LABEL, ABOUT HIS HEART CRYING BECAUSE OF HIS LONELINESS AND HOPING YOU'LL RETURN.
A) I'M SO LONESOME I COULD CRY
B) LONELY BOY
C) TEEN ANGEL
D) LONELY TEARDROPS

22. **1 x 1**

JACKIE WILSON ALSO RECORDED ANOTHER THAT IF YOU CALLED HIM EVEN JUST ONCE A DAY HE WOULD BE SO CONTENTED.
A) I'LL BE SATISFIED
B) ONCE IN AWHILE
C) YOU'VE GOT WHAT IT TAKES
D) THAT'S MY DESIRE

23. **1 x 1**

JERRY BUTLER, THE POPULAR SINGER OUT OF CHICAGO, HAD THIS CHERISHED LOVE SONG ABOUT WHAT YOUR LOVE MEANT TO HIM AND WANTING TO HEAR THAT YOU'LL ALWAYS BE HIS.
A) WE BELONG TOGETHER
B) FOR YOUR PRECIOUS LOVE
C) DEVOTED TO YOU
D) THE END

24. **1 x 1**

CHOOSE THE GROUP *JERRY BUTLER* EVOLVED FROM AND WHO WOULD ALSO DO THE BACK UP ON THAT ROMANTIC SONG ABOVE.
A) THE IMPRESSIONS
B) THE MOONGLOWS
C) THE DRIFTERS
D) THE JORDANAIRES

25. **1 x 1**

WHAT WAS *JERRY BUTLER'S* GIVEN NICKNAME?
A) THE ICE MAN
B) THE KILLER
C) BOOM BOOM
D) MR PERSONALITY

26. **1 x 1**

CHUCK WILLIS, THE SINGER/SONGWRITER FOR THE ATLANTIC RECORDS LABEL COMPANY, CHARTED THIS SONG BELOW ABOUT A CERTAIN RIDER.
A) LOW RIDER
B) C.C. RIDER
C) RIDE CAPTAIN RIDE
D) LIL' RED RIDING HOOD

27. **1 x 1**

CHUCK WILLIS HAD ANOTHER THAT QUESTIONED HIS EXISTENCE. ONE THAT *PAT BOONE* WOULD COVER AND GAIN HIGHER RECOGNITION FOR AT THE TIME.
A) LIFE IS BUT A DREAM
B) WHAT AM I LIVING FOR
C) WHAT NOW MY LOVE
D) WHERE OR WHEN

28. **1 x 1**

IN 1958 *THE DANLEERS*, THE TEEN GROUP WITH *JIMMY WESTON* IN LEAD, HAD THIS ROMANTIC DOO WOP BALLAD ABOUT FALLING IN LOVE ONE HOT NIGHT UNDER THE MOON UP ABOVE. IT WOULD BECOME A SUMMER CLASSIC WHICH WAS ALSO THEIR MAJOR CLAIM TO FAME SONG.
A) ONE SUMMER NIGHT
B) HERE COMES SUMMER
C) LITTLE STAR
D) FOR YOUR LOVE

29. **1 x 1**

BOBBY FREEMAN RECORDED WHAT SONG QUESTIONING IF YOU WOULD LIKE TO GET ON THE DANCE FLOOR AND MAYBE, JUST MAYBE HUG AND KISS, WELL DO YA? IT'S A SONG THAT *THE BEACH BOYS* WOULD RECORD IN THE MID 60'S AND *BETTE MIDLER* IN THE EARLY 70'S, HER VERSION AT A MUCH SLOWER AND MORE ROMANTIC PACE.
A) THERE GOES MY BABY
B) A LOVER'S QUESTION
C) DO YOU WANT TO DANCE
D) LET'S DANCE

30. **1 x 1**

BOBBY DAY, THE SINGER/SONGWRITER AND TRUE NAME ROBERT BYRD, CHARTED THIS POPULAR SONG THAT LITTLE *MICHAEL JACKSON* WOULD ALSO RECORD IN THE EARLY 70'S ABOUT A BIRD THAT DOES SOMETHING ALL DAY.
A) ROCKIN' ROBIN
B) TWEEDLEE DEE
C) LITTLE BITTY PRETTY ONE
D) BIRD DOG

31. **1 x 1**

DEE CLARK, THE MALE SINGER, CHARTED THIS NOTABLE HIT IN 1959 ABOUT A SMALL GIRL WHO WORE A CERTAIN SWEATER, WHOM HE WANTED TO KNOW AND SOCIALIZE WITH.
A) LITTLE BITTY PRETTY ONE
B) HEY LITTLE GIRL
C) LET THE LITTLE GIRL DANCE
D) LITTLE DARLIN'

32. **1 x 1**

THE ISLEY BROTHERS, A TRIO OF BROTHERS, HAD A POPULAR DANCE HIT IN 1959 THAT WOULD MAKE A COMEBACK IN THE LATE 70'S FOR THE MOVIE SOUNDTRACK OF 'ANIMAL HOUSE' STARRING JOHN BELUSHI AND TIM MATHESON. WHAT WAS THAT DANCE HIT AND PLEASE YELL IT OUT IF YOU CAN?
A) LOUIE LOUIE
B) SHOUT (PARTS 1 AND 2)
C) DON'T LET GO
D) SAVE THE LAST DANCE FOR ME

33. **1 x 1**

THE CLOVERS, THE POPULAR GROUP, CHARTED COUNTLESS OF R&B HITS FOR THE ATLANTIC RECORDS LABEL. THIS INCLUDED A SONG THAT ANOTHER ARTIST, *BOBBY VEE,* WOULD GO ON TO RECORD IN THE EARLY 60'S ABOUT A GIRL WITH A DUAL PERSONALITY WHOM HE LOVED JUST THE SAME.

A) GYPSY WOMAN
B) DEVIL OR ANGEL
C) BLACK MAGIC WOMAN
D) (YOU'RE THE) DEVIL IN DISGUISE

34. **1 x 1**

THE CLOVERS HAD ANOTHER, A NOVELTY SONG, THAT WOULD BE RECORDED BY ANOTHER GROUP, THIS TIME *THE SEARCHERS,* IN THE MID 60'S ABOUT A MAGIC POTION THAT HAD HIM KISSING EVERYBODY. WHAT WAS THAT SONG THAT WOULD BECOME THE TITLE OF A MOVIE OF THE SAME NAME STARRING SANDRA BULLOCK AND TATE DONOVAN IN THE EARLY 90'S THAT FEATURED *THE CLOVERS'* ORIGINAL VERSION?

A) POISON IVY
B) MISTY
C) LOVE POTION NO. 9
D) (YOU'VE GOT) THAT MAGIC TOUCH

35. **1 x 1**

JOE TURNER, THE PRE-ROCK 'N ROLLER ALSO FROM THE ATLANTIC RECORDS LABEL, HAD THIS POPULAR SONG IN 1954 ABOUT A GIRL HE WANTED IN THE HOUSE TO DO HER CHORES WHICH INCLUDED THOSE KITCHEN UTENSILS. IT WAS A SONG *BILL HALEY AND HIS COMETS* WOULD ALSO COVER AND GAIN GREATER RECOGNITION OVER *TURNER'S.*

A) YAKETY YAK
B) MAYBELLENE
C) CHANTILLY LACE
D) SHAKE, RATTLE AND ROLL

36. **1 x 1**

JOE TURNER RECORDED ANOTHER ABOUT A GIRL NAMED CORRINA THAT HE LOVED AND WANTED ALL TO KNOW THAT HE DID. *RAY PETERSON,* THE POP SINGER, WOULD ALSO RECORD IT IN THE EARLY 60'S WITH THE NAMES OF THE TITLE SPELLED SLIGHTLY DIFFERENT. NAME IT.

________________ , ________________

37. **1 x 1**

BO DIDDLEY, THE FAMED BLUES GUITARIST, CHARTED A SONG THAT *BUDDY HOLLY* AND COUNTLESS OTHERS WOULD GO ON TO RECORD ABOUT THAT RING AND THE HELP THEY MIGHT REQUIRE FROM THE PRIVATE EYE. CHOOSE IT BELOW.

A) OH, BOY!
B) PETER GUNN
C) BO DIDDLEY
D) RING OF FIRE

38. **1 x 1**

THE RAYS, THE ALL MALE GROUP, RECORDED THIS POPULAR SONG ABOUT LOVERS SNUGGLED UP IN AN EMBRACE BEHIND THE SHADES. A SONG THAT THE BRITISH GROUP, *HERMAN'S HERMITS,* WOULD ALSO GO ON TO CHART IN THE MID 60'S EQUALLY AS GOOD.

A) I'M INTO SOMETHING GOOD
B) SILHOUETTES
C) PUT YOUR HEAD ON MY SHOULDER
D) BEHIND CLOSED DOORS

39. **1 x 1**

THE EL DORADOS CHARTED A SONG IN 1955 ABOUT HIS INSANE WOMAN WHO WAS ALWAYS KNOCKING ON HIS DOOR.

A) BEHIND CLOSED DOORS
B) AT MY FRONT DOOR
C) GREEN DOOR
D) LITTLE DARLIN'

40. **1 x 1**

THE SHOWMAN HAD A POPULAR HIT ABOUT WHAT WOULD LIVE ON FOREVER? IT WOULD BE THEIR CLAIM TO FAME SONG.

A) IT WILL STAND
B) ROCK AND ROLL IS HERE TO STAY
C) FOR YOUR LOVE
D) THE END

41. **1 x 1**

SONNY TIL & THE ORIOLES, ANOTHER PRE-ROCK 'N ROLL GROUP, HAD THIS ONE BIG ROMANTIC HIT IN 1953 THAT *ELVIS* WOULD CHART IN THE MID 60'S ABOUT TEARDROPS OF HAPPINESS AND GOING DOWN ON THEIR KNEES. WHAT WAS THAT JOYFUL HIT CALLED?

A) CRYING IN THE CHAPEL
B) CHAPEL OF LOVE
C) CRYING IN THE RAIN
D) CRYING

42. **1 x 1**

THE CHORDS, ANOTHER WELL KNOWN R&B GROUP, ORIGINALLY RECORDED THIS SONG IN THE 1954 THAT *THE CREW-CUTS* WOULD GO ON TO COVER ALMOST SIMULTANEOUSLY AS A POP HIT, ABOUT WHAT LIFE COULD BE IF YOU CHOSE HIM. MANY CONSIDER *THE CHORDS* VERSION TO BE THE FIRST TRUE SONG OF THE ROCK 'N ROLL ERA OVER *BILL HALEY'S* "(WE'RE GONNA)ROCK AROUND THE CLOCK".

A) DREAM LOVER
B) SH-BOOM
C) SUNDAY KIND OF LOVE
D) MR DREAM MERCHANT

43. **4 x 1**

THE MOONGLOWS, A QUARTET GROUP OF GUYS WITH *BOBBY LESTER* AND *HARVEY FUQUA* SWITCHING ON LEAD, CHARTED NUMEROUS HITS INCLUDING THESE FOUR IN THE 50'S.
ONE, ABOUT THAT GENUINE FEELING BECAUSE HE LOVES YOU DEARLY. THIS SONG WOULD BE COVERED BY *THE MCGUIRE SISTERS* WHICH WAS THE STANDARD PRACTICE OF THE DAY, RECORDING POPULAR R&B MUSIC BY WHITE ARTISTS.
TWO, ABOUT THE TEN RULES OF LOVE, A SONG *PEACHES & HERB* WOULD ALSO GO ON TO RECORD IN THE 60'S.
THREE, WHAT YOUR LOVE IS, UP ONE MOMENT, DOWN THE NEXT, LIKE A CHILD'S PLAY THING FOUND IN A PARK FROM MONDAY THROUGH SUNDAY.
FOUR, ABOUT BEING A PAIR BECAUSE THEY HAVE SIMILAR DESIRES AND HOPEFULLY GO STEADY AND THEN SOMEDAY WEAR HIS WEDDING RING.
NAME THEM.

1) ____________________
2) ____________________________
3) ____________
4) ____________________

44. **1 x 1**

RAY CHARLES, THE GIFTED TALENTED BLIND ARTIST, HAD THIS SONG ABOUT A WOMAN WHO'S BEEN GOOD TO HIM.

A) PARTY DOLL
B) VENUS
C) EARTH ANGEL
D) I GOT A WOMAN

45. **1 x 1**

RAY CHARLES CHARTED ANOTHER ABOUT SOMETHING HE WOULD SAY TO A WOMAN IN RED AND ABOUT THAT STATE OF ARKANSAS.

A) I'M WALKIN'
B) WHAT'D I SAY (PT 1)
C) KANSAS CITY
D) HIT THE ROAD JACK

46. **1 x 1**

THE SILHOUETTES, THE MALE QUARTET GROUP, HAD A POPULAR CLASSIC HIT IN THE LATE 50'S ABOUT CHECKING THROUGH THE NEWSPAPERS LOOKING FOR WORK. IT WOULD BE THEIR ONLY BIG MAJOR RECORDING BUT WOULD REACH TO THE TOP OF THE CHARTS FOR GOOD MEASURE, AND DON'T GO ASKING ANY OF THOSE GUYS FROM *SHA NA NA* FOR ANY CLUES.

A) GET A JOB
B) HELP ME MAKE IT THROUGH THE NIGHT
C) WHAT AM I LIVING FOR
D) GOODNIGHT, SWEETHEART, GOODNIGHT

47. **1 x 1**

THIS BLACK R&B ARTIST OUT OF NEW ORLEANS WAS ONE OF THE TRUE FOUNDING FATHERS OF ROCK 'N ROLL DURING THE EARLY 50'S. HIS SONGS WERE COVERED BY MANY WHITE ARTISTS INCLUDING *PAT BOONE* AND *LITTLE RICKY NELSON.* WHO WAS HE?

A) JOHNNIE RAY
B) ANTOINE 'FATS' DOMINO
C) LLOYD PRICE
D) LITTLE RICHARD

48. **1 x 1**

THE DEL-VIKINGS RECORDED THIS SONG BELOW ASKING HIS DARLING TO ACCOMPANY HIM BECAUSE HE TRULY NEEDED HER AND THAT HE WOULD NEVER PART FROM. IT WOULD BE FEATURED IN THE MOVIE SOUNDTRACK OF 'STAND BY ME' DURING THE MID 80'S.

A) LITTLE DARLIN'
B) DARLING LORRAINE
C) DON'T LET GO
D) COME GO WITH ME

49. **1 x 1**

THE DEL-VIKINGS CHARTED YET ANOTHER ABOUT CERTAIN TYPES OF BELLS THAT CAN REUNITE HIM WITH HIS BABY. IT TOO, WOULD BE FEATURED IN THAT SOUNDTRACK MOVIE ABOVE THAT CO-STARRED RIVER PHOENIX, COREY FELDMAN, KIEFER SUTHERLAND, JOHN CUSACK AND RICHARD DREYFUSS.

A) WEDDING BELL BLUES
B) WHISPERING BELLS
C) CHURCH BELLS MAY RING
D) CHAPEL OF LOVE

50. **1 x 1**

THE BOBBETTES, A QUINTET GROUP OF TEENAGE GIRLS, HAD WHAT POPULAR HIT SONG ABOUT A CERTAIN GUY NAMED LEE WHO THEY THOUGHT WAS NOT ONLY GOOD LOOKING BUT THE SWEETEST OF THEM ALL?

A) HEY, GOOD LOOKIN'
B) SWEETEST ONE
C) SWEET NOTHIN'S
D) MR LEE

51. **1 x 1**

THE GENIES ARE BEST REMEMBERED FOR CHARTING A SONG IN 1958 THAT QUESTIONED THE IDENTITY OF THAT PERSON KNOCKING ON THEIR DOOR. IT WOULD BE THEIR ONLY CLAIM TO FAME SONG AND A CLASSIC TO THIS DAY.

A) KNOCK ON WOOD
B) LET 'EM IN
C) WHO'S THAT KNOCKIN'
D) LET ME IN

52. **1 x 1**

CHOOSE THE MALE ARTIST BELOW WHO WAS ONCE A MEMBER OF *BILLY WARD AND HIS DOMINOES* AND THEN AS THE LEAD SINGER WITH THE ORIGINAL *DRIFTERS.*

A) BEN E KING
B) CLYDE MCPHATTER
C) JERRY BUTLER
D) JACKIE WILSON

53. **1 x 1**

THE JACKS, WHO ALSO RECORDED AS *THE CADETS,* HAD THIS BALLAD BELOW IN 1955 ASKING SOMEONE TO WRITE HIM.

A) EDDIE MY LOVE
B) LOVE LETTERS IN THE SAND
C) WHY DON'T YOU WRITE ME?
D) SEALED WITH A KISS

54. **1 x 1**

THE CLEFTONES UNDER THE LEAD OF *HERBIE COX,* CHARTED A SONG IN THE MID 50'S ABOUT HIS FINE LOOKING GIRL THAT HE WON'T LET GO BECAUSE SHE'S ALWAYS ON HIS MIND.

A) PRETTY LITTLE ANGEL EYES
B) LITTLE GIRL OF MINE
C) SO FINE
D) LITTLE STAR

55. **2 x 1**

BENJAMIN EARL NELSON WENT ON TO JOIN A NEW GROUP IN 1958 AND GIVEN A NEW IDENTITY NAME. ONE YEAR LATER THEY RECORDED "THERE GOES MY BABY" WITH HIM IN LEAD. NAME HIS GROUP AND ALSO HIS NEW IDENTITY NAME.

1) ____________________
2) ______________

56. **1 x 1**

THE SHIELDS ARE MOSTLY REMEMBERED FOR THIS SONG IN THE LATE 50'S ABOUT DECEIT AND LIES WHEN SHE CLAIMED THAT SHE LOVED ONLY HIM.

A) ONLY YOU (AND YOU ALONE)
B) YOU CHEATED
C) LAST KISS
D) DON'T PLAY THAT SONG (YOU LIED)

57. **4 x 1**

NAME THESE FOUR BIG HITS BY *SAM COOKE*, THE LEGENDARY GOSPEL AND R&B SINGER/SONGWRITER.
ONE, HIS BIG NUMBER SIXTEEN HIT SONG THAT *DR HOOK* WOULD GO ON TO RECORD IN THE 70'S.
TWO, SOMETHING HE DID SENTIMENTALLY.
THREE, ABOUT A CERTAIN LATIN DANCE THAT EVERYBODY LIKES TO DO, BUT NOT HIS BABY, CAUSE SHE DIDN'T KNOW HOW. AND NOW A ONE, TWO.
FOUR, WHAT HIS DARLING HONESTLY DOES TO HIM. A SONG BOTH *TERESA BREWER* WOULD RECORD IN THE 50'S AND *THE MANHATTANS* IN THE 80'S WHO ALSO FEATURED IT IN A MUSIC VIDEO AS WELL.

1) ________________
2) ____
3) ____________________________, ,
4) ________________

58. **3 x 1**

NAME THESE THREE SONGS BELOW BY *LEE ANDREWS AND THE HEARTS*.
ONE, ABOUT THOSE LONELY EVENINGS HE HAD TO ENDURE EVER SINCE THE DAY YOU LEFT HIM.
TWO, ABOUT DOING THE IMPOSSIBLE.
THREE, CERTAIN DROPS CAUSED BY LOST ROMANCE AS A RESULT OF DOING HER WRONG BY BEING WITH ANOTHER AND NOW HAVING TO PAY THE PRICE.

1) _______________________
2) _______________________
3) ______________

59. **1 x 1**

THE DIABLOS, ANOTHER PRE-MOTOWN GROUP FROM DETROIT WITH *NOLAN STRONG* IN LEAD, RECORDED THIS SONG BELOW ABOUT ONE OF THE FORCES OF NATURE. WHAT WAS THAT HIT?

A) STORMY WEATHER
B) THE WIND
C) THE WAYWARD WIND
D) RAINDROPS

60. **4 x 1**

THE FIVE KEYS, YOU GUESSED IT, FIVE GUYS, RECORDED THESE FOUR POPULAR DOO WOP HITS BELOW.
ONE, ABOUT THE KNOWLEDGE OF A FOOL.
TWO, ABOUT THE TWO REASONS ONE CAN EASILY FORGET ONE EVER EXISTED.
THREE, ABOUT THE PRAISE OF LOVE.
FOUR, ABOUT THAT CHINA MAN IN THE RESTAURANT WHO SANG "TIE-SA-MOKE-UM-BOOT-A-YAY" AND WHO WAS NEVER WRONG.
NAME THEM.

1) _____________________
2) _______________________________
3) ________________
4) _____________________

61. **1 x 1**

THE TURBANS, WITH *AL BANKS* IN LEAD, RECORDED WHAT DANCE NUMBER THAT WHENEVER YOU SQUEEZED HER, YOU COULD FEEL THE WARMTH OF HER TOUCH?

A) DO YOU WANT TO DANCE
B) SAVE THE LAST DANCE FOR ME
C) DON'T LET GO
D) WHEN YOU DANCE

62. **1 x 1**

THE MONOTONES HAD THIS ONE MAJOR HIT ABOUT HOW THEY WONDERED WHO WROTE THE CHAPTERS IN THE REGISTRY OF LOVE, THAT QUOTED CHAPTERS ONE THROUGH FOUR. IT WAS A SONG THAT WOULD BE FEATURED IN THE MOVIE SOUNDTRACK 'AMERICAN GRAFFITI' DURING THE EARLY 70'S THAT CO-STARRED RON HOWARD, RICHARD DREYFUSS, CINDY WILLIAMS, MACKENZIE PHILLIPS, HARRISON FORD AND WOLFMAN JACK. WHAT WAS THAT SONG AND PLEASE DON'T WONDER TOO LONG?

A) LOVE LETTERS
B) I WONDER WHY
C) BOOK OF LOVE
D) THE DIARY

63. **1 x 1**

THURSTON HARRIS CHARTED THIS POPULAR SONG BELOW ABOUT SOMEONE EXTREMELY SMALL AND GOOD LOOKING. IT'S A SONG THAT *THE JACKSON FIVE* WOULD ALSO GO ON TO RECORD IN THE EARLY 70'S. WHAT WAS THAT DOUBLE HITTER CALLED?

A) ROCKIN' ROBIN
B) LITTLE BITTY PRETTY ONE
C) LITTLE STAR
D) GO AWAY LITTLE GIRL

64. **1 x 1**

THE NUTMEGS, THE POPULAR DOO WOP GROUP, HAD A HIT SONG IN 1955 ABOUT A STORY THAT WAS NEVER REVEALED CONCERNING A GIRL WHO LEFT HIM OUT IN THE COLD AND HE HOPED AND PRAYED WOULD COME BACK INTO HIS LIFE. *THE CREW-CUTS,* THE WHITE POP GROUP OUT OF CANADA, WOULD GO ON TO COVER IT AND RECEIVE GREATER ATTENTION FOR IT AT THE TIME. TO THIS DAY *THE NUTMEGS* VERSION IS CONSIDERED BY FAR THE BETTER OF THE TWO WITH IT'S GREAT A CAPPELLA SOUND.

A) STORY UNTOLD
B) MY TRUE STORY
C) MY PRAYER
D) LIFE IS BUT A DREAM

65. **1 x 1**

JESSE BELVIN, THE MALE SINGER/SONGWRITER, HAD THIS ONE BIG MAJOR HIT ABOUT DEPARTING FROM HIS LOVED ONE AND BIDDING HER SWEET DREAMS. BOTH *PAUL* ANKA IN THE 60'S AND *GLORIA ESTEFAN* IN THE 90'S WOULD GO ON TO RECORD IT. WHAT WAS THAT TRIPLE HITTER CALLED?

A) GOODNIGHT, SWEETHEART, GOODNIGHT
B) GOODNIGHT MY LOVE
C) DREAM LOVER
D) OH WHAT A NITE

66. **1 x 1**

AHMET AND NESUHI ERTEGUN, BROTHERS, FORMED A NEW RECORD LABEL COMPANY BACK IN THE LATE 40'S AND BUILT IT INTO A MUSICAL EMPIRE. AHMET WOULD OVERSEE THE R&B PRODUCTION AND EVEN WRITE SONGS WHILE NESUHI OVERLOOKED THE JAZZ PRODUCTION. TO FURTHER EXPAND THEIR R&B EXPOSURE THEY SIGNED *RUTH BROWN*, *JOE TURNER* AND *THE DRIFTERS* WOULD FOLLOW. WHAT WAS THE NAME OF THAT LABEL COMPANY THEY FOUNDED?

A) MOTOWN
B) ATLANTIC RECORDS
C) CHESS
D) REPRISE

67. **1 x 1**

THE FALCONS, THE PRE-MOTOWN GROUP FROM DETROIT WITH *JOE STUBBS* IN LEAD, ARE MOSTLY REMEMBERED FOR RECORDING THIS SONG BELOW ABOUT SOMEONE WHO MAKES THEM TALK AND WALK ONLY ABOUT HER AND WHOSE KISS IS REALLY FINE.

A) GLORIA
B) EARTH ANGEL
C) YOU'RE SO FINE
D) BABY TALK

68. **1 x 1**

THE FIESTAS ALSO HAD A FINE SONG OF THEIR OWN ABOUT A FABULOUS GIRL WHO SENDS THESE CERTAIN FEELINGS UP THROUGH HIS SPINE.

A) SO FINE
B) SWEET LITTLE SIXTEEN
C) ONE FINE DAY
D) AIN'T SHE SWEET

69. **3 x 1**

NAME THESE THREE HITS BY *LLOYD PRICE,* THE POPULAR R&B SINGER WHO STARTED CHARTING DURING THE PRE-ROCK 'N ROLL ERA.
ONE, ABOUT THAT SOREHEAD LOSER NAMED LEE WHO LOST ALL HIS MONEY AND EVEN HIS PRECIOUS HAT TO BOOT.
TWO, QUESTIONING YOUR WHEREABOUTS WHILE HE WAS STRANDED AT THE ALTAR
THREE, HIS NAME TO FAME SONG ABOUT TRYING TO PROCLAIM HIS LOVE TO YOU WITH ALL THE CHARMS AND OTHER FINE QUALITIES ONE COULD ONLY ASK FOR.

1) ________________
2) ________________________________**?**
3) ________________

70. **1 x 1**

LLOYD PRICE CHARTED TWO OTHER HITS BELOW. WHICH ONE WAS **NOT** HIS?

A) LAWDY MISS CLAWDY
B) LONG TALL SALLY
C) I'M GONNA GET MARRIED

71. **1 x 1**

THIS FEMALE ARTIST, WHO LATER BECAME AN ACTRESS AND STARRED IN THE TV SERIES 'TOUCHED BY AN ANGEL', WOULD CHART THE BIGGEST HIT OF HER CAREER IN 1959 THAT JUST BARELY MISSED THE TOP OF THE CHARTS WITH "DON'T YOU KNOW". WHO WAS THAT ANGEL?

A) GLADYS KNIGHT
B) SARAH VAUGHAN
C) DELLA REESE
D) NANCY WILSON

72. **1 x 1**

THE SCHOOLBOYS, A TEEN GROUP, CHARTED THIS HIGHLY UNDERATED OVERLOOKED SONG BEGGING THEIR GIRL TO SAY SOMETHING THAT THEY REALLY WANTED TO HEAR. THE SONG HAS BECOME A CLASSIC DUE TO ITS TRUE VALUE AND MIGHT HAVE HAD POTENTIAL.

A) BABY TALK
B) I WANT YOU TO BE MY GIRL
C) PLEASE SAY YOU WANT ME
D) I PROMISE TO REMEMBER

73. **6 x 1**

NAME THESE SIX HITS BY THE GRAND DADDY OF THEM ALL, *CHUCK BERRY*.
ONE, ABOUT A CERTAIN SIXTEEN YEAR OLD GAL.
TWO, ABOUT A NEW TYPE OF MUSIC IF YOU WOULD LIKE TO GET ON THE DANCE FLOOR WITH HIM.
THREE, ABOUT A MUSICIAN NAMED JOHNNY DOWN BY THE TRACKS.
FOUR, ABOUT A GIRL WHO COULDN'T BE TRUE.
FIVE, HIS BIG BEETHOVEN HIT SONG.
SIX, HIS RETURN TO THE STATES SONG THAT *LINDA RONDSTADT* WOULD ALSO RECORD IN THE 70'S.

1) ______________________________
2) ________________________
3) ________________________
4) ________________
5) ______________________________
6) ________________________

74. **1 x 1**

CHUCK BERRY ALSO CHARTED THREE OTHER HITS BELOW. WHICH ONE WAS **NOT** HIS?
A) SCHOOL DAY
B) CHARLIE BROWN
C) ALMOST GROWN
D) CAROL

TOTAL POINTS. **100 x 1 = 100**

R&B ROCKERS-QUIZ # 2

1. **1 x 2**

ROY HAMILTON HAD A MAJOR HIT SONG BELOW ABOUT BEING HELD TIGHT AND PLEADING NOT TO BE RELEASED.
A) DON'T LET GO
B) HOLD ME TIGHT
C) HOLD ME, THRILL ME, KISS ME
D) FOR THE GOOD TIMES

2. **1 x 2**

WILBERT HARRISON IS BEST REMEMBERED FOR CHARTING THIS POPULAR SONG BELOW ABOUT GOING TO A CERTAIN CITY TO GET HIMSELF A LADY EVEN IF IT MEANT WALKING TO THAT DESTINATION.
A) KANSAS CITY
B) I'M WALKIN'
C) A WALKIN' MIRACLE
D) EL PASO

3. **3 x 2**

THE DUBS LED BY *RICHARD BLANDON,* HAD THESE THREE ROMANTIC DOO WOP HITS BELOW.
ONE, QUESTIONING IF THEIR LOVE WAS THE RESULT OF MAGIC OR WHAT.
TWO, ABOUT NOT WANTING TO BE LONELY.
THREE, ABOUT A CHAPEL OF ILLUSIONS.
NAME THEM.
1) ______________________
2) ____________________________
3) __________________

4. **5 x 2**

NAME THESE FIVE BIG ROCKING HITS BY *LITTLE RICHARD,* THE POPULAR R&B SINGER, PIANIST AND ONE OF THE TRUE FOUNDING FATHERS OF ROCK 'N ROLL.
ONE, ABOUT A GIRL THAT *KENNY ROGERS* WOULD ALSO SING ABOUT IN THE 70'S BUT WITH DIFFERENT LYRICS.
TWO, ABOUT THAT LADY NAMED MOLLY.
THREE, ABOUT A GIRL NAMED JENNY.
FOUR, ABOUT NOT COMING IN NO MATTER HOW MANY TIMES YOU KNOCKED, BUT MAYBE YOU'LL HAVE LUCK TOMORROW.
FIVE, ABOUT A TALL GAL NAMED SALLY, THAT *PAT BOONE* WOULD GO ON TO COVER.
1) __________
2) ____________________________
3) _______________
4) ___________________
5) ___________________

5. **1 x 2**

LITTLE RICHARD HAD THESE THREE OTHER HITS BELOW. WHICH ONE WAS **NOT** HIS?
A) TUTTI FRUTTI
B) RIP IT UP
C) JOHNNY B. GOODE
D) SLIPPIN' & SLIDIN' (PEEPIN' AND HIDIN')

6. **1 x 2**

LAVERN BAKER, THE POPULAR FEMALE SINGER OUT OF THE ATLANTIC RECORDS LABEL COMPANY, HAD A BIG HIT ABOUT A GUY NAMED JIM WHO'S ALWAYS DOING HEROIC FEATS INCLUDING SAVING DAMSELS IN DISTRESS.
A) JIMMY MACK
B) RESCUE ME
C) DON'T MESS AROUND WITH JIM
D) JIM DANDY

7. **1 x 2**

LAVERN BAKER ALSO CHARTED ANOTHER ABOUT A GUY NAMED DEE WHO BRINGS HER HAPPINESS AND CAUSES HER HEART TO BEAT ABNORMALLY.
A) LITTLE STAR
B) TWEEDLE DEE
C) ROCKIN' ROBIN
D) ZIP-A-DEE-DOO-DAH

8. **1 x 2**

"WILLIE AND THE HAND JIVE" WAS A POPULAR DANCE NUMBER PUT TOGETHER BY THIS TALENTED SHOWMAN IN THE LATE 50'S. IT'S A SONG *ERIC CLAPTON* WOULD ALSO RECORD IN THE MID 70'S. WHO WAS THAT TALENTED SHOWMAN?
A) JOHNNY OTIS SHOW
B) ED SULLIVAN
C) DICK CLARK
D) ALAN FREED

9. **1 x 2**

WILLIE MAE **(***BIG MAMA) THORNTON* HAD THIS R&B HIT IN 1953 THAT *ELVIS* WOULD RECORD YEARS LATER AT A MUCH FASTER PACE AND MUCH ADDED LYRICS. WHAT WAS THAT DOUBLE HITTER?
A) LOVE ME TENDER
B) HOUND DOG
C) SUSPICION
D) PEACE IN THE VALLEY

10. **1 x 2**

CHOOSE THE LEAD SINGER OF *THE DRIFTERS* WHO RECORDED "MONEY HONEY" AND "HONEY LOVE" AND LATER WOULD START HIS OWN BIG SOLO CAREER.
A) BEN E KING
B) CLYDE MCPHATTER
C) RUDY LEWIS
D) JACKIE WILSON

11. **1 x 2**

JOHNNIE RAY WAS A WHITE MALE SINGER WHO WOULD BECOME THE FIRST NON-BLACK SINGER TO HAVE A NUMBER ONE HIT ON THE R&B CHARTS. WHAT WAS THAT SONG IN 1952 ABOUT THE HEARTACHE PAIN CAUSED BY HIS SWEETHEART AND NOT HAVING SHAME FOR WHAT HE DID?
A) CRY
B) HEARTACHES BY THE NUMBERS
C) BYE BYE LOVE
D) CRYING TIME

12. **1 x 2**

JOHNNIE RAY HAD WHAT OTHER ABOUT DOING SOMETHING IN THE RAIN?
A) CRYING
B) IN THE RAIN
C) JUST WALKING IN THE RAIN
D) RAINDROPS

13. 5 x 2

NAME THESE FIVE BIG HITS BY *FRANKIE LYMON AND THE TEENAGERS*, THE POPULAR R&B TEEN GROUP FROM NYC.
ONE, ABOUT FOOLS IN LOVE, A SONG *DIANA ROSS* WOULD RECORD IN THE 80'S.
TWO, ABOUT THE ABC'S.
THREE, HOORAY HE BROKE YOUR HEART, BECAUSE WHAT GOES AROUND, COMES AROUND.
FOUR, ABOUT WHAT HE WANTED THAT GIRL TO BE.
FIVE, WHAT HE PROMISED TO DO.

1) ______________________________
2) ________________________
3) ________________
4) ______________________________
5) ________________________

14. 3 x 2

EARL LEWIS AND THE CHANNELS HAD THESE THREE BIG HITS BELOW.
ONE, ABOUT HIS DESIRE.
TWO, ABOUT SOMETHING OF HIS THAT WILL NEVER KEEL OVER.
THREE, THE REASON HIS LOVE GROWS STRONGER EVERYDAY.
NAME THEM.

1) ______________________
2) ___________________________
3) ______________________

15. 3 x 2

CLYDE MCPHATTER CHARTED THESE THREE SOLO HITS BELOW.
ONE, A QUESTION THAT WHEN THEY KISS DOES SHE MUTUALLY FEEL WHAT HE'S GOING THROUGH.
TWO, A GOLDMINE FOUND ONLY IN YOUR HEART, STRONGER AND MORE PRECIOUS THAN ANY TYPE OF ROCK.
THREE, A SONG THAT *TOM JONES* WOULD ALSO RECORD IN THE 60'S, THAT WITHOUT TRUE PASSION NOTHING ELSE MATTERS.
NAME THEM.

1) ________________________
2) _____________________
3) ______________________________

16. 1 x 2

THE CHARTS, A TEEN GROUP OUT OF HARLEM, ARE MOSTLY REMEMBERED FOR RECORDING WHAT DOO WOP HIT SONG BELOW NAMED AFTER A GIRL AND ALSO WRITTEN BY THEIR SEVENTEEN YEAR OLD LEAD SINGER *JOE GRIER*.

A) PEGGY SUE
B) DESERIE
C) DONNA
D) RUBY

17. 1 x 2

ZOLA TAYLOR WAS THE ONLY FEMALE MEMBER OF THIS VERY POPULAR QUINTET SINGING GROUP. WHAT WAS THE NAME OF THAT GROUP KNOWN FOR CHARTING COUNTLESS ROMANTIC BALLADS IN THE 50'S AND 60'S?

A) THE SKYLINERS
B) THE FLAMINGOS
C) THE PLATTERS
D) THE MOONGLOWS

18. 1 x 2

THE ROMANTIC BALLAD "IT'S ALL IN THE GAME" ABOUT LOVE WITH IT'S UPS AND DOWNS WITH KISSING AND CARESSING THE END RESULT, WAS RECORDED BY WHICH MALE ARTIST BELOW IN 1958 WHICH GAVE HIM HIS PREMIER STARDOM?

A) JACKIE WILSON
B) SAM COOKE
C) PAUL ANKA
D) TOMMY EDWARDS

19. 2 x 2

THIS ARTIST WAS BELIEVED TO HAVE KILLED HIMSELF WHILE PLAYING RUSSIAN ROULETTE. SHORTLY AFTER, HIS SONG ABOUT PROFESSING HIS LOVE AND MAKING YOU HAPPY WAS RELEASED AND BECAME A POSTHUMOUS HIT. WHAT WAS HIS NAME AND THAT POSTHUMOUS HIT SONG?

1) ______________
2) ____________________

20. 4 x 2

MATCH THESE 'BIRD NAMED' GROUPS WITH THE SONG THEY CHARTED.

	BIRD GROUP		SONG		
1.	THE PENGUINS	A)	I ONLY HAVE EYES FOR YOU	1.	
2.	THE FALCONS	B)	EARTH ANGEL	2.	
3.	THE FLAMINGOS	C)	YOU'RE SO FINE	3.	
4.	THE ORIOLES	D)	CRYING IN THE CHAPEL	4.	

21. 1 x 2

THE ROBINS, ANOTHER BIRD TITLED GROUP AND THE NUCLEUS OF A NEW GROUP TO BE, *THE COASTERS*, HAD THIS HIT SONG BELOW ABOUT A CERTAIN CAFÉ. IN THE 90'S IT WOULD BECOME THE NAME OF A BROADWAY MUSICAL.

A) SMOKEY JOE'S CAFE
B) GREASE
C) HAIR
D) VIVA LAS VEGAS

22. 1 x 2

THE SHIRELLES, THE VERY POPULAR GIRL GROUP FROM PASSAIC, NJ, CHARTED A SONG ABOUT A GUY SHE ENCOUNTERED ON A CERTAIN DAY OF THE WEEK.

A) SUNDAY TO MONDAY
B) BLUE MONDAY
C) I MET HIM ON A SUNDAY
D) I WANT A SUNDAY KIND OF LOVE

23. 1 x 2

THE DUO OF *SHIRLEY & LEE* EARNED THEIR PLACE IN MUSIC HISTORY BY RECORDING WHAT CLASSIC SONG BACK IN 1956 ABOUT THE WONDERFUL TIMES WHEN THEY WOULD ROCK ALL THROUGH THE NIGHT?

A) LET THE GOOD TIMES ROLL
B) FOR THE GOOD TIMES
C) MEMORIES ARE MADE OF THIS
D) TWISTIN' THE NIGHT AWAY

24. **1 x 2**

BILLY WARD AND HIS DOMINOES HAD THESE TWO LEAD SINGERS WHO LATER MADE NAMES FOR THEMSELVES. ONE BECAME THE LEAD SINGER OF THE 'EARLY' *DRIFTERS* AND LATER WOULD HAVE HIS OWN BIG SOLO CAREER AND THE OTHER CHARTED A NUMBER OF SONGS INCLUDING "LONELY TEARDROPS". WHO WERE THOSE TWO MUSICAL GIANTS BELOW?

A) CLYDE MCPHATTER & BEN E KING
B) BEN E KING & JACKIE WILSON
C) JERRY BUTLER & SAM COOKE
D) CLYDE MCPHATTER & JACKIE WILSON

25. **6 x 2**

THIS ARTIST IS CALLED *'THE FAT MAN'*. NAME HIM AND THESE FIVE CHARTED HITS BELOW, NUMBERS TWO THROUGH SIX.
ONE, HIS NAME.
TWO, ABOUT IT BEING A SHAME BECAUSE YOU LEFT HIM HEARTBROKEN, A SONG *PAT BOONE* AND *LITTLE RICKY NELSON* WOULD EACH GO ON TO COVER.
THREE, ABOUT A THRILL UP ON A CERTAIN HILL THAT FULLFILLED HIS DREAMS. THIS WAS ORIGINALLY A HIT SONG BY *GLENN MILLER* BACK IN 1940.
FOUR, ABOUT WHAT HE'LL BE DOING IN HOPES THAT YOU MIGHT COME BACK.
FIVE, HE'S GOT A WHOLE BUNCH OF WHAT FOR YOU?
SIX, ABOUT WHAT HE WANTS TO DO BY YOUR SIDE.

1) ______________
2) ______________________
3) ___________________
4) ______________
5) ______________________
6) _____________________________

26. **1 x 2**

THE FAT MAN ABOVE WOULD ALSO CHART THREE OF THE FOUR HITS BELOW. WHICH ONE WAS **NOT** HIS?

A) GOOD GOLLY, MISS MOLLY
B) MY BLUE HEAVEN
C) BLUE MONDAY
D) I'M READY

27. **1 x 2**

FRANKIE FORD IS MOSTLY REMEMBERED FOR WHAT BIG HIT IN 1959 ABOUT HIS DESIRE FOR YOU TO GO WITH HIM ON A CERTAIN JOURNEY?

A) BEYOND THE SEA
B) OVER THE MOUNTAIN, ACROSS THE SEA
C) SEA CRUISE
D) SEA OF LOVE

TOTAL POINTS. **50 x 2 = 100**

R&B ROCKERS-QUIZ # 3

1. **10 x 5**

THE PLATTERS, THE POPULAR ROMANTIC QUINTET GROUP WHO LED THE WAY FOR CHARTING NUMEROUS HITS IN BOTH THE R&B CHARTS AND IN THE POP CHARTS AS A CROSSOVER, CHARTED THESE TEN BIG HITS BELOW. NAME THEM.
ONE, YOU BEING IN HIS HEART WHILE HE PRAYS, THAT WAS ORIGINALLLY RECORDED BY *THE INK SPOTS* ALSO IN THE 50'S.
TWO, YOU ARE HIS DESTINY, THE ONE AND ONLY.
THREE, ABOUT PRETENDING TO BE OK.
FOUR, ABOUT SOMETHING IN YOUR EYES.
FIVE, HE PRAYS DAILY FOR EVENINGS TO BE WITH YOU.
SIX, ABOUT YOUR SPECIAL TOUCH THAT MAKES HIM GLOW.
SEVEN, APOLOGIZING FOR WHAT HE'S DONE.
EIGHT, YOU GET THIS WAY WHEN YOU TOUCH A STAR.
NINE, ABOUT WHAT YOU MADE FOR YOU AND I.
TEN, ABOUT MEMORIES WHEN HE LOVED YOU THEN AND STILL DOES.

1) ______________
2) ______________
3) _________________________
4) ______________________________
5) ____________________
6) ______________________________
7) ______________
8) ______________
9) ____________________
10) ___________________

2. **1 x 5**

THE PLATTERS ALSO CHARTED TWO OF THE THREE HITS BELOW. WHICH ONE WAS **NOT** THEIRS?
A) ONE IN A MILLION
B) HARBOR LIGHTS
C) OUT OF SIGHT, OUT OF MIND

3. **1 x 5**

THE VELOURS ARE MOSTLY REMEMBERED FOR CHARTING THIS SONG BELOW THAT QUESTIONED IF HE COULD DO WHAT AT YOUR PLACE.
A) LET THE GOOD TIMES ROLL
B) TONITE, TONITE
C) CAN I COME OVER TONIGHT
D) SORRY (I RAN ALL THE WAY HOME)

4. **1 x 5**

THE CROWS, ANOTHER PRE-ROCK 'N ROLL GROUP, RECORDED WHAT SONG BELOW ABOUT THE REASON HE LOVES THAT GIRL, AND YOU DON'T HAVE TO BE A WHIZ TO FIGURE THIS ONE OUT?
A) TEN COMMANDMENTS OF LOVE
B) GEE
C) SWEET LITTLE SIXTEEN
D) LITTLE STAR

5. **1 x 5**

WHO MANAGED *THE PLATTERS* AND MOLDED THEM INTO ONE OF THE MOST POPULAR GROUPS OF THE 50'S AND 60'S AND WAS BY TRADE, A SONGWRITER AND MUSIC ARRANGER?
A) ALAN FREED
B) BUCK RAM
C) COLONEL TOM PARKER
D) ZOLA TAYLOR

50'S

6. **1 x 5**

JACKIE BRENSTON AND THE IKE TURNER BAND CHARTED THIS PRE-ROCK 'N ROLL SONG IN 1951 ABOUT A CERTAIN CAR WITH AWESOME POWER AND LOOKS TO SPARE FOR THE SUN LABEL. SOME CONSIDER IT TO BE THE FIRST TRUE ROCK 'N ROLL SONG OF THE ROCK ERA OVER "(WE'RE GONNA) ROCK AROUND THE CLOCK" WHO HOLDS THAT HONOR. IRONICALLY *BILL HALEY* ALSO DID A COVER VERSION OF THAT PRE-ROCKER HIT AS WELL.

A) ROCKET 88
B) SH-BOOM
C) GOOD ROCKIN' TONIGHT
D) GEE

7. **1 x 5**

"(I'M YOUR) HOOCHIE COOCHIE MAN" WAS A PRE-ROCK AND ROLL HIT SONG BY WHAT INFLUENTIAL BLUES ARTIST BELOW?

A) BO DIDDLEY
B) CHUCK BERRY
C) WILLIE MAE 'BIG MAMA' THORNTON
D) MUDDY WATERS

8. **1 x 5**

IN 1950 *NAT 'KING' COLE* RECORED THIS SONG BELOW ABOUT A WOMAN WHO WAS A MASTERPIECE OF FINE ART. LEONARDO DA VINCI, THE FAMED ARTIST WOULD PROBABLY HAVE BEEN IMPRESSED. CHOOSE THAT PRE-ROCK 'N ROLL SONG STILL ACTIVE ON OLDIES RADIO STATIONS TODAY. THE SONG WOULD BE FEATURED IN A JULIA ROBERTS 2004 MOVIE, TITLE SLIGHTLY CHANGED.

A) AVE MARIA
B) GLORIA
C) MONA LISA
D) PEGGY SUE

9. **1 x 5**

IN 1951 *NAT 'KING' COLE* CHARTED ANOTHER ABOUT WHAT PEOPLE WERE SAYING ABOUT THEIR RELATIONSHIP, THAT IT WAS BOUND TO DOOM. WHAT WAS THAT PRE-ROCKER, THAT SOUNDS AS IF IT WERE RECORDED YESTERDAY?

A) BORN TOO LATE
B) JUST A DREAM
C) TOO YOUNG
D) DON'T

10. **1 x 5**

BILLY WILLIAMS WILL ALWAYS BE REMEMBERED FOR RECORDING THIS *FAT'S WALLER* 1930'S SONG BELOW ABOUT A LETTER WHICH HE PRETENDED WAS WRITTEN BY YOU. NAME IT BY COMPLETING THE INITIALS PROVIDED BELOW.

I'- G---A S-T R---T D--N A-D W---E M----F A L----R

11. **1 x 5**

DINAH WASHINGTON CHARTED THIS CLASSIC HIT THAT HAS BEEN RECORDED BY NUMEROUS ARTISTS INCLUDING *NAT KING COLE* IN THE FORTIES ABOUT WHAT YOU ARE AND HOW INCREDIBLE IT IS FOR THINKING I AM TOO. IN THE EARLY 90'S *NATALIE COLE, NAT'*S DAUGHTER, WOULD DO A DUET WITH HER DAD ON THIS SONG BY MEANS OF MODERN TECHNOLOGY. (NAT DIED IN 1965) WHAT WAS THAT CLASSIC HIT CALLED?

A) UNFORGETTABLE
B) LET IT BE ME
C) DEVOTED TO YOU
D) MONA LISA

TOTAL POINTS. 20 x 5 = 100 50'S

R&B ROCKERS-QUIZ # 4

1. **1 x 5**

THE SPANIELS, A QUINTET GROUP OF GUYS, CHARTED WHAT BIG CLASSIC SONG IN 1954 ABOUT DEPARTING FROM THEIR SWEETHEART FOR THE NIGHT? THE OLDIES GROUP *SHA-NA-NA* WOULD ALSO USE IT IN THEIR ACT.

A) OH WHAT A NITE
B) THEN YOU CAN TELL ME GOODBYE
C) GOODNIGHT, SWEETHEART, GOODNIGHT
D) BEYOND THE SEA

2. **1 x 5**

PHIL PHILLIPS WITH THE TWILIGHTS HAD A SONG WHERE HE WANTED TO PROFESS HIS IMMENSE LOVE FOR YOU AND TO COME JOIN HIM ON A SEA VENTURE. IT WAS A SONG THAT *THE HONEYDRIPPERS* WOULD ALSO CHART IN THE MID 80'S AND ALSO BECOME THE TITLE OF AN AL PACINO MOVIE CO-STARRING ELLEN BARKIN, JOHN GOODMAN AND SAMUEL L JACKSON IN THE LATE 80'S THAT FEATURED THE *PHIL PHILLIPS* ORIGINAL VERSION.

A) BEYOND THE SEA
B) SEA OF LOVE
C) COME GO WITH ME
D) WHISPERING BELLS

3. **1 x 5**

IN 1954 *THE PENGUINS* LED BY *CLEVELAND DUNCAN* CHARTED THEIR CLAIM TO FAME SONG ABOUT A MORTAL ANGEL WHO THEY ADORED AND WISHED WOULD BE THEIRS. IT'S A SONG THAT *THE CREW-CUTS* WOULD GO ON TO COVER AND GAIN RECOGNITION FOR IT AT THE TIME. WHAT WAS THE NAME OF THAT ROMANTIC BALLAD THAT HAS MADE *THE PENGUINS* VERSION ONE OF THE MOST POPULAR SONGS OF THE EARLY ROCK ERA AND CONSTANTLY PLAYED ON THE OLDIES RADIO STATIONS TODAY?

A) EARTH ANGEL
B) MY SPECIAL ANGEL
C) THE ANGELS LISTENED IN
D) TEEN ANGEL

4. **1 x 5**

THE PASTELS RECORDED THIS SONG ABOUT THAT CERTAIN TIME WHEN HE SQUEEZED YOU TIGHT AND KISSED YOU GOODNIGHT. WHAT WAS THAT SONG THAT BROUGHT BACK THOSE FOND MEMORIES OF LONG AGO?

A) BEEN SO LONG
B) LONG LONELY NIGHTS
C) GOODNIGHT, SWEETHEART, GOODNIGHT
D) OH WHAT A NITE

5. **1 x 5**

THIS VERY POPULAR ENTERTAINER OUT OF DETROIT NOT ONLY SANG BUT DANCED IN HIS PERFORMANCES. HE WAS CALLED '*MR EXCITEMENT*' BY MANY.

A) SAM COOKE
B) JACKIE WILSON
C) CHUCK BERRY
D) JOHNNY MATHIS

6. **1 x 5**

BILLY WARD AND HIS DOMINOES CHARTED THIS ROMANTIC BALLAD WITH *EUGENE MUNFORD* IN LEAD WITH WHAT STAR TITLED SONG BELOW?

A) CATCH A FALLING STAR
B) WHEN YOU WISH UPON A STAR
C) LITTLE STAR
D) STARDUST

7.

1 x 5

LITTLE WILLIE JOHN RECORDED THIS SONG ABOUT SOMETHING THAT CAUSES THE TEMPERATURE TO RISE. *PEGGY LEE* WOULD GO ON TO DO A COVER VERSION OF IT IN THE 50'S, *THE MCCOYS* IN THE 60'S, AND *MADONNA* IN THE 90'S.
A) SUMMERTIME BLUES
B) FEVER
C) CHAIN GANG
D) 16 TONS

8.

1 x 5

LITTLE WILLIE JOHN CHARTED ANOTHER PLEADING FOR SOMEONE TO CONVERSE WITH HIM. WHAT WAS THE NAME OF THAT SONG?
A) BABY TALK
B) TALK TO ME, TALK TO ME
C) TALK THAT TALK
D) TALKING ABOUT MY BABY

9.

1 x 5

IN 1954 *THE CADILLACS* CHARTED THE ORIGINAL VERSION OF AN A CAPPELLA SONG WITH A GIRL'S NAME. IF IT'S NOT THAT GIRL MARIE, THEN WHO COULD IT BE? THIS SONG HAS BEEN RECORDED BY COUNTLESS OTHERS BUT ONLY A HANDFULL INCLUDING *EARL LEWIS* AND *THE CHANNELS*, *THE PASSIONS* AND *VITO BALSAMO & THE SALUTATIONS* CAN RIGHTFULLY BOAST IT WAS ONCE THEIRS TOO.
A) OH! CAROL
B) CAROL
C) DONNA
D) GLORIA

10.

1 x 5

HARRY BELAFONTE, THE SINGER TURNED ACTOR, RECORDED A SONG ABOUT THE APPEARANCE OF A NEW DAY APPROACHING WITH THE SUNRISE. IT WOULD RESURFACE IN THE 80'S AS THE RESULT OF BEING FEATURED IN THE MOVIE SOUNDTRACK OF 'BEETLEJUICE' STARRING MICHAEL KEATON, ALEC BALDWIN AND GEENA DAVIS. NAME THAT POPULAR CALYPSO HIT THAT IS OFTEN PLAYED AT MAJOR LEAGUE BASEBALL GAMES.
A) EARTH ANGEL
B) BANANA BOAT (DAY-O)
C) IN THE STILL OF THE NIGHT
D) EBB TIDE

11.

1 x 5

BILLY WARD AND HIS DOMINOES HAD ANOTHER ABOUT A GUY WHO CLAIMED HE HAD ENDURANCE AND COULD ROCK ALL THROUGH THE NIGHT.
A) (WE'RE GONNA) ROCK AROUND THE CLOCK
B) SIXTY MINUTE MAN
C) LET THE GOOD TIMES ROLL
D) ROCKIN' ROBIN

12.

1 x 5

ONE OF THE GROUPS BELOW, FROM HARLEM, NY, ARE BEST REMEMBERED FOR CHARTING THE SONG "CHURCH BELLS MAY RING" BACK IN 1956. WHAT WAS THAT GROUP CALLED?
A) THE DEL VIKINGS
B) THE WILLOWS
C) THE PLATTERS
D) THE MOONGLOWS

13. **1 x 5**

DINAH WASHINGTON, THE JAZZ AND R&B SINGER, CHARTED THE SONG "WHAT A DIFFERENCE A DAY MAKES". SHE WAS KNOWN FOR RECORDING DUETS WITH A POPULAR MALE ARTIST BELOW? WHO WAS HER CO-SINGER?

A) JERRY BUTLER
B) BROOK BENTON
C) JOHNNY MATHIS
D) TONY WILLIAMS

14. **1 x 5**

AL HIBBLER, BLIND AT BIRTH AND A ONE TIME MEMBER OF *DUKE ELLINGTONS' BAND,* HAD A HIT WITH A THEME SONG FOR THE MOVIE 'UNCHAINED' STARRING ELROY HIRSCH AND BARBARA HALE IN 1955. A SONG *VITO AND THE SALUTATIONS* AND *THE RIGHTEOUS BROTHERS* WOULD EACH GO ON TO RECORD IN THE 60'S. WHAT WAS THAT POPULAR SONG WHICH BECAME *AL HIBBLERS'* FIRST MAJOR HIT, ABOUT WHAT HE HUNGERED FOR?

A) HE
B) UNCHAINED MELODY
C) FOR YOUR LOVE
D) PEANUT BUTTER

15. **1 x 5**

SARAH VAUGHAN, THE JAZZ SINGER, HAD ONE OF HER BIGGEST HITS FROM THE BROADWAY SHOW 'DAMN YANKEES' WITH THIS LOLA SONG IN THE EARLY 50'S ABOUT WHAT SHE WANTED AND ALWAYS GETS, INCLUDING YOU. NAME IT.

____

16. **2 x 5**

IVORY JOE HUNTER, THE MALE R&B SINGER/SONGWRITER, CHARTED THESE TWO POPULAR HITS BELOW.
ONE, ABOUT WHAT ALMOST HAPPENED TO HIM AS A RESULT OF LOSING THAT GIRL. A SONG *PAT BOONE* WOULD COVER AND GAIN WIDER RECOGNITION FOR.
TWO, A SONG THAT *FREDDIE FENDER* WOULD RECORD IN THE 70'S ABOUT A GIRL WHO CHANGED HIS LIFE AFTER MEETING UP.
NAME THEM.

1) _____________________________
2) __________________________

17. **1 x 5**

IN 1956 THIS ARTIST WITH HIS GROUP WOULD GAIN HIS FIRST BIG CHARTED HIT CALLED "PLEASE, PLEASE, PLEASE". WHO WAS THIS GUY THAT WOULD AMASS WELL OVER ONE HUNDRED R&B HITS TO HIS CREDIT DURING HIS LIFETIME, ALSO KNOWN AS THE HARDEST WORKING MAN IN SHOW BUSINESS STILL PERFORMING TODAY, NOW IN HIS FIFTH DECADE?

A) JACKIE WILSON
B) ROY HAMILTON
C) JAMES BROWN
D) OTIS REDDING

18. **1 x 5**

WHAT WAS THE NICKNAME GIVEN TO *LLOYD PRICE*?

A) THE FAT MAN
B) MR PERSONALITY
C) THE ICE MAN
D) THE KILLER

19.

1 x 5

NAME THIS CLASSIC HIT IN 1957 BY THE DUO OF *MICKEY AND SYLVIA* ABOUT SOMETHING BEING STRANGE. ANOTHER DUO, *PEACHES & HERB,* WOULD ALSO GO ON TO RECORD IT IN THE LATE 60'S. IN THE LATE 80'S THE ORIGINAL VERSION WOULD BE FEATURED IN THE BLOCKBUSTER MOVIE 'DIRTY DANCING'.

A) AT MY FRONT DOOR (CRAZY LITTLE MAMA)
B) LOVE IS STRANGE
C) PEOPLE ARE STRANGE
D) WITCH DOCTOR

TOTAL POINTS. **20 x 5 = 100**

POP ROCKERS-QUIZ # 1

1. **1 x 1**

THE CRESTS, THE GROUP OUT OF NYC CONSISTING OF A MULTI-INTEGRATED BAND OF FOUR GUYS, CHARTED A TOP NUMBER TWO HIT WITH WHAT BIG CLASSIC BIRTHDAY SONG FOR A SIXTEEN YEAR OLD TEEN QUEEN THAT HE LOVED TO NO END.

A) SWEET LITTLE SIXTEEN
B) HAPPY, HAPPY BIRTHDAY BABY
C) 16 CANDLES
D) HAPPY BIRTHDAY, SWEET SIXTEEN

2. **2 x 1**

THE CRESTS ALSO RECORDED THESE TWO OTHER HITS BELOW. NAME THEM.
ONE, ABOUT THE REACTION OF THE ANGELS AFTER HEARING HIM PRAY.
TWO, ABOUT THE NUMBER OF DAYS THAT HE LONGS FOR YOU WITH THE SEVENTH HOLDING YOU IN HIS ARMS AT THE WEEKLY SATURDAY DANCE.

1) ______________________________
2) _______________________

3. **1 x 1**

THE SKYLINERS, OUT OF PITTSBURGH, CONSISTING OF FOUR GUYS AND ONE GIRL AND LED BY *JIMMY BEAUMONT*, HAD THIS ROMANTIC BALLAD ABOUT NOT HAVING YOU OR ANY HAPPINESS SINCE THEY'VE PARTED. WHAT WAS THAT ROMANTIC HIT CALLED?

A) WE BELONG TOGETHER
B) SINCE I DON'T HAVE YOU
C) SINCE I FELL FOR YOU
D) SINCE I LOST MY BABY

4. **1 x 1**

THE SKYLINERS ALSO CHARTED WHAT OTHER SONG ABOUT A SACRED VOW THAT HIS LOVE FOR YOU WILL LAST FOR ETERNITY?

A) THIS I SWEAR
B) THE END
C) DEDICATED TO THE ONE I LOVE
D) MY LOVE WILL NEVER DIE

5. **1 x 1**

THE FIREFLYS ARE BEST REMEMBERED FOR RECORDING THIS SONG BELOW ABOUT SOMETHING SO GRAND THAT USED TO BE, BUT SADLY TO SAY NO LONGER SO.

A) OH, WHAT A NITE
B) WE BELONG TOGETHER
C) YOU WERE MINE
D) OVER THE MOUNTAIN, ACROSS THE SEA

6. **5 x 1**

NAME THESE FIVE HITS BY THE LEGENDARY POP SINGER *JOHNNY MATHIS*.
ONE, A SONG THAT WOULD BECOME IN THE 80'S THE LOVE THEME SONG AND ALSO THE MOVIE TITLE STARRING CYBILL SHEPHERD, ROBERT DOWNEY JR., RYAN O'NEAL AND MARY STUART MASTERSON ABOUT SOMETHING AWFULLY GOOD.
TWO, ABOUT HOW MUCH HE LOVED HER, MUST HE DRAW YOU A PICTURE?
THREE, ABOUT THE POSSIBILITY OF NEVER MEETING AGAIN, NOT WITHIN HIS CONTROL.
FOUR, ABOUT WHEN THEY WALK HOLDING HANDS BY THE OCEAN SIDE IT'S QUITE SO GRAND.
FIVE, ABOUT A PARTICULAR SMILE.

1) ________________
2) _______________________
3) ___________________________________
4) ____________!_______________!
 5) _______________________

7. **1 x 1**

IN 'TAMMY AND THE BACHELOR', STARRING *DEBBIE REYNOLDS,* LESLIE NEILSEN, FAY WRAY AND WALTER BRENNAN, DEBBIE NURSES AN INJURED PILOT BACK TO HEALTH. NAME HER TOP HIT SONG FEATURED IN THE MOVIE ABOUT HER BEING IN LOVE.

____

8. **1 x 1**

THE THREE GROUPS*, THE CHORDETTES, THE TEEN QUEENS* AND *THE FONTANE SISTERS,* EACH CHARTED THIS SONG DURING THE SAME POINT IN TIME IN 1956 ABOUT A GUY NAMED EDDIE WHO THEY LOVED SO DEARLY. NAME THAT SONG WHICH HAD THE *FONTANE SISTERS* JUST BARELY AHEAD OF THE PACK.

____

9. **5 x 1**

NAME THESE FIVE POPULAR HITS BY *PAUL ANKA*, THE YOUNG TALENTED SINGER/SONGWRITER.
ONE, ABOUT A GIRL HE HAD A CRUSH ON AND THOUGH SHE WAS MUCH OLDER HOPED WOULD BE BY HIS SIDE, RECORDED AT THE TENDER AGE OF FIFTEEN.
TWO, ABOUT A CERTAIN BOY WHO'S GOT THE BLUES, ALONE, AND LOOKING FOR THAT ONE TO CALL HIS OWN.
THREE, PLEADING ABOUT YOU BEING HIS WISH COME TRUE AND MEANT TO BE.
FOUR, WHISPERING WORDS HE LONGS TO HEAR.
FIVE, WHEN YOU'RE HEARTBROKEN DUE TO HER DEPARTURE IT'S TIME TO DO WHAT?

1) __________
2) __________
3) __________
4) __________
5) __________

10. **6 x 1**

THIS POPULAR 'BLUE EYES' CROONER TURNED ACTOR, SINCE THE BIG BAND ERA OF THE 40'S, HAD MANY HITS INCLUDING "(LOVE IS) THE TENDER TRAP", AND "LEARNIN' THE BLUES". NAME HIM AND FIVE OF HIS OTHER HITS BELOW, NUMBERS TWO THROUGH SIX.
ONE, HIS NAME.
TWO, A SONG THAT IN THE 80'S AND 90'S WOULD BE USED AS THE THEME FOR A TV COMEDY SHOW STARRING THE BUNDYS, ALSO RECORDED BY *DINAH SHORE*, THE FEMALE POP SINGER.
THREE, ABOUT A CERTAIN JEALOUS PERSON.
FOUR, ABOUT SOMETHING THAT IS TABOO.
FIVE, ABOUT THAT INSECT WITH THE RUBBER TREE.
SIX, ABOUT HAVING YOUR LOVE TOTALLY AND NOT JUST HALF THE WAY, LIKE THE VERY TALLEST OR THE DEEPEST AND NOTHING LESS.

1) __________
2) __________
3) __________
4) __________
5) __________
6) __________

11. **1 x 1**

THE BELL TONES' ONLY MAJOR RECORDING WAS THIS SONG BELOW CHARTED IN 1959 WHERE THEY PROCLAIMED THEY'VE HAD ENOUGH.
A) DON'T
B) I'VE HAD IT
C) STOP THE MUSIC
D) YOU CHEATED

12. **1 x 1**

THE MYSTICS HAD THEIR CLAIM TO FAME SONG IN 1959 ASKING CERTAIN ANGELS TO WATCH OVER THEIR LOVED ONE. WHAT WAS IT CALLED?

A) HUSHABYE
B) THE ANGELS LISTENED IN
C) MY SPECIAL ANGEL
D) LITTLE STAR

13. **1 x 1**

THE MELLO-KINGS, ANOTHER TEEN GROUP WITH THE SOULFUL SOUND, CHARTED THIS CLASSIC HIT ABOUT WISHING TONIGHT FOR A MIRACLE THAT HE WOULD HAVE YOU BY HIS SIDE AND LOVE YOU 'TIL THEY PART. WHAT WAS THAT CLASSIC HIT CALLED, STILL VERY POPULAR TODAY?

A) TEEN ANGEL
B) LITTLE STAR
C) MY SPECIAL ANGEL
D) TONITE, TONITE

14. **3 x 1**

DION AND THE BELMONTS, THE POP GROUP FROM NYC, BELMONT STREET IN THE BRONX, CHARTED THESE THREE BIG HITS BELOW.
ONE, QUESTIONING WHY HE LOVED YOU SO.
TWO, ABOUT A TEENAGER IN A CERTAIN MOOD WHO FEELS THREATENED AND ASKS FOR SOME GUIDANCE.
THREE, THAT NO ONE KNEW OF HIS HEARTACHE.
NAME THEM.

1) ______________
2) ______________________
3) ________________

15. **1 x 1**

THE TUNE WEAVERS LED BY *MARGO SYLVIA* WILL ALWAYS BE REMEMBERED FOR RECORDING THIS SONG BELOW WISHING HER FORMER BABE A JOYFUL BIRTHDAY EVEN THOUGH HE'S WITH ANOTHER. WHAT WAS THAT CLASSIC HIT BELOW?

A) 16 CANDLES
B) HAPPY, HAPPY BIRTHDAY BABY
C) CELEBRATION
D) HAPPY BIRTHDAY, SWEET SIXTEEN

16. **1 x 1**

THE PASSIONS FROM BROOKLYN, NY, WITH *JIMMY GALLAGHER* IN LEAD, RECORDED THIS SONG BELOW THAT THERE WAS NOTHING HE WOULDN'T DO IN ORDER TO HAVE YOU.

A) WE BELONG TOGETHER
B) 'TIL
C) JUST TO BE WITH YOU
D) FOR YOUR PRECIOUS LOVE

17. **1 x 1**

IN 1959 *BOBBY RYDELL* RECORDED THIS SONG BELOW THAT DEALT WITH THE SUBJECT MATTER OF KISSING. IT WOULD BE HIS FIRST AND EARN HIM HIS PREMIER STARDOM.

A) KISSIN' TIME
B) KISSIN' COUSINS
C) KISS ME GOODBYE
D) THEN YOU CAN TELL ME GOODBYE

18. 1 x 1

"GRADUATION DAY" AND "FROM A SCHOOL RING TO A WEDDING RING" WERE CHARTED BY WHICH POP MALE GROUP BELOW?
A) THE ROVER BOYS
B) THE EVERLY BROTHERS
C) LITTLE ANTHONY AND THE IMPERIALS
D) THE CRESTS

19. 1 x 1

THE FOUR ACES, A TRADITIONAL POP GROUP OF GUYS ORIGINATING DURING THE PRE-ROCK ERA WITH *AL ALBERTS* IN LEAD, HAD A HIT FROM A MOVIE THEME SONG ABOUT COINS THROWN INTO A WISHING WELL WITH ONE BEING GRANTED, STARRING CLIFTON WEBB, DOROTHY MCGUIRE, LOUIS JORDAN AND ROSSANO BRAZZI. *FRANK SINATRA* HAD THE DISTINCTION OF RECORDING THE ORIGINAL MOVIE VERSION. WHAT WAS THAT DOUBLE HITTER CALLED?
A) THREE COINS IN THE FOUNTAIN
B) WHEN YOU WISH UPON A STAR
C) I WISH THAT WE WERE MARRIED
D) THE WAYWARD WIND

20. 1 x 1

THE FOUR ACES ALSO CHARTED THE TITLE SONG OF A MOVIE STARRING WILLIAM HOLDEN AND JENNIFER JONES THAT LOVE IS THE REASON FOR LIVING AND GIVING. IT WOULD BE THEIR BIGGEST AND LAND THEM ON TOP OF THE CHARTS IN 1955.
A) TAMMY
B) HIGH HOPES
C) TOWN WITHOUT PITY
D) LOVE IS A MANY SPLENDORED THING

21. 1 x 1

THE FOUR PREPS HAD THEIR BIGGEST HIT WITH THEIR FIRST RECORDING ABOUT THE CITY OF SANTA CATALINA. NAME IT.

______________ (____________________)

22. 1 x 1

THE FOUR PREPS RECORDED ANOTHER ABOUT WANTING HER FORGIVENESS FOR THE WORDS HE HAD SAID BECAUSE SHE WAS THE REASON FOR BEING WHAT HE WAS.
A) I'M SORRY
B) BIG MAN IN TOWN
C) BIG MAN
D) BIG HUNK O' LOVE

23. 1 x 1

PEGGY LEE, THE TALENTED JAZZ SINGER/TURN ACTRESS OUT OF NORTH DAKOTA, CHARTED WHAT COVER SONG BELOW? IT WAS A *LITTLE WILLIE JOHN* TUNE THAT MENTIONED THE HEROIC DEED OF POCAHONTAS.
A) FEVER
B) THE BATTLE OF NEW ORLEANS
C) GOOD TIMIN'
D) COLORS OF THE WIND

24. 1 x 1

'TENNESSEE' ERNIE FORD, THE POPULAR COUNTRY AND GOSPEL SINGER, RECORDED A BIG HIT ABOUT HOW HE WAS AGING AND FALLING BEHIND IN HIS BILLS. NAME THAT BIG HEAVY HIT THAT WOULD ALSO CLIMB TO THE TOP OF THE CHARTS.

____

25. **1 x 1**

GOGI GRANT SANG ABOUT A GUY WHO TRIED SETTLING DOWN WITH HER, BUT LIKE THE WIND, WAS RESTLESS AND THEIR RELATIONSHIP FAILED.
A) THE WAYWARD WIND
B) THE WIND
C) BLOWIN' IN THE WIND
D) IT'S JUST A MATTER OF TIME

26. **1 x 1**

THIS BEARDED GENTLEMAN BELOW CHARTED WITH THE SONG "THE YELLOW ROSE OF TEXAS". LATER HE HAD HIS OWN TV VARIETY SHOW WHERE THE VIEWERS COULD SEE THE LYRICS FLASHED AT THE BOTTOM OF THE SCREEN AND THEY COULD SING ALONG. WHO WAS THAT BEARDED GENTLEMAN?
A) LAWRENCE WELK
B) MITCH MILLER
C) STEVE ALLEN
D) PERRY COMO

27. **1 x 1**

"QUE SERA, SERA (WHATEVER WILL BE, WILL BE") WAS A BIG HIT RECORDED BY WHAT FEMALE ARTIST WHO CO-STARRED WITH JIMMY STEWART AND PETER LORE IN THE MOVIE 'THE MAN WHO KNEW TOO MUCH' THAT FEATURED THAT SONG? SHE ALSO CO-STARRED IN MANY MOVIES OPPOSITE THAT HUDSON FELLA. CAN YOU NAME HER NOW, LIKE MAYBE THIS DAY.

____

28. **1 x 1**

THE FEMALE ARTIST ABOVE ALSO CHARTED ANOTHER ABOUT WHO SHE LOVES. IT WOULD ALSO BE RECORDED BY *THE SHIRELLES* IN THE EARLY 60'S.
A) EVERYBODY LOVES SOMEBODY
B) EVERYBODY LOVES A LOVER
C) APRIL LOVE
D) TAMMY

29. **1 x 1**

THIS MALE ARTIST, TRUE NAME *DINO CROCETTI*, HAD A HIT WITH AN ITALIAN TITLED SONG CALLED "THAT'S AMORE" SUNG BOTH IN ENGLISH AND ITALIAN LYRICS. WHAT WAS HIS PROFESSIONAL NAME?
A) JERRY LEWIS
B) DANNY THOMAS
C) DEAN MARTIN
D) PERRY COMO

30. **1 x 1**

THIS ALL ROUND ENTERTAINER, SINGER/COMEDIAN/TURNED ACTOR, WOULD GO ON TO STAR IN THE MATT HELM SERIES. HE CHARTED THE SONG "RETURN TO ME" AND WAS A MEMBER OF THE RAT PACK. NAME THAT TALENTED ENTERTAINER

____

31. **1 x 1**

PHIL SPECTOR, THE SINGER/SONGWRITER AND A MEMBER OF *THE TEDDY BEARS* WHEN THEY RECORDED THIS SONG BELOW IN 1958, WHICH HE WROTE, ABOUT A GUY THEY KNEW AND LOVED. HE WOULD BECOME A VERY SUCCESSFUL RECORD PRODUCER AND HAVE HIS OWN RECORD LABEL COMPANY CALLED PHILLES. WHAT WAS THAT *TEDDY BEARS* HIT SONG WITH *ANNETTE LEIB* IN LEAD?
A) COLOR HIM FATHER
B) I LOVE HOW YOU LOVE ME
C) LOVE ME WITH ALL YOUR HEART (CUANDO CALIENTA EL SOL)
D) TO KNOW HIM, IS TO LOVE HIM

32. **1 x 1**

THE CHORDETTES, THE POPULAR FEMALE GROUP, RECORDED THIS SONG BELOW ABOUT A MAN THEY CALLED ON TO GRANT THEM A WISH TO END THEIR LONELINESS.

A) EARTH ANGEL
B) MR SANDMAN
C) MR LEE
D) MR BLUE

33. **2 x 1**

THE CHORDETTES ALSO CHARTED THESE TWO OTHER HITS BELOW.
ONE, WHAT SHE CALLED HER MAN, LIKE CANDY TO LICK ON WHO'S SO GREAT, IT WOULD BECOME A TOP NUMBER TWO AND WOULD BE FEATURED IN THE MOVIE SOUNDTRACK OF 'STAND BY ME' IN THE 80'S.
TWO, A COVER SONG OF *THE TEEN QUEENS* ABOUT HER MAN EDDIE WHO THEY LOVED SO DEARLY. ALSO RECORDED BY *THE FONTANE SISTERS* AS A COVER.
NAME THEM.

1) ____________
2) __________________

34. **1 x 1**

RITCHIE VALENS, THE TEEN POP LATIN ROCK SENSATION, CHARTED A POPULAR SONG ABOUT A GIRL THAT LEFT HIM BROKENHEARTED AND SADDENED EVER SINCE. IT WOULD BE THE FIRST AND BIGGEST OF HIS SHORT LIVED CAREER. WHAT WAS THAT POPULAR SONG?

A) PEGGY SUE
B) GLORIA
C) DONNA
D) DONNA THE PRIMA DONNA

35. **1 x 1**

'THE IDOLMAKER' STARRING RAY SHARKEY, PORTRAYED BOB MARCUCCI THE PRESIDENT OF CHANCELLOR RECORDS WHO DISCOVERED TWO TEEN IDOLS. NAME THESE TWO KIDS WHO BROKE AWAY FROM THEIR MENTOR TO BECOME ROCK SINGERS AND THEN ACTORS. ONE HAD A HIT WITH "VENUS" AND THE OTHER WITH "TURN ME LOOSE".

A) FRANKIE AVALON & FABIAN
B) FRANKIE AVALON & LITTLE RICKY NELSON
C) PAT BOONE & FABIAN
D) LITTLE RICKY NELSON & FABIAN

36. **1 x 1**

WHAT POP CROONER THAT HAD A MAJOR HIT WITH "ROUND AND ROUND" BESIDES COUNTLESS OTHERS INCLUDING MANY IN THE PRE-ROCK AND ROLL ERA?

A) PERRY COMO
B) FRANK SINATRA
C) DEAN MARTIN
D) 'TENNESSEE' ERNIE FORD

37. **2 x 1**

THE CROONER ABOVE CHARTED THESE TWO OTHER HITS BELOW.
ONE, ABOUT WHAT PAPA REALLY LOVES THAT CAN HELP YOU STAY TRIM BY DOING IT WITH MAMA.
TWO, ABOUT WHAT ONE SHOULD HOPE TO CATCH AND NEVER RELEASE. HAD THE BACKING OF '*THE RAY CHARLES SINGERS*'.
NAME THEM.

1) __________________
2) ________________________

38. **8 x 1**

THIS YOUNG MALE ACTOR TURNED TO SINGING WHILE ON HIS PARENTS WEEKLY TV SITCOM. NAME HIM AND THESE SEVEN HITS BELOW, NUMBERS TWO THROUGH EIGHT.
ONE, HIS NAME.
TWO, ABOUT A BABY WHO'S GOT LOTS OF RHYTHM AND SPUNK.
THREE, SHE LEFT HIM WAITING AND BROKEN HEARTED ONCE MORE.
FOUR, A GIRL WHO LEFT HIM NOT ONLY HEARTBROKEN BUT A CERTAIN FOOL.
FIVE, A CERTAIN LOCATION IN THE NEIGHBORHOOD WHERE LOVERS GO TO RELEASE AND DWELL OVER THEIR MISERIES.
SIX, THE FEAR OF HER DAD BEING MAD BECAUSE OF THEIR TARDINESS AND HOPING THIS WON'T TURN OUT TO BE THEIR LAST DATE.
SEVEN, A SONG FEATURED ON HIS PARENTS' SHOW HOPING THAT SHE'LL RETURN TO HIM. THIS WAS ORIGINALLY *FATS DOMINO* R&B HIT TUNE.
EIGHT, HOW YOU COULD NEVER BE SECOND TO NONE WHILE HE'S ALIVE ON THIS EARTH.

1) ____________________________
2) ____________________
3) ________________
4) ________________________
5) ____________________
6) ________________
7) ____________________
8) ____

39. **1 x 1**

JOAN WEBER CHARTED A SONG PLEADING WITH HER LOVER TO BE TURNED LOOSE AND FREE OF HIS SPELL.
A) RELEASE ME (AND LET ME LOVE AGAIN)
B) LET ME GO LOVER
C) I CAN'T STOP LOVING YOU
D) THE WAYWARD WIND

40. **1 x 1**

THE *PONI-TAILS*, A GIRL TRIO GROUP, CHARTED THEIR MOST MEMORABLE HIT OF THEIR CAREER IN 1958 WITH THIS TRAGIC LOVE SONG ABOUT BEING TOO YOUNG TO HAVE A RELATIONSHIP WITH THIS MUCH OLDER GUY WHO THEY DEEPLY ADMIRED.
A) SO YOUNG
B) POOR LITTLE FOOL
C) A MILLION TO ONE
D) BORN TOO LATE

41. **1 x 1**

THIS QUARTET GROUP OUT OF NYC FIRST STARTED OUT AS A QUINTET CONSISTING OF MULTI-INTEGRATED MEMBERS, FOUR GUYS AND ONE GIRL. ONE ITALIAN MALE, WHO WAS THE LEAD SINGER, TWO BLACK MALES, ONE PUERTO RICAN MALE AND ONE BLACK FEMALE. *PATRICIA VAN DROSS* WAS THE SOLE FEMALE MEMBER, SISTER OF LITTLE *LUTHER VAN DROSS* WHO WOULD BECOME A LEGEND OF HIS OWN YEARS TO COME. *PATRICIA* WOULD DROP OUT OF THE GROUP DUE TO THE FACT THAT SHE WAS UNABLE TO TOUR ACROSS THE COUNTRY AS THEY STARTED TO ACHIEVE THEIR FAME. WHO WAS THAT GROUP THAT CHARTED "SWEETEST ONE" AND "MY JUANITA" INITIALLY BEFORE HITTING IT BIG WITH THEIR OTHER HITS?
A) THE TEDDY BEARS
B) THE PLATTERS
C) THE CRESTS
D) THE MIRACLES

42. **1 x 1**

"COME SOFTLY TO ME" AND "MR BLUE" WERE BOTH CHART TOPPERS FOR WHAT POP TRIO GROUP BELOW WHICH CONSISTED OF TWO GIRLS AND ONE GUY?
A) THE CADILLACS
B) THE FLEETWOODS
C) THE SKYLINERS
D) DAWN

43. **1 x 1**

JERRY KELLER IS MOSTLY REMEMBERED FOR RECORDING WHAT SUMMER HIT SONG IN 1959 WHICH WAS HIS ONE CLAIM TO FAME SONG?
A) SUMMERTIME BLUES
B) HERE COMES SUMMER
C) SUMMERTIME
D) THEME FROM 'A SUMMER PLACE'

44. **1 x 1**

JODY REYNOLDS, A MALE SINGER, ALSO HAD A TRAGIC LOST LOVE HIT SONG ABOUT WANTING TO JOIN HIS DEPARTED LOVED ONE. WHAT WAS THAT TRAGIC HIT CALLED?
A) ENDLESS SLEEP
B) THE END
C) LAST KISS
D) TELL LAURA I LOVE HER

45. **5 x 1**

THIS POPULAR FEMALE, MULTI-LINGUELED SINGER TURNED ACTRESS HAD A BIG HIT WITH "MY HAPPINESS". NAME HER AND THESE FOUR OTHER HITS BELOW, NUMBERS TWO THROUGH FIVE.
ONE, HER NAME.
TWO, ABOUT A BROKEN HEART IN HER TROPHIES.
THREE, ABOUT A HEART NOW DUE FOR A-BREAKING.
-FOUR, JUMPING LIKE AN INSANE CLOWN.
FIVE, ABOUT WHAT SHE FOUND ON YOUR SHIRT THAT CAUSED THEIR BREAKUP.
1) ____________________
2) ________________________
3) ______________________
4) __________________
5) ________________________________

46. **1 x 1**

JIMMY CLANTON, OUT OF LOUISIANA THE HOME STATE OF MANY BLUES AND JAZZ ARTISTS, RECORDED A SONG IN IN THE LATE 50'S ABOUT A FANTASY WHEREBY THEIR PLANS WERE DOOMED AND THEIR RELATIONSHIP WOULD NEVER LAST. CHOOSE IT BELOW WHICH WAS HIS FIRST AND THE BIGGEST OF HIS CAREER.
A) JUST A DREAM
B) HIGH HOPES
C) DREAMIN'
D) ALL I HAVE TO DO IS DREAM

47. **1 x 1**

JIMMY CLANTON RECORDED WHAT OTHER BIG HIT ABOUT THAT SWEET TALKING GUY ON THE GO, AS SHE PUT IT?
A) JIMMY MACK
B) GO, JIMMY, GO
C) MR LEE
D) SWEET TALKIN' GUY

48. **1 x 1**

VINCE MARTIN WITH *THE TARRIERS* RECORDED WHAT SONG BELOW ABOUT A GIRL WHOSE LOVER JOINS THE NAVY. IT'S A SONG THAT *EDDIE FISHER* WOULD ALSO GO ON TO CHART ALMOST SIMULTANEOUSLY AND COMPETE FOR SUPREMACY, WITH *VINCE* WINNING OUT BY ONE NOTCH.

A) CINDY, OH CINDY
B) NAVY BLUE
C) COMING HOME SOLDIER
D) SOLDIER BOY

49. **4 x 1**

NAME THESE FOUR BIG HITS BY *BOBBY DARIN,* THE VERY TALENTED SINGER/SONGWRITER TURNED ACTOR.
ONE, ABOUT WHAT HE WAS DOING SATURDAY NIGHT.
TWO, ABOUT HIS LITTLE QUEEN WHO WEARS SHORTS AND DIGS ROCK AND ROLL.
THREE, ABOUT HIS NIGHTLY PRAYERS AND FANTASIES FOR A LOVER OF HIS VERY OWN.
FOUR, ABOUT THAT FEARLESS GUY KNOWN AS MACKIE WHO'S RUMOURED TO BE BACK IN THE CITY. THIS WAS FROM THE 1928 'THE THREEPENNY OPERA' REWORDED IN ENGLISH LYRICS IN 1954 AND REARRANGED BY *LOUIS ARMSTRONG* WHO ALSO CHARTED IT IN 1957 AND THEN RECORDED BY *BOBBY DARIN* WHO TOOK IT TO HIGHER LEVEL AND INTO A MONSTER OF A HIT.

1) ____________________
2) ____________________
3) ____________________
4) ____________________

50. **6 x 1**

PAT BOONE, THE SINGER TURNED ACTOR, CHARTED THESE SIX HITS BELOW.
ONE, HIS COVER VERSION OF A *FATS DOMINO* SONG ABOUT SHAME.
TWO, ANOTHER COVER TUNE, THIS TIME OF A *FLAMINGOS* SONG ABOUT HOME.
THREE, HIS COVER VERSION OF A *IVY JOE HUNTER* SONG ABOUT SOMETHING HE ALMOST LOST AS A RESULT OF LOSING HIS BABY.
FOUR, A SONG FEATURED IN HIS MOVIE 'BERNARDINE' OPPOSITE TERRY MOORE AND DEAN JAGGER ABOUT A VOW THAT YOU WOULD BE TRUE AND WRITTEN SO. IT WAS ORIGINALLY A 1931 HIT FOR RUSS COLUMBO BROUGHT BACK FOR THIS MOVIE.
FIVE, ANOTHER ORIGINAL SONG BY HIM THAT THIS PARTICULAR LOVE IS MAINLY FOR THE YOUNG.
SIX, A COVER VERSION OF A LITTLE RICHARD SONG ABOUT THAT GIRL SALLY.
NAME THEM.

1) ____________________
2) ____________________
3) ____________________
4) ____________________
5) ____________________
6) ____________________

51. **1 x 1**

PAT BOONE ALSO HAD FOUR OTHER HITS BELOW EITHER AS A COVER OR AS AN ORIGINAL. WHICH ONE BELOW WAS **NOT** HIS?

A) FRIENDLY PERSUASION (THEE I LOVE)
B) LONG TALL SALLY
C) 16 CANDLES
D) TUTTI FRUTTI
E) DON'T FORBID ME

52. 1 x 1

FABIAN, ONE OF THE TEEN IDOLS, HAD THREE OF THE FOUR HITS BELOW. WHICH ONE WAS **NOT** HIS?
A) TIGER
B) TURN ME LOOSE
C) PARTY DOLL
D) HOUND DOG MAN

53. 1 x 1

THOMAS WAYNE IS BEST REMEMBERED FOR RECORDING THIS TRAGIC LOVE SONG BELOW BACK IN THE LATE 50'S.
A) TELL LAURA I LOVE HER
B) YOU CAN HAVE HER
C) THE END
D) TRAGEDY

54. 1 x 1

CHOOSE THE FEMALE MOUSEKETEER BELOW WHO HAD A HIT WITH "TALL PAUL" WITH THE BACKING OF *THE AFTERBEATS* AND WOULD GO ON TO DO BEACH PARTY MOVIES IN THE 60'S OPPOSITE *FRANKIE AVALON*.
A) CONNIE FRANCIS
B) SHELLEY FABARES
C) GALE STORM
D) ANNETTE FUNICELLO

55. 1 x 1

ANDY WILLIAMS RECORDED THIS ROMANTIC SONG BELOW ABOUT THEIR JOINING TOGETHER AS ONE ON THIS VERY SPECIAL OCCASION AND VOWING HE WOULD LOVE HER UNTIL FOREVER.
A) THE HAWAIIAN WEDDING SONG (KE KALI NEI AU)
B) CHAPEL OF LOVE
C) TO THE AISLE
D) I WISH THAT WE WERE MARRIED

56. 1 x 1

ANDY WILLIAMS CHARTED YET ANOTHER ABOUT WHAT HE CALLED HER BECAUSE OF HER FLYING AROUND AND WHAT HE WOULD DO TO HER TO MAKE HER STAY PUT, HOPEFULLY IN HIS ARMS.
A) DEVIL OR ANGEL
B) GOOD GOLLY, MISS MOLLY
C) LITTLE ANGEL EYES
D) BUTTERFLY

57. 1 x 1

TERESA BREWER CHARTED A SONG ABOUT WHAT FELL WHEN SHE FOUND HIM WITH ANOTHER AND HE THEN TOLD HER THAT THEIR LOVE AFFAIR WAS OVER.
A) CRY
B) TEARS ON MY PILLOW
C) LONELY TEARDROPS
D) A TEAR FELL

58. 2 x 1

TERESA BREWER ALSO RECORDED THESE TWO OTHER HITS BELOW.
ONE, WITH A COVER SONG OF *SAM COOKE'S,* ABOUT WHAT YOU HONESTLY DID.
AND THE OTHER, A TUNE OF *JOAN WEBER'S* ABOUT A LOVER WHO THEY WANTED TO BE FREE FROM.
NAME THOSE TWO HITS.
1) ________________
2) ______________________

59. **3 x 1**

THIS POP IDOL/TURNED ACTOR HAD NUMEROUS HITS INCLUDING "WHY" IN 1959 WHICH CLIMBED TO THE TOP OF THE CHARTS. NAME HIM, KNOWN FOR HIS BEACH PARTY MOVIES WITH ANNETTE FUNICELLO IN THE 60'S, AND THESE TWO OTHER BIG HITS BELOW, NUMBERS TWO AND THREE.
ONE, HIS NAME.
TWO, ABOUT WHEN A YOUNG GIRL GROWS UP AND STARTS WEARING NYLONS.
THREE, ABOUT A GODDESS WITH CHARM AND LOVE THAT HE'LL BE TRUE TO.

1) ________________
2) ______________________
3) ________

60. **1 x 1**

THE TEMPOS RECORDED THE ONLY MEMORABLE HIT OF THEIR CAREER THAT ANOTHER GROUP, *THE HAPPENINGS,* WOULD ALSO GO ON TO CHART IN THE 60'S ABOUT A SUMMER VACATION COMING TO AN END.

A) HERE COMES SUMMER
B) SEE YOU IN SEPTEMBER
C) SUMMERTIME
D) C'MON EVERYBODY

TOTAL POINTS. **100 x 1 = 100**

POP ROCKERS-QUIZ # 2

1. **1 x 5**

JOHNNY MATHIS RECORDED WHAT SONG BELOW REFERRING TO HIMSELF AS A HELPLESS KITTEN?

A) STARDUST
B) MISTY
C) FOR YOUR LOVE
D) MISTY BLUE

2. **1 x 5**

THE FOUR ACES HAD THIS SONG BELOW ABOUT WHAT THEY WERE DOING AS THE GIRLS PASSED BY. IT WAS ORIGINALLY A *MILLS BROTHERS* RECORDING ALSO DURING THE 50'S.

A) WISHIN' AND HOPIN'
B) STANDING ON THE CORNER
C) A PRAYER AND A JUKEBOX
D) THERE GOES MY BABY

3. **1 x 5**

JO STAFFORD, A POP FEMALE ARTIST IN THE EARLY 50'S, CHARTED WHAT SONG THAT *DEAN MARTIN* WOULD ALSO RECORD, BUT WOULD GAIN MORE POPULARITY BY *THE DUPREES* IN THE EARLY 60'S ABOUT YOU BEING THEIRS?

A) YOU WERE MINE
B) WE BELONG TOGETHER
C) YOU BELONG TO ME
D) VOLARE

4. **1 x 5**

"THE TENNESSEE WALTZ" WAS ALSO A PRE-ROCKER ABOUT PAINFUL MEMORIES OF LOSING HER DARLING TO AN OLD FRIEND. WHO WAS THE FEMALE ARTIST WHO WOULD GAIN HER INITIAL RECOGNITION FROM IT?

A) DEBBIE REYNOLDS
B) DELLA REESE
C) BRENDA LEE
D) PATTI PAGE

5. **1 x 5**

ROBIN LUKE ACHIEVED HIS STARDOM BY RECORDING THIS SONG BELOW ABOUT THAT CHARMING GIRL IN HIS DREAMS WHO LEFT HIM AND HE'S SO EMPTY WITHOUT AND HOPES SHE'LL RETURN TO HIM.

A) LITTLE DARLIN'
B) DARLING LORRAINE
C) SUSIE DARLIN'
D) WAKE UP LITTLE SUSIE

6. **2 x 5**

TONY BENNETT, THE POP AND JAZZ SINGER OF THE PRE-ROCK AND ROLL ERA, CHARTED THESE TWO SONGS BELOW.
ONE, ABOUT SOMETHING THAT KEEPS US APART AND SO VERY COLD. IT WAS ORIGINALLY A *HANK WILLIAMS* COUNTRY HIT SONG.
TWO, ABOUT HIS RISE FROM MEAGER BELONGINGS TO FORTUNE.
NAME THEM.

1) ____________________
2) ________________

7. **1 x 5**

GALE STORM, THE ACTRESS, WOULD ACHIEVE HER MUSICAL STARDOM WITH WHAT SONG BELOW ABOUT THE KNOCK ON HER DOOR THAT SHE REFUSED TO OPEN? IN THE EARLY 70'S *DAVE EDMUNDS* WOULD GO ON TO RECORD HIS RENDITION OF IT.

A) KNOCK THREE TIMES
B) I HEAR YOU KNOCKING
C) KNOCKIN' ON HEAVENS' DOOR
D) KEEP A KNOCKIN'

8. **1 x 5**

CARL DOBKINS JR CHARTED THE BIGGEST HIT OF HIS CAREER IN THE LATE 50'S WHERE HE PROCLAIMED TO HIS DARLING THAT HIS LOVE WAS TRUE AND THAT HE LOVED NO OTHER DESPITE WHAT THAT ENVIOUS FELLA HAD TOLD HER.

A) BIRD DOG
B) MY HEART IS AN OPEN BOOK
C) BOOK OF LOVE
D) IT'S ONLY MAKE BELIEVE

9. **1 x 5**

WHAT WHITE FEMALE ARTIST HAD A BUNCH OF HITS IN THE MID TO LATE 50'S INCLUDING THESE TWO COVER SONGS, "TWEEDLE DEE" ORIGINALLY BY *LAVERN BAKER* AND "DANCE WITH ME HENRY (WALLFLOWER)", TITLE CHANGED FROM "ROLL WITH ME HENRY" THAT WAS AN *ETTA JAMES* RECORDING?

A) DEBBIE REYNOLDS
B) GEORGIA GIBBS
C) CONNIE FRANCIS
D) LESLIE GORE

10. **1 x 5**

JIM LOWE WILL ALWAYS BE REMEMBERED FOR CHARTING THIS SONG BELOW BACK IN 1956 ABOUT A CERTAIN DOOR.

A) THE GREEN DOOR
B) BEHIND CLOSED DOORS
C) AT MY FRONT DOOR (CRAZY LITTLE MAMA)
D) WHO'S THAT KNOCKIN'

11. **1 x 5**

THE FOUR FRESHMAN RECORDED WHAT SONG THAT WAS ALSO CHARTED BY *THE ROVER BOYS* ABOUT A CERTAIN CELEBRATION?

A) TO THE AISLE
B) HAVING A PARTY
C) PAPA LOVES MAMBO
D) GRADUATION DAY

12. **1 x 5**

THE ELEGANTS FROM STATEN ISLAND, NY, RECORDED A SONG BASED ON A NURSERY RHYME ABOUT GRANTING HIM A WISH WITH A LOVER OF HIS OWN. THOUGH IT WOULD BE THEIR ONE AND ONLY, IT HAD THE DISTINCTION OF REACHING THE TOP OF THE CHARTS AND ELEVATING THEM TO STARDOM.

A) THE ANGELS LISTENED IN
B) LITTLE STAR
C) WHEN YOU WISH UPON A STAR
D) WISHIN' AND HOPIN'

13. **1 x 5**

KAY STARR'S BIGGEST CHARTED HIT WAS THIS ROCK AND ROLL TITLED SONG BELOW BACK IN 1956.
A) ROCK AND ROLL WALTZ
B) ROCK AND ROLL IS HERE TO STAY
C) (WE'RE GONNA) ROCK AROUND THE CLOCK
D) ROCK & ROLL MUSIC

14. **4 x 5**

THE CREW-CUTS, A WHITE QUARTET GROUP OUT OF CANADA, WERE MOST NOTABLE FOR THEIR COVER RENDITIONS OF R&B SONGS. MATCH THESE FOUR COVER SONGS WITH THE ORIGINAL R&B ARTIST.

	SONG		ORIGINAL R&B ARTIST		
1.	**SH-BOOM**	**A)**	**THE PENGUINS**	1.	
2.	**EARTH ANGEL**	**B)**	**AL HIBBLER**	2.	
3.	**A STORY UNTOLD**	**C)**	**THE CHORDS**	3.	
4.	**UNCHAINED MELODY**	**D)**	**THE NUTMEGS**	4.	

15. **2 x 5**

THE MCGUIRE SISTERS, THREE FAMILY MEMBERS, *PHYLLIS, CHRISTINE* AND *DOROTHY*, CHARTED NUMEROUS SONGS IN THE 50'S INCLUDING THESE TWO NUMBER ONE HITS BELOW.
ONE, AN ORIGINAL *MOONGLOWS* HIT SONG WHICH THEY DID AS A COVER ABOUT THE GENUINE FEELING THAT THEY HAD FOR THEIR GUY.
TWO, ABOUT WHAT THEY HAD IN THE MORNING AND EVENING THAT THEY COMPARED TO HONEY.
1) ____________
2) ____________

TOTAL POINTS. **20 x 5 = 100**

POP ROCKERS-BONUS

1.

"THE BIG HURT" WAS A SONG BY WHAT FEMALE ARTIST BELOW ABOUT HEART BREAK ROMANCE?
A) TIMI YURO
B) BRENDA LEE
C) MISS TONI FISHER
D) CONNIE FRANCIS

COUNTRY ROCKERS

1. **4 x 2**

NAME THESE FOUR HITS BY *BILL HALEY AND HIS COMETS,* THE COUNTRY & WESTERN GROUP, AND ONE OF THE FOUNDING FATHERS OF ROCK 'N ROLL.
ONE, WHAT HE TOLD HIS GATOR THE NEXT TIME THEY MET, A POPULAR SLANG EXPRESSION.
TWO, A CLOCK TITLED SONG THAT WAS FEATURED IN THE MOVIE 'BLACKBOARD JUNGLE' STARRING GLENN FORD, SIDNEY POITIER AND VIC MORROW THAT BECAME THE FIRST NUMBER ONE SONG OF THE ROCK AND ROLL ERA. ALSO THE THEME SONG FOR 'THE HAPPY DAY' TV SITCOM STARRING HENRY WINKLER AND RON HOWARD IN THE 80'S.
THREE, WITH A COVER SONG OF *JOE TURNER'S,* ABOUT A GIRL WHO HE DEMANDED WORK THOSE POTS AND PANS.
FOUR, ABOUT HIS CRAZY CHICK WHO HE CLAIMED WASN'T SKINNY BUT SIMPLY TALL.

1) ____________________
2) ____________________
3) ____________________
4) ____________________

2. **1 x 2**

DON GIBSON, THE SINGER/SONGWRITER, CHARTED THIS COUNTRY HIT THAT *RAY CHARLES* WOULD GO ON TO RECORD IN THE 60'S ABOUT HIS STRONG DESIRE FOR YOU THAT HE COULDN'T STOP NO HOW.

A) I CAN'T STOP LOVING YOU
B) OH LONESOME ME
C) LONESOME TOWN
D) I WANT TO WALK YOU HOME

3. **4 x 2**

IN THE 50'S THE SUN RECORD LABEL HAD THE 'MILLION DOLLAR QUARTET'. NAME THOSE FOUR GUYS BY COMPLETING THE INITIALS PROVIDED BELOW.

1) E P - 1) ____________________
2) C P - 2) ____________________
3) J L L - 3) ____________________
4) J C - 4) ____________________

4. **1 x 2**

"THE BATTLE OF NEW ORLEANS" WAS A POPULAR HIT BY THIS MALE ARTIST WHO WOULD GO ON TO RECORD SMASH HITS FOR OTHER SOUNDTRACK MOVIES INCLUDING "SINK THE BISMARCK" AND "NORTH TO ALASKA" IN THE 60'S.

A) JOHNNY HORTON
B) GENE PITNEY
C) JOHNNY CASH
D) FREDDY CANNON

5. **1 x 2**

THE COUNTRY SINGER *SONNY JAMES* AND THE ACTOR *TAB HUNTER,* SEPARATELY CHARTED THE SAME SONG ALMOST SIMULTANEOUSLY. CHOOSE IT, ABOUT FIRST LOVE AND WHAT ONE KISS CAN REVEAL. *TAB'S* VERSION WOULD REACH TO THE TOP OF THE CHARTS WITH *SONNY'S* VERSION AT THE NUMBER TWO SPOT.

A) YOUNG LOVE
B) DEVOTED TO YOU
C) KISSES SWEETER THAN WINE
D) IT'S ALL IN THE GAME

6. **1 x 2**

WHAT ARE THE FIRST NAMES OF *THE EVERLY BROTHERS*, THE POPULAR COUNTRY DUO?

__________&__________

7. **1 x 2**

WHAT WAS THE NICKNAME BESTOWED UPON *JERRY LEE LEWIS*?
A) THE ICE MAN
B) MR EXCITEMENT
C) THE KILLER
D) MR PERSONALITY

8. **1 x 2**

BILL HAYES HAD A WALT DISNEY TV THEME SONG ABOUT THAT FAMOUS AMERICAN FRONTIERSMAN. *FESS PARKER,* THE ACTOR TO PLAY THE CHARACTER PART, WOULD ALSO RECORD IT. NAME THIS BALLAD SONG ABOUT THE KING OF THE FRONTIER WHO WOULD LATER DIE AT THE ALAMO.

____

9. **1 x 2**

LINK WRAY & HIS RAY MEN HAD THIS TV THEME SONG BELOW ABOUT A WESTERN WHICH GAVE CLINT EASTWOOD HIS PREMIER STARDOM. IT WOULD ALSO BE PERFORMED BY *DAN ACKROYD* AND *JOHN BELUSHI* IN THEIR BLOCKBUSTER MOVIE 'THE BLUES BROTHERS' IN THE EARLY 80'S.
A) WESTERN MOVIES
B) THE BALLAD OF PALADIN
C) RAW-HIDE
D) THE MAGNIFICENT SEVEN

10. **1 x 2**

CHOOSE THE MALE ARTIST BELOW WHO HAD A MAJOR HIT WITH "IT'S ONLY MAKE BELIEVE" ABOUT HIS HOPES AND DREAMS ONLY FOR YOU. HE WOULD GO ON TO BECOME A BIG COUNTRY ARTIST LASTING CLOSE TO FOUR DECADES.
A) TIM CONWAY
B) CONWAY TWITTY
C) MARTY ROBBINS
D) BUDDY HOLLY

11. **1 x 2**

IN 1959 *JERRY WALLACE* CHARTED THE BIGGEST HIT OF HIS CARRER WITH WHAT SONG BELOW?
A) KANSAS CITY
B) EL PASO
C) PRIMROSE LANE
D) TALLAHASSEE LASSIE

12. **1 x 2**

PATSY CLINE HAD THIS ONE MAJOR HIT IN THE LATE 50'S ABOUT HER STROLLING LATE ONE EVENING HOPING TO FIND YOU. IT WOULD BE FEATURED IN THE SOUNDTRACK MOVIE 'SWEET DREAMS' IN 1985 STARRING JESSICA LANGE AS PATSY AND ED HARRIS AS PATSY'S HUSBAND.
A) I WANT TO WALK YOU HOME
B) WALKIN' AFTER MIDNIGHT
C) IN THE MIDNIGHT HOUR
D) I'M WALKIN'

13. **1 x 2**

BUDDY KNOX WITH THE RHYTHM ORCHIDS CHARTED A NUMBER ONE HIT SONG IN 1957 THAT ALL MEN MUST HAVE A PARTY GAL. CHOOSE THAT NUMBER ONE HIT.
A) PEANUTS
B) QUEEN OF THE HOP
C) GOOD LUCK CHARM
D) PARTY DOLL

14. **1 x 2**

ROY ORBISON WROTE A SONG AS A TRIBUTE TO HIS WIFE CALLED "CLAUDETTE". NAME THE YOUNG DUO WHO WOULD RECORD IT.
A) JOHNNY & JOE
B) THE EVERLY BROTHERS
C) EYDIE GORME & STEVE LAWRENCE
D) DON & JUAN

15. **5 x 2**

NAME THESE FIVE HITS BY THE LEGENDARY *BUDDY HOLLY AND THE CRICKETS,* WHO WERE A BIG INFLUENCE ON MANY ARTISTS INCLUDING *THE BEATLES*.
ONE, ABOUT THE DAY HE CLAIMED WOULD NEVER BE.
TWO, ABOUT HIS LOVE AND KISSES THAT YOU'LL BE LACKING.
THREE, ABOUT A LOVE THAT WILL ENDURE AND NOT DISAPPEAR.
FOUR, ABOUT THAT GUY AND THE DIAMOND RING THAT MIGHT NOT SHINE, AND THE ACTIONS HE WOULD HAVE TO TAKE.
FIVE, ABOUT A PRETTY GIRL THAT MAKES HIM BLUE BECAUSE HE WANTS HER SO BADLY.
1) ____________________________
2) ____________!
3) _____________________
4) _________________
5) _________________

16. **1 x 2**

BUDDY HOLLY CHARTED THREE OTHER HITS BELOW. WHICH ONE WAS **NOT** HIS?
A) SHOUT (PARTS 1 AND 2)
B) RAVE ON
C) MAYBE BABY
D) EVERYDAY

17. **7 x 2**

NAME THESE SEVEN POPULAR HITS BY *THE EVERLY BROTHERS* IN THE 50'S.
ONE, ABOUT A GIRL NAMED SUSIE WHO WITH HER BOYFRIEND FELL ASLEEP AT THE MOVIE THEATRE.
TWO, ABOUT THAT SMART ALECK WHO'S A CERTAIN DOG.
THREE, WORRIES CAUSED BY MY LOVE FOR NOT BEING TRUE.
FOUR, ABOUT A DREAM TO MAKE YOU MINE.
FIVE, ABOUT BEING DEDICATED AND FAITHFUL TO YOU TIL THE END OF TIME.
SIX, ABOUT THAT KISS WHICH TURNED HIS LIFE AROUND.
SEVEN, ABOUT DEPARTED LOVE BECAUSE SHE LEFT HIM FOR ANOTHER AND IT MADE HIM BLUE AND IN TEARS.
1) _____________________________
2) ______________
3) ______________
4) ______________________________________
5) ______________________
6) _________________________
7) ___________________

18. **1 x 2**

ROY ORBISON, THE SINGER/SONGWRITER, HAD AN EARLY COUNTRY HIT WITH WHAT SONG BELOW IN 1956 WITH THE SUN RECORD LABEL COMPANY BEFORE HIS DEPARTURE TO JOIN THE MONUMENT LABEL?
A) OOBY DOOBY
B) BURNING BRIDGES
C) SUGARTIME
D) I WALK THE LINE

19. **3 x 2**

NAME THESE THREE POPULAR HITS BY *JERRY LEE LEWIS*, THE COUNTRY ROCKER WELL KNOWN FOR HIS PIANO PLAYING ABILITIES.
ONE, A FLAMING HIT SONG ABOUT WANTING TO LOVE YOU THE WAY YOU SHOULD.
TWO, ABOUT A CONTINUOUS MOTION AND SOME WIGGLING AS WELL.
THREE, HOW YOU LEAVE HIM OUT OF BREATH.
1) ____________________
2) ____________________________________
3) ______________

20. **1 x 2**

JOHNNY CASH, THE POPULAR COUNTRY SINGER, CHARTED WHAT SONG PROCLAIMING THAT YOUR LOVE WAS HIS MOTIVATION FOR DOING RIGHT?
A) WALK RIGHT IN
B) I WALK THE LINE
C) WALK LIKE A MAN
D) I WANT TO WALK YOU HOME

21. **1 x 2**

WHO WERE THE OTHER TWO ARTISTS WHO DIED ALONG SIDE OF *BUDDY HOLLY* IN THAT FATEFUL CRASH ON FEBRUARY 3, 1959, THE DAY THE MUSIC DIED?
A) RITCHIE VALENS & DION
B) THE BIG BOPPER & WAYLON JENNINGS
C) THE BIG BOPPER & RITCHIE VALENS
D) RITCHIE VALENS & JOHNNY HORTON

22. **1 x 2**

IN THE LATE 50'S *BOBBY HELMS* WITH THE BACKING OF *'THE ANITA KERR SINGERS'* CHARTED HIS FIRST BIG HIT ABOUT SOMEONE SPECIAL BROUGHT DOWN TO KEEP AN EYE OVER HIM. IT'S A SONG THAT *THE VOGUES* WOULD ALSO RECORD IN THE 60'S EQUALLY POPULAR.
A) DREAM LOVER
B) MY SPECIAL ANGEL
C) FOR YOUR LOVE
D) THE ANGELS LISTENED IN

23. **1 x 2**

BOBBY HELMS CHARTED ANOTHER WITH THIS CLASSIC CHRISTMAS SONG BELOW THAT WOULD BECOME THE BIGGEST OF HIS CAREER.
A) ROCKIN' AROUND THE CHRISTMAS TREE
B) THE LITTLE DRUMMER BOY
C) JINGLE BELL ROCK
D) THE CHRISTMAS SONG "CHESTNUTS ROASTING ON AN OPEN FIRE"

50'S

24. **1 x 2**

EDDIE COCHRAN HAD A MAJOR HIT ABOUT WORKING DURING THE SUMMER TO EARN SOME MONEY.

A) SUMMERTIME BLUES
B) WORKING IN THE COAL MINE
C) SUMMER IN THE CITY
D) HERE COMES SUMMER

25. **1 x 2**

GENE VINCENT AND HIS BLUE CAPS RECORDED THIS SONG BELOW THAT BECAME A POPULAR DANCE NUMBER ABOUT HIS BABY LOVE.

A) BE-BOP BABY
B) BE-BOP-A-LULA
C) AT THE HOP
D) SHIMMY, SHIMMY, KO-KO-BOP

26. **1 x 2**

DON GIBSON THE SINGER/SONGWRITER CHARTED THIS SONG ABOUT A CERTAIN BLUE FEELING THAT HE COULDN'T GET RID OF.

A) I CAN'T STOP LOVING YOU
B) BLUE BAYOU
C) OH LONESOME ME
D) SINGING THE BLUES

27. **1 x 2**

"A WHITE SPORT COAT (AND A PINK CARNATION)" WAS A TOP NUMBER TWO FOR THIS POPULAR COUNTRY ARTIST. THE SONG "EL PASO" WOULD BE ANOTHER BIG HIT FOR HIM TWO AND A HALF YEARS LATER. WHO WAS THAT POPULAR COUNTRY ARTIST BELOW?

A) JOHNNY HORTON
B) MARTY ROBBINS
C) JOHNNY CASH
D) GENE PITNEY

28. **1 x 2**

IN 1956 *CARL PERKINS* RECORDED WHAT SONG THAT *ELVIS* WOULD ALSO GO ON TO CHART IN THE SAME YEAR, WHERE YOU CAN DO ALMOST ANYTHING BUT STAY CLEAR AWAY FROM HIS PRECIOUS SHOES? *ELVIS'* VERSION HELPED GENERATE A LOT OF ROYALTY FOR *PERKINS* WHO WAS THE SONGWRITER.

A) BLUE SUEDE SHOES
B) PINK SHOE LACES
C) BOOGIE SHOES
D) THESE BOOTS ARE MADE FOR WALKIN'

29. **4 x 2**

HANK WILLIAMS, THE VERY POPULAR COUNTRY SINGER/SONGWRITER, RECORDED MANY COUNTRY HITS PRIOR TO HIS EARLY DEATH. NAME THESE FOUR BELOW.
ONE, ABOUT A CERTAIN FROZEN HEART, THAT *TONY BENNETT* WOULD ALSO CHART.
TWO, HIS LONESOME HIT SONG THAT CAN BRING ON TEARS. IT WOULD BE RECORDED BY *BJ THOMAS* IN THE 60'S AND THEN BY *ELVIS* IN THE 70'S.
THREE, ABOUT AN UNFAITHFUL LOVER WITH A ROAMING HEART.
FOUR, ABOUT A CERTAIN GAL WHOSE HOT AND GOT IT GOING ON AND THE MAIN REASON FOR HIM TO DITCH THAT LITTLE BLACK BOOK.

1) ____________________
2) ______________________________
3) ______________________
4) ____________________

50'S **TOTAL POINTS.** **50 x 2 = 100**

COUNTRY ROCKERS BONUS

1.

THIS MOVIE FEATURED A SONG OF THE SAME TITLE STARRING GARY COOPER, GRACE KELLY, LLOYD BRIDGES AND SHEB WOOLEY. *TEX RITTER,* THE COUNTRY SINGER AND COWBOY ACTOR, WAS THE ORIGINAL ARTIST TO CHART THE MOVIE THEME SONG IN THE EARLY 50'S AND THEN *FRANKIE LAINE* SHORTLY AFTER AND STILL LATER BY *CONNIE FRANCES* IN THE 60'S. CHOOSE THAT TRIPLE HITTER BELOW.

A) WESTERN MOVIES
B) HIGH NOON (DO NOT FORSAKE ME)
C) RAW-HIDE
D) RUNNING BEAR

2.

THE BROWNS, A FAMILY ACT CONSISTING OF TWO SISTERS AND ONE BROTHER, RECORDED THIS BELL TITLED SONG BELOW. IT WAS THEIR FIRST AND ALSO BIGGEST THAT WOULD REACH THE TOP OF THE CHARTS IN THE LATE 50'S.

A) CHURCH BELLS MAY RING
B) THE THREE BELLS
C) WHISPERING BELLS
D) THE BELLS OF ST CECILA

3.

BILLY GRAMMER RECORDED THIS SONG BELOW ABOUT WHAT HE CLAIMED THAT HE HAD TO DO.

A) I WALK THE LINE
B) I'M WALKIN'
C) GOTTA TRAVEL ON
D) DON'T LET GO

ROCKERS

1. **1 x 10**

FREDDY CANNON CHARTED A SONG ABOUT A CERTAIN GAL OF HIS WHO LIKES TO DO THE BOP, THE STROLL AND EVEN ROCK AND ROLL.
A) QUEEN OF THE HOP
B) TALLAHASSEE LASSIE
C) MY ANGEL BABY
D) AT THE HOP

2. **1 x 10**

FREDDY CANNON HAD ANOTHER BIG HIT WITH WHAT NEW ORLEANS TITLED SONG BELOW?
A) THE BATTLE OF NEW ORLEANS
B) NEW ORLEANS
C) WAY DOWN YONDER IN NEW ORLEANS
D) WALKING TO NEW ORLEANS

3. **1 x 10**

GUY MITCHELL RECORDED A TOP OF THE CHARTS HIT SONG ABOUT WHAT SHE HAD HIM DOING, SOMETHING HE THOUGHT HE'D NEVER LOSE NOR STAY WITHOUT THAT HAD HIM CRYING ALL NIGHT LONG. WHAT WAS THAT CHART TOPPER?
A) SINGING THE BLUES
B) BLUE MOON
C) BLUE MOON OVER KENTUCKY
D) I ALMOST LOST MY MIND

4. **1 x 10**

GUY MITCHELL ALSO CHARTED WHAT OTHER NUMBER ONE HIT SONG ABOUT HEARTACHES?
A) HEARTACHE TONIGHT
B) HEARTACHES BY THE NUMBER
C) HEARTBREAKER
D) HEARTBREAK HOTEL

5. **4 x 10**

NAME THESE FOUR POPULAR HITS BY *JIMMIE RODGERS*.
ONE, ABOUT WHAT THE LORD CREATED.
TWO, SOMETHING SHE HAD THAT WAS SWEETER THAN A CERTAIN ALCOHOLIC DRINK.
THREE, ABOUT A HOUSE ON A SLOPE.
FOUR, ASKING THE REASONS THEY HAVE TO MEET IN HIDING WHENEVER THEY KISS.
1) ______________
2) ________________________________
3) ______________
4) ______________

6. **2 x 10**

DANNY & THE JUNIORS CHARTED THESE TWO BIG PARTY HITS BELOW.
ONE, THEIR ROCK ANTHEM SONG ABOUT WHAT THEY CLAIMED WOULD LIVE ON FOREVER IN HISTORY.
TWO, ABOUT THAT PLACE WHERE ONE CAN GO TO ROCK AND ROLL AND DO ALL THE DANCES AND THE MUSIC IS JUST RIGHT.
NAME THOSE TWO BIG PARTY HITS.
1) ____________________________________
2) ________________

TOTAL POINTS. **10 x 10 = 100**

ROCKERS-BONUS

1.

JACK SCOTT'S BIGGEST CHARTED HIT IN THE 50'S WAS THIS ROMANTIC SONG ABOUT HIS PRAYERS BEING FULFILLED BECAUSE THE ALMIGHTY HAD SENT YOU. WHAT WAS THAT ROMANTIC HIT?

A) MY TRUE LOVE
B) MY LOVE
C) THE ANGELS LISTENED IN
D) MY PRAYER

2.

THE IMPALAS HAD THIS ONE BIG CLAIM TO FAME SONG THAT WOULD REACH THE NUMBER TWO SPOT ABOUT RUNNING HOME TO APOLOGIZE AND HOPING THAT HE WOULD BE ALLOWED TO STAY. WHAT WAS THAT RUNNERUP HIT?

A) RUNAWAY
B) STAY
C) SORRY (I RAN ALL THE WAY HOME)
D) I'M SORRY

MISC (NOVELTY, FOLK, FOREIGN & INSTRUMENTALS)-QUIZ # 1

1. **1 x 2**

THE KINGSTON TRIO, THE LEGENDARY FOLK BAND, CHARTED A POPULAR SONG ABOUT A MOUNTAINEER WHO WAS DOOMED TO BE HUNG FOR MURDER. IT WOULD BE THEIR FIRST AND MOST NOTABLE THAT WOULD RACE TO THE TOP OF THE CHARTS IN 1958.

A) TOWN WITHOUT PITY
B) NORTH TO ALASKA
C) TOM DOOLEY
D) BIG BAD JOHN

2. **1 x 2**

LAURIE LONDON, A TEENAGE BOY, IS PRIMARILY REMEMBERED FOR CHARTING THIS NUMBER TWO HIT SONG ON THE CHARTS ABOUT SOMETHING HE HAD IN HIS HANDS. THE SONG, A GOSPEL STANDARD, WAS ORIGINALLY FEATURED DECADES EARLIER IN THAT OLD CLASSIC MOVIE 'SERGEANT YORK' STARRING GARY COOPER AND WALTER BRENNAN.

A) HE'S GOT THE WHOLE WORLD (IN HIS HANDS)
B) SWING LOW, SWEET CHARIOT
C) AMAZING GRACE
D) HE

3. **4 x 2**

DURING THE 50'S THERE WERE AT LEAST FOUR POPULAR HITS WITH THE NUMBER 16 IN THE TITLE OF THE SONG. FROM THE RECORDING ARTIST BELOW NAME THEIR 16 TITLED HIT SONG.

ARTIST		16 HIT SONG
1) CHUCK BERRY	-	**1)** ____________________
2) THE CRESTS	-	**2)** __________
3) SAM COOKE	-	**3)** ____________
4) 'TENNESSEE' ERNIE FORD	-	**4)** _________

4. **8 x 2**

MATCH THE ARTIST WITH THEIR 'ROCK' OR 'ROCK 'N' ROLL' TITLED SONG.

	ARTIST		'ROCK' TITLED SONG		
1.	**KAY STARR**	**A)**	**(WE'RE GONNA) ROCK AROUND THE CLOCK**	1.	
2.	**BOBBY HELMS**	**B)**	**JAILHOUSE ROCK**	2.	
3.	**DANNY & THE JUNIORS**	**C)**	**ROCK & ROLL MUSIC**	3.	
4.	**ELVIS**	**D)**	**JINGLE BELL ROCK**	4.	
5.	**BILL HALEY & HIS COMETS**	**E)**	**ROCK AND ROLL IS HERE TO STAY**	5.	
6.	**CHUCK BERRY**	**F)**	**REELIN' AND ROCKIN'**	6.	
7.	**JERRY LEWIS**	**G)**	**ROCK-A-BYE YOUR BABY WITH A DIXIE MELODY**	7.	
8.	**CHUCK BERRY**	**H)**	**ROCK AND ROLL WALTZ**	8.	

5. **1 x 2**

SANTO & JOHNNY, A BROTHER DUO ACT, RECORDED WHAT BIG INSTRUMENTAL NUMBER BELOW ABOUT A CERTAIN WALK.

A) I'M WALKIN'
B) SLEEP WALK
C) I WANT TO WALK YOU HOME
D) WALK IN THE BLACK FOREST

6. 1 x 2

THE '*HARRY SIMEONE CHORALE*' CHARTED A POPULAR CHRISTMAS SONG THAT HAD THE INFANT 'JESUS' SMILING.
A) THE CHRISTMAS SONG
B) JINGLE BELL ROCK
C) THE LITTLE DRUMMER BOY
D) RUDOLPH THE RED NOSED REINDEER

7. 6 x 2

MATCH THESE SIX 'CAR' TITLED GROUPS WITH THE SONG THEY CHARTED IN THE 50'S.

	CAR GROUP		SONG		
1.	THE EL DORADOS	A)	TEARS ON MY PILLOW	1.	
2.	THE CADILLACS	B)	SORRY (I RAN ALL THE WAY HOME)	2.	
3.	THE FLEETWOODS	C)	AT MY FRONT DOOR	3.	
4.	THE IMPALAS	D)	SPEEDO	4.	
5.	THE IMPERIALS	E)	MR BLUE	5.	
6.	THE CAPRIS	F)	THERE'S A MOON OUT TONIGHT	6.	

8. 1 x 2

IN 1956 *BUCHANAN & GOODMAN,* ACTING AS REPORTERS, HAD THIS NOVELTY SONG ABOUT SPACE CREATURES VISITING EARTH DURING PRESIDENT EISENHOWER'S REIGN AND FEATURING PARTS OF ROCK AND ROLL HIT SONGS OF THE DAY.
A) THE CHIPMUNK SONG
B) THE FLYING SAUCER (PARTS 1 & 2)
C) THE PURPLE PEOPLE EATER
D) SEE YOU LATER, ALLIGATOR

9. 1 x 2

THIS MEXICAN FOLK TUNE WAS MADE POPULAR BY *RITCHIE VALENS* IN 1959. IT WOULD ALSO BE RECORDED IN THE LATE 80'S BY THE '*LOS LOBOS*' FOR THE MOVIE SOUNDTRACK OF *RITCHIE*'S LIFE STORY, STARRING LOU DIAMOND PHILLIPS AS *RITCHIE VALENS*. BOTH VERSIONS SUNG TOTALLY IN SPANISH. WHAT WAS THAT POPULAR FOLK TUNE?
A) LA BAMBA
B) ERES TU
C) EL WATUSI
D) QUE SERA, SERA (WHATEVER WILL BE, WILL BE)

10. 1 x 2

WHAT WAS THE NAME OF THIS POPULAR ITALIAN SONG RECORDED BY *DOMENICO MODUGNO* THAT WOULD CLIMB TO THE TOP OF THE CHARTS AND THAT BOTH *DEAN MARTIN* WOULD CHART IN THE 50'S BILINGUALLY, ENGLISH AND ITALIAN, AND *BOBBY RYDELL* IN THE 60'S TOTALLY IN THE ENGLISH VERSION?
A) PEPINO THE ITALIAN MOUSE
B) NEL BLU DIPINTO DI BLU (VOLARE)
C) PAPA LOVES MAMBO
D) LAZY MARY

11. **1 x 2**

THE TV WESTERN 'HAVE GUN WILL TRAVEL', STARRING RICHARD BOONE, FEATURED A THEME SONG RECORDED BY *JOHNNY WESTERN*. NAME THAT BALLAD SONG THAT WAS SUNG BY THE YOUNG BOYS, RIVER PHOENIX, COREY FELDMAN AND JERRY O'CONNELL, IN THE MOVIE 'STAND BY ME' IN THE MID 80'S.
A) BALLAD OF PALADIN
B) THE BALLAD OF DAVY CROCKETT
C) ZORRO
D) WHEN JOHNNY COMES MARCHING HOME

12. **1 x 2**

IN THE 50'S THERE WERE A NUMBER OF TV SHOWS THAT FEATURED AMATEUR TALENT SHOWS THAT HELPED DISCOVER FUTURE STARS SUCH AS *LITTLE GLADYS KNIGHT, STEVE LAWRENCE, TONY BENNETT, PATSY CLINE* AND SO FORTH. CHOOSE BELOW THE TV PROGRAM THAT WAS **NOT** USED FOR THIS PURPOSE.
A) ARTHUR GODFREY TALENT SCOUT SHOW
B) TED MACK'S AMATEUR HOUR
C) ED SULLIVAN'S 'TOAST OF THE TOWN'
D) YOUR HIT PARADE

13. **1 x 2**

WHAT WAS *JOHNNY PRESTON'S* TOP OF THE CHARTS HIT SONG ABOUT HIS AFFECTION FOR LITTLE WHITE DOVE?
A) RUNNING BEAR
B) MR CUSTER
C) BIRD DOG
D) FEVER

14. **1 x 2**

SCREAMIN' JAY HAWKINS RECORDED THIS SONG BELOW THAT HE WOULD PERFORM COMING OUT OF A COFFIN PROCLAIMING WHAT HE COULD DO TO YOU.
A) WITCH DOCTOR
B) LOVE POTION NO. 9
C) I PUT A SPELL ON YOU
D) WITCHCRAFT

15. **1 x 2**

'MY FAIR LADY' WAS ORIGINALLY A BROADWAY MUSICAL IN THE 50'S CO-STARRING JULIE ANDREWS AND REX HARRISON, AND LATER MADE INTO A MOVIE. WHAT WAS THE NAME OF THE SONG THAT WAS FEATURED IN THAT MUSICAL ABOUT DANCE?
A) I COULD HAVE DANCED ALL NIGHT
B) WHEN YOU DANCE
C) DANCE WITH ME
D) DO YOU WANT TO DANCE

16. **1 x 2**

IN 1958 *AUGIE RIOS* CHARTED BELOW THIS POPULAR CHRISTMAS SONG THAT CONTAINED BOTH ENGLISH AND SPANISH LYRICS.
A) ROCKIN' AROUND THE CHRISTMAS TREE
B) JINGLE BELL ROCK
C) DONDE ESTA' SANTA CLAUS
D) THE LITTLE DRUMMER BOY

17. 1 x 2

THIS POPULAR DISC JOCKEY ORIGINALLY FROM CLEVELAND, OHIO, HELPED TO COIN AND PUSH THE PHRASE 'ROCK AND ROLL' INTO MAINSTREAM AMERICA. HE MC'D CONCERTS ALL OVER THE COUNTRY AND WAS LATER CHARGED WITH A PAYOLA SCANDLE THAT WOULD END HIS CAREER. WHO WAS HE?

A) ALAN FREED
B) MURRAY THE K
C) JOCKO HENDERSON
D) 'COUSIN' BRUCE MORROW

18. 1 x 2

PEREZ PRADO, THE BANDLEADER, HAD AT LEAST TWO BIG INSTRUMENTAL HITS IN THE 50'S. WHICH ONE BELOW WAS **NOT** HIS?

A) PATRICIA
B) CHERRY PINK AND APPLE BLOSSOM WHITE
C) SLEEP WALK

19. 1 x 2

DAVID SEVILLE, THE NOVELTY SINGER, HAD A TOP OF THE CHARTS HIT SONG ABOUT HIS FRIEND, A MEDICINE MAN, WHO ADVISED HIM ON WHAT ACTIONS TO TAKE.

A) MR CUSTER
B) LOVE POTION NO. 9
C) WITCH DOCTOR
D) MR LEE

20. 1 x 2

THIS GROUP BELOW HAD A BIG INSTRUMENTAL HIT CALLED "TEQUILA" THAT WOULD BE THEIR FIRST AND ALSO CLIMB TO THE TOP OF THE CHARTS. WHO WERE THEY?

A) PEREZ PRADO & HIS ORCHESTRA
B) THE CHAMPS
C) DUANE EDDY
D) SANTO & JOHNNY

21. 3 x 2

DAVID SEVILLE WAS THE CREATOR OF *THE CHIPMUNKS*. NAME THE THREE CHIPMUNKS BY COMPLETING THE INITIALS PROVIDED BELOW.

1) T - 1) ______________
2) A - 2) ________
3) S - 3) ________

22. 1 x 2

RAY ANTHONY, THE TALENTED TRUMPET PLAYER AND TV PERSONALITY, HAD A TV THEME HIT IN 1959 ABOUT A PRIVATE EYE, STARRING CRAIG STEVENS, WHOSE FIRST NAME WAS PETER. NAME IT.

____

23. 1 x 2

MARTIN DENNY HAD THIS POPULAR INSTRUMENTAL HIT BELOW THAT CONSISTED OF BIRD AND OTHER JUNGLE SOUNDS. CHOOSE IT BELOW.

A) QUIET VILLAGE
B) ROCKIN' ROBIN
C) ROCKIN' IN THE JUNGLE
D) THE LION SLEEPS TONIGHT

24. **1 x 2**

THE PLAYMATES HAD A BIG NOVELTY SONG ABOUT AN UNINTENTIONAL RACE BETWEEN A CADILLAC AND A LITTLE NASH RAMBLER. ALL THAT THE RAMBLER DRIVER WANTED WAS HELP TO CHANGE GEARS AND NOTHING ELSE.
A) HEY LITTLE COBRA
B) BEEP BEEP
C) 409
D) FUN, FUN, FUN

25. **1 x 2**

JAN & DEAN, THE TEEN DUO, CHARTED THIS SONG BELOW THAT CONTAINED INFANT BABBLING.
A) A WALKIN' MIRACLE
B) LITTLE BITTY PRETTY ONE
C) BABY TALK
D) BABY LOVE

26. **1 x 2**

THE *'ROYAL TEENS'* RECORDED THIS GIRL'S FASHION SONG ABOUT A CRAZY CHICK AND WHAT SHE WORE.
A) ITSY BITSY TEENIE WEENIE YELLOW POLKADOT BIKINI
B) HOT PANTS
C) SHORT SHORTS
D) DEVIL WITH A BLUE DRESS ON & GOOD GOLLY MISS MOLLY

27. **1 x 2**

THIS POPULAR TV HOST PREMIERED IN PHILADELPHIA ON JULY 9, 1956 WITH A PROGRAM THAT INFLUENCED US ALL WITH THIS NEW MUSIC KNOWN AS ROCK AND ROLL. HE WOULD SHOWCASE NEW SONGS, THE STARS OF THOSE NEW SONGS AND INTRODUCED US TO THE CURRENT DANCES AND UNAVOIDABLY THE NEW FASHION TRENDS THAT THE KIDS WERE SPORTING. THE SHOW WOULD THEN GO NATIONAL ON AUGUST 5, 1957. WHO WAS THIS EVERLASTING TEENAGER THAT REPLACED BOB HORN AND CHANGED THE NAME OF THE SHOW FROM 'BANDSTAND' TO 'AMERICAN BANDSTAND' FOR THE ABC NETWORK?
A) CLAY COLE
B) ALAN FREED
C) MURRAY THE K
D) DICK CLARK

28. **1 x 2**

THE DIAMONDS, THE POPULAR CANADIAN MALE GROUP, RECORDED A COVER SONG OF A *MAURICE WILLIAMS & THE ZODIACS* R&B TUNE ABOUT A DARLING HE PROMISED TO ONLY LOVE AND NEVER BETRAY AGAIN. IT WOULD GAIN THEM WIDER RECOGNITION OVER *THE ZODIACS* VERSION.
A) STAY
B) POETRY IN MOTION
C) LITTLE DARLIN'
D) DARLING LORRAINE

29. **1 x 2**

THE DIAMONDS ALSO CHARTED A POPULAR DANCE NUMBER SEEN MANY TIMES ON 'AMERICAN BANDSTAND'. THE KIDS WOULD FORM TWO LINES AND A COUPLE AT A TIME WOULD WALK DOWN THE MIDDLE OF THE FLOOR DOING THIS PARTICULAR DANCE STEP.
A) AT THE HOP
B) WILLIE AND THE HAND JIVE
C) THE STROLL
D) SPLISH SPLASH

30. **1 x 2**

CHOOSE THE TALENTED PIANIST BELOW WHO WAS CREDITED WITH CHARTING "AUTUMN LEAVES".

A) LIBERACE
B) DAVID ROSE
C) ROGER WILLIAMS
D) MERV GRIFFIN

31. **1 x 2**

ED BYRNES AND *CONNIE STEVENS,* BOTH OF '77 SUNSET STRIP' TV FAME, HAD THIS DUET SONG ABOUT ED'S CHARACTER PART WHO'S CONSTANTLY COMBING HIS HAIR. NAME THEIR KOOKIE TITLED HIT SONG.

____

32. **1 x 2**

ARCHIE BLEYER HAD A BIG TANGO HIT SONG ABOUT A PLACE ONE CAN GO UN-NOTICED AND WHISPER SWEET NOTHINGS AND TALK OF LOVE, OLE'. WHAT WAS THAT TANGO HIT SONG?

A) HERNANDO'S HIDEAWAY
B) MAMBO # 5
C) SO RARE
D) PATRICIA

33. **1 x 2**

JULIUS LA ROSA CHARTED THIS ITALIAN NOVELTY SONG BELOW DURING THE PRE-ROCK AND ROLL ERA.

A) EH CUMPARI
B) VOLARE
C) PEPINO THE ITALIAN MOUSE
D) QUE SERA SERA (WHATEVER WILL BE WILL BE)

TOTAL POINTS. **50 x 2 = 100**

MISC (NOVELTY, FOLK, FOREIGN & INSTRUMENTALS)-QUIZ # 2

1. **1 x 5**

IN 1958 THIS TALENTED BLACK JAZZ MUSICIAN, DRUMMER FOR VARIOUS GROUPS INCLUDING *CAB CALLOWAY*, HIT IT BIG WITH "TOPSY PT II". HE ALSO CHARTED WITH PARTS 1 AND III BUT NOT AS POPULAR. WHO WAS THAT TALENTED DRUMMER?
A) BUDDY RICH
B) BO DIDDLEY
C) COZY COLE
D) GENE CRUPA

2. **1 x 5**

BILL DOGGETT THE TALENTED MUSICIAN WHO PLAYED PIANO AND ORGAN FOR SOME OF THE JAZZ LEGENDS INCLUDING COUNT BASIE, CHARTED THE BIGGEST HIT OF HIS CAREER WITH WHAT INSTRUMENTAL NUMBER BELOW THAT WOULD JUST BARELY MISS HITTING THE TOP OF THE CHARTS AND LAND ON THE NUMBER TWO SPOT?
A) SLEEP WALK
B) HONKY TONK (PARTS 1 & 2)
C) PATRICIA
D) THE STRIPPER

3. **1 x 5**

THE OLYMPICS RECORDED WHAT SONG ABOUT THE WESTERNS THAT THEIR BABY JUST ADORED? WHICH INCLUDED CHEYENNE, MARSHALL DILLON, SUGAR FOOT, AND WYATT EARP, JUST TO NAME A FEW.
A) HAPPY TRAILS
B) WESTERN MOVIES
C) THE BALLAD OF PALADIN
D) THE MAGNIFICENT SEVEN

4. **1 x 5**

THE ETERNALS CHARTED THIS SONG ABOUT WHAT WAS HAPPENING IN THE JUNGLE. CHOOSE IT BELOW.
A) ROCKIN' ROBIN
B) THE LION SLEEPS TONIGHT
C) QUIET VILLAGE
D) ROCKIN' IN THE JUNGLE

5. **1 x 5**

THE ETERNALS HAD ANOTHER ABOUT A CERTAIN GUY AT HIS WEDDING.
A) WHERE WERE YOU (ON OUR WEDDING DAY)?
B) I'M GONNA GET MARRIED
C) BABALU'S WEDDING DAY
D) WHEN WE GET MARRIED

6. **1 x 5**

"BUZZ-BUZZ-BUZZ" WAS A NOVELTY SONG BY WHAT TINSELTOWN GROUP LED BY ROBERT BYRD, LATER TO BE KNOWN AS *BOBBY DAY*, THE SINGER/SONGWRITER WHO HAD A SOLO HIT WITH "ROCKIN' ROBIN" YEARS LATER?
A) BUDDY HOLLY WITH THE CRICKETS
B) THE HOLLYWOOD ARGYLES
C) THE HOLLYWOOD FLAMES
D) THE PENGUINS

7. **1 x 5**

THE BIG BOPPER, TRUE NAME *J P RICHARDSON,* CHARTED A BIG NOVELTY HIT SONG IN 1958 ABOUT A GIGGLING, WIGGLING GIRL WITH A PRETTY FACE WHO BLEW HIS MIND. NAME IT.

8. **1 x 5**

THIS GROUP OUT OF THE ATLANTIC RECORDS LABEL COMPANY, CHARTED MANY NOVELTY SONGS. THEY WERE CONSIDERED THE CLOWNS OF ROCK 'N ROLL. WHO WERE THEY? AND DON'T CALL JONES OR THAT BROWN FELLA FOR ANY CLUES.
A) THE DRIFTERS
B) THE COASTERS
C) BILL HALEY AND HIS COMETS
D) MAURICE WILLIAMS & THE ZODIACS

9. **1 x 5**

IN 1956 *THE JAYHAWKS* AND *THE CADETS,* TWO SEPARATE GROUPS, EACH RECORDED WHAT SONG BELOW THAT WOULD COMPETE ON THE CHARTS SIMULTANEOUSLY WITH THE *CADETS,* WHO ALSO SANG AS *THE JACKS,* SLIGHTLY AHEAD?
A) STRANDED IN THE JUNGLE
B) KEEP A KNOCKIN'
C) ROCKIN' ROBIN
D) GO, JIMMY, GO

10. **1 x 5**

THE AMES BROTHERS WERE A POPULAR QUARTET OF SINGERS WHO WERE ALL RELATED, BROTHERS. THEY CHARTED WHAT SONG ABOUT A GAL WHO WAS THE TALK OF THE TOWN WITH HER FLIRTING, CONSTANT DRINKING, AND OTHER GOING ON'S?
A) THE LADY'S A TRAMP
B) TAMMY
C) THE NAUGHTY LADY OF SHADY LANE
D) HARD HEADED WOMAN

11. **5 x 5**

NAME THESE FIVE POPULAR HITS BY THE FABULOUS '*COASTERS*' FORMERLY KNOWN AS *THE ROBINS.*
ONE, HE'LL LOCATE HER EVEN IF HE HAS TO SWIM OR CLIMB HIGH PEAKS.
TWO, ABOUT A CERTAIN FELLA WHO ACTS LIKE A CLOWN AND ALWAYS INTO MISCHIEF.
THREE, ABOUT SOMETHING YOU CAN SEE BUT NEVER TOUCH.
FOUR, ABOUT A GUY NAMED JONES AND QUITE THE HERO.
FIVE, THAT YOU CAN'T HANG OUT TONIGHT AND DON'T YOU DARE TRY ANSWERING BACK.

1) ____________
2) _______________
3) ____________
4) ___________________
5) ____________

12. **1 x 5**

PAUL EVANS CHARTED THIS LONG TITLED SONG IN 1959 ABOUT A CERTAIN NUMBER OF GIRLS SMOOCHING WITH FRED. COMPLETE THE INITIALS PROVIDED BELOW TO HELP YOU NAME THAT HIT.

S---N L----E G---S S-----G I- T-E B--K S--T K-----G A-D H-----G W--H F--D

13. **1 x 5**

PATTI PAGE CHARTED A SONG ABOUT A CERTAIN ANIMAL WITH A WAGGETY TAIL UP FOR SALE. NAME THAT PRE-ROCK AND ROLL POP HIT SONG.

____

14. **1 x 5**

DODIE STEVENS, A YOUNG FEMALE ARTIST, RECORDED HER ONE CLAIM TO FAME SONG ABOUT HER ECCENTRIC GUY NAMED DOOLEY WHO WORE NOTICEABLE CLOTHING, TAN FOOTWEAR WITH CERTAIN COLORED SHOELACES, A VEST, AND A HAT TO BOOT. NAME IT.

A) TOM DOOLEY
B) BLUE SUEDE SHOES
C) STAGGER LEE
D) PINK SHOE LACES

15. **1 x 5**

IN 1957 *LARRY WILLIAMS* RECORDED THE FIRST AND BIGGEST HIT OF HIS CAREER WITH THIS SONG BELOW ABOUT SOMEONE SHORT WHO WAS HIS VERY OWN LITTLE TUTTI FRUTTI.

A) SHORT SHORTS
B) SHORT FAT FANNIE
C) LITTLE DARLIN'
D) LITTLE ANGEL EYES

16. **1 x 5**

LARRY WILLIAMS ALSO HAD ANOTHER IN 1957 ABOUT A SKINNY CALENDAR TYPE OF GIRL WHO HE LOVES AND WANTS TO MARRY THOUGH SHE'S JUST A BAG OF BONES.

A) CHANTILLY LACE
B) BONY MORONIE
C) LONG TALL SALLY
D) CALENDAR GIRL

TOTAL POINTS. **20 x 5 = 100**

MATCH THE GROUP WITH THE LEAD SINGER IN THE 50'S

	GROUP		LEAD SINGER	
1	THE CRESTS	A	HANK BALLARD	1
2	THE MOONGLOWS	B	BUDDY HOLLY	2
3	THE PLATTERS	C	SONNY TIL	3
4	THE DRIFTERS	D	EARL LEWIS	4
5	THE DRIFTERS	E	FRED PARRIS	5
6	THE TEENAGERS	F	HARVEY FUQUA	6
7	THE CADILLACS	G	AELENE SMITH	7
8	THE SKYLINERS	H	JOHNNY MAESTRO	8
9	THE CHANNELS	I	CLYDE MCPHATTER	9
10	THE CHANTELS	J	TONY WILLIAMS	10
11	THE IMPERIALS	K	BILL HALEY	11
12	THE COASTERS	L	BEN E KING	12
13	COMETS	M	EARL 'SPEEDO' CARROL	13
14	THE ORIOLES	N	FRANKIE LYMON	14
15	THE MIDNIGHTERS	O	JIMMY BEAUMONT	15
16	THE FIVE SATINS	P	LITTLE ANTHONY GOURDINE	16
17	THE JUNIORS	Q	CORNELL GUNTHER	17
18	THE CRICKETS	R	DANNY RAPP	18
19	THE BELMONTS	S	RICHARD BLANDON	19
20	THE HEARTS	T	RUDY WEST	20
21	THE HARPTONES	U	DION DIMUCCIO	21
22	THE ELEGANTS	V	VITO PICONE	22
23	THE PENGUINS	W	WILLIE WINFIELD	23
24	THE FIVE KEYS	X	CLEVELAND DUNCAN	24
25	THE DUBS	Y	LEE ANDREWS	25
			TOTAL POINTS.	25 x 4 = 100

MATCH THE GROUP WITH THEIR SONG IN THE 50'S

	GROUP		SONG	
1	THE CRESTS	A	THE CLOSER YOU ARE	1
2	THE MOONGLOWS	B	POISON IVY	2
3	THE PLATTERS	C	TRY THE IMPOSSIBLE	3
4	THE DRIFTERS	D	EARTH ANGEL	4
5	THE DRIFTERS	E	SEE YOU LATER, ALLIGATOR	5
6	THE TEENAGERS	F	LITTLE STAR	6
7	THE CADILLACS	G	CRYING IN THE CHAPEL	7
8	THE SKYLINERS	H	I WANT A SUNDAY KIND OF LOVE	8
9	THE CHANNELS	I	I WONDER WHY	9
10	THE CHANTELS	J	IN THE STILL OF THE NIGHT	10
11	THE IMPERIALS	K	SINCERELY	11
12	THE COASTERS	L	DANCE WITH ME	12
13	COMETS	M	MY PRAYER	13
14	THE ORIOLES	N	COULD THIS BE MAGIC	14
15	THE MIDNIGHTERS	O	THE ANGELS LISTENED IN	15
16	THE FIVE SATINS	P	OUT OF SIGHT, OUT OF MIND	16
17	THE JUNIORS	Q	GLORIA	17
18	THE CRICKETS	R	WORK WITH ME ANNIE	18
19	THE BELMONTS	S	THIS I SWEAR	19
20	THE HEARTS	T	GOODY GOODY	20
21	THE HARPTONES	U	TEARS ON MY PILLOW	21
22	THE ELEGANTS	V	HONEY LOVE	22
23	THE PENGUINS	W	PEGGY SUE	23
24	THE FIVE KEYS	X	MAYBE	24
25	THE DUBS	Y	AT THE HOP	25

TOTAL POINTS. 25 x 4 = 100

MATCH THE INSTRUMENTAL HIT WITH THE ARTIST IN THE 50'S

	INSTRUMENTAL HIT		ARTIST	
1	SLEEP WALK	A	DAVE 'BABY' CORTEZ	1
2	TEQUILA	B	FRANCK POURCEL & HIS ORCHESTRA	2
3	SO RARE	C	MARTIN DENNY	3
4	THEME FROM 'PETER GUNN'	D	SANTO & JOHNNY	4
5	RAW-HIDE	E	PEREZ PRADO & HIS ORCHESTRA	5
6	QUIET VILLAGE	F	JIMMY DORSEY ORCHESTRA	6
7	THE HAPPY ORGAN	G	ROGER WILLIAMS	7
8	ONLY YOU	H	THE CHAMPS	8
9	PATRICIA	I	RAY ANTHONY	9
10	AUTUMN LEAVES	J	LINK WRAY & HIS RAY MEN	10
			TOTAL POINTS.	10 x 10 = 100

50/16

MATCH THE DUOS AND ALSO THEIR HIT SONG IN THE 50'S

	1ST DUO		2ND DUO		SONG	
1	DON EVERLY	A	DEAN	AA	SLEEP WALK	1 ,
2	JOHNNIE	B	PHIL EVERLY	BB	LOVE IS STRANGE	2 ,
3	SHIRLEY	C	CONNIE STEVENS	CC	LET THE GOOD TIMES ROLL	3 ,
4	SANTO	D	JOE	DD	BIRD DOG	4 ,
5	MICKEY	E	JOHNNY	EE	OVER THE MOUNTAIN, ACROSS THE SEA	5 ,
6	ROBERT	F	GOODMAN	FF	THE FLYING SAUCER (PARTS 1 & 2)	6 ,
7	JAN	G	SYLVIA	GG	BYE BYE LOVE	7 ,
8	ED BURNS	H	DON EVERLY	HH	WE BELONG TOGETHER	8 ,
9	BUCHANAN	I	JOHNNY	II	KOOKIE, KOOKIE (LEND ME YOUR COMB)	9 ,
10	PHIL EVERLY	J	LEE	JJ	BABY TALK	10 ,
					TOTAL POINTS.	20 x 5 =100

50/17

MATCH THE ARTIST WITH MOVIE/TV SHOW SONG IN THE 50'S

	ARTIST		SONG	
1	BILL HALEY AND HIS COMETS	A	TAMMY	1
2	DORIS DAY	B	APRIL LOVE	2
3	DEBBIE REYNOLDS	C	LOVE LETTERS IN THE SAND	3
4	PAT BOONE	D	THEME FROM 'PETER GUNN'	4
5	THE FOUR ACES	E	I'M WALKING	5
6	ELVIS	F	WHATEVER WILL BE, WILL BE (QUE SERA, SERA)	6
7	ELVIS	G	(WE'RE GONNA) ROCK AROUND THE CLOCK	7
8	LITTLE RICKY NELSON	H	(LET ME BE YOUR) TEDDY BEAR	8
9	PAT BOONE	I	JAILHOUSE ROCK	9
10	RAY ANTHONY	J	LOVE IS A MANY SPLENDORED THING	10

TOTAL POINTS. 10 x 10 = 100

50/18

MATCH THE SONG WITH THE MOVIE/TV SHOW IN THE 50'S

	SONG		MOVIE/TV SHOW	
1	LOVE IS A MANY SPLENDORED THING	AA	BERNARDINE	1
2	APRIL LOVE	BB	TAMMY AND THE BACHELOR	2
3	WHATEVER WILL BE, WILL BE (QUE SERA, SERA)	CC	LOVE IS A MANY SPLENDORED THING	3
4	THEME FROM 'PETER GUNN'	DD	JAILHOUSE ROCK	4
5	TAMMY	EE	BLACKBOARD JUNGLE	5
6	(LET ME BE YOUR) TEDDY BEAR	FF	THE MAN WHO KNEW TOO MUCH	6
7	LOVE LETTERS IN THE SAND	GG	PETER GUNN	7
8	I'M WALKING	HH	LOVING YOU	8
9	JAILHOUSE ROCK	II	APRIL LOVE	9
10	(WE'RE GONNA) ROCK AROUND THE CLOCK	JJ	THE ADVENTURES OF OZZIE & HARRIET	10

TOTAL POINTS. 10 x 10 = 100

(50'S ANSWER SHEETS)

50/1 ELVIS-QUIZ # 1

1. D. LOVE ME TENDER
2. JAILHOUSE ROCK
3. A. LOVING YOU
4. D. ED SULLIVAN
5. B. SUN RECORDS
6. C. IKE TURNER
7. C. HOUND DOG
8. B. THE JORDANAIRES
9. A. BLUE SUEDE SHOES
10. C. HEARTBREAK HOTEL
11. 1) B. ARTHUR CRUDUP
    2) C. ROY BROWN
    3) A. WILLIE MAE (BIG MAMA) THORNTON
12. B. COLONEL TOM PARKER
13. C. GRACELAND
14. ELVIS ARON PRESLEY
15. C. THE DEL SATINS
16. B. RCA
17. C. THE MEMPHIS MAFIA
18. C. 17

50/2 ELVIS-QUIZ # 2

1. 1) HEARTBREAK HOTEL
   2) BLUE SUEDE SHOES
   3) I WANT YOU, I NEED YOU, I LOVE YOU
   4) DON'T BE CRUEL
   5) HOUND DOG
   6) LOVE ME TENDER
   7) LOVE ME
   8) TOO MUCH
   9) ALL SHOOK UP
   10) (LET ME BE YOUR) TEDDY BEAR
   11) LOVING YOU
   12) JAILHOUSE ROCK
   13) TREAT ME NICE
   14) DON'T
   15) I BEG OF YOU
   16) WEAR MY RING AROUND YOUR NECK
   17) HARD HEADED WOMAN
   18) ONE NIGHT
   19) I GOT STUNG
   20) (NOW AND THEN THERE'S) A FOOL SUCH AS I
   21) I NEED YOUR LOVE TONIGHT
   22) A BIG HUNK O' LOVE
   23) GOOD ROCKIN' TONIGHT
   24) THAT'S ALL RIGHT
   25) MYSTERY TRAIN

50/3 R&B ROCKERS-QUIZ # 1

1. 1) LOVERS NEVER SAY GOODBYE
   2) I ONLY HAVE EYES FOR YOU
   3) I'LL BE HOME
2. D. I WANT A SUNDAY KIND OF LOVE

3. B. LIFE IS BUT A DREAM
4. A. MAYBE
5. B. EVERY NIGHT (I PRAY)
6. C. SPEEDO
7. I'M SORRY
8. D. THERE GOES MY BABY
9. A. DANCE WITH ME
10. 1) TEARS ON MY PILLOW
    2) A PRAYER AND A JUKEBOX
    3) THE DIARY
    4) TWO PEOPLE IN THE WORLD
    5) SO NEAR AND YET SO FAR
    6) WHEN YOU WISH UPON A STAR
11. B. THE END
12. A. WE BELONG TOGETHER
13. B. IT'S JUST A MATTER OF TIME
14. C. OH WHAT A NITE
15. D. SO YOUNG
16. B. EVERYDAY OF THE WEEK
17. B. A THOUSAND MILES AWAY
18. B. FOR YOUR LOVE
19. C. IN THE STILL OF THE NIGHT
20. B. TO THE AISLE
21. D. LONELY TEARDROPS
22. A. I'LL BE SATISFIED
23. B. FOR YOUR PRECIOUS LOVE
24. A. THE IMPRESSIONS
25. A. THE ICE MAN
26. B. C.C. RIDER
27. B. WHAT AM I LIVING FOR
28. A. ONE SUMMER NIGHT
29. C. DO YOU WANT TO DANCE
30. A. ROCKIN' ROBIN
31. B. HEY LITTLE GIRL
32. B. SHOUT (PARTS 1 AND 2)
33. B. DEVIL OR ANGEL
34. C. LOVE POTION NO. 9
35. D. SHAKE, RATTLE AND ROLL
36. CORRINE, CORRINA
37. C. BO DIDDLEY
38. B. SILHOUETTES
39. B. AT MY FRONT DOOR
40. A. IT WILL STAND
41. A. CRYING IN THE CHAPEL
42. B. SH-BOOM
43. 1) SINCERELY
    2) TEN COMMANDMENTS OF LOVE
    3) SEE SAW
    4) WE GO TOGETHER
44. D. I GOT A WOMAN
45. B. WHAT'D I SAY (PT 1)
46. A. GET A JOB
47. B. ANTOINE 'FATS' DOMINO
48. D. COME GO WITH ME
49. B. WHISPERING BELLS
50. D. MR LEE
51. C. WHO'S THAT KNOCKIN'
52. B. CLYDE MCPHATTER

53. C. WHY DON'T YOU WRITE ME?
54. B. LITTLE GIRL OF MINE
55. 1) THE DRIFTERS
    2) BEN E KING
56. B. YOU CHEATED
57. 1) ONLY SIXTEEN
    2) (I LOVE YOU) FOR SENTIMENTAL REASONS
    3) EVERYBODY LIKES TO CHA, CHA, CHA
    4) YOU SEND ME
58. 1) LONG LONELY NIGHTS
    2) TRY THE IMPOSSIBLE
    3) TEARDROPS
59. B. THE WIND
60. 1) WISDOM OF A FOOL
    2) OUT OF SIGHT, OUT OF MIND
    3) GLORY OF LOVE
    4) LING, TING, TONG
61. D. WHEN YOU DANCE
62. C. BOOK OF LOVE
63. B. LITTLE BITTY PRETTY ONE
64. A. STORY UNTOLD
65. B. GOODNIGHT MY LOVE
66. B. ATLANTIC RECORDS
67. C. YOU'RE SO FINE
68. A. SO FINE
69. 1) STAGGER LEE
    2) WHERE WERE YOU (ON OUR WEDDING DAY)?
    3) PERSONALITY
70. B. LONG TALL SALLY
71. C. DELLA REESE
72. C. PLEASE SAY YOU WANT ME
73. 1) SWEET LITTLE SIXTEEN
    2) ROCK & ROLL MUSIC
    3) JOHNNY B. GOODE
    4) MAYBELLENE
    5) ROLL OVER BEETHOVEN
    6) BACK IN THE U.S.A.
74. B. CHARLIE BROWN

50/4 R&B ROCKERS-QUIZ # 2

1. A. DON'T LET GO
2. A. KANSAS CITY
3. 1) COULD THIS BE MAGIC
   2) DON'T ASK ME TO BE LONELY
   3) CHAPEL OF DREAMS
4. 1) LUCILLE
   2) GOOD GOLLY, MISS MOLLY
   3) JENNY, JENNY
   4) KEEP A KNOCKIN'
   5) LONG TALL SALLY
5. C. JOHNNY B. GOODE
6. D. JIM DANDY
7. B. TWEEDLE DEE
8. A. JOHNNY OTIS SHOW
9. B. HOUND DOG
10. B. CLYDE MCPHATTER
11. A. CRY

12. C. JUST WALKING IN THE RAIN
13. 1) WHY DO FOOLS FALL IN LOVE
    2) THE A.B.C.'S OF LOVE
    3) GOODY GOODY
    4) I WANT YOU TO BE MY GIRL
    5) I PROMISE TO REMEMBER
14. 1) THAT'S MY DESIRE
    2) MY LOVE WILL NEVER DIE
    3) THE CLOSER YOU ARE
15. 1) A LOVER'S QUESTION
    2) TREASURE OF LOVE
    3) WITHOUT LOVE (THERE IS NOTHING)
16. B. DESERIE
17. C. THE PLATTERS
18. D. TOMMY EDWARDS
19. 1) JOHNNY ACE
    2. PLEDGING MY LOVE
20. 1) B. EARTH ANGEL
    2) C. YOU'RE SO FINE
    3) A. I ONLY HAVE EYES FOR YOU
    4) D. CRYING IN THE CHAPEL
21. A. SMOKEY JOE'S CAFE
22. C. I MET HIM ON A SUNDAY
23. A. LET THE GOOD TIMES ROLL
24. D. CLYDE MCPHATTER & JACKIE WILSON
25. 1) FATS DOMINO
    2) AIN'T THAT A SHAME
    3) BLUEBERRY HILL
    4) I'M WALKIN'
    5) WHOLE LOTTA LOVING
    6) I WANT TO WALK YOU HOME
26. A. GOOD GOLLY, MISS MOLLY
27. C. SEA CUISE

50/5 R&B ROCKERS-QUIZ # 3

1. 1) MY PRAYER
    2) ONLY YOU
    3) THE GREAT PRETENDER
    4) SMOKE GETS IN YOUR EYES
    5) TWILIGHT TIME
    6) (YOU'VE GOT) THE MAGIC TOUCH
    7) I'M SORRY
    8) ENCHANTED
    9) HEAVEN ON EARTH
    10) REMEMBER WHEN
2. C. OUT OF SIGHT, OUT OF MIND
3. C. CAN I COME OVER TONIGHT
4. B. GEE
5. B. BUCK RAM
6. A. ROCKET 88
7. D. MUDDY WATERS
8. C. MONA LISA
9. C. TOO YOUNG
10. I'M GONNA SIT RIGHT DOWN AND WRITE MYSELF A LETTER
11. A. UNFORGETTABLE

50/6 R&B ROCKERS-QUIZ # 4

1. C. GOODNIGHT, SWEETHEART, GOODNIGHT
2. B. SEA OF LOVE
3. A. EARTH ANGEL
4. A. BEEN SO LONG
5. B. JACKIE WILSON
6. D. STARDUST
7. B. FEVER
8. B. TALK TO ME, TALK TO ME
9. D. GLORIA
10. B. BANANA BOAT (DAY-O)
11. B. SIXTY MINUTE MAN
12. B. THE WILLOWS
13. B. BROOK BENTON
14. B. UNCHAINED MELODY
15. WHATEVER LOLA WANTS
16. 1) I ALMOST LOST MY MIND
    2) SINCE I MET YOU BABY
17. C. JAMES BROWN
18. B. MR PERSONALITY
19. B. LOVE IS STRANGE

50/7 POP ROCKERS-QUIZ # 1

1. C. 16 CANDLES
2. 1) THE ANGELS LISTENED IN
   2) SIX NIGHTS A WEEK
3. B. SINCE I DON'T HAVE YOU
4. A. THIS I SWEAR
5. C. YOU WERE MINE
6. 1) CHANCES ARE
   2) THE TWELFTH OF NEVER
   3) IT'S NOT FOR ME TO SAY
   4) WONDERFUL! WONDERFUL!
   5) A CERTAIN SMILE
7. TAMMY
8. EDDIE MY LOVE
9. 1) DIANA
   2) LONELY BOY
   3) YOU ARE MY DESTINY
   4) PUT YOUR HEAD ON MY SHOULDER
   5) IT'S TIME TO CRY
10. 1) FRANK SINATRA
    2) LOVE AND MARRIAGE
    3) HEY! JEALOUS LOVER
    4) WITCHCRAFT
    5) HIGH HOPES
    6) ALL THE WAY
11. B. I'VE HAD IT
12. A. HUSHABYE
13. D. TONITE, TONITE
14. 1) I WONDER WHY
    2) A TEENAGER IN LOVE
    3) NO ONE KNOWS
15. B. HAPPY, HAPPY BIRTHDAY BABY
16. C. JUST TO BE WITH YOU
17. A. KISSIN' TIME

18. A. THE ROVER BOYS
19. A. THREE COINS IN THE FOUNTAIN
20. D. LOVE IS A MANY SPLENDORED THING
21. 26 MILES (SANTA CATALINA)
22. C. BIG MAN
23. A. FEVER
24. 16 TONS
25. A. THE WAYWARD WIND
26. B. MITCH MILLER
27. DORIS DAY
28. B. EVERYBODY LOVES A LOVER
29. C. DEAN MARTIN
30. DEAN MARTIN
31. D. TO KNOW HIM, IS TO LOVE HIM
32. B. MR SANDMAN
33. 1) LOLLIPOP
    2) EDDIE MY LOVE
34. C. DONNA
35. A. FRANKIE AVALON & FABIAN
36. A. PERRY COMO
37. 1) PAPA LOVES MAMBO
    2) CATCH A FALLING STAR
38. 1) LITTLE RICKY NELSON
    2) BE BOP BABY
    3) STOOD UP
    4) POOR LITTLE FOOL
    5) LONESOME TOWN
    6) IT'S LATE
    7) I'M WALKIN'
    8) NEVER BE ANYONE ELSE BUT YOU
39. B. LET ME GO LOVER
40. D. BORN TOO LATE
41. C. THE CRESTS
42. B. THE FLEETWOODS
43. B. HERE COMES SUMMER
44. A. ENDLESS SLEEP
45. 1) CONNIE FRANCIS
    2) AMONG MY SOUVENIRS
    3) WHO'S SORRY NOW
    4) STUPID CUPID
    5) LIPSTICK ON YOUR COLLAR
46. A. JUST A DREAM
47. B. GO, JIMMY, GO
48. A. CINDY, OH CINDY
49. 1) SPLISH SPLASH
    2) QUEEN OF THE HOP
    3) DREAM LOVER
    4) MACK THE KNIFE
50. 1) AIN'T THAT A SHAME
    2) I'LL BE HOME
    3) I ALMOST LOST MY MIND
    4) LOVE LETTERS IN THE SAND
    5) APRIL LOVE
    6) LONG TALL SALLY
51. C. 16 CANDLES
52. C. PARTY DOLL
53. D. TRAGEDY
54. D. ANNETTE FUNICELLO

55. A. THE HAWAIIAN WEDDING SONG (KE KALI NEI AU)
56. D. BUTTERFLY
57. D. A TEAR FELL
58. 1) YOU SEND ME
    2) LET ME GO LOVER
59. 1) FRANKIE AVALON
    2) BOBBY SOX TO STOCKINGS
    3) VENUS
60. B. SEE YOU IN SEPTEMBER

50/8 POP ROCKERS-QUIZ # 2

1. B. MISTY
2. B. STANDING ON THE CORNER
3. C. YOU BELONG TO ME
4. D. PATTI PAGE
5. C. SUSIE DARLIN'
6. 1) COLD, COLD HEART
    2) RAGS TO RICHES
7. B. I HEAR YOU KNOCKING
8. B. MY HEART IS AN OPEN BOOK
9. B. GEORGIA GIBBS
10. A. THE GREEN DOOR
11. D. GRADUATION DAY
12. B. LITTLE STAR
13. A. ROCK AND ROLL WALTZ
14. 1) C. THE CHORDS
    2) A. THE PENGUINS
    3) D. THE NUTMEGS
    4) B. AL HIBBLER
15. 1) SINCERELY
    2) SUGARTIME

POP ROCKERS-BONUS

1. C. MISS TONI FISHER

50/9 COUNTRY ROCKERS

1. 1) SEE YOU LATER, ALLIGATOR
    2) (WE'RE GONNA) ROCK AROUND THE CLOCK
    3) SHAKE, RATTLE AND ROLL
    4) SKINNY MINNIE
2. A. I CAN'T STOP LOVING YOU
3. 1) ELVIS PRESLEY
    2) CARL PERKINS
    3) JERRY LEE LEWIS
    4) JOHNNY CASH
4. A. JOHNNY HORTON
5. A. YOUNG LOVE
6. DON & PHIL
7. C. THE KILLER
8. THE BALLAD OF DAVY CROCKETT
9. C. RAW-HIDE
10. B. CONWAY TWITTY
11. C. PRIMROSE LANE
12. B. WALKIN' AFTER MIDNIGHT
13. D. PARTY DOLL

14. B. THE EVERLY BROTHERS
15. 1) THAT'LL BE THE DAY
    2) OH, BOY!
    3) NOT FADE AWAY
    4) BO DIDDLEY
    5) PEGGY SUE
16. A. SHOUT (PARTS 1 AND 2)
17. 1) WAKE UP LITTLE SUSIE
    2) BIRD DOG
    3) PROBLEMS
    4) ALL I HAVE TO DO IS DREAM
    5) DEVOTED TO YOU
    6) (TIL) I KISSED YOU
    7) BYE, BYE LOVE
18. A. OOBY DOOBY
19. 1) GREAT BALLS OF FIRE
    2) WHOLE LOT OF SHAKIN' GOING ON
    3) BREATHLESS
20. B. I WALK THE LINE
21. C. THE BIG BOPPER & RITCHIE VALENS
22. B. MY SPECIAL ANGEL
23. C. JINGLE BELL ROCK
24. A. SUMMERTIME BLUES
25. B. BE-BOP-A-LULA
26. C. OH LONESOME ME
27. B. MARTY ROBBINS
28. A. BLUE SUEDE SHOES
29. 1) COLD, COLD HEART
    2) I'M SO LONESOME I COULD CRY
    3) YOUR CHEATIN' HEART
    4) HEY, GOOD LOOKIN'

COUNTRY ROCKERS-BONUS

1. B. HIGH NOON (DO NOT FORSAKE ME)
2. B. THE THREE BELLS
3. C. GOTTA TRAVEL ON

50/10 ROCKERS

1. B. TALLAHASSEE LASSIE
2. C. WAY DOWN YONDER IN NEW ORLEANS
3. A. SINGING THE BLUES
4. B. HEARTACHES BY THE NUMBER
5. 1) HONEY COMB
   2) KISSES SWEETER THAN WINE
   3) BIMBOMBEY
   4) SECRETLY
6. 1) ROCK AND ROLL IS HERE TO STAY
   2) AT THE HOP

ROCKERS-BONUS

1. A. MY TRUE LOVE
2. C. SORRY (I RAN ALL THE WAY HOME)

50/11 MISC (NOVELTY, FOLK, FOREIGN & INSTRUMENTALS)-QUIZ # 1

1. C. TOM DOOLEY
2. A. HE'S GOT THE WHOLE WORLD (IN HIS HANDS)
3. 1) SWEET LITTLE SIXTEEN
   2) 16 CANDLES
   3) ONLY SIXTEEN
   4) 16 TONS
4. 1) H. ROCK AND ROLL WALTZ
   2) D. JINGLE BELL ROCK
   3) E. ROCK AND ROLL IS HERE TO STAY
   4) B. JAILHOUSE ROCK
   5) A. (WE'RE GONNA) ROCK AROUND THE CLOCK
   6) C. ROCK & ROLL MUSIC
   7) G. ROCK-A-BYE YOUR BABY WITH A DIXIE MELODY
   8) F. REELIN' AND ROCKIN'
5. B. SLEEP WALK
6. C. THE LITTLE DRUMMER BOY
7. 1) C. AT MY FRONT DOOR
   2) D. SPEEDO
   3) E. MR BLUE
   4) B. SORRY (I RAN ALL THE WAY HOME)
   5) A. TEARS ON MY PILLOW
   6) F. THERE'S A MOON OUT TONIGHT
8. B. THE FLYING SAUCER {PARTS 1 & 2)
9. A. LA BAMBA
10. B. NEL BLU DIPINTO DI BLU (VOLARE)
11. A. BALLAD OF PALADIN
12. C. ED SULLIVAN'S 'TOAST OF THE TOWN'
13. A. RUNNING BEAR
14. C. I PUT A SPELL ON YOU
15. A. I COULD HAVE DANCED ALL NIGHT
16. C. DONDE ESTA' SANTA CLAUS
17. A. ALAN FREED
18. C. SLEEP WALK
19. C. WITCH DOCTOR
20. B. THE CHAMPS
21. 1) THEODORE
    2) ALVIN
    3) SIMON
22. PETER GUNN THEME
23. A. QUIET VILLAGE
24. B. BEEP BEEP
25. C. BABY TALK
26. C. SHORT SHORTS
27. D. DICK CLARK
28. C. LITTLE DARLIN'
29. C. THE STROLL
30. C. ROGER WILLIAMS
31. KOOKIE, KOOKIE (LEND ME YOUR COMB)
32. A. HERNANDO'S HIDEAWAY
33. A. EH CUMPARI

50/12 MISC (NOVELTY, FOLK, FOREIGN & INSTRUMENTALS)-QUIZ # 2

1. C. COZY COLE
2. B. HONKY TONK (PARTS 1 & 2)
3. B. WESTERN MOVIES

4. D. ROCKIN' IN THE JUNGLE
5. C. BABALU'S WEDDING DAY
6. C. THE HOLLYWOOD FLAMES
7. CHANTILLY LACE
8. B. THE COASTERS
9. A. STRANDED IN THE JUNGLE
10. C. THE NAUGHTY LADY OF SHADY LANE
11. 1) SEARCHIN'
    2) CHARLIE BROWN
    3) POISON IVY
    4) ALONG CAME JONES
    5) YAKETY YAK
12. SEVEN LITTLE GIRLS SITTING IN THE BACK SEAT KISSING AND HUGGING WITH FRED
13. HOW MUCH IS THAT DOGGIE IN THE WINDOW
14. D. PINK SHOE LACES
15. B. SHORT FAT FANNIE
16. B. BONY MORONIE

50/13 MATCH THE GROUP WITH THE LEAD SINGER IN THE 50'S

1. H. JOHNNY MAESTRO
2. F. HARVEY FUQUA
3. J. TONY WILLIAMS
4. I. CLYDE MCPHATTER
5. L. BEN E KING
6. N. FRANKIE LYMON
7. M. EARL 'SPEEDO' CARROLL
8. O. JIMMY BEAUMONT
9. D. EARL LEWIS
10. G. ARLENE SMITH
11. P. LITTLE ANTHONY GOURDINE
12. Q. CORNELL GUNTHER
13. K. BILL HALEY
14. C. SONNY TIL
15. A. HANK BALLARD
16. E. FRED PARRIS
17. R. DANNY RAPP
18. B. BUDDY HOLLY
19. U. DION DIMUCCIO
20. Y. LEE ANDREWS
21. W. WILLIE WINFIELD
22. V. VITO PICONE
23. X. CLEVELAND DUNCAN
24. T. RUDY WEST
25. S. RICHARD BLANDON

50/14 MATCH THE GROUP WITH THEIR SONG IN THE 50'S

1. O. THE ANGELS LISTENED IN
2. K. SINCERELY
3. M. MY PRAYER
4. L. DANCE WITH ME
5. V. HONEY LOVE
6. T. GOODY GOODY
7. Q. GLORIA
8. S. THIS I SWEAR
9. A. THE CLOSER YOU ARE

10. X. MAYBE
11. U. TEARS ON MY PILLOW
12. B. POISON IVY
13. E. SEE YOU LATER, ALLIGATOR
14. G. CRYING IN THE CHAPEL
15. R. WORK WITH ME ANNIE
16. J. IN THE STILL OF THE NIGHT
17. Y. AT THE HOP
18. W. PEGGY SUE
19. I. I WONDER WHY
20. C. TRY THE IMPOSSIBLE
21. H. I WANT A SUNDAY KIND OF LOVE
22. F. LITTLE STAR
23. D. EARTH ANGEL
24. P. OUT OF SIGHT, OUT OF MIND
25. N. COULD THIS BE MAGIC

50/15 MATCH THE INSTRUMENTAL HIT WITH THE ARTIST IN THE 50'S

1. D. SANTO & JOHNNY
2. H. THE CHAMPS
3. F. JIMMY DORSEY ORCHESTRA
4. I. RAY ANTHONY
5. J. LINK WRAY & HIS RAY MEN
6. C. MARTIN DENNY
7. A. DAVE 'BABY' CORTEZ
8. B. FRANCK POURCEL & HIS ORCHESTRA
9. E. PEREZ PRADO & HIS ORCHESTRA
10. G. ROGER WILLIAMS

50/16 MATCH THE DUOS AND ALSO THEIR HIT SONG IN THE 50'S

1. B,DD. PHIL EVERLY, BIRD DOG
2. D,EE. JOE/ OVER THE MOUNTAIN, ACROSS THE SEA
3. J,CC. LEE, LET THE GOOD TIMES ROLL
4. E,AA. JOHNNY, SLEEP WALK
5. G,BB. SYLVIA, LOVE IS STRANGE
6. I,HH. JOHNNY, WE BELONG TOGETHER
7. A,JJ. DEAN, BABY TALK
8. C,II. CONNIE STEVENS/ KOOKIE, KOOKIE (LEND ME YOUR COMB)
9. F,FF. GOODMAN, THE FLYING SAUCER (PARTS 1 & 2)
10. H,GG. DON EVERLY, BYE BYE LOVE

50/17 MATCH THE ARTIST WITH MOVIE/TV SHOW SONG IN THE 50'S

1. G. (WE'RE GONNA) ROCK AROUND THE CLOCK
2. F. WHATEVER WILL BE, WILL BE (QUE SERA, SERA)
3. A. TAMMY
4. B. APRIL LOVE
5. J. LOVE IS A MANY SPLENDORED THING
6. H. (LET ME BE YOUR) TEDDY BEAR
7. I. JAILHOUSE ROCK
8. E. I'M WALKING
9. C. LOVE LETTERS IN THE SAND
10. D. THEME FROM 'PETER GUNN'

50/18 MATCH THE SONG WITH THE MOVIE/TV SHOW IN THE 50'S

1. CC. LOVE IS A MANY SPLENDORED THING
2. II. APRIL LOVE
3. FF. THE MAN WHO KNEW TOO MUCH
4. GG. PETER GUNN
5. BB. TAMMY AND THE BACHELOR
6. HH. LOVING YOU
7. AA. BERNARDINE
8. JJ. THE ADVENTURES OF OZZIE & HARRIET
9. DD. JAILHOUSE ROCK
10. EE. BLACKBOARD JUNGLE

THE SIXTIES

THE DECADE OF THE SIXTIES KNOWN AS THE TURBULENT SIXTIES BROUGHT US AN EVEN GREATER DIVERSIFIED SOUND OF MUSIC THROUGH DOO-WOP, A CAPPELLA, MOTOWN, ATLANTIC, BROADWAY SHOW HITS AND THE RISE OF SMALL INDEPENDENT RECORD LABELS. ELVIS STILL KNOWN AS THE KING OF ROCK 'N ROLL, CONTINUED WHERE HE LEFT OFF CHARTING HIT AFTER HIT AND STARRING IN A NUMBER OF MOVIES THAT SHOWCASED A LOT OF THOSE HITS. MEANWHILE THE COLD WAR RAGED ON. IT LED TO THE CUBAN MISSILE CRISIS WHICH HAD THE WORLD ON THE EDGE. ASSASINATIONS, DEMONSTRATIONS AND RIOTS WERE QUITE FREQUENT. DION SUMMED IT BEST WITH HIS 'ABRAHAM, MARTIN AND JOHN' HIT SONG. FOLK SINGERS LIKE BOB DYLAN, PETER, PAUL & MARY AND ESPECIALLY BARRY MCGUIRE WITH HIS 'EVE OF DESTRUCTION' HIT SONG FORETOLD OF THE DANGERS IN OUR WORLD AND OUR SOCIETY'S ILLS. THE VIETNAM WAR CONTINUED TO ESCALATE DURING THE JOHNSON ADMINISTRATION BRINGING UNTOLD CASUALTIES AND CIVIL UNREST. THE CIVIL RIGHTS MOVEMENT FINALLY LED TO THE PASSAGE OF CIVIL RIGHTS LAWS THAT WERE INEVITABLE AND AT THE SAME TIME COSTLY IN TERMS OF LOSS OF LIVES INCLUDING THAT OF MARTIN LUTHER KING JR. MEANWHILE ON THE MUSIC FRONT WE EXPERIENCED THE ARRIVAL OF THE BRITISH INVASION LED BY THE FAB FOUR, THE BEATLES, IN 1964. AMERICAN GROUPS SUCH AS THE FOUR SEASONS, THE BEACH BOYS, THE SOUND OF YOUNG AMERICA, MOTOWN, LED BY IT'S FOUNDER BERRY GORDY, THE STAX SOUND WITH OTIS AT THE HELM AND THE DRIFTERS WITH THE REST OF THEIR ATLANTIC LABEL COMPETED WELL AGAINST THE LIKES OF THE ROLLING STONES, DAVE CLARK FIVE, THE ANIMALS, HERMAN'S HERMITS, PETULA CLARK, THE ZOMBIES, ETC. R&B WAS NOW CALLED BY MANY, SOUL MUSIC AND YOU DIDN'T HAVE TO BE BLACK TO HAVE IT, JUST ASK THE RIGHTEOUS BROTHERS OR TOM JONES WITH THEIR SOULFUL RENDITIONS. THE DANCES CONTINUED TO EVOLVE DURING THIS PERIOD IN TIME. THANKS TO CHUBBY CHECKER BY WAY OF HANK BALLARD, THE TWIST, THE LIMBO, THE PONY, THE SWIM ETC. WE LEARNED TO DANCE THE LOCOMOTION, THE MASHED POTATO, THE HULLY GULLY AND DID THE WAH-TUSI WITH LINDA. WE DID THE MONKEY, THE JERK, THE BOSSA NOVA AND SO ON. ROCK 'N ROLL PROVED IT WAS HERE TO STAY AND THE FOLLOWING REPRESENTS THAT ERA, THE SIXTIES.

THE 60'S - QUIZZES IN THIS SECTION

No.	Quiz	Part	Questions
60/1	ELVIS		(20 QUESTIONS = 100)
60/2	BEATLEMANIA	QUIZ # 1	(10 QUESTIONS = 100)
60/3	BEATLEMANIA	2	(50 QUESTIONS = 100)
	BEATLEMANIA	BONUS	2
60/4	THE REST OF THE BRITISH INVASION	QUIZ # 1	(100 QUESTIONS = 100)
60/5	THE REST OF THE BRITISH INVASION	2	(25 QUESTIONS = 100)
	THE REST OF THE BRITISH INVASION	BONUS	2
60/6	MOTOWN ROCKERS	QUIZ # 1	(100 QUESTIONS = 100)
60/7	MOTOWN ROCKERS	2	(20 QUESTIONS = 100)
60/8	R&B ROCKERS	QUIZ # 1	(100 QUESTIONS = 100)
60/9	R&B ROCKERS	2	(100 QUESTIONS = 100)
60/10	R&B ROCKERS	3	(50 QUESTIONS = 100)
60/11	R&B ROCKERS	4	(100 QUESTIONS = 100)
	R&B ROCKERS	BONUS	3
60/12	POP ROCKERS	QUIZ # 1	(100 QUESTIONS = 100)
60/13	POP ROCKERS	2	(100 QUESTIONS = 100)
60/14	POP ROCKERS	3	(100 QUESTIONS = 100)
	POP ROCKERS	BONUS	2
60/15	COUNTRY ROCKERS	QUIZ # 1	(50 QUESTIONS = 100)
60/16	ROCKERS	QUIZ # 1	(25 QUESTIONS = 100)
60/17	ROCKERS	2	(100 QUESTIONS = 100)
60/18	MISC (NOVELTY, FOLK, FOREIGN & INSTRMTLS)	# 1	(50 QUESTIONS = 100)
60/19	MISC (NOVELTY, FOLK, FOREIGN & INSTRMTLS)	2	(25 QUESTIONS = 100)
60/20	MISC (NOVELTY, FOLK, FOREIGN & INSTRMTLS)	3	(25 QUESTIONS = 100)
	MISC (NOVELTY, FOLK, FOREIGN & INSTRMTLS)	BONUS	8
60/21	MATCH THE WOODSTOCK ARTIST WITH THEIR SONG		(20 QUESTIONS = 100)
60/22	MATCH THE DANCE HIT WITH THE ARTIST		(20 QUESTIONS = 100)
60/23	MATCH THE LEAD SINGER WITH THE GROUP PT 1		(25 QUESTIONS = 100)
60/24	MATCH THE GROUP WITH THEIR SONG PT 1		(25 QUESTIONS = 100)
60/25	MATCH THE LEAD SINGER WITH THE GROUP PT II		(25 QUESTIONS = 100)
60/26	MATCH THE GROUP WITH THEIR SONG PT II		(25 QUESTIONS = 100)
60/27	MATCH THE LEAD SINGER WITH THE GROUP PT III		(20 QUESTIONS = 100)
60/28	MATCH THE GROUP WITH THEIR SONG PT III		(20 QUESTIONS = 100)
60/29	MATCH THE DUOS AND ALSO THEIR HIT SONG		(50 QUESTIONS = 100)
60/30	MATCH THE ARTIST WITH MOVIE/TV SHOW SONG PT 1		(25 QUESTIONS = 100)
60/31	MATCH THE SONG WITH THE MOVIE/TV SHOW PT 1		(25 QUESTIONS = 100)
60/32	MATCH THE ARTIST WITH MOVIE/TV SHOW SONG PT II		(20 QUESTIONS = 100)
60/33	MATCH THE SONG WITH THE MOVIE/TV SHOW PT II		(20 QUESTIONS = 100)
60/34	MATCH THE INSTRUMENTAL HIT WITH ARTIST PT 1		(20 QUESTIONS = 100)
60/35	MATCH THE INSTRUMENTAL HIT WITH ARTIST PT II		(20 QUESTIONS = 100)

35 TOTAL QUIZZES

ELVIS

1. **18 x 5**

NAME THESE EIGHTEEN GIANT HITS BY *ELVIS* DURING THE 60'S.
ONE, ABOUT BEING STUCK TO SOMEONE.
TWO, LONESOME BECAUSE WE'RE APART.
THREE, ABOUT GIVING UP.
FOUR, A CERTAIN CHARM THAT SHE IS TO HIM.
FIVE, A VEGAS SONG THAT WAS FEATURED IN A MOVIE OF THE SAME NAME CO-STARRING *ANN-MARGARET,* WILLIAM DEMAREST AND JACK CARTER WITH *ELVIS* PORTRAYING A RACECAR DRIVER.
SIX, A LOVE SONG FEATURED IN THE MOVIE 'BLUE HAWAII' CO-STARRING ANGELA LANSBURY AS HIS MOTHER ABOUT SOMETHING HE COULDN'T HELP DOING.
SEVEN, A LETTER RETURNED WITH NO WHERE TO GO THAT WAS FEATURED IN HIS MOVIE 'GIRLS! GIRLS! GIRLS!' CO-STARRING STELLA STEVENS.
EIGHT, ABOUT SOMEONE EVIL IN DISGUISE.
NINE, HIS COVER SONG OF THE R&B GROUP, *THE ORIOLES,* ABOUT A CHAPEL.
TEN, HIS COMEBACK HIT SONG WHY HE COULDN'T WALK OUT YET STILL HAD DOUBTS ABOUT HER.
ELEVEN, A CHICAGO MOM CRYING FOR HER NEWLY BORN.
TWELVE, A DREAM HIT THAT HE WOULD OFTEN USE TO CLOSE HIS SHOWS.
THIRTEEN, ABOUT HIS FLAME AND NO IT'S NOT THAT GIRL GLORIA.
FOURTEEN, A CERTAIN BURNING STAR THAT WAS ALSO FEATURED IN HIS MOVIE OF THE SAME NAME CO-STARRING BARBARA EDEN AND DELORES DEL RIO WHERE HE PORTRAYS A HALF-BREED INDIAN.
FIFTEEN, FOLLOW WHAT?
SIXTEEN, A PUT UP OR SHUT UP HIT SONG.
SEVENTEEN, ABOUT A LITTLE SIBLING.
EIGHTEEN, THOUGHTS HE CAN'T FORGET.

1) ________________
2) ____________________________?
3) ________________
4) __________________
5) ________________
6) _____________________________
7) __________________
8) ___________________________________
9) _____________________
10) ____________________
11) _________________
12) _________________
13) _______________________________________
14) _________________
15) ____________________
16) ____________________
17) _________________
18) __________

2. **1 x 5**

THE SONG "BOSSA NOVA BABY" WAS FEATURED IN THIS 1963 MOVIE BELOW CO-STARRING URSULA ANDRESS WHERE *ELVIS* PORTRAYS A LIFEGUARD JUST SOUTH OF THE BORDER. WHAT WAS THAT MOVIE CALLED?

A) KID GALAHAD
B) BLUE HAWAII
C) FUN IN ALCAPULCO
D) WILD IN THE COUNTRY

3. **1 x 5**

ON DECEMBER 3, 1968 *ELVIS* IS FEATURED IN A TV VARIETY SHOW ON NBC PERFORMING MANY OF HIS SONGS, INCLUDING TO AN AUDIENCE MOSTLY OF GIRLS, WHILE DRESSED UP IN ALL BLACK LEATHER. IT WOULD HAVE A REPEAT AIRING ON AUGUST 17, 1969. WHAT WAS IT CALLED?

A) THE ED SULLIVAN SHOW
B) VIVA LAS VEGAS
C) BLUE HAWAII
D) ELVIS '68 COMEBACK SPECIAL

TOTAL POINTS. **20 x 5 = 100**

BEATLEMANIA-QUIZ # 1

1. **1 x 10**

THE PLASTIC ONO BAND, CONSISTING OF *JOHN LENNON AND YOKO ONO*, RECORDED A SONG WHILE IN BED THAT HAD *THE SMOTHERS BROTHERS*, *MURRAY THE K* AND TIMOTHY LEARY DOING BACKUP ABOUT WHAT THEY HAD TO SAY REGARDING PEACE. WHAT WAS THAT BED-IN HIT SONG?

A) MY SWEET LORD
B) PEOPLE GOT TO BE FREE
C) PEACE TRAIN
D) GIVE PEACE A CHANCE

2. **4 x 10**

NAME THE FOUR *BEATLES* BY COMPLETING THE INITIALS PROVIDED BELOW.

1) J L - 1) _______________
2) P M - 2) __________________
3) G H - 3) __________________
4) R S - 4) _______________

3. **1 x 10**

WHICH MOVIE DID **NOT** FEATURE *THE BEATLES*?

A) YELLOW SUBMARINE
B) HELP!
C) THUNDERBALL
D) A HARD DAY'S NIGHT

4. **1 x 10**

IN THIS MOVIE, *RINGO* UNKNOWINGLY POSSESSED A SACRIFICIAL RING THAT A RELIGIOUS CULT HAD TO HAVE AT ANY COST. WHAT WAS THAT SONG WHICH WAS ALSO THE MOVIE TITLE?

A) A HARD DAY'S NIGHT
B) YELLOW SUBMARINE
C) HELP!
D) GOLDFINGER

5. **1 x 10**

DURING THE BEATLEMANIA PERIOD *THE CAREFREES*, A BRITISH GROUP, HAD A SONG THAT EXPRESSED THEIR LOVE FOR THE FAB FOUR. NAME THAT SONG.

____

6. **1 x 10**

IN FEBRUARY OF 1964 *THE BEATLES* CAME TO THE UNITED STATES AND PERFORMED ON WHAT TV VARIETY SHOW WHICH HELPED TO BOOSTER THEIR PRESENCE WORLDWIDE BECAUSE OF IT'S HUGE VIEWING AUDIENCE?

A) THE STEVE ALLEN SHOW
B) THE ED SULLIVAN SHOW
C) THE JOHNNY CARSON TONIGHT SHOW
D) THE DINAH SHORE SHOW

7. **1 x 10**

WHAT WAS THE SONG ORIGINALLY RECORDED BY *THE ISLEY BROTHERS* THAT *THE BEATLES* WOULD ALSO GO ON TO CHART AND MAYBE LOUDER?

A) SHOUT (PARTS 1 AND 2)
B) MONEY (THAT'S WHAT I WANT)
C) PLEASE, PLEASE, PLEASE
D) TWIST AND SHOUT

TOTAL POINTS. **10 x 10 = 100**

BEATLEMANIA-QUIZ # 2

1. 46 x 2

NAME THESE 46 SONGS OF *THE BEATLES*, BY COMPLETING THE INITIALS PROVIDED BELOW.

1 I W--T T- H--D Y--R H--D

2 I S-W H-R S------G T---E

3 S-E L---S Y-U

4 P----E P----E M-

5 M---Y (T---'S W--T I W--T) (MOTOWN SONG)

6 C--'T B-Y M- L--E

7 S-------G

8 D- Y-U W--T T- K--W A S----T

9 R--L O--R B-------N (CHUCK BERRY TUNE)

10 P.S. I L--E Y--

11 A H--D D--S N---T

12 A-D I L--E H-R

13 I F--L F--E

14 S--'S A W---N

15 E---T D--S A W--K

16 T----T T- R--E

17 M---Y (T--T'S W--T I W--T)

18 D---E M- C-R

19 W- C-N W--K I- O-T

20 D-Y T-----R

21 N-----E M-N

22 P-------K W----R

23 Y----W S-------E

24 E-----R R---Y

25 P---Y L--E

26 S--------Y F----S F-----R

27 A-L Y-U N--D I- L--E

28 H---O G-----E

29 L--Y M-----A

30 R--------N

31 G-T B--K

32 D--'T L-T M- D--N

33 T-E B----D O- J--N A-D Y--O

34 C--E T------R

35 F--M M- T- Y-U

36 H-Y J--E

37 A-L M- L----G

38 Y--'VE G-T T- H--E Y--R L--E A--Y

39 Y--'-E G---G T- L--E T--T G--L

40 I- I F--L

41 I- W--'T B- L--G

42 G--D D-Y S------E

43 T--S B-Y

44 T--L T---E W-S Y-U

45 W--H A L----E H--P F--M M- F-----S

46 N- R---Y

47. **1 x 2**

WHAT SONG HAD THE DISTINCTION OF BEING RECORDED BY ONE SOLO *BEATLE*, *PAUL MCCARTNEY*, AND ALSO BE THE MOST COVERED SONG IN HISTORY AS PER THE GUINNESS BOOK OF WORLD RECORDS?
A) I WANT TO HOLD YOUR HAND
B) EIGHT DAYS AWEEK
C) YESTERDAY
D) LOVE ME DO

48. **1 x 2**

THIS POPULAR SONG OUT OF THE 'RUBBER SOUL' ALBUM WAS A HIT BASED ON A FRENCH TUNE SUNG WITH BOTH ENGLISH AND FRENCH LYRICS. WHAT WAS THAT POPULAR SONG BY *PAUL MCCARTNEY*?
A) MICHELLE
B) MY CHERIE AMOUR
C) MA BELLE AMIE
D) NOWHERE MAN

49. **1 x 2**

THE BEATLES FIRST MAJOR HIT BELOW WAS RECORDED IN 1962 PRIOR TO THEIR NOTORIETY THROUGHOUT THE WORLD BUT WOULD BE RE-RELEASED IN 1964 AND CLIMB TO THE TOP OF THE CHARTS.

A) HELP!
B) HEY JUDE
C) LOVE ME DO
D) REVOLUTION

50. **1 x 2**

IN THE 60'S *RINGO STARR* HAD THE LEAD ON WHAT SONG THAT WAS ORIGINALLY A *BUCK OWENS'* COUNTRY HIT?

A) HELP
B) ACT NATURALLY
C) PENNY LANE
D) NO NO SONG

TOTAL POINTS. **50 x 2 = 100**

BEATLEMANIA-BONUS

1.

CHOOSE BELOW THE MANAGER OF *THE BEATLES* WHO GUIDED THEM TO FAME AND FORTUNE AND WHO WOULD DIE IN 1967 DUE TO AN OVERDOSE OF DRUGS.

A) COLONEL TOM PARKER
B) BRIAN EPSTEIN
C) BUCK RAM
D) QUINCY JONES

2.

RINGO STARR WOULD REPLACE WHAT DRUMMER BELOW?

A) GINGER BAKER
B) BUDDY RICH
C) PETE BEST
D) SAL MINEO

THE REST OF THE BRITISH INVASION-QUIZ # 1

1. **1 x 1**

IN 1965 *WAYNE FONTANA & THE MINDBENDERS* CHARTED A SONG ABOUT THE OBJECTIVE OF A MAN AND THAT OF A WOMAN EVER SINCE THE TIME OF ADAM AND EVE. IT WOULD BE *WAYNES'* BIGGEST MAJOR HIT OF HIS CAREER.
A) GAME OF LOVE
B) GAMES PEOPLE PLAY
C) WHEN A MAN LOVES A WOMAN
D) SHOW ME

2. **6 x 1**

PETULA CLARK THE POPULAR ENGLISH FEMALE SINGER CHARTED A NUMBER OF HITS DURING THE 60'S THAT INCLUDED "DOWNTOWN", "A SIGN OF THE TIMES", AND "COLOR MY WORLD". NAME THESE SIX OF HER OTHER HITS BELOW.
ONE, ABOUT A PLACE WE CAN GO THAT SHE KNEW.
TWO, ABOUT A FEELING MUCH DEEPER THAN ANY SEA.
THREE A TUNE TO SERENADE YOU WITH.
FOUR, ABOUT A DEPARTING KISS BECAUSE YOU'VE MET SOMEONE NEW.
FIVE, SOMETHING YOU SHOULDN'T DO IN THE SUBWAY.
SIX, NOT BEING ABLE TO SURVIVE WITHOUT YOU.
1) ____________________
2) ___________
3) ________________________
4) ________________________
5) ________________________________
6) ____

3. **1 x 1**

WHAT ENGLISH ARTIST PLAYED THE GUITAR, THE HARMONICA AND DRESSED ALOT LIKE *BOB DYLAN*? "ATLANTIS" WAS ONE OF HIS BIG HITS.
A) DAVE CLARK
B) ERIC BURDON
C) DONOVAN
D) BARRY GIBB

4. **1 x 1**

MANFRED MANN RECORDED THIS SONG THAT WOULD CLIMB TO THE TOP OF THE CHARTS ABOUT A GIRL SINGING AS SHE WAS STROLLING DOWN THE STREET. IT WAS AN ORIGINAL TUNE BY *THE EXCITERS*, THE R&B GROUP, BACK IN 1963.
A) DO WAH DIDDY DIDDY
B) I'D LIKE TO TEACH THE WORLD TO SING (IN PERFECT HARMONY)
C) WALK ON BY
D) SINGING THE BLUES

5. **1 x 1**

THE ROLLING STONES GAVE A FREE OUTDOOR CONCERT AT THE ALTAMONT SPEEDWAY IN SAN FRANCISCO ON DECEMBER 6, 1969. JOINING THEM WERE *CROSBY, NASH & YOUNG, SANTANA, JEFFERSON AIRPLANE*, ETC. THE HELLS ANGELS WERE HIRED AS SECURITY GUARDS. DURING THE EVENT A MAN WAS STABBED TO DEATH, AND A SHAKEN *MICK JAGGER* IS SEEN PLEADING WITH THE AUDIENCE TO BEHAVE. NAME THE DOCUMENTARY MOVIE THAT WAS PUT TOGETHER FOR THIS SHOW THAT DREW CLOSE TO 300,000 SPECTATORS.
A) THE WOODSTOCK FESTIVAL
B) GIMME SHELTER
C) THE MONTEREY INTERNATIONAL POP FESTIVAL
D) THE NEWPORT FOLK FESTIVAL

6. **3 x 1**

COMPLETE THE NAMES OF THE *'BEE GEES'* FROM THE INITIALS BELOW.

1) B G - 1) ______________
2) M G - 2) __________________
3) R G - 3) ______________

7. **14 x 1**

NAME THESE FOURTEEN HITS CHARTED BY *THE ROLLING STONES* IN THE 60'S.
ONE, WHAT HE COULDN'T GET. A SONG *OTIS REDDING* WOULD ALSO CHART.
TWO, ABOUT A CLOUD THEY WANTED YOU OUT OF.
THREE, ABOUT PAINTING SOMETHING BLACK.
FOUR, ABOUT A CERTAIN TUESDAY.
FIVE, A SONG THAT IN THE 80'S WOULD BE USED FOR A WHOOPI GOLDBERG MOVIE AS PART OF THE MOVIE PLOT ABOUT JACK.
SIX, ABOUT WHAT'S ON HIS SIDE THAT HE KNOWS YOU'LL BE BACK.
SEVEN, ABOUT MOM'S SPECIAL HELPER.
EIGHT, ABOUT A CERTAIN BAR ROOM TYPE OF WOMAN.
NINE, SOMETHING ON THE WAY THAT CAN BE NERVE RACKING AND QUITE REPETITIOUS FOR THAT INSANE GIRL.
TEN, THEIR VERSION OF A *MARIANNE FAITHFULL* SONG ABOUT TEARS.
ELEVEN, ABOUT A CERTAIN HEART THAT SHE'LL NEVER BREAK.
TWELVE, ABOUT SOMEONE HE ONCE LOVED BUT NO LONGER SO.
THIRTEEN, WHAT HE WANTED TO HEAR FROM SOMEONE WHO WALKED OUT ON HIM.
FOURTEEN, THE POSSIBILITY THIS COULD BE THE END OF OUR RELATIONSHIP.

1) ______________________________
2) __________________
3) __________________
4) _______________
5) _______________________
6) _______________________
7) _______________________
8) __________________
9) _______________________
10) _________________
11) _________________
12) ______________________
13) ______________________________
14) _________________

8. **1 x 1**

THE TROGGS RECORDED THIS ORIGINAL TUNE THAT THE GROUP, *WET, WET, WET* WOULD ALSO GO ON TO RECORD IN THE 90'S FOR THE MOVIE SOUNDTRACK OF 'FOUR WEDDINGS AND A FUNERAL' STARRING HUGH GRANT AND ANDIE MACDOWELL ABOUT LOVE BEING EVERYWHERE.

A) LOVE IS IN THE AIR
B) LOVE IS ALL AROUND
C) LOVE MAKES THE WORLD GO ROUND
D) EVERYBODY NEEDS SOMEBODY TO LOVE

9. **1 x 1**

THE TROGGS CHARTED ANOTHER ABOUT WHO HE LOVES THAT CAUSES A GROOVY FEELING TO OCCUR. IT WAS LATER RECORDED BY *JIMI HENDRIX,* AND ALSO AS A NOVELTY HIT BY *SENATOR BOBBY*. WHAT WAS THAT TRIPLE HITTER CALLED?

A) LIL' RED RIDING HOOD
B) A GROOVY KIND OF LOVE
C) BABY IT'S YOU
 D) WILD THING

10. **1 x 1**

THE SEARCHERS HAD THIS HEARTBREAK HIT SONG THAT MENTIONED SEWING UTENSILS THAT CAN REALLY HURT AND LEAVE ONE ON THE EDGE. NAME IT.

____

11. **1 x 1**

THE SEARCHERS CHARTED AGAIN IN 1964 WITH A RE-MAKE SONG OF *THE CLOVERS* THAT WAS ORIGINALLY RECORDED BACK IN THE LATE 50'S REGARDING A CERTAIN POTION THAT BLINDED HIM WITH DESIRE. THE SONG WOULD BE MADE INTO A MOVIE STARRING SANDRA BULLOCK AND TATE DONOVAN IN 1992 FEATURING THE *CLOVERS'* VERSION. WHAT WAS THAT DOUBLE HITTER BELOW?

A) WITCH DOCTOR
B) DEVIL OR ANGEL
C) WITCHCRAFT
D) LOVE POTION NUMBER NINE

12. **1 x 1**

"YOU'VE GOT TO HIDE YOUR LOVE AWAY" WAS FIRST RECORDED BY *THE BEATLES* FOR THEIR 'HELP' ALBUM AND SHORTLY AFTER BY WHAT OTHER GROUP BELOW?

A) THE ROLLING STONES
B) THREE DOG NIGHT
C) THE SILKIE
D) THE ANIMALS

13. **1 x 1**

MARIANNE FAITHFULL, THE ONE TIME GIRL FRIEND OF *MICK JAGGER,* CHARTED A SONG THAT *THE STONES* WOULD ALSO GO ON TO CHART THE FOLLOWING YEAR.

A) JUMPIN' JACK FLASH
B) THOSE WERE THE DAYS
C) AS TEARS GO BY
D) GIMME SOME LOVIN'

14. **1 x 1**

"I'M TELLING YOU NOW" AND "DO THE FREDDIE" WERE TWO RECORDED HITS BY WHAT ENGLISH GROUP BELOW?

A) THE ROLLING STONES
B) HERMAN'S HERMITS
C) GERRY AND THE PACEMAKERS
D) FREDDIE AND THE DREAMERS

15. **1 x 1**

PROCOL HARUM CHARTED THIS SONG BELOW THAT IN THE 80'S WOULD BE FEATURED IN THE MOVIE SOUNDTRACK OF 'THE BIG CHILL' STARRING TOM BERINGER, GLENN CLOSE, JEFF GOLDBLUM AND MEG TILLY, TO NAME A FEW, ABOUT A CERTAIN COLOR.

A) SILHOUETTES
B) A WHITER SHADE OF PALE
C) BLACK IS BLACK
D) COLOR HIM FATHER

16. **1 x 1**

GERRY AND THE PACEMAKERS HAD THESE TWO HITS BELOW. WHICH ONE WAS **NOT** THEIRS?

A) DON'T LET THE SUN CATCH YOU CRYING
B) FERRY CROSS THE MERSEY
C) RUBY TUESDAY

17. **1 x 1**

THE MINDBENDERS LESS *WAYNE FONTANA* CHARTED A TOP NUMBER TWO HIT SONG ABOUT A CERTAIN TYPE OF LOVE. IT WOULD BE FEATURED IN THE *PHIL COLLINS* MOVIE 'BUSTER' IN THE LATE 80'S RECORDED BY *PHIL*. WHAT WAS THAT DOUBLE HITTER BELOW?

A) GAME OF LOVE
B) GROOVIN'
C) YOU CAN'T HURRY LOVE
D) A GROOVY KIND OF LOVE

18. **8 x 1**

NAME THESE EIGHT CHARTED HITS BY *HERMAN'S HERMITS,* WITH *PETER HERMAN NOONE* IN LEAD.
ONE, ABOUT A CERTAIN LADY WHO HAD A GORGEOUS DAUGHTER.
TWO, A CERTAIN BEAT THAT YOU COULD HEAR.
THREE, ABOUT SOMETHING SWELL THAT HE WAS INTO.
FOUR, ABOUT KING HENRY AND WHAT HE CLAIMED TO BE.
FIVE, THEIR VERSION OF A *SAM COOKE* TUNE ABOUT WHAT HE TOO CLAIMED NOT TO BE.
SIX, ABOUT LISTENING TO WHAT HE HAS TO SAY.
SEVEN, ABOUT A CERTAIN HUSH THROUGHOUT THE WORLD THAT *THE CARPENTERS* WOULD ALSO RECORD IN THE 70'S.
EIGHT, THEIR RECORDING OF AN ORIGINAL HIT SONG OF *THE RAYS* CHARTED IN THE 50'S ABOUT TWO SHADOWS BEHIND THE WINDOW SHADE IN AN EMBRACE.

1) ______________________________
2) ______________________
3) ___________________
4) _______________
5) ____________
6) ___________
7) ___________________
8) ___________

19. **8 x 1**

NAME THESE EIGHT POPULAR HITS BY THE '*DAVE CLARK FIVE*'.
ONE, THEIR BIG DOUBLE OVER TITLED HIT SONG THAT WAS ORIGINALLY WRITTEN AND RECORDED BY *BOBBY DAY* IN THE LATE 50'S.
TWO, ABOUT THE GLAD FEELING HE HAD BECAUSE SHE WAS HIS.
THREE, ABOUT BEING SHATTERED INTO MANY BITS AND PARTS BECAUSE SHE'S GONE AND LEFT HIM ALL ALONE.
FOUR, THEIR RENDITION OF A *MARV JOHNSON* TUNE RECORDED A FEW YEARS LATER ABOUT SOMETHING YOU GOT.
FIVE, THEIR COVER VERSION OF A *CHRIS KENNER* SONG ABOUT WHO THEY WERE GONNA TAKE, JUST ASK SALLY OR SUE.
SIX, IT'S SO OBVIOUS THAT SHE'S MINE AND FOR SO LONG.
SEVEN, THE ONLY OBVIOUS REASON HE LOVES YOU AND WANTS THAT CHANCE TO BE BY YOUR SIDE.
EIGHT, ABOUT WANTING YOU TO CHASE THEM LIKE IN A CHILDS' GAME.

1) ___________
2) ___________
3) _____________
4) _________________
5) _______________
6) ______________________
7) ______
8) _______________

20. **5 x 1**

NAME THE FIVE ORIGINAL MEMBERS OF *THE ROLLING STONES* BY COMPLETING THE INITIALS PROVIDED BELOW.

1) M J - 1) ____________
2) K R - 2) __________________
3) B J - 3) ____________
4) C W - 4) __________________
5) B W - 5) ____________

21. **4 x 1**

NAME THESE FOUR HITS BY *DUSTY SPRINGFIELD,* THE FEMALE SINGER.
ONE, ABOUT HER WANTING TO SPEND EVERY MOMENT WITH YOU, A SONG *BAY CITY ROLLERS* WOULD RECORD IN THE 70'S AND *SAMANTHA FOX* IN THE 80'S.
TWO, HOW DREAMING AND PRAYING WON'T BE ENOUGH TO GET INTO HIS HEART.
THREE, WHAT YOU WOULDN'T HAVE TO SAY NOR DO FOR LONG.
FOUR, ABOUT THE PREACHER'S SON AND WHAT HE WAS ABLE TO DO.

1) ______________________________
2) ______________________
3) ______________________________________
4) ___________________________

22. **3 x 1**

THE ZOMBIES CHARTED THESE THREE BIG HITS IN THE 60'S.
ONE, WHAT THEY DIDN'T KNOW ABOUT THAT GIRL AND THE LACK OF HER PRESENCE.
TWO, ABOUT A CERTAIN TIME.
THREE, WHAT HE WANTED YOU TO TELL THAT GIRL BECAUSE SHE STILL BELONGED TO HIM RIGHT OR WRONG. IT WAS A SONG *JUICE NEWTON* WOULD ALSO GO ON TO RECORD IN THE EARLY 80'S.
NAME THEM.

1) __________________
2) ______________________
3) _______________

23. **1 x 1**

IN 1965 *THE YARDBIRDS* RECORDED THIS SONG BELOW ABOUT WHAT THEY WOULD DO TO HAVE YOUR LOVE. IT WOULD GAIN THEM THEIR INITIAL STARDOM.

A) FOR YOUR PRECIOUS LOVE
B) FOR YOUR LOVE
C) YOU BELONG TO ME
D) YOU WERE MINE

25. **1 x 1**

NAME THE ROCK BAND BELOW RESPONSIBLE FOR CHARTING NUMEROUS HITS INCLUDING "A WELL RESPECTED MAN" AND "YOU REALLY GOT ME".

A) THE ROLLING STONES
B) DAVE CLARK FIVE
C) THE ANIMALS
D) THE KINKS

25. **1 x 1**

THE GROUP ABOVE HAD ANOTHER ABOUT WANTING TO BE WITH A GIRL DAY IN AND DAY OUT, 24/7, ALL THE TIME. WHAT WAS THAT HIT BELOW?

A) I ONLY WANT TO BE WITH YOU
B) TIME WON'T LET ME
C) ALL DAY AND ALL OF THE NIGHT
D) A GIRL LIKE YOU

26. **3 x 1**

NAME THESE THREE CHARTED HITS BY *THE ANIMALS* WITH *ERIC BURDON* IN LEAD.
ONE, ABOUT A CERTAIN HOUSE THAT HAS DAMAGED MANY A GUY. A SONG THAT *FRIJID PINK* WOULD ALSO RECORD IN THE EARLY 70'S.
TWO, ABOUT HAVING TO VACATE A CERTAIN PLACE.
THREE, ABOUT WANTING TO CONTROL HIS OWN DESTINY AS HE SEES FIT.

1) ______________________________
2) ___________________________________
3) ________________

27. **1 x 1**

WHAT POPULAR ROCK BAND WITH NUMEROUS HITS TO THEIR BELTS RECORDED THESE TWO, "I CAN SEE FOR MILES" AND "PINBALL WIZARD"?
A) LED ZEPPLIN
B) ALICE COOPER
C) THE WHO
D) THE ROLLING STONES

28. **1 x 1**

IN 1968 THE GROUP *CREAM* CHARTED TWO BIG HITS. "SUNSHINE OF YOUR LOVE" WAS THEIR FIRST. WHAT WAS THE OTHER ABOUT THE COLOR WHITE?
A) WHITE ROOM
B) A WHITER SHADE OF PALE
C) WHITE RABBIT
D) NIGHTS IN WHITE SATIN

29. **19 x 1**

COMPLETE THE NAMES OF THESE NINETEEN POPULAR BRITISH ACTS IN THE 60'S FROM THE INITIALS PROVIDED BELOW.

1) THE B-----S - 1) _______________
2) C--D & J----Y - 2) __________________
3) D--E C---K F--E - 3) _____________________
4) D-----N - 4) __________
5) THE A-----S - 5) ______________
6) THE F------S - 6) ________________
7) G---Y AND THE P--------S - 7) ____________________________
8) THE H-----S - 8) ______________
9) THE K---S - 9) ___________
10) M-----D M--N - 10) ________________
11) P---R AND G----N - 11) __________________
12) THE R-----G S----S - 12) ______________________
13) THE Z-----S - 13) _____________
14) H-----'S H-----S - 14) ___________________
15) THE T----S - 15) _______________
16) S-----R D---S G---P - 16) __________________________
17) P----A C---K - 17) ________________
18) D---Y S---------D - 18) ________________________
19) F-----E AND THE D------S - 19) ______________________________

30. **1 x 1**

"SMILE A LITTLE SMILE FOR ME", WAS RECORDED BY WHICH GROUP BELOW IN 1969 THAT WOULD BECOME THEIR ONLY CLAIM TO FAME SONG?
A) THE IMPRESSIONS
B) THE DRIFTERS
C) BROOKLYN BRIDGE
D) THE FLYING MACHINE

31. **1 x 1**

LULU, THE YOUNG SINGER TURNED ACTRESS, HAD WHAT POPULAR SONG IN 1967 THAT WAS FEATURED IN A MOVIE OF THE SAME NAME STARRING SIDNEY POITIER AS A SCHOOL MASTER, BETTER KNOWN AS SIR, WHO EVENTUALLY WINS THE CONFIDENCE AND TRUST AND LOVE OF ALL HIS STUDENTS?

A) MR LEE
B) (WE'RE GONNA) ROCK AROUND THE CLOCK
C) TO SIR WITH LOVE
D) AMEN

32. **1 x 1**

*THE FORTUNES C*HARTED WHAT MAJOR HIT BELOW THAT WOULD PROPELL THEM TO STARDOM ABOUT WHAT WE ALL HAVE, AND THAT WOULD INCLUDE YOU AND I?

A) I GOT RHYTHM
B) YOU'VE GOT YOUR TROUBLES
C) I'VE GOT YOU UNDER MY SKIN
D) I GOT YOU BABE

33. **1 x 1**

CHAD & JEREMY CHARTED A SONG ABOUT THE SUMMER AND HOW IT HURTS TO SEE IT GO BUT BY DREAMING YOU CAN HELP PROLONG IT.

A) A SUMMER SONG
B) SUMMERTIME
C) HERE COMES SUMMER
D) SUMMER IN THE CITY

34. **2 x 1**

THIS MALE ARTIST, *ENGELBERT HUMPERDINCK* BY WAY OF ENGLAND, CHARTED THESE TWO SONGS BELOW.
ONE, HIS RENDITION OF AN *ESTHER PHILLIPS* SONG ABOUT WANTING TO BE SET FREE BY THE ONE HE NO LONGER LOVES, HIS VERSION TITLE EXTENDED.
TWO, ANOTHER RENDITION SONG, THIS TIME OF A *DEBBY REYNOLDS* TUNE, QUESTIONING HOW EASILY ONE CAN BE FORGOTTEN.
NAME THEM.

1) ______________________________________
2) ____________________________

35. **1 x 1**

BILLY J. KRAMER WITH THE DAKOTAS HAD A HIT WITH WHAT SONG BELOW ABOUT KIDS, THAT HE HOPED THEY WOULDN'T SQUEAL ON THEIR OLDER SISTER WHO WAS CAUGHT KISSING HIM?

A) MOTHER'S LITTLE HELPER
B) LITTLE CHILDREN
C) O-O-H CHILD
D) TWO LITTLE KIDS

36. **1 x 1**

BILLY J. KRAMER WITH THE DAKOTAS RECORDED ANOTHER ABOUT HIS INTENTIONS TO KEEP YOU FOR GOOD AS LONG AS YOU DIDN'T TREAT HIM BAD. WHAT WAS THAT HIT?

A) DON'T LET ME DOWN
B) BE MY BABY
C) BAD TO ME
D) THINK

TOTAL POINTS. **100 x 1 = 100**

THE REST OF THE BRITISH INVASION-QUIZ # 2

1. **1 x 4**

JONATHAN KING IS MOSTLY REMEMBERED FOR RECORDING THIS SONG BELOW IN 1965 WHERE HE CLAIMED EVERYONE HAD BEEN TO THIS PARTICULAR PLACE UP ABOVE.

A) BLUE MOON
B) BLUE MOON OVER KENTUCKY
C) THERE'S A MOON OUT TONIGHT
D) EVERYONE'S GONE TO THE MOON

2. **3 x 4**

THE DUO OF *PETER AND GORDON* WOULD RECORD THESE THREE HITS BELOW.
ONE, WHAT HE GOES THROUGH EVERYTIME HIS BABE PASSES BY.
TWO, ABOUT THAT CERTAIN LADY ON A HORSE.
THREE, ABOUT REFUSING TO LIVE IN THIS WORLD WITHOUT WHAT?
NAME THEM.

1) ____________________
2) ________________
3) ___________________________

3. **6 x 4**

DONOVAN, THE SINGER/SONGWRITER, CHARTED THESE SIX BIG HITS BELOW.
ONE, ABOUT THE SUPER HEROES WHO HAVE NOTHING ON HIM.
TWO, ABOUT THAT GREEK MYTH OF AN ISLAND THOUGHT TO HAVE DISAPPEARED BY SINKING.
THREE, ABOUT HIS GIRLS, INCLUDING SAFRON AND FRAUNTINE AND WHAT THEY CALLED HIM THAT WAS QUITE SOOTHING.
FOUR, HIS MOUNTAIN HIT SONG.
FIVE, ABOUT A CERTAIN MAN WHO SANG SONGS OF PASSION.
SIX, ABOUT HIS FRENCH LASSIE, JUNIPER.
NAME THEM.

1) ____________________
2) ___________
3) __________________
4) ____________________________
5) __________________
6) ____________________

4. **1 x 4**

IN THE 60'S THIS MALE ARTIST WAS A MEMBER OF *THE YARDBIRDS* AND THEN WITH THE GROUP *CREAM,* IN THE 70'S PART OF *DEREK AND THE DOMINOS,* AND AS A SOLOIST IN THE 80'S AND STILL IS. HE OFTEN PLAYED THE BLUES AND HAD A BIT PART IN THE *CHUCK BERRY* MOVIE 'HAIL! HAIL! ROCK 'N' ROLL'. WHO IS HE, STILL PERFORMING HERE IN THE 21ST CENTURY?

A) ROD STEWART
B) KEITH RICHARDS
C) ERIC CLAPTON
D) RON WOOD

5. **3 x 4**

THE '*BEE GEES*', THE TRIO BROTHER ACT, HAD A BUNCH OF HITS INCLUDING "WORDS" AND "MASSACHUSETTS". NAME THESE THREE OTHER HITS BELOW.
ONE, TO LOVE WHO? ALSO RECORDED BY *MICHAEL BOLTON* IN THE EARLY 90'S.
TWO, ABOUT A MESSAGE HE MUST DELIVER.
THREE, SOMETHING HE STARTED.

1) ____________________
2) ____________________________________
 3) ____________________

6. **1 x 4**

TEN YEARS AFTER RECORDED A SONG THAT WAS FEATURED IN 'THE WOODSTOCK FESTIVAL' ABOUT WHERE HE WAS GOING. WHAT WAS THAT FEATURED HIT?
A) GOING UP THE COUNTRY
B) COMING HOME SOLDIER
C) I'M GOING HOME
D) UP ON THE ROOF

7. **1 x 5**

THE HOLLIES RECORDED THIS SONG BELOW ABOUT A CERTAIN STOP WHERE THEY WAIT FOR ONE ANOTHER AND WHEN NECESSARY SHARE AN UMBRELLA. HOPEFULLY ONE DAY THEY WILL GET TO SHARE THE SAME NAME.
A) BUS STOP
B) HOMEWARD BOUND
C) AT MY FRONT DOOR
D) LAST TRAIN TO CLARKSVILLE

8. **1 x 4**

THE HOLLIES CHARTED TWO OTHER HITS BELOW. WHICH ONE WAS **NOT** THEIRS?
A) SUGAR, SUGAR
B) CARRIE ANNE
C) STOP STOP STOP

9. **1 x 4**

IN 1968 *THE FOUNDATIONS* RECORDED THEIR FIRST MAJOR HIT WITH THIS SONG ABOUT NEVER LETTING YOU GO.
A) I'M INTO SOMETHING GOOD
B) BABY, NOW THAT I'VE FOUND YOU
C) YOU CAN'T HURRY LOVE
D) PLEASE STAY

10. **1 x 4**

A YEAR LATER *THE FOUNDATIONS* HAD ANOTHER WHICH WAS THE BIGGEST OF THEIR SHORT SPANNED CAREER ABOUT A BUTTERCUP. IN THE LATE 90'S IT WOULD BE FEATURED IN THE SOUNDTRACK MOVIE 'WHAT ABOUT MARY' STARRING CAMERON DIAZ AND BEN STILLER. NAME THAT ONE BELOW.
A) PEANUTS
B) PEANUT BUTTER
C) BUILD ME UP BUTTERCUP
D) BREAD AND BUTTER

11. **1 x 4**

THE TREMELOES CHARTED THEIR RENDITION OF A *FOUR SEASONS* SONG ABOUT SILENCE AND HOW PRECIOUS IT CAN BE. WHAT WAS THAT DOUBLE HITTER?
A) QUIET VILLAGE
B) BIG GIRLS DON'T CRY
C) DAWN (GO AWAY)
D) SILENCE IS GOLDEN

12. **1 x 4**

THE *'SPENCER DAVIS GROUP'* WITH *STEVE WINWOOD* IN LEAD HAD THIS BIG LOVING HIT SONG THAT WOULD BE FEATURED IN A JULIA ROBERTS AND HUGH GRANT MOVIE CALLED 'NOTTING HILL' IN THE LATE 90'S ABOUT WHAT HE WANTED. GIVE ME THE NAME OF THAT BIG HIT.
A) GIMME GIMME GOOD LOVIN'
B) BABY I NEED YOUR LOVING
C) GIMME SOME LOVIN'
D) TO LOVE SOMEBODY

13. **1 x 4**

'THE CRAZY WORLD OF ARTHUR BROWN' CHARTED A TOP NUMBER TWO HIT SONG IN 1968 ABOUT WHERE HE WAS GOING TO TAKE YOU TO BURN. WHAT WAS THAT NUMBER TWO HIT SONG?
A) SOMETHING'S BURNING
B) FIRE
C) WE GOTTA GET OUT OF THIS PLACE
D) SUMMERTIME BLUES

14. **1 x 4**

IN 1965 *THE MOODY BLUES* RECORDED A RE-MAKE OF A 1964 *BESSIE BANKS* SONG ABOUT WHAT THEY WANTED YOU TO DO, ASAP. IT WOULD BE THEIR FIRST MAJOR HIT AND CATAPULT THEM TO THEIR INITIAL STARDOM THAT WOULD LAST FOR THREE DECADES.
A) FOR YOUR LOVE
B) SHAKE ME, WAKE ME (WHEN IT'S OVER)
C) GO NOW!
D) (JUST LIKE) ROMEO & JULIET

15. **1 x 4**

IAN WHITCOMB & BLUESVILLE CHARTED THIS CLAIM TO FAME SONG ABOUT THE EXCITEMENT HIS BABY GIVES HIM. WHAT WAS THAT CLAIM TO FAME SONG?
A) TURN ON YOUR LOVE LIGHT
B) SUGAR SUGAR
C) FEVER
D) YOU TURN ME ON (TURN ON SONG)

16. **1 x 4**

THE SWINGING BLUE JEANS HAD A HIT WITH THIS DANCE NUMBER WHERE THEY TAUGHT US HOW TO DO IT IN THE LYRICS, WHERE YOU SHAKE IT TO THE LEFT, THEN TO THE RIGHT, AND WITH ALL YOUR MIGHT. WHAT WAS THAT DANCE NUMBER BELOW THAT WOULD BE THEIR CLAIM TO FAME SONG?
A) TIGHTEN UP
B) DOUBLE SHOT OF MY BABY'S LOVE
C) HIPPY HIPPY SHAKE
D) SHAKE

TOTAL POINTS. 25 x 4 = 100

THE REST OF THE BRITISH INVASION-BONUS

1.

THE HONEYCOMBS RECORDED THIS SONG BELOW THAT QUESTIONED THEIR RIGHT TO DO SOMETHING. IT WAS THEIR BIGGEST MAJOR ENTRY INTO THE CHARTS.
A) HAVE I THE RIGHT
B) RIGHT PLACE WRONG TIME
C) RIGHT TIME OF THE NIGHT
D) RIGHT BACK WHERE WE STARTED FROM

2.

THE SONG "HUSH" WAS RECORDED BY THIS HARD ROCK BAND BELOW ABOUT THAT GIRL WHO BROKE HIS HEART YET HE LOVES HER JUST THE SAME. IN THE 70'S THEY WOULD HAVE ANOTHER BIG HIT WITH "SMOKE ON THE WATER". NAME THAT HARD ROCK BAND BELOW.
A) HERMAN'S HERMITS
B) THE MYSTICS
C) DEEP PURPLE
D) THE TROGGS

MOTOWN ROCKERS-QUIZ # 1

1. **9 x 1**

THIS GROUP CONSISTING OF FOUR GUYS AND ONE GIRL OUT OF THE STAPLES OF THE MOTOWN LABEL HAD A BIG NUMBER OF HITS INCLUDING: "THE LOVE I SAW IN YOU WAS JUST A MIRAGE", "BABY, BABY DON'T CRY", "SPECIAL OCCASION", "COME 'ROUND HERE) I'M THE ONE YOU NEED" AND "MORE LOVE". NAME THEM AND EIGHT OF THEIR OTHER HITS BELOW, NUMBERS TWO THROUGH NINE.

ONE, GROUP NAME.

TWO, WHAT HIS MOTHER TOLD HIM TO DO THAT *THE CAPTAIN & TENNILLE* WOULD ALSO SING ABOUT IN THE 70'S.

THREE, ABOUT WHAT HE WOULD SECOND.

FOUR, ABOUT TRACKS OF EMOTIONAL PAIN SINCE YOU LEFT HIM. A SONG BOTH *JOHNNY RIVERS* IN THE 60'S AND *LINDA RONSTADT* IN THE 70'S WOULD ALSO RECORD.

FIVE, ABOUT BUILDING HER A FORTRESS AND TRYING OTHER THINGS IF NEED BE.

SIX, A HOLD SHE HAS ON HIM EVEN THOUGH SHE TREATED HIM SO BADLY.

SEVEN, ABOUT A GUY NAMED MICKEY SHOWCASING A NEW DANCE STEP.

EIGHT, THEIR BIG GO-GO HIT SONG.

NINE, A SONG THAT *LINDA RONSTADT* WOULD ALSO RECORD ABOUT CRYING BECAUSE YOU DID YOUR BABY WRONG.

1) ____________________
2) ______________
3) __________________________
4) __________________________
5) __________________________
6) ________________________________
7) ____________________
8) ____________________
9) ____________________

2. **1 x 1**

THIS GENTLEMAN STARTED OUT WORKING AT A FORD MOTOR ASSEMBLY PLANT AS A CHROME TRIMMER. DURING HIS SPARE TIME HE WOULD WRITE OR CO-WRITE SONGS. THIS INCLUDED *JACKIE WILSONS'* "REET PETITE", "TO BE LOVED", AND "LONELY TEARDROPS". FOR *THE MIRACLES* "SHOP AROUND", AND FOR *THE CONTOURS* "DO YOU LOVE ME" AND GOD ONLY KNOWS HOW MANY MORE. WHO WAS THIS GENTLEMAN WHO FOUNDED ONE OF THE GREATEST RECORD LABELS OF ALL TIME WHOSE PRODUCTIVITY COULD NEVER BE MATCHED AGAIN?

____

3. **1 x 1**

WHICH HIT TUNE BELOW WAS **NOT** AN ORIGINAL *DENNIS EDWARDS* SONG AS A MEMBER OF *THE TEMPTATIONS* DURING THE 60'S?

A) CLOUD NINE
B) DON'T LET THE JONESES GET YOU DOWN
C) MY GIRL
D) I CAN'T GET NEXT TO YOU

4. **2 x 1**

WHAT DID *MARY WELLS* SING ABOUT IN TWO OF HER BIGGEST HITS?

ONE, SOMETHING THAT SHE'S GOT AND LOVES EQUALLY.

TWO, SOMETHING OF HERS, THAT NOTHING CAN TAKE HIM AWAY.

NAME THEM.

1) _______________
2) __________

5. **1 x 1**

CINDY BIRDSONG, ORIGINALLY A MEMBER OF *THE BLUE BELLES*, BECAME A REPLACEMENT FOR WHAT ORIGINAL MEMBER OF THE *SUPREMES?*

A) FLORENCE BALLARD
B) JEAN TERRELL
C) DIANA ROSS
D) MARY WILSON

6. **14 x 1**

THIS POPULAR QUINTET MALE GROUP OUT OF MOTOWN CHARTED NUMEROUS HITS, INCLUDING: "RUN AWAY CHILD, RUNNING WILD", "DON'T LET THE JONESES GET YOU DOWN", "LONELINESS MADE ME REALIZE) IT'S YOU THAT I NEED" AND "GIRL (WHY YOU WANNA MAKE ME BLUE". NAME THEM, AND THESE THIRTEEN OTHER HITS BELOW, NUMBERS TWO THROUGH FOURTEEN.
ONE, THEIR NAME.
TWO, LIKE THE FISH THAT GOT AWAY AND THE AMOUNT OF LOVE THAT HE HAS FOR YOU.
THREE, NOT BEING ASHAMED TO HAVE TO DO THIS IF IT MEANS HAVING YOU.
FOUR, ABOUT LEAVING THEIR TROUBLES AND NOT DWELLING ON THEM.
FIVE, TELLING HER TO BE PREPARED BECAUSE HE'S ON HIS WAY WITH HIS LOVING.
SIX, SINCE SHE LEFT HIM HE'S BEEN SEARCHING ALL OVER FOR HER.
SEVEN, ABOUT LOOKS BEING OK BUT HE'D RATHER HAVE A GIRL WITH SINCERITY AND GOOD PERSONALITY ANYTIME.
EIGHT, ABOUT HOPING THE BLUE SKIES WOULD DISAPPEAR SO HE COULD CRY IN DISGUISE WITH THE DOWNPOUR.
NINE, ABOUT A CERTAIN GIRL IN MAY. THIS SONG WOULD BE FEATURED IN THE MOVIE SOUNDTRACK OF 'THE BIG CHILL' IN THE 80'S.
TEN, ABOUT A GIRL THAT COULD HAVE SUCCEEDED IN ANYTHING SHE DESIRED AND MADE HIM FEEL SO CONTENT. A SONG *UB40* WOULD GO ON TO RECORD IN THE EARLY 90'S.
ELEVEN, ABOUT THE WORLD OF POVERTY AND THE CLOUD THAT CHANGES THINGS SUPPOSEDLY FOR THE BETTER.
TWELVE, WHAT YOU ARE THAT MOTIVATES HIM TO WANT ONLY YOU.
THIRTEEN, ABOUT A LOVE AFFAIR COMING TO AN END AND THERE NEVER BEING ANOTHER WHO COULD REPLACE HER.
FOURTEEN, WHAT HE KNEW ABOUT YOUR PLANS AND THAT WAS FOR ANOTHER.

1) ____________________
2) ________________
3) _________________________
4) ____________________
5) ____________
6) _________________________
7) _________________________________
8) _________________________
9) __________
10) ____
11) ______________
12) ________________________
13) ____
14) ______________________________

7. **1 x 1**

THE ORIGINALS CHARTED WHAT ROMANTIC SONG BELOW ABOUT BEING SINCERE ON HOW MUCH HE LOVES YOU AND WANTS TO BE YOUR ONLY ONE?
A) BABY, I'M YOURS
B) BABY, I'M FOR REAL
C) I DO LOVE YOU
D) SINCERELY

8. **1 x 1**

DAVID RUFFIN, THE FORMER MEMBER AND SOMETIME LEAD SINGER OF *THE TEMPTATIONS*, RECORDED A SONG ABOUT HIS WORLD BEING SHATTERED, BECAUSE WITHOUT YOU, IT WOULD BE SO MEANINGLESS.
A) BREAKING UP IS HARD TO DO
B) HELP ME MAKE IT THROUGH THE NIGHT
C) MY WHOLE WORLD ENDED (THE MOMENT YOU LEFT ME)
D) WHAT BECOMES OF THE BROKENHEARTED

9. **6 x 1**

THIS YOUNGSTER ALSO FROM THE MOTOWN LABEL CHARTED LOTS OF HITS INCLUDING: "A PLACE IN THE SUN", "UPTIGHT (EVERYTHING'S ALRIGHT)", "NOTHING'S TOO GOOD FOR MY BABY", AND "I'M WONDERING". NAME HIM, AND THESE FIVE OTHER HITS BELOW, NUMBERS TWO THROUGH SIX.
ONE, HIS NAME.
TWO, A SONG RECORDED LIVE AT THE TENDER AGE OF 12, PARTS 1 AND 2, WITH THE CONDUCTOR ASKING "WHAT KEY" NEAR THE END OF THE SONG.
THREE, ABOUT FINALLY HAVING FOUND SOMEONE.
FOUR, WHAT HE WAS MADE TO DO.
FIVE, HIS VERSION OF A *BOB DYLAN* TUNE ABOUT THE WIND, THAT WAS ALSO A BIG *PETER, PAUL & MARY* HIT SONG.
SIX, ABOUT HIS AMOUR.
1) ______________________________
2) ______________________________
3) ______________________________
4) ______________________________
5) ______________________________
6) _______________________

10. **1 x 1**

BARRETT STRONG, THE SINGER/SONGWRITER FOR MOTOWN, HAD A POPULAR SONG ABOUT SOMETHING HE COULDN'T GET ENOUGH OF, IT'S ALL HE WANTED, LOTS OF IT. IN FACT, ACCORDING TO 'THE MOTOWN STORY' IT BECAME ONE OF MOTOWN'S EARLY RECORDED HITS FOR MR BERRY GORDY WHICH HELPED TO EXPAND HIS EMPIRE.
A) ALL YOU NEED IS LOVE
B) PENNIES FROM HEAVEN
C) MONEY (THAT'S WHAT I WANT)
D) GIRL WATCHER

11. **1 x 1**

JIMMY RUFFIN, THE BROTHER OF *DAVID RUFFIN,* RECORDED A SONG ABOUT HIS QUESTIONING THE PATH OF DEPARTED ROMANCE. *PAUL YOUNG*, THE ENGLISHMAN, WOULD RECORD IT IN THE 90'S FOR THE MOVIE SOUNDTRACK OF "FRIED GREEN TOMATOES", STARRING MARY STUART MASTERSON, KATHY BATES AND JESSICA TANDY.
A) WHAT BECOMES OF THE BROKENHEARTED
B) MY WHOLE WORLD ENDED (THE MOMENT YOU LEFT ME)
C) SEALED WITH A KISS
D) SEE YOU IN SEPTEMBER

12. **13 x 1**

THIS VERY SUCCESSFUL FEMALE TRIO GROUP OUT OF MOTOWN CHARTED HIT AFTER HIT. THIS INCLUDED: "WHERE DID OUR LOVE GO", "COME SEE ABOUT ME", "BABY LOVE", "LOVE IS HERE AND NOW YOU'RE GONE", "IN AND OUT OF LOVE", "WHEN THE LOVELIGHT STARTS SHINING THROUGH HIS EYES", AND "FOREVER CAME TODAY". NAME THEM, AND THESE TWELVE OTHER HITS BELOW, NUMBERS TWO THROUGH THIRTEEN.
ONE, THEIR NAME.
TWO , ABOUT COMPARING WHAT, TO AN ITCHING THAT SHE WAS UNABLE TO STOP.
THREE, WHEN YOU'RE NEAR, A MELODY IS WHAT THEY HEAR.
FOUR, HOLDING ON, ONLY TO BE USED BY HIM.
FIVE, GRATEFUL THAT YOU'RE BACK ONCE MORE.
SIX, STOP OR YOU'LL BREAK HER HEART.
SEVEN, HER LIFE SO MEANINGLESS AND EMPTY WITHOUT HIM.
EIGHT, WHAT MAMA SAID ABOUT LOVE NOT ALWAYS BEING EASY. ALSO RECORDED BY *PHIL COLLINS* IN THE 80'S.
NINE, HEARTACHES IS ALL HE BRINGS AND SHE CAN'T BREAK AWAY.
TEN, ABOUT A CHILD BORN OUT OF WEDLOCK NOT MEANT TO BE. A SONG THE FEMALE GROUP *SWEET SENSATION* WOULD ALSO RECORD IN THE EARLY 90'S.
ELEVEN, A SONG THAT WOULD BE USED AS THE THEME FOR THE 'CHINA BEACH' TV SERIES STARRING DANA DELANEY ABOUT THE WAY LIFE USED TO BE OR A MIRROR OF IT.
TWELVE, ABOUT BEING ASHAMED OF HER UNKEMPT MOTHER WHO SHE NOW MISSES SINCE HER DEATH AND WISHING SHE COULD BEG FOR HER FORGIVENESS.
THIRTEEN, ABOUT HAVING LOVE ONE DAY AND UNEXPECTINGLY LOSING IT THE NEXT. THIS WAS ALSO THE TITLE OF THE MOVIE STARRING ANTHONY QUINN.

1) ____________________
2) ____
3) ________________________
4) _________________________________
5) ______________________________
6) _________________________________
7) ____
8) ______________________________
9) ______________________________
10) ___________________
11) ___________________
12) ____________________________
13) ___________________

13. **1 x 1**

CHOOSE THIS FINAL *SUPREMES* HIT SONG WITH *DIANA ROSS* IN LEAD BEFORE HER DEPARTURE FROM THE GROUP TO GO IT ALONE. IT DEALT WITH THE POSSIBILITY OF SOMETHING OCCURRING IN THE FUTURE.
A) MAYBE
B) COME BACK WHEN YOU GROW UP
C) TOGETHER
D) SOMEDAY WE'LL BE TOGETHER

14. **1 x 1**

WHAT SONG DID *EDWIN STARR* CHART IN THE 60'S ABOUT THAT REMAINING DISTANCE HE'S GOT TO WALK BEFORE HE CAN HOLD THAT WOMAN IN HIS ARMS?
A) 500 MILES
B) A THOUSAND MILES AWAY
C) 25 MILES
D) 26 MILES (SANTA CATALINA)

15. **5 x 1**

COMPLETE THE NAMES OF THE *TEMPTATIONS* IN THE EARLY 60'S FROM THE INITIALS PROVIDED BELOW.

1) O W - 1) ____________________
2) P W - 2) ____________________
3) M F - 3) ________________________
4) E K - 4) ________________________
5) D R - 5) ____________________

16. **1 x 1**

MARVIN GAYE RECORDED DUETS WITH AT LEAST FOUR FEMALE CO-SINGERS. WHO BELOW WAS **NOT** FORTUNATE TO HAVE THAT PLEASURE?

A) DIANA ROSS
B) TAMMI TERRELL
C) MARY WELLS
D) KIM WESTON
E) BETTY EVERETT

17. **8 x 1**

NAME THESE EIGHT SOLO HITS BY *MARVIN GAYE*.
ONE, ABOUT A SWEET SENSATION HE GETS KNOWING THAT YOU LOVE HIM. ALSO RECORDED SHORTLY AFTERWARDS BY *JUNIOR WALKER & THE ALL STARS* AND EVEN LATER BY *JAMES TAYLOR* IN THE 70'S
TWO, THE REASONS HE'LL BE FAR GONE.
THREE, SOMETHING MIGHTY PECULIAR EVEN AFTER BEING WRONGED THAT HE'S STILL CARES FOR HER.
FOUR, HIS VERSION OF A *GLADYS KNIGHT* TUNE ABOUT WHAT HE HEARD THAT WAS FEATURED IN THE MOVIE SOUNDTRACK 'THE BIG CHILL' IN THE 80'S STARRING GLENN CLOSE, TOM BERENGER, MEG TILLY, WILLIAM HURT AND JEFF GOLDBLUM.
FIVE, ABOUT NOT HAVING TIME FOR ANYTHING OTHER THAN TO THINK ABOUT SOMEONE WHOSE ALWAYS ON HIS MIND AND SO WONDERFUL AT THAT.
SIX, WHAT SHE WAS TO HIM THAT HE WOULD TELL THE WORLD.
SEVEN, ABOUT YOUR WONDERFUL BEHAVIOR, WITH YOUR CONCERNS AND LOVE.
EIGHT, ABOUT THE LESSONS OF LOVE HE WAS TRYING TO INSTILL UPON HER THAT DEPARTED ROMANCE SHOULD NOT BE THE END NOR LET IT GET THE BEST OF YOU BECAUSE THAT'S LIFE AND JUST ANOTHER ROAD WE HAVE TO TRAVEL ON.

1) ____
2) ______________________
3) ___________________________
4) ____
5) ______________________________________
6) ______________________
7) ___________________________
8) ___________________________

18. **1 x 1**

THE TEMPTATIONS AND *THE SUPREMES* RECORDED A DUET ABOUT WHAT THEY WERE GONNA DO TO WIN YOUR LOVE AND NEVER TIRE OF THE OTHER EVEN IF BY HOOK OR CROOK. WHAT WAS THAT DUET HIT?

A) I'LL TRY SOMETHING NEW
B) WHAT DOES IT TAKE (TO WIN YOUR LOVE)
C) I WAS MADE TO LOVE HER
D) I'M GONNA MAKE YOU LOVE ME

19. **7 x 1**

NAME THESE SEVEN POPULAR HITS BY *MARTHA REEVES & THE VANDELLAS*, THE ALL GIRL GROUP.
ONE, DANCING TO MUSIC ALL OVER THE USA.
TWO, ABOUT MEMORIES THAT SHE DIDN'T WANT THAT YOU CAN HAVE.
THREE, QUESTIONING HER JIMMY FELLA ABOUT HIS RETURN.
FOUR, HIS PRESENCE DRAWS HER CLOSER AND DEEPER INTO LOVE.
FIVE, ABOUT A BURNING SENSATION SHE GETS WHEN SHE'S NEAR HIM.
SIX, ABOUT THAT PLACE WHERE HE COULDN'T RUN NOR HIDE.
SEVEN, ABOUT HER TWO TIMING HONEY THAT SHE LOVES JUST THE SAME.

1) ______________________
2) __________________________
3) _____________
4) _____________
5) ___________
6) __________________
7) _____________

20. **9 x 1**

THIS QUADRUPLE GROUP OF GUYS WITH COUNTLESS HITS TO THEIR BELTS FOR MOTOWN CHARTED THESE HITS: "IT'S THE SAME OLD SONG", "SEVEN ROOMS OF GLOOM", "BERNADETTE", "LOVING YOU IS SWEETER THEN EVER", AND "STANDING IN THE SHADOWS OF LOVE". NAME THEM, AND EIGHT OF THEIR OTHER HITS BELOW, NUMBERS TWO THROUGH NINE.
ONE, GROUP NAME.
TWO, ABOUT HIS SUGAR THAT'S SECOND TO NONE.
THREE, WHAT HE NEEDS BECAUSE WITHOUT IT HE COULDN'T GO ON AND END UP SO EMPTY AND SO LONELY.
FOUR, HE'S SO LONELY BECAUSE OF THE LOVE HE COULDN'T REGAIN.
FIVE, ABOUT EXTENDING OUT TO HIM WHEN YOU NEED A HELPING HAND.
SIX, WHAT CAUSES HIM TO LOVE YOU MORE AND MORE.
SEVEN, WHAT HE WANTED YOU TO DO WHEN IT WAS OVER.
EIGHT, THEIR VERSION OF A *BOBBY DARIN* HIT SONG, *BOBBY* RECORDED IN THE 60'S ABOUT YOU BEING HIS LADY.
NINE, ABOUT A GIRL NAMED RENEE, THAT WAS AN ORIGINAL HIT FOR *THE LEFT BANKE* ALSO IN THE 60'S.

1) _______________
2) ____________________
3) ________________________
4) _______________
5) ________________________
6) ____________________
7) _________________________________
8) ________________________
9) ___________________

21. **1 x 1**

WHAT SONG BY *THE ISLEY BROTHERS* WAS THEIR ONLY RECORDED HIT WHILE AT MOTOWN, DURING THEIR BRIEF STAY, ABOUT A HEART THAT KEEPS BREAKING EACH TIME SHE PARTS FROM HIM? IN THE 90'S IT WOULD BECOME A DUET HIT FOR *ROD STEWART* AND *RONALD ISLEY*.
A) LOVE IS A HURTIN' THING
B) THIS OLD HEART OF MINE (IS WEAK FOR YOU)
C) TWIST AND SHOUT
D) ONLY LOVE CAN BREAK A HEART

22. **1 x 1**

THE CONTOURS CHARTED THIS ONE MAJOR HIT FOR THE MOTOWN LABEL THAT WOULD MAKE A COMEBACK AND CHART ONCE AGAIN AS A RESULT OF BEING FEATURED IN 'THE DIRTY DANCING' MOVIE SOUNDTRACK IN THE 80'S. WHAT WAS THAT HIT, NOW THAT HE CAN DANCE?

A) DO YOU WANT TO DANCE
B) DANCE, DANCE, DANCE
C) HE'S THE GREATEST DANCER
D) DO YOU LOVE ME

23. **7 x 1**

NAME THESE SEVEN BIG HITS BY *THE MARVELETTES*, THE MOTOWN TEEN GIRL GROUP WITH THE TWO LEAD SINGERS, *GLADYS HORTON* AND *WANDA YOUNG*.
ONE, QUESTIONING THE POSTMAN IF HE HAD SOMETHING FOR HER, LIKE MAYBE A CORRESPONDENCE FROM HER BOYFRIEND, ANYTHING WILL DO. IT WAS A SONG THAT *THE CARPENTERS* WOULD ALSO GO ON TO RECORD IN THE 70'S.
TWO, TELLING THIS ROMEO TO STAY AWAY FROM HER DOOR.
THREE, ABOUT A TELEPHONE NUMBER IN THE BEECHWOOD AREA CODE.
FOUR, ADVISING OTHERS TO STAY AWAY FROM HER GUY BILL.
FIVE, ABOUT A HUNTER WHO GETS HIS OWN TREATMENT.
SIX, THE ADVISE OF NOT WASTING TIME ON SOMEONE WHO DOESN'T REALLY WANT YOU, THERE'S PLENTY OTHERS ALL AROUND TO CHOOSE FROM.
SEVEN, ABOUT HER MAGICIAN WITH THE MAGIC TOUCH.

1) ______________________
2) __________
3) ______________________
4) _________________________
5) ______________________________________
6) ____________________________
7) _______________________________

24. **1 x 1**

WHICH GROUP BELOW CONSISTING OF HIGHLY TALENTED MUSICIANS WERE THE BACK-UP PLAYERS FOR COUNTLESS HITS AT MOTOWN, INCLUDING OVER TWO HUNDRED NUMBER ONE HIT SONGS JUST FOR STARTERS? A DOCUMENTARY CALLED 'STANDING IN THE SHADOWS OF MOTOWN' FINALLY GAVE THEM THEIR DUE JUSTICE OF RECOGNITION INCLUDING THOSE WHO HAVE PASSED AWAY.

A) THE TIJUNA BRASS
B) THE VENTURES
C) THE FUNK BROTHERS
D) BOOKER T AND THE MG'S

25. **6 x 1**

MATCH THE MOTOWN SONG WITH THE MOTOWN ARTIST AND THE NEW COVER ARTIST

MOTOWN SONG	MOTOWN ARTIST	COVER ARTIST	
1) YOU KEEP ME HANGIN' ON	A) THE CONTOURS	AA) JOHNNY RIVERS	**1)** ,
2) BABY I NEED YOUR LOVING	B) THE SUPREMES	BB) VANILLA FUDGE	**2)** ,
3) DO YOU LOVE ME	C) THE FOUR TOPS	CC) DAVE CLARK FIVE	**3)** ,

TOTAL POINTS. **100 x 1 = 100**

MOTOWN ROCKERS-QUIZ # 2

1. **1 x 5**

SHORTY LONG AND *PIGMEAT MARKHAM,* SEPARATELY, RECORDED A NOVELTY SONG THAT WAS FREQUENTLY FEATURED IN THE 'LAUGH-IN' COMEDY TV SERIES WITH *SAMMY DAVIS JR.* DRESSED AS A JUDGE. NAME THIS DOUBLE HITTER.

____

2. **1 x 5**

BERRY GORDY, THE FOUNDER OF MOTOWN, HAD VARIOUS SUBSIDIARY LABEL NAMES IN HIS MOTOWN ORGANIZATION. WHICH LABEL BELOW WAS **NOT** HIS?

A) TAMLA
B) GORDY
C) SOUL
D) ATCO
E) MOTOWN

3. **1 x 5**

IN 1964 *BRENDA HOLLOWAY* RECORDED HER BIGGEST HIT FOR MOTOWN WITH A SONG ABOUT WHAT HURTS.

A) HURT
B) HURTS SO BAD
C) EVERY LITTLE BIT HURTS
D) YOU'RE GONNA HURT YOURSELF

4. **3 x 5**

JUNIOR WALKER & THE ALL STARS CHARTED THESE THREE HITS BELOW.
ONE, ABOUT A DEADLY RIFLE THEY WERE GOING TO PURCHASE DOWNTOWN.
TWO, THE CHANCES OF WINNING YOUR LOVE.
THREE, WITH A *MARVIN GAYE* TUNE ABOUT HOW SWELL IT FEELS TO BE LOVED, ALSO TO BE RECORDED BY *JAMES TAYLOR* IN THE MID 70'S.
NAME THEM.

1) ______________
2) ____?
3) ____

5. **4 x 5**

GLADYS KNIGHT & THE PIPS, A FAMILY GROUP, HAD AT LEAST FOUR BIG HITS IN THE 60'S WHICH INCLUDED THREE FOR THE MOTOWN RECORD LABEL.
ONE, A HEART BEAT HIT SONG ABOUT YOU BEING HER INSPIRATION AND WHAT KEEPS HER GOING. IT WOULD BE THEIR FIRST MAJOR RECORDING AND FOR THE VEE JAY LABEL.
TWO, A SONG *MARVIN GAYE* WOULD ALSO RECORD ABOUT WHAT HE HEARD.
THREE, THEIR BIG GRITTY TITLED HIT SONG.
FOUR, ABOUT A FRIENDLY TRAIN.
NAME THEM.

1) ______________________________
2) ____
3) ______________________
4) ______________________

6. **1 x 5**

MARVIN GAYE CHARTED THIS SONG BELOW AS A DUET WITH *KIM WESTON* ABOUT THE REQUIREMENTS TO MAKE THINGS RIGHT, THAT ONE ALONE CAN'T DO.

A) LET'S GET IT ON
B) TOO BUSY THINKING ABOUT MY BABY
C) IT TAKES TWO
D) THINGS

7. **5 x 5**

MARVIN GAYE ALSO RECORDED THESE FIVE OTHER HITS BELOW WITH *TAMMI TERRELL*.
ONE, ABOUT NO OBSTACLE HIGH, LOW OR WIDE ENOUGH THAT CAN KEEP THEM APART.
TWO, WHAT WAS SENT DOWN FROM HIGH ABOVE BECAUSE OF THE JOY AND INSPIRATION YOU HAVE BROUGHT TO EACH OTHER.
THREE, THAT IF THEY HAD THE POWER TO REARRANGE THIS WORLD, THEY WOULD INSERT LOTS OF JOY, LOVE AND HAPPINESS ALL AROUND YOU.
FOUR, THAT PHOTOS AND MEMORIES WON'T DO UNLESS IT'S THE ACTUAL PHYSICAL THING.
FIVE, WHAT YOU WOULD NEED TO CARRY ON BECAUSE IT WAS MEANT TO BE AND ALSO RIGHT FOR EACH OTHER.
NAME THEM.

1) ____________________
2) ____________________
3) ____________________
4) ____________________
5) ____________________

8. **1 x 5**

IN 1968 *DAVID RUFFIN* LEFT *THE TEMPTATIONS* FOR A SOLO CAREER. WHO WOULD REPLACE HIM?
A) BILLY GRIFFIN
B) SMOKEY ROBINSON
C) DENNIS EDWARDS
D) BEN E KING

9. **1 x 5**

WHO WAS THE SOLE FEMALE MEMBER OF *THE MIRACLES* WHO WOULD LATER MARRY ONE OF IT'S MEMBERS?
A) DIANA ROSS
B) CLAUDETTE ROGERS
C) ETTA JAMES
D) MARTHA REEVES

10. **1 x 5**

WHO WAS THAT LUCKY MEMBER SHE WOULD MARRY?
A) RONNIE WHITE
B) LEVI STUBBS
C) SMOKEY ROBINSON
D) JUNIOR WALKER

11. **1 x 5**

THIS FELLA WAS AN IMPORTANT ASSET TO BERRY GORDY'S MOTOWN LABEL. NOT ONLY WAS HE THE LEAD SINGER OF ONE OF THE GROUPS, BUT A TERRIFIC SONGWRITER WHO *BOB DYLAN* ONCE CALLED A POET, AND ALSO BECAME A MOTOWN VICE PRESIDENT. IN THE MID 70'S HE DEPARTED FROM THE GROUP TO GO IT ALONE AND CHARTED A NUMBER OF HITS OF HIS OWN. WHO WAS THAT FELLA?

____

TOTAL POINTS. **20 x 5 = 100**

R&B ROCKERS-QUIZ # 1

1. **8 x 1**

NAME THESE EIGHT BIG HITS BY *LITTLE ANTHONY AND THE IMPERIALS*, THE POPULAR R&B GROUP FROM BROOKLYN, NY.
ONE, ABOUT BEING ON THE OUTS TRYING TO GET BACK INTO YOUR HEART.
TWO, ABOUT LOSING HIS MIND BECAUSE HE CAN'T THINK OF ANYTHING OTHER THAN YOU.
THREE, ABOUT AN ENORMOUS PAIN HE GETS JUST TO SEE YOU. A SONG *LINDA RONSTADT* WOULD GO ON TO RECORD IN THE EARLY 80'S.
FOUR, BEGGING HIS DARLING ON HIS KNEES TO DO WHAT?
FIVE, ABOUT A GIRL WHO SHOWED HIM HOW TO DO THE KO-KO BOP.
SIX, ABOUT WHO HE MISSES BECAUSE HE'LL ALWAYS LOVE HER AND HOPES THAT SHE'LL HAVE HIM BACK.
SEVEN, ABOUT THE PAIN YOU CAUSED HIM BY LIES AND DECEIT, AN ORIGINAL BIG HIT FOR *TIMI YURO*.
EIGHT, ABOUT A SONG MEANT ONLY FOR US.

1) ____
2) __________________________
3) _______________
4) _________________
5) _________________________________
6) _________________
7) ________
8) ______________

2. **1 x 1**

THE CHANTELS, THE EVER POPULAR GIRL GROUP OUT OF THE BRONX, NY, CHARTED WHAT ROMANTIC SONG ABOUT LOOKING DEEP INTO HER EYES AND LETTING HER KNOW WHAT YOU FELT.

A) LOOK IN MY EYES
B) TURN AROUND, LOOK AT ME
C) THE LOOK OF LOVE
D) THESE EYES

3. **8 x 1**

NAME THESE EIGHT BIG HITS BY *THE SHIRELLES* DURING THE 60'S.
ONE, HER BIG DEDICATION HIT SONG TO SOMEONE SHE LOVES. ALSO RECORDED BY *THE MAMAS* AND *THE PAPAS* IN THE 60'S.
TWO, ABOUT TONIGHT POSSIBLY BEING THAT SPECIAL NIGHT.
THREE, QUESTIONING IF YOU WILL CONTINUE TO LOVE HER AFTER THIS NIGHT OF PASSION OR WILL YOU BE LONG GONE.
FOUR, ABOUT HER SPECIAL LITTLE SOLDIER WHOM SHE PROMISED TO BE FAITHFUL.
FIVE, ABOUT WHAT HER MOTHER SAID.
SIX, ABOUT A CERTAIN LITTLE GIRL WHO MADE HIM GO AWAY BROKENHEARTEDLY AND NOW IT'S TOO LATE TO WIN HIM BACK.
SEVEN, WHAT EVERYBODY LOVES THAT WAS ORIGINALLY A *DORIS DAY* HIT SONG IN THE LATE 50'S.
EIGHT, THEIR SUMMATION THAT IT'S NOT ONLY YOUR SMILE, OR KISS, IT'S THE FULL PACKAGE, YOU. A SONG THE GROUP, *SMITH*, WOULD ALSO RECORD.

1) ___________________________________
2) ________________________
3) ___________________________________
4) __________________
5) ______________
6) __________________
7) ______________________________
 8) __________________

4. **11 x 1**

NAME THESE ELEVEN GIANT HITS BY *THE DRIFTERS* IN THE 60'S.
ONE, A TUNE ABOUT A FINAL DANCE AND WHO'LL BE ESCORTING YOU HOME.
TWO, ABOUT THAT PEACEFUL PLACE AT THE VERY END OF THE STAIRS TO GET AWAY FROM THE HUSTLE AND BUSTLE AND LOSE YOUR CARES AWAY.
THREE, UNDER WHAT, LYING NEXT TO HIS BABY AND HAVING FUN.
FOUR, ABOUT A CERTAIN PLACE IN TOWN WHERE THE NEON LIGHTS SHINE. A SONG *GEORGE BENSON* WOULD ALSO RECORD IN THE LATE 70'S FOR THAT BOB FOSSE MOVIE, 'ALL THAT JAZZ', STARRING ROY SCHEIDER, JESSICA LANGE AND BEN VEREEN.
FIVE, SOMETHING MAGICAL OCCURRING WHENEVER HE HOLDS YOU TIGHT.
SIX, WHAT HE'S BEEN DOING THAT WAS PAINFUL SINCE YOU'VE BEEN GONE AND FOUND SOMEONE ELSE.
SEVEN, SOMETHING WONDERFUL HAPPENS WHEN YOU TOUCH HIS HAND.
EIGHT, ABOUT SOMETHING AWFULLY SWEET FOR HIS BABY.
NINE, A PLACE THEY GO TO ON SATURDAYS WHERE THEY CAN HUG, KISS AND MOST LIKEY EAT POPCORN LIKE THE REST OF THE PATRONS.
TEN, PLEADING ON HIS KNEES FOR HER NOT TO GO. A SONG *AARON NEVILLE* WOULD ALSO GO ON TO RECORD IN THE 90'S.
ELEVEN, A SONG THEY DID AS A FOLLOW UP TO NUMBER THREE ABOVE ABOUT WHAT HE HAD IN HIS SHOES.

1) ______________________________
2) __________________
3) _________________________
4) ________
5) __________________
6) __________________
7) _________________________
8) _______________________
9) _______________________________
10) ______________
11) ______________________________

5. **1 x 1**

FREDDIE SCOTT RECORDED A SONG ABOUT HEARTBREAK LOVE. THAT HE WOULD MISS YOU SO DEARLY IF YOU WENT AWAY. IT WAS A SONG THAT *BILLY JOEL* WOULD ALSO RECORD IN THE 90'S FOR HIS GREATEST HITS VOLUME III.
A) HEY, GIRL
B) LOVE IS A HURTIN' THING
C) SINCE I FELL FOR YOU
D) DON'T LET GO

6. **1 x 1**

BARBARA LEWIS CHARTED THIS LOVE SONG ABOUT GREETING A STRANGER SHE HASN'T SEEN FOR QUITE SOME TIME. A SONG THAT *YVONNE ELLIMAN* WOULD ALSO GO ON TO RECORD IN THE 70'S EQUALLY ROMANTIC.
A) STRANGER ON THE SHORE
B) (SWEET SWEET BABY) SINCE YOU'VE BEEN GONE
C) HELLO STRANGER
D) WHAT'S NEW PUSSYCAT?

7. **1 x 1**

BARBARA LEWIS RECORDED ANOTHER LOVE SONG ABOUT BELONGING TO HER BABY 'TIL THE STARS CEASED SHINING.
A) BE MY BABY
B) WE BELONG TOGETHER
C) YOU BELONG TO ME
D) BABY, I'M YOURS

8. **1 x 1**

BARBARA MASON, FROM PHILLY, HAD A BIG HIT ABOUT HER BEING WILLING AND ABLE NOW TO DO ALL THE THINGS LOVERS NORMALLY DO. A SONG *KC* OF *THE SUNSHINE BAND* WOULD CHART AS A DUET WITH *TERI DESARIO* IN THE EARLY 80'S.
A) HOLD ME, THRILL ME, KISS ME
B) YES, I'M READY
C) HOLD ME TIGHT
D) I DO LOVE YOU

9. **1 x 1**

THE DUO OF *JAMES & BOBBY PURIFY,* A FAMILY ACT, ARE WELL REMEMBERED FOR CHARTING THIS ROMANTIC SONG BELOW, THAT ALL SHE HAD TO DO WAS BE GOOD TO HIM AND HE'LL LET HER PULL THOSE STRINGS FOR WHATEVER SHE ASKED.
A) I'M YOUR PUPPET
B) BABY, I'M YOURS
C) BABY IT'S YOU
D) BACKFIELD IN MOTION

10. **3 x 1**

NAME THESE THREE HITS BY *THE RIGHTEOUS BROTHERS,* THE BLUE-EYED SOUL SENSATION OF *BILL MEDLEY* AND *BOBBY HATFIELD.*
ONE, WITHOUT HIS BABY WHAT GOOD IS HE.
TWO, ABOUT A LOST SENSATION THAT HE'D GO ON HIS KNEES JUST TO WIN HER BACK.
THREE, A ROMANTIC BALLAD ORIGINALLY RECORDED BY *AL HIBBLER* IN 1955, THEN BY *VITO AND THE SALUTATIONS* IN 1963 WHO HAD AN UPTEMPO LIVELIER WOO WOP VERSION, ALL ABOUT WHAT HE HUNGERED FOR. THE BROTHERS VERSION WOULD RESURFACE IN 1990 FOR THE SOUNDTRACK MOVIE 'GHOSTS', STARRING PATRICK SWAYZE, DEMI MOORE AND WHOOPI GOLDBERG.
1) ______________________________________
2) ___________________________________
3) _____________________

11. **1 x 1**

THE AD LIBS CHARTED A SONG ABOUT A GUY FROM THE BIG APPLE WHO WAS TALL, FINE, WITH PLENTY OF DOUGH, AND ALL THAT A GIRL COULD EVER WANT, AND HOPING HE WOULD BE HERS. IT'S A SONG THAT *THE MANHATTAN TRANSFER* WOULD GO ON TO RECORD IN THE EARLY 80'S.
A) EL WATUSI
B) HE'S SO FINE
C) THE BOY FROM NEW YORK CITY
D) HE'S SURE THE BOY I LOVE

12. **3 x 1**

THE INTRUDERS, OUT OF PHILLY, WENT ON TO RECORD THESE THREE BALLADS BELOW. NAME THOSE BALLADS.
ONE, REMINISCING HOW AS A KID HE PLAYED WESTERN CHARACTERS AND CHASED THE GIRLS AROUND.
TWO, SOMEONE'S SAD BECAUSE HE BROKE HER HEART.
THREE, ABOUT BEING STRANDED IN A REMOTE AREA OR ANY OTHER PLACE FOR THAT MATTER AS LONG AS IT'S JUST YOU AND HIM, RICH OR POOR. A SONG THAT THE GROUP *TIERRA* WOULD ALSO GO ON TO CHART IN THE EARLY 80'S.
1) ____________________
2) ____________

 3) ____________

13. **1 x 1**

THE HIT SONG "DUKE OF EARL" WAS RECORDED BY WHAT MALE ARTIST BELOW WHO WOULD DRESS IN TAILS, TOP HAT, AND A CANE IN HAND TO PROMOTE THE SONG? IN THE 70'S HE WOULD HAVE ANOTHER POPULAR HIT CALLED "GROOVY SITUATION".

A) ROGER MILLER
B) GENE CHANDLER
C) BEN E KING
D) JAMES BROWN

14. **1 x 1**

WHAT POPULAR SOUL SINGER BELOW GAINED A LOT OF FAME FROM HIS APPEARANCE AT THE MONTEREY INTERNATIONAL POP FESTIVAL IN 1967 PERFORMING A *SAM COOKE* TUNE CALLED "SHAKE"?

A) LOU RAWLS
B) OTIS REDDING
C) JACKIE WILSON
D) JAMES BROWN

15. **1 x 1**

CHUBBY CHECKER CHARTED A NUMBER OF DANCE HITS IN THE 60'S. WHICH ONE BELOW WAS **NOT** ONE TO HIS CREDIT?

A) THE TWIST
B) THE PONY
C) LIMBO ROCK
D) MASHED POTATO TIME

16. **1 x 1**

MAURICE WILLIAMS, THE SINGER/SONGWRITER, *& THE ZODIACS* RECORDED A SONG IN THE 60'S THAT WOULD RESURFACE ONCE AGAIN IN THE 80'S AS A RESULT OF BEING FEATURED IN THE 'DIRTY DANCING' SOUNDTRACK MOVIE, STARRING PATRICK SWAYZE, JENNIFER GREY AND JERRY ORBACH. CHOOSE BELOW THEIR POPULAR HIT SONG THAT *THE FOUR SEASONS* WOULD ALSO RECORD IN THE 60'S THAT HAD THEM PLEADING FOR HER TO DO SOMETHING A LITTLE WHILE LONGER.

A) STAY
B) PLEASE STAY
C) PLEASE DON'T GO
D) HE'LL HAVE TO GO

17. **1 x 1**

THIS TEEN GROUP OF BOYS, *RONNIE AND THE HI-LITES,* WOULD ACHIEVE THEIR STARDOM IN 1962 BY CHARTING WHAT SONG BELOW ABOUT HIS DESIRE TO BE MARRIED?

A) I WISH THAT WE WERE MARRIED
B) WHEN WE GET MARRIED
C) THAT'S MY DESIRE
D) SO YOUNG

18. **1 x 1**

IN 1969 *THE FRIENDS OF DISTINCTION,* A QUARTET GROUP CONSISTING OF TWO GUYS AND TWO GIRLS, RECORDED A SONG ABOUT MOTHER NATURE AND IT'S AFFECT ON GRASS THAT WE CAN ALL DIG. IT WOULD BE THEIR FIRST AND BIGGEST AND CATAPULT THEM TO STARDOM.

A) STONE SOUL PICNIC
B) BABY, I'M FOR REAL
C) GREEN, GREEN GRASS OF HOME
D) GRAZING IN THE GRASS

19. **1 x 1**

THE FRIENDS OF DISTINCTION CHARTED ANOTHER POPULAR HIT ABOUT HOW SHE'S GOT HIM ROLLING LIKE A TOY ON A STRING.

A) SPINNING WHEEL
B) GOING IN CIRCLES
C) I'M YOUR PUPPET
D) TELL IT LIKE IT IS

20. **8 x 1**

NAME THESE EIGHT HITS BY *SAM COOKE,* THE LEGENDARY GOSPEL/R&B SINGER.
ONE, ABOUT NOT CLAIMING TO BE AN HONOR ROLL STUDENT. A SONG THAT THE BRITISH GROUP, *HERMAN'S HERMITS,* WOULD ALSO RECORD IN THE MID 60'S.
TWO, A REMAKE OF A *BOBBY SCOTT* 1956 SONG ABOUT DOING TIME THAT INVOLVED HARD LABOR.
THREE, ABOUT WANTING THE ARROW TO PENETRATE HIS LOVERS' HEART.
FOUR, WHERE TO BRING YOUR SWEET LOVING.
FIVE, A TWISTING HIT THAT *ROD STEWART* WOULD ALSO RECORD IN THE 90'S.
SIX, DANCING TO THE MUSIC WHILE AT A PARTY.
SEVEN, A SONG *CAT STEVENS* WOULD ALSO CHART IN THE 70'S ABOUT GETTING PAID AND STILL NO ONE HE CAN CONVERSE WITH.
EIGHT, ABOUT THAT NEW DANCE WHERE YOU MOVE YOUR BODY AS YOU WOULD TO A SOUP, WITH ALL YOUR MIGHT AND WHIP IT ALL AROUND.

1) ____________________
2) _______________
3) _________
4) ____________________________
5) _________________________________
6) ____________________
7) ____________________________
8) _________

21. **1 x 1**

IN 1969 *MEL AND TIM* WOULD ACHIEVE THEIR INITIAL STARDOM BY CHARTING WHAT SONG BELOW ABOUT MOTION?

A) TOSSIN' AND TURNIN'
B) BACKFIELD IN MOTION
C) POETRY IN MOTION
D) GOING IN CIRCLES

22. **1 x 1**

THE CAPITOLS WERE BEST KNOWN FOR RECORDING THIS POPULAR SONG BELOW IN 1966 ABOUT A CERTAIN CAT WHO THEY THOUGHT WAS QUITE HIP. IT WOULD BECOME THEIR CLAIM TO FAME SONG.

A) ALLEY-OOP
B) COOL JERK
C) MR BIG STUFF
D) ALONG CAME JONES

23. **1 x 1**

IN 1963 *JIMMY SOUL* ACHIEVED HIS PLACE IN MUSIC HISTORY FOR CHARTING WHAT SONG THAT ALL A MAN HAD TO DO TO GAIN FULFILLMENT WAS TO GET HITCHED TO AN UGLY CHICK? IT WOULD BE A CHART TOPPER AND BE FEATURED IN THE MOVIE 'MY BEST FRIEND'S WEDDING' STARRING JULIA ROBERTS AND CAMERON DIAZ IN THE 90'S.

A) HAPPY TOGETHER
B) I WISH THAT WE WERE MARRIED
C) IF YOU WANNA BE HAPPY
 D) MOTHER-IN-LAW

24. **1 x 1**

WHO WAS THIS TALENTED FEMALE SOUL SINGER, DAUGHTER OF A BAPTIST MINISTER, ALSO KNOWN AS LADY SOUL, WHO GREW UP IN HER FATHER'S CHURCH SINGING IN THE CHOIR?

A) DIONNE WARWICK
B) GLADYS KNIGHT
C) ARETHA FRANKLIN
D) MAHALIA JACKSON

25. **1 x 1**

CLARENCE CARTER RECORDED THIS LOVE TRIANGLE HIT SONG ABOUT WHAT HE WOULD DO TO HAVE YOU NEAR, BECAUSE HE DESPERATELY NEEDS YOU. WHAT WAS THAT LOVE TRIANGLE HIT CALLED?

A) DRIFT AWAY
B) SLIP AWAY
C) GET ON UP
D) SLIP SLIDIN' AWAY

26. **1 x 1**

LEE DORSEY, A MALE SINGER FROM NEW ORLEANS, HAD A HIT SONG CALLED "YA YA". HE THEN RECORDED WHAT OTHER, ABOUT THE BACKBREAKING JOB THAT HE HAD TO ENDURE?

A) 16 TONS
B) WORKING IN THE COAL MINE
C) CHAIN GANG
D) WE GOTTA GET OUT OF THIS PLACE

27. **1 x 1**

IN 1964 *MILLI SMALL* CHARTED THE BIGGEST HIT OF HER CAREER ABOUT SOMEONE THAT SHE WOULD CALL HER BOY LIKE ON A STICK.

A) MR LEE
B) LOLLIPOP
C) SUGAR, SUGAR
D) MY BOY LOLLIPOP

28. **2 x 1**

MATCH THE REGIONAL MUSIC SOUND WITH THEIR RESPECTIVE MUSIC LABEL.

MUSIC SOUND	**MUSIC LABEL**	
1) THE DETROIT SOUND	A) SUN RECORDS	**1)**
2) THE MEMPHIS SOUND	B) CHESS RECORDS	**2)**
	C) STAX/VOLT RECORDS	
	D) MOTOWN	
	E) LAURIE RECORDS	
	F) CAPITOL RECORDS	

29. **1 x 1**

THIS R&B ARTIST, AN AMERICAN LEGEND, BLINDED SINCE CHILDHOOD, WENT ON TO EXPANDED HIS HORIZONS IN MUSIC BY SINGING COUNTRY SONGS. ALSO HIS RENDITION OF "AMERICA" IS SECOND TO NONE. WHO IS THIS LEGEND STILL ACTIVE TODAY HERE IN THE 21ST CENTURY?

A) AL HIBBLER
B) LITTLE STEVIE WONDER
C) RAY CHARLES
D) CLARENCE CARTER

30. **1 x 1**

THE PARLIAMENTS WITH *GEORGE CLINTON* AT THE HELM CHARTED THIS SONG BELOW ABOUT WHAT HE WANTED TO PROCLAIM TO THE WORLD OF THE SWEET LOVING SHE BROUGHT HIM THAT WAS LIKE HONEY AND SECOND TO NONE. WHAT WAS THAT SONG?

A) THE BIRDS AND THE BEES
B) GOOD LOVIN'
C) (I WANNA) TESTIFY
D) SHE'S A LADY

31. **1 x 1**

IN 1969 *JOE JEFFREY GROUP* RECORDED THIS ONE MAJOR HIT ABOUT A PLEDGE. WHAT WAS IT CALLED?

A) PLEDGING MY LOVE
B) WITH THIS RING
C) MY PLEDGE OF LOVE
D) TEN COMMANDMENTS OF LOVE

32. **1 x 1**

THE DELLS HAD A RE-MAKE HIT WITH ONE OF THEIR PREVIOUS RECORDINGS DONE BACK IN THE 50'S ABOUT A SPECIAL NIGHT AND WHY HE LOVES HER SO, TITLE SLIGHTLY CHANGED AND WITH AN OPENING VERBAL MONOLOGUE.

A) MIDNIGHT SPECIAL
B) REMEMBER THEN
C) ONE SUMMER NIGHT
D) OH, WHAT A NIGHT

33. **1 x 1**

THE DELLS CHARTED ANOTHER ABOUT A DARLING THAT HE LOVED AND PLEADING FOR HER TO STAY BY HIS SIDE. *JOHNNY CARTER*, THE LEAD SINGER, IS WELL KNOWN FOR BEING ABLE TO HOLD A NOTE IF NOT BETTER THAN ANY AROUND AS ILLUSTRATED IN THIS PARTICULAR SONG. WHAT WAS THAT SONG?

A) I WISH THAT WE WERE MARRIED
B) STAY IN MY CORNER
C) DARLIN' BE HOME SOON
D) STAY

34. **2 x 1**

THIS MALE ARTIST HAD A HIT THAT ENDURED FOR OVER TWO YEARS, GOING TO THE TOP OF THE CHARTS TWICE. IT ALSO HELPED TO INSPIRE OTHERS TO RECORD SONGS ON THAT SUBJECT MATTER. NAME BOTH THE ARTIST AND THE SONG THAT TAUGHT US A NEW DANCE, WHICH IS PROBABLY THE REASON FOR ITS' POPULARITY AND LONGEVITY.

1) ____________________
2) _____________

35. **1 x 1**

THE ARTIST ABOVE ALSO RECORDED ANOTHER ABOUT DOING SOMETHING AGAIN WHICH PERTAINED TO THAT ORIGINAL HIT.

A) THE FLY
B) PEPPERMINT TWIST (PT 1)
C) LET'S TWIST AGAIN
D) TWISTIN' THE NIGHT AWAY

36. **8 x 1**

NAME THESE EIGHT POPULAR HITS BY THE GENIOUS HIMSELF, *RAY CHARLES*.
ONE, ABOUT A CERTAIN LADY THAT WAS ON HIS MIND.
TWO, ABOUT JACK BEING TOLD WHERE TO GO.
THREE, ABOUT UNLOCKING HIS HEART AND LETTING HIM GO FREE.
FOUR, SOMETHING HE COULDN'T STOP DOING EVEN IF IT MEANT A LIFE OF UNPLEASANTRY. IT WAS WRITTEN AND RECORDED BY *DON GIBSON* IN THE 50'S.
FIVE, ABOUT BEING BROKE.
SIX, CRYING BECAUSE SHE'S LEAVING HIM AGAIN.
SEVEN, GOING TO GET BLASTED OUT OF HIS MIND.
EIGHT, HIS SOULFUL VERSION OF AN ORIGINAL *BEATLE* SONG ABOUT ELEANOR THAT *ARETHA FRANKLIN* WOULD ALSO RECORD.

1) ______________________
2) ______________________
3) ____________________
4) ____________________________
5) __________
6) _______________
7) ______________________
8) _________________

37. **1 x 1**

RAY CHARLES HAD THESE THREE OTHER HITS BELOW. WHICH ONE WAS **NOT** HIS?
A) DON'T LOOK BACK
B) HERE WE GO AGAIN
C) TAKE THESE CHAINS FROM MY HEART
D) YOUR CHEATING HEART

38. **1 x 1**

BILLY BLAND GAINED HIS PREMIER STARDOM BY CHARTING WHAT SONG BELOW PLEADING TO ALLOW THAT GIRL TO DANCE?
A) LET THE LITTLE GIRL DANCE
B) HEY LITTLE GIRL
C) DO YOU WANT TO DANCE
D) DANCE, DANCE, DANCE

39. **1 x 1**

"PONY TIME" WAS A NUMBER ONE HIT IN 1961 BY WHICH ARTIST BELOW?
A) CHUBBY CHECKER
B) DEE DEE SHARP
C) LITTLE EVA
D) RUFUS THOMAS

40. **4 x 1**

SAM & DAVE, THE SOULFUL DUO OUT OF THE STAX LABEL, CHARTED THESE FOUR BIG HITS BELOW.
ONE, ABOUT A CERTAIN TYPE OF MAN THAT HE WAS, STRAIGHT FROM THE HEART.
TWO, ABOUT HOLDING ON BECAUSE HE'S ON HIS WAY BACK.
THREE, LIKE HIS BABY, HE TOO FEELS WHAT SHE FEELS. A SONG THAT *AARON NEVILLE* AND *LINDA RONSTADT* WOULD GO ON TO RECORD IN THE EARLY 90'S.
FOUR, EXPRESSING THEIR PERSONAL GRATITUDE.
NAME THEM.

1) _____________
2) ________________________
3) ____
4) ________________

41. **1 x 1**

THE EDWIN HAWKINS SINGERS GAINED THEIR RECOGNITION BY CHARTING WHAT POPULAR GOSPEL LIKE TYPE OF SONG BELOW?
A) OH HOW HAPPY
B) HAPPY TOGETHER
C) OH HAPPY DAY
D) YOU MADE ME SO VERY HAPPY

42. **1 x 1**

IN 1960 *LITTLE CAESAR AND THE ROMANS* WOULD GAIN THEIR PLACE IN MUSIC HISTORY BY RECORDING THIS ONE HIT WONDER SONG ABOUT THOSE CLASSIC HITS THAT BROUGHT BACK FOND MEMORIES.
A) MEMORIES ARE MADE OF THIS
B) IT'S THE SAME OLD SONG
C) THOSE OLDIES BUT GOODIES (REMIND ME OF YOU)
D) YESTERDAY

43. **1 x 1**

JJ JACKSON CHARTED THIS SONG BELOW ABOUT HOW HE FELT, ONE FINE DAY SHE'LL GET HERS AND REALIZE THE HURT THAT WAS INFLICTED ON HIM, BECAUSE WHAT GOES AROUND, COMES AROUND. IT'S A SONG *HUEY LEWIS AND THE NEWS* WOULD GO ON TO RECORD IN THE 90'S EQUALLY SOULFUL.
A) HURT
B) BUT IT'S ALRIGHT
C) GOIN' OUT OF MY HEAD
D) ONE FINE DAY

44. **1 x 1**

THE JARMELS CHARTED WHAT MAJOR HIT IN 1961 ABOUT SOMETHING THAT COULD NEVER DO?
A) NEVER MY LOVE
B) A LITTLE BIT OF SOAP
C) A LITTLE BIT O' SOUL
D) A LITTLE BIT OF ME, A LITTLE BIT OF YOU

45. **8 x 1**

NAME THIS POPULAR ALL GIRL GROUP WHO HAD VARIOUS LEAD SINGERS DURING THEIR CAREER AND THEIR SEVEN HITS BELOW, NUMBERS TWO THROUGH EIGHT.
ONE, GROUP NAME.
TWO, ABOUT A REBEL.
THREE, WHAT HE DID AFTER WALKING HER HOME?
FOUR, ABOUT A BOY THAT SHE'S BEEN DREAMING OF.
FIVE, ABOUT PENETRATING DEEP INTO HER EYES AND LETTING HER KNOW HOW YOU FEEL. ORIGINALLY RECORDED BY *THE CHANTELS* A FEW YEARS EARLIER.
SIX, HOW SHE GOT TO KNOW BILL ON A MONDAY. THIS SONG WAS ALSO RECORDED BY *SHAUN CASSIDY* IN THE 70'S ABOUT WALKING YOU HOME.
SEVEN, ABOUT NO ONE ELSE LIKE HER BABE?
EIGHT, ABOUT THAT UPPER PART OF TOWN WHERE HE'S A KING AND SHE WAITS FOR HIM.

1) ____________________
2) ____________________
3) ____________________________
4) _________________________________
5) ____________________________
6) ____
7) ____
 8) _______________

46. **1 x 1**

JOHNNY THUNDER IS WELL REMEMBERED FOR RECORDING WHAT SONG BELOW IN 1963 TAKEN PART FROM A NURSERY RHYME.

A) LIL' RED RIDING HOOD
B) LITTLE STAR
C) SALLY, GO 'ROUND THE ROSE
D) LOOP DE LOOP

TOTAL POINTS. **100 x 1 = 100**

R&B ROCKERS-QUIZ # 2

1. **3 x 1**

NAME THESE THREE BIG HITS BY *THE CHIFFONS*, THE ALL GIRL GROUP. ONE, DESCRIBING THAT HANDSOME, SOFT SPOKEN, SHY GUY WHO SHE PLANNED TO HAVE FOR HER OWN. A SONG *JANE OLIVER* WOULD ALSO RECORD IN THE 70'S AT A MUCH SLOWER AND ROMANTIC PACE, BOTH EXCEPTIONALLY FINE. TWO, ONE DAY YOU MAY REALIZE THAT YOU'LL WANT HER FOR YOURSELF. THREE, ABOUT A SWEET CONNIVING KIND OF GUY.

1) ________________
2) ________________
3) ______________________

2. **1 x 1**

ESTHER PHILLIPS, FORMERLY KNOWN AS *LITTLE ESTHER,* WHO WAS DISCOVERED BY *JOHNNY OTIS* AT THE TENDER AGE OF FIFTEEN AND WORKED IN HIS REVIEW SHOWS BACK IN THE EARLY 50'S WOULD GO ON TO RECORD THIS HEARTBREAKER OF A HIT SONG THAT *ENGELBERT HUMPERDINCK* WOULD ALSO CHART A FEW YEARS LATER WITH THE TITLE EXTENDED, ABOUT DESIRING TO BE SET FREE TO LOVE ANOTHER. WHAT WAS THAT DOUBLE HITTER CALLED?

A) LET ME GO, LOVER
B) AFTER THE LOVIN'
C) RELEASE ME
D) DON'T LET GO

3. **5 x 1**

NAME THIS FORMER *DRIFTER* MEMBER WHO LEFT TO GO IT ALONE AND FOUR OF HIS BIG HITS BELOW, NUMBERS TWO THROUGH FIVE.
ONE, HIS NEW ADOPTED NAME.
TWO, ABOUT WANTING HIS LOVED ONE TO STAND BY HIS SIDE TO GIVE HIM STRENGTH AND COURAGE. IN THE 80'S IT WOULD BECOME THE TITLE OF A BOB REINER MOVIE THAT FEATURED THIS SONG AND COUNTLESS OTHERS.
THREE, ABOUT A CERTAIN FLOWER IN A CERTAIN ETHNIC PART OF HARLEM. A SONG *ARETHA FRANKLIN* WOULD ALSO GO ON TO RECORD IN THE 70'S.
FOUR, PLEADING NOT TO DO SOMETHING THAT MAY BRING BACK MEMORIES HE'D RATHER FORGET. AGAIN RECORDED BY *ARETHA FRANKLIN* IN THE 70'S.
FIVE, A HEARTBREAK HIT SONG ABOUT SOMEONE WHO HAS NOTHING. A SONG THAT *TOM JONES* WOULD GO ON TO RECORD IN THE 70'S.

1) ______________
2) ______________
3) ___________________
4) _____________________________________
5) __________________________

4. **1 x 1**

CHOOSE THE POPULAR SONG BELOW BY *THE ESSEX* ABOUT HOW TALKING CAN BE CHEAP. IT WOULD BE THEIR FIRST MAJOR HIT AND RACE TO THE TOP OF THE CHARTS GIVING THEM THEIR INITIAL STARDOM.

A) YOU TALK TOO MUCH
B) TALK TO ME, TALK TO ME
C) EASIER SAID THAN DONE
D) YOU AIN'T SEEN NOTHING YET

5. **1 x 1**

THE ESSEX ALSO RECORDED WHAT OTHER, THAT DEALT WITH A LIVING MARVEL?

A) HE'S SO FINE
B) A WALKIN' MIRACLE
C) SWEET TALKIN' GUY
D) MY BOY LOLLIPOP

6. **1 x 1**

"COLOR HIM FATHER" WAS THEIR ONLY MAJOR RECORDING ABOUT THAT MAN WHO BECAME AN INSTANT SAVIOR AND A FATHER SENT FROM HEAVEN THAT BROUGHT LOVE AND GUIDANCE JUST IN TIME. WHAT GROUP WAS RESPONSIBLE FOR IT?
A) THE WINSTONS
B) THE IMPRESSIONS
C) THE FOUR TOPS
D) THE TEMPTATIONS

7. **1 x 1**

CHOOSE BELOW THIS YOUNG MALE ARTIST WHO RECORDED "A MILLION TO ONE" WHICH WAS HIS ONLY CLAIM TO FAME SONG.
A) GENE CHANDLER
B) JIMMY CHARLES
C) LARRY GRAHAM
D) TONY ORLANDO

8. **1 x 1**

CANNIBAL AND THE HEADHUNTERS CHARTED "LAND OF A THOUSAND DANCES". WHAT WICKED MALE ARTIST WOULD GO ON TO RECORD IT SHORTLY THEREAFTER?
A) JERRY BUTLER
B) GENE CHANDLER
C) WILSON PICKETT
D) SCREAMIN' JAY HAWKINS

9. **1 x 1**

JOHNNIE TAYLOR CHARTED A SONG ABOUT THE ADVISE HE GAVE THAT QUESTIONED THE CHEATING SIDE OF LOVE, WHAT GOES AROUND, COMES AROUND, SOMETHING HE KNEW SO WELL FIRST HAND.
A) TAKE A LETTER MARIA
B) WHO'S MAKING LOVE
C) BY THE TIME I GET TO PHOENIX
D) ANY DAY NOW (MY WILD BEAUTIFUL BIRD)

10. **2 x 1**

IN 1966 THIS ARTIST RECORDED A SONG THAT TWENTYONE YEARS LATER WOULD BE FEATURED IN THE MOVIE 'THE BIG EASY' STARRING DENNIS QUAID AND ELLEN BARKIN. IN 1989 HE RECORDED WITH *LINDA RONSTADT* ON A BUNCH OF HITS. NAME HIM AND THAT SONG ABOUT NOT BEING A CHILD OR A PLAY THING.
1) ____________________
2) ____________________________

11. **1 x 1**

WHAT *DEON JACKSON* SONG RECORDED IN 1966 BECAME HIS CLAIM TO FAME SONG THAT REVEALS WHAT LOVE CAN DO TO EVERY BOY AND GIRL?
A) MAKE THE WORLD GO AWAY
B) LOVE MAKES THE WORLD GO ROUND
C) SUNNY
D) ONLY LOVE CAN BREAK A HEART

12. **2 x 1**

NAME THESE TWO HITS BY *THE ISLEY BROTHERS,* ONE BEFORE AND ONE AFTER THEIR BRIEF STAY AT MOTOWN DURING THE 60'S.
ONE, A POPULAR TWIST SONG WHICH WAS LATER RECORDED BY *THE BEATLES*.
TWO, ABOUT WHAT YOU POSSESSED THAT'S TOTALLY UNDER YOUR CONTROL.
1) _______________________
2) _______________________

13. **3 x 1**

NAME THESE THREE HIT SONGS BY *JOE TEX* IN THE 60'S.
ONE, ABOUT HOLDING ONTO SOMETHING THAT YOU POSSESS.
TWO, A NOVELTY SONG ABOUT A SKINNY LADY AND THAT GUY NAMED LEROY.
THREE, ABOUT WANTING TO SEE AN EXAMPLE OF A GOOD WOMAN AND A GOOD MAN.

1) ______________________
2) ______________________
3) __________

14. **3 x 1**

NAME THESE THREE HITS BY *MAXINE BROWN*.
ONE, ABOUT SOMETHING SHE HAD ON HER MIND.
TWO, A JOKE THAT MADE HER LAUGH BECAUSE SHE'S OVER YOU.
THREE, PLEADING THAT HER BABY'S NOT LIKE THE REST OF THEM.

1) _________________
2) ________
3) ____________________

15. **1 x 1**

CHRIS KENNER RECORDED A POPULAR SONG ABOUT HIM TAKING A CERTAIN GIRL AND YOU A CERTAIN OTHER. IT WOULD BE RECORDED BY THE BRITISH GROUP *'DAVE CLARK FIVE'* ALSO IN THE 60'S. NAME THAT DOUBLE HITTER BELOW.

A) WHAT'S YOUR NAME
B) I LIKE IT LIKE THAT
C) RUNAROUND SUE
D) PEGGY SUE

16. **1 x 1**

IN 1963 *RUBY AND THE ROMANTICS* CHARTED THE BIGGEST HIT OF THEIR CAREER WITH WHAT SONG BELOW THAT *FRANKIE VALLI* WOULD ALSO GO ON TO RECORD IN THE 70'S ABOUT OUR TIME COMING?

A) TIME HAS COME
B) TIME WON'T LET ME
C) ANY DAY NOW (MY WILD BEAUTIFUL BIRD)
D) OUR DAY WILL COME

17. **1 x 1**

SONNY CHARLES AND THE CHECKMATES LTD HAD THIS POPULAR SONG BELOW ABOUT A GEM OF A GIRL WHO'S WORKED A LIFETIME CARING FOR OTHERS AND NOW HER TIME HAS COME.

A) DIAMONDS AND PEARLS
B) BLACK PEARL
C) MY BABY MUST BE A MAGICIAN
D) LITTLE STAR

18. **1 x 1**

THE SHELLS RECORDED THEIR ONLY MAJOR HIT ABOUT A BABE HE WAS MADLY IN LOVE WITH AND NEEDED SO. IN FACT, THERE WAS NOTHING THAT HE WOULDN'T DO TO SATISFY HER. WHAT WAS THAT MAJOR HIT?

A) FOR YOUR LOVE
B) BABY OH BABY
C) THE END
D) EARTH ANGEL

19. **1 x 1**

HAROLD DORMAN HAD THIS MOUNTAIN OF A HIT THAT *JOHNNY RIVERS* WOULD GO ON TO CHART A FEW YEARS LATER. WHAT WAS THAT MOUNTAIN OF A HIT?
A) AIN'T NO MOUNTAIN HIGH ENOUGH
B) OVER THE MOUNTAIN, ACROSS THE SEA
C) MOUNTAIN'S HIGH
D) MOUNTAIN OF LOVE

20. **1 x 1**

THE O'KAYSIONS, AN ALL MALE WHITE GROUP WITH THE SOULFUL SOUND, CHARTED WHAT POPULAR SONG ABOUT WATCHING THE FEMALES STROLL BY?
A) CAN'T YOU HEAR MY HEART BEAT
B) GIRL WATCHER
C) WONDERFUL WORLD
D) STANDING ON THE CORNER

21. **5 x 1**

NAME THESE FIVE BIG HITS BY *THE 5TH DIMENSION* DURING THE 60'S.
ONE, A MEDLEY TUNE FROM THE BROADWAY ROCK MUSICAL 'HAIR' ABOUT ASTROLOGICAL SIGNS AND SUNSHINE.
TWO, ABOUT A PICNIC WITH LOTS OF WINE.
THREE, ABOUT THEIR PRETTY BALLOON.
FOUR, ABOUT WEDDING VOWS THAT BILL WOULDN'T COMMIT TO, LEAVING HER WITH THE BLUES.
FIVE, ABOUT THAT GRAPEVINE WHERE THEY CAN DRINK DADDY'S BOOZE, BUT DON'T LET HIM KNOW.
1) ______________________
2) ______________________
3) ______________________
4) ______________________
5) ______________________

22. **1 x 1**

CHOOSE THE *DORIS TROY* SONG THAT *LINDA RONSTADT* WOULD ALSO RECORD IN THE 80'S ABOUT A CERTAIN LOOK THAT KNOCKED THEM OFF THEIR FEET WHEN THEY SAW YOU.
A) THE LOOK OF LOVE
B) FOR WHAT IT'S WORTH (STOP, HEY WHAT'S THAT SOUND)
C) LOOK IN MY EYES
D) JUST ONE LOOK

23. **1 x 1**

THIS LEGENDARY ROCKER OF THE 50'S CHARTED THESE THREE BIG HITS DURING THE 60'S: "NADINE (IS IT YOU?)", "NO PARTICULAR PLACE TO GO", AND "YOU NEVER CAN TELL". WHO WAS THAT LEGENDARY ROCKER?
A) FATS DOMINO
B) LITTLE RICHARD
C) CHUCK BERRY
D) BO DIDDLEY

24. **1 x 1**

THE SHIRELLES WERE ORIGINALLY MADE UP OF FOUR GIRLS. WHO WAS **NOT** A MEMBER OF THAT FABULOUS GROUP?
A) SHIRLEY ALSTON
B) BEVERLY LEE
C) DORIS KENNER
D) MICKI HARRIS
E) MARY WILSON

25. **1 x 1**

IN 1963 *INEZ FOXX* WITH *CHARLIE FOXX,* A SISTER AND BROTHER ACT, CHARTED WHAT SONG BELOW THAT *JAMES TAYLOR* AND HIS WIFE AT THE TIME, *CARLY SIMON,* WOULD GO ON TO RECORD ELEVEN YEARS LATER?

A) MOCKINGBIRD
B) BIRD DOG
C) THE BIRDS AND THE BEES
D) ROCKIN' ROBIN

26. **9 x 1**

IN 2003 THIS FEMALE SINGER WAS VOTED BY VH1, THE GREATEST DIVA OF ALL TIME. SHE CHARTED NUMEROUS HITS THAT INCLUDED: "CHAIN OF FOOLS", "BABY I LOVE YOU", "(SWEET SWEET BABY) SINCE YOU'VE BEEN GONE", "DR FEELGOOD", "SEE SAW" AND "THE WEIGHT". NAME HER, AND THESE EIGHT OTHER HITS BELOW, NUMBERS TWO THROUGH NINE.

ONE, HER NAME.
TWO, ABOUT WHAT JACK BUILT THROUGH LOVE AND SHE WANTS HIM BACK.
THREE, AN ORIGINAL *OTIS REDDING* TUNE OF WHAT SHE NEEDED WHEN YOU GOT HOME.
FOUR, A FEELING HE HELPED TO RESTORE TO HER AND MAKE WHOLE ONCE MORE. IT WOULD BE FEATURED IN THE MOVIE 'THE BIG CHILL' IN THE 80'S.
FIVE, A PRAYER HIT SONG FIRST RECORDED BY *DIONNE WARWICK.*
SIX, HER COPY VERSION OF A *BEATLE* SONG ABOUT ELEANOR, ALSO RECORDED BY *RAY CHARLES* DONE SOULFULLY.
SEVEN, ABOUT LOVING A MAN LIKE NO OTHER THAT JUST THE THOUGHT OF HIM WOULDN'T LET HER SLEEP.
EIGHT, HER PLEADING SONG ABOUT WANTING TO BE RESCUED, EVEN BRUCE LEE WOULD DO.
NINE, ABOUT WHAT SHE WANTED YOU TO RECONSIDER IF YOU WANTED TO BE WITH HER.

1) ____________________
2) ______________________________
3) _____________
4) ____
5) __________________________
6) _______________
7) ____
8) _____________
9) _______

27. **1 x 1**

"I LOVE YOU A THOUSAND TIMES" AND "WITH THIS RING" WERE SONGS BY WHAT POPULAR QUINTET ACT 'NAME' OF THE FIFTIES BUT NOW CONSISTING OF A NEW SET OF MEMBERS WHO WERE ALL REPLACEMENTS, INCLUDING *SONNY TURNER* FOR *TONY WILLIAMS*?

A) THE DRIFTERS
B) THE PLATTERS
C) THE COASTERS
D) THE CADILLACS

28. **1 x 1**

DARLENE LOVE, A FORMER MEMBER OF *THE CRYSTALS* AND THEIR PARTTIME LEAD SINGER, HAD A SOLO HIT WITH WHAT BOBBY TITLED SONG BELOW?

A) BOBBY SOX TO STOCKINGS
B) ME AND BOBBY MCGEE
C) BOBBY'S GIRL
D) WAIT TIL' MY BOBBY GETS HOME

29. **1 x 1**

WHAT WAS THE NICKNAME GIVEN TO *PEACHES & HERB?*
A) PEARL
B) BOOM BOOM
C) THE SWEETHEARTS OF SOUL
D) THE KILLER

30. **1 x 1**

"MASHED POTATO TIME" WAS A BIG DANCE NUMBER BY WHICH TEEN FEMALE ARTIST IN 1962 THAT WOULD BE HER BIGGEST AND CLIMB TO THE NUMBER TWO SPOT ON THE CHARTS?
A) THE MIRACLES
B) LITTLE EVA
C) DEE-DEE SHARP
D) CHUBBY CHECKER

31. **1 x 1**

"MY TRUE STORY" AND "WHAT TIME IS IT" WERE RECORDED BY *THE JIVE FIVE*, FROM BROOKLYN, NY. THEY WENT ON TO CHART A THIRD POPULAR SONG ABOUT WHAT HIS BABY MADE HIM FEEL. WHAT WAS THAT THIRD SONG?
A) I FEEL FINE
B) I'M A HAPPY MAN
C) YOU'VE MADE ME SO VERY HAPPY
D) FOR YOUR LOVE

32. **6 x 1**

NAME THESE SIX BIG FUNKY HITS BY *SLY & THE FAMILY STONE*.
ONE, ABOUT REACHING UP AND CELEBRATING ALONG WITH THE MUSIC.
TWO, ABOUT THE DIFFERENT TYPES OF PEOPLE LEARNING TO COEXIST REGARDLESS OF THEIR BELIEFS, LOOKS OR THE COLOR OF THEIR SKINS.
THREE, ABOUT THE BEST TIME TO BE HAD, DURING THE HOT SUMMER SEASON.
FOUR, ABOUT THE NEED TO WAKE UP AND DO THE THINGS TO ACHIEVE YOUR GOALS.
FIVE, ABOUT EACH AND EVERYONE OF US RISING UP AND TAKING PART IN LIFE.
SIX, WHERE THEY WANTED TO TAKE YOU.

1) ______________________
2) __________________
3) _____________________________
4) _____________________________
5) _________**!**
6) _____________________________

33. **1 x 1**

THE SONG "SALLY, GO 'ROUND THE ROSES" WAS RECORDED BY WHAT FEMALE GROUP BELOW WHO NARROWLY MISSED GOING TO THE TOP OF THE CHARTS BACK IN 1963? IT WOULD TURN OUT TO BE THEIR ONLY CLAIM TO FAME SONG.
A) THE SUPREMES
B) THE JAYNETTS
C) THE MARVELETTES
D) THE CHIFFONS

34. **1 x 1**

THE TAMS ALSO CHARTED THEIR CLAIM TO FAME SONG ABOUT NOT BEING A FOOL AND REFUSING TO BE HER SECOND FIDDLE.
A) WHY DO FOOLS FALL IN LOVE
B) WHAT KIND OF FOOL (DO YOU THINK I AM)
C) FOOL # 1
D) THE FOOL ON THE HILL

35. **1 x 1**

WHAT GROUP BELOW WERE THE BACK UP SINGERS FOR MANY OF *CHUBBY CHECKER'S* RECORDINGS INCLUDING "THE TWIST"? THEY WOULD GO ON TO CHART THE BIGGEST HIT OF THEIR CAREER WITH THE SONG "WHEN WE GET MARRIED" THAT *THE INTRUDERS,* ANOTHER GROUP, WOULD ALSO RECORD IN THE EARLY 70'S. WHO WERE THOSE BACK UP SINGERS?

A) THE DOVELLS
B) THE DREAMLOVERS
C) THE FUNK BROTHERS
D) THE IMPERIALS

36. **1 x 1**

THE CLEFTONES, FROM QUEENS, NY, LED BY *HERBIE COX,* HAD A SONG ABOUT THAT MAGICAL NIGHT WHEN SHE HELD HIM AND SWIPED A KISS, A SONG THAT *JAN & DEAN* WOULD ALSO RECORD SHORTLY THEREAFTER.

A) HEART OF GOLD
B) HEART AND SOUL
C) HEART OF THE NIGHT
D) DON'T GO BREAKING MY HEART

37. **1 x 1**

NANCY WILSON RECORDED THE BIGGEST HIT OF HER CAREER WITH WHAT SONG BELOW ABOUT WHAT SHE COULDN'T STOP DOING WHICH WAS SO JOYFUL THAT ONLY AN ARTIST OR A POET COULD DESCRIBE THOSE TYPE OF FEELINGS?

A) DON'T YOU KNOW
B) (YOU DON'T KNOW) HOW GLAD I AM
C) I CAN'T STOP LOVING YOU
D) GLAD ALL OVER

38. **1 x 1**

IN 1962 *THE MAJORS'* ALSO HAD THEIR ONLY BIG HIT ABOUT WHAT SHE HAD LAST NIGHT IN HER SLEEP. HOW YOU HELD HER AND KISSED HER AND SHE HOPED IT WOULD TURN OUT SO TRUE.

A) JUST A DREAM
B) DREAM LOVER
C) ALL I HAVE TO DO IS DREAM
D) A WONDERFUL DREAM

39. **4 x 1**

THIS VERY POPULAR MALE ARTIST, RECORDING PROFESSIONALLY SINCE THE 50'S, CHARTED NUMEROUS HITS IN THE 60'S INCLUDING: "A WOMAN, A LOVER, A FRIEND", "DOGGIN' AROUND", AND "WHISPERS (GETTIN' LOUDER)". NAME HIM AND THESE THREE OTHER HITS BELOW, NUMBERS TWO THROUGH FOUR.
ONE, HIS NAME.
TWO, ABOUT A WORKOUT ON THE DANCE FLOOR.
THREE, ABOUT AN UPLIFTING EMOTION THAT'S ELEVATED HIM TO A LEVEL THAT HE'S NEVER BEEN, CAUSED BY YOU AND SO GRATEFUL TO HAVE MET YOU.
FOUR, ABOUT HOW YOU SHOULD SEE HIS BABY IN ACTION, TALKING AND WALKING JUST FOR STARTERS.

1) ____________________
2) ________________
3) ____
4) ____________________

40. **7 x 1**

NAME THIS DUO WHO WERE KNOWN AS 'THE SWEETHEARTS OF SOUL' AND THESE SIX CHARTED HITS BELOW DURING THE 60'S, NUMBERS TWO THROUGH SEVEN.
ONE, THEIR NAME, KNOWN ONLY BY THEIR FIRST NAMES.
TWO, ABOUT THEIR PLEA TO FALL IN ECSTACY BECAUSE IT'S MEANT TO BE.
THREE, SHUTTING YOUR EYES TO WHISPER AND PRETEND IF NEED BE YOUR PLEDGE OF LOVE TO ME. A SONG ORIGINALLY RECORDED BY *THE FIVE KEYS* BACK IN THE 50'S.
FOUR, THEIR VERSION OF AN *ED TOWNSEND* RECORDING ABOUT WHAT THEY WOULD DO FOR EACH OTHER'S LOVE AND SWEET KISS.
FIVE, THEIR VERSION THIS TIME OF A *MICKEY & SILVIA* TUNE ABOUT WHAT WAS STRANGE. THAT WHEN YOU HAVE IT, YOU DON'T WANT TO LET IT GO.
SIX, ABOUT TWO CHILDHOOD FRIENDS GROWING UP TO EVENTUALLY BECOME LOVERS.
SEVEN, THEIR RENDITION OF A *MOONGLOW* RECORDING ABOUT A CERTAIN SET OF RULES AND HOW IT'LL BRING YOU JOY AND GOODNESS, TITLE SLIGHTLY EXTENDED.

1) ____________ & __________
2) ________________________
3) ________________________
4) ________________
5) ____________________
6) ____________________
7) ___________________________________

41. **11 x 1**

NAME THIS GENTLEMAN WHO WAS COOL AS ICE AND HIS TEN BIG HITS BELOW, NUMBERS TWO THROUGH ELEVEN.
ONE, HIS NAME.
TWO, CLAIMING WHO WOULD BREAK HER HEART BECAUSE HE'S HAD A LOT OF PRACTICE.
THREE, HIS VERSION OF A SONG FEATURED IN 'BREAKFAST AT TIFFANYS' IN THE EARLY 60'S STARRING AUDREY HEPBURN, GEORGE PEPPARD, PATRICIA NEAL AND MICKEY ROONEY ABOUT HIS HUCKLEBERRY FRIEND.
FOUR, A SONG THAT *THE WALKER BROS* WOULD ALSO RECORD WITH A PLEAD TO HER TO BREAK AWAY QUICKLY TO AVOID THE STRESS AND PAIN THAT CAN FOLLOW.
FIVE, HIS BIG WESTERN UNION HIT SONG.
SIX, ABOUT THE ADVISE FROM HIS MOTHER ABOUT THE SURVIVAL OF THE FITTEST.
SEVEN, QUESTIONING THE PURPOSE OF BREAKING UP.
EIGHT, ABOUT SOMEONE WHO IS MOODY BUT STILL HAS IT TOGETHER.
NINE, ABOUT NOT GIVING UP ON YOU NO MATTER WHAT YOU DO.
TEN, ABOUT A CERTAIN MAN THAT CAN MAKE HIS DREAMS COME TRUE.
ELEVEN, ABOUT DIGGING ON YOU BECAUSE YOU'RE THAT SPECIAL ONE.

1) ___________________
2) ______________________________
3) _______________
4) __________________________
5) __________________________
6) ______________________________
7) ___________________________________
8) ________________
9) ______________________
10) _____________________
11) ___________________

42. **9 x 1**

NAME THESE NINE BIG HITS BY *THE IMPRESSIONS* WITH *CURTIS MAYFIED* AT THE HELM.
ONE, ABOUT THAT TRAIN RIDE TO JORDAN FOR THOSE PEOPLE HAVING FAITH.
TWO, ABOUT THE NEED TO KEEP STRIVING TO REACH YOUR GOAL.
THREE, ABOUT A WINNER.
FOUR, A SONG FEATURED IN THE MOVIE 'LILLIES OF THE FIELD', STARRING SIDNEY POITIER AS A HANDY MAN BUILDING A CHAPEL FOR A BUNCH OF NUNS, AND THAT SONG OF BIBLICAL HISTORY RELATING TO THE MESSIAH.
FIVE, ABOUT THE LOVE HE FELT FOR THAT CERTAIN WOMAN THAT HYPNOTIZED HIM WITH LOVE.
SIX, ABOUT THE PRIDE THAT HE FEELS FOR YOU.
SEVEN, THAT IT'S OK TO HAVE FUN AND TO CLAP HANDS.
EIGHT, WHO HE WANTS TO TALK ABOUT THAT HAS THAT CERTAIN WALK, TALK AND GORGEOUS SMILE.
NINE, ABOUT HIS NEED FOR A WOMAN WITH A CERTAIN ATTRIBUTE THAT COMES FROM WITHIN THE HEART.

1) ______________________
2) ____________________
3) ____________________
4) ________
5) ______________
6) ________________
7) ________________
8) _______________________
9) _____________________

43. **1 x 1**

"TRAMP" AND "KNOCK ON WOOD" WERE DUET HITS BY *CARLA THOMAS* AND WHAT SUPER STAR MALE ARTIST WHO WOULD PERISH IN A PLANE CRASH?
A) JOHHNY ACE
B) OTIS REDDING
C) JIM CROCE
D) BUDDY HOLLY

44. **1 x 1**

IN 1958 THE MANAGER/OWNER, GEORGE TREADWELL, OF THIS WELL KNOWN GROUP WHO WERE NO LONGER PRODUCING HITS, FIRED THE MEMBERS OF THE GROUP AND REPLACED THEM WITH MEMBERS OF *THE CROWNS* FORMERLY KNOWN AS *THE FIVE CROWNS*. THEY INCLUDED *CHARLIE THOMAS, BENJAMIN EARL NELSON, DOC GREEN*, AND *ELSBEARY HOBBS*. WHAT WAS THE NAME OF THAT GROUP WITH THE NEW LINEUP AND SOON TO PRODUCE BIG HITS ONCE AGAIN?

____

TOTAL POINTS. **100 x 1 = 100**

R&B ROCKERS-QUIZ # 3

1. **1 x 2**

DEE CLARK, THE MALE ARTIST, RECORDED WHAT NUMBER TWO HIT SONG IN 1961 ABOUT THOSE DROPS FROM ABOVE, SO HE CLAIMS, BECAUSE MEN AREN'T SUPPOSE TO CRY?
A) I DON'T WANT TO CRY
B) WALKING IN THE RAIN
C) IN THE RAIN
D) RAINDROPS

2. **1 x 2**

THIS SONG BELOW, ORIGINALLY RECORDED BY *EDDIE FLOYD,* THEN AS A DUET BY *CARLA THOMAS* AND *OTIS REDDING,* AND DURING THE NEXT DECADE BY *AMII STEWART* ABOUT A SILLY SUPERSTITION THAT ONE DOES IN HOPES OF NOT HAVING BAD LUCK. IN THIS CASE NOT PUTTING AN END TO THIS LOVE AFFAIR. WHAT WAS THAT TRIPLE HITTER CALLED?
A) KNOCKIN' ON HEAVEN'S DOOR
B) KNOCK THREE TIMES
C) KNOCK ON WOOD
D) LOVE POTION NO. 9

3. **1 x 2**

THE MARVELLOS CHARTED THEIR CLAIM TO FAME SONG ABOUT WANTING YOU BY HIS SIDE PERMANENTLY AS HIS BRIDE SINCE HE LOVED YOU WITH ALL OF HIS HEART. WHAT WAS THAT CLAIM TO FAME SONG?
A) I WISH THAT WE WERE MARRIED
B) WHEN WE GET MARRIED
C) I DO LOVE YOU
D) I DO

4. **1 x 2**

"RAMA LAMA DING DONG" WAS A POPULAR SONG BY WHAT GROUP IN 1961 THAT WOULD ALSO BECOME THEIR MAJOR CLAIM TO FAME SONG? IN REALITY IT WAS A RE-MAKE OF THEIR PREVIOUS RECORDING IN THE LATE 50'S WITH ANOTHER LABEL THAT HAD LITTLE OR NO PROMOTION TO GET IT GOING UP THE CHARTS, WITH TITLE SLIGHTLY CHANGED.
A) THE EDSELS
B) THE CRYSTALS
C) THE TEMPTATIONS
D) THE DREAMLOVERS

5. **1 x 2**

THE VELVETS RECORDED WHAT SONG IN 1961 ABOUT THE POSSIBILITY OF WHAT COULD OCCUR TONIGHT?
A) OH, WHAT A NIGHT
B) TONIGHT (COULD BE THE NIGHT)
C) MAKIN' WHOOPEE
D) TONIGHT'S THE NIGHT

6. **1 x 2**

RUFUS THOMAS, THE FATHER OF *CARLA THOMAS,* RECORDED WHAT SONG BELOW ABOUT SHOWING YOU HOW TO DO WHAT IF YOU DIDN'T ALREADY KNOW HOW TO?
A) SHOW ME
B) WALKING THE DOG
C) I'LL TAKE YOU THERE
D) SHOW AND TELL

7. **1 x 2**

THE TOYS, AN ALL GIRL TRIO GROUP, HAD A POPULAR NUMBER TWO HIT SONG ABOUT THE WAY MOTHER NATURE WORKED HER MAGIC, CAUSING THE BIRDS TO SING A MELODY, AND SHE IN YOUR ARMS HEARING YOU PLEDGE YOUR LOVE TO HER ONCE MORE. WHAT WAS THAT POPULAR SONG?

A) A LOVER'S CONCERTO
B) THE BIRDS AND THE BEES
C) WHERE HAVE ALL THE FLOWERS GONE
D) THIS IS MY SONG

8. **1 x 2**

THE FANTASTIC JOHHNY C CHARTED A FUNKY HIT SONG ABOUT WHAT HE WANTED HIS BABY TO DO ALL NIGHT THAT WASN'T HARD TO DO AND HAVE A GOOD TIME AT THAT.

A) BOOGALOO BLUES
B) FUNKY BROADWAY
C) BOOGALOO DOWN BROADWAY
D) FUNKY NASSAU

9. **1 x 2**

"ANGEL BABY" WAS A ROMANTIC SONG BACK IN 1960 LED BY *ROSIE*. WHAT WAS THE GROUP *ROSIE* FRONTED WITH ON THAT ROMANTIC HIT?

A) THE IMPERIALS
B) THE ORIGINALS
C) THE MOONGLOWS
D) THE PIPS

10. **1 x 2**

LINDA JONES CHARTED WHAT MAJOR HIT BELOW ABOUT A CERTAIN STATE OF BEING THAT LEFT HER HELPLESS AND DAZED, WHERE SHE WAS NOW UNDER HIS FULL COMMAND?

A) MY BABY MUST BE A MAGICIAN
B) HYPNOTIZED
C) CRAZY
D) HELP!

11. **1 x 2**

BOBBY 'BLUE' BLAND CHARTED THE MOST MEMORABLE SONG OF HIS CAREER IN THE EARLY 60'S ABOUT A CERTAIN LIGHT THAT HE WANTED HER TO SHINE ON HIM. WHAT WAS THAT SONG?

A) PARTY LIGHTS
B) LIGHT MY FIRE
C) TURN ON YOUR LOVE LIGHT
D) STARSHINE

12. **1 x 2**

THE DRIFTERS HAD NUMEROUS LEAD SINGERS DURING THEIR HISTORICAL CAREER. WHO BELOW DID NOT HAVE THE PRIVILGE OF LEADING THEM?

A) BEN E KING
B) CLYDE MCPHATTER
C) RUDY LEWIS
D) JACKIE WILSON
E) JOHNNY MOORE
F) CHARLIE THOMAS
G) BILL PINKNEY

13. **1 x 2**

NAME THE POPULAR MALE ARTIST WHO GAINED RECOGNITION FOR THE SONG "LIMBO ROCK" WHICH WAS ORIGINALLY CHARTED BY *THE CHAMPS* BETTER KNOWN FOR THEIR BIG HIT "TEQUILA".

A) DEAN MARTIN
B) HANK BALLARD
C) JOE TEX
D) CHUBBY CHECKER

14. **1 x 2**

KETTY LESTER, A FEMALE SINGER/TURNED ACTRESS, CHARTED THIS ROMANTIC SONG IN 1962 ABOUT PASSIONATE WORDS WRITTEN BY HER DARLING FROM WITHIN HIS HEART. IT WOULD BE HER ONLY MAJOR HIT. THE SONG WAS ORIGINALLY A THEME FOR A MOVIE OF THE SAME NAME BY VICTOR YOUNG IN 1945 STARRING JENNIFER JONES AND JOSEPH COTTON. WHAT WAS THAT ROMANTIC HIT?

A) APRIL LOVE
B) LOVE LETTERS IN THE SAND
C) LET IT BE ME
D) LOVE LETTERS

15. **1 x 2**

THE BLUE BELLES HAD A HIT WITH "I SOLD MY HEART TO THE JUNKMAN". NAME THEIR LEAD SINGER WHO WOULD GO ON TO CHART MORE HITS WITH THE GROUP, THEN AS A SOLOIST, AND ON RARE OCCASIONS AS A PART OF A DUO.

A) GLADYS KNIGHT
B) MARY WELLS
C) PATTI LABELLE
D) DIANA ROSS

16. **1 x 2**

THE BLUE BELLES CHARTED ANOTHER, THIS TIME WITH A ROMANTIC BALLAD ABOUT WALKING DOWN THAT CEREMONIAL PATH WITH EXCHANGES OF RINGS AND VOWS 'TIL DEATH DO THEY PART.

A) CRYING IN THE CHAPEL
B) WITH THIS RING
C) DOWN THE AISLE (WEDDING SONG)
D) CHAPEL OF LOVE

17. **1 x 2**

ROBERT KNIGHT CHARTED WHAT SONG IN 1967 ABOUT AN ENDURING LOVE THAT WOULD BE RECORDED BY *CARL CARLTON* IN THE 70'S, AS A DUET BY *REX SMITH* AND *RACHEL SWEET* IN THE 80'S, AND BY *GLORIA ESTEFAN* IN THE 90'S?

A) WHEN WE GET MARRIED
B) ALWAYS
C) EVERLASTING LOVE
D) 'TIL

18. **1 x 2**

IN 1968 *OC SMITH,* A MALE R&B SINGER, RECORDED WHAT FRUIT TITLED SONG BELOW THAT WAS JUST ONE NOTCH SHY OF REACHING THE TOP OF THE CHARTS ABOUT IMAGINING WHAT GOD DIDN'T CREATE AND WHAT NEVER HAPPENS OR DOESN'T EXIST? CHOOSE IT BELOW.

A) APPLES, PEACHES, PUMPKIN PIE
B) GREEN, GREEN GRASS OF HOME
C) LITTLE GREEN APPLES
D) WATERMELON MAN

19. **1 x 2**

IN 1966 *ROBERT PARKER* HAD THIS DANCE NUMBER THAT ONE WOULD ATTEMPT TO DO WITH NO SHOES ON. CHOOSE THAT DANCE NUMBER BELOW.
A) SNAP YOUR FINGERS
B) MICKEY'S MONKEY
C) BAREFOOTIN'
D) MASHED POTATO TIME

20. **1 x 2**

"THE JERK" WAS A DANCE NUMBER CHARTED BY WHICH SOUL GROUP BELOW IN 1964 THAT HE WAS GONNA TEACH YOU HOW. JUST WATCH HIM WORK AND MOVE THOSE HIPS. IT WOULD BE THEIR ONLY MAJOR HIT.
A) THE MIRACLES
B) THE LARKS
C) THE COASTERS
D) CANNIBAL AND THE HEADHUNTERS

21. **1 x 2**

"KIDDEO" WAS A SONG RECORDED BY WHAT POPULAR MALE ARTIST BELOW?
A) BROOK BENTON
B) SAM COOKE
C) JIMMY JONES
D) CHUCK BERRY

22. **1 x 2**

ROCHELLE AND THE CANDLES HAD THIS BEAUTIFUL BALLAD IN THE EARLY 60'S WHICH BECAME THEIR MAJOR CLAIM TO FAME SONG. CHOOSE THAT BEAUTIFUL BALLAD BELOW.
A) ONE FINE DAY
B) MY BABY MUST BE A MAGICIAN
C) ONCE IN AWHILE
D) ONCE UPON A TIME

23. **1 x 2**

THE R&B GROUP, *THE BLUE JAYS,* RECORDED THIS SONG IN THE EARLY 60'S WHICH ALSO BECAME THEIR ONE CLAIM TO FAME SONG. CHOOSE THAT ONE.
A) LOVER'S CONCERTO
B) LOVE LETTERS IN THE SAND
C) LOVER'S ISLAND
D) GYPSY WOMAN

24. **1 x 2**

THIS BLACK FEMALE ARTIST CHARTED NUMEROUS SONGS DURING HER CAREER. ONE OF HER MOST IMPRESSIVE AND YET UNDERRATED WAS A SONG CALLED "AT LAST". SHE WAS KNOWN FOR HER DYED BLONDE HAIR AND HER NICKNAME 'MISS PEACHES'. WHO IS SHE THAT STILL PERFORMS TODAY?
A) ETTA JAMES
B) DEE DEE SHARP
C) DIONNE WARWICK
D) MAHALIA JACKSON

25. **1 x 2**

ROY HAMILTON CHARTED WHAT SONG ABOUT A GIRL WHO WANTED TO ONLY USE HIM AND HE WOULD RATHER BE LAID OUT IN THE GROUND THAN TO BE WITH?
A) YOU DON'T OWN ME
B) YOU CAN HAVE HER
C) WE GOTTA GET OUT OF THIS PLACE
 D) WHAT KIND OF FOOL (DO YOU THINK I AM)

26. **1 x 2**

LENNY WELCH RECORDED WHAT CLASSIC LOVE BALLAD BELOW THAT GAINED HIM HIS PREMIER STARDOM ABOUT WHAT HE LOST AS A RESULT OF FALLING FOR YOU, AND NOW THAT YOU HAVE LEFT HIM, HE'S LIVING IN MISERY?

A) SINCE YOU'RE GONE
B) SINCE I DON'T HAVE YOU
C) I CAN'T GET NEXT TO YOU
D) SINCE I FELL FOR YOU

27. **1 x 2**

LOUIS ARMSTRONG, THE GREAT JAZZ AND BLUES MUSICIAN KNOWN FOR HIS TRUMPET PLAYING ABILITIES, HAD A TOP OF THE CHARTS HIT SONG FROM A POPULAR BROADWAY MUSICAL ABOUT DOLLY, THE MATCH MAKER, STARRING CAROL CHANNING WHO WAS THE ORIGINAL ARTIST OF THIS SONG. LATER IT WOULD BE ADAPTED INTO A MOVIE STARRING *BARBRA STREISAND,* WALTER MATTHAU AND *LOUIS* MAKING IT HIS VERY OWN AND A NUMBER ONE HIT.

__________, _________!

28. **1 x 2**

THE LEGENDARY *NAT 'KING' COLE* CHARTED WHAT SUMMER TITLED SONG BELOW?

A) SUMMERTIME
B) HERE COMES SUMMER
C) ONE SUMMER NIGHT
D) THOSE LAZY HAZY CRAZY DAYS OF SUMMER

29 **2 x 2**

NAT 'KING' COLE ALSO HAD THESE TWO OTHER POPULAR HITS.
ONE, ABOUT A RAMBLING GIRL WHO DID EXACTLY THAT, RAMBLED ALL DAY, YET HE LOVES HER JUST THE SAME.
TWO, A ROMANTIC SONG THAT SPELLS OUT A FOUR LETTER WORD WITH EACH LETTER INDICATING WHAT IT MEANS TO HIM AND HIS LOVE.
NAME THEM.

1) ____________'_______
2) ___.___.___.___

30. **7 x 2**

THIS POPULAR FEMALE ARTIST HAD BUNCHES OF HITS INCLUDING: "(THEME FROM) VALLEY OF THE DOLLS", "PROMISES, PROMISES", "THIS GIRL'S IN LOVE WITH YOU", AND "ALFIE". NAME HER AND THESE SIX OTHER HITS, NUMBERS TWO THROUGH SEVEN.
ONE, HER NAME.
TWO, ONLY SOMEONE WITH A HEART THAT CAN EMBRACE HER.
THREE, ASKING HER FORMER LOVER TO WALK PAST HER SHOULD SHE BREAK DOWN TO CRY WHENEVER THEY MEET.
FOUR, ABOUT A MESSAGE FOR SOMEONE.
FIVE, ABOUT A PRAYER THAT SHE WILL QUOTE THROUGHOUT THE DAY, HOPING THAT THEY WILL NEVER PART. IT'S A SONG *ARETHA FRANKLIN* WOULD ALSO RECORD.
SIX, ASKING DIRECTIONS TO GET TO THAT CERTAIN CITY IN CALIFORNIA.
SEVEN, ABOUT A MAKE OVER THAT SHE DIDN'T WANT.

1) ____________________
2) ____________________________
3) _______________
4) ________________________
5) ____________________________
6) ______________________________________?
7) ________________________

31. **1 x 2**

WHAT FEMALE TEENAGER CHARTED THE SONG "THE LOCO-MOTION" WHICH WOULD CLIMB TO THE TOP OF THE CHARTS IN 1962 ABOUT THAT NEW DANCE THAT WAS EASY TO DO?
A) LITTLE EVA
B) LITTLE PEGGY MARCH
C) LESLIE GORE
D) SKEETER DAVIS

32. **1 x 2**

THE DIXIEBELLES, A TRIO OF GIRLS, CHARTED WHAT SONG BELOW ABOUT PAPA? IT WOULD BE THEIR ONE CLAIM TO FAME SONG.
A) PAPA WAS A ROLLIN' STONE
B) PAPA LOVES MAMBO
C) (DOWN AT) PAPA JOE'S
D) PAPA'S GOT A BRAND NEW BAG

33. **1 x 2**

B.B. KING, THE BLUES SINGER AND FAMED GUITARIST, HAD A HIT ABOUT A CERTAIN GOOD FEELING THAT HE NO LONGER HAD, THAT LEFT HIM SO LONELY BUT ALSO FREE OF HER SPELL.
A) I GOT YOU (I FEEL GOOD)
B) I FEEL FINE
C) THE THRILL IS GONE
D) LOVE IS A HURTIN' THING

34. **1 x 2**

BROOK BENTON AND *DINAH WASHINGTON* CHARTED A DUET WITH THIS ROCKING HIT BELOW.
A) ROCKIN' ROBIN
B) A ROCKIN' GOOD WAY (TO MESS AROUND AND FALL IN LOVE)
C) ROCKIN' AROUND THE CHRISTMAS TREE
D) ROCK & ROLL MUSIC

35. **1 x 2**

BARBARA GEORGE HAD THIS LOST LOVE HIT SONG WHERE SHE ADMITTED KNOWING HE NO LONGER WANTED HER.
A) I KNOW (YOU DON'T LOVE ME NO MORE)
B) I CAN'T GET NEXT TO YOU
C) (I KNOW) I'M LOSING YOU
D) RELEASE ME (AND LET ME LOVE AGAIN)

36. **1 x 2**

WHAT SONG DO *SOLOMAN BURKE* AND *WILSON PICKETT* HAVE IN COMMON?
A) EVERYBODY PLAYS THE FOOL
B) EVERYBODY'S TALKIN'
C) EVERYBODY'S SOMEBODY'S FOOL
D) EVERYBODY NEEDS SOMEBODY TO LOVE

37. **2 x 2**

NAME THESE TWO HITS BY *CHUCK JACKSON*.
ONE, A SONG *ELVIS* WOULD RECORD IN THE 70'S AND *RONNIE MILSAP* IN THE 80'S ABOUT THE FEAR OF HEARING GOODBYE FOR THE VERY LAST TIME DUE TO PARTED LOVE.
TWO, WHAT HE DIDN'T WANT TO DO THAT WAS SO PAINFULL.
1) ______________________________________

 2) ______________________

38. **1 x 2**

GARNET MIMMS & THE ENCHANTERS RECORDED WHAT HURT SONG ABOUT A MAN WHO LEFT HIS BABY TO CRY?
A) CRYING TIME
B) CRY BABY
C) CRYING
D) I WISH IT WOULD RAIN

39. **1 x 2**

ARTHUR CONLEY CHARTED A POPULAR SONG THAT WAS A TRIBUTE TO THE VARIOUS SOUL SINGERS OF THE DAY WHICH INCLUDED THE LIKES OF *LOU RAWLS, SAM & DAVE, THE WICKED PICKETT, OTIS REDDING* AND THE MEANEST OF ALL, *JAMES BROWN*. WHAT WAS THAT SOULFUL HIT CALLED?
A) STAND BY ME
B) WOMAN'S GOT SOUL
C) SWEET SOUL MUSIC
D) (YOU'RE MY) SOUL AND INSPIRATION

40. **1 x 2**

ARCHIE BELL & THE DRELLS, FROM TEXAS, RECORDED THIS SONG BELOW THAT TAUGHT US A NEW DANCE NUMBER THROUGH THE LYRICS AND THE VARIOUS INSTRUMENTS, WHICH INCLUDED THE DRUMS, BASE, GUITAR, AND ORGAN ALL COMING TOGETHER TO CREATE THIS SOUND. IT TOO WOULD BE THEIR FIRST MAJOR HIT AND GIVE THEM THEIR PREMIER STARDOM.
A) FINGER POPPIN' TIME
B) TIGHTEN UP
C) MASHED POTATO TIME
D) BAREFOOTIN'

41. **1 x 2**

*JOE SIMON C*HARTED A HIT WITH WHAT SONG BELOW WHERE YOUR LOVE WAS FRIGHTENING TO SAY THE LEAST, YET HE LOVED YOU JUST THE SAME?
A) THE CHOKIN' KIND
B) I CAN'T STOP LOVING YOU
C) (I BELIEVE) THERE'S NOTHING STRONGER THAN OUR LOVE
D) I CAN'T HELP MYSELF

42. **1 x 2**

SHEP AND THE LIMELITES, WITH *JIM SHEPPARD* IN LEAD, CHARTED THIS POPULAR HIT SONG ABOUT COMING HOME TO BE BY HIS ANGEL FOR GOOD. IT WOULD BE THEIR BIGGEST AND REACH THE NUMBER TWO SPOT ON THE CHARTS IN 1961. *JERMAINE JACKSON,* OF *THE JACKSON FIVE,* WOULD GO ON TO RECORD IT FOR THE MOTOWN LABEL AS A SOLO IN THE EARLY 70'S. WHAT WAS THAT DOUBLE HITTER?
A) DADDY'S HOME
B) COLOR HIM FATHER
C) SUGAR DADDY
D) I'LL BE HOME

TOTAL POINTS. **50 x 2 = 100**

R&B ROCKERS-QUIZ # 4

1. **1 x 1**

BROOK BENTON AND *DINAH WASHINGTON* CHARTED A DUET ABOUT SOMETHING THEY EACH CLAIMED THE OTHER HAD. WHAT WAS THAT DUET HIT BELOW?
A) BABY, I'M YOURS
B) BABY (YOU'VE GOT WHAT IT TAKES)
C) I GOT RHYTHM
D) BABY, I'M FOR REAL

2. **1 x 1**

IN 1966 *PERCY SLEDGE* RECORDED THE BIGGEST HIT OF HIS CAREER THAT INITIALLY GAVE HIM HIS STARDOM WITH THIS ROMANTIC SONG BELOW ABOUT THE GENUINE FEELINGS THAT A MAN HAS FOR A WOMAN THAT HE WOULD GIVE UP ANYTHING JUST TO HAVE HER. A SONG *MICHAEL BOLTON* WOULD GO ON TO RECORD IN THE 90'S.
A) SINCE I FELL FOR YOU
B) TO LOVE SOMEBODY
C) WHEN A MAN LOVES A WOMAN
D) YOU SEND ME

3. **1 x 1**

PERCY SLEDGE CHARTED ANOTHER ABOUT A GIRL HE FOUND AND THE ADVISE HE DIDN'T TAKE PRIOR TO MARRYING HER FROM HIS MAMA AND HIS PREACHER.
A) LISTEN PEOPLE
B) THINK
C) ALL IN MY MIND
D) TAKE TIME TO KNOW HER

4. **3 x 1**

NAME THESE THREE BIG SOLO HITS BY *BROOK BENTON*.
ONE, ABOUT AN INSECT THAT CHOSE HIS FARM TO LIVE AND CREATE HAVOC.
TWO, ABOUT A CERTAIN HOTEL THAT HE'S MAKING RESERVATIONS TO.
THREE, PLEADING FOR YOU TO RECONSIDER BEFORE DECIDING.
1) ____________________
2) ____________________
3) ____________________

5. **6 x 1**

NAME THESE SIX HITS BY THE LATE GREAT *OTIS REDDING*.
ONE, A SONG THAT *ARETHA FRANKLIN* WOULD ALSO SING, ABOUT WHAT THEY WANTED, EVEN IF JUST A LITTLE BIT, AT THEIR POINT OF ARRIVAL AT HOME.
TWO, HIS VERSION OF A *SAM COOKE* TUNE ABOUT WHAT YOU CAN DO LIKE YOU WOULD TO A SOUP.
THREE, HIS SOULFUL COVER VERSION OF A *ROLLING STONE* SONG ABOUT SOMETHING HE COULDN'T GET, TITLE SHORTENED.
FOUR, ABOUT THE LENGTH OF TIME HE'S LOVED YOU.
FIVE, A SONG THAT THE GROUP *THREE DOG NIGHT* WOULD ALSO RECORD SOULFULLY ABOUT APPLYING SOME TENDERNESS TO SATISFY HER NEEDS.
SIX, HIS BIG POSTHUMOUS HIT ABOUT A PLACE IN THE BAY THAT HE CAN ESCAPE TO, WHERE SHIPS MIGHT ROLL IN AND OUT OF, RECORDED DAYS BEFORE HIS DEATH.
1) ____________________
2) ____________________
3) ____________________
4) ____________________
5) ____________________
6) ____________________

6. **1 x 1**

WHO IS KNOWN AS SOUL BROTHER NUMBER ONE AND THE HARDEST WORKING MAN IN SHOW BUSINESS, STILL PERFORMING AND DOING WALK ON'S IN MOVIES HERE IN THE 21ST CENTURY, AS IN 'THE TUXEDO MAN' WITH JACKIE CHAN?

A) JAMES BROWN
B) CHUCK BERRY
C) LOU RAWLS
D) SMOKEY ROBINSON

7. **1 x 1**

R.B. GREAVES, THE NEPHEW OF *SAM COOKE*, CHARTED WHAT MARRIAGE BREAK-UP HIT SONG IN 1969, A TOP NUMBER TWO, ABOUT THE TIME HE CAUGHT HIS WIFE WITH ANOTHER? IT WOULD GAIN HIM HIS INITIAL STARDOM.

A) BY THE TIME I GET TO PHOENIX
B) TAKE TIME TO KNOW HER
C) TAKE A LETTER MARIA
D) YOU CHEATED

8. **8 x 1**

NAME THESE SEVEN CHARTED HITS BY *WILSON 'THE WICKED' PICKETT.*
ONE, ABOUT A CERTAIN TIME OF THE NIGHT THAT HIS LOVE COMES ROLLING ON DOWN.
TWO, A NUMBER WHERE YOU CAN REACH HIM ANY TIME.
THREE, HIS SOULFUL RENDITION OF A *CANNIBAL AND THE HEADHUNTERS* HIT SONG ABOUT THAT LAND WHERE YOU CAN DO THE PONY, MASHED POTATO, THE ALLIGATOR, AND EVEN THE WATUSI.
FOUR, ABOUT A GIRL NAMED SALLY RIDING ALL OVER TOWN IN HER NEW FORD.
FIVE, HIS BIG FUNKY HIT SONG ABOUT A STREET AND CLUB THAT EVERY TOWN POSSESSES.
SIX, WHAT EVERYBODY NEEDS ALL THE TIME.
SEVEN, WHAT HE CLAIMED TO HAVE FOUND, PT 1.
EIGHT, WHAT HE WAS DEEPLY IN THAT HE WANTED THE WORLD TO KNOW.

1) ________________________
2) ____________
3) ______________________________
4) __________________
5) __________________
6) __________________________________
7) __________________
8) _______________

9. **1 x 1**

BETTY EVERETT RECORDED A SONG PROCLAIMING THAT IF HE LOVES HER, HIS KISS WOULD REVEAL IT SO. IT IS A SONG THAT *CHER* WOULD ALSO RECORD IN THE 90'S FOR THE MOVIE SOUNDTRACK 'MERMAIDS' IN WHICH SHE CO-STARRED WITH WINONA RYDER.

A) (TIL) I KISSED YOU
B) THE SHOOP, SHOOP SONG (IT'S IN HIS KISS)
C) KISSES SWEETER THAN WINE
D) GIVE HIM A GREAT BIG KISS

10. **2 x 1**

NAME THE TWO ARTISTS THAT WOULD EVOLVE OUT OF *THE IMPRESSIONS*. ONE WOULD GO ON TO CHART NUMEROUS ROMANTIC COOL HITS AND THE OTHER WAS INVOLVED WITH THE '*SUPER FLY*' SOUNDTRACK MOVIE IN THE EARLY 70'S.

1) _______________
2) ___________________

11. **1 x 1**

JACKIE LEE WILL BE MOSTLY REMEMBERED FOR HIS ONE HIT WONDER SONG OF THIS BIRD TUNE THAT ONE WOULD PROBABLY ASSOCIATE WITH *CHUCK BERRY* WITH HIS STAGE WALK. WHAT WAS THAT HIT?

A) ROCKIN' ROBIN
B) DO THE BIRD
C) THE DUCK
D) TWEEDLEE DEE

12. **1 x 1**

IN 1964 *THE JELLY BEANS,* A QUINTET GROUP OF FOUR GIRLS AND ONE GUY, CHARTED THEIR CLAIM TO FAME SONG ABOUT THE INTENSE LOVE THAT THEY HAD FOR THIS GUY NAMED JIM WHO THEY WANTED THE CHANCE TO MAKE HIM HAPPY IF ONLY HE WOULD GIVE THEM THE TIME. WHAT WAS THAT FAME SONG?

A) GIMME GIMME GOOD LOVIN'
B) FOR YOUR LOVE
C) I WANNA LOVE HIM SO BAD
D) LOVE IS A HURTIN' THING

13. **1 x 1**

BILL MEDLEY, FORMERLY OF THE *RIGHTEOUS BROTHERS* AND STILL WITH THE SOULFUL SOUND, CHARTED WHAT SOLO HIT SONG ABOUT PEACE?

A) A PIECE OF MY HEART
B) PEACE IN THE VALLEY
C) PEACE TRAIN
D) PEACE BROTHER PEACE

14. **1 x 1**

BILL MEDLEY RECORDED STILL ANOTHER ABOUT A CERTAIN WOMAN WITH CERTAIN COLORED EYES WHO HE WANTED NO PART OF.

A) BROWN EYED GIRL
B) BROWN EYED WOMAN
C) BROWN SUGAR
D) AMERICAN WOMAN

15. **1 x 1**

BRENDA & THE TABULATIONS, THE GROUP FROM PHILLY, CHARTED A SONG TELLING HER BABY TO WIPE AWAY THOSE TEARS.

A) TEARS ON MY PILLOW
B) CRY BABY
C) DRY YOUR EYES
D) RAINDROPS

16. **1 x 1**

THE COOKIES WHO HAD A HIT WITH "CHAINS" IN 1962 PLEADED IN ANOTHER NOT TO PUT THEIR BABY DOWN. WHAT WAS THAT ONE CALLED?

A) DON'T LET ME DOWN
B) DON'T SAY NOTHIN' BAD (ABOUT MY BABY)
C) DON'T HANG UP
D) DON'T LET THE JONESES GET YOU DOWN

17. **1 x 1**

JOE HENDERSON HAD HIS BIG MOMENT IN TIME WHEN HE RECORDED WHAT SNAPPING HIT SONG BELOW?

A) FINGER POPPIN' TIME
B) BAREFOOTIN'
C) SNAP YOUR FINGERS
 D) TIGHTEN UP

18. **1 x 1**

IN 1966 *BOBBY HEBB* CHARTED THE BIGGEST HIT OF HIS CAREER ABOUT SOMEONE WHO EASED THE HURT INSIDE. WHAT WAS THAT SONG CALLED?
A) HURT SO BAD
B) HURT
C) GOOD MORNING STARSHINE
D) SUNNY

19. **1 x 1**

IN THE 60'S *MEL CARTER* RECORDED THIS ROMANTIC SONG ABOUT A NEVER ENDING EMBRACE, AN ORIGINAL HIT FOR *KAREN CHANDLER* AS A POP HIT YEARS EARLIER. IN THE 90'S *GLORIA ESTEFAN* WOULD ALSO RECORD IT FOR HER CLASSIC HITS ALBUM OF THE SAME NAME. CHOOSE THAT ROMANTIC TRIPLE HITTER BELOW.
A) HOLD ME TIGHT
B) THE THRILL IS GONE
C) HOLD ME, THRILL ME, KISS ME
D) DON'T LET GO

20. **1 x 1**

THE TYMES HAD WHAT TOP OF THE CHARTS HIT SONG BELOW ABOUT TWO LOVERS STROLLING ALONG AND EXPRESSING THEIR LOVE TO ONE ANOTHER? IN THE BACKGROUND ONE COULD HEAR BIRD CALLS AND OTHER SEASHORE SOUNDS. IN THE 90'S THE GROUP *ALL-4-ONE* WOULD GO ON TO RECORD THEIR VERSION OF IT, EQUALLY ROMANTIC.
A) (SITTIN' ON) THE DOCK OF THE BAY
B) THE STROLL
C) SILHOUETTES
D) SO MUCH IN LOVE

21. **1 x 1**

THE TYMES ALSO RECORDED ANOTHER WHICH WAS THEIR VERSION OF A *JOHNNY MATHIS* TUNE ABOUT SOMETHING SO GRAND.
A) WONDERFUL WORLD
B) WONDERFUL! WONDERFUL!
C) OH HAPPY DAY
D) OH HOW HAPPY

22. **1 x 1**

THE ROYALETTES, A FEMALE GROUP, CHARTED A SONG ABOUT WHAT IT'LL TAKE TO HAVE YOUR LOVE BECAUSE SHE'S STILL CRAZY FOR YOU, A SONG *DENIECE WILLIAMS* WOULD GO ON TO RECORD IN THE EARLY 80'S.
A) GIVE HIM A GREAT BIG KISS
B) HE'S SO FINE
C) (TODAY I MET) THE BOY I'M GONNA MARRY
D) IT'S GONNA TAKE A MIRACLE

23. **1 x 1**

THE DIXIE CUPS, A TRIO FEMALE GROUP OF TWO SISTERS AND ONE COUSIN, HAD WHAT CHART TOPPER IN 1964 ABOUT A PLACE THEY WERE GOING, TO EXCHANGE VOWS, END UP AS ONE, AND CARRY A NEW NAME?
A) CHAPEL OF LOVE
B) CRYING IN THE CHAPEL
C) WHEN WE GET MARRIED
D) TO THE AISLE

24. **2 x 1**

THE DIXIE CUPS WOULD ALSO CHART TWO MORE IN THE MID 60'S. NAME THEM. ONE, WHAT THE PEOPLE WERE GOSSIPING ABOUT, THAT THEIR RELATIONSHIP WAS ONLY A SUMMER FLING.
TWO, A NOVELTY SONG ABOUT WHAT ONE GRANDMOTHER DID TO ANOTHER GRANDMOTHER.

1) ________________

2) ___________

25. **1 x 1**

IN 1965 *JEWEL AKENS* WOULD HAVE HIS ONE CLAIM TO FAME SONG ABOUT THE STORY OF MOTHER NATURE AND THE COLOR OF YOUR EYES.

A) BROWN EYED GIRL
B) BROWN EYED WOMAN
C) THE BIRDS AND THE BEES
D) ELUSIVE BUTTERFLY

26. **1 x 1**

BARBARA LYNN IS MOSTLY REMEMBERED FOR WHAT SONG BELOW THAT SHE CHARTED BACK IN 1962 THAT *FREDDIE FENDER* WOULD ALSO RECORD IN THE 70'S ABOUT WHAT YOU CAN END UP LOSING THAT'S QUITE GOOD?

A) I KNOW (I'M LOSING YOU)
B) SINCE I LOST MY BABY
C) YOU'LL LOSE A GOOD THING
D) I ALMOST LOST MY MIND

27. **3 x 1**

ALSO IN 1962 THESE TWO GUYS RECORDED A CLASSIC HIT ABOUT HOW THEY WANTED TO KNOW A CERTAIN GIRL'S NAME AND TRIED GUESSING IT. NAME BOTH THE SONG AND THE DUO KNOWN ONLY BY THEIR FIRST NAMES.

1) ______________________

2) _______

3) _________

28. **1 x 1**

BOBBY LEWIS RECORDED A TOP OF THE CHARTS HIT SONG BACK IN 1961 ABOUT HIS TWISTING AND TURNING BECAUSE HE COULDN'T SLEEP.

A) (LAST NIGHT) I DIDN'T GET TO SLEEP AT ALL
B) TOSSIN' AND TURNIN'
C) TWISTIN' THE NIGHT AWAY
D) SHAKE

29. **1 x 1**

THE *'CORSAIRS'* CHARTED THIS ONE MAJOR HIT WHICH LEFT THEIR MARK IN MUSIC HISTORY ABOUT A CERTAIN PLACE WHERE THEY COULD MEET.

A) SMOKEY JOE'S CAFE
B) SMOKEY PLACES
C) HERNANDO'S HIDEAWAY
D) ON BROADWAY

30. **1 x 1**

THE SENSATIONS WOULD ALSO HAVE THEIR DAY IN MUSIC HISTORY WHEN THEY RECORDED A SONG BACK IN 1962 PLEADING TO BE ALLOWED IN.

A) HELP!
B) I'M ON THE OUTSIDE (LOOKING IN)
C) LET ME IN
D) WHO'S THAT KNOCKIN'

31. **1 x 1**

JOE JONES CHARTED THIS SONG ABOUT SOMEONE WHO WAS CONSTANTLY TALKING WHICH NOT ONLY ANNOYED HIM BUT HIS PET AS WELL.

A) TALK THAT TALK
B) YOU TALK TOO MUCH
C) TALK TO ME, TALK TO ME
D) TALKING ABOUT MY BABY

32. **1 x 1**

THE VIBRATIONS CHARTED TWO BIG HITS IN THE EARLY 60'S. ONE WAS CALLED "THE WATUSI" WHICH WAS THEIR FIRST BIG MAJOR RECORDING THAT WOULD GIVE THEM THEIR STAR POWER. WHAT WAS THE OTHER ABOUT A GIRL THEY LOVED? IT WOULD BE RECORDED BY *THE MCCOYS,* THE POP GROUP, TITLE SLIGHTLY CHANGED, WHO WOULD TAKE IT TO THE TOP OF THE CHARTS.

A) MY BABY
B) MY GIRL SLOOPY
C) MY GIRL
D) BABY LOVE

33. **1 x 1**

THE VIBRATIONS HAD ANOTHER ABOUT A CERTAIN FOOD ITEM THAT ONE CAN EAT ANYTIME WITH BREAD. THIS SONG WAS CONTROVERSIAL BECAUSE IT WOULD BE RELEASED AS ANOTHER GROUP NAME, CALLED *THE MARATHONS,* AND FOR ANOTHER LABEL WHICH RESULTED IN A CONFLICT OF INTEREST DISPUTE AND COURT ACTIONS.

A) BREAD AND BUTTER
B) PEANUT BUTTER
C) PEANUTS
D) ON TOP OF SPAGHETTI

34. **1 x 1**

GARY U.S. BONDS HAD A BUNCH OF HITS IN THE EARLY 60'S WHICH INCLUDED FOUR BELOW. WHICH ONE UNFORTUNATELY WAS **NOT** HIS?

A) QUARTER TO THREE
B) NEW ORLEANS
C) SCHOOL IS OUT
D) TWIST, TWIST SENORA
E) TWISTIN' THE NIGHT AWAY

35. **1 x 1**

CHOOSE FROM BELOW THIS ROCK 'N ROLL LEGEND WHO INSPIRED MANY. HE SANG ABOUT CARS, MUSIC, ROMANCE, SCHOOL ETC.

A) LITTLE RICKY NELSON
B) LITTLE RICHARD
C) CHUCK BERRY
D) FATS DOMINO

36. **1 x 1**

"C'MON AND SWIM" WAS A DANCE NUMBER BY WHICH POPULAR SINGER BELOW WHO WAS GONNA SHOW YOU HOW THAT INVOLVED A LOT OF THE DANCES STEPS CURRENTLY AROUND, THE MONKEY, THE TWIST, THE HULLY GULLY, AND THE DOG, ALL DONE LIKE IF YOU WERE IN THE WATER?

A) BOBBY DARIN
B) BOBBY FREEMAN
C) JACKIE WILSON
D) SAM COOKE

37. **1 x 1**

CLAUDINE CLARK CHARTED THIS POPULAR SONG BELOW ABOUT THOSE CERTAIN LIGHTS WHICH GAVE HER THE INDICATION THAT A PARTY WAS IN PROGRESS AND SHE DESPERATELY WANTED TO ATTEND.
A) PARTY LIGHTS
B) HAVING A PARTY
C) GOING TO A GO-GO
D) TWISTIN' THE NIGHT AWAY

38. **1 x 1**

GENE MCDANIELS RECORDED WHAT SONG ABOUT HOW THE ALMIGHTY TOOK A CERTAIN AMOUNT OF CLAY TO CREATE SOMETHING GRAND FOR A MAN?
A) BUILD ME UP BUTTERCUP
B) A WOMAN, A LOVER, A FRIEND
C) A HUNDRED POUNDS OF CLAY
D) YOUNG GIRL

39. **1 x 1**

GENE MCDANIELS CHARTED ANOTHER ABOUT THAT TOWER THAT HE COULD NEVER BECOME. CHOOSE THAT ONE.
A) STAND TALL
B) BIG MAN IN TOWN
C) TOWER OF STRENGTH
D) MR DREAM MERCHANT

40. **1 x 1**

IN 1961 *ERNIE K-DOE* HAD A POPULAR SONG THAT REACHED THE TOP OF THE CHARTS AND BROUGHT HIM HIS DAY OF FAME. IN THE SONG HE BELIEVED HIS WIFE'S MOTHER WAS THE CAUSE OF THEIR MARITAL PROBLEMS AND BIG TIME STRESS.
A) MOTHER-IN-LAW
B) MAMA DIDN'T LIE
C) MAMA SAID
D) YAKETY YAK

41. **1 x 1**

JERRY BUTLER RECORDED "LET IT BE ME" AS A DUET WITH WHAT FEMALE ARTIST BELOW?
A) MARY WELLS
B) DINAH WASHINGTON
C) JEAN TERRELL
D) BETTY EVERETT

42. **1 x 1**

CHOOSE THIS *FONTELLA BASS* SONG BELOW IN WHICH SHE WOULD BE SAVED AND HELD IN HIS ARMS TO END HER LONELINESS.
A) RESCUE ME
B) HOLD ME TIGHT
C) HOLD ME, THRILL ME, KISS ME
D) ALONG CAME JONES

43. **1 x 1**

CLARENCE 'FROGMAN' HENRY HAD THIS POPULAR SONG ABOUT SOMETHING HE COULDN'T FIGURE OUT, BUT NEVERTHELESS WAS FINALLY ABLE TO.
A) I DON'T KNOW WHY I LOVE YOU (BUT I DO)
B) I THINK I LOVE YOU
C) (IF LOVING YOU IS WRONG) I DON'T WANT TO BE RIGHT
 D) (IF YOU LET ME MAKE LOVE TO YOU THEN) WHY CAN'Y I TOUCH YOU?

44. **2 x 1**

"THE IN CROWD" WAS A POPULAR HIT FOR TWO ARTISTS.
ONE, AS AN INSTRUMENTAL HIT FOR THIS JAZZY TRIO GROUP LED BY *RAMSEY*.
TWO, AS A VOCAL HIT FOR THIS MALE SINGER WHO WOULD ALSO CHART IN THE 70'S WITH THAT BLOCKBUSTER HIT "DRIFT AWAY".
NAME THEM BOTH.

1) ______________________

2) _____________

45. **1 x 1**

CHOOSE THE GIRL GROUP BELOW THAT FEATURED THESE THREE DIFFERENT LEAD SINGERS IN THE 60'S, *BARBARA ALSTON, LA LA BROOKS* AND *DARLENE LOVE*. ALL RECORDED FOR PHIL SPECTORS' PHILLES LABEL AND AT HIS SAY SO.

A) THE CRYSTALS
B) THE RONETTES
C) THE SUPREMES
D) THE VANDELLAS

46. **1 x 1**

MAJOR LANCE HAD TWO BIG HITS. ONE WAS CALLED "UM, UM, UM, UM, UM, UM". NAME THE OTHER, A POPULAR DANCE TUNE ABOUT WHERE THE PEOPLE UPTOWN GATHERED TO DO THAT DANCE.

A) MICKEY'S MONKEY
B) THE MONKEY TIME
C) DO YOU LOVE ME
D) GOING TO A GO-GO

47. **1 x 1**

THE CHAMBERS BROTHERS, A FAMILY GROUP, HAD THIS ONE MAJOR HIT BELOW ABOUT TIME. IT WOULD BE FEATURED IN THE MOVIE SOUNDTRACK OF 'COMING HOME' WITH ITS DRUM ROLLING EFFECT STARRING JON VOIGHT, JANE FONDA AND BRUCE DERN IN THE LATE 70'S.

A) TIME HAS COME TODAY
B) TIME IS ON MY SIDE
C) TIME WON'T LET ME
D) TIME OF THE SEASON

48. **1 x 1**

JAY AND THE TECHNIQUES HAD A MAJOR HIT IN 1967 WITH THIS FRUIT TITLED SONG BELOW ABOUT THE GIRL HE WAS GONNA MARRY TO PREVENT HER FROM ROAMING ANYMORE. IT WOULD BECOME THE MOST POPULAR OF THEIR SHORT LIVED CAREER.

A) LITTLE GREEN APPLES
B) APPLES, PEACHES, PUMPKIN PIE
C) ONE BAD APPLE
D) WATERMELON MAN

49. **1 x 1**

HANK BALLARD AND THE MIDNIGHTERS WERE THE ORIGINAL SINGERS OF THE SONG, 'THE TWIST', ALSO WRITTEN BY *HANK*. WHAT WAS THE NAME OF THAT OTHER MALE ARTIST WHO WOULD RECORD IT AND RECEIVE ALL THE ATTENTION AND GLORY FOR THE SONG?

A) SAM COOKE
B) JOEY DEE & THE STARLITERS
C) GARY U.S. BONDS
D) CHUBBY CHECKER

50. **3 x 1**

NAME THESE THREE CHARTED HITS IN THE 60'S BY *FATS DOMINO,* THE POPULAR R&B SINGER/SONGWRITER AND PIANIST.
ONE, ABOUT THE FOUR WINDS.
TWO, ABOUT WALKING TO HIS HOMETOWN.
THREE, ABOUT A GIRL NAMED JOSEPHINE.

1) ______________________________

2) _________________________

3) ____________________

51. **1 x 1**

WHAT SONG DID *THE ESQUIRES* RECORD IN 1967 WHICH WAS THE BIGGEST HIT OF THEIR CAREER ABOUT PICKING YOURSELF UP?

A) GET ON UP
B) GET ON YOUR FEET
C) GET ON THE GOOD FOOT
D) KEEP ON PUSHING

52. **1 x 1**

JIMMY JONES HAD A POPULAR SONG THAT BOTH *DEL SHANNON* IN THE 60'S AND *JAMES TAYLOR* IN THE 70'S WOULD GO ON TO RECORD ABOUT A MAN WHO REPAIRS GIRLS' HEARTS BY WHISPERING SWEET NOTHINGS. *JONES'* VERSION WOULD REACH THE NUMBER TWO SPOT ON THE CHARTS. CHOOSE THAT HIT.

A) HELP ME, RHONDA
B) SWEET NOTHIN'S
C) HANDY MAN
D) RUNAWAY

53. **1 x 1**

JIMMY JONES CHARTED ANOTHER ABOUT HOW TIMING GOT THEM TOGETHER AND HELPED DEFEAT GOLIATH.

A) TOGETHER
B) GOOD TIMIN'
C) HAPPY TOGETHER
D) GOOD LUCK CHARM

54. **1 x 1**

LOU RAWLS WOULD ACHIEVE HIS PREMIER STARDOM IN 1966 RECORDING THIS SONG BELOW ABOUT A PAINFUL LOVE.

A) LOVE IS A HURTIN' THING
B) GOIN' OUT OF MY HEAD
C) TAKE ME BACK
D) HURT SO BAD

55. **1 x 1**

LOU RAWLS CHARTED YET ANOTHER ABOUT A MEAN DEADLY STREET IN CHICAGO THAT ENDS UP GOING NOWHERE. CHOOSE IT.

A) HEARTBREAK HOTEL
B) DEAD END STREET
C) NOWHERE TO RUN
D) TOBACCO ROAD

56. **1 x 1**

JAN BRADLEY, A FEMALE ARTIST, HAD A POPULAR SONG ABOUT THE ADVISE HER MOTHER TOLD HER ABOUT MEN THAT WAS SO, SO, TRUE.

A) MAMA SAID
B) MAMA DIDN'T LIE
C) MAMA TOLD ME NOT TO COME
 D) YOU CAN'T HURRY LOVE

57. **1 x 1**

JOHNNY NASH CHARTED THIS SONG BELOW PLEADING TO BE HELD WITH A FIRM GRIP.
A) HOLD ME, THRILL ME, KISS ME
B) HOLD ME TIGHT
C) DON'T LET GO
D) TIGHTEN UP

58. **1 x 1**

BRENTON WOOD HAD THE BIGGEST HIT OF HIS CAREER ASKING THIS GIRL TO GIVE HIM SOME KIND OF SIGNAL IF SHE WANTED TO BE HIS.
A) GIMME LITTLE SIGN
B) SHOW ME
C) FOR YOUR LOVE
D) SIMON SAYS

59. **1 x 1**

HANK BALLARD AND THE MIDNIGHTERS RECORDED WHAT PARTY SONG BELOW THAT HAD EVERYBODY POPPING AND WEAVING TO IT?
A) THE MONKEY TIME
B) MICKEY'S MONKEY
C) FINGER POPPIN' TIME
D) SNAP YOUR FINGERS

60. **1 x 1**

HANK BALLARD AND THE MIDNIGHTERS CHARTED YET ANOTHER ABOUT GOING UP THE HILL TO GET A THRILL. WHAT WAS THAT OTHER HIT?
A) BIMBOMBEY
B) BRISTOL STOMP
C) LET'S GO, LET'S GO, LET'S GO
D) BLUEBERRY HILL

61. **1 x 1**

THE DELFONICS OUT OF PHILLY, HAD THIS ROMANTIC SONG ABOUT HIS STRONG FEELINGS FOR THIS GIRL AND LETTING HER KNOW HOW HE TRULY FELT AND HOPING THAT SHE WOULD REACH OUT TO HIM. NAME THIS LA, LA TITLED SONG THAT *THE JETS,* A FAMILY GROUP, WOULD ALSO GO ON TO RECORD IN THE LATE 80'S.

____

62. **3 x 1**

NAME THESE THREE POPULAR HITS BY *BILLY STEWART*.
ONE, ABOUT A CERTAIN SEASON IN THE YEAR, AND NO IT'S NOT CHUCK. ORIGINALLY FEATURED IN THE 'PORGY AND BESS' FOLK OPERA IN 1935.
TWO, EXPRESSING HIS LOVE FOR YOU AND HE'S NEVER GONNA LET YOU GO, NEVER.
THREE, ABOUT WAITING ON A BENCH AND WONDERING IF SHE'S GONNA COME.
1) ______________
2) ______________
3) ______________

63. **1 x 1**

WHAT WAS *BILLY STEWART'S* NICKNAME?
A) THE KILLER
B) FAT BOY
C) BOOM BOOM
D) MR PERSONALITY

64. **3 x 1**

NAME THESE THREE BIG CHARTED HITS BY *THE ORLONS,* THE GROUP THAT CONSISTED OF THREE GIRLS AND ONE GUY.
ONE, THEIR BIG WATUSI DANCE HIT.
TWO, ABOUT A CERTAIN STREET LOCATION WHERE THE HIPPIES GO.
THREE, PLEADING NOT TO DO SOMETHING WITH THE TELEPHONE.

1) ________________
2) ________________
3) ________________

65. **4 x 1**

THIS ARTIST IS CALLED '*THE GODFATHER OF SOUL*'. NAME HIM, AND HIS THREE HITS BELOW, NUMBERS TWO THROUGH FOUR.
ONE, HIS NAME.
TWO, WHAT PAPA'S GOT, PART 1.
THREE, A TRIPLE MAN TITLED SONG HOW HE COULD END UP WITHOUT A GIRL.
FOUR, ABOUT BEING BLACK AND PROUD TO LET IT BE KNOWN ALSO PART 1.

1) ________________
2) ____ **(PART 1)**
3) ____
4) ____ **(PART 1)**

66. **1 x 1**

THE GODFATHER HAD TWO OTHER HITS BELOW. WHICH ONE WAS **NOT** HIS?
A) I GOT YOU (I FEEL GOOD)
B) LOVE IS A HURTIN' THING
C) COLD SWEAT (PART 1)

67. **1 x 1**

THE MARCELS CHARTED THIS POPULAR SONG IN 1961 THAT BROUGHT THEM WIDE ACCLAIM ABOUT A CERTAIN COLORED MOON. IN THE EARLY 80'S IT WOULD BE FEATURED IN THE MOVIE 'AN AMERICAN WEREWOLF IN LONDON' DIRECTED BY JOHN LANDIS.
A) EVERYONE'S GONE TO THE MOON
B) ONE SUMMER NIGHT
C) BLUE MOON
D) BLUE MOON OVER KENTUCKY

68. **1 x 1**

WHAT ROMANTIC SONG DID *THE PARADONS* RECORD IN 1960 ABOUT NOT WANTING PRECIOUS STONES BUT ONLY YOUR LOVE? IT WOULD BE THEIR ONE CLAIM TO FAME SONG AND A CLASSIC AT THAT.
A) TREASURE OF LOVE
B) FOR YOUR LOVE
C) DIAMONDS AND PEARLS
D) HONEY LOVE

69. **1 x 1**

THE EXCITERS, ANOTHER QUARTET, THIS TIME CONSISTING OF THREE GIRLS AND ONE GUY, ARE MOSTLY REMEMBERED FOR CHARTING WHAT SONG IN 1962 THAT IF YOU WANT THAT GUY, TAKE THEIR ADVISE AND LET HIM KNOW, AND TO BE THERE BY HIS SIDE? IT WOULD BE FEATURED IN THE MOVIE SOUNDTRACK OF 'THE BIG CHILL' IN THE 80'S.
A) TELL HIM
B) I DO LOVE YOU
C) ANY DAY NOW (MY WILD BEAUTIFUL BIRD)
 D) MY SONG

70. **1 x 1**

OSCAR TONEY JR RECORDED HIS MAJOR CLAIM TO FAME SONG IN 1967 WITH HIS RENDITION OF WHAT *JERRY BUTLER* TUNE THAT STARTS OUT WITH A LONG VERBAL MONOLOGUE THAT FINALLY LEADS INTO THE SONG ABOUT YOUR CHERISHED LOVE?

A) FOR YOUR LOVE
B) FOR YOUR PRECIOUS LOVE
C) LET IT BE ME
D) HE WILL BREAK YOUR HEART

71. **1 x 1**

CARLA THOMAS, THE POPULAR SINGER/SONGWRITER, HAD THIS BIG HIT ABOUT A GUY SHE FELT WAS AWFULLY NICE, EVERYTHING A GIRL COULD WANT. IT WOULD BE HER BIGGEST CHARTED HIT AND ALSO HER ONLY RECORDING FOR THE ATLANTIC LABEL BEFORE SWITCHING OVER TO THE STAX LABEL.

A) WOULDN'T IT BE NICE
B) THEN HE KISSED ME
C) HE'S SURE THE BOY I LOVE
D) GEE WHIZ (LOOK AT HIS EYES)

72. **1 x 1**

CARLA THOMAS RECORDED WHAT OTHER ABOUT HER BABE WHO MAKES THINGS RIGHT?

A) MY BABY MUST BE A MAGICIAN
B) B-A-B-Y
C) BABY LOVE
D) HONEY CHILE

TOTAL POINTS. **100 x 1 = 100**

R&B ROCKERS-BONUS

1.

SAMMY DAVIS JR, THE BLACK ALL ROUNDED ENTERTAINER, HAD A BIG HIT BELOW ABOUT SOMETHING HE HAD TO BE. IT WAS BRIEFLY FEATURED IN THAT TOM HANKS AND SHELLY LONG MOVIE 'MONEY PIT' IN THE MID 80'S.

A) I AM A ROCK
B) I GOTTA BE ME
C) MR BOJANGLES
D) FOOL # 1

2.

IN 1964 *THE SAPPHIRES*, A TRIO GROUP, RECORDED A HIT WITH THIS SONG BELOW WANTING TO KNOW WHO THAT PLAYBOY TRULY LOVED, OR WAS MOTHERS' ADVISE RIGHT AND HE WAS ONLY LEADING HER ON, SOMETHING SHE HAD TO KNOW.

A) SWEET TALKIN' GUY
B) HOW CAN I BE SURE
C) HONEY CHILE
D) WHO DO YOU LOVE

3.

THE SWEET INSPIRATIONS, A GROUP OF GIRLS THAT INCLUDED *CISSY HOUSTON, WHITNEYS'* MOM, CHARTED THEIR NAME TO CLAIM SONG BELOW ABOUT WHAT THEY WANTED EVERY HOUR OF THE DAY, 24/7. CHOOSE IT BELOW.

A) ALL DAY AND ALL OF THE NIGHT
B) GOOD LOVIN'
C) RESPECT
D) SWEET INSPIRATION

POP ROCKERS-QUIZ # 1

1. **6 x 1**

NAME THESE SIX HITS BY *BOBBY VEE*, THE POPULAR SINGER FROM NORTH DAKOTA.
ONE, ABOUT A CERTAIN BALL THAT REBOUNDS BACK.
TWO, TELLING THIS GUY TO TAKE PROPER CARE OF HIS FORMER BABE OR ELSE SHIP HER BACK TO HIM.
THREE, HIS VERSION OF *THE CLOVERS* ORIGINAL HIT SONG FIRST RECORDED IN THE 50'S ABOUT A GIRL WITH A DUAL PERSONALITY, SOMETIMES BAD AND SOMETIMES GOOD.
FOUR, ABOUT ALLOWING YOU TO RUN TO SOME OTHER GUY IF HE CAN DO ANY BETTER.
FIVE, SOMETHING THAT HAS AN ENORMOUS NUMBER OF EYES.
SIX, WHAT YOU SHOULD DO WHEN YOU FINALLY GROW UP.

1) ______________
2) ______________________________
3) __________________
4) ______________
5) __________________________________
6) ________________________________

2. **1 x 1**

TONY BENNETT CHARTED HIS TRADEMARK HIT SONG ABOUT A CERTAIN CITY LOCATED IN A CALIFORNIA BAY AREA WHERE HE LEFT SOMETHING SO DEAR TO HIM. WHAT WAS THAT TRADEMARK HIT SONG?

A) I LEFT MY HEART IN SAN FRANCISCO
B) CALIFORNIA SUN
C) LEAVING ON A JET PLANE
D) CALIFORNIA GIRLS

3. **1 x 1**

THE WALKER BROS, A MALE TRIO GROUP, HAD THIS HEARTBREAKER HIT SONG BELOW ABOUT LONELINESS AND EMPTINESS CREATED BY NOT BEING WITH YOU, AND NOT CARING IF THE HEAVENS ABOVE FUNCTIONED AS IT ALWAYS HAS.

A) AQUARIUS/LET THE SUNSHINE IN
B) 'TIL
C) BLUE MOON
D) THE SUN AIN'T GONNA SHINE (ANYMORE)

4. **1 x 1**

THE WALKER BROS CHARTED ANOTHER WITH THIS BREAKUP HIT SONG, A RE-MAKE OF A *JERRY BUTLER* TUNE, THAT HAD HIM PLEADING TO HIS FORMER BABE NOT TO BURDEN HERSELF AND TO BREAK AWAY QUICKLY TO AVOID THE STRESS AND PAIN THAT CAN POSSIBLY FOLLOW.

A) EASY TO BE HARD
B) FOR YOUR PRECIOUS LOVE
C) MAKE IT EASY ON YOURSELF
D) RUN TO HIM

5. **1 x 1**

THE EXCELLENTS RECORDED THEIR ONLY CLAIM TO FAME SONG ABOUT A PRETTY LITTLE BABE IN ONE OF THE POPULAR BEACHES IN BROOKLYN, NEW YORK WHO HE ADMIRED TO NO END AND HOPED SHE WOULD BE HIS FOREVER. CHOOSE IT BELOW.

A) ITSY BITSY TEENIE WEENIE YELLOW POLKADOT BIKINI
B) BEACH BABY
C) TALLAHASSIE LASSIE
D) CONEY ISLAND BABY

6. **2 x 1**

THE LETTERMEN CHARTED A MEDLEY OF TWO SONGS. ONE FROM *LITTLE ANTHONY AND THE IMPERIALS* ABOUT LOSING HIS MIND AND THE OTHER FROM *FRANKIE VALLI* ABOUT HIS EYES AND WHAT YOU ARE TO TOUCH. NAME THEM BOTH.

1) ______________________

2) ____________________________

7. **2 x 1**

THE LETTERMEN RECORDED TWO OTHER ROMANTIC HITS. ONE ABOUT YOUR APPEARANCE TONIGHT WHICH WAS CHARTED BY MANY OTHERS INCLUDING *ROD STEWART* IN THE 90'S. THE OTHER SONG WAS ABOUT THAT BIG EVENT, THAT WHEN IT FINALLY OCCURS, IT'LL BE EVERLASTING. THIS SONG WAS ORIGINALLY RECORDED BY *NAT KING COLE* AND COUNTLESS OTHERS INCLUDING HIS DAUGHTER *NATALIE COLE* AND *CELINE DION*. CHOOSE THOSE TWO HITS BELOW.

A) TONIGHT'S THE NIGHT
B) SHE'S JUST MY STYLE
C) THE WAY YOU LOOK TONIGHT
D) TOGETHER
E) WHEN I FALL IN LOVE
F) WHEN WE GET MARRIED
G) EVERLASTING LOVE

8. **1 x 1**

B J THOMAS CHARTED WHAT *HANK WILLIAMS SR* SONG ABOUT LONELINESS AND HOW IT MAKES HIM FEEL LIKE CRYING?

A) CRYING
B) I'M SO LONESOME I COULD CRY
C) CRYING TIME
D) COLD, COLD HEART

9. **1 x 1**

B J THOMAS RECORDED ANOTHER ABOUT A CERTAIN FEELING HE WAS STUCK ON. A SONG THAT THE GROUP *BLUE SWEDE* WOULD ALSO GO ON TO RECORD IN THE MID 70'S.

A) I FEEL FINE
B) HOOKED ON A FEELING
C) I GOT YOU (I FEEL GOOD)
D) STUCK ON YOU

10. **1 x 1**

NILSSON CHARTED A THEME SONG FOR THE MOVIE 'MIDNIGHT COWBOY' STARRING DUSTIN HOFFMAN AND JON VOIGHT ABOUT WHAT EVERYBODY WAS DOING. IT WOULD GAIN HIM HIS PREMIER STARDOM.

A) EVERYBODY LOVES A LOVER
B) EVERYBODY LOVES SOMEBODY
C) EVERYBODY NEEDS SOMEBODY TO LOVE
D) EVERYBODY'S TALKIN'

11. **1 x 1**

CLASSICS IV, WITH *DENNIS YOST* IN LEAD, HAD THIS BIG HIT ABOUT MEMORIES OF HAPPIER DAYS WITH LETTERS AND PHOTOS AND THE HOPE THAT YOU'LL COME BACK TO HIM. IT WOULD BECOME THEIR BIGGEST AND REACH THE NUMBER TWO SPOT ON THE CHARTS. CHOOSE THAT BIG HIT BELOW.

A) TRACES
B) APRIL LOVE
C) YESTERDAY
D) HAPPY TOGETHER

12. **1 x 1**

CLASSICS 1V CHARTED TWO OTHER HITS BELOW. WHICH ONE WAS **NOT** THEIRS?
A) SUGAR, SUGAR
B) SPOOKY
C) STORMY

13. **1 x 1**

BOBBY SHERMAN, THE POPULAR STAR FROM 'HERE COME THE BRIDES' TV SERIES BACK IN THE 60'S ALSO CO-STARRING DAVID SOUL OF STARSKY & HUTCH FAME, HAD A HIT WITH THIS WOMAN TITLED SONG BELOW.
A) OH, PRETTY WOMAN
B) LITTLE WOMAN
C) GYPSY WOMAN
D) BLACK MAGIC WOMAN

14. **1 x 1**

"GREEN TAMBOURINE" WAS A SONG CHARTED BY WHICH GROUP BELOW BACK IN 1967 WHICH BECAME THEIR ONLY MAJOR CLAIM TO FAME SONG?
A) THE FOUR SEASONS
B) THE MAMAS & THE PAPAS
C) THE LEMON PIPERS
D) THE LOVIN' SPOONFUL

15. **1 x 1**

THE CUFF LINKS HAD THEIR MAJOR CLAIM TO FAME SONG IN 1969 ABOUT A GIRL THEY WANTED TO BE HELD IN HER ARMS FOR ETERNITY WHO THEY VOWED TO MAKE HAPPY. WHAT WAS THAT CLAIM TO FAME SONG?
A) TRACY
B) SHERRY
C) DIANA
D) HELLO MARY LOU

16. **6 x 1**

NAME THESE SIX CHARTED HITS IN THE 60'S BY *BOBBY DARIN,* THE SINGER SONGWRITER TURNED ACTOR.
ONE, ABOUT THE SEA.
TWO, ASSUMING THAT YOU WERE A KNOCKOUT AS A BABY BECAUSE YOU STILL HAVE THAT GEORGEOUS LOOK EVEN NOW.
THREE, ABOUT A GUY NAMED BILL WHO WOULDN'T COME HOME.
FOUR, A CERTAIN TYPE OF FLOWERS THAT SHE MADE.
FIVE, WHAT HE TOLD HER ABOUT THE POSSIBILITY OF BEING A TRADESMAN AND THE MARRIAGE PROPOSAL AT HAND.
SIX, REMINISCING OF THE VARIOUS FUN ACTIVITIES THAT THEY USED TO DO. LIKE TAKING A BOAT RIDE, OR EVEN A STROLL, OR MAYBE JUST KISSING, BUT IT'S ONLY MEMORIES OF PAST EVENTS NO LONGER DONE.

1) ____________________
2) ____
3) ____
4) ________________________
5) _____________________________
6) __________

17. **1 x 1**

BOBBY DARIN ALSO HAD TWO OTHER HITS BELOW. WHICH ONE WAS **NOT** HIS?
A) SUMMER WIND
B) LAZY RIVER
 C) CLEMENTINE

18. **1 x 1**

SKIP & FLIP, A POP DUO, HAD WHAT FRUIT TITLED SONG BELOW IN 1960?
A) CHERRY PIE
B) APPLES, PEACHES, PUMPKIN PIE
C) WATERMELON MAN
D) BANANA BOAT (DAY-O)

19. **1 x 1**

IN 1962 *ERNIE MARESCA,* THE SINGER/SONGWRITER, RECORDED WHAT SHOUTING HIT SONG BELOW?
A) SHOUT (PARTS 1 AND 2)
B) SHOUT! SHOUT! (KNOCK YOURSELF OUT)
C) TWIST AND SHOUT
D) LOUIE LOUIE

20. **1 x 1**

CHOOSE THE TALENTED MALE COMPOSER WHO WITH HAL DAVID WOULD COMPOSE MOST OF THE HIT SONGS FOR *DIONNE WARWICK.*
A) HENRY MANCINI
B) SMOKEY ROBINSON
C) DAVID ROSE
D) BURT BACHARACH

21. **1 x 1**

WHAT POPULAR YOUNG ACTOR/TURNED SINGER, STARRED IN THE WESTERN MOVIE 'RIO BRAVO' OPPOSITE JOHN WAYNE AND *DEAN MARTIN*? HE GREW UP ON HIS PARENTS TV SERIES IN THE 50'S AND 60'S AND MANY THOUGHT HE WAS JUST A TRAVELING MAN.
A) DAVID NELSON
B) RICKY NELSON
C) ELVIS
D) FABIAN

22. **1 x 1**

SOUL SURVIVORS, THE ALL WHITE MALE BAND WITH THE SOULFUL SOUND, CHARTED THIS POPULAR SONG BELOW ABOUT HIS EFFORTS TO GET TO YOU, BECAUSE YOU WERE ALL HE THOUGHT ABOUT, CONSTANTLY 24/7.
A) EXPRESSWAY (TO YOUR HEART)
B) LOVE ON A TWO WAY STREET
C) YOU WERE ON MY MIND
D) SUMMER IN THE CITY

23. **1 x 1**

BRIAN HYLAND CHARTED ABOUT A SUMMER ROMANCE COMING TO AN END AND A VOW TO SEND HIS LOVE DAILY THROUGH THE MAIL.
A) THE LETTER
B) SEALED WITH A KISS
C) SEE YOU IN SEPTEMBER
D) WHY DON'T YOU WRITE ME?

24. **1 x 1**

STEAM, THE ONE HIT WONDER GROUP, HAD THIS KISS AND DEPARTING HIT SONG THAT WOULD ALSO BE RECORDED BY *THE NYLONS* IN THE LATE 80'S, BUT WITH THE TITLE SHORTENED. WHAT WAS THAT DOUBLE HITTER CALLED?
A) KISS ME GOODBYE
B) SEE YOU IN SEPTEMBER
C) NA NA HEY HEY KISS HIM GOODBYE
D) SEALED WITH A KISS

25. **3 x 1**

NANCY SINATRA, FRANK'S LITTLE GIRL, HAD A SUCCESSFUL CAREER OF HER OWN. NAME THESE THREE BIG HITS BELOW.
ONE, ABOUT THOSE BOOTS THAT WILL WALK RIGHT OVER YOU.
TWO, ABOUT THAT SWEET TOWN WHERE SHE'S PROTECTED FROM THE RAIN.
THREE, AS PART OF A DUET WITH HER FAMOUS DAD ABOUT SOMETHING SILLY.

1) ____________________________________
2) ______________
3) ______________________

26. **1 x 1**

WHAT IS *FREDDY CANNON'S* NICKNAME?
A) THE KILLER
B) BOOM BOOM
C) THE POLISH PRINCE
D) THE ICE MAN

27. **1 x 1**

THIS YOUNG ACTRESS STARRED IN THE WEEKLY TV DETECTIVE SERIES '77 SUNSET STRIP' AND HAD A BIG HIT WITH "SIXTEEN REASONS". WHO IS SHE?
A) DEBBIE REYNOLDS
B) CONNIE STEVENS
C) ANN MARGARET
D) CONNIE FRANCIS

28. **1 x 1**

THE SAFARIS HAD THEIR ONLY MAJOR HIT OF THEIR CAREER IN 1960 ABOUT SLEEPLESS MIGHTS AND DREAMING OF A GIRL THAT HE HOPED TO FIND. THE SONG STARTS OUT WITH THE SOUND OF A CLOCK TIC TOCKING AWAY. WHAT WAS THAT ONE HIT WONDER SONG CALLED?
A) IT'S ONLY MAKE BELIEVE
B) ANGEL BABY
C) IMAGE OF A GIRL
D) DREAMIN'

29. **1 x 1**

BOBBY RYDELL CHARTED TWO OF THE THREE BIG HITS BELOW. WHICH ONE WAS **NOT** HIS?
A) WILD ONE
B) VOLARE
C) PALISADES PARK

30. **1 x 1**

IN 1966 *CHER* RECORDED WHAT TOP NUMBER TWO HIT SONG AS A SOLO, ABOUT WHAT HER BABY DID TO MAKE HER FALL TO THE GROUND?
A) TWO LITTLE KIDS
B) COWBOYS TO GIRLS
C) DOUBLE SHOT (OF MY BABY'S LOVE)
D) BANG, BANG (MY BABY SHOT ME DOWN)

31. **1 x 1**

JACKIE DESHANNON, THE FEMALE SINGER/SONGWRITER, CHARTED THIS SONG BELOW ABOUT WHAT THE WORLD TRULY LACKED.
A) MORE LOVE
B) ALL YOU NEED IS LOVE
C) IF I HAD A HAMMER (THE HAMMER **SONG)**
D) WHAT THE WORLD NEEDS NOW IS LOVE

32. **1 x 1**

JACKIE DESHANNON RECORDED ANOTHER ABOUT WHAT YOUR HEART COULD REALLY USE. CHOOSE IT BELOW.
A) CUPID
B) PUT A LITTLE LOVE IN YOUR HEART
C) A LITTLE BIT OF YOU, A LITTLE BIT OF ME
D) A LOVER'S CONCERTO

33. **1 x 1**

CHRIS MONTEZ HAD HIS FIRST MAJOR HIT AND THE BIGGEST OF HIS CAREER WITH WHAT SONG BELOW ABOUT HIS DESIRE TO GO DANCING WITH YOU? IT WOULD BE FEATURED IN THE 'ANIMAL HOUSE' SOUNDTRACK MOVIE STARRING JOHN BELUSHI, TIM MATHESON AND KEVIN BACON IN THE LATE 70'S.
A) WHEN YOU DANCE
B) SAVE THE LAST DANCE FOR ME
C) DO YOU WANT TO DANCE
D) LET'S DANCE

34. **5 x 1**

THIS SINGER/SONGWRITER HAD A BUNCH OF HITS IN THE EARLY TO MID 60'S. "KEEP SEARCHIN' (WE'LL FOLLOW THE SUN)" WAS ONE OF THEM. NAME HIM AND THESE FOUR OTHER HITS BELOW, NUMBERS TWO THROUGH FIVE.
ONE, HIS NAME.
TWO, HOPING FOR HER RETURN, TO END HIS MISERY.
THREE, ABOUT TIPPING HIS HAT TO LARRY FOR WHAT HE DID TO HER, BECAUSE WHAT GOES AROUND, COMES AROUND. BUT CRAZY AS IT SOUNDS HE'LL HAVE HER BACK.
FOUR, ABOUT WHAT SHE WAS KNOWN THROUGHOUT THE TOWN.
FIVE, HIS VERSION OF A *JIMMY JONES* TUNE ABOUT A HANDY PERSON WHO REPAIRS BROKEN HEARTS ALSO RECORDED BY *JAMES TAYLOR* IN THE 70'S.

1) ______________
2) ____________
3) ______________________
4) ______________________
5) ______________

35. **8 x 1**

NEIL DIAMOND, THE TALENTED SINGER/SONGWRITER, CHARTED THESE EIGHT BIG HITS BELOW.
ONE, ABOUT A SWEET GIRL REACHING OUT.
TWO, ABOUT A GIRL TRANSFORMING INTO A WOMAN.
THREE, THANKING THE LORD FOR WHAT?
FOUR, ABOUT A KENTUCKY LADY THAT LOVES HIM.
FIVE, ABOUT A SALVATION SHOW ON THE ROAD.
SIX, ABOUT A GIRL NAMED CHERRY.
SEVEN, HIS BIG HOLY HIT SONG.
EIGHT, WHAT SHE WAS ABLE TO DO TO HIM.
NAME THEM.

1) ____
2) ___________________________________
3) ____
4) ___________________
5) ____
6) ___________________
7) _______________
8) ___________________

36. **1 x 1**

TIMI YURO, THE FEMALE SINGER, RECORDED A SONG ABOUT THE AWFUL PAIN YOU CAUSED HER, ABOUT THE LIE THAT YOU WOULD NEVER PART, AND ABOUT YOU FINDING SOMEONE NEW. ALSO TO BE RECORDED BY *ELVIS* IN THE 70'S.
A) HURT
B) LOVE IS A HURTIN' THING
C) LOVE IS BLUE
D) LOVE IS HERE AND NOW YOU'RE GONE

37. **2 x 1**

PAUL ANKA WROTE THIS POPULAR SONG FOR 'OLE BLUE EYES' ABOUT DOING THINGS HE PERSONALLY DESIRED. IT WAS ALSO RECORDED BY *ELVIS* BUT ONLY RELEASED AFTER HIS DEATH IN 1977. NAME THE SONG AND 'OLE BLUE EYES'.
1) ____________
2) __________________

38. **1 x 1**

"DAYS OF WINE AND ROSES" WAS A MOVIE INSTRUMENTAL THEME HIT FOR *HENRY MANCINI AND HIS ORCHESTRA* STARRING JACK LEMMON AND LEE REMICK. WHO WAS THE POP MALE ARTIST TO CHART IT AS A VOCAL HIT?
A) ROGER WILLIAMS
B) ROGER MILLER
C) ANDY WILLIAMS
D) PERRY COMO

39. **1 x 1**

THE FIVE AMERICANS, OBVIOUSLY A GROUP CONSISTING OF FIVE GUYS, RECORDED THIS SONG BELOW WITH THE DOTS AND DASHES AND THE MESSAGE THAT READ YOU WOULD CHANGE YOUR WAYS. CHOOSE IT BELOW.
A) HEY, WESTERN UNION MAN
B) WESTERN UNION
C) MORSE CODE OF LOVE
D) THE LETTER

40. **1 x 1**

BOB LIND CHARTED WHAT POPULAR HIT IN 1966 WITH A FLYING INSECT TITLED SONG THAT WOULD BE HIS ONLY CLAIM TO FAME?
A) THE BIRDS AND THE BEES
B) ELUSIVE BUTTERFLY
C) THE BOLL WEEVIL SONG
D) THE FLY

41. **1 x 1**

'RAY CHARLES SINGERS', NO RELATION TO THE R&B SINGER, HAD THIS ROMANTIC HIT BELOW CONDUCTED BY *CHARLES RAYMOND OFFENBERG* ABOUT LOVING YOU NOT JUST FOR A MOMENT OR EVEN AN HOUR BUT FOR ETERNITY.
A) THE TWELFTH OF NEVER
B) CHANCES ARE
C) LOVE ME WITH ALL YOUR HEART (CUANDO CALIENTA EL SOL)
D) WHAT NOW MY LOVE

42. **1 x 1**

JAMES DARREN RECORDED WHAT SONG BELOW ABOUT THE CRUEL CONDITIONS THAT HE LIVED IN AND HOW HE WAS GOING TO LEAVE AND HOOK UP WITH THE CIRCUS TO HELP HIM FORGET THAT VICIOUS WOMAN?
A) EVE OF DESTRUCTION
B) WE GOTTA GET OUT OF THIS PLACE
C) GOODBYE CRUEL WORLD
D) THE END OF THE WORLD

43. **2 x 1**

NEIL DIAMOND WROTE AND SANG THESE TWO SONGS BELOW THAT WOULD BECOME MORE POPULAR BY TWO OTHER GROUPS. THE FIRST SONG WAS RECORDED BY *THE MONKEES* IN THE 60'S ABOUT WHAT HE BECAME AFTER WHAT HE SAW. THE SECOND SONG WAS RECORDED BY *UB40* IN THE 90'S ABOUT SOMETHING RED. NAME THOSE TWO GIANT RESURRECTED HITS.

1) ____________________

2) ________________

44. **1 x 1**

"98.6" IS WHAT HE CALLS HIS BABY BECAUSE SHE GIVES HIM LOVING AND BRINGS OUT ALL THE GOOD IN HIM. WHAT MALE ARTIST WOULD GO ON TO RECORD IT AND MAKE IT THE BIGGEST OF HIS CAREER?

A) NEIL DIAMOND
B) KEITH
C) LEN BARRY
D) SIMON & GARFUNKEL

45. **1 x 1**

IN 1960 *JOHNNY TILLOTSON* CHARTED WHAT SONG BELOW ABOUT WHAT HE SAW IN HIS BABY, SOMETHING IN MOTION THAT HE LOVED AND WOULDN'T CHANGE? IT WOULD BE HIS FIRST MAJOR HIT AND A TOP NUMBER TWO ON THE CHARTS.

A) BACKFIELD IN MOTION
B) SWEET LITTLE SIXTEEN
C) LET THE LITTLE GIRL DANCE
D) POETRY IN MOTION

46. **1 x 1**

JOHNNY TILLOTSON HAD ANOTHER ABOUT THE HURT SHE INFLICTED ON HIM THE DAY SHE LEFT. LEAVING HIM BROKENHEARTED AND UNABLE TO GO ON. WHAT WAS THAT HURT SONG?

A) LOVE IS A HURTING THING
B) HURT SO BAD
C) IT KEEPS RIGHT ON-A-HURTIN'
D) HURT

47. **1 x 1**

SHELLY FABARES RECORDED THE BIGGEST HIT OF HER CAREER WITH WHAT ANGEL SONG IN 1962 ABOUT WHO SHE COULDN'T RESIST AND WONDERING WHAT LIFE COULD BE TOGETHER AS ONE?

A) JOHNNY ANGEL
B) BLUE ANGEL
C) ANGEL BABY
D) ANGEL OF THE MORNING

48. **4 x 1**

NAME THESE FOUR BIG HITS BY *THE ASSOCIATION*.
ONE, ABOUT A GIRL NAMED MARY ON THE GO.
TWO, HIS LOVE NEVER TIRING NOR LOSING DESIRE FOR YOU.
THREE, ABOUT THAT GIRL WITH THE STORMY EYES AND WINGS THAT FLY OVER THE CLOUDS.
FOUR, ONE ROMANTIC WORD TO DESCRIBE HIS FEELINGS FOR YOU.

1) ____________________

2) ________________

3) _________

4) __________

49. **1 x 1**

ROBIN WARD, A FEMALE SINGER, HAD WHAT SUMMER HIT SONG ABOUT THANKING HIM FOR THE BEST TIME SHE'S EVER EXPERIENCED IN HER LIFE REGARDLESS THAT THEY HAVE TO PART?

A) HERE COMES SUMMER
B) SUMMERTIME
C) SEE YOU IN SEPTEMBER
D) WONDERFUL SUMMER

50. **1 x 1**

MARK DINNING WOULD ACHIEVE HIS FAME BY RECORDING WHAT TRAGIC ANGEL HIT BELOW?

A) BLUE ANGEL
B) TEEN ANGEL
C) DEVIL OR ANGEL
D) ANGEL OF THE MORNING

51. **1 x 1**

CURTIS LEE WITH *THE HALOS*, AND WITH THE SOULFUL SOUND, HAD A MAJOR HIT WITH WHAT SONG BELOW ABOUT A GIRL SO HEAVENLY TO TOUCH AND SENT TO HIM FROM UP ABOVE?

A) CAN'T TAKE MY EYES OFF YOU
B) OH, PRETTY WOMAN
C) PRETTY LITTLE ANGEL EYES
D) MY GIRL

52. **1 x 1**

JACK JONES CHARTED A BIG HIT OF HIS CAREER WITH THE ADVISE TO ALWAYS TREAT YOUR MAN SPECIAL BY CATERING TO HIS EVERY NEED BY MAKING HIM FEEL WANTED, AND KNOWING WHEN IT'S TIME TO MAKE PASSIONATE LOVE.

A) IT'S NOW OR NEVER
B) GET ON UP
C) WIVES AND LOVERS
D) TONIGHT'S THE NIGHT

53. **1 x 1**

JACK JONES ALSO RECORDED ANOTHER SONG FEATURED IN THE BROADWAY MUSICAL 'MAN OF LA MANCHA' ABOUT SOMETHING UNLIKELY. ONE THAT *THE TEMPTATIONS* WOULD ALSO RECORD FOR THEIR 'MELLOW MOOD' HIT ALBUM.

A) EASY TO BE HARD
B) ALFIE
C) THE IMPOSSIBLE DREAM (THE QUEST)
D) SOMEWHERE, MY LOVE

54. **1 x 1**

THE QUOTATIONS, A GROUP OF TEENS, RECORDED THIS CLASSIC DOO WOP HIT BELOW ABOUT SOMETHING IN HIS SUBCONSCIOUS. IT WAS HIS WHAT?

A) DREAMIN'
B) ALL I HAVE TO DO IS DREAM
C) IMAGINATION
D) CAN'T YOU HEAR MY HEART BEAT

55. **1 x 1**

RAL DONNER RECORDED A SONG ABOUT HOW ONE CAN TAKE THINGS EASILY FOR GRANTED UNTIL IT'S GONE. CHOOSE THAT ONE.

A) SINCE YOU'RE GONE
B) SINCE I DON'T HAVE YOU
C) COME BACK WHEN YOU GROW UP
D) YOU DON'T KNOW WHAT YOU'VE GOT (UNTIL YOU LOSE IT)

56. **1 x 1**

THIS DUO, *NINO TEMPO & APRIL STEVENS*, SIBLINGS, CHARTED A NUMBER ONE HIT SONG IN 1963 THAT *DONNY* AND *MARIE OSMOND,* ANOTHER SET OF SIBLINGS, WOULD ALSO GO ON TO RECORD IN THE MID 70'S. WHAT WAS THAT DOUBLE HITTER CALLED?
A) PAINT IT BLACK
B) DEEP PURPLE
C) BLACK IS BLACK
D) BLACK AND WHITE

57. **1 x 1**

HARPERS BIZARRE, AN ALL MALE GROUP, RECORDED A GROOVY SONG ABOUT THIS STEEL STRUCTURE WHICH CONNECTS QUEENS TO MANHATTAN, TWO BOROUGHS IN NYC.
A) GROOVIN'
B) GROOVY KIND OF LOVE
C) THE 59TH STREET BRIDGE SONG (FEELIN' GROOVY)
D) GROOVY SITUATION

58. **1 x 1**

"BLAME IT ON THE BOSSA NOVA" WAS A POPULAR HIT IN 1963 BY WHAT FEMALE ARTIST BELOW WHO IS MARRIED TO *STEVE LAWRENCE*, THE POP SINGER? IT WOULD BECOME HER HIGHEST CHARTED HIT OF HER CAREER.
A) EYDIE GORME
B) VIKKI CARR
C) DELLA REESE
D) PETULA CLARK

59. **1 x 1**

"RED RUBBER BALL" WAS A SONG BY WHAT GROUP BELOW THAT WAS BRIEFLY MANAGED BY BRIAN EPSTEIN, *THE BEATLES* LATE BELOVED MANAGER, ABOUT THE LESSON HE JUST LEARNED FROM THE GIRL WHO DID HIM WRONG? LIKE THE NEW DAY APPROACHING, HE TOO WILL MOVE ON.
A) BADFINGER
B) THE SILKIE
C) THE CYRKLE
D) THE HOLLIES

60. **1 x 1**

THE REGENTS WERE THE ORIGINAL ARTISTS TO RECORD WHAT SONG BELOW ABOUT A GIRL HE MET AT A DANCE WHO HE HOPED TO ROMANCE, THAT THE OTHERS THERE WOULDN'T DO? IT IS A SONG *THE BEACH BOYS* WOULD ALSO RECORD AS A LIVE HIT.
A) BARBARA ANN
B) DONNA
C) PEGGY SUE
D) CHANTILLY LACE

61. **1 x 1**

SMITH, A ONE HIT WONDER GROUP, RECORDED THEIR VERSION OF *A SHIRELLES* HIT SONG ABOUT WHAT ATTRACTED YOU TO HIM. BOTH WERE CHARTED DURING THE 60'S.
A) THE WAY YOU LOOK TONIGHT
B) THE WAY YOU DO THE THINGS YOU DO
C) SOLDIER BOY
D) BABY IT'S YOU

62. **1 x 1**

THE DUO OF *BOBBY HART* AND *TOMMY BOYCE* CHARTED WHAT SONG BELOW THAT QUESTIONED HER WHEREABOUTS, EVEN THOUGH HE HAD NO RIGHTS TO HER SINCE HE WAS NOT ROMANTICALLY LINKED.

A) HAVE YOU SEEN HER
B) THE WONDER OF YOU
C) I WONDER WHAT SHE'S DOING TONITE
D) LITTLE STAR

63. **1 x 1**

"MR DIEINGLY SAD" WAS A BIG HIT BY *THE CRITTERS* WITH *DON CICCONE* IN LEAD. THEY RECORDED ANOTHER ABOUT THAT BROWN EYED GIRL WHO KEEPS ROLLING IN HIS MIND THAT HE PREFERS TO BE HER MAN RATHER THAN HAVE A BIG BROTHER RELATIONSHIP.

A) YOUNGER GIRL
B) BROWN EYED WOMAN
C) BROWN EYED GIRL
D) YOU WERE ON MY MIND

64. **5 x 1**

NAME THESE FIVE POPULAR HITS BY *ROY ORBISON*, THE SINGER/SONGWRITER.
ONE, A SONG THAT WAS RE-RELEASED FOR A SOUNDTRACK MOVIE OF THE SAME NAME STARRING RICHARD GERE AND JULIA ROBERTS IN THE 90'S ABOUT A GORGEOUS WOMAN.
TWO, A RELATION THAT'S OVER BECAUSE SHE DOESN'T LOVE HIM ANY MORE.
THREE, A CERTAIN COLORED ANGEL WHO'S IN PAIN BECAUSE OF A LOST LOVE.
FOUR, SOMETHING HE WAS DOING OVER YOU BECAUSE YOU DIDN'T LOVE HIM ANYMORE.
FIVE, SOMEONE EQUALLY LONELY WOULD KNOW THE MISERY THAT HE ENDURES.

1) ____________________
2) ____________
3) ____________
4) __________
5) ____________________________________

65. **1 x 1**

ROY ORBISON CHARTED TWO OTHER HITS BELOW. WHICH ONE UNFORTUNATELY WAS **NOT** HIS?

A) DREAM BABY (HOW LONG MUST I DREAM)
B) TREAT HER RIGHT
C) RUNNING SCARED

66. **1 x 1**

RANDY & THE RAINBOWS, THE GROUP FROM QUEENS, NY, WITH *RANDY SAFUTO* IN LEAD, RECORDED THIS POPULAR SONG BELOW ABOUT A CERTAIN GIRL HE'S IN LOVE WITH AND IT'S LIKE BEING IN ECSTACY WHENEVER THEY'RE TOGETHER.

A) SHERRY
B) DENISE
C) GLORIA
D) SHEILA

TOTAL POINTS. **100 x 1 = 100**

POP ROCKERS-QUIZ # 2

1. **6 x 1**

NAME THESE SIX BIG HITS BY *NEIL SEDAKA*, THE SINGER/SONGWRITER.
ONE, ABOUT HIS PIN UP GIRL THROUGHOUT THE YEAR.
TWO, ABOUT A STAIRWAY TO ECSTACY.
THREE, ABOUT AN ANNIVERSARY DAY FOR A SWEET SIXTEEN YEAR OLD.
FOUR, SOMETHING THAT IS HARD TO DO THAT CAN ONLY LEAVE HIM WITH THE BLUES. A SONG THAT HE WOULD RE-RECORD IN THE 70'S AT A SLOWER PACE.
FIVE, HABITATING NEXT DOOR TO SOMEONE VERY SPECIAL SENT FROM HEAVEN.
SIX, ABOUT A MEAN LITTLE GIRL THAT HE'S GONNA REFORM INTO AN ANGEL FOR HIMSELF.

1) ________________
2) ____________________
3) ___________________________________
4) ____________________________
5) ________________________
6) ________________

2. **10 x 1**

THE FOUR SEASONS RECORDED NUMEROUS HITS DURING THE 60'S INCLUDING: "SAVE IT FOR ME", "I'VE GOT YOU UNDER MY SKIN", "BYE, BYE BABY (BABY GOOD BYE)", "RONNIE", "BEGGIN", "OPUS 17 (DON'T WORRY 'BOUT ME)" AND "C'MON MARIANNE". NAME THESE TEN OTHERS BELOW.
ONE, ABOUT A GIRL THAT THEY WANTED OUT TONIGHT IN HER RED DRESS.
TWO, WHAT HIS FATHER TOLD HIM TO DO AS A MAN AND TO WALK AWAY FROM HER.
THREE, WHAT OLDER GIRLS NEVER SEEM TO DO ESPECIALLY WHEN DUMPED.
FOUR, ABOUT A CERTAIN DOLL WHO WORE HANDMEDOWNS.
FIVE, ABOUT A GIRL THAT HE HAD TO SEND AWAY BECAUSE HE'S GOT NO FUTURE.
SIX, HIS PREDICTION THAT ONE DAY HE'LL BECOME A SOMEBODY IN TOWN.
SEVEN, ABOUT OUR HOLDING ON.
EIGHT, PLANNING TO COME BACK BECAUSE IT'S SO LONELY WITHOUT YOU. A SONG THE '*SPINNERS*' WOULD RECORD AS A MEDLEY HIT IN THE EARLY 80'S.
NINE, HIS SWEET THING WHO'S SO DEVINE AND LOVES TO THE VERY END.
TEN, TELL YOUR PROBLEMS TO WHOM MIGHT CARE.

1) ________
2) ___________________
3) ________________________
4) ____________
5) __________________
6) __________________
7) __________________**!**
8) __________________________________
9) _____________
10) _______________________

3. **1 x 1**

THE ARBORS CHARTED WHAT SONG MADE POPULAR BY *THE BOX TOPS* ABOUT A WRITTEN CORRESPONDENCE FROM HIS BABE, THAT *JOE COCKER* WOULD ALSO RECORD IN THE EARLY 70'S.

A) WHY DON'T YOU WRITE
B) LOVE LETTERS IN THE SAND
C) THE LETTER
D) LOVE LETTERS

4. **2 x 1**

SALVATORE BONO AND CHER LaPIERE BETTER KNOWN AS *SONNY & CHER,* THE POPULAR HUSBAND AND WIFE DUO, CHARTED THESE TWO BIG HITS BELOW. ONE, ABOUT WHAT THEY EACH CLAIMED ABOUT THE OTHER, THAT WOULD RESURFACE ONCE AGAIN IN THE 80'S AFTER BEING FEATURED IN THE SOUNDTRACK MOVIE 'BUSTER' STARRING *PHIL COLLINS*.
TWO, ABOUT A CONTINUOUS BEAT.
NAME THEM.

1) ____________________

2) _________________________

5. **1 x 1**

SONNY & CHER RECORDED WHAT OTHER, A PLEA TO HIS PRETTY BABY ABOUT WHAT NOT TO DO BECAUSE HE TRULY LOVES HER SO?

A) STAY
B) PLEASE STAY
C) BABY DON'T GO
D) STAY IN MY CORNER

6. **1 x 1**

ANDY KIM CHARTED A HIT WITH WHAT BABY TITLED SONG BELOW?

A) BABY, I LOVE YOU
B) BABY LOVE
C) BE MY BABY
D) MY BABY MUST BE A MAGICIAN

7. **4 x 1**

NAME THESE FOUR SONGS BY *TOMMY ROE*.
ONE, ABOUT A SWEET LITTLE GIRL THAT DRIVES HIM INSANE.
TWO, ABOUT A CERTAIN PEA.
THREE, ABOUT A GIRL NAMED HAZEL.
FOUR, A CERTAIN STATE OF MIND THAT LEFT HIM DISORIENTED.

1) _____________

2) ________________

3) ______________________

4) _____________

8. **1 x 1**

VIKKI CARR HAD THE BIGGEST HIT OF HER CAREER IN 1967 ABOUT A CALL SHE WAS EXPECTING, AND BELIEVING THAT ALL THE INCOMING CALLS WERE FROM HIM. WHAT WAS THAT HIT?

A) CALL ME
B) IT MUST BE HIM
C) BEECHWOOD 4-5789
D) TELL IT LIKE IT IS

9. **3 x 1**

NAME THESE THREE CHARTED HITS BY *THE HAPPENINGS*.
ONE, ABOUT A CERTAIN BEAT THAT HE'S GOT.
TWO, ABOUT A SUMMER LOVE COMING TO A CLOSE IN SEPTEMBER WHICH WAS AN ORIGINAL HIT FOR *THE TEMPOS* IN THE LATE 50'S.
THREE, THEIR VERSION OF A *STEVE LAWRENCE* TUNE ABOUT SENDING SOMEBODY AWAY BECAUSE HE'S ALREADY COMMITTED TO ANOTHER.

1) ___________________

2) ________________________

3) _____________________________

10. **5 x 1**

NAME THESE FIVE SONGS BY *THE MAMAS & THE PAPAS*, THE QUARTET GROUP CONSISTING OF TWO GIRLS AND TWO GUYS.
ONE, THEIR BIG MONDAY HIT SONG ABOUT NEVER KNOWING HOW THAT DAY WILL TURN OUT BUT IT CAN USUALLY LEAVE HIM IN TEARS.
TWO, ABOUT THE STATE OF CALIFORNIA AND THE CONDITION THEY WERE IN.
THREE, ABOUT THAT ALLEY IN LA WHERE JOHN'S TRYING TO GET HIGHER.
FOUR, WHO THEY SAW LAST NIGHT ONCE MORE.
FIVE, THEIR VERSION OF A DEDICATION HIT SONG THAT WAS ORIGINALLY RECORDED BY *THE SHIRELLES* ALSO IN THE 60'S.

1) ____________________
2) __________________________
3) _________________
4) ____________________
5) _________________________________

11. **1 x 1**

MAMA CASS CHARTED A SONG WITH THE BACKING OF THE OTHER MEMBERS OF THE GROUP ABOUT WHAT SHE HOPED YOU WOULD DO THAT INVOLVED HER.
A) DREAM LOVER
B) DREAM A LITTLE DREAM OF ME
C) MR DREAM MERCHANT
D) DREAMIN'

12. **2 x 1**

PHIL SPECTOR, THE RECORD PRODUCER AND LABEL OWNER, MARRIED AND LATER DIVORCED ONE OF HIS LEADING LADIES. NAME HER AND HER GROUP.

1) ___________
2) __________________

13. **1 x 1**

1910 FRUITGUM CO. HAD THIS BIG HIT BELOW ABOUT A CHILDS GAME ONE PLAYS THAT'S NOT HARD TO DO, WHERE YOU RAISE YOUR HANDS UP IN THE AIR, DOWN TO YOUR HIPS, AND SHAKE FROM SIDE TO SIDE, JUST FOLLOW THE LEADS' INSTRUCTIONS.
A) GAMES PEOPLE PLAY
B) CATCH US IF YOU CAN
C) SIMON SAYS
D) RUBBER BALL

14. **1 x 1**

MERRILLEE RUSH & THE TURNABOUTS CHARTED WHAT SONG THAT *JUICE NEWTON* WOULD ALSO GO ON TO RECORD IN THE 80'S? SHE STATED THAT NOTHING COULD BIND HIM PHYSICALLY IF SHE COULDN'T HAVE HIS HEART.
A) HEART OF STONE
B) HOLD ME TIGHT
C) ANGEL OF THE MORNING
D) SEALED WITH A KISS

15. **1 x 1**

FRIEND AND LOVER, A HUSBAND AND WIFE DUO, ARE BEST KNOWN FOR RECORDING THIS REACH OUT HIT TUNE BELOW THAT WOULD BECOME A ONE HIT WONDER SONG.
A) REACH OUT OF THE DARKNESS
B) REACH OUT I'LL BE THERE
C) REACH OUT AND TOUCH (SOMEBODY'S HAND)
D) HOLD ME TIGHT

16. **1 x 1**

WHAT ARTIST BELOW WAS **NOT** A MEMBER OF *THE MONKEES*?
A) DAVY JONES
B) MICKEY DOLENZ
C) JOHNNY MAESTRO
D) PETER TORK
E) MICHAEL NESMITH

17. **1 x 1**

JOANIE SOMMERS IS BEST REMEMBERED FOR HER RECORDING OF WHAT SONG BELOW ABOUT HER JOHNNY?
A) WHEN JOHNNY COMES MARCHING HOME
B) JOHNNY ANGEL
C) JOHNNY B. GOODE
D) JOHNNY GET ANGRY

18. **1 x 1**

CHOOSE THE SONG THAT WAS A HIT FOR *THE CASCADES* DURING THE 60'S AND AGAIN FOR *DAN FOGELBERG* IN THE 90'S ABOUT LISTENING TO THE FALLING OF WHAT DURING INCLEMENT WEATHER AS A RESULT OF HEART BREAK LOVE.
A) BABY THE RAIN MUST FALL
B) RAINDROPS KEEP FALLIN' ON MY HEAD
C) RHYTHM OF THE RAIN
D) RAINDROPS

19. **2 x 1**

THIS GROUP HAD THE FOLLOWING TWO HITS: "TURN AROUND, LOOK AT ME" AND "FIVE O'CLOCK WORLD". NAME THEM AND ANOTHER OF THEIR HITS BELOW.
ONE, GROUP NAME.
TWO, THEIR VERSION OF A *BOBBY HELMS* TUNE ABOUT AN ANGEL FROM ABOVE.
1) ______________
2) ___________________

20. **1 x 1**

THE SKYLINERS WITH *JIMMY BEAUMONT* IN LEAD CHARTED ONCE AGAIN WITH A HEAVEN TITLED SONG THAT DEALT WITH COPPER CURRENCY. IT WAS A RE-MAKE OF A *MILLS BROTHERS* RECORDING OF THE LATE 30'S. NAME THAT SONG.

____

21. **1 x 1**

VIC DANA RECORDED WHAT POPULAR SONG BELOW ABOUT SENDING FLOWERS TO A SWEET LADY IN HOPES IT WILL TAKE HER BLUES AWAY? IT WAS A BIG INSTRUMENTAL HIT FOR *BERT KAEMPFERT & HIS ORCHESTRA* AND HAD *WAYNE NEWTON* COMPETING WITH *VIC DANA* ON THE CHARTS SIMULTANEOUSLY.
A) ROSES ARE RED
B) BLUE ON BLUE
C) BLUE VELVET
D) RED ROSES FOR A BLUE LADY

22. **1 x 1**

VITO AND THE SALUTATIONS CHARTED AN UPTEMPO DOO WOP VERSION OF AN *AL HIBBLER* TUNE OF THE 50'S THAT *THE RIGHTEOUS BROTHERS* WOULD GO ON TO RECORD IN THE MID 60'S. NAME THAT SONG WHERE HE HUNGERED FOR YOU.
A) YOU'VE LOST THAT LOVIN' FEELIN'
B) UNCHAINED MELODY
C) TOUCH ME
D) HUNGRY

23. **1 x 1**

FREDDY CANNON STILL ACTIVE SINCE THE LATE 50'S WHEN HE CHARTED "TALLAHASSEE LASSIE" AND "WAY DOWN YONDER IN NEW ORLEANS" CHARTED THIS SONG ABOUT A CERTAIN PARK LOCATED IN NEW JERSEY WITH ITS ROLLER COASTER RIDES, FERRIS WHEELS AND HOT DOG STANDS. WHAT WAS THAT HIT?
A) THE RAIN, THE PARK & OTHER THINGS
B) I'VE GOT SAND IN MY SHOES
C) UNDER THE BOARDWALK
D) PALISADES PARK

24. **1 x 1**

THE FOUR SEASONS RECORDED THE SONG "DON'T THINK TWICE" UNDER A 'PSEUDO NAME' THAT HAD EVERYONE GUESSING THEIR TRUE IDENTITY. CHOOSE THAT PSEUDO NAMED GROUP BELOW THAT WOULD GO DOWN IN MUSIC HISTORY AS A ONE HIT WONDER GROUP.
A) THE GUESS WHO
B) THE WHO
C) THE WONDER WHO?
D) ?(QUESTION MARK) & THE MYSTERIANS

25. **1 x 1**

THE CASINOS ARE MOSTLY REMEMBERED FOR CHARTING THIS ROMANTIC SONG BELOW ABOUT BEING KISSED FOR AN ENORMOUS NUMBER OF YEARS AND THEN IF NOT TOTALLY SATISFIED BY THEN YOU CAN BID HIM FAREWELL. IT TOO WOULD BECOME A ONE HIT WONDER GROUP SONG.
A) KISS AND SAY GOODBYE
B) KISS YOU ALL OVER
C) A MILLION TO ONE
D) THEN YOU CAN TELL ME GOODBYE

26. **1 x 1**

IN 1964 *TERRY STAFFORD* HAD A POPULAR HIT WITH A RE-MAKE OF AN ORIGINAL *ELVIS* RECORDING. IT WAS ABOUT THIS GIRL THAT EVERYTIME SHE KISSED AND HELD HIM, HE WAS STILL DOUBTFUL THAT SHE CARED. THIS IS ONE OF THE RARE TIMES THAT *ELVIS* WAS OUTCLASSED WITH ONE OF HIS OWN ORIGINAL SONGS. WHAT WAS THAT POPULAR HIT?
A) YOU CHEATED
B) SUSPICION
C) GO NOW!
D) I KNOW (YOU DON'T LOVE NO MORE)

27. **1 x 1**

KATHY YOUNG WITH THE INNOCENTS RECORDED THEIR CLAIM TO FAME SONG IN 1960 WITH THIS BIG ROMANTIC CLASSIC ABOUT THESE THINGS IN THE SKY, VISIBLE ONLY AT NIGHT, AND THAT SHE COULD NEVER LOVE ANY OTHER BUT YOU.
A) ONE SUMMER NIGHT
B) A THOUSAND STARS
C) THERE'S A MOON OUT TONIGHT
D) LITTLE STAR

28. **1 x 1**

WHAT WAS THIS BIG TRAGIC HIT BY *RAY PETERSON* ABOUT A MESSAGE THAT TOMMY WANTED YOU TO RELAY TO LAURA PROFESSING HIS UNDYING LOVE?
A) NEVER GIVE YOU UP
B) NEVER CAN SAY GOODBYE
C) TELL LAURA I LOVE HER
D) NEVER MY LOVE

29. **1 x 1**

RAY PETERSON CHARTED ANOTHER ABOUT A GIRL NAMED CORINNA THAT HE LOVED SO MUCH. IT WAS A SONG *JOE TURNER* PREVIOUSLY RECORDED IN THE MID 50'S, TITLE SPELLING SLIGHTLY CHANGED. NAME IT.

____________, ____________

30. **4 x 1**

NAME THESE FOUR HITS BY *GENE PITNEY*, THE SINGER/SONGWRITER.
ONE, A SONG FEATURED IN A MOVIE OF THE SAME NAME IN 1961 ABOUT A TOWN THAT SHOWED NO SORROW, STARRING KIRK DOUGLAS AS A MILITARY LAWYER DEFENDING GI'S IN A RAPE CASE, ALSO CO-STARRING ROBERT BLAKE AND CHRISTINE KAUFMANN.
TWO, ABOUT WHAT HE CLAIMED LOVE CAN DO TO YOUR HEART THAT HE WANTED A CHANCE TO MAKE UP.
THREE, THAT HE'S GONNA BE TOUGH AND LET YOU GO YOUR OWN WAY. IT WAS A SONG *JUICE NEWTON* WOULD ALSO RECORD IN THE 80'S.
FOUR, ABOUT THE PAIN TO BE IN LOVE DAY AND NIGHT.

1) ____________________

2) ______________________________

3) ____________________

4) ________________________

31. **1 x 1**

GENE PITNEY CHARTED THESE THREE OTHERS BELOW. WHICH ONE WAS **NOT** HIS?
A) MECCA
B) POOR LITTLE FOOL
C) TWENTY FOUR HOURS FROM TULSA
D) (THE MAN WHO SHOT) LIBERTY VALANCE

32. **1 x 1**

WE FIVE, A GROUP CONSISTING OF A GIRL AND FOUR GUYS, RECORDED A POPULAR HIT SONG ABOUT WHO WAS ON THEIR MIND WHEN THEY HAD AWAKEN.
A) ALL IN MY MIND
B) JUST TO BE WITH YOU
C) GOOD LOVIN'
D) YOU WERE ON MY MIND

33. **1 x 1**

JOSE FELICIANO, THE GIFTED BLIND PUERTO RICAN ARTIST, CHARTED A SONG THAT WAS AN ORIGINAL HIT FOR *THE DOORS* ABOUT TRYING TO DO SOMETHING TO THE NIGHT. BOTH WERE RECORDED IN THE 60'S, ALMOST ONE YEAR APART. NAME IT BELOW.
A) NIGHTS IN WHITE SATIN
B) LIGHT MY FIRE
C) TOUCH ME
D) ONE SUMMER NIGHT

34. **1 x 1**

THE SONG "SAN FRANCISCO (BE SURE TO WEAR FLOWERS IN YOUR HAIR)" WAS RECORDED BY WHAT ARTIST BELOW IN 1967 WHICH WAS HIS FIRST MAJOR HIT AND ALSO HIS BIGGEST?
A) THE MAMAS AND THE PAPAS
B) THREE DOG NIGHT
C) SCOTT MCKENZIE
D) TONY BENNETT

35. **1 x 1**

CATHY JEAN AND THE ROOMMATES RECORDED A SONG THAT *BOBBY VINTON* WOULD ALSO RECORD ABOUT A PLEA FOR SOMETHING TO LAST FOR ETERNITY.

A) TILL THEN
B) PLEASE STAY
C) PLEASE LOVE ME FOREVER
D) 'TIL

36. **9 x 1**

JOHNNY RIVERS WAS KNOWN FOR RECORDING RE-MAKE HITS OF OTHER ARTISTS. NAME THESE NINE HITS BELOW, INCLUDING SOME RE-MAKES.
ONE, A *CHUCK BERRY* TUNE ABOUT A CERTAIN GIRL WHO COULDN'T BE TRUE, SPELLING SLIGHTLY DIFFERENT.
TWO, ANOTHER *CHUCK BERRY* TUNE ABOUT A CERTAIN CITY IN TENNESSEE AND THAT GIRL MARIE. ALSO DONE AS AN INSTRUMENTAL BY *LONNIE MACK* ONE YEAR PRIOR TO *RIVERS* VERSION.
THREE, AN ORIGINAL *PAUL EVANS* TUNE ABOUT SOMETHING SPECIAL, TITLE SPELLING SLIGHTLY CHANGED. IT WOULD BECOME THE THEME SONG FOR DON KERSHNER'S WEEKLY TV ROCK CONCERT SHOW.
FOUR, A *HAROLD DORMAN* TUNE ABOUT A CERTAIN MOUNTAIN.
FIVE, A THEME SONG FROM A TV SERIES OF THE SAME NAME ABOUT AN UNDERCOVER AGENT.
SIX, HIS VERSION OF A *FOUR TOPS* HIT SONG ABOUT NEEDING YOUR LOVE AND LONGING TO HOLD.
SEVEN, HIS RENDITION OF A *SMOKEY ROBINSON AND THE MIRACLES* HIT TUNE ABOUT THE TRACKS OF SOMETHING THAT OCCURS WHEN YOU'RE IN EMOTIONAL PAIN RECORDED IN THE 60'S AND ALSO TO BE RECORDED BY *LINDA RONSTADT* IN THE MID 70'S.
EIGHT, A SONG THAT STATED YOU WERE THE GREATEST AND HE CAN'T GO ON WITHOUT YOU.
NINE, HE'S DEFINITELY THE ONE, AND THE SEVENTH AT THAT.

1) ________________
2) ___________
3) ____________________
4) ____________________
5) ____________________
6) _____________________________
7) _____________________________
8) ______________________
9) ________________

37. **5 x 1**

NAME THESE FIVE HITS BY *SIMON & GARFUNKEL*, THE POPULAR DUO FROM QUEENS, NY.
ONE, ABOUT THE TYPE OF SOUNDS AND GRAFFITI FOUND IN THE SUBWAYS.
TWO, A SONG FEATURED IN THE MOVIE 'THE GRADUATE', STARRING DUSTIN HOFFMAN, KATHERINE ROSS AND ANN BANKROFT, ABOUT A MARRIED WOMAN.
THREE, SOMEONE BOUND FOR HOME.
FOUR, ABOUT A ROCK THAT HE CLAIMED TO BE.
FIVE, ABOUT THE BOY WHO WAS FORCED TO BE A FIGHTER TO SURVIVE.

1) _________________________
2) __________________
3) ____________________
4) __________________
5) ______________

38. **1 x 1**

ACCORDING TO *THE TOKENS* WHOM WAS SLEEPING IN THE ALL MIGHTY JUNGLE? IT WOULD RESURFACE FOR THE ANIMATION MOVIE OF 'THE LION KING' IN THE 90'S THAT FEATURED THE VOICES OF JAMES EARL JONES, NATHANE LANE, WHOOPI GOLDBERG AND NUMEROUS OTHERS ABOUT A LION CUB DESTINED TO BE KING OF THE JUNGLE SOMEDAY. THIS WAS AN OLD AFRICAN FOLK SONG REWORDED BY *THE WEAVERS* IN 1951 AND REWORDED ONCE AGAIN FOR *THE TOKENS*. NAME THAT COMEBACK HIT SONG.

____

39. **1 x 1**

CHOOSE BELOW ANOTHER BY *THE TOKENS* ABOUT WHAT HAPPENED TONIGHT.
A) TONIGHT'S THE NIGHT
B) WILL YOU LOVE ME TOMORROW
C) TONIGHT I FELL IN LOVE
D) OH, WHAT A NIGHT

40. **1 x 1**

JOHNNY CRAWFORD, THE SON OF CHUCK CONNORS IN THE TV SERIES 'THE RIFLEMAN' IN THE 60'S, RECORDED WHAT BIRTHDAY SONG BELOW?
A) HAPPY BIRTHDAY, SWEET 16
B) CINDY'S BIRTHDAY
C) 16 CANDLES
D) HAPPY, HAPPY BIRTHDAY BABY

41. **1 x 1**

"EVERYBODY LOVES SOMEBODY" WAS RECORDED BY THIS ALL ROUNDED MALE ENTERTAINER AND USED AS THE THEME SONG FOR HIS WEEKLY TV VARIETY SHOW. WHO WAS THAT ALL ROUNDED ENTERTAINER?
A) PERRY COMO
B) TOM JONES
C) DEAN MARTIN
D) CHUBBY CHECKER

42. **3 x 1**

NAME THESE THREE BIG HITS BY *LOU CHRISTIE*.
ONE, ABOUT A GYPSY IN TEARS WHO HE WENT TO SEE FOR CONSULTATION OF THE HEART WITH SAD RESULTS.
TWO, ABOUT A GUY WITH TWO FACES.
THREE, ABOUT THE LIGHTENING SHE CAUSES WHENEVER THEY'RE TOGETHER TRYING TO MAKE TIME.

1) ____________________
2) ____________________
3) ____________________

43. **1 x 1**

LOU CHRISTIE ALSO CHARTED TWO OTHERS. WHICH ONE BELOW WAS **NOT** HIS?
A) THIS DIAMOND RING
B) RHAPSODY IN THE RAIN
C) I'M GONNA MAKE YOU MINE

44. **1 x 1**

THE SPIRAL STAIRCASE, A ONE HIT WONDER GROUP, RECORDED WHAT SONG BELOW THAT DEALT WITH THEIR LOVE GROWING MORE AND MORE EACH DAY?
A) LOVE GROWS (WHERE MY ROSEMARY GOES)
B) IT'S GROWING
C) I DO LOVE YOU
D) MORE TODAY THAN YESTERDAY

45. **1 x 1**

IN 1961 *TONY ORLANDO* CHARTED WHAT SONG BELOW ABOUT A PARADISE SO NEAR? IT WAS SUCH AN UNDERRATED SONG FOR ITS TRUE POTENTIAL BUT NEVERTHELESS HAS BECOME AN EVERLASTING CLASSIC. IT IS ALSO THE NAME OF HIS INSPIRING AUTOBIOGRAPHY BOOK IN 2002.

A) HEAVEN ON EARTH
B) EARTH ANGEL
C) HALFWAY TO PARADISE
D) SO NEAR AND YET SO FAR

46. **1 x 1**

TONY ORLANDO RECORDED ANOTHER ABOUT A GIRL THAT LOVES HIM AND HE BLESSES HER AND EVERY MOMENT FOR IT.

A) (YOU'RE MY) SOUL AND INSPIRATION
B) BLESS YOU
C) CUPID
D) MY SPECIAL ANGEL

47. **1 x 1**

BARRY DEVORZON AND THE TAMERLANES CHARTED THIS SONG BELOW WONDERING THE WHEREABOUTS OF A GIRL HE BELIEVED COULD DO WITHOUT AND SORRY FOR MAKING THAT MISTAKE ALL TOGETHER. IT WAS A SIMILAR TITLED SONG OF A *TOMMY BOYCE AND BOBBY HART* TUNE, SPELLING SLIGHTLY DIFFERENT AND WITH UNRELATED LYRICS. WHAT WAS THAT HIT?

A) I'M SORRY
B) I WONDER WHAT SHE'S DOING TONIGHT
C) LITTLE STAR
D) I WONDER WHY

48. **1 x 1**

WHAT SONG DID *MARCIE BLANE* RECORD IN 1962 ABOUT LONGING TO BE SOMEBODY'S GIRL? SOMETHING SHE'S BEEN PRAYING FOR AND IF IT SHOULD HAPPEN SHE'D BE GRATEFUL AND SO LOYAL.

A) JOHNNY ANGEL
B) JIMMY MACK
C) BOBBY'S GIRL
D) JOHNNY B. GOODE

49. **1 x 1**

"(JUST LIKE) ROMEO & JULIET" WAS A BIG HIT FOR WHAT WHITE MALE GROUP WITH THAT SOULFUL SOUND?

A) THE O'KAYSIONS
B) JAY & THE AMERICANS
C) THE REFLECTIONS
D) THE KNOCKOUTS

50. **1 x 1**

ANDY WILLIAMS CHARTED WHAT SONG BELOW IN 1963 ABOUT WHAT HE COULDN'T STOP DOING BECAUSE NO MATTER WHAT HE TRIED, HIS LOVE FOR YOU COULD NEVER END? IT JUST BARELY MISSED REACHING THE TOP OF THE CHARTS WHERE IT SETTLED AT NUMBER TWO.

A) (YOU'RE MY) SOUL AND INSPIRATION
B) CAN'T GET USED TO LOSING YOU
C) I CAN'T STOP LOVING YOU
D) I DO LOVE YOU

51. **1 x 1**

MIKE DOUGLAS, THE VERY POPULAR TV HOST PERSONALITY, CHARTED WHAT SONG BELOW, A ONE HIT WONDER SONG FOR HIM IN THE ROCK ERA ABOUT A LITTLE GIRL SO DEAR TO HIM?
A) LITTLE CHILDREN
B) LITTLE BITTY PRETTY ONE
C) HEY LITTLE GIRL
D) THE MEN IN MY LITTLE GIRL'S LIFE

52. **1 x 1**

THE GROUP, *EVERY MOTHER'S SON,* RECORDED A SONG ABOUT A GUY WHO WANTED THIS GIRL TO SAIL IN HIS BOAT, BUT SHE WAS RESTRICTED ONLY TO THE DOCK. IT TOO WOULD BECOME A ONE HIT WONDER SONG FOR THE GROUP.
A) 26 MILES (SANTA CATALINA)
B) COME ON DOWN TO MY BOAT
C) SLOOP JOHN B
D) (SITTIN' ON) THE DOCK OF THE BAY

53. **1 x 1**

STEVE LAWRENCE CHARTED THIS SONG BELOW THAT HE WOULD SING ON NATIONAL TV TO A LITTLE GIRL WHO WAS AFFLICTED WITH MUSCULAR DYSTROPHY DURING THE ANNUAL TV FUNDRAISER. BOTH *THE HAPPENINGS* IN THE 60'S AND *DONNY OSMOND* IN THE 70'S WOULD ALSO DO A VERSION OF THEIR OWN. WHAT WAS THAT TRIPLE HITTER?
A) YOU'LL NEVER WALK ALONE
B) GO AWAY LITTLE GIRL
C) HAPPY TOGETHER
D) IT AIN'T ME BABE

54. **1 x 1**

STEVE LAWRENCE ALSO HAD A HIT WITH WHAT SONG BELOW ABOUT WHAT OF HIS LOVER?
A) PORTRAIT OF MY LOVE
B) LOVER PLEASE
C) MY BABY LOVES LOVIN'
D) TWO LOVERS

55. **2 x 1**

THE CRESTS, LED BY *JOHNNY MAESTRO*, CHARTED TWO MORE BIG HITS PRIOR TO THEIR BREAKUP IN THE EARLY 60'S. NAME THEM.
ONE, ABOUT THE SEVEN OR MORE STEPS ONE FOLLOWS WHEN TRYING TO WIN HER LOVE FOR GOOD, ONE BY ONE.
TWO, ABOUT THE DANGERS IN PARADISE CAUSED BY THAT DEVIL WITH HIS PACK OF LIES, AND ASKING FOR HELP FROM THE ANGELS OR ANYTHING UP ABOVE.
1) ________________
2) __________________________

56. **1 x 1**

DIANE RENAY HAD A BIG HIT WITH THIS SAILOR BOY SONG BELOW ABOUT THE BLUE FEELING SHE WAS EXPERIENCING BECAUSE HER LOVER BOY WAS SHIPPING AHOY.
A) SOLDIER BOY
B) NAVY BLUE
C) COMING HOME SOLDIER
D) THE BALLAD OF THE GREEN BERETS

TOTAL POINTS. **100 x 1 = 100**

POP ROCKERS-QUIZ # 3

1. **1 x 1**

THE DUO OF *PAUL & PAULA*, CHARTED WHAT POPULAR SONG IN THE 60'S THAT WOULD REACH THE TOP OF THE CHARTS ABOUT WANTING TO MARRY YOU AND NO OTHER WOULD DO? IT WOULD ALSO BE FEATURED IN THE 'ANIMAL HOUSE' SOUNDTRACK MOVIE STARRING JOHN BELUCHI AND TIM MATHESON IN THE 70'S.

A) WHEN WE GET MARRIED
B) I WISH THAT WE WERE MARRIED
C) HEY PAULA
D) TO THE AISLE

2. **1 x 1**

THE CHIMES FROM BROOKLYN, NY, WITH *LENNY COCCO* IN LEAD, HAD A BIG CLASSIC HIT ABOUT THE THOUGHT OF ME NOW AND THEN EVEN THOUGH WE HAVE PARTED.

A) REMEMBER THEN
B) HE'LL HAVE TO GO
C) I THINK WE'RE ALONE NOW
D) ONCE IN AWHILE

3. **1 x 1**

THIS GROUP CONSISTED OF THE FORMER LEAD SINGER OF *THE CRESTS* AND SOME MEMBERS OF THE OF *THE DEL SATINS*. WHAT WAS THE NAME OF THAT NEW GROUP?

A) JAY & THE AMERICANS
B) THE EARLS
C) BROOKLYN BRIDGE
D) THE FIVE SATINS

4. **4 x 1**

NAME THESE FOUR RECORDED HITS BY THE GROUP ABOVE.
ONE, WHAT HE HEARD ABOUT HER THAT HE WANTED NO PART OF SINCE HE WAS NOT THE MARRYING KIND AND IT COULD ONLY DESTROY HIM.
TWO, LONELY IS HIS NAME.
THREE, WHAT ABOUT OUR SPOUSES?
FOUR, ABOUT THE RAIN BEING SACRED.

1) ______________________________
2) __________________
3) ________________________
4) ________________________

5. **1 x 1**

THE CAPRIS, THE DOO WOP GROUP, CHARTED WHAT CLASSIC SONG BELOW ABOUT THE MOON AND ABOUT THE DESIRE TO GO STROLLING TOGETHER?

A) SO MUCH IN LOVE
B) THAT'S MY DESIRE
C) ONE SUMMER NIGHT
D) THERE'S A MOON OUT TONIGHT

6. **1 x 1**

IN 1963 *THE CLASSICS* HAD THIS SONG BELOW ASKING HIS LOVED ONE TO PLEASE WAIT AND PRAY BECAUSE ONE DAY THEY'LL BE REUNITED WITH THEIR DREAMS AND LOVE FULFILLED. IT WAS A RE-MAKE OF A *MILLS BROTHERS* ORIGINAL RECORDING BACK IN THE EARLY 50'S. WHAT WAS THAT DOUBLE HITTER?

A) TILL THEN
B) DARLIN' BE HOME SOON
C) PLEASE STAY
D) COMING HOME SOLDIER

7. **3 x 1**

THIS ALL MALE GROUP WENT ON TO CHART A SONG CALLED "MY OWN TRUE LOVE". NAME THEM AND TWO OF THEIR OTHER HITS BELOW, NUMBERS TWO AND THREE.
ONE, GROUP NAME.
TWO, ABOUT ENJOYING YOUR TRAVELS AND TO DO AS YOU PLEASE, BUT WITH THE END RESULT THAT YOU'LL STILL BE MINE. A SONG ORIGINALLY RECORDED BY *JO STAFFORD* IN THE 50'S AND LATER BY *DEAN MARTIN*.
THREE, QUESTIONING WHO'S SHE WITH AND DO I KNOW HIM, ORIGINALLY A *JONI JAMES* RECORDING.

1) ________________
2) ________________________
3) ____________________

8. **1 x 1**

THE EARLS, WITH *LARRY CHANCE* IN LEAD, CHARTED WHAT POPULAR SONG BELOW ABOUT THOSE SPECIAL FOND MEMORIES OF AN UNFORGETTABLE SUMMER NIGHT OF PASSION.
A) 'TIL
B) LITTLE STAR
C) REMEMBER THEN
D) MEMORIES

9. **1 x 1**

THE EARLS RECORDED ANOTHER ABOUT WHAT HE THOUGHT WHEN IT RAINED. IT WOULD END UP AS A TRIBUTE SONG TO A FORMER FALLEN MEMBER OF THE GROUP WHO WOULD DIE DURING THE VIETNAM WAR.
A) A LOVER'S CONCERTO
B) I BELIEVE
C) RAINDROPS
D) ALL IN MY MIND

10. **1 x 1**

IN 1960 *THE DEMENSIONS* HAD THEIR ONLY MAJOR HIT WITH A RENDITION OF A 'WIZARD OF OZ' MOVIE SONG ORIGINALLY RECORDED BY *JUDY GARLAND* IN 1939. WHAT WAS THAT DOUBLE HITTER CALLED?
A) OVER THE RAINBOW
B) THE END
C) WHEN YOU WISH UPON A STAR
D) THE TIN MAN

11. **1 x 1**

THE HONDELLS CHARTED WHAT CAR TITLED SONG IN 1964 THAT BECAME A BIG HIT AND THEIR ONLY CLAIM TO FAME SONG?
A) MAYBELLENE
B) MUSTANG SALLY
C) LITTLE HONDA
D) BEEP BEEP

12. **1 x 1**

HERB ALPERT, THE LEADER OF *THE TIJUANA BRASS,* RECORDED A ROMANTIC SOLO HIT THAT SHOWCASED HIS SINGING ABILITIES ABOUT A GUY IN LOVE AND HAPPY TO HAVE KNOWN HER.
A) I DO LOVE YOU
B) I DO
C) THIS GUY'S IN LOVE WITH YOU
D) WITH THIS RING

13. **1 x 1**

DALE & GRACE HAD THIS TOP OF THE CHARTS HIT SONG ABOUT LETTING YOU DECIDE THE OUTCOME OF THEIR FUTURE. IT'S A SONG THAT UNFORTUNATELY WOULD LOSE SOME OF ITS APPEAL WHILE THE WORLD WOULD BE IN A STATE OF SHOCK AND MOURNING DURING THIS PERIOD OF THE JFK ASSASSINATION.

A) I'M LEAVING IT UP TO YOU
B) IT'S NOW OR NEVER
C) DID YOU EVER HAVE TO MAKE UP YOUR MIND?
D) YOU'RE THE ONE

14. **5 x 1**

NAME THESE FIVE CHARTED HITS BY *FRANK SINATRA,* THE LEGENDARY CROONER TURNED ACTOR.
ONE, ABOUT STRANGERS WHO BECAME LOVERS.
TWO, A SONG WRITTEN BY *PAUL ANKA* AND LATER RECORDED BY *ELVIS* ABOUT DOING THINGS AS HE SAW FIT.
THREE, ABOUT LIFE, ONE DAY YOU COULD BE UP AND THE NEXT DAY DOWN.
FOUR, ABOUT A CERTAIN WIND IN A PARTICULAR SEASON.
FIVE, ABOUT IT BEING A VERY PRODUCTIVE YEAR.

1) ______________________________
2) ___________
3) ________________
4) ________________
5) ___________________________________

15. **1 x 1**

IN THE 60'S *PAUL ANKA* HAD THESE TWO BIG HITS. WHICH ONE WAS **NOT** HIS?

A) MY HOMETOWN
B) PUPPY LOVE
C) YOU WERE MINE

16. **4 x 1**

THE RONETTES, A FAMILY TRIO OF GIRLS, HAD THESE FOUR POPULAR HITS BELOW.
ONE, ABOUT THAT FIRST ENCOUNTER WHEN THEY MET AND HOW SHE WANTED YOU TO BE HER BABE. IT WOULD BE FEATURED IN THE BLOCKBUSTER SOUNDTRACK MOVIE OF "DIRTY DANCING" IN THE LATE 80'S STARRING *PATRICK SWAYZEE*, JENNIFER GREY AND JERRY ORBACH.
TWO, HOW SHE LOVES EVERYTHING ABOUT YOU.
THREE, ABOUT THE UPS AND DOWNS AND THE ACT OF RECONCILIATION.
FOUR, DOING SOMETHING IN THE RAIN, A SONG *JAY & THE AMERICANS* WOULD ALSO RECORD IN THE EARLY 70'S.
NAME THEM.

1) ________________
2) __________________________
3) ___________________________________
4) __________________________

17. **1 x 1**

THE ANGELS, A FEMALE TRIO GROUP, FORETOLD THE ARRIVAL OF HER BOYFRIEND AND THE POSSIBILITY OF TROUBLE BREWING THROUGH WHAT SONG BELOW?

A) YOU'VE GOT YOUR TROUBLES
B) MY BOYFRIEND'S BACK
C) YOU BETTER RUN
D) YOU AIN'T SEEN NOTHING YET

18. **1 x 1**

THE ANGELS WOULD ALSO CHART WITH WHAT CLASSIC HIT BELOW ABOUT THE POSSIBILITY OF SOMETHING OCCURRING, AND THAT'S ONLY IF THE MOON DISAPPEARS FROM THE SKY?

A) BLUE MOON
B) TILL THEN
C) 'TIL
D) MAYBE

19. **1 x 1**

LITTLE PEGGY MARCH WOULD GAIN HER PREMIER STARDOM WITH THIS POPULAR SONG ABOUT FOLLOWING SOMEONE AND THAT NO OBSTACLE COULD KEEP HER AWAY FROM HIM. IT WOULD BE HER FIRST AND RACE TO THE TOP OF THE CHARTS IN 1963 WHEN SHE WAS JUST BARELY FIFTEEN YEARS OLD.

A) OVER THE MOUNTAIN, ACROSS THE SEA
B) AIN'T NO MOUNTAIN HIGH ENOUGH
C) RIVER DEEP, MOUNTAIN HIGH
D) I WILL FOLLOW HIM

20. **1 x 1**

BARBRA STREISAND ACHIEVED HER STARDOM IN 1964 WITH WHAT SONG ABOUT OUR NEEDING OTHERS AND BEING VERY LUCKY FOR IT? IT WOULD BE FEATURED IN HER MUSICAL 'FUNNY GIRL' CO-STARRING OMAR SHARIF.

A) HAPPY TOGETHER
B) PEOPLE
C) GET TOGETHER
D) FOR ONCE IN MY LIFE

21. **1 x 1**

IN 1961 *DICK AND DEEDEE*, WITH THE SOULFUL SOUND, CHARTED THE FIRST MAJOR HIT OF THEIR CAREER WITH WHAT SONG BELOW ABOUT A HIGH PEAK AND DEEP VALLEY. IT WOULD JUST BARELY MISS THE TOP OF THE CHARTS, REACHING AT NUMBER TWO.

A) RIVER DEEP, MOUNTAIN HIGH
B) AIN'T NO MOUNTAIN HIGH ENOUGH
C) THE MOUNTAIN'S HIGH
D) I WILL FOLLOW HIM

22. **1 x 1**

BOBBY GOLDSBORO, THE POPULAR SINGER/SONGWRITER AND TV PERSONALITY CHARTED THESE FOUR HITS BELOW. WHICH ONE WAS **NOT** HIS?

A) HONEY
B) SEE THE FUNNY LITTLE CLOWN
C) LITTLE THINGS
D) AUTUMN OF MY LIFE
E) ONLY THE LONELY

23. **1 x 1**

THE NEWBEATS HAD THIS BIG HIT ABOUT A FOOD ITEM THAT THEY CRAVED. IT TOO WOULD CLIMB TO THE NUMBER TWO SPOT ON THE CHARTS. CHOOSE IT BELOW.

A) PEANUTS
B) MASHED POTATO TIME
C) BREAD AND BUTTER
D) ON TOP OF SPAGHETTI

24. **6 x 1**

NAME THESE SIX BIG HITS BY *GARY LEWIS AND THE PLAYBOYS.*
ONE, SHE TOOK IT OFF HER HAND AND NO IT'S NOT FOR *BO DIDDLEY.*
TWO, DON'TCHA KNOW THAT.
THREE, ABOUT WHO'S GONNA MISS HER PRESENCE.
FOUR, WHAT EVERYBODY LOVES THAT WEARS A SILLY COSTUME AND MAKEUP.
FIVE, WHAT HE WANTED YOU TO SAVE FOR HIM.
SIX, ABOUT WHO YOU CAN COUNT ON.

1) ____________________
2) ________________________
3) ________________________
4) ____________________________
5) ______________________________
6) _______________

25. **1 x 1**

THE KNOCKOUTS, A WHITE GROUP WITH THE SOULFUL SOUND, RECORDED WHAT SONG ABOUT AN ANGEL OUT OF HEAVEN WHO HE HOPED THEY WOULD NEVER PART AND HIS REASON FOR LIVING?

A) DREAM LOVER
B) LITTLE STAR
C) WHAT AM I LIVING FOR
D) DARLING LORRAINE

26. **1 x 1**

WHICH GIRL SONG BELOW WAS **NOT** A *FOUR SEASONS* RECORDING?

A) C'MON MARIANNE
B) RONNIE
C) DAWN (GO AWAY)
D) BARBARA ANN

27. **3 x 1**

THE MONKEES, THE POPULAR QUADRUPLE GROUP, CHARTED "PLEASANT VALLEY SUNDAY" AND "DAYDREAM BELIEVER". NAME THEIR THREE OTHER HITS BELOW.
ONE, ASKING HER TO MEET HIM AT A CERTAIN TRAIN STATION.
TWO, ABOUT FINALLY BELIEVING IN THE POWER OF LOVE AFTER HE TOOK A LOOK AT HER FACE.
THREE, APOLOGIZING AND BEGGING HER NOT TO LEAVE HIM BECAUSE WHEN IT COMES DOWN TO IT, IT'S A LITTLE OF BOTH.

1) ______________________________
2) ____________________
3) ____

28. **3 x 1**

NAME THESE THREE CHARTED HITS BY *THE SHANGRI-LAS*, THE POPULAR ALL GIRL GROUP.
ONE, THE MEMORY OF WALKING HAND IN HAND BY THE SEA.
TWO, ABOUT THAT REBEL LEADER NAMED JIMMY THAT SHE MET AT THE PENNY AND DIME STORE.
THREE, ABOUT A BIG KISS.

1) ___________________________________
2) _____________________
3) ______________________________

29. **1 x 1**

CHOOSE BELOW THIS MALE SINGER OF GREEK AND PUERTO RICAN DESCENT WHO FIRST RECORDED AS A SOLOIST IN THE EARLY 60'S AND THEN AS A LEAD SINGER WITH TWO BACKUP GIRL SINGERS AS A TRIO GROUP IN THE 70'S.

A) JOSE FELICIANO
B) TONY ORLANDO
C) RICKY MARTIN
D) FREDDIE PRINZE

30. **1 x 1**

LINDA SCOTT, THE TEEN SINGER, HAD A POPULAR HIT IN 1961 WITH WHAT STAR TITLED SONG BELOW?

A) LITTLE STAR
B) A THOUSAND STARS
C) I'VE TOLD EVERY LITTLE STAR
D) WHEN YOU WISH UPON A STAR

31. **1 x 1**

LINDA SCOTT WOULD CHART ANOTHER ADVISING NOT TO WAGER ANY MONEY ON IT. CHOOSE THAT ONE BELOW.

A) MONEY (THAT'S WHAT I WANT)
B) DON'T BET MONEY HONEY
C) 25 OR 6 TO 4
D) EASY COME, EASY GO

32. **1 x 1**

THE CASTAWAYS, A ONE HIT WONDER GROUP, CHARTED THIS SONG BELOW IN 1965 ABOUT ONE WHO DECEIVES. WHAT WAS IT CALLED?

A) LIAR, LIAR
B) YOU'RE NO GOOD
C) YOU CHEATED
D) (YOU'RE THE) DEVIL IN DISGUISE

33. **7 x 1**

NAME THESE SEVEN POPULAR HITS BY *DION,* THE POP MALE SINGER FROM NYC, BELMONT STREET IN THE BRONX.
ONE, ABOUT AN UNFAITHFUL GIRL NAMED SUE WHO RAN ALL OVER TOWN. LATER CHARTED BY *LEIF GARRETT,* THE ACTOR TURNED SINGER IN THE LATE 70'S.
TWO, WHAT THEY CALLED HIM BECAUSE HE ROAMED THROUGHOUT THE TOWN.
THREE, HIS VERSION OF *THE DRIFTERS* SONG ABOUT RUBY.
FOUR, ABOUT A CERTAIN TEENAGER WITH THE BLUES.
FIVE, ABOUT A CERTAIN GIRL WHO THINKS SHE'S ZSA ZSA GABOR.
SIX, A TRIBUTE SONG TO THREE GUYS, AND WHERE HAVE THEY DISAPPEARED?
SEVEN, ABOUT LOVERS WHO GO ASTRAY.

1) ____________________
2) ________________
3) ______________
4) ________________
5) _________________________
6) ______________________________
7) _____________________

34. **1 x 1**

DION WOULD ALSO CHART FOUR OTHER HITS BELOW. WHICH ONE WAS **NOT** HIS?

A) WHERE OR WHEN
B) BARBARA ANN
C) LOVE CAME TO ME
D) LITTLE DIANA
E) DRIP DROP

35. **1 x 1**

FRANKIE VALLI RECORDED THIS BIG SOLO HIT ABOUT WHAT HE COULDN'T STOP DOING. IT WOULD BE FEATURED IN THE MEL GIBSON AND JULIA ROBERTS MOVIE "CONSPIRACY THEORY" IN THE LATE 90'S ALSO CO-STARRING PATRICK STEWART.

A) I CAN'T STOP LOVING YOU
B) GOIN' OUT OF MY HEAD
C) CAN'T GET USED TO LOSING YOU
D) CAN'T TAKE MY EYES OFF YOU

36. **1 x 1**

FRANKIE VALLI ALSO CHARTED ANOTHER ABOUT THE POSSIBILITY OF YOU GETTING HURT. WHAT WAS THAT OTHER HIT BELOW?

A) LOVE IS A HURTIN' THING
B) (YOU'RE GONNA) HURT YOURSELF
C) HURT
D) HURT SO BAD

37. **1 x 1**

OLIVER RECORDED A SONG FEATURED IN THE OFF BROADWAY MUSICAL 'HAIR' THAT WOULD GAIN HIM HIS INITIAL STARDOM ABOUT THE POWER OF THE SUNLIGHT WITH IT'S MAGICAL AFFECTS HERE ON EARTH WITH LOVE, LAUGHTER, AND SONG. CHOOSE THAT HIT BELOW.

A) HAIR
B) SEE ME, FEEL ME
C) EASY TO BE HARD
D) GOOD MORNING STARSHINE

38. **1 x 1**

OLIVER ALSO HAD WHAT OTHER, THAT WOULD BE FEATURED IN THE MOVIE 'THE PRIME OF MISS JEAN BRODIE' STARRING MAGGIE SMITH AND ROBERT STEPHENS IN 1969?

A) NORTH TO ALASKA
B) JEAN
C) TOWN WITHOUT PITY
D) (THE MAN WHO SHOT) LIBERTY VALANCE

39. **1 x 1**

THE BELMONTS CHARTED A SONG ABOUT THEIR DESIRE TO KNOW THE REASONS HE LOVES THAT GIRLIE SO.

A) WHY DO FOOLS FALL IN LOVE
B) WHY DO LOVERS BREAK EACH OTHER'S HEART
C) LITTLE STAR
D) TELL ME WHY

40. **1 x 1**

CHOOSE THIS POPULAR MALE ARTIST BELOW WHO LIKE *ELVIS* AND *FRANK SINATRA* COULD PACK THE FANS INTO VEGAS, AND WHO HAD A BIG HIT WITH THE SONG "DANKE SCHOEN".

A) DEAN MARTIN
B) SAMMY DAVIS JR
C) TOM JONES
D) WAYNE NEWTON

41. **6 x 1**

BOBBY VINTON CHARTED NUMEROUS HITS DURING THE 60'S INCLUDING "I LOVE HOW YOU LOVE ME" AND "THERE! I'VE SAID IT AGAIN". NAME THESE SIX OTHERS BELOW.
ONE, WHAT HE CLAIMED ABOUT ROSES.
TWO, BLUE CAUSED BY HEARTACHE AND LOST LOVE.
THREE, HIS BEAUTIFUL RENDITION OF AN ORIGINAL *MOONGLOWS* RECORDING ABOUT A CERTAIN COLORED VELVET THAT SHE WORE.
FOUR, ABOUT A FORGOTTEN LONELY SOLDIER.
FIVE, AGAIN ABOUT A SOLDIER, ON HIS WAY HOME.
SIX, ABOUT LOVING HIM FOR ETERNITY.

1) ____________________
2) ________________
3) ________________
4) ____________
5) _______________________
6) ___________________________

42. **1 x 1**

WHAT SONG DID THE GROUP *MERCY* RECORD IN 1969 THAT WOULD BECOME THEIR ONLY MAJOR HIT ABOUT THE POSSIBILITY OF LOVE BRINGING YOU HAPPINESS, TO SHARE, HAVE AND TO HOLD UNTIL FOREVER, A TOP NUMBER TWO UP ON THE CHARTS?

A) LOVE (CAN MAKE YOU HAPPY)
B) MAYBE
C) OH HOW HAPPY
D) OH HAPPY DAY

43. **1 x 1**

NAME THIS TRAGIC LOVE SONG BY *J FRANK WILSON AND THE CAVALIERS* ABOUT A GUY THAT WAS INVOLVED IN A FATAL CAR CRASH AND HIS FINAL ACT. A SONG THAT THE GROUP *PEARL JAM* WOULD ALSO RECORD IN THE LATE 90'S.

A) SINCE I LOST MY BABY
B) TEEN ANGEL
C) TELL LAURA I LOVE HER
D) LAST KISS

44. **2 x 1**

NAME THE TWO DIFFERENT GROUPS WHO BACKED *DION* ON MANY OF HIS SONGS.

1) ________________
2) _____________________

45. **2 x 1**

NAME THESE TWO BIG HITS BY *LITTLE RICKY NELSON* IN THE EARLY 60'S.
ONE, ABOUT HIS TRAVELS THROUGHOUT WITH A GIRL AT EVERY PORT, INCLUDING HIS CHINA BABE.
TWO, ABOUT GREETING HIS MARY WHO HE KNEW THEY WOULD NEVER PART.

1) _________________
2) ______________________

46. **1 x 1**

WHAT IS *BOBBY VINTON'S* NICKNAME?

A) THE KILLER
B) THE POLISH PRINCE
C) THE ICE MAN
D) MR PERSONALITY

47. **6 x 1**

THIS TEENAGE FEMALE ARTIST HAD A HIT WITH "MAYBE I KNOW". NAME HER, AND HER FIVE OTHER HITS BELOW, NUMBERS TWO THROUGH SIX.
ONE, HER NAME.
TWO, ABOUT A CERTAIN PARTY WHERE SHE CAN DO WHATEVER SHE WANTS, RECORDED AT THE TENDER AGE OF SIXTEEN.
THREE, ABOUT THAT GIRL JUDY WHOSE TIME HAS COME BECAUSE JOHNNY'S BACK IN MY ARMS AGAIN.
FOUR, ABOUT WHAT SHE IS FOR TREATING HER GUY SO CRUEL AND DOING HIM WRONG.
FIVE, WHY YOU CAN'T ORDER HER AROUND, SHE'S FREE TO DO AS SHE PLEASES, NOT YOUR PLAY THING.
SIX, HOW YOUNG BOYS BEHAVE.

1) ______________
2) _________________
3) __________________
4) __________________
5) ______________________
6) ___________________________

48. **1 x 1**

THE TEENAGER ABOVE ALSO CHARTED ANOTHER ABOUT WHAT HER LIFE IS WHEN THEY'RE TOGETHER AND SO IN LOVE?
A) PARTY LIGHTS
B) MY BOY LOLLIPOP
C) SUNSHINE, LOLLIPOPS AND RAINBOWS
D) HAPPY TOGETHER

49. **8 x 1**

NAME THESE EIGHT BIG HITS BY *CONNIE FRANCIS*, THE SINGER/ACTRESS.
ONE, A SONG FEATURED IN A MOVIE OF THE SAME NAME STARRING *CONNIE*, GEORGE HAMILTON AND MANY OTHERS ABOUT WHERE THE GUYS HANG OUT.
TWO, ABOUT A BROKEN HEART AMONG HER TROPHIES.
THREE, ABOUT A FOOL.
FOUR, ABOUT A SUMMER RECESS SPELLED OUT IN THE SONG.
FIVE, ANOTHER SONG FEATURED IN A MOVIE OF THE SAME NAME, STARRING *CONNIE* AGAIN AND PAULA PRENTICE ABOUT FOLLOWING WHO AROUND?
SIX, DON'T BREAK WHAT, THAT LOVES YOU?
SEVEN, BREAKING IN SOMETHING NEW.
EIGHT, ABOUT THE THINGS THEY'VE SHARED AS ONE.

1) ______________________
2) ______________________
3) __________________________________
4) _______________
5) _____________________
6) ____
7) ____
8) ______________

50. **1 x 1**

PAUL EVANS RECORDED THIS SONG IN 1960 THAT *JOHNNY RIVERS* WOULD ALSO CHART FIVE YEARS LATER, TITLE SPELLING SLIGHTLY CHANGED, ABOUT SOMETHING SPECIAL. IT WOULD BECOME THE THEME SONG FOR THE DON KERSHNER WEEKLY TV CONCERT IN THE 70'S. WHAT WAS THAT DOUBLE HITTER?
A) SOMETHING
B) MIDNITE SPECIAL
C) SPECIAL OCCASION
D) SPECIAL LADY

51. **1 x 1**

BRUCE CHANNEL HAD THIS CHART TOPPER IN 1962 WITH THE HARMONICA BACKING WANTING TO KNOW IF SHE WOULD BE HIS GIRL. IT WOULD RESURFACE ONCE AGAIN AFTER BEING FEATURED IN THE MOVIE SOUNDTRACK OF 'DIRTY DANCING' IN THE 80'S. WHAT WAS THAT NUMBER ONE AND HIS ONLY CLAIM TO FAME SONG?
A) BE MY BABY
B) BABY LOVE
C) HEY! BABY
D) DO YOU LOVE ME

52. **1 x 1**

GALE GARNETT CHARTED A SONG ABOUT AN UNCOMMITTED RELATION THAT WOULD LAST TILL SHE'S READY TO GO ON HER WAY, BUT IN THE MEANTIME THEY'LL DO WHAT EVERY DAY?
A) WALK LIKE A MAN
B) JUST LIKE ROMEO AND JULIET
C) WE'LL SING IN THE SUNSHINE
D) YOU WERE ON MY MIND

53. **1 x 1**

ANITA BRYANT RECORDED A SONG ABOUT THOSE IMITATION FLOWERS THAT ARE NO DIFFERENT THAN THE LOVE YOU HAVE FOR HER. IT'S A SONG THAT LITTLE *MARIE OSMOND* WOULD GO ON TO CHART IN THE 70'S EQUALLY AS FINE.
A) IT'S ONLY MAKE BELIEVE
B) ARTIFICIAL FLOWERS
C) PAPER ROSES
D) THE YELLOW ROSE OF TEXAS

54. **1 x 1**

SANDY POSEY, A FEMALE ARTIST, RECORDED WHAT SONG BELOW ABOUT HOW HER GENDER WERE BORN, WITH NO CHOICE ON THEIR PART, TO BE ABUSED AND UNDER THE CONTROL OF A MAN, BUT IN THE LONG RUN SHE WAS GLAD FOR IT ESPECIALLY WHEN HE GOT HOME?
A) BORN TO BE WILD
B) BORN A WOMAN
C) BORN FREE
D) GLAD ALL OVER

TOTAL POINTS. 100 x 1 = 100

POP ROCKERS BONUS

1.

THIS GROUP OF GUYS CHARTED THE FOLLOWING HIT SONGS: "LET'S LIVE FOR TODAY", "MIDNIGHT CONFESSIONS", AND "I'D WAIT A MILLION YEARS". WHO WERE THOSE BOYS?
A) CREEDENCE CLEARWATER REVIVAL
B) GARY PUCKETT AND THE UNION GAP
C) STEAM
D) THE GRASS ROOTS

2.

BOB KUBAN AND THE IN MEN RECORDED THIS SONG BELOW ABOUT THAT DECEITFUL CLOWN WHO USES GIRLS AND THEN LETS THEM DOWN, THAT HOPEFULLY ONE DAY HE'LL GET HIS OWN. CHOOSE IT BELOW.
A) PLAYBOY
B) MR BIG STUFF
C) THE CHEATER
 D) KOOL JERK

COUNTRY ROCKERS-QUIZ # 1

1. **1 x 2**

JOE SOUTH CHARTED WHICH SONG BELOW ABOUT WHAT PEOPLE LIKED TO DO?
A) GAMES PEOPLE PLAY
B) GAME OF LOVE
C) I LIKE IT LIKE THAT (PT 1)
D) SIMON SAYS

2. **1 x 2**

CHOOSE THE *BILLY JOE ROYAL* SONG ABOUT THE BAD PART OF TOWN WHERE HE WAS BORN, RAISED AND WOULD HOPEFULLY CLIMB OUT OF SOMEDAY.
A) NORTH TO ALASKA
B) DOWN IN THE BOONDOCKS
C) (SITTIN' ON) THE DOCK OF THE BAY
D) POOR SIDE OF TOWN

3. **1 x 2**

ROY CLARK, OF 'HEE HAW' FAME, RECORDED WHAT SONG BELOW ABOUT THE MEMORIES OF HIS YOUNGER DAYS?
A) YOUNG LOVE
B) YESTERDAY
C) YESTERDAY, WHEN I WAS YOUNG
D) REMEMBER THEN

4. **2 x 2**

KENNY ROGERS AND THE FIRST EDITION CHARTED THESE TWO HITS "BUT YOU KNOW I LOVE YOU" AND "RUBEN JAMES". NAME THESE TWO OTHERS BELOW. ONE, WHAT HE DIDN'T WANT RUBY TO DO THAT WOULD BE UNFAITHFUL. TWO, ABOUT THE CONDITION HE PERSONALLY NEEDED TO KNOW.
1) ______________________________
2) ______________________________

5. **1 x 2**

EDDIE ARNOLD CHARTED WHAT SONG BELOW ABOUT WANTING SOMETHING TO GO AWAY AND OFF HIS SHOULDERS WITH THOSE WORDS SHE USED TO SAY? IT'S A SONG *ELVIS* WOULD LATER RECORD.
A) MAKE THE WORLD GO AWAY
B) GO AWAY LITTLE GIRL
C) GO NOW!
D) RELEASE ME (AND LET ME LOVE AGAIN)

6. **1 x 2**

IN 1965 *ROY HEAD* CHARTED WHAT TOP NUMBER TWO HIT SONG ABOUT THE CORRECT MANNER TO HANDLE A WOMAN IF YOU WANT HER TO LOVE YOU IN RETURN? AFTERWARDS HE WOULD BECOME A FULL FLEDGED COUNTRY ARTIST.
A) TREAT HER RIGHT
B) TREAT HER LIKE A LADY
C) TREAT ME NICE
D) TAKE GOOD CARE OF MY BABY

7. **1 x 2**

WHAT WAS THAT POPULAR SONG BY *JIMMY DEAN* ABOUT A HEROIC GUY WHO WAS OVER SIX FEET TALL, SKINNY, AND YET STRONG? AN UNKNOWN GENTLE DRIFTER THAT NO ONE DARED TO MESS WITH.
A) JOHNNY ANGEL
B) SKINNY MINNIE
C) DUKE OF EARL
D) BIG BAD JOHN

8. **1 x 2**

BRENDA LEE CHARTED WHAT CLASSIC HOLIDAY SONG IN 1960 THAT IS STILL VERY POPULAR AT CHRISTMAS TIME EACH YEAR?

A) THE CHRISTMAS SONG
B) DONDE ESTA SANTA CLAUS?
C) ROCKIN' AROUND THE CHRISTMAS TREE
D) JINGLE BELL ROCK

9. **1 x 2**

WHAT WAS *BRENDA LEE'S* NICKNAME WHICH WAS ALSO THE NAME OF HER AUTOBIOGRAPHY IN 2002?

A) THE QUEEN OF SOUL
B) BOOM BOOM
C) LITTLE MISS MUFFIN
D) LITTLE MISS DYNAMITE

10. **1 x 2**

THE STATLER BROTHERS CHARTED A SONG ABOUT FLOWERS AND THAT KANGEROO FELLA. CHOOSE IT BELOW.

A) YOU DON'T BRING ME FLOWERS
B) FLOWERS ON THE WALL
C) TIP TOE THROUGH THE TULIPS WITH ME
D) WHERE HAVE ALL THE FLOWERS GONE

11. **1 x 2**

CHOOSE BELOW THIS SONGWRITER WHO HAD A BIG HIT WITH "POLK SALAD ANNIE" AND MADE HIM A ONE HIT WONDER ARTIST AS A SINGER. IT'S A SONG *ELVIS* WOULD RECORD YEARS LATER.

A) BROOK BENTON
B) TONY ORLANDO
C) BOBBY DARIN
D) TONY JOE WHITE

12. **1 x 2**

FARON YOUNG, THE COUNTRY AND WESTERN SINGER, CHARTED WHAT SONG IN 1961 WRITTEN BY *WILLIE NELSON*?

A) HELLO WALLS
B) RINGO
C) EL PASO
D) CRAZY

13. **1 x 2**

JIMMY CLANTON CHARTED THIS SONG BELOW ABOUT HIS MODERN DAY TEEN GIRL THAT HE COMPARES TO A GODDESS, HIS VERY OWN SENT FROM HEAVEN ABOVE.

A) VENUS
B) VENUS IN BLUE JEANS
C) THE MOST BEAUTIFUL GIRL
D) ISN'T SHE LOVELY

14. **1 x 2**

JEANNIE C RILEY HAD A HIT SONG ABOUT A WIDOW WHOSE LOCAL PTA OBJECTED TO HER SOCIAL ACTIVITIES AND DRESS CODE, BUT IN REALITY THEY WERE THE ONES WHO NEEDED MORAL CORRECTING. IT WOULD BE MADE INTO A MOVIE STARRING BARBARA EDEN, RONNIE COX, NANETTE FABRAY AND PAT PAULSEN IN THE LATE 70'S.

A) WITCHCRAFT
B) HARPER VALLEY P.T.A.
C) ODE TO BILLIE JOE
D) MARIA

15. **5 x 2**

NAME THESE FIVE BIG HITS BY *THE EVERLY BROTHERS* DURING THE 60'S.
ONE, ABOUT A PAINFUL ACT ONE WOULD PERFORM IN THE RAIN.
TWO, ABOUT THAT CLOWN HE DOESN'T WANT TO BE KNOWN AS ANYMORE, MORE SO SINCE THEY'RE NOT TOGETHER.
THREE, A TUNE *JERRY BUTLER* AND *BETTY EVERETT* WOULD ALSO CHART, WITH A PLEA THAT THEY'LL ALWAYS CHOOSE EACH OTHER BECAUSE WITHOUT YOU LIFE WOULD BE SO EMPTY.
FOUR, QUESTIONING WHEN WILL THEY FIND TRUE LOVE BECAUSE THEY'VE BEEN DONE WRONG, MISTREATED AND LEFT BROKEN HEARTED EVERYTIME, A SONG *LINDA RONSTADT* WOULD ALSO RECORD IN THE MID 70'S.
FIVE, WISHING THAT SHE'LL FOOT RIGHT ON BACK TO HIM.

1) ______________________
2) ________________
3) ______________
4) __________________________
5) ________________

16. **1 x 2**

THIS TOP OF THE CHARTS HIT SONG BY *MARTY ROBBINS* DEALS WITH A COWBOY IN LOVE WITH A MEXICAN MAIDEN AND HOW HE WOULD END UP DYING TRAGICALLY AT THE END OF THE SONG. CHOOSE THAT HIT NAMED AFTER A GREAT CITY IN THE STATE OF TEXAS.

A) SAN ANTONIO ROSE
B) DEEP IN THE HEART OF TEXAS
C) EL PASO
D) YELLOW ROSE OF TEXAS

17. **1 x 2**

SKEETER DAVIS, THE FEMALE SINGER, HAD A POPULAR NUMBER TWO HIT SONG ON THE CHARTS ABOUT THE WORLD WE LIVED IN, AND THE POSSIBILITY OF ITS DESTRUCTION FOREVER. CHOOSE THAT POPULAR HIT BELOW.

A) THE END
B) MAKE THE WORLD GO AWAY
C) EVE OF DESTRUCTION
D) THE END OF THE WORLD

18. **4 x 2**

NAME THESE FOUR HITS BY *GLEN CAMPBELL*.
ONE, ABOUT THAT TOWN IN TEXAS AND A GIRL HE LEFT BEHIND.
TWO, ABOUT HIS ARRIVAL IN THE CITY OF PHOENIX, THAT TWO YEARS LATER *ISAAC HAYES* WOULD DO A FINE SOULFUL VERSION OF IN RAP FORM.
THREE, ABOUT A CERTAIN LINEMAN IN NEED OF THAT GIRL FOR ALL TIME.
FOUR, ABOUT USING SOME KINDNESS.

1) ______________
2) _________________________________
3) ____________________
4) ___________________________

19. **1 x 2**

JOHNNY HORTON RECORDED THE THEME SONG FOR A JOHN WAYNE MOVIE CONCERNING THE GOLD RUSH UP IN ALASKA, THAT CO-STARRED STEWART GRANGER, ERNIE KOVACS AND FABIAN. WHAT WAS THAT THEME SONG?

A) ALL THE GOLD IN CALIFORNIA
B) DIAMONDS AND PEARLS
C) TREASURE OF LOVE
D) NORTH TO ALASKA

20. **1 x 2**

JOHNNY HORTON ALSO CHARTED A MOVIE THEME SONG IN 1960 ABOUT A GERMAN NAVY VESSEL CALLED THE BISMARCK, WHICH HAD TO BE DESTROYED AT ANY COST STARRING A CAST OF BRITISH ACTORS. NAME IT.

____

21. **3 x 2**

JOHNNY CASH, THE FAMED COUNTRY SINGER/SONGWRITER, AND GUITARIST CHARTED BELOW THESE THREE BIG HITS IN THE 60'S.
ONE, ABOUT SOMEBODY NAMED SUE WHO WAS FORCED TO GROW UP TOUGH.
TWO, ABOUT A CERTAIN FIRE.
THREE, ABOUT A MEAN PRISON FULL OF BLUES.
NAME THEM.

1) __________________________
2) _____________________
3) ______________________________

22. **2 x 2**

NAME THESE TWO BIG HITS BY *ROGER MILLER,* THE VERY POPULAR SINGER, SONGWRITER AND TV PERSONALITY KNOWN FOR HIS NOVELTY HIT SONGS.
ONE, ABOUT A CERTAIN KING WHO LACKED CIGARETTES AND A WHOLE LOT MORE BOUND FOR MAINE.
TWO, WHAT THEY SHOULD DO WITH A ROPE TO THAT SON OF A GUN.

1) _________________________
2) ________________

23. **1 x 2**

ROGER MILLER HAD THREE OTHER HITS BELOW. WHICH ONE WAS **NOT** HIS?
A) ENGINE ENGINE # 9
B) CHUG-A-LUG
C) DUKE OF EARL
D) ENGLAND SWINGS

24. **1 x 2**

"ODE TO BILLIE JOE" WAS A CHART TOPPER RECORDED IN 1967. IN 1976 IT WOULD BE MADE INTO A MOVIE OF THE SAME NAME STARRING ROBBY BENSON AND GLYNNIS O'CONNOR. WHO WAS THE FEMALE ARTIST RESPONSIBLE FOR IT?
A) BRENDA LEE
B) PEGGY LEE
C) CONNIE FRANCIS
D) BOBBIE GENTRY

25. **4 x 2**

NAME THESE FOUR POPULAR SONGS BY *PATSY CLINE* BEFORE HER UNTIMELY DEATH IN AN AIRPLANE CRASH ON MARCH 5, 1963.
ONE, ABOUT WHAT HAPPENS TO HER WHEN SHE FALLS.
TWO, WHAT SHE'S GOT THAT I HAVEN'T.
THREE, ABOUT CERTAIN DREAMS WHICH WAS ALSO THE NAME OF THE MOVIE OF HER LIFE STORY, STARRING JESSICA LANGE, ED HARRIS AND JOHN GOODMAN.
FOUR, ABOUT WHAT SHE WAS, MESMERIZED AND IN LOVE, WRITTEN AND RECORDED BY *WILLIE NELSON*, ANOTHER COUNTRY SINGER/SONGWRITER.

1) __________________________
2) ______________________
3) ___________________
4) _____________

26. **8 x 2**

NAME THESE EIGHT POPULAR SAD LOVE SONGS BY *LITTLE BRENDA LEE*.
ONE, HER BIG APOLOGETIC SONG ABOUT THE WRONG SHE COMMITTED AND HOPING YOU WOULD ACCEPT.
TWO, ABOUT THAT HEARTBREAKER WHO'S PROBABLY MADE HER ONE OF THE BIGGEST FOOLS OF THEM ALL.
THREE, ABOUT BREAKING THE NEWS GRADUALLY SO AS NOT TO HURT HER SO BADLY. A SONG *JUICE NEWTON* WOULD ALSO GO ON TO RECORD IN THE 80'S.
FOUR, WHAT SHE'S BEEN EVER SINCE YOU LEFT, LIVING IN MISERY AND WITH ONLY MEMORIES.
FIVE, WHISPERING WHAT IN HER EARS THAT SHE LIKED TO HEAR?
SIX, WHAT SHE WANTED FROM THAT SOMEONE DESTINED FOR HER.
SEVEN, A UNIQUE BOOK THAT DESCRIBES HER HEARTBREAK AFFAIR WITH COLORS, FROM GRAY, BLUE, GREEN AND GONE.
EIGHT, WHAT SHE KNEW THAT WAS UNAVOIDABLE BECAUSE YOU CHANGED AND OF THAT OTHER YOU HAD FOUND.

1) ____________
2) ____________
3) ____________________________
4) ___________________
5) ___________________
6) ________________________
7) ___________________
8) _____________

27. **1 x 2**

BRENDA LEE CHARTED FOUR OTHER HITS BELOW. WHICH ONE WAS **NOT** HERS?
A) DOWNTOWN
B) EMOTIONS
C) YOU CAN DEPEND ON ME
D) EVERYBODY LOVES ME BUT YOU
E) THAT'S ALL YOU GOTTA DO

28. **1 x 2**

JOHNNY BURNETTE RECORDED THIS POPULAR SONG BELOW ABOUT HIS FANTASIZING, WHICH HE WAS GONNA KEEP ON DOING TIL IT TURNED OUT SO TRUE. IT WOULD BE HIS FIRST MAJOR HIT AND CATAPULT HIM INTO STARDOM.
A) IT'S ONLY MAKE BELIEVE
B) GET OFF MY CLOUD
C) CALIFORNIA DREAMIN'
D) DREAMIN'

29. **1 x 2**

JOHNNY BURNETTE CHARTED ANOTHER ABOUT A GIRL WHO'S SIXTEEN, GORGEOUS AND TOTALLY HIS. IT'S A SONG *RINGO STARR* WOULD ALSO GO ON TO RECORD IN 1974 AFTER THE BREAKUP OF *THE BEATLES*.
A) HAPPY BIRTHDAY, SWEET SIXTEEN
B) YOU'RE SIXTEEN
C) SWEET LITTLE SIXTEEN
D) MY GIRL

TOTAL POINTS. **50 x 2 = 100**

COUNTRY ROCKERS-BONUS

1.

CLAUDE KING HAD A HIT WITH THIS MOUNTAIN TALE ABOUT A GIRL WITH LIPS SWEETER THAN HONEY WHOM HE WANTED TO POSSESS BUT WOULD HAVE TO FACE HER GUN TOTING, KNIFE WEILDING, MEAN OLD DAD. WHAT WAS THAT HIT?
A) MOUNTAIN'S HIGH
B) MOUNTAIN OF LOVE
C) KISSES SWEETER THAN WINE
D) WOLVERTON MOUNTAIN **60'S**

ROCKERS-QUIZ # 1

1. **5 x 4**

THIS GROUP WITH *JOHN SEBASTIAN* IN LEAD HAD THESE TWO BIG HITS, "YOU DIDN'T HAVE TO BE SO NICE" AND "DAYDREAM". NAME THE GROUP *JOHN* FRONTED WITH AND THESE FOUR OTHER HITS BELOW, NUMBERS TWO THROUGH FIVE.

ONE, GROUP NAME.
TWO, A SUMMER TITLED SONG WITH THE SOUNDS OF TRAFFIC JAMS IN THE CITY.
THREE, QUESTIONING YOUR BELIEF IN MAGIC.
FOUR, QUESTIONING YOUR DECISION MAKING.
FIVE, A SONG *JOE COCKER* WOULD ALSO GO ON TO RECORD ABOUT WHAT HE TOLD HIS DARLING.
NAME THEM.

1) ______________________________
2) ______________________________
3) __________________________________
4) ____?
5) ______________________________

2. **1 x 4**

JOEY DEE & THE STARLITERS RECORDED WHAT POPULAR DANCE NUMBER IN 1961 WHERE YOU CONTINUOUSLY SHAKE IT ALL AROUND AND UP AND DOWN? IT WOULD BE A CHART TOPPER AND PARTIALLY NAMED AFTER THAT FAMOUS LOUNGE IN MID MANHATTAN?

A) LET'S TWIST AGAIN
B) PEPPERMINT TWIST (PT 1)
C) TWISTIN' THE NIGHT AWAY
D) TWIST AND SHOUT

3. **1 x 4**

IN 1961 *THE DOVELLS* CHARTED WHAT BIG DANCE HIT WHICH GAVE THEM THEIR PREMIER STARDOM WHEN IT CLIMBED TO THE NUMBER TWO SPOT ON THE CHARTS?

A) MASHED POTATO TIME
B) FINGER POPPIN' TIME
C) BRISTOL STOMP
D) PEPPERMINT TWIST (PT 1)

4. **1 x 4**

THE DOVELLS RECORDED ANOTHER ABOUT WHAT YOU COULDN'T DO BECAUSE EVERYBODY THERE WAS DANCING AND GROOVING AND NO REASON TO BE IDLE. WHAT WAS THAT OTHER HIT BELOW?

A) TOSSIN' AND TURNIN'
B) YOU BETTER SIT DOWN KIDS
C) YOU CAN'T HURRY LOVE
D) YOU CAN'T SIT DOWN

5. **1 x 4**

"1-2-3" WAS A BIG NUMBER TWO HIT SONG ON THE CHARTS FOR THE FORMER LEAD SINGER OF *THE DOVELLS* ABOUT HOW EASY IT IS TO FALL IN LOVE. WHO WAS THAT FORMER LEAD SINGER?

A) JIMMY HART
B) JOHNNY MAESTRO
C) LEN BARRY
D) JACKIE WILSON

6. **1 x 4**

BOB FULLER FOUR HAD A HIT WITH WHAT SONG BELOW ABOUT THEIR FIGHT WITH THE LAW AND THE OBVIOUS OUTCOME, ANOTHER WIN FOR THE GOOD GUYS?
A) NOWHERE TO RUN
B) I FOUGHT THE LAW
C) WE'RE A WINNER
D) THE GOOD, THE BAD AND THE UGLY

7. **1 x 4**

RONNY & THE DAYTONAS CHARTED WHAT CAR TITLED SONG BELOW IN 1964 WHICH WAS THE BIGGEST OF THEIR BRIEF CAREER?
A) G-T-O
B) LITTLE RED CORVETTE
C) FAST CAR
D) PINK CADILLAC

8. **5 x 4**

THIS POPULAR ALL MALE GROUP WITH *GARY* IN LEAD HAD A BIG HIT WITH THE SONG "OVER YOU". NAME THEM, AND FOUR OF THEIR OTHER HITS BELOW, NUMBERS TWO THROUGH FIVE
ONE, GROUP'S FULL NAME.
TWO, ABOUT A CERTAIN WOMAN HE KNEW WAS NOT BEING FAITHFUL.
THREE, ABOUT A YOUNGSTER HE WANTS TOTALLY OUT OF HIS MIND BECAUSE SHE'S QUITE TOO YOUNG FOR HIM.
FOUR, GIVING THIS CERTAIN LADY AN ULTIMATUM LIKE *ELVIS* ONCE DID.
FIVE, ABOUT A GIRL WHO'S GROWN UP AND PUT AWAY HER CHILDISH THINGS TO BECOME A WOMAN.
1) ____________________________________
2) ________________
3) ______________
4) ____________________
5) ______________________________

9. **1 x 4**

PAUL REVERE AND THE RAIDERS CHARTED THESE THREE HITS BELOW. WHICH ONE WAS **NOT** THEIRS?
A) KICKS
B) HUNGRY
C) GOOD THING
D) MIDNIGHT SPECIAL

10. **1 x 4**

IN 1964 *THE RIP CHORDS* RECORDED WHAT SONG ABOUT A CAR RACE THAT INVOLVED THEIR AUTOMOBILE THAT COULD EASILY SHUT OUT THE OPPONENTS WHICH INCLUDED STINGRAYS AND XKE'S ONCE THEY SHIFTED INTO GEAR?
A) MUSTANG SALLY
B) HEY LITTLE COBRA
C) FUN, FUN, FUN
D) BEEP BEEP

11. **1 x 4**

THE OUTSIDERS, AN ALL MALE GROUP WITH *SONNY GERACI* IN LEAD, ACHIEVED THEIR INITIAL STARDOM IN 1966 BY RECORDING WHAT SONG ABOUT TIME AND WHAT IT WOULDN'T ALLOW THEM TO DO?
A) TIME IS ON MY SIDE
B) TIME OF THE SEASON
C) TIME HAS COME TODAY
D) TIME WON'T LET ME

12. **1 x 4**

JAN & DEAN RECORDED A SURFING HIT SONG, A NUMBER ONE, THAT HAD *BRIAN WILSON* OF *THE BEACH BOYS* AS A BACK-UP SINGER.

A) SURF CITY
B) CALIFORNIA SUN
C) SURFIN' U.S.A.
D) SURFIN' SAFARI

13. **1 x 4**

JAN & DEAN CHARTED ANOTHER ABOUT THAT LADY, A/K/A GRANNY, FROM PASADENA WHO WAS A TERROR ON THE ROAD. WHAT WAS THAT OTHER HIT?

A) HIT THE ROAD JACK
B) LADY GODIVA
C) THE LITTLE OLD LADY (FROM PASADENA)
D) NADINE (IS IT YOU?)

14. **1 x 4**

THE FIRE BALLS, LESS *JIMMY GILMER*, CHARTED A SONG ABOUT A CERTAIN ALCOHOLIC BEVERAGE THAT HAD A TERRIBLE HOLD ON THEM WHICH KEPT THEM FROM GETTING HOME. CHOOSE IT BELOW.

A) RED RED WINE
B) BOTTLE OF WINE
C) SCOTCH AND SODA
D) LOVE ON THE ROCKS

15. **1 x 4**

THE SHADOWS OF KNIGHT RECORDED THIS GIRL TITLED SONG IN WHICH THEY WOULD SPELL HER NAME THROUGH THE LYRICS OF THE SONG. CHOOSE THAT POPULAR HIT THAT *THE CADILLACS* SANG ABOUT IN THE 50'S AND *LAURA BRANIGAN* WOULD IN THE 80'S.

A) MARIA
B) RONNIE
C) GLORIA
D) DARLING LORRAINE

16. **1 x 4**

WHO WAS **NOT** A MEMBER OF *THE RASCALS,* FORMERLY KNOWN AS *THE YOUNG RASCALS*?

A) FELIX CAVALIERE
B) JOHNNY MAESTRO
C) GENE CORNISH
D) DINO DANELLI
E) EDDIE BRIGATI

17. **1 x 4**

THIS YOUNG MALE GROUP CONSISTING OF THREE BROTHERS, ONE COUSIN AND ONE FRIEND OUT OF CALIFORNIA WERE ALREADY AND STILL WERE BIG STARS WITH THE ARRIVAL OF THE BRITISH INVASION. WHO WERE THOSE BOYS?

A) THE BEACH BOYS
B) THE FOUR SEASONS
C) JAY & THE AMERICANS
D) THE RIGHTEOUS BROTHERS

TOTAL POINTS. **25 x 4 = 100**

ROCKERS-QUIZ # 2

1. **2 x 1**

JEFFERSON AIRPLANE, WITH *GRACE SLICK* IN LEAD, RECORDED THESE TWO BIG HITS BELOW.
ONE, ABOUT A CERTAIN COLORED RABBIT.
TWO, ABOUT WHAT EVERYBODY NEEDS AND IF YOU DON'T HAVE IT, YOU BETTER GO FIND ONE.
NAME THEM.

1) ________________

2) ____________________

2. **1 x 1**

THE KNICKERBOCKERS WHO SOUNDED LIKE 'THE FAB FOUR' IN THIS SONG BELOW, DEALT ABOUT A GIRL WHO WAS SO UNTRUSTWORTHY WITH HER CONSTANTING FIBBING. CHOOSE THAT HIT BELOW.

A) YOU CHEATED
B) HOW CAN I BE SURE
C SUSPICION
D) LIES

3. **1 x 1**

THE 'STONE PONEYS' RECORDED THE SONG "DIFFERENT DRUM" IN 1967. CHOOSE THE FEMALE LEAD SINGER BELOW WHO WOULD GAIN HER PREMIER STARDOM AS A RESULT OF THIS RECORDING.

A) TINA TURNER
B) LINDA RONSTADT
C) DOLLY PARTON
D) JANIS JOPLIN

4. **1 x 1**

THE STANDELLS, ANOTHER ONE HIT WONDER GROUP, CHARTED BELOW THEIR ONLY MAJOR HIT OF THEIR CAREER THAT DESCRIBED HOW UNFIT THE SAINT JAMES RIVER WATER WAS.

A) DIRTY WATER
B) BLACK WATER
C) PAINT IT BLACK
D) PLEASE COME TO BOSTON

5. **3 x 1**

NAME THESE THREE BIG HITS BY *THE BUCKINGHAMS* THAT WERE ALL CHARTED IN 1967.
ONE, PLAYING THEIR TUNE.
TWO, THEIR VERBAL RENDITION OF A *CANNONBALL ADDERLY* BIG INSTRUMENTAL HIT ABOUT THAT FINE LOOKING GIRL WHO CAN LOVE HIM LIKE NO OTHER AND KNOCK HIM OUT WITH PASSION, LORD HAVE MERCY.
THREE, A DRAG FEELING WHEN SHE BIDS HIM FAREWELL.

1) _______________________________________

2) _________,__________,_________

3) __________________

6. **1 x 1**

IN 1964 *THE RIVIERAS*, ALSO A ONE HIT WONDER GROUP, RECORDED WHAT BIG HIT THAT HAD EXCELLENT BACKGROUND MUSIC ABOUT A PLACE WHERE THEY BELONG, HEADED FOR, AND THE GIRLS WERE THE MOST?

A) CALIFORNIA GIRLS
B) CALIFORNIA SUN
C) CALIFORNIA DREAMIN'
D) SURF CITY

7. **1 x 1**

? QUESTION MARK & THE MYSTERIANS, AN ALL MALE ROCK GROUP, CHARTED THIS SONG BELOW ABOUT TEARS?
A) AS TEARS GO BY
B) 96 TEARS
C) LONELY TEARDROPS
D) THE TRACKS OF MY TEARS

8. **1 x 1**

WHAT BLACK 'HARD ROCK' MALE ARTIST WOULD BE THE LAST PERFORMER AT 'THE WOODSTOCK FESTIVAL' AND DIE AT AN EARLY AGE DUE TO A DRUG OVERDOSE? HE WAS WELL KNOWN FOR HIS ELECTRICFYING GUITAR SKILLS.
A) RICHIE HAVENS
B) SAM COOKE
C) JIMI HENDRIX
D) JOHNNY NASH

9. **1 x 1**

THE ARTIST ABOVE RECORDED THREE OF THE FOUR SONGS BELOW. WHICH ONE WAS **NOT** HIS?
A) PURPLE HAZE
B) WILD THING
C) STAR SPANGLED BANNER
D) HOLLY HOLY

10. **5 x 1**

NAME THESE FIVE SONGS BY *JOHN FOGERTY* IN LEAD WITH *CREEDENCE CLEARWATER REVIVAL* DURING THE 60'S.
ONE, A SONG *IKE & TINA TURNER* WOULD ALSO RECORD ABOUT MARY, THE RIVERBOAT.
TWO, ABOUT A CERTAIN MOON RISING THAT INDICATES TERRIBLE WEATHER IS UPON US.
THREE, ABOUT THE STREET CORNER WHERE THE BOYS WERE JAMMING.
FOUR, ABOUT A WELL OFF SON THAT HE'S NOT.
FIVE, ABOUT THAT GIRL SUSIE AND THE WAY SHE WALKS AND TALKS, PART 1.
1) ________________
2) ______________________
3) ________________________
4) ______________________
5) ______________________**(PART 1)**

11. **3 x 1**

NAME THESE THREE BIG HITS BY THE GROUP *BLOOD, SWEAT & TEARS* WITH *DAVID CLAYTON THOMAS* IN LEAD.
ONE, SOMEONE WHO ENTERED HIS LIFE AND BROUGHT HIM HAPPINESS.
TWO, ABOUT A WHEEL THAT GOES UP AND DOWN.
THREE, ABOUT NOT BEING AFRAID TO DIE BUT HOPING IT WILL BE HARMLESS.
1) ____________________________________
2) ______________________
3) ______________________

12. **1 x 1**

"JUDY IN DISGUISE (WITH GLASSES)" WAS A CHART TOPPER BY WHAT BAND IN 1967 THAT WOULD ALSO BE THEIR ONE AND ONLY?
A) LITTLE ANTHONY AND THE IMPERIALS
B) BROOKLYN BRIDGE
C) JOHN FRED & HIS PLAYBOY BAND
D) RANDY & THE RAINBOWS

13. **1 x 1**

THE KINGSMEN HAD THIS ROCK 'N ROLL CLASSIC HIT THAT WOULD BARELY MISS REACHING THE TOP AND LAND ON THE NUMBER TWO SPOT. IN THE LATE 70'S IT WOULD BE FEATURED IN THE MOVIE SOUNDTRACK 'ANIMAL HOUSE' STARRING JOHN BELUSHI, TIM MATHESON, DONALD SUTHERLAND AND KEVIN BACON. WHAT WAS THAT CLASSIC HIT?

A) FOOTLOOSE
B) BLACK IS BLACK
C) GOING TO A GO-GO
D) LOUIE LOUIE

14. **1 x 1**

CRAZY ELEPHANT WERE BEST KNOWN FOR CHARTING THIS SONG ABOUT SOMETHING GOOD. IT WAS WHAT THEY DESPERATELY WANTED. NOW GIMME THE NAME OF THAT SONG BELOW.

A) GIMME SOME LOVIN'
B) GIMME GIMME GOOD LOVIN'
C) GIMME LITTLE SIGN
D) GOOD LOVIN'

15. **1 x 1**

THE ALL MALE ROCK BAND, *SYNDICATE OF SOUND,* CHARTED WHAT SONG BELOW ABOUT A CERTAIN GIRL, WHICH WAS THEIR ONLY MAJOR CLAIM TO FAME SONG AND PUT THEM IN THE CATEGORY AS A ONE HIT WONDER GROUP?

A) A GIRL LIKE YOU
B) YOUNG GIRL
C) GIRL, YOU'LL BE A WOMAN SOON
D) LITTLE GIRL

16. **1 x 1**

THE FENDERMEN, CONSISTING *OF* A MALE DUO, HAD A BIG HIT WITH THIS SONG ABOUT A CERTAIN BLUES THAT HAD THEM ALSO AS A ONE HIT WONDER GROUP. CHOOSE THAT HIT BELOW.

A) THE THRILL IS GONE
B) SINGING THE BLUES
C) HEARTACHES BY THE NUMBERS
D) MULE SKINNER BLUES

17. **1 x 1**

CANNED HEAT, THE ALL MALE ROCK BAND, RECORDED THIS COUNTRY SONG THAT WOULD BE FEATURED IN 'THE WOODSTOCK FESTIVAL' IN 1969. WHAT WAS THAT FESTIVAL HIT?

A) WITH A LITTLE HELP FROM MY FRIENDS
B) GOING UP THE COUNTRY
C) THIS LAND IS YOUR LAND
D) I'M GOING HOME

18. **3 x 1**

NAME THESE THREE CHARTED HITS BY *THE TURTLES*.
ONE, A *BOB DYLAN* TUNE THAT ADAMANTLY EXPRESSED THAT HE WASN'T THE ONE TO BE MANIPULATED IN ANY WHICH WAY SHE SAW FIT.
TWO, ABOUT THE JOY OF BEING A TWOSOME WITH THE ONLY GIRL HE LOVES THAT NO OTHER COULD EVER DO.
THREE, ABOUT WHO THAT GIRL WOULD RATHER STAY WITH.

1) ______________________
2) __________________
3) ____________________________

19. **2 x 1**

THIS POPULAR MALE ROCK GROUP HAD THE FOLLOWING HITS: "PEOPLE ARE STRANGE", "HELLO, I LOVE YOU", "LOVE ME TWO TIMES", AND "TOUCH ME". NAME THEM, AND THEIR FIRST MAJOR HIT THAT WOULD RACE TO THE TOP OF THE CHARTS IN 1967 AND GIVE THEM THEIR INITIAL STARDOM. THE SONG WOULD ALSO BE RECORDED BY *JOSE FELICIANO* THE FOLLOWING YEAR.

1) ____________

2) ____________________

20. **4 x 1**

THREE DOG NIGHT CHARTED THESE FOUR POPULAR HITS IN THE 60'S.
ONE, ABOUT SOMETHING HARD, WHICH WAS FEATURED IN THE OFF BROADWAY MUSICAL 'HAIR'.
TWO, ABOUT A CERTAIN NUMBER ALL BY ITSELF.
THREE, ABOUT THAT CERTAIN GUY ON HIS WAY IN.
FOUR, THEIR TENDER AND SOULFUL RENDITION OF AN *OTIS REDDING* SONG.
NAME THEM.

1) ______________________

2) _____

3) ______________

4) ____________________________

21. **1 x 1**

"BURNING BRIDGES" WAS AN ATTEMPT TO FORGET A GIRL BY BURNING HER LETTERS AND MOVING FAR AWAY AND CHARTED BY WHAT ARTIST BELOW WHO WAS JUST AS POPULAR IN THE 50'S?

A) PAT BOONE
B) CONWAY TWITTY
C) JACK SCOTT
D) SIMON & GARFUNKEL

22. **1 x 1**

THE BOX TOPS HAD THIS BIG NUMBER TWO HIT SONG THAT REMINDED HIM OF THE LOVE HE ONCE HAD AND HOW ITS MEMORY DRIVES HIM TO TEARS. WHAT WAS THAT NUMBER TWO HIT SONG?

A) CRY LIKE A BABY
B) CRY BABY
C) CRYING TIME
D) REMEMBER THEN

23. **1 x 1**

THE BOX TOPS CHARTED ANOTHER THAT *THE ARBORS* AND *JOE COCKER* WOULD ALSO RECORD ABOUT A CERTAIN CORRESPONDENCE FROM HIS BABE WHICH STATED SHE COULDN'T GO ON WITHOUT HIM. CHOOSE THAT TRIPLE HITTER BELOW.

A) TELL HIM
B) THE LETTER
C) I KNOW (YOU DON'T LOVE ME NO MORE)
D) I'VE GOTTA GET A MESSAGE TO YOU

24. **1 x 1**

THE POPULAR HARD ROCK BAND *STEPPENWOLF* RECORDED THIS BIG HIT ABOUT WHAT THEY WERE BORN TO DO, LOOKING FOR EXCITEMENT, THAT WOULD BE THEIR FIRST AND BIGGEST AND GAIN THEM STAR POWER. WHAT WAS THAT FIRST HIT?

A) WILD ONE
B) WILD THING
C) WILD WORLD
D) BORN TO BE WILD

25. **1 x 1**

STEPPENWOLF RECORDED ANOTHER ABOUT A MAGIC ITEM THAT HE WANTED TO PUT THAT LITTLE GIRL ON.

A) DO YOU BELIEVE IN MAGIC
B) MAGIC CARPET RIDE
C) PUFF THE MAGIC DRAGON
D) ABRACADABRA

26. **7 x 1**

NAME THESE SEVEN BIG HITS BY *JAY & THE AMERICANS*.
ONE, ABOUT THAT TOWN FLIRT THAT BELONGS TO JOSE, SOUTH OF THE BORDER.
TWO, ABOUT THAT PLACE OF PLENTY WHERE EVEN A POOR BOY HAS A CHANCE TO REACH THE SKIES AND BECOME SOMEONE IMPORTANT, ORIGINALLY PLANNED TO BE CHARTED BY *THE DRIFTERS* BUT SECOND THOUGHTS OF THE SONG MEANING WAS GIVEN TO *JAY* INSTEAD.
THREE, ABOUT CLOSING THE DOOR AND DISCARDING THE KEY IN ORDER TO KISS AND DO MUCH MORE.
FOUR, THEIR VERSION OF *THE DRIFTERS* SONG ABOUT MAGIC WHEN HE KISSED AND HELD HER CLOSE.
FIVE, WHAT SHE EMOTIONALLY DID AFTER HE INFORMED HER THAT THEIR ROMANCE WAS OVER BECAUSE HE HAD FOUND ANOTHER.
SIX, ANOTHER REMAKE HIT, THIS TIME OF *ROY ORBISON'S* ABOUT WHAT HE WAS DOING BECAUSE OF YOUR ACTIONS, LEAVING HIM ALONE AND FOR GOOD.
SEVEN, ABOUT A CERTAIN CARA GIRL WHO HE'LL LOVE FOR ETERNITY.

1) ______________________________
2) ___________________
3) ____
4) _______________________
5) _______________
6) ____________
7) _______________

27. **1 x 1**

JAY & THE AMERICANS ALSO HAD TWO OF THE THREE HITS BELOW. WHICH ONE UNFORTUNATELY WAS **NOT** THEIRS?

A) SUNDAY AND ME
B) ON BROADWAY
C) SOME ENCHANTED EVENING

28. **2 x 1**

THE CANADIAN GROUP, *THE GUESS WHO*, WITH *BURTON CUMMINGS* IN LEAD CHARTED THESE TWO BIG HITS BELOW DURING THE 60'S.
ONE, ABOUT WHAT HE'S SEEN THAT BROUGHT TEARS TO HIS EYES BECAUSE SHE BROKE HIS HEART AND HE KNEW NO ONE COULD EVER REPLACE HER.
TWO, WHAT SHE WAS DOING THAT NOT ONLY SURPRISED HIM BUT LEFT HIM IN A WORLD OF PAIN.
NAME THEM.

1) _________________
2) ____________

29. **1 x 1**

JIMMY GILMER AND THE FIREBALLS RECORDED THIS TOP OF THE CHARTS HIT SONG ABOUT A CERTAIN COFFEEHOUSE THE OTHER SIDE OF THE TRACKS. WHAT WAS THAT CHART TOPPER?

A) SUGAR, SUGAR
B) BREAD AND BUTTER
C) WORKING MY WAY BACK TO YOU
D) SUGAR SHACK

30. **1 x 1**

"DEVIL WITH A BLUE DRESS ON & GOOD GOLLY MISS MOLLY", "SOCK IT TO ME-BABY", AND "JENNY TAKE A RIDE" WERE ALL CHARTED BY WHAT MALE GROUP BELOW?

A) TOMMY JAMES AND THE SHONDELLS
B) THE FOUR SEASONS
C) MITCH RYDER AND THE DETROIT WHEELS
D) THE KINGSMEN

31. **15 x 1**

NAME THESE FIFTEEN POPULAR HITS BY *THE BEACH BOYS*.
ONE, ABOUT WHAT HE DOES IN HIS CAR TO MOVE AROUND.
TWO, THEIR BIG SURFING THROUGHOUT THE COUNTRY HIT SONG.
THREE, A TRIPLE FUN TITLED SONG UNTIL SHE LOSES HER T-BIRD.
FOUR, ABOUT A GIRL NAMED RHONDA WHO WOULD COME TO HIS RESCUE TO FORGET THAT OTHER GIRL.
FIVE, ABOUT THEIR CALIFORNIA BABES, SECOND TO NONE, THROUGHOUT THE WORLD.
SIX, ABOUT CERTAIN VIBRATIONS THAT SHE GENERATES AND WANTING THEM TO OCCUR CONTINOUSLY BECAUSE THEY FEEL SO GOOD.
SEVEN, ABOUT THE BIG SAFARI THEY WERE TAKING YOU ON, STARTING FROM HAWAII.
EIGHT, ABOUT A SURFER BABE THAT HE LOVES AND WANTS TO TAKE WHEREVER HE GOES.
NINE, ABOUT THE SAILING SHIP JOHN B. AND THE TRIP HE WANTED TO PUT AN END TO BY RETURNING HOME.
TEN, THEIR VERSION OF *THE REGENTS* HIT SONG ABOUT A GIRL NAMED BARBARA RECORDED LIVE AND THAT HAD *JAN*, OF *JAN & DEAN*, SINGING ALONG SIDE.
ELEVEN, WOULDN'T IT BE WHAT, LIVING TOGETHER AND SO HAPPILY.
TWELVE, ABOUT BEING TRUE TO YOUR ALMA MATER.
THIRTEEN, ABOUT A ROOM.
FOURTEEN, THEIR TRIPLE DANCE TITLED HIT SONG THAT THEY LOVED TO DO.
FIFTEEN, ABOUT HOW ONLY THE ALMIGHTY COULD EVER KNOW THE OUTCOME OF LIFE WITHOUT HER.

1) ________________
2) ________________
3) ______,_______,_______
4) ________________
5) ________________
6) ________________
7) ________________
8) ________________
9) ________________
10) ________________
11) ________________________
12) ______________________________
13) _____________
14) _______, _________,_________
15) ___________________

32. **1 x 1**

THE HUMAN BEINZ, A ROCK BAND OUT OF OHIO, RECORDED WHAT SONG IN 1968 THAT WOULD BE THEIR ONLY MAJOR HIT ABOUT NO ONE ABLE TO SHINGALING, SKATE OR BOOGALOO LIKE YOU KNOW WHO?

A) ONLY YOU (AND YOU ALONE)
B) NOBODY BUT ME
C) LAND OF 1000 DANCES
 D) MUSTANG SALLY

33. **1 x 1**

OHIO EXPRESS RECORDED THE BIGGEST HIT OF THEIR CAREER WITH THIS SONG ABOUT SOMETHING GOOD IN THEIR TUMMY. NAME THEIR TRIPLE TITLED YUMMY HIT SONG.

________, ________, ________

34. **2 x 1**

THE COWSILLS, A FAMILY GROUP ACT, CHARTED THESE TWO BIG HITS BELOW THAT WOULD EACH OCCUPY THE NUMBER TWO SPOT ON THE CHARTS.
ONE, ABOUT A FLOWER GIRL IN THE RAIN WHO MADE HIM SO HAPPY.
TWO, A SONG FEATURED IN AN OFF BROADWAY MUSICAL OF THE SAME NAME DURING THE HIPPY ERA WHERE EVERYONE POSSESSED LONG SLICKED HAIR.
NAME THEM.

1) ________________________________

2) ________

35. **1 x 1**

THE MCCOYS CHARTED A SONG ABOUT A GIRL NAMED SLOOPY THAT HE'S IN LOVE WITH, WHICH WOULD REACH THE TOP OF THE CHARTS. IT WAS A RE-MAKE OF *THE VIBRATIONS*, AKA, *THE MARATHONS,* WHO CHARTED "PEANUT BUTTER" IN THE EARLY 60'S. NAME THIS DOUBLE HITTER.

____

36. **1 x 1**

THE MCCOYS ALSO HAD ANOTHER, THEIR RENDITION OF A *PEGGY LEE* SONG ABOUT WHAT CAUSES THE BODY TEMPERATURE TO RISE. NAME IT BELOW.

A) 98.6
B) GOOD LOVIN'
C) FEVER
D) HEATWAVE

37. **1 x 1**

BLUES MAGOOS, ALSO A ONE HIT WONDER GROUP, RECORDED WHAT SONG ABOUT NOT HAVING ACHIEVED THEIR GOALS AS OF YET BECAUSE NOTHING'S GONNA HOLD THEM DOWN FOREVER?

A) AIN'T NO MOUNTAIN HIGH ENOUGH
B) HALF WAY TO PARADISE
C) KING OF THE ROAD
D) (WE AIN'T GOT) NOTHIN' YET

38. **1 x 1**

THE HOMBRES HAD THEIR ONE AND ONLY CLAIM TO FAME SONG ABOUT ALLOWING SOMETHING TO OCCUR, AND ALL THE WAY AT THAT. WHAT WAS THAT CLAIM TO FAME SONG?

A) LET'S HANG ON
B) LET IT OUT (LET IT ALL HANG OUT)
C) LET IT BE
D) LET'S GO GET STONED

39. **1 x 1**

THE MUSIC EXPLOSION, THE ROCK BAND, ARE BEST REMEMBERED FOR WHAT TOP NUMBER TWO HIT SONG THAT WAS ALSO THEIR ONLY MAJOR RECORDING ABOUT WHAT YOU NEED WHEN YOU'RE DOWN IN ORDER TO PICK YOURSELF UP?

A) WOMAN'S GOT SOUL
B) LITTLE BIT O' SOUL
C) (YOU'RE MY) SOUL AND INSPIRATION
D) GET ON UP

40. **9 x 1**

THIS YOUNG GROUP OF BOYS FROM NYC RECORDED NUMEROUS HITS. NAME THEM AND EIGHT OF THOSE HITS BELOW, NUMBERS TWO THROUGH NINE.
ONE, GROUP NAME.
TWO, ABOUT WHAT HIS MD WAS ABLE TO DIAGNOSE THAT ONLY HIS BABE COULD CURE. IT WOULD BE FEATURED IN THAT BLOCKBUSTER SOUNDTRACK MOVIE OF 'THE BIG CHILL' IN 1983 STARRING TOM BERENGER, GLEN CLOSE, JEFF GOLDBLUM, MEG TILLY AND SO FORTH.
THREE, ABOUT SOMETHING BEAUTIFUL.
FOUR, ABOUT BEING LONELY AND NOT ABLE TO GO ON.
FIVE, ABOUT A SITUATION ON A CERTAIN WEEKEND AFTERNOON.
SIX, ABOUT THE TRAIN LOOKING FOR PASSENGERS SEEKING TO BE FREE.
SEVEN, ABOUT A GIRL HE WANTS BUT STILL NOT SURE OF HER HONESTY.
EIGHT, ABOUT A GIRL WHO ENTERED HIS LIFE THAT SATIFIES HIS EVERY NEED AND PUTS HIM IN A WORLD OF ECSTACY.
NINE, WHAT HE'S NOT GONNA DO ANY LONGER.

1) ______________________
2) ______________
3) ___________________
4) __________________________
5) _________
6) _______________________
7) ___________________
8) ________________
9) ____

41. **1 x 1**

SWINGIN' MEDALLIONS CHARTED THIS PARTY SONG BELOW THAT WAS A RE-MAKE OF *DICK HOLLER & THE HOLIDAYS* ABOUT A LOVE HANGOVER CAUSED BY HIS BABY BECAUSE SHE LOVED HIM SO LONG, SO HARD AND SO RIGHT THAT IT KNOCKED HIM OUT. IT TOO WOULD BE THEIR ONLY CLAIM TO FAME SONG.

A) BABY LOVE
B) COME SEE ABOUT ME
C) DOUBLE SHOT (OF MY BABY'S LOVE)
D) BABY, NOW THAT I'VE FOUND YOU

42. **1 x 1**

IN 1965 *THE GENTRYS* OUT OF MEMPHIS RECORDED THIS POPULAR SONG BELOW ABOUT DANCING CONTINUOUSLY WHICH WOULD BE THEIR ONLY MAJOR HIT.

A) DANCE, DANCE, DANCE
B) DANCING IN THE STREET
C) LET'S DANCE
D) KEEP ON DANCING

43. **1 x 1**

THE SONG "SUGAR, SUGAR" WAS A CHART TOPPER ABOUT YOU BEING HIS CANDY GIRL AND RUMORED TO BE SUNG BY WHAT CARTOON NAMED CHARACTERS BELOW?

A) THE FLINTSTONES
B) THE JETSONS
C) THE ARCHIES
D) SCOOBY DOO AND SHAGGY

44. **1 x 1**

IN 1966 *THE LEFT BANKE* RECORDED A SONG THAT *THE FOUR TOPS* WOULD ALSO GO ON TO RECORD TWO YEARS LATER ABOUT A GIRL NAMED RENEE. NAME THAT DOUBLE HITTER.

____

60'S

45. **1 x 1**

THE AMERICAN BREED CHARTED A SONG ABOUT A GUY WHO DIDN'T CARE WHAT SHE DID TO HIM AS LONG AS SHE KEPT HIM BY HER SIDE AND LOVED HIM.

A) BEND ME, SHAPE ME
B) FOOLISH LITTLE GIRL
C) HE'S A REBEL
D) TOWER OF STRENGTH

46. **5 x 1**

THIS ALL MALE GROUP, WITH *TOMMY* IN LEAD AND ALSO THE SONGWRITER, RECORDED THE FOLLOWING HITS: "CRIMSON AND CLOVER", "SWEET CHERRY WINE", "BALL OF FIRE", AND "MIRAGE". GIVE THE FULL NAME OF GROUP AND THESE FOUR OTHER HITS BELOW, NUMBERS TWO THROUGH FIVE.
ONE, GROUPS' FULL NAME.
TWO, ABOUT WHAT HIS BABY DOES.
THREE, ABOUT WHAT HE THOUGHT, A SONG *TIFFANY* WOULD RECORD IN THE 80'S AND BRING ALL THE WAY TO THE TOP OF THE CHARTS.
FOUR, A MONY HIT SONG THAT *BILLY IDOL* WOULD ALSO GO ON TO RECORD IN THE LATE 80'S AND TAKE TO THE TOP AS WELL.
FIVE, ABOUT A CERTAIN COLORED PERSUASION.

1) ______________________________
2) _____________
3) ________________________
4) _____________
5) ________________________

47. **1 x 1**

"*INCENSE & PEPPERMINTS*" WAS A SONG RECORDED BY WHICH GROUP BELOW IN 1967 THAT WOULD RACE TO THE TOP OF THE CHARTS?

A) JOEY DEE & THE STARLITERS
B) STRAWBERRY ALARM CLOCK
C) THE IMPRESSIONS
D) THE FOUR SEASONS

48. **2 x 1**

BIG BROTHER & THE HOLDING COMPANY WITH A FEMALE IN LEAD, HAD A HIT SONG ABOUT A PORTION OF THEIR HEART. SHE WAS ONE OF THE PERFORMERS AT 'THE WOODSTOCK FESTIVAL' AND WOULD DIE AT AN EARLY AGE DUE TO DRUG AND ALCOHOL ABUSE ON OCTOBER 4, 1970. NAME HER AND THAT HIT.

1) _______________
2) ____________________

49. **1 x 1**

WHAT WAS THE NICKNAME GIVEN TO THAT FEMALE LEAD SINGER ABOVE?

A) LITTLE MISS DYNAMITE
B) THE QUEEN OF SOUL
C) PEARL
D) BOOM BOOM

50. **1 x 1**

WHAT GROUP OF GANG MEMBERS LED BY A FEMALE CHARTED THESE TWO BIG HITS, "SUNDAY WILL NEVER BE THE SAME" AND "LIKE TO GET TO KNOW YOU"?

A) JEFFERSON AIRPLANE
B) JOAN JETT & THE BLACKHEARTS
C) SPANKY AND OUR GANG
D) STONE PONEYS

TOTAL POINTS. **100 x 1 = 100**
60'S

MISC (NOVELTY, FOLK, FOREIGN & INSTRUMENTALS)-QUIZ # 1

1.

1 x 2

RAY BARRETTO HAD THIS GIANT LATIN HIT THAT WAS RECORDED TOTALLY IN SPANISH WITH A MIX OF RHYTHM AND BLUES AND EXCELLENT BACKUP MUSIC. CHOOSE THAT GIANT HIT BELOW ABOUT BEING "GRANDE Y FEO".

A) WATERMELON MAN
B) EL WATUSI
C) OYE COMO VA
D) BANG, BANG

2.

2 x 2

PAUL MAURIAT AND HIS ORCHESTRA RECORDED AN INSTRUMENTAL HIT ABOUT HEARTBREAK LOVE. CHOOSE THAT BLUE TITLED SONG BELOW THAT *THE DELLS* WOULD ALSO SING AS PART OF A SONG MEDLEY.

A) BLUE ON BLUE
B) LOVE IS BLUE
C) BLUE VELVET
D) BLUE ANGEL

3.

2 x 2

THE GROUP *THEM,* LED BY *VAN MORRISON,* CHARTED THESE TWO HITS BELOW. ONE, ABOUT THE NIGHT APPROACHING.
TWO, A GIRL TITLED SONG THAT THE *CADILLACS* HAD PREVIOUSLY CHARTED IN THE 50'S BUT WITH DIFFERENT LYRICS.
NAME THOSE TWO HITS.

1) ________________________
2) __________

4.

1 x 2

JUDY COLLINS, THE FOLK SINGER, HAD THIS SAD LOVE SONG THAT *NEIL DIAMOND* WOULD ALSO RECORD LIVE FROM THE TROUBADOUR CLUB FOR HIS GOLD ALBUM ABOUT EXPERIENCING ROMANCE FROM INSIDE OUT.

A) TWO LOVERS
B) WE CAN WORK IT OUT
C) BOTH SIDES NOW
D) DON'T LOOK BACK

5.

1 x 2

IN 1969 *DESMON DEKKER & THE ACES* HAD A HIT WITH WHAT BIBLICAL SONG AND ALSO NOT WANTING TO END UP LIKE BONNIE AND CLYDE. IT WOULD NOT ONLY BE HIS BIGGEST CLAIM TO FAME SONG BUT ALSO HAVE THE DISTINCTION OF BEING THE FIRST REGGAE ARTIST TO HAVE A HIT WITH HIS BUDDY *BOB MARLEY* TO FOLLOW SHORTLY AFTER.

A) ISRAELITES
B) EXODUS
C) EVE OF DESTRUCTION
D) PEACE TRAIN

6.

1 x 2

IN 1967 *SENATOR BOBBY,* A ONE HIT WONDER GROUP, CHARTED THIS NOVELTY VERSION OF A SONG ORIGINALLY MADE POPULAR BY *THE TROGGS* THAT IMITATED THE VOICE OF NEW YORK SENATOR ROBERT KENNEDY. CHOOSE IT BELOW.

A) WILD ONE
B) WILD THING
C) ALLEY-OOP
D) SPIDERS & SNAKES

7. **1 x 2**

CHOOSE BELOW THIS BIG NOVELTY SONG BY *ROLF HARRIS*, THE AUSTRALIAN, IN 1963 THAT WOULD BE AT LEAST HIS ONLY AMERICAN CHARTED HIT.
A) TIE ME KANGAROO DOWN, SPORT
B) ALLEY-OOP
C) CHARLIE BROWN
D) LOVE POTION NO. 9

8. **1 x 2**

GLENN YARBROUGH RECORDED THIS RAIN TITLED SONG BELOW THAT WAS ALSO THE NAME OF A MOVIE ABOUT SOMETHING THAT WAS BOUND TO HAPPEN, STARRING STEVE MCQUEEN, LEE REMICK AND DON MURRAY IN THE MID 60'S.
A) HAVE YOU EVER SEEN THE RAIN
B) WHO'LL STOP THE RAIN
C) IN THE RAIN
D) BABY THE RAIN MUST FALL

9. **1 x 2**

"THEY'RE COMING TO TAKE ME AWAY, HA-HAAA!", A NOVELTY SONG, WAS RECORDED BY WHICH MALE ARTIST BELOW IN 1966 THAT WOULD ALSO BE HIS ONE AND ONLY?
A) RAY STEVENS
B) NAPOLEAN X1V
C) DAVID SEVILLE
D) BIG BOPPER

10. **1 x 2**

TOM GLAZER, A SINGER/SONGWRITER, *AND THE DO-RE-MI CHILDREN'S CHORUS* HAD A NOVELTY SING-A-LONG HIT SONG ABOUT A MEATBALL ON THE RUN THAT WOULD EVENTUALLY GROW INTO A TREE. NAME THIS ONE HIT WONDER SONG.

____

11. **1 x 2**

THE TV THEME SONG "THE BALLAD OF JED CLAMPETT" STARRING THE BEVERLY HILLBILLIES WAS A HIT FOR WHAT VERY POPULAR COUNTRY BLUEGRASS DUO?
A) THE EVERLY BROTHERS
B) FLATT & SCRUGGS
C) SANTO & JOHNNY
D) DON & JUAN

12. **1 x 2**

ZAGER & EVANS, A ROCK DUO, HAD WHAT BIG MAJOR HIT IN 1969 THAT DESCRIBED THE FUTURE IF ANY, OF MANKIND IN A CERTAIN YEAR YET TO COME? IT WOULD BE A CHART TOPPER AND THEIR ONE AND ONLY HIT EVER.
A) EVE OF DESTRUCTION
B) WE GOTTA GET OUT OF THIS PLACE
C) IN THE YEAR 2525
D) ALSO SPRACH ZARATHUSTRA (2001)

13. **1 x 2**

KYU SAKAMOTO, A JAPANESE SINGER, HAD HIS ONE CLAIM TO FAME SONG HERE IN AMERICA SUNG ENTIRELY IN JAPANESE THAT IRONICALLY WOULD REACH THE TOP OF THE CHARTS. IN THE 80'S IT WOULD BE RECORDED BY THE GROUP *A TASTE OF HONEY* WITH ENGLISH LYRICS. CHOOSE THAT DOUBLE HITTER BELOW.
A) VOLARE
B) SUKIYAKI
C) DOMINIQUE
D) GUANTANAMERA

14. **1 x 2**

THE ROOFTOP SINGERS CHARTED WHAT POPULAR SONG BELOW THAT WOULD REACH THE TOP OF THE CHARTS ABOUT HOW EVERYBODY'S TALKING AND WALKING? A SONG THAT *DR HOOK* WOULD ALSO RECORD FOR HIS GREATEST HITS ALBUM IN THE 80'S.

A) EVERYBODY'S TALKIN'
B) WALK RIGHT IN
C) TALKING IN YOUR SLEEP
D) TALK THAT TALK

15. **1 x 2**

MARY HOPKIN HAD A POPULAR SONG ABOUT THOSE DAYS IN THE PAST WHERE THEY WOULD SING AND DANCE ALL NIGHT LONG AND SEEMED TO NEVER END. A SONG THAT ARCHIE AND EDITH BUNKER WOULD SING AS THE THEME SONG FOR THEIR TV SITCOM IN THE 80'S. WHAT WAS THAT POPULAR HIT?

A) THOSE OLDIES BUT GOODIES (REMIND ME OF YOU)
B) THOSE WERE THE DAYS
C) OH HAPPY DAY
D) COME AND GET THESE MEMORIES

16. **1 x 2**

IN 1962 *NELSON RIDDLE AND HIS ORCHESTRA* CHARTED A TV THEME HIT ABOUT TWO YOUNG MEN WHO FOUND ROMANCE AND ADVENTURE WHILE DRIVING ACROSS AMERICA IN THEIR CORVETTE STARRING MARTIN MILNER AND GEORGE MAHARIS. CHOOSE IT BELOW.

A) ROUTE 66 THEME
B) BORN TO BE WILD
C) KING OF THE ROAD
D) BACK IN THE U.S.A.

17. **2 x 2**

NAME THESE TWO BIG HITS BY *TRINI LOPEZ* THAT WERE ORIGINALLY CHARTED BY *PETER, PAUL* & *MARY*.
ONE, ABOUT WHAT HE WOULD DO WITH A HAMMER THROUGHOUT THE LAND.
TWO, ABOUT A CERTAIN LOVELY TREE WHOSE FRUIT IS INEDIBLE.

1) ____________________
2) ________________

18. **1 x 2**

LOU MONTE HAD WHAT NOVELTY SONG ABOUT HIS PET? BOTH WERE FREQUENT GUESTS OF 'ED SULLIVAN' ON HIS WEEKLY VARIETY SHOW WHERE AT THE END OF THEIR MONOLOGUE THE PET WOULD ASK EDDIE IN A SHY MANNER TO KISS HIM GOODNIGHT.

A) WITCH DOCTOR
B) LAZY MARY
C) PEPINO THE ITALIAN MOUSE
D) VOLARE

19. **1 x 2**

ALLAN SHERMAN RECORDED A NOVELTY SONG ABOUT HIS SUMMER EXPERIENCES AS A CHILD AT CAMP AND WRITING A LETTER TO HIS PARENTS ABOUT HIS FIRST DAY THERE. IT WOULD REACH THE NUMBER TWO SPOT WAY UP ON THE CHARTS.

A) HELLO MUDDUH, HELLO FADDUH! (A LETTER FROM CAMP)
B) SEALED WITH A KISS
C) HERE COMES SUMMER
D) SEE YOU IN SEPTEMBER

20. **1 x 2**

THE SEEKERS RECORDED THIS GIRL TITLED SONG THAT WAS FEATURED IN A MOVIE OF THE SAME NAME ABOUT GEORGY, STARRING JAMES MASON AND LYNN REDGRAVE. NAME IT.

____

21. **1 x 2**

THE SEEKERS ALSO HAD ANOTHER ABOUT THE CHANCES OF REPLACING YOU. CHOOSE THAT ONE.

A) IT MUST BE HIM
B) I'LL NEVER FIND ANOTHER YOU
C) BE MY BABY
D) BABY IT'S YOU

22. **1 x 2**

In 1962 *THE NEW CHRISTY MINSTRELS* RECORDED THIS POPULAR FOLK SONG ABOUT THIS COUNTRY OF OURS, FROM ONE END TO THE OTHER. IT WAS AN ORIGINAL *WOODY GUTHRIE* SONG.

A) 500 MILES
B) IF I HAD A HAMMER
C) THIS LAND IS YOUR LAND
D) MOUNTAIN OF LOVE

23. **1 x 2**

THE NEW CHRISTY MINSTRELS, FEATURING *BARRY McGUIRE* IN THE LEAD, CHARTED ANOTHER ABOUT THE COLOR GREEN.

A) LITTLE GREEN APPLES
B) GREEN DOOR
C) GREEN, GREEN
D) GREEN TAMBOURINE

24. **1 x 2**

THE BUFFALO SPRINGFIELD RECORDED A SONG IN THE LATE 60'S THAT WOULD BE FEATURED IN THE MOVIE 'COMING HOME', STARRING JON VOIGHT AND JANE FONDA IN THE LATE 70'S ABOUT THE VIOLENCE ONE CAN HEAR OCCURRING ALL AROUND US.

A) EVE OF DESTRUCTION
B) ABRAHAM, MARTIN AND JOHN
C) TIME HAS COME TODAY
D) FOR WHAT IT'S WORTH (STOP, HEY WHAT'S THAT SOUND)

25. **1 x 2**

DAVID CROSBY WAS A MEMBER OF WHAT GROUP BEFORE JOINING UP TO FORM *CROSBY, STILLS, NASH & YOUNG*? "MR TAMBOURINE MAN" WAS A BIG HIT FOR THAT GROUP.

A) DEREK AND THE DOMINOS
B) THE BYRDS
C) CREAM
D) THE T-BONES

26. **1 x 2**

LONNIE DONEGAN, THE POPULAR ENGLISH ARTIST, HAD A NOVELTY HIT SONG ABOUT CHEWING GUM AND WHAT CAN HAPPEN TO IT OVERNIGHT. FILL IN THE INITIALS PROVIDED TO COMPLETE THE NAME OF THAT SONG BELOW.

D--S Y--R C-----G G-M L--E I-'S F----R (O- T-E B-----T O--R N---T)

27. **8 x 2**

NAME THESE EIGHT BIG HITS BELOW BY *PETER, PAUL & MARY* THE LEGENDARY FOLK TRIO GROUP.
ONE, A JET PLANE SONG WRITTEN BY *JOHN DENVER* THAT SHE WAS BOUND TO LEAVE AND ALREADY LONESOME FOR YOU.
TWO, ABOUT THAT MAGIC DRAGON FROM HANNAHLEE.
THREE, A *BOB DYLAN* TUNE ABOUT THE WIND AND THE MANY UNANSWERABLE QUESTIONS LEFT UP IN THE AIR, ALSO RECORDED *BY LITTLE STEVIE WONDER*.
FOUR, ABOUT A CERTAIN FRUIT TREE THAT IS LOVELY BUT AT THE SAME TIME IT'S FRUIT IMPOSSIBLE TO INGEST. A SONG *TRINI LOPEZ* WOULD ALSO GO ON TO RECORD.
FIVE, A HAMMER SONG THAT THEY WOULD USE TO RING JUSTICE, FREEDOM AND LOVE. ALSO RECORDED BY *TRINI LOPEZ.*
SIX, ABOUT A CERTAIN NUMBER OF MILES, NOT ONE, NOT TWO, BUT FIVE.
SEVEN, ABOUT A DEPARTING ROMANCE AND NO NEED TO DO SOMETHING TWICE BECAUSE IT'LL TURN OUT OK, A SONG ORIGINALLY SUNG BY *BOB DYLAN*.
EIGHT, ABOUT WHAT THEY DIG THAT INCLUDED THOSE OF *THE MAMAS & THE PAPAS.*

1) ______________________________
2) __________________________
3) __________________________
4) ________________
5) ______________________
6) _____________
7) ____________________________________
8) ______________________________

28. **6 x 2**

BOB DYLAN ALSO A LEGENDARY FOLK SINGER AND SONGWRITER AS WELL CHARTED MANY HITS DURING THE 60'S INCLUDING "JUST LIKE A WOMAN", "RAINY DAY WOMAN # 12 & 35", "SUBTERRANEAN HOMESICK BLUES", "I WANT YOU", AND "THE TIMES THEY ARE-A-CHANGIN'". NAME THESE SIX OTHER HITS BELOW.
ONE, ABOUT HAVING TO BE ON HER OWN LIKE A STONE THAT GATHERS NO MOSS.
TWO, HIS FOURTH STREET TITLED SONG ABOUT A HYPOCRITE WHO CAUSES NOTHING BUT PAIN, LIES, AND IS SIMPLY A BACKSTABBER.
THREE, HIS BIG LADY HIT SONG.
FOUR, HIS WIND SONG ABOUT WHERE THE ANSWER CAN BE FOUND. A SONG THAT A TRIO GROUP AND THEN A MOTOWN YOUNGSTER WOULD ALSO RECORD, ALL DURING THE DECADE OF THE 60'S.
FIVE, A SONG ALSO RECORDED BY *THE TURTLES* CLAIMING IT WASN'T HIM THAT YOU NEEDED, TO BE USED DAY IN AND DAY OUT AT YOUR BECKONING CALL.
SIX, A TAMBOURINE HIT SONG ALSO RECORDED BY *THE BYRDS* ABOUT A CERTAIN JINGLE MAN THAT HE WANTED TO HEAR AND FOLLOW.

1) ________________________
2) ______________________________
3) ________________
4) ________________________
5) ____________________
6) ____________________

29. **1 x 2**

THE KINGSTON TRIO, THE POPULAR FOLK SINGERS, HAD A HIT WITH WHAT FLOWER SONG BELOW?

A) ROSES ARE RED
B) YELLOW ROSE OF TEXAS
C) WHERE HAVE ALL THE FLOWERS GONE
D) FLOWERS ON THE WALL

30. **3 x 2**

NAME THESE THREE INSTRUMENTAL HITS BY *HERB ALPERT & THE TIJUANA BRASS.*
ONE, ABOUT A SAD BULL.
TWO, ABOUT A CERTAIN SWEET FLAVOR.
THREE, ABOUT A GREEK MAN FROM THE MOVIE SOUNDTRACK OF THE SAME NAME ORIGINALLY SUNG BY *MELINA MERCOURIE* AND STARRING ANTHONY QUINN.

1) ____________________
2) ________________
3) ____________________

31. **1 x 2**

"SNOOPY VS THE RED BARON" WAS A NOVELTY SONG CHARTED BY WHICH GROUP BELOW IN 1966 ABOUT THAT DOG FIGHT IN THE SKY WHERE PREVIOUSLY EIGHTY MEN HAD DIED AT THE HANDS OF THAT BLOODY BARON? IT WAS THEIR FIRST MAJOR HIT AND REACH THE NUMBER TWO SPOT ON THE CHARTS.

A) THE ROYAL GUARDSMEN
B) THE TURTLES
C) THE ARCHIES
D) THE MCCOYS

32. **1 x 2**

VAN MORRISON RECORDED A SOLO HIT ABOUT A GIRL WITH CERTAIN COLORED EYES AND TO HIS AMAZEMENT HAS GROWN UP. IT TOO WOULD BE FEATURED IN THE MOVIE 'COMING HOME' STARRING JON VOIGHT, JANE FONDA AND BRUCE DERN IN THE LATE 70'S.

A) DRY YOUR EYES
B) BROWN EYED GIRL
C) PRETTY LITTLE ANGEL EYES
D) BROWN EYED WOMAN

33. **1 x 2**

BARRY McGUIRE, THE FORMER MEMBER OF *THE NEW CHRISTY MINSTRELS,* CHARTED A TOP OF THE CHARTS HIT SONG THAT HE BELIEVED WE WERE ON THE EVE OF SOMETHING SO TERRIBLE. THE HATRED, VIOLENCE AND DESTRUCTION WERE BECOMING A THREAT TO OUR HUMANITY AND EXISTENCE NOT ONLY HERE IN OUR COUNTRY BUT IN THE REST OF THE WORLD. WHAT WAS THAT HIT?

A) WE GOTTA GET OUT OF THIS PLACE
B) ABRAHAM, MARTIN AND JOHN
C) EVE OF DESTRUCTION
D) THE END OF THE WORLD

34. **1 x 2**

BRIAN HYLAND, THE TEENAGE SINGING SENSATION, RECORDED THIS NOVELTY SONG ABOUT A GIRL WHO WORE A CERTAIN TYPE OF BATHING SUIT AND WAS TOO FRIGHTENED TO GET OUT. NAME THIS SONG WHICH WAS HIS FIRST MAJOR HIT AND ALSO HIS BIGGEST BY COMPLETING THE INITIALS PROVIDED BELOW.

I--Y B---Y T----E W---I Y----W P------T B----I

TOTAL POINTS. 50 x 2 = 100 60'S

MISC (NOVELTY, FOLK, FOREIGN & INSTRUMENTALS)-QUIZ # 2

1.

1 x 4

WHICH ARTIST BELOW CHARTED "HEY, LEROY, YOUR MAMA'S CALLIN' YOU" BACK IN 1967?

A) RAY BARRETTO
B) JIMMY CASTOR
C) JOE CUBA
D) JOE TEX

2.

1 x 4

"THE UNICORN" WAS A NOVELTY HIT CHARTED BY WHAT IRISH GROUP BELOW ABOUT WHAT YOU'LL NEVER SEE THAT WOULD BE GREEN, ALWAYS HIDING AND PLAYING?

A) THE CREW-CUTS
B) THE FOUR SEASONS
C) THE IRISH ROVERS
D) U2

3.

1 x 4

MASON WILLIAMS, THE VERY POPULAR COMEDIAN, SONGWRITER, HAD THIS BIG CLASSICAL INSTRUMENTAL NUMBER BELOW.

A) ROLL OVER BEETHOVEN
B) CLASSICAL GAS
C) A FIFTH OF BEETHOVEN
D) LITTLE STAR

4.

1 x 4

CLIFF NOBLES & CO CHARTED THEIR ONE BIG MAJOR RECORDING WITH WHAT BIG INSTRUMENTAL DANCE NUMBER BELOW? IT WOULD JUST BARELY MISS REACHING THE TOP OF THE CHARTS AND STAY AT NUMBER TWO.

A) THE HORSE
B) THE DUCK
C) MICKEY'S MONKEY
D) WALKING THE DOG

5.

1 x 4

YOUNG-HOLT UNLIMITED RECORDED WHAT SOULFUL INSTRUMENTAL HIT BELOW IN 1968 WHICH BECAME THEIR BIGGEST TO DATE?

A) SOULFUL STRUT
B) (YOU'RE MY) SOUL AND INSPIRATION
C) MEMPHIS SOUL STEW
D) SOUL FINGER

6.

1 x 4

SPYDER TURNER'S ONLY MAJOR HIT WAS WHAT NOVELTY SONG IN 1967 IN WHICH HE IMITATED THE TOP ARTISTS OF THE DAY? INCLUDING *BEN E KING, JACKIE WILSON, JAMES BROWN, EDDIE KENDRICKS, MELVIN FRANKLIN, DAVID RUFFIN, BILLY STEWART, SAM COOKE, SMOKEY ROBINSON,* AND *CHUCK JACKSON* SINGING THIS *BEN E KING* TUNE.

A) STAND BY ME
B) SPANISH HARLEM
C) AMOR
D) I (WHO HAVE NOTHING)

7.

1 x 4

THE RIVINGTONS WERE KNOWN FOR TWO OF THE THREE NOVELTY SONGS BELOW IN THE 60'S. WHICH ONE UNFORTUNATELY WAS **NOT** THEIRS?

A) THE BIRD'S THE WORD
B) PAPA-OOM-MOW-MOW
C) THE NAME GAME

8. **1 x 4**

KING CURTIS RECORDED A MEMPHIS TITLED SONG WITH BAND MEMBERS JOINING IN ONE AT A TIME TO CREATE A SOULFUL HIT SOUND THAT WAS THE SPECIAL OF THE DAY. FIRST THE BASS, THEN THE DRUMS, THE GUITAR, THE ORGAN AND FINALLY THE HORN. WITH A LITTLE OF THIS, A LITTLE OF THAT, AND SO ON. WHAT WAS THAT SOULFULL MEMPHIS HIT?

A) MEMPHIS SOUL STEW
B) MEMPHIS
C) A LITTLE BIT OF ME, A LITTLE BIT OF YOU
D) WALKING IN MEMPHIS

9. **1 x 4**

THE *'MAR-KEYS'* WHOSE MEMBERS WOULD BECOME PART OF THE HOUSE BAND FOR THE STAX LABEL CHARTED THIS INSTUMENTAL NUMBER IN 1961. THE MUSIC WITH ITS OOH'S AND AAH'S AND GIRL MOANING SOUNDS WAS PROBABLY USED IN STRIP JOINTS WHERE IT WOULD FIT THE ATMOSPHERE PRESENT THERE.

A) TEQUILA
B) LAST NIGHT
C) HONKY TONK WOMAN
D) PHYSICAL

10. **1 x 4**

THE SONG "SOUL FINGER" WAS CHARTED BY WHICH MALE GROUP BELOW THAT WOULD LOSE MOST OF ITS MEMBERS ALONG SIDE OF *OTIS REDDING* IN THAT FATEFUL CRASH ON DECEMBER 10, 1967?

A) THE TAMS
B) BOOKER T & THE MG'S
C) BAR-KAYS
D) THE IMPRESSIONS

11. **1 x 4**

TINY TIM HAD THIS ONE HIT WONDER FLOWER SONG THAT HE WOULD PERFORM ON THE JOHNNY CARSON 'TONIGHT SHOW'. CHOOSE THAT FLOWER SONG BELOW.

A) RED ROSES FOR A BLUE LADY
B) ROSES ARE RED
C) FLOWERS ON THE WALL
D) TIP TOE THRU' THE TULIPS WITH ME

12. **1 x 4**

IN 1964 *THE DEVOTIONS* CHARTED THEIR ONE CLAIM TO FAME SONG BELOW THAT DEALT WITH A FAIRY TALE ABOUT A CERTAIN GUY WHO SLEPT FOR A LONG PERIOD OF TIME. IT'S ANOTHER EXAMPLE OF A UNDERRATED HIT THAT NEVER REACHED ITS REAL POTENTIAL BUT NOW STANDS AS A CLASSIC.

A) YOU WERE ON MY MIND
B) RIP VAN WINKLE
C) THE LION SLEEPS TONIGHT
D) ENDLESS SLEEP

13. **1 x 4**

IN 1963 *LONNIE MACK* CHARTED THIS INSTRUMENTAL VERSION OF A *CHUCK BERRY* TUNE ORIGINALLY RECORDED IN THE LATE 50'S, TITLE SHORTENED ABOUT THAT TOWN IN TENNESSEE. A YEAR LATER *JOHNNY RIVERS* WOULD ALSO GO ON TO RECORD IT, TAKING IT TO THE NUMBER TWO SPOT ON THE CHARTS. WHAT WAS THAT TRIPLE HITTER?

A) TENNESSEE WALTZ
B) KENTUCKY WOMAN
C) MEMPHIS SOUL STEW
D) MEMPHIS

14. **1 x 4**

SHIRLEY ELLIS WAS STRICTLY KNOWN FOR HER NOVELTY SONGS. WHICH ONE BELOW WAS **NOT** HERS?
A) THE NAME GAME
B) ALLEY-OOP
C) THE NITTY GRITTY
D) THE CLAPPING SONG (CLAP PAT CLAP SLAP)

15. **1 x 4**

THIS PIANO DUO CHARTED NUMEROUS INSTRUMENTAL MOVIE AND STAGE TUNES WHICH INCLUDED THE FOLLOWING TWO HITS, "EXODUS" FEATURED IN A MOVIE OF THE SAME NAME STARRING PAUL NEWMAN AND EVA MARIE SAINT, AND THE OTHER HIT "TONIGHT" WHICH WAS A ROMANTIC SONG FROM THE BROADWAY SHOW AND LATER MADE INTO A MOVIE, 'WEST SIDE STORY' STARRING NATALIE WOOD AND RICHARD BEYMER. CHOOSE THOSE TWO TALENTED PIANISTS BELOW.
A) FERRANTE & TEICHER
B) BURT BACHARACH & HAL DAVID
C) ROGER WILLIAMS & HENRY MANCINI
D) STEVE ALLEN & LIBERACE

16. **1 x 4**

MIRIAM MAKEBA HAD THIS HIT BELOW ABOUT THAT DANCE THEY DO EVERY FRIDAY AND SATURDAY NIGHT IN JOHANNESBURG THAT HAD HER MAKING POPPING SOUNDS WITH HER MOUTH. CHOOSE THAT HIT BELOW.
A) SHOUT (PARTS 1 AND 2)
B) PATA, PATA
C) PAPA-OOM-MOW-MOW
D) BANG, BANG

17. **3 x 4**

NAME THESE THREE INSTRUMENTAL HITS BY *BOOKER T & THE MG'S* FOR THE STAX LABEL.
ONE, ABOUT A GREEN VEGETABLE THAT IS QUITE PUNGENT.
TWO, A THEME SONG FOR A CLINT EASTWOOD WESTERN MOVIE THAT CO-STARRED HIS ACTING BUDDY PAT HINGLE, AND ALSO INGER STEVENS, ED BEGLEY, DENNIS HOPPER AND BRUCE DERN IN THE LATE 60'S.
THREE, ABOUT WHAT TIME IS.
1) ________________
2) ________________
3) ________________

18. **1 x 4**

IN 1967, THE AUSTRALIAN BAND, *THE EASYBEATS,* CHARTED A SONG ABOUT A CERTAIN DAY OF THE WEEK THAT WAS ALWAYS IN THEIR SUBCONSCIENCE. IT WOULD BECOME THE MOST NOTABLE HIT OF THEIR SHORT CAREER AND LABEL THEM AS A ONE HIT WONDER GROUP. WHAT WAS THAT SONG?
A) EVERYDAY OF THE WEEK
B) RUBY TUESDAY
C) MONDAY, MONDAY
D) FRIDAY ON MY MIND

19. **1 x 4**

MONGO SANTAMARIA, THE POPULAR CONGA PLAYER, HAD A BIG HIT WITH THIS LATIN R&B SONG ABOUT A CERTAIN GUY.
A) EL WATUSI
B) BANG, BANG
C) HEY, LEROY, YOUR MAMA'S CALLIN' YOU
D) WATERMELON MAN

20. **1 x 4**

CHOOSE THIS NOVELTY SONG BELOW BY *LARRY VERNE* IN 1960 ABOUT A CALVARY SOLDIER'S COMICAL CRY TO HIS GENERAL THAT HE DIDN'T WANT TO FIGHT OR DIE. IT WOULD BE HIS ONLY CLAIM TO FAME SONG AND ALSO REACH THE TOP OF THE CHARTS FOR GOOD MEASURE.

A) HELP!
B) RUNAWAY
C) WE GOTTA GET OUT OF THIS PLACE
D) MR CUSTER

21. **1 x 4**

IN 1963 *THE CHANTAYS,* THE ROCK BAND FROM CALIFORNIA, CHARTED THEIR ONLY CLAIM TO FAME WITH THIS BIG INSTRUMENTAL SURFING NUMBER BELOW. WHAT WAS THAT INSTRUMENTAL CALLED?

A) PIPELINE
B) TEQUILA
C) SLEEP WALK
D) WALK DON'T RUN

22. **1 x 4**

SAM THE SHAM AND THE PHAROAHS RECORDED TWO BIG NOVELTY HIT SONGS THAT WOULD BOTH CLIMB TO THE SECOND TOP SPOT ON THE CHARTS. THE FIRST WAS CALLED "WOOLY BULLY". NAME THE SECOND, ABOUT A CUTE LOOKING GIRL ON HER WAY TO GRANDMA'S THROUGH THOSE DANGEROUS WOODED ROADS.

A) YOU MUST HAVE BEEN A BEAUTIFUL BABY
B) MARY'S LITTLE LAMB
C) LIL' RED RIDING HOOD
D) HEY! LITTLE GIRL

23. **1 x 4**

THE VENTURES, THE VERY TALENTED INSTRUMENTAL GROUP, HAD THIS TV THEME HIT ABOUT A POLICE SERIES STARRING JACK LORD, WHICH TOOK PLACE OFF THE MAINLAND AND ALWAYS ENDED WITH "BOOK-EM DANO". NOW NAME IT.

____

TOTAL POINTS. **25 x 4 = 100**

MISC (NOVELTY, FOLK, FOREIGN & INSTRUMENTALS)-QUIZ # 3.

1. **1 x 4**

THE BYRDS RECORDED A TOP OF THE CHARTS HIT WITH WHAT INSTRUMENT TITLED SONG WRITTEN AND ALSO RECORDED BY *BOB DYLAN* ABOUT A CERTAIN JINGLE MAN WHO THEY WANTED TO HEAR AND FOLLOW?

A) MR TAMBOURINE MAN
B) DIFFERENT DRUM
C) LET THERE BE DRUMS
D) GREEN TAMBOURINE

2. **1 x 4**

THE BYRDS CHARTED ANOTHER ABOUT THERE BEING A TIME FOR EVERYTHING, LIKE FOR DANCING, SINGING AND SO FORTH. IT TOO WOULD REACH THE TOP OF THE CHARTS. CHOOSE THAT ONE BELOW.

A) TIME OF THE SEASON
B) OUR DAY WILL COME
C) TURN! TURN! TURN! (TO EVERYTHING THERE IS A SEASON)
D) SOMEDAY WE'LL BE TOGETHER

3. **1 x 4**

RAY STEVENS, THE POPULAR NOVELTY SINGER, HAD AT LEAST TWO BIG HITS IN THE 60'S. WHICH SONG BELOW WAS **NOT** HIS?

A) WITCH DOCTOR
B) AHAB, THE ARAB
C) GITARZAN

4. **1 x 4**

SERGIO MENDES & BRASIL '66 RECORDED THEIR FIRST MAJOR HIT THAT WOULD CATAPULT THEM TO FAME AND GLORY ABOUT A LOOK THAT SAYS IT ALL. IT WAS A REMAKE OF AN ORIGINAL *DUSTY SPRINGFIELD* SONG FEATURED IN THE MOVIE 'CASINO ROYALE' BACK IN 1967 STARRING DAVID NIVEN, WOODY ALLEN AND URSULA ANDRES.

A) TURN AROUND, LOOK AT ME
B) WORDS
C) THE LOOK OF LOVE
D) LOOK IN MY EYES

5. **1 x 4**

IN 1968 *SERGIO MENDES & BRASIL '66* HAD ANOTHER, THIS TIME WITH AN ORIGINAL *BEATLES* SONG ABOUT A FOOL THAT THE FAB FOUR HAD RECORDED THE PREVIOUS YEAR. CHOOSE THAT ONE AS WELL.

A) FOOL # 1
B) THE FOOL ON THE HILL
C) FOOLS RUSH IN
D) FOOLISH LITTLE GIRL

6. **1 x 4**

THE HOLLYWOOD ARGYLES CHARTED A NOVELTY SONG THAT ONE WOULD NORMALLY ASSOCIATE WITH CAVEMEN. A SONG THAT *DANTE & THE EVERGREENS* WOULD ALSO RECORD SIMULTANEOUSLY BUT WITH THE *ARGYLES* VERSION ON TOP. NAME THAT NOVELTY SONG.

____

7. **1 x 4**

WHAT NOVELTY SONG BELOW BY *BOBBY 'BORIS' PICKETT AND THE CRYPT KICKERS* WAS A POPULAR MONSTER HIT AND STILL IS ON HALLOWEEN?

A) MONSTER MASH
B) YAKETY YAK
C) GREEN EYED LADY
D) ALLEY-OOP

8. **1 x 4**

TOM JONES RECORDED THESE FIVE BIG HITS BELOW. WHICH ONE WAS **NOT** HIS?
A) AFTER THE LOVIN'
B) IT'S NOT UNUSUAL
C) DELILAH
D) WHAT'S NEW PUSSYCAT?
E) GREEN GREEN GRASS OF HOME
F) I'LL NEVER FALL IN LOVE AGAIN

9. **1 x 4**

THE YOUNGBLOODS CHARTED THIS ONE HIT WONDER SONG, ASKING PEOPLE TO UNITE BY CARING FOR ONE ANOTHER AND THAT A SMILE CAN BE THE KEY TO IT ALL. THE SONG WOULD BE RECORDED BY THE COUNTRY SINGER *GARTH BROOKS* IN THE 90'S AS PART OF A MEDLEY SONG.
A) PEOPLE GOT TO BE FREE
B) PEACE TRAIN
C) STAND BY ME
D) GET TOGETHER

10. **1 x 4**

IN 1966 *STAFF SERGEANT BARRY SADLER*, A GREEN BERET HIMSELF, HAD A BIG HIT WITH A TRIBUTE SONG TO HIS FALLEN ELITE FIGHTING SOLDIERS DURING THE VIETNAM WAR. NAME HIS BALLAD HIT THAT WAS A CHART TOPPER, CLIMBING TO NUMBER ONE.

____

11. **1 x 4**

LORNE GREEN OF 'BONANZA' FAME, BEN CARTWRIGHT, CHARTED THIS WESTERN HIT THAT COINCIDENTALLY SHARES THE SAME FIRST NAME OF ONE OF *THE BEATLES*. IT WOULD BE HIS ONE AND ONLY CLAIM TO FAME SONG OF HIS MUSICAL CAREER. WHAT WAS THAT WESTERN HIT?
A) BIG BAD JOHN
B) JOHNNY YUMA
C) RINGO
D) GEORGY PORGIE

12. **1 x 4**

HUGO MONTENEGRO AND HIS ORCHESTRA RECORDED WHAT BIG INSTRUMENTAL THEME HIT FOR A POPULAR CLINT EASTWOOD SPAGHETTI WESTERN THAT CO-STARRED ELI WALLACH AND LEE VAN CLIFF? IT WOULD REACH THE NUMBER TWO SPOT HIGH UP ON THE CHARTS.
A) HANG 'EM HIGH
B) RAW-HIDE
C) THE GOOD, THE BAD AND THE UGLY
D) THE MAGNIFICENT SEVEN

13. **1 x 4**

DAVID ROSE AND HIS ORCHESTRA HAD A BIG INSTRUMENTAL HIT WITH THIS TUNE THAT DANCERS IN A STRIP JOINT MIGHT TAKE THEIR CLOTHES OFF TO. IT WOULD CLIMB TO THE TOP OF THE CHARTS. WHAT WAS THAT INSTRUMENTAL HIT BELOW?
A) QUIET VILLAGE
B) THE STRIPPER
C) WATERMELON MAN
D) GREEN ONIONS

14. **1 x 4**

THE SONG "MACARTHUR PARK" ABOUT A CAKE IN THE RAIN WAS ORIGINALLY RECORDED BY AN ACTOR. BOTH *THE FOUR TOPS* AND *DONNA SUMMER* WOULD EVENTUALLY RECORD A VERSION OF THEIR OWN. CHOOSE THAT ACTOR BELOW WHO NOT ONLY CHARTED HIS ONE MAJOR CLAIM TO FAME SONG BUT IT WOULD CLIMB WAY UP TO THE NUMBER TWO SPOT AS WELL.

A) LEE MARVIN
B) RICHARD HARRIS
C) CLINT EASTWOOD
D) DEAN MARTIN

15. **1 x 4**

"MR BASS MAN" WAS A NOVELTY SONG ABOUT THE ROCK 'N ROLL BASS SINGERS. CHOOSE THE ARTIST WHO WISHED TO BE ONE HIMSELF.

A) HERB ALPERT
B) SAM THE SHAM
C) JOHNNY CYMBAL
D) MELVIN FRANKLIN

16. **1 x 4**

THESE TWO SONGS,"OUT OF LIMITS" AND "THE BATMAN THEME", WERE RECORDED BY WHICH INSTRUMENTAL GROUP BELOW?

A) HERB ALPERT & THE TIJUANA BRASS
B) THE MARKETTS
C) THE VENTURES
D) HENRY MANCINI AND HIS ORCHESTRA

17. **1 x 4**

THE T-BONES RECORDED AN INSTRUMENTAL HIT THAT ALKA SELTZER WOULD USE IN THEIR COMMERCIALS FEATURING STOMACHS. IT WOULD BE THEIR ONE AND ONLY AND PUT THEM AS A ONE HIT WONDER GROUP. CHOOSE THAT HIT BELOW.

A) WALK DON'T RUN
B) NO MATTER WHAT SHAPE (YOUR STOMACH'S IN)
C) THE STRIPPER
D) WIPEOUT

18. **1 x 4**

CANNONBALL ADDERLEY, THE TALENTED SAXOPHONIST, HAD THIS INSTRUMENTAL HIT THAT *THE BUCKINGHAMS* WOULD CHART AS A VOCAL SONG. NAME THIS TRIPLE MERCY TITLED DOUBLE HITTER.

________,________,________

19. **1 x 4**

WHAT WAS THE NAME OF THAT THREE DAY FESTIVAL OF PEACE, LOVE, AND ROCK THAT ATTRACTED OVER A HALF MILLION FANS IN 1969 IN UPSTATE NY?

A) GIMME SHELTER
B) THE MONTEREY INTERNATIONAL POP FESTIVAL
C) NEWPORT FOLK FESTIVAL
D) THE WOODSTOCK FESTIVAL

20. **1 x 4**

CHOOSE BELOW THE 'JAMES BOND' MOVIE THEME SONG BY *SHIRLEY BASSEY* IN 1965 ABOUT A FELLA WITH THE MIDAS TOUCH WHO LOVES ONLY GOLD STARRING SEAN CONNERY AND GERT FROBE (GOLDFINGER CHARACTER).

A) THUNDERBALL
B) HELP!
C) YOU ONLY LIVE TWICE
D) GOLDFINGER

21. **1 x 4**

THE DUO OF *RENE & RENE*, CONSISTING OF TWO GUYS, RECORDED THIS LATIN HIT SONG BELOW ABOUT THEIR LOVE GROWING MORE ALL THE TIME.
A) IT'S GROWING
B) LO MUCHO QUE TE QUIERO (THE MORE I LOVE YOU)
C) BANG, BANG
D) MORE TODAY THAN YESTERDAY

22. **1 x 4**

THIS FOLK GROUP, CONSISTING OF FOUR GUYS, KNOWN AS *THE BROTHERS FOUR* RECORDED THIS SONG BELOW ABOUT SOMETHING GREEN THAT WAS BLESSED WITH A KISS BY THE SUN. CHOOSE IT BELOW.
A) GREEN ONIONS
B) GREEN TAMBOURINE
C) LITTLE GREEN APPLES
D) GREENFIELDS

23. **1 x 4**

THE SINGING NUN, TRUE NAME SISTER LUC-GABRIELLE, CHARTED WHAT SONG IN 1963 THAT WOULD REACH TO THE TOP OF THE CHARTS?
A) AMEN
B) AVE MARIA
C) AMAZING GRACE
D) DOMINIQUE

24. **1 x 4**

IN 1963 *THE ROCKY FELLERS*, A FAMILY ACT, CHARTED THIS SONG BELOW ABOUT THAT GUY WITH MARIE ON THE DANCE FLOOR.
A) MARIE'S THE NAME (HIS LATEST FLAME)
B) DO YOU WANT TO DANCE
C) LET THE LITTLE GIRL DANCE
D) KILLER JOE

25. **1 x 4**

LOS BRAVOS, A ONE HIT WONDER GROUP, HAD THIS ONE BIG CLAIM TO FAME SONG BACK IN 1966 ABOUT WANTING HIS GIRL BACK EVER SINCE SHE WENT AWAY. CHOOSE THAT COLORED TITLED SONG BELOW.
A) A WHITER SHADE OF PALE
B) PAINT IT BLACK
C) BLACK IS BLACK
D) BLUE ON BLUE

TOTAL POINTS. 25 x 4 = 100

MISC (NOVELTY, FOLK, FOREIGN & INSTRUMENTALS)-BONUS

1.

"WHO PUT THE BOMP (IN THE BOMP, BOMP, BOMP)" WAS A HIT SONG THAT MADE THE RELATIONSHIP WITH HIS GIRL MUCH STRONGER. WHAT MALE SINGER/SONGWRITER BELOW WAS RESPONSIBLE FOR IT BACK IN 1961?
A) JERRY BUTLER
B) DION
C) JOHNNY MAESTRO
D) BARRY MANN

2.

JOE HARNELL AND HIS ORCHESTRA CHARTED WHAT INSTRUMENTAL NUMBER IN 1963 ABOUT FLYING HIM TO SOMEWHERE IN SPACE?
A) EVERYONE'S GONE TO THE MOON
B) FLY ME TO THE MOON-BOSSA NOVA
C) TRAVELIN' MAN
D) UP-UP AND AWAY

3\.

THE SANDPIPERS, A MALE TRIO GROUP, HAD THE BIGGEST HIT OF THEIR CAREER WITH THIS SONG BELOW ABOUT A CERTAIN TOWN WHERE THE PALMS GROW. IT WAS SUNG IN BOTH ENGLISH AND SPANISH LYRICS.
A) THE GIRL FROM IPANEMA
B) QUE SERA, SERA (WHATEVER WILL BE, WILL BE)
C) GUANTANAMERA
D) TALLAHASSEE LASSIE

4\.

"LITTLE OLE MAN (UPTIGHT-EVERYTHING'S ALRIGHT)" WAS A BIG NOVELTY HIT IN 1967, A PARODY OF A *STEVIE WONDER* HIT SONG. WHO WAS THE COMEDIAN TURNED ACTOR RESPONSIBLE FOR IT ABOUT THE HERD OF ELEPHANTS AND TRAIN THAT RAN THAT OLD MAN DOWN?
A) FLIP WILSON
B) RED FOXX
C) RICHARD PRYOR
D) BILL COSBY

5\.

THE SERENDIPITY SINGERS CHARTED A NOVELTY HIT IN 1964 WITH THIS RAIN SONG THAT THEY FEARED WOULD DROWN THEM OUT OF THEIR HOME WITH THAT HOLE IN THE ROOF. WHAT WAS THAT NOVELTY HIT?
A) UP ON THE ROOF
B) DON'T LET THE RAIN COME DOWN (CROOKED LITTLE MAN)
C) DRIP DROP
D) RAIN RAIN GO AWAY

6\.

JANIS IAN RECORDED HER FIRST MAJOR HIT ABOUT AN INTERACIAL RELATIONSHIP THAT WOULD END DUE TO OUTSIDE PRESSURE AND THE RACIAL TENTIONS BACK THEN. WHAT WAS THAT FIRST MAJOR HIT?
A) LOUIE LOUIE
B) THINK
C) SOCIETY'S CHILD (BABY I'VE BEEN THINKING)
D) WHY CAN'T WE LIVE TOGETHER

7\.

THE DUO OF *STAN GETZ AND ASTRID GILBERTO,* MUSICIAN AND LYRIST RESPECTIVELY, HAD THIS JAZZY LATIN HIT ABOUT THAT GIRL BY THE SEA WHO WAS BLIND TO THE FACT THAT HE'S IN LOVE WITH HER. CHOOSE IT BELOW.
A) GIRL LIKE YOU
B) THE GIRL FROM IPANEMA
C) GIRL WATCHER
D) MY GIRL

8\.

THE '*SHADES OF BLUE*', A WHITE GROUP WITH A SOULFUL SOUND, CHARTED THIS HAPPY TITLED SONG ABOUT WHAT YOU HAVE DONE BECAUSE THEIR LOVE HAS GROWN STRONGER, BROUGHT JOY, AND MADE THINGS PERFECT. IT WOULD TURN OUT TO BE THEIR ONLY CLAIM TO FAME SONG.
A) OH HOW HAPPY
B) HAPPY TOGETHER
C) OH HAPPY DAY
D) YOU MADE ME SO VERY HAPPY

60'S | 60/21

MATCH THE WOODSTOCK MUSIC FESTIVAL ARTIST WITH THE THEIR SONG

	ARTIST		SONG	
1	RICHIE HAVENS	A	I WANT TO TAKE YOU HIGHER	1
2	COUNTRY JOE MCDONALD	B	I-FEEL-LIKE-I'M-FIXIN'-TO-DIE	2
3	COUNTRY JOE AND THE FISH	C	STAR SPANGLED BANNER	3
4	JOHN SEBASTIAN	D	WITH A LITTLE HELP FROM MY FRIENDS	4
5	ARLO GUTHRIE	E	FREEDOM	5
6	JOAN BAEZ	F	GOING UP THE COUNTRY	6
7	SANTANA	G	ROCK AND SOUL MUSIC	7
8	CANNED HEAT	H	YOUNGER GENERATION	8
9	JANIS JOPLIN	I	WORK ME, LORD	9
10	SLY & THE FAMILY STONE	J	SOUL SACRIFICE	10
11	THE WHO	K	JOE HILL	11
12	JEFFERSON AIRPLANE	L	COMING INTO LOS ANGELES	12
13	JOE COCKER & THE GREASE BAND	M	AT THE HOP	13
14	TEN YEARS AFTER	N	SUITE: JUDY BLUE EYES	14
15	CROSBY, STILLS & NASH	O	I'M GOING HOME	15
16	SHA NA NA	P	WON'T YOU TRY	16
17	JIMI HENDRIX	Q	WE'RE NOT GOING TO TAKE IT	17
18	CROSBY, STILLS, NASH & YOUNG	R	PURPLE HAZE	18
19	JIMI HENDRIX	S	SWING LOW SWEET CHARIOT	19
20	JOAN BAEZ	T	WOODSTOCK ****	20

TOTAL POINTS. 20 x 5 = 100

**** WRITTEN & RECORDED AFTER THE FESTIVAL

60'S | 60/22

MATCH THE DANCE HIT WITH THE ARTIST IN THE 60'S

	SONG		ARTIST	
1	PONY TIME	A	THE DOVELLS	1
2	THE TWIST	B	SAM COOKE	2
3	THE FLY	C	THE ORLONS	3
4	PEPPERMINT TWIST (PART 1)	D	THE ISLEY BROTHERS	4
5	LIMBO ROCK	E	CHUBBY CHECKER	5
6	TWISTIN' THE NIGHT AWAY	F	CHUBBY CHECKER	6
7	BRISTOL STOMP	G	LITTLE EVA	7
8	MICKEY'S MONKEY	H	JOEY DEE & THE STARLITERS	8
9	WALKING THE DOG	I	THE VIBRATIONS	9
10	FINGER POPPIN' TIME	J	THE MIRACLES	10
11	THE HUCKLEBUCK	K	CHUBBY CHECKER	11
12	LET'S TWIST AGAIN	L	WILSON PICKETT	12
13	THE WATUSI	M	CHUBBY CHECKER	13
14	THE LOCO-MOTION	N	CANNIBAL AND THE HEADHUNTERS	14
15	THE WAH WATUSI	O	MAJOR LANCE	15
16	TWIST AND SHOUT	P	CHUBBY CHECKER	16
17	MASHED POTATO TIME	Q	HANK BALLARD AND THE MIDNIGHTERS	17
18	THE MONKEY TIME	R	CHUBBY CHECKER	18
19	LAND OF 1000 DANCES	S	RUFUS THOMAS	19
20	LAND OF 1000 DANCES	T	DEE DEE SHARP	20

TOTAL POINTS. 20 x 5 = 100

60'S

MATCH THE LEAD SINGER WITH THE GROUP PT 1 IN THE 60'S

	LEAD SINGER		GROUP	
1	DIANA ROSS	A	SLY & THE FAMILY STONE	1
2	MICK JAGGER	B	THE CRYSTALS	2
3	SMOKEY ROBINSON	C	THE ANIMALS	3
4	JOHN SEBASTIAN	D	THE DRIFTERS	4
5	DAVID RUFFIN	E	THE DRIFTERS	5
6	JOHNNY MAESTRO	F	THE TEMPTATIONS	6
7	LEVI STUBBS	G	THE TEMPTATIONS	7
8	LEN BARRY	H	THE AMERICANS	8
9	JOHN FOGERTY	I	BLOOD, SWEAT & TEARS	9
10	DARLENE LOVE	J	THE CRESTS	10
11	RUDY LEWIS	K	THE SUPREMES	11
12	JIM MORRISON	L	THE LOVIN' SPOONFUL	12
13	ERIC BURDON	M	BROOKLYN BRIDGE	13
14	JOHNNY MAESTRO	N	THE ROLLING STONES	14
15	PETER NOONE	O	THE DOVELLS	15
16	SYLESTER STEWART	P	THE VANDELLAS	16
17	MARTHA REEVES	Q	THE MIRACLES	17
18	DARLENE LOVE	R	THE UNION GAP	18
19	JOHNNY MOORE	S	THE FOUR TOPS	19
20	BEN E KING	T	HERMAN'S HERMITS	20
21	GARY PUCKETT	U	THE DOORS	21
22	JAY BLACK	V	THE LIMELITES	22
23	DENNIS EDWARDS	W	CREEDENCE CLEARWATER REVIVAL	23
24	ADAM CLAYTON THOMAS	X	THE DRIFTERS	24
25	JIM SHEPPARD	Y	BOB B. SOXX AND THE BLUE JEANS	25

TOTAL POINTS. 25 x 4 = 100

MATCH THE GROUP WITH THEIR HIT SONG PT 1 IN THE 60'S

	GROUP		SONG	
1	SLY & THE FAMILY STONE	AA	DADDY'S HOME	1
2	THE CRYSTALS	BB	ZIP-A-DEE-D0-DAH	2
3	THE ANIMALS	CC	PROUD MARY	3
4	THE DRIFTERS	DD	EVERYDAY PEOPLE	4
5	THE DRIFTERS	EE	YOUNG GIRL	5
6	THE TEMPTATIONS	FF	I CAN'T GET NEXT TO YOU	6
7	THE TEMPTATIONS	GG	HELLO, I LOVE YOU	7
8	JAY & THE AMERICANS	HH	HE'S A REBEL	8
9	BLOOD, SWEAT & TEARS	II	UNDER THE BOARDWALK	9
10	THE CRESTS	JJ	MY GIRL	10
11	THE SUPREMES	KK	SHOP AROUND	11
12	THE LOVIN' SPOONFUL	LL	STEP BY STEP	12
13	BROOKLYN BRIDGE	MM	SAVE THE LAST DANCE FOR ME	13
14	THE ROLLING STONES	NN	I CAN'T HELP MYSELF	14
15	THE DOVELLS	OO	WHERE DID OUR LOVE GO?	15
16	THE VANDELLAS	PP	SOME KIND OF WONDERFUL	16
17	THE MIRACLES	QQ	BRISTOL STOMP	17
18	THE UNION GAP	RR	WORST THAT COULD HAPPEN	18
19	THE FOUR TOPS	SS	THE HOUSE OF THE RISING SUN	19
20	HERMAN'S HERMITS	TT	JIMMY MACK	20
21	THE DOORS	UU	SHE CRIED	21
22	THE LIMELITES	VV	YOU MADE ME SO VERY HAPPY	22
23	CREEDENCE CLEARWATER REVIVAL	WW	MRS BROWN YOU'VE GOT A LOVELY DAUGHTER	23
24	THE DRIFTERS	XX	SUMMER IN THE CITY	24
25	BOB B. SOXX AND THE BLUE JEANS	YY	(I CAN'T GET NO) SATISFACTION	25

TOTAL POINTS. 25 x 4 = 100

MATCH THE LEAD SINGER WITH THE GROUP PT II IN THE 60'S

	LEAD SINGER		GROUP	
1	LITTLE ANTHONY GOURDINE	A	THE EARLS	1
2	ARLENE SMITH	B	THE COASTERS	2
3	ARCHIE BELL	C	THE NEW CHRISTY MINSTRELS	3
4	SERGIO MENDES	D	SPENCER DAVIS GROUP	4
5	CURTIS MAYFIELD	E	THE CHECKMATES LTD.	5
6	RONNIE SPECTOR	F	THE SKYLINERS	6
7	TOMMY JAMES	G	THE FIREBALLS	7
8	GARNET MIMMS	H	THE DRELLS	8
9	WAYNE FONTANA	I	THE PLAYBOYS	9
10	SHIRLEY ALSTON	J	THE PIPS	10
11	MARK LINDSAY	K	THE JIVE FIVE	11
12	SONNY CHARLES	L	BIG BROTHER & THE HOLDING COMPANY	12
13	MAURICE WILLIAMS	M	THE RAIDERS	13
14	LARRY CHANCE	N	THE ALL STARS	14
15	JUNIOR WALKER	O	THE INNOCENTS	15
16	CORNELL GUNTHER	P	THE IMPERIALS	16
17	BARRY MCGUIRE	Q	BRASIL '66	17
18	STEVE WINWOOD	R	THE MINDBENDERS	18
19	KATHY YOUNG	S	THE IMPRESSIONS	19
20	EUGENE PITT	T	THE RONETTES	20
21	JIMMY GILMER	U	THE CHANTELS	21
22	GLADYS KNIGHT	V	THE SHIRELLES	22
23	JIMMY BEAUMONT	W	THE SHONDELLS	23
24	GARY LEWIS	X	THE ENCHANTERS	24
25	JANIS JOPLIN	Y	THE ZODIACS	25
			TOTAL POINTS.	25 x 4 = 100

MATCH THE GROUP WITH THEIR HIT SONG PT II IN THE 60'S

	GROUP		SONG	
1	THE EARLS	A	SOLDIER BOY	1
2	THE COASTERS	B	KICKS	2
3	THE NEW CHRISTY MINSTRELS	C	SUGAR SHACK	3
4	SPENCER DAVIS GROUP	D	CRY BABY	4
5	THE CHECKMATES LTD.	E	LOOK IN MY EYES	5
6	THE SKYLINERS	F	THE LOOK OF LOVE	6
7	THE FIREBALLS	G	CHARLIE BROWN	7
8	THE DRELLS	H	MY TRUE STORY	8
9	THE PLAYBOYS	I	GIMME SOME LOVIN'	9
10	THE PIPS	J	HANKY PANKY	10
11	THE JIVE FIVE	K	BE MY BABY	11
12	BIG BROTHER & THE HOLDING COMPANY	L	PIECE OF MY HEART	12
13	THE RAIDERS	M	PENNIES FROM HEAVEN	13
14	THE ALL STARS	N	IT'S ALRIGHT	14
15	THE INNOCENTS	O	EVERY BEAT OF MY HEART	15
16	THE IMPERIALS	P	A THOUSAND STARS	16
17	BRASIL '66	Q	THIS DIAMOND RING	17
18	THE MINDBENDERS	R	GOIN' OUT OF MY HEAD	18
19	THE IMPRESSIONS	S	TIGHTEN UP	19
20	THE RONETTES	T	GREEN, GREEN	20
21	THE CHANTELS	U	SHOTGUN	21
22	THE SHIRELLES	V	THE GAME OF LOVE	22
23	THE SHONDELLS	W	BLACK PEARL	23
24	THE ENCHANTERS	X	STAY	24
25	THE ZODIACS	Y	REMEMBER THEN	25
			TOTAL POINTS.	25 x 4 = 100

MATCH THE LEAD SINGER WITH THE GROUP PT III IN THE 60'S

	LEAD SINGER		GROUP	
1	LENNY COCCO	A	PLAYBOY BAND	1
2	FRANKIE VALLI	B	THE PHAROAHS	2
3	CHUCK NEGRON	C	THE BLUE BELLES	3
4	KENNY ROGERS	D	THE ROMANTICS	4
5	HERB ALPERT	E	STONE PONEYS	5
6	MITCH RDYER	F	THE RAINBOWS	6
7	HANK BALLARD	G	THE HI-LITES	7
8	RUBY NASH CURTIS	H	THE CHIMES	8
9	LINDA RONSTADT	I	THE TIJUANA BRASS	9
10	JAY PROCTOR	J	THE DREAMERS	10
11	PATTI LABELLE	K	THE WHO	11
12	JIMMY HART	L	THE FOUR SEASONS	12
13	DOMINICK RANDY SAFUTO	M	THE TECHNIQUES	13
14	SONNY TURNER	N	THE GENTRYS	14
15	FREDDIE GARRITY	O	THREE DOG NIGHT	15
16	ROGER DALTRY	P	THE PLATTERS	16
17	DOMINGO SAM SAMUDIO	Q	THE MIDNIGHTERS	17
18	JOHN FRED GOURRIER	R	THE FIRST EDITION	18
19	RONNIE GOODSON	S	THE DETROIT WHEELS	19
20	GRACE SLICK	T	JEFFERSON AIRPLANE	20

TOTAL POINTS. 20 x 5 = 100

60/28

MATCH THE GROUP WITH THEIR HIT SONG PT III IN THE 60'S

	GROUP		SONG	
1	PLAYBOY BAND	A	PINBALL WIZARD	1
2	THE PHAROAHS	B	I WISH THAT WE WERE MARRIED	2
3	THE BLUE BELLES	C	DENISE	3
4	THE ROMANTICS	D	KEEP ON DANCING	4
5	THE STONE PONEYS	E	WITH THIS RING	5
6	THE RAINBOWS	F	FINGER POPPIN' TIME	6
7	THE HI-LITES	G	JUST DROPPED IN (TO SEE WHAT CONDITION MY CONDITION WAS IN)	7
8	THE CHIMES	H	ELI'S COMING	8
9	THE TIJUANA BRASS	I	THE LONELY BULL	9
10	THE DREAMERS	J	JUDY IN DIGUISE (WITH GLASSES)	10
11	THE WHO	K	OUR DAY WILL COME	11
12	THE FOUR SEASONS	L	ONCE IN AWHILE	12
13	THE TECHNIQUES	M	SHERRY	13
14	THE GENTRYS	N	DIFFERENT DRUM	14
15	THREE DOG NIGHT	O	I'M TELLING YOU NOW	15
16	THE PLATTERS	P	APPLES, PEACHES, PUMPKIN PIE	16
17	THE MIDNIGHTERS	Q	I SOLD MY HEART TO THE JUNKMAN	17
18	THE FIRST EDITION	R	WHITE RABBIT	18
19	THE DETROIT WHEELS	S	WOLLY BULLY	19
20	JEFFERSON AIRPLANE	T	DEVIL WITH A BLUE DRESS ON & GOOD GOLLY MISS MOLLY	20

TOTAL POINTS. 20 x 5 = 100

MATCH THE DUOS AND ALSO THEIR HIT SONG IN THE 60'S

	1ST DUO		2ND DUO		SONG		
1	BROOK BENTON	A	DEEDEE	AA	CATHY'S CLOWN	1	,
2	PAUL SIMON	B	EVANS	BB	HEY PAULA	2	,
3	BILL MEDLEY	C	PAULA	CC	DEEP PURPLE	3	,
4	THE BEATLES	D	PHIL EVERLY	DD	SURF CITY	4	,
5	INEZ FOXX	E	GORDON	EE	I'M YOUR PUPPET	5	,
6	ZAGER	F	JUAN	FF	I'M LEAVING IT UP TO YOU	6	,
7	SONNY	G	CHER	GG	YOUR PRECIOUS LOVE	7	,
8	MARVIN GAYE	H	HERB	HH	BABY YOU'VE GOT WHAT IT TAKES	8	,
9	JERRY BUTLER	I	DINAH WASHINGTON	II	THE MOUNTAIN'S HIGH	9	,
10	NINO TEMPO	J	TINA	JJ	YOU'VE LOST THAT LOVIN' FEELIN'	10	,
11	NANCY SINATRA	K	BOBBY PURIFY	KK	MRS ROBINSON	11	,
12	PAUL	L	BOBBY HATFIELD	LL	CLOSE YOUR EYES	12	,
13	DON EVERLY	M	ART GARFUNKEL	MM	I'M GONNA MAKE YOU LOVE ME	13	,
14	JAN	N	CHARLIE FOXX	NN	I GOT YOU BABE	14	,
15	DALE	O	OTIS REDDING	OO	IN THE YEAR 2525	15	,
16	PETER	P	TEICHER	PP	GET BACK	16	,
17	THE SUPREMES	Q	TAMMI TERRELL	QQ	LET IT BE ME	17	,
18	DICK	R	APRIL STEVENS	RR	SOMETHIN' STUPID	18	,
19	JAMES PURIFY	S	DAVE	SS	MOCKINGBIRD	19	,
20	PEACHES	T	BETTY EVERETT	TT	EXODUS	20	,
21	FERRANTE	U	GRACE	UU	A WORLD WITHOUT LOVE	21	,
22	DON	V	FRANK SINATRA	VV	SOUL MAN	22	,
23	SAM	W	DEAN	WW	RIVER DEEP, MOUNTAIN HIGH	23	,
24	IKE	X	THE TEMPTATIONS	XX	TRAMP	24	,
25	CARLA THOMAS	Y	BILLY PRESTON	YY	WHAT'S YOUR NAME	25	,

TOTAL POINTS. 50 x 2 = 100

MATCH THE ARTIST WITH MOVIE/TV SHOW SONG PT 1 IN THE 60'S

	ARTIST		SONG	
1	LULU	A	HELLO, DOLLY!	1
2	SIMON & GARFUNKEL	B	RETURN TO SENDER	2
3	THE BEATLES	C	WHERE THE BOYS ARE	3
4	THE BEATLES	D	CAN'T HELP FALLING IN LOVE	4
5	LOUIS ARMSTRONG	E	NORTH TO ALSAKA	5
6	THE SUPREMES	F	TO SIR WITH LOVE	6
7	JOHNNY HORTON	G	HELP!	7
8	JOHNNY HORTON	H	THE HAPPENING	8
9	ELVIS	I	MRS ROBINSON	9
10	ELVIS	J	SINK THE BISMARCK	10
11	ELVIS	K	A HARD DAY'S NIGHT	11
12	ELVIS	L	THE THEME FROM 'A SUMMER PLACE'	12
13	ELVIS	M	OVER THE RAINBOW	13
14	GENE PITNEY	N	TOWN WITHOUT PITY	14
15	CONNIE FRANCIS	O	MOON RIVER	15
16	AL CAIOLA AND HIS ORCHESTRA	P	THE MAGNIFICENT SEVEN	16
17	PERCY FAITH AND HIS ORCHESTRA	Q	FLAMING STAR	17
18	THE DEMENSIONS	R	THEME FROM 'EXODUS'	18
19	FERRANTE & TEICHER	S	VIVA LAS VEGAS	19
20	BOB B. SOXX AND THE BLUE JEANS	T	DAYS OF WINE AND ROSES	20
21	GENE PITNEY	U	THEME FROM 'VALLEY OF THE DOLLS'	21
22	HENRY MANCINI AND HIS ORCHESTRA	V	THEME FROM 'THE PINK PANTHER'	22
23	ANDY WILLIAMS	W	FOLLOW THAT DREAM	23
24	DIONNE WARWICK	X	ZIP-A-DEE-DOO-DAH	24
25	HENRY MANCINI AND HIS ORCHESTRA	Y	THE MAN WHO SHOT LIBERTY VALANCE	25

TOTAL POINTS. 25 x 4 = 100

MATCH THE SONG WITH THE MOVIE/TV SHOW PT 1 IN THE 60'S

	SONG		MOVIE/TV SHOW	
1	HELLO, DOLLY!	A	HELP!	1
2	RETURN TO SENDER	B	THE HAPPENING	2
3	WHERE THE BOYS ARE	C	BLUE HAWAII	3
4	CAN'T HELP FALLING IN LOVE	D	NORTH TO ALASKA	4
5	NORTH TO ALASKA	E	TO SIR WITH LOVE	5
6	TO SIR WITH LOVE	F	HELLO, DOLLY!	6
7	HELP!	G	GIRLS, GIRLS, GIRLS	7
8	THE HAPPENING	H	SINK THE BISMARCK	8
9	MRS ROBINSON	I	WHERE THE BOYS ARE	9
10	SINK THE BISMARCK	J	A HARD DAY'S NIGHT	10
11	A HARD DAY'S NIGHT	K	THE GRADUATE	11
12	THE THEME FROM 'A SUMMER PLACE'	L	EXODUS	12
13	OVER THE RAINBOW	M	THE MAGNIFICENT SEVEN	13
14	TOWN WITHOUT PITY	N	A SUMMER PLACE	14
15	MOON RIVER	O	WIZARD OF OZ	15
16	THE MAGNIFICENT SEVEN	P	FOLLOW THAT DREAM	16
17	FLAMING STAR	Q	VIVA LAS VEGAS	17
18	THEME FROM 'EXODUS'	R	THE MAN WHO SHOT LIBERTY VALANCE	18
19	VIVA LAS VEGAS	S	BREAKFAST AT TIFFANY'S	19
20	DAYS OF WINE AND ROSES	T	TOWN WITHOUT PITY	20
21	THEME FROM 'VALLEY OF THE DOLLS'	U	SONG OF THE SOUTH	21
22	THEME FROM 'PINK PANTHER'	V	FLAMING STAR	22
23	FOLLOW THAT DREAM	W	DAYS OF WINE AND ROSES	23
24	ZIP-A-DEE-DOO-DAH	X	THE PINK PANTHER	24
25	THE MAN WHO SHOT LIBERTY VALANCE	Y	VALLEY OF THE DOLLS	25

TOTAL POINTS. 25 x 4 = 100

60/32

MATCH THE ARTIST WITH THE MOVIE/TV SHOW PT II IN THE 60'S

	ARTIST		MOVIE/TV SHOW	
1	AL CAIOLA AND HIS ORCHESTRA	A	TRUE GRIT	1
2	TOM JONES	B	GEORGY GIRL	2
3	SHIRLEY BASSEY	C	THE PRIDE OF MISS JEAN BRODIE	3
4	NANCY SINATRA	D	YELLOW SUBMARINE	4
5	NILSSON	E	CASINO ROYALE	5
6	GLENN YARBROUGH	F	NEVER ON SUNDAY	6
7	LESLEY GORE	G	BABY THE RAIN MUST FALL	7
8	MELINA MELCOURI	H	BONANZA	8
9	BARBRA STREISAND	I	YOU ONLY LIVE TWICE	9
10	JERRY BUTLER	J	THUNDERBALL	10
11	THE SEEKERS	K	FUNNY GIRL	11
12	THE BEATLES	L	ZORBA THE GREEK	12
13	GLEN CAMPBELL	M	HELP!	13
14	THE BEATLES	N	GOLDFINGER	14
15	OLIVER	O	BREAKFAST AT TIFFANY'S	15
16	BOOKER T & THE MG'S	P	MIDNIGHT COWBOY	16
17	HERB ALPERT & THE TIJUANA BRASS	Q	SKI PARTY	17
18	DUSTY SPRINGFIELD	R	HANG 'EM HIGH	18
19	ROGER WILLIAMS	S	BORN FREE	19
20	RAY CONIFF AND THE SINGERS	T	DR. ZHIVAGO	20
			TOTAL POINTS.	20 x 5 =100

60/33

MATCH THE SONG WITH THE MOVIE/TV SHOW PT II IN THE 60'S

	SONG		MOVIE/TV SHOW	
1	TRUE GRIT	A	THUNDERBALL	1
2	GEORGY GIRL	B	HANG 'EM HIGH	2
3	JEAN	C	ZORBA THE GREEK	3
4	YELLOW SUBMARINE	D	HELP!	4
5	THE LOOK OF LOVE	E	BONANZA	5
6	NEVER ON SUNDAY	F	FUNNY GIRL	6
7	BABY THE RAIN MUST FALL	G	THE PRIDE OF MISS JEAN BRODIE	7
8	THEME FROM 'BONANZA'	H	MIDNIGHT COWBOY	8
9	YOU ONLY LIVE TWICE	I	BABY THE RAIN MUST FALL	9
10	THUNDERBALL	J	CASINO ROYALE	10
11	PEOPLE	K	YELLOW SUBMARINE	11
12	ZORBA THE GREEK	L	TRUE GRIT	12
13	TICKET TO RIDE	M	GEORGY GIRL	13
14	GOLDFINGER	N	NEVER ON SUNDAY	14
15	MOON RIVER	O	SKI PARTY	15
16	EVERYBODY'S TALKIN'	P	BREAKFAST AT TIFFANY'S	16
17	SUNSHINE, LOLLIPOPS AND RAINBOWS	Q	YOU ONLY LIVE TWICE	17
18	HANG 'EM HIGH	R	GOLDFINGER	18
19	BORN FREE	S	BORN FREE	19
20	SOMEWHERE, MY LOVE	T	DR. ZHIVAGO	20
			TOTAL POINTS.	20 x 5 = 100

MATCH THE INSTRUMENTAL HIT WITH THE ARTIST PT 1 IN THE 60'S

	INSTRUMENTAL HIT		ARTIST	
1	GRAZING IN THE GRASS	A	PERCY FAITH AND HIS ORCHESTRA	1
2	THE 'IN' CROWD	B	THE T-BONES	2
3	THE STRIPPER	C	THE SURFARIS	3
4	TASTE OF HONEY	D	THE MARKETTS	4
5	WATERMELON MAN	E	PAUL MAURIAT AND HIS ORCHESTRA	5
6	GREEN ONIONS	F	THE VENTURES	6
7	OUT OF LIMITS	G	JOE HARNELL AND HIS ORCHESTRA	7
8	ROUTE 66 THEME	H	FERRANTE & TEICHER	8
9	WALK, DON'T RUN	I	MR ACKER BILL	9
10	THE THEME FROM 'A SUMMER PLACE'	J	MONGO SANTAMARIA	10
11	SOULFUL STRUT	K	RAMSEY LEWIS TRIO	11
12	NO MATTER WHAT SHAPE (YOUR STOMACH'S IN)	L	NELSON RIDDLE AND HIS ORCHESTRA	12
13	EXODUS	M	YOUNG-HOLT UNLIMITED	13
14	WIPEOUT	N	HERB ALPERT & THE TIJUANA BRASS	14
15	MUSIC TO WATCH GIRLS BY	O	DAVID ROSE AND HIS ORCHESTRA	15
16	FLY ME TO THE MOON-BOSSA NOVA	P	HUGO MONTENEGRO, HIS ORCHESTRA AND CHORUS	16
17	LOVE THEME FROM 'ROMEO & JULIET'	Q	BOB CREWE GENERATION	17
18	THE GOOD, THE BAD & THE UGLY	R	BOOKER T. & THE MG'S	18
19	STRANGERS ON THE SHORE	S	HUGH MASEKELA	19
20	LOVE IS BLUE	T	HENRY MANCINI AND HIS ORCHESTRA	20

TOTAL POINTS. 20 x 5 = 100

60/35

MATCH THE INSTRUMENTAL HIT WITH THE ARTIST PT II IN THE 60'S

	INSTRUMENTAL HIT		ARTIST	
1	CLASSICAL GAS	A	AL CAIOLA AND HIS ORCHESTRA	1
2	THE LONELY BULL	B	MAR-KEYS	2
3	LAST DATE	C	DON COSTA AND HIS ORCHESTRA AND CHORUS	3
4	NEVER ON SUNDAY	D	RAY CONIFF AND THE SINGERS	4
5	THEME FROM 'BONANZA'	E	MASON WILLIAMS	5
6	MERCY, MERCY, MERCY	F	HERB ALPERT & THE TIJUANA BRASS	6
7	LAST NIGHT	G	HERB ALPERT & THE TIJUANA BRASS	7
8	SOMEWHERE, MY LOVE	H	THE VENTURES	8
9	HANG 'EM HIGH	I	CANNONBALL ADDERLY	9
10	ZORBA THE GREEK	J	BOOKER T. & THE MG'S	10
11	TELSTAR	K	HENRY MANCINI AND HIS ORCHESTRA	11
12	BORN FREE	L	THE MARKETTS	12
13	MIDNIGHT COWBOY	M	THE CHANTAYS	13
14	HAWAII FIVE-O	N	THE TORNADOES	14
15	MEMPHIS	O	KING CURTIS & HIS BAND	15
16	THE HORSE	P	ROGER WILLIAMS	16
17	MOON RIVER	Q	FERRANTE & TEICHER	17
18	PIPELINE	R	LONNIE MACK	18
19	MEMPHIS SOUL STEW	S	CLIFF NOBLES	19
20	THE BATMAN THEME	T	FLOYD CRAMER	20

TOTAL POINTS. 20 x 5 = 100

(60'S ANSWER SHEET)

60/1 ELVIS

1. 1) STUCK ON YOU
   2) ARE YOU LONESOME TONIGHT?
   3) SURRENDER
   4) GOOD LUCK CHARM
   5) VIVA LAS VEGAS
   6) CAN'T HELP FALLING IN LOVE
   7) RETURN TO SENDER
   8) (YOU'RE THE) DEVIL IN DISGUISE
   9) CRYING IN THE CHAPEL
   10) SUSPICIOUS MINDS
   11) IN THE GHETTO
   12) IF I CAN DREAM
   13) (MARIE'S THE NAME) HIS LATEST FLAME
   14) FLAMING STAR
   15) FOLLOW THAT DREAM
   16) IT'S NOW OR NEVER
   17) LITTLE SISTER
   18) MEMORIES
2. C. FUN IN ALCAPULCO
3. D. ELVIS '68 COMEBACK SPECIAL

60/2 BEATLEMANIA-QUIZ # 1

1. D. GIVE PEACE A CHANCE
2. 1) JOHN LENNON
   2) PAUL MCCARTNEY
   3) GEORGE HARRISON
   4) RINGO STARR
3. C. THUNDERBALL
4. C. HELP!
5. WE LOVE YOU BEATLES
6. B. THE ED SULLIVAN SHOW
7. D. TWIST AND SHOUT

60/3 BEATLEMANIA-QUIZ # 2

1. I WANT TO HOLD YOUR HAND
2. I SAW HER STANDING THERE
3. SHE LOVES YOU
4. PLEASE PLEASE ME
5. MONEY (THAT'S WHAT I WANT)
6. CAN'T BUY ME LOVE
7. SOMETHING
8. DO YOU WANT TO KNOW A SECRET
9. ROLL OVER BEETHOVEN
10. P.S. I LOVE YOU
11. A HARD DAYS NIGHT
12. AND I LOVE HER
13. I FEEL FINE
14. SHE'S A WOMAN
15. EIGHT DAYS A WEEK
16. TICKET TO RIDE
17. HELP!
18. DRIVE MY CAR
19. WE CAN WORK IT OUT

20. DAY TRIPPER
21. NOWHERE MAN
22. PAPERBACK WRITER
23. YELLOW SUBMARINE
24. ELEANOR RIGBY
25. PENNY LANE
26. STRAWBERRY FIELDS FOREVER
27. ALL YOU NEED IS LOVE
28. HELLO GOODBYE
29. LADY MADONNA
30. REVOLUTION
31. GET BACK
32. DON'T LET ME DOWN
33. THE BALLAD OF JOHN AND YOKO
34. COME TOGETHER
35. FROM ME TO YOU
36. HEY JUDE
37. ALL MY LOVING
38. YOU'VE GOT TO HIDE YOUR LOVE AWAY
39. YOU'RE GOING TO LOSE THAT GIRL
40. IF I FELL
41. IT WON'T BE LONG
42. GOOD DAY SUNSHINE
43. THIS BOY
44. TILL THERE WAS YOU
45. WITH A LITTLE HELP FROM MY FRIENDS
46. NO REPLY
47. C. YESTERDAY
48. A. MICHELLE
49. C. LOVE ME DO
50. B. ACT NATURALLY

BEATLEMANIA BONUS

1. B. BRIAN EPSTEIN
2. C. PETE BEST

60/4 THE REST OF THE BRITISH INVASION-QUIZ # 1

1. A. GAME OF LOVE
2. 1) I KNOW A PLACE
   2) MY LOVE
   3) THIS IS MY SONG
   4) KISS ME GOODBYE
   5) DON'T SLEEP IN THE SUBWAY
   6) I COULDN'T LIVE WITHOUT YOUR LOVE
3. C. DONOVAN
4. A. DO WAH DIDDY DIDDY
5. B. GIMME SHELTER
6. 1) BARRY GIBB
   2) MAURICE GIBB
   3) ROBIN GIBB
7. 1) (I CAN'T GET NO) SATISFACTION
   2) GET OFF MY CLOUD
   3) PAINT IT, BLACK
   4) RUBY TUESDAY
   5) JUMPIN' JACK FLASH
   6) TIME IS ON MY SIDE

7) MOTHER'S LITTLE HELPER
8) HONKY TONK WOMAN
9) 19TH NERVOUS BREAKDOWN
10) AS TEARS GO BY
11) HEART OF STONE
12) IT'S ALL OVER NOW
13) TELL ME (YOU'RE COMING BACK)
14) THE LAST TIME

8. B. LOVE IS ALL AROUND
9. D. WILD THING
10. NEEDLES AND PINS
11. D. LOVE POTION NUMBER NINE
12. C. THE SILKIE
13. C. AS TEARS GO BY
14. D. FREDDIE AND THE DREAMERS
15. B. A WHITER SHADE OF PALE
16. C. RUBY TUESDAY
17. D. A GROOVY KIND OF LOVE
18. 1) MRS BROWN YOU GOT A LOVELY DAUGHTER
2) CAN'T YOU HEAR MY HEARTBEAT
3) I'M INTO SOMETHING GOOD
4) I'M HENRY THE VIII, I AM
5) WONDERFUL WORLD
6) LISTEN PEOPLE
7) THERE'S A KIND OF HUSH
8) SILHOUETTES
19. 1) OVER AND OVER
2) GLAD ALL OVER
3) BITS AND PIECES
4) YOU GOT WHAT IT TAKES
5) I LIKE IT LIKE THAT
6) CAN'T YOU SEE THAT SHE'S MINE
7) BECAUSE
8) CATCH US IF YOU CAN
20. 1) MICK JAGGER
2) KEITH RICHARDS
3) BRIAN JONES
4) CHARLIE WATTS
5) BILL WYMAN
21. 1) I ONLY WANT TO BE WITH YOU
2) WISHIN' AND HOPIN'
3) YOU DON'T HAVE TO SAY YOU LOVE ME
4) SON OF A PREACHER MAN
22. 1) SHE'S NOT THERE
2) TIME OF THE SEASON
3) TELL HER NO
23. B. FOR YOUR LOVE
24. D. THE KINKS
25. C. ALL DAY AND ALL OF THE NIGHT
26. 1) THE HOUSE OF THE RISING SUN
2) WE GOTTA GET OUT OF THIS PLACE
3) IT'S MY LIFE
27. C. THE WHO
28. A. WHITE ROOM
29. 1) THE BEATLES
2) CHAD & JEREMY
3) DAVE CLARK FIVE
4) DONOVAN

5) THE ANIMALS
6) THE FORTUNES
7) GERRY AND THE PACEMAKERS
8) THE HOLLIES
9) THE KINKS
10) MANFRED MANN
11) PETER AND GORDON
12) THE ROLLING STONES
13) THE ZOMBIES
14) HERMAN'S HERMITS
15) THE TROGGS
16) SPENCER DAVIS GROUP
17) PETULA CLARK
18) DUSTY SPRINGFIELD
19) FREDDIE AND THE DREAMERS

30\. D. THE FLYING MACHINE
31\. C. TO SIR WITH LOVE
32\. B. YOU'VE GOT YOUR TROUBLES
33\. A. A SUMMER SONG
34\. 1) RELEASE ME (AND LET ME LOVE AGAIN)
2) AM I THAT EASY TO FORGET
35\. B. LITTLE CHILDREN
36\. C. BAD TO ME

60/5 THE REST OF THE BRITISH INVASION-QUIZ # 2

1\. D. EVERYONE'S GONE TO THE MOON
2\. 1) I GO TO PIECES
2) LADY GODIVA
3) A WORLD WITHOUT LOVE
3\. 1) SUNSHINE SUPERMAN
2) ATLANTIS
3) MELLOW YELLOW
4) THERE IS A MOUNTAIN
5) HURDY GURDY MAN
6) JENNIFER JUNIPER
4\. C. ERIC CLAPTON
5\. 1) TO LOVE SOMEBODY
2) I'VE GOTTA GET A MESSAGE TO YOU
3) I STARTED A JOKE
6\. C. I'M GOING HOME
7\. A. BUS STOP
8\. A. SUGAR, SUGAR
9\. B. BABY, NOW THAT I'VE FOUND YOU
10\. C. BUILD ME UP BUTTERCUP
11\. D. SILENCE IS GOLDEN
12\. C. GIMME SOME LOVIN'
13\. B. FIRE
14\. C. GO NOW!
15\. D. YOU TURN ME ON (TURN ON SONG)
16\. C. HIPPY HIPPY SHAKE

THE REST OF THE BRITISH INVASION-BONUS

1\. A. HAVE I THE RIGHT
2\. C. DEEP PURPLE

60/6 MOTOWN ROCKERS

1\. 1) THE MIRACLES
   2) SHOP AROUND
   3) I SECOND THAT EMOTION
   4) THE TRACKS OF MY TEARS
   5) I'LL TRY SOMETHING NEW
   6) YOU'VE REALLY GOT A HOLD ON ME
   7) MICKEY'S MONKEY
   8) GOING TO A GO-GO
   9) OOH BABY BABY
2\. BERRY GORDY JR
3\. C. MY GIRL
4\. 1) TWO LOVERS
   2) MY GUY
5\. A. FLORENCE BALLARD
6\. 1) THE TEMPTATIONS
   2) IT'S GROWING
   3) AIN'T TOO PROUD TO BEG
   4) DON'T LOOK BACK
   5) GET READY
   6) SINCE I LOST MY BABY
   7) BEAUTY IS ONLY SKIN DEEP
   8) I WISH IT WOULD RAIN
   9) MY GIRL
   10) THE WAY YOU DO THE THINGS YOU DO
   11) CLOUD NINE
   12) YOU'RE MY EVERYTHING
   13) I COULD NEVER LOVE ANOTHER (AFTER LOVING YOU)
   14) (I KNOW) I'M LOSING YOU
7\. B. BABY, I'M FOR REAL
8\. C. MY WHOLE WORLD ENDED (THE MOMENT YOU LEFT ME)
9\. 1) LITTLE STEVIE WONDER
   2) FINGER TIPS (PT II)
   3) FOR ONCE IN MY LIFE
   4) I WAS MADE TO LOVE HER
   5) BLOWIN' IN THE WIND
   6) MY CHERIE AMOUR
10\. C. MONEY (THAT'S WHAT I WANT)
11\. A. WHAT BECOMES OF THE BROKENHEARTED
12\. 1) THE SUPREMES
   2) LOVE IS LIKE AN ITCHING IN MY HEART
   3) I HEAR A SYMPHONY
   4) YOU KEEP ME HANGIN' ON
   5) BACK IN MY ARMS AGAIN
   6) STOP! IN THE NAME OF LOVE
   7) MY WORLD IS EMPTY WITHOUT YOU
   8) YOU CAN'T HURRY LOVE
   9) NOTHING BUT HEARTACHES
   10) LOVE CHILD
   11) REFLECTIONS
   12) I'M LIVING IN SHAME
   13) THE HAPPENING
13\. D. SOMEDAY WE'LL BE TOGETHER
14\. C. 25 MILES
15\. 1) OTIS WILLIAMS
   2) PAUL WILLIAMS
   3) MELVIN FRANKLIN

4) EDDIE KENDRICKS
5) DAVID RUFFIN

16. E. BETTY EVERETT
17. 1) HOW SWEET IT IS TO BE LOVED BY YOU
2) I'LL BE DOGGONE
3) AIN'T THAT PECULIAR
4) I HEARD IT THROUGH THE GRAPEVINE
5) TOO BUSY THINKING ABOUT MY BABY
6) PRIDE AND JOY
7) YOU'RE A WONDERFUL ONE
8) THAT'S THE WAY LOVE IS
18. D. I'M GONNA MAKE YOU LOVE ME
19. 1) DANCING IN THE STREET
2) COME AND GET THESE MEMORIES
3) JIMMY MACK
4) QUICKSAND
5) HEATWAVE
6) NOWHERE TO RUN
7) HONEY CHILE
20. 1) FOUR TOPS
2) I CAN'T HELP MYSELF
3) BABY I NEED YOUR LOVING
4) ASK THE LONELY
5) REACH OUT I'LL BE THERE
6) SOMETHING ABOUT YOU
7) SHAKE ME, WAKE ME (WHEN IT'S OVER)
8) IF I WERE A CARPENTER
9) WALK AWAY RENEE
21. B. THIS OLD HEART OF MINE (IS WEAK FOR YOU)
22. D. DO YOU LOVE ME
23. 1) PLEASE MR POSTMAN
2) PLAYBOY
3) BEECHWOOD 4-5789
4) DON'T MESS WITH BILL
5) THE HUNTER GETS CAPTURED BY THE GAME
6) TOO MANY FISH IN THE SEA
7) MY BABY MUST BE A MAGICIAN
24. C. THE FUNK BROTHERS
25. 1) B, BB THE SUPREMES, VANILLA FUDGE
2) C, AA THE FOUR TOPS, JOHNNY RIVERS
3) A, CC THE CONTOURS, DAVE CLARK FIVE

60/7 MOTOWN ROCKERS-QUIZ # 2

1. HERE COMES THE JUDGE
2. D. ATCO
3. C. EVERY LITTLE BIT HURTS
4. 1) SHOTGUN
2) WHAT DOES IT TAKE (TO WIN YOUR LOVE)?
3) HOW SWEET IT IS (TO BE LOVED BY YOU)
5. 1) EVERY BEAT OF MY HEART
2) I HEARD IT THROUGH THE GRAPEVINE
3) THE NITTY GRITTY
4) FRIENDSHIP TRAIN
6. C. IT TAKES TWO
7. 1) AIN'T NO MOUNTAIN HIGH ENOUGH
2) YOUR PRECIOUS LOVE
3) IF I COULD BUILD MY WHOLE WORLD AROUND YOU

4) AIN'T NOTHING LIKE THE REAL THING
5) YOU'RE ALL I NEED TO GET BY

8. C. DENNIS EDWARDS
9. B. CLAUDETTE ROGERS
10. C. SMOKEY ROBINSON
11. SMOKEY ROBINSON

60/8 R&B ROCKERS-QUIZ # 1

1. 1) I'M ON THE OUTSIDE (LOOKING IN)
   2) GOIN' OUT OF MY HEAD
   3) HURT SO BAD
   4) TAKE ME BACK
   5) SHIMMY, SHIMMY, KO-KO-BOP
   6) I MISS YOU SO
   7) HURT
   8) OUR SONG
2. A. LOOK IN MY EYES
3. 1) DEDICATED TO THE ONE I LOVE
   2) TONIGHTS THE NIGHT
   3) WILL YOU LOVE ME TOMORROW
   4) SOLDIER BOY
   5) MAMA SAID
   6) FOOLISH LITTLE GIRL
   7) EVERYBODY LOVES A LOVER
   8) BABY IT'S YOU
4. 1) SAVE THE LAST DANCE FOR ME
   2) UP ON THE ROOF
   3) UNDER THE BOARDWALK
   4) ON BROADWAY
   5) THIS MAGIC MOMENT
   6) I COUNT THE TEARS
   7) SOME KIND OF WONDERFUL
   8) SWEETS FOR MY SWEET
   9) SATURDAY NIGHT AT THE MOVIES
   10) PLEASE STAY
   11) I'VE GOT SAND IN MY SHOES
5. A. HEY, GIRL
6. C. HELLO STRANGER
7. D. BABY, I'M YOURS
8. B. YES, I'M READY
9. A. I'M YOUR PUPPET
10. 1) (YOU'RE MY) SOUL AND INSPIRATION
    2) YOU'VE LOST THAT LOVIN' FEELIN'
    3) UNCHAINED MELODY
11. C. THE BOY FROM NEW YORK CITY
12. 1) COWBOYS TO GIRLS
    2) SAD GIRL
    3) TOGETHER
13. B. GENE CHANDLER
14. B. OTIS REDDING
15. D. MASHED POTATO TIME
16. A. STAY
17. A. I WISH THAT WE WERE MARRIED
18. D. GRAZING IN THE GRASS
19. B. GOING IN CIRCLES
20. 1) WONDERFUL WORLD
    2) CHAIN GANG

3) CUPID
4) BRING IT ON HOME TO ME
5) TWISTIN' THE NIGHT AWAY
6) HAVING A PARTY
7) ANOTHER SATURDAY NIGHT
8) SHAKE

21. B. BACKFIELD IN MOTION
22. B. COOL JERK
23. C. IF YOU WANNA BE HAPPY
24. C. ARETHA FRANKLIN
25. B. SLIP AWAY
26. B. WORKING IN THE COAL MINE
27. D. MY BOY LOLLIPOP
28. 1) D. MOTOWN
    2) C. STAX/VOLT RECORDS
29. C. RAY CHARLES
30. C. (I WANNA) TESTIFY
31. C. MY PLEDGE OF LOVE
32. D. OH, WHAT A NIGHT
33. B. STAY IN MY CORNER
34. 1) CHUBBY CHECKER
    2) THE TWIST
35. C. LET'S TWIST AGAIN
36. 1) GEORGIA ON MY MIND
    2) HIT THE ROAD JACK
    3) UNCHAIN MY HEART
    4) I CAN'T STOP LOVING YOU
    5) BUSTED
    6) CRYING TIME
    7) LET'S GO GET STONED
    8) ELEANOR RIGBY
37. A. DON'T LOOK BACK
38. A. LET THE LITTLE GIRL DANCE
39. A. CHUBBY CHECKER
40. 1) SOUL MAN
    2) HOLD ON! I'M A COMIN'
    3) WHEN SOMETHING IS WRONG WITH MY BABY
    4) I THANK YOU
41. C. OH HAPPY DAY
42. C. THOSE OLDIERS BUT GOODIES (REMIND ME OF YOU)
43. B. BUT IT'S ALRIGHT
44. B. A LITTLE BIT OF SOAP
45. 1) THE CRYSTALS
    2) HE'S A REBEL
    3) THEN HE KISSED ME
    4) HE'S SURE THE BOY I LOVE
    5) LOOK IN MY EYES
    6) DA DOO RON RON (WHEN HE WALKED ME HOME)
    7) THERE'S NO OTHER (LIKE MY BABY)
    8) UPTOWN
46. D. LOOP DE LOOP

60/9 R&B ROCKERS-QUIZ # 2

1. 1) HE'S SO FINE
   2) ONE FINE DAY
   3) SWEET TALKIN' GUY
2. C. RELEASE ME

3. 1) BEN E KING
2) STAND BY ME
3) SPANISH HARLEM
4) DON'T PLAY THAT SONG (YOU LIED)
5) I (WHO HAVE NOTHING)
4. C. EASIER SAID THAN DONE
5. B. A WALKIN' MIRACLE
6. A. THE WINSTONS
7. B. JIMMY CHARLES
8. C. WILSON PICKETT
9. B. WHO'S MAKING LOVE
10. 1) AARON NEVILLE
2) TELL IT LIKE IT IS
11. B. LOVE MAKES THE WORLD GO ROUND
12. 1) TWIST AND SHOUT
2) IT'S YOUR THING
13. 1) HOLD WHAT YOU'VE GOT
2) SKINNY LEGS AND ALL
3) SHOW ME
14. 1) ALL IN MY MIND
2) FUNNY
3) OH NO NOT MY BABY
15. B. I LIKE IT LIKE THAT
16. D. OUR DAY WILL COME
17. B. BLACK PEARL
18. B. BABY OH BABY
19. D. MOUNTAIN OF LOVE
20. B. GIRL WATCHER
21. 1) AQUARIUS/LET THE SUNSHINE IN
2) STONED SOUL PICNIC
3) UP-UP AND AWAY
4) WEDDING BELL BLUES
5) SWEET BLINDNESS
22. D. JUST ONE LOOK
23. C. CHUCK BERRY
24. E. MARY WILSON
25. A. MOCKINGBIRD
26. 1) ARETHA FRANKLIN
2) THE HOUSE THAT JACK BUILT
3) RESPECT
4) A NATURAL WOMAN (YOU MAKE ME FEEL LIKE)
5) I SAY A LITTLE PRAYER
6) ELEANOR RIGBY
7) I NEVER LOVED A MAN (THE WAY I LOVE YOU)
8) SAVE ME
9) THINK
27. B. THE PLATTERS
28. D. WAIT TIL' MY BOBBY GETS HOME
29. C. THE SWEETHEARTS OF SOUL
30. C. DEE-DEE SHARP
31. B. I'M A HAPPY MAN
32. 1) DANCE TO THE MUSIC
2) EVERYDAY PEOPLE
3) HOT FUN IN THE SUMMERTIME
4) YOU CAN MAKE IT IF YOU TRY
5) STAND!
6) I WANT TO TAKE YOU HIGHER
33. B. THE JAYNETTS

34. B. WHAT KIND OF FOOL (DO YOU THINK I AM)
35. B. THE DREAMLOVERS
36. B. HEART AND SOUL
37. B. (YOU DON'T KNOW) HOW GLAD I AM
38. D. A WONDERFUL DREAM
39. 1) JACKIE WILSON
    2) BABY WORKOUT
    3) (YOUR LOVE KEEPS LIFTING ME) HIGHER AND HIGHER
    4) TALK THAT TALK
40. 1) PEACHES & HERB
    2) LET'S FALL IN LOVE
    3) CLOSE YOUR EYES
    4) FOR YOUR LOVE
    5) LOVE IS STRANGE
    6) TWO LITTLE KIDS
    7) THE TEN COMMANDMENTS OF LOVE
41. 1) JERRY BUTLER
    2) HE WILL BREAK YOUR HEART
    3) MOON RIVER
    4) MAKE IT EASY ON YOURSELF
    5) HEY, WESTERN UNION MAN
    6) ONLY THE STRONG SURVIVE
    7) WHAT'S THE USE OF BREAKING UP
    8) MOODY WOMAN
    9) NEVER GIVE YOU UP
    10) MR DREAM MERCHANT
    11) I DIG YOU BABY
42. 1) PEOPLE GET READY
    2) KEEP ON PUSHING
    3) WE'RE A WINNER
    4) AMEN
    5) GYPSY WOMAN
    6) I'M SO PROUD
    7) IT'S ALL RIGHT
    8) TALKING ABOUT MY BABY
    9) WOMAN'S GOT SOUL
43. B. OTIS REDDING
44. THE DRIFTERS

60/10 R&B ROCKERS-QUIZ # 3

1. D. RAINDROPS
2. C. KNOCK ON WOOD
3. D. I DO
4. A. THE EDSELS
5. B. TONIGHT (COULD BE THE NIGHT)
6. B. WALKING THE DOG
7. A. A LOVER'S CONCERTO
8. C. BOOGALOO DOWN BROADWAY
9. B. THE ORIGINALS
10. B. HYPNOTIZED
11. C. TURN ON YOUR LOVE LIGHT
12. D. JACKIE WILSON
13. D. CHUBBY CHECKER
14. D. LOVE LETTERS
15. C. PATTI LABELLE
16. C. DOWN THE AISLE (WEDDING SONG)
17. C. EVERLASTING LOVE

18. C. LITTLE GREEN APPLES
19. C. BAREFOOTIN'
20. B. THE LARKS
21. A. BROOK BENTON
22. D. ONCE UPON A TIME
23. C. LOVER'S ISLAND
24. A. ETTA JAMES
25. B. YOU CAN HAVE HER
26. D. SINCE I FELL FOR YOU
27. HELLO, DOLLY!
28. D. THOSE LAZY HAZY CRAZY DAYS OF SUMMER
29. 1) RAMBLIN' ROSE
    2) L.O.V.E.
30. 1) DIONNE WARWICK
    2) ANYONE WHO HAD A HEART
    3) WALK ON BY
    4) MESSAGE TO MICHAEL
    5) I SAY A LITTLE PRAYER
    6) DO YOU KNOW THE WAY TO SAN JOSE?
    7) DON'T MAKE ME OVER
31. A. LITTLE EVA
32. C. (DOWN AT) PAPA JOE'S
33. C. THE THRILL IS GONE
34. B. A ROCKIN' GOOD WAY (TO MESS AROUND AND FALL IN LOVE)
35. A. I KNOW (YOU DON'T LOVE ME NO MORE)
36. D. EVERYBODY NEEDS SOMEBODY TO LOVE
37. 1) ANY DAY NOW (MY WILD AND BEAUTIFUL BIRD)
    2) I DON'T WANT TO CRY
38. B. CRY BABY
39. C. SWEET SOUL MUSIC
40. B. TIGHTEN UP
41. A. THE CHOKIN' KIND
42. A. DADDY'S HOME

60/11 R&B ROCKERS-QUIZ # 4

1. B. BABY (YOU'VE GOT WHAT IT TAKES)
2. C. WHEN A MAN LOVES A WOMAN
3. D. TAKE TIME TO KNOW HER
4. 1) THE BOLL WEEVIL SONG
   2) HOTEL HAPPINESS
   3) THINK TWICE
5. 1) RESPECT
   2) SHAKE
   3) SATISFACTION
   4) I'VE BEEN LOVING YOU TOO LONG (TO STOP NOW)
   5) TRY A LITTLE TENDERNESS
   6) (SITTIN' ON) THE DOCK OF THE BAY
6. A. JAMES BROWN
7. C. TAKE A LETTER MARIA
8. 1) IN THE MIDNIGHT HOUR
   2) 634-5789
   3) LAND OF A THOUSAND DANCES
   4) MUSTANG SALLY
   5) FUNKY BROADWAY
   6) EVERYBODY NEEDS SOMEBODY TO LOVE
   7) I FOUND A LOVE
   8) I'M IN LOVE

9. B. THE SHOOP, SHOOP SONG (IT'S IN HIS KISS)
10. 1) JERRY BUTLER
    2) CURTIS MAYFIELD
11. C. THE DUCK
12. C. I WANNA LOVE HIM SO BAD
13. D. PEACE BROTHER PEACE
14. B. BROWN EYED WOMAN
15. C. DRY YOUR EYES
16. B. DON'T SAY NOTHIN' BAD (ABOUT MY BABY)
17. C. SNAP YOUR FINGERS
18. D. SUNNY
19. C. HOLD ME, THRILL ME, KISS ME
20. D. SO MUCH IN LOVE
21. B. WONDERFUL! WONDERFUL!
22. D. IT'S GONNA TAKE A MIRACLE
23. A. CHAPEL OF LOVE
24. 1) PEOPLE SAY
    2) IKO IKO
25. C. THE BIRDS AND THE BEES
26. C. YOU'LL LOSE A GOOD THING
27. 1) WHAT'S YOUR NAME
    2) DON
    3) JUAN
28. B. TOSSIN' AND TURNIN'
29. B. SMOKEY PLACES
30. C. LET ME IN
31. B. YOU TALK TOO MUCH
32. B. MY GIRL SLOOPY
33. B. PEANUT BUTTER
34. E. TWISTIN' THE NIGHT AWAY
35. C. CHUCK BERRY
36. B. BOBBY FREEMAN
37. A. PARTY LIGHTS
38. C. A HUNDRED POUNDS OF CLAY
39. C. TOWER OF STRENGTH
40. A. MOTHER-IN-LAW
41. D. BETTY EVERETT
42. A. RESCUE ME
43. A. I DON'T KNOW WHY I LOVE YOU (BUT I DO)
44. 1) RAMSEY LEWIS TRIO
    2) DOBIE GRAY
45. A. THE CRYSTALS
46. B. THE MONKEY TIME
47. A. TIME HAS COME TODAY
48. B. APPLES, PEACHES, PUMPKIN PIE
49. D. CHUBBY CHECKER
50. 1) LET THE FOUR WINDS BLOW
    2) WALKING TO NEW ORLEANS
    3) MY GIRL JOSEPHINE
51. A. GET ON UP
52. C. HANDY MAN
53. B. GOOD TIMIN'
54. A. LOVE IS A HURTIN' THING
55. B. DEAD END STREET
56. B. MAMA DIDN'T LIE
57. B. HOLD ME TIGHT
58. A. GIMME LITTLE SIGN
59. C. FINGER POPPIN' TIME

60. C. LET'S GO, LET'S GO, LET'S GO
61. LA LA MEANS I LOVE YOU
62. 1) SUMMERTIME
2) I DO LOVE YOU
3) SITTING IN THE PARK
63. B. FAT BOY
64. 1) THE WAH WATUSI
2) SOUTH STREET
3) DON'T HANG UP
65. 1) JAMES BROWN
2) PAPA'S GOT A BRAND NEW BAG (PART 1)
3) IT'S A MAN'S, MAN'S, MAN'S WORLD
4) SAY IT LOUD-I'M BLACK AND I'M PROUD (PART 1)
66. B. LOVE IS A HURTIN' THING
67. C. BLUE MOON
68. C. DIAMONDS AND PEARLS
69. A. TELL HIM
70. B. FOR YOUR PRECIOUS LOVE
71. D. GEE WHIZ (LOOK AT HIS EYES)
72. B. B-A-B-Y

R&B ROCKERS-BONUS

1. B. I GOTTA BE ME
2. D. WHO DO YOU LOVE
3. D. SWEET INSPIRATION

60/12 POP ROCKERS-QUIZ # 1

1. 1) RUBBER BALL
2) TAKE GOOD CARE OF MY BABY
3) DEVIL OR ANGEL
4) RUN TO HIM
5) THE NIGHT HAS A THOUSAND EYES
6) COME BACK WHEN YOU GROW UP
2. A. I LEFT MY HEART IN SAN FRANCISCO
3. D. THE SUN AIN'T GONNA SHINE (ANYMORE)
4. C. MAKE IT EASY ON YOURSELF
5. D. CONEY ISLAND BABY
6. 1) GOIN' OUT OF MY HEAD
2) CAN'T TAKE MY EYES OFF YOU
7. C. THE WAY YOU LOOK TONIGHT
E. WHEN I FALL IN LOVE
8. B. I'M SO LONESOME I COULD CRY
9. B. HOOKED ON A FEELING
10. D. EVERYBODY'S TALKIN'
11. A. TRACES
12. A. SUGAR, SUGAR
13. B. LITTLE WOMAN
14. C. THE LEMON PIPERS
15. A. TRACY
16. 1) BEYOND THE SEA
2) YOU MUST HAVE BEEN A BEAUTIFUL BABY
3) BILL BAILEY, WON'T YOU COME HOME
4) ARTIFICIAL FLOWERS
5) IF I WERE A CARPENTER
6) THINGS
17. A. SUMMER WIND

18. A. CHERRY PIE
19. B. SHOUT! SHOUT! (KNOCK YOURSELF OUT)
20. D. BURT BACHARACH
21. B. RICKY NELSON
22. A. EXPRESSWAY (TO YOUR HEART)
23. B. SEALED WITH A KISS
24. C. NA NA HEY HEY KISS HIM GOODBYE
25. 1) THESE BOOTS ARE MADE FOR WALKIN'
    2) SUGAR TOWN
    3) SOMETHIN' STUPID
26. B. BOOM BOOM
27. B. CONNIE STEVENS
28. C. IMAGE OF A GIRL
29. C. PALISADES PARK
30. D. BANG, BANG (MY BABY SHOT ME DOWN)
31. D. WHAT THE WORLD NEEDS NOW IS LOVE
32. B. PUT A LITTLE LOVE IN YOUR HEART
33. D. LET'S DANCE
34. 1) DEL SHANNON
    2) RUNAWAY
    3) HATS OFF TO LARRY
    4) LITTLE TOWN FLIRT
    5) HANDY MAN
35. 1) SWEET CAROLINE (GOOD TIMES NEVER SEEMED SO GOOD)
    2) GIRL, YOU'LL BE A WOMAN SOON
    3) I THANK THE LORD FOR THE NIGHT TIME
    4) KENTUCKY WOMAN
    5) BROTHER LOVE'S TRAVELLING SALVATION SHOW
    6) CHERRY, CHERRY
    7) HOLLY HOLY
    8) YOU GOT TO ME
36. A. HURT
37. 1) MY WAY
    2) FRANK SINATRA
38. C. ANDY WILLIAMS
39. B. WESTERN UNION
40. B. ELUSIVE BUTTERFLY
41. C. LOVE ME WITH ALL YOUR HEART (CUANDO CALIENTA EL SOL)
42. C. GOODBYE CRUEL WORLD
43. 1) I'M A BELIEVER
    2) RED RED WINE
44. B. KEITH
45. D. POETRY IN MOTION
46. C. IT KEEPS RIGHT ON-A-HURTIN'
47. A. JOHNNY ANGEL
48. 1) ALONG COMES MARY
    2) NEVER MY LOVE
    3) WINDY
    4) CHERISH
49. D. WONDERFUL SUMMER
50. B. TEEN ANGEL
51. C. PRETTY LITTLE ANGEL EYES
52. C. WIVES AND LOVERS
53. C. THE IMPOSSIBLE DREAM (THE QUEST)
54. C. IMAGINATION
55. D. YOU DON'T KNOW WHAT YOU'VE GOT (UNTIL YOU LOSE IT)
56. B. DEEP PURPLE

57. C. THE 59TH STREET BRIDGE SONG (FEELIN' GROOVY)
58. A. EYDIE GORME
59. C. THE CYRKLE
60. A. BARBARA ANN
61. D. BABY IT'S YOU
62. C. I WONDER WHAT SHE'S DOING TONITE
63. A. YOUNGER GIRL
64. 1) OH, PRETTY WOMAN
    2) IT'S OVER
    3) BLUE ANGEL
    4) CRYING
    5) ONLY THE LONELY (KNOW HOW I FEEL)
65. B. TREAT HER RIGHT
66. B. DENISE

60/13 POP ROCKERS-QUIZ # 2

1. 1) CALENDAR GIRL
   2) STAIRWAY TO HEAVEN
   3) HAPPY BIRTHDAY, SWEET SIXTEEN
   4) BREAKING UP IS HARD TO DO
   5) NEXT DOOR TO AN ANGEL
   6) LITTLE DEVIL
2. 1) SHERRY
   2) WALK LIKE A MAN
   3) BIG GIRLS DON'T CRY
   4) RAG DOLL
   5) DAWN (GO AWAY)
   6) BIG MAN IN TOWN
   7) LET'S HANG ON!
   8) WORKING MY WAY BACK TO YOU
   9) CANDY GIRL
   10) TELL IT TO THE RAIN
3. C. THE LETTER
4. 1) I GOT YOU BABE
   2) THE BEAT GOES ON
5. C. BABY DON'T GO
6. A. BABY, I LOVE YOU
7. 1) SHEILA
   2) SWEET PEA
   3) HOORAY FOR HAZEL
   4) DIZZY
8. B. IT MUST BE HIM
9. 1) I GOT RHYTHM
   2) SEE YOU IN SEPTEMBER
   3) GO AWAY LITTLE GIRL
10. 1) MONDAY, MONDAY
    2) CALIFORNIA DREAMIN'
    3) CREEQUE ALLEY
    4) I SAW HER AGAIN
    5) DEDICATED TO THE ONE I LOVE
11. B. DREAM A LITTLE DREAM OF ME
12. 1) RONNIE
    2) THE RONETTES
13. C. SIMON SAYS
14. C. ANGEL OF THE MORNING
15. A. REACH OUT OF THE DARKNESS
16. C. JOHNNY MAESTRO

17. D. JOHNNY GET ANGRY
18. C. RHYTHM OF THE RAIN
19. 1) THE VOGUES
    2) MY SPECIAL ANGEL
20. PENNIES FROM HEAVEN
21. D. RED ROSES FOR A BLUE LADY
22. B. UNCHAINED MELODY
23. D. PALISADES PARK
24. C. THE WONDER WHO?
25. D. THEN YOU CAN TELL ME GOODBYE
26. B. SUSPICION
27. B. A THOUSAND STARS
28. C. TELL LAURA I LOVE HER
29. CORRINA, CORRINA
30. 1) TOWN WITHOUT PITY
    2) ONLY LOVE CAN BREAK A HEART
    3) I'M GONNA BE STRONG
    4) IT HURTS TO BE IN LOVE
31. B. POOR LITTLE FOOL
32. D. YOU WERE ON MY MIND
33. B. LIGHT MY FIRE
34. C. SCOTT MCKENZIE
35. C. PLEASE LOVE ME FOREVER
36. 1) MAYBELLINE
    2) MEMPHIS
    3) MIDNIGHT SPECIAL
    4) MOUNTAIN OF LOVE
    5) SECRET AGENT MAN
    6) BABY I NEED YOUR LOVING
    7) THE TRACKS OF MY TEARS
    8) POOR SIDE OF TOWN
    9) SEVENTH SON
37. 1) THE SOUNDS OF SILENCE
    2) MRS ROBINSON
    3) HOMEWARD BOUND
    4) I AM A ROCK
    5) THE BOXER
38. THE LION SLEEPS TONIGHT
39. C. TONIGHT I FELL IN LOVE
40. B. CINDY'S BIRTHDAY
41. C. DEAN MARTIN
42. 1) THE GYPSY CRIED
    2) TWO FACES HAVE I
    3) LIGHTNIN' STRIKES
43. A. THIS DIAMOND RING
44. D. MORE TODAY THAN YESTERDAY
45. C. HALFWAY TO PARADISE
46. B. BLESS YOU
47. B. I WONDER WHAT SHE'S DOING TONIGHT
48. C. BOBBY'S GIRL
49. C. THE REFLECTIONS
50. B. CAN'T GET USED TO LOSING YOU
51. D. THE MEN IN MY LITTLE GIRL'S LIFE
52. B. COME ON DOWN TO MY BOAT
53. B. GO AWAY LITTLE GIRL
54. A. PORTRAIT OF MY LOVE
55. 1) STEP BY STEP
    2) TROUBLE IN PARADISE

56. B. NAVY BLUE

60/14 POP ROCKERS-QUIZ # 3

1. C. HEY PAULA
2. D. ONCE IN AWHILE
3. C. BROOKLYN BRIDGE
4. 1) WORST THAT COULD HAPPEN
   2) WELCOME ME LOVE
   3) YOUR HUSBAND, MY WIFE
   4) BLESSED IS THE RAIN
5. D. THERE'S A MOON OUT TONIGHT
6. A. TILL THEN
7. 1) THE DUPREES
   2) YOU BELONG TO ME
   3) HAVE YOU HEARD
8. C. REMEMBER THEN
9. B. I BELIEVE
10. A. OVER THE RAINBOW
11. C. LITTLE HONDA
12. C. THIS GUY'S IN LOVE WITH YOU
13. A. I'M LEAVING IT UP TO YOU
14. 1) STRANGERS IN THE NIGHT
    2) MY WAY
    3) THAT'S LIFE
    4) SUMMER WIND
    5) IT WAS A VERY GOOD YEAR
15. C. YOU WERE MINE
16. 1) BE MY BABY
    2) BABY, I LOVE YOU
    3) (THE BEST PART OF) BREAKIN' UP
    4) WALKIN' IN THE RAIN
17. B. MY BOYFRIEND'S BACK
18. C. 'TIL
19. D. I WILL FOLLOW HIM
20. B. PEOPLE
21. C. THE MOUNTAIN'S HIGH
22. E. ONLY THE LONELY
23. C. BREAD AND BUTTER
24. 1) THIS DIAMOND RING
    2) SHE'S JUST MY STYLE
    3) SURE GONNA MISS HER
    4) EVERYBODY LOVES A CLOWN
    5) SAVE YOUR HEART FOR ME
    6) COUNT ME IN
25. D. DARLING LORRAINE
26. D. BARBARA ANN
27. 1) LAST TRAIN TO CLARKSVILLE
    2) I'M A BELIEVER
    3) A LITTLE BIT OF ME, A LITTLE BIT OF YOU
28. 1) REMEMBER (WALKIN' IN THE SAND)
    2) LEADER OF THE PACK
    3) GIVE HIM A GREAT BIG KISS
29. B. TONY ORLANDO
30. C. I'VE TOLD EVERY LITTLE STAR
31. B. DON'T BET MONEY HONEY
32. A. LIAR, LIAR
33. 1) RUNAROUND SUE

2) THE WANDERER
3) RUBY BABY
4) LONELY TEENAGER
5) DONNA THE PRIMA DONNA
6) ABRAHAM, MARTIN AND JOHN
7) LOVERS WHO WANDER
34. B. BARBARA ANN
35. D. CAN'T TAKE MY EYES OFF YOU
36. B. (YOU'RE GONNA) HURT YOURSELF
37. D. GOOD MORNING STARSHINE
38. B. JEAN
39. D. TELL ME WHY
40. D. WAYNE NEWTON
41. 1) ROSES ARE RED
2) BLUE ON BLUE
3) BLUE VELVET
4) MR LONELY
5) COMING HOME SOLDIER
6) PLEASE LOVE ME FOREVER
42. A. LOVE (CAN MAKE YOU HAPPY)
43. D. LAST KISS
44. 1) THE BELMONTS
2) THE DEL SATINS
45. 1) TRAVELIN' MAN
2) HELLO MARY LOU
46. B. THE POLISH PRINCE
47. 1) LESLIE GORE
2) IT'S MY PARTY
3) JUDY'S TURN TO CRY
4) SHE'S A FOOL
5) YOU DON'T OWN ME
6) THAT'S THE WAY BOYS ARE
48. C. SUNSHINE, LOLLIPOPS AND RAINBOWS
49. 1) WHERE THE BOYS ARE
2) AMONG MY SOUVENIRS
3) EVERYBODY'S SOMEBODY'S FOOL
4) VACATION
5) FOLLOW THE BOYS
6) DON'T BREAK THE HEART THAT LOVES YOU
7) BREAKIN' IN A BRAND NEW BROKEN HEART
8) TOGETHER
50. B. MIDNITE SPECIAL
51. C. HEY! BABY
52. C. WE'LL SING IN THE SUNSHINE
53. C. PAPER ROSES
54. B. BORN A WOMAN

POP ROCKERS-BONUS

1. D. THE GRASS ROOTS
2. C. THE CHEATER

60/15 COUNTRY ROCKERS

1. A. GAMES PEOPLE PLAY
2. B. DOWN IN THE BOONDOCKS
3. C. YESTERDAY, WHEN I WAS YOUNG
4. 1) RUBY, DON'T TAKE YOUR LOVE TO TOWN
2) JUST DROPPED IN (TO SEE WHAT CONDITION MY CONDITION WAS IN)

5. A. MAKE THE WORLD GO AWAY
6. A. TREAT HER RIGHT
7. D. BIG BAD JOHN
8. C. ROCKIN' AROUND THE CHRISTMAS TREE
9. D. LITTLE MISS DYNAMITE
10. B. FLOWERS ON THE WALL
11. D. TONY JOE WHITE
12. A. HELLO WALLS
13. B. VENUS IN BLUE JEANS
14. B. HARPER VALLEY P.T.A.
15. 1) CRYING IN THE RAIN
    2) CATHY'S CLOWN
    3) LET IT BE ME
    4) WHEN WILL I BE LOVED
    5) WALK RIGHT BACK
16. C. EL PASO
17. D. THE END OF THE WORLD
18. 1) GALVESTON
    2) BY THE TIME I GET TO PHOENIX
    3) WICHITA LINEMAN
    4) TRY A LITTLE KINDNESS
19. D. NORTH TO ALASKA
20. SINK THE BISMARCK
21. 1) A BOY NAMED SUE
    2) RING OF FIRE
    3) FOLSOM PRISON BLUES
22. 1) KING OF THE ROAD
    2) DANG ME
23. C. DUKE OF EARL
24. D. BOBBIE GENTRY
25. 1) I FALL TO PIECES
    2) SHE'S GOT YOU
    3) SWEET DREAMS
    4) CRAZY
26. 1) I'M SORRY
    2) FOOL # 1
    3) BREAK IT TO ME GENTLY
    4) ALL ALONE AM I
    5) SWEET NOTHIN'S
    6) I WANT TO BE WANTED
    7) MY COLORING BOOK
    8) LOSING YOU
27. A. DOWNTOWN
28. D. DREAMIN'
29. B. YOU'RE SIXTEEN

COUNTRY ROCKER-BONUS

1. D. WOLVERTON MOUNTAIN

60/16 ROCKERS-QUIZ # 1

1. 1) THE LOVIN' SPOONFUL
   2) SUMMER IN THE CITY
   3) DO YOU BELIEVE IN MAGIC
   4) DID YOU EVER HAVE TO MAKE UP YOUR MIND?
   5) DARLING BE HOME SOON
2. B. PEPPERMINT TWIST (PT 1)

3. C. BRISTOL STOMP
4. D. YOU CAN'T SIT DOWN
5. C. LEN BARRY
6. B. I FOUGHT THE LAW
7. A. G-T-O
8. 1) GARY PUCKETT AND THE UNION GAP
   2) WOMAN, WOMAN
   3) YOUNG GIRL
   4) LADY WILLPOWER
   5) THIS GIRL IS A WOMAN NOW
9. D. MIDNIGHT SPECIAL
10. B. HEY LITTLE COBRA
11. D. TIME WON'T LET ME
12. A. SURF CITY
13. C. THE LITTLE OLD LADY (FROM PASADENA)
14. B. BOTTLE OF WINE
15. C. GLORIA
16. B. JOHNNY MAESTRO
17. A. THE BEACH BOYS

60/17 ROCKERS-QUIZ # 2

1. 1) WHITE RABBIT
   2) SOMEBODY TO LOVE
2. D. LIES
3. B. LINDA RONSTADT
4. A. DIRTY WATER
5. 1) HEY BABY (THEY'RE PLAYING OUR SONG)
   2) MERCY, MERCY, MERCY
   3) KIND OF A DRAG
6. B. CALIFORNIA SUN
7. B. 96 TEARS
8. C. JIMI HENDRIX
9. D. HOLLY HOLY
10. 1) PROUD MARY
    2) BAD MOON RISING
    3) DOWN ON THE CORNER
    4) FORTUNATE SON
    5) SUZIE Q. (PART 1)
11. 1) YOU'VE MADE ME SO VERY HAPPY
    2) SPINNING WHEEL
    3) AND WHEN I DIE
12. C. JOHN FRED & HIS PLAYBOY BAND
13. D. LOUIE LOUIE
14. B. GIMME GIMME GOOD LOVIN'
15. D. LITTLE GIRL
16. D. MULE SKINNER BLUES
17. B. GOING UP THE COUNTRY
18. 1) IT AIN'T ME BABE
    2) HAPPY TOGETHER
    3) SHE'D RATHER BE WITH ME
19. 1) THE DOORS
    2) LIGHT MY FIRE
20. 1) EASY TO BE HARD
    2) ONE
    3) ELI'S COMING
    4) TRY A LITTLE TENDERNESS
21. C. JACK SCOTT

22. A. CRY LIKE A BABY
23. B. THE LETTER
24. D. BORN TO BE WILD
25. B. MAGIC CARPET RIDE
26. 1) COME A LITTLE BIT CLOSER
    2) ONLY IN AMERICA
    3) LET'S LOCK THE DOOR (AND THROW AWAY THE KEY)
    4) THIS MAGIC MOMENT
    5) SHE CRIED
    6) CRYING
    7) CARA, MIA
27. B. ON BROADWAY
28. 1) THESE EYES
    2) LAUGHING
29. D. SUGAR SHACK
30. C. MITCH RYDER AND THE DETROIT WHEELS
31. 1) I GET AROUND
    2) SURFIN' U.S.A.
    3) FUN, FUN, FUN
    4) HELP ME, RHONDA
    5) CALIFORNIA GIRLS
    6) GOOD VIBRATIONS
    7) SURFIN' SAFARI
    8) SURFER GIRL
    9) SLOOP JOHN B
    10) BARBARA ANN
    11) WOULDN'T IT BE NICE
    12) BE TRUE TO YOUR SCHOOL
    13) IN MY ROOM
    14) DANCE, DANCE, DANCE
    15) GOD ONLY KNOWS
32. B. NOBODY BUT ME
33. YUMMY, YUMMY, YUMMY
34. 1) THE RAIN, THE PARK & OTHER THINGS
    2) HAIR
35. HANG ON SLOOPY
36. C. FEVER
37. D. (WE AIN'T GOT) NOTHIN' YET
38. B. LET IT OUT (LET IT ALL HANG OUT)
39. B. LITTLE BIT O' SOUL
40. 1) THE YOUNG RASCALS
    2) GOOD LOVIN'
    3) A BEAUTIFUL MORNING
    4) I'VE BEEN LONELY TOO LONG
    5) GROOVIN'
    6) PEOPLE GOT TO BE FREE
    7) HOW CAN I BE SURE
    8) A GIRL LIKE YOU
    9) I AIN'T GONNA EAT OUT MY HEART ANY MORE
41. C. DOUBLE SHOT (OF MY BABY'S LOVE)
42. D. KEEP ON DANCING
43. C. THE ARCHIES
44. WALK AWAY RENEE
45. A. BEND ME, SHAPE ME
46. 1) TOMMY JAMES AND THE SHONDELLS
    2) HANKY PANKY
    3) I THINK WE'RE ALONE NOW
    4) MONY MONY

5) CRYSTAL BLUE PERSUASION
47. B. STRAWBERRY ALARM CLOCK
48. 1) JANIS JOPLIN
2) PIECE OF MY HEART
49. C. PEARL
50. C. SPANKY AND OUR GANG

60/18 MISC (NOVELTY, FOLK, FOREIGN & INSTRUMENTALS)-QUIZ # 1

1. B. EL WATUSI
2. B. LOVE IS BLUE
3. 1) HERE COMES THE NIGHT
2) GLORIA
4. C. BOTH SIDES NOW
5. A. ISRAELITES
6. B. WILD THING
7. A. TIE ME KANGAROO DOWN, SPORT
8. D. BABY THE RAIN MUST FALL
9. B. NAPOLEAN XIV
10. ON TOP OF SPAGHETTI
11. B. FLATT & SCRUGGS
12. C. IN THE YEAR 2525
13. B. SUKIYAKI
14. B. WALK RIGHT IN
15. B. THOSE WERE THE DAYS
16. A. ROUTE 66 THEME
17. 1) IF I HAD A HAMMER
2) LEMON TREE
18. C. PEPINO THE ITALIAN MOUSE
19. A. HELLO MUDDUH, HELLO FADDUH! (A LETTER FROM CAMP)
20. GEORGY GIRL
21. B. I'LL NEVER FIND ANOTHER YOU
22. C. THIS LAND IS YOUR LAND
23. C. GREEN, GREEN
24. D. FOR WHAT IT'S WORTH (STOP, HEY WHAT'S THAT SOUND)
25. B. THE BYRDS
26. DOES YOUR CHEWING GUM LOSE ITS FLAVOR(ON THE BEDPOST OVER NIGHT)
27. 1) LEAVING ON A JET PLANE
2) PUFF THE MAGIC DRAGON
3) BLOWIN' IN THE WIND
4) LEMON TREE
5) IF I HAD A HAMMER
6) 500 MILES
7) DON'T THINK TWICE, IT'S ALL RIGHT
8) I DIG ROCK AND ROLL MUSIC
28. 1) LIKE A ROLLING STONE
2) POSITIVELY FOURTH STREET
3) LAY LADY LAY
4) BLOWIN' IN THE WIND
5) IT AIN'T ME BABE
6) MR TAMBOURINE MAN
29. C. WHERE HAVE ALL THE FLOWERS GONE
30. 1) THE LONELY BULL
2) TASTE OF HONEY
3) ZORBA THE GREEK
31. A. THE ROYAL GUARDSMEN
32. B. BROWN EYED GIRL
33. C. EVE OF DESTRUCTION

34. ITSY BITSY TEENIE WEENIE YELLOW POLKADOT BIKINI

60/19 MISC (NOVELTY, FOLK, FOREIGN & INSTRUMENTALS)-QUIZ # 2

1. B. JIMMY CASTOR
2. C. THE IRISH ROVERS
3. B. CLASSICAL GAS
4. A. THE HORSE
5. A. SOULFUL STRUT
6. A. STAND BY ME
7. C. THE NAME GAME
8. A. MEMPHIS SOUL STEW
9. B. LAST NIGHT
10. C. BAR-KAYS
11. D. TIP TOE THRU' THE TULIPS WITH ME
12. B. RIP VAN WINKLE
13. D. MEMPHIS
14. B. ALLEY-OOP
15. A. FERRANTE & TEICHER
16. B. PATA, PATA
17. 1) GREEN ONIONS
    2) HANG 'EM HIGH
    3) TIME IS TIGHT
18. D. FRIDAY ON MY MIND
19. D. WATERMELON MAN
20. D. MR CUSTER
21. A. PIPELINE
22. C. LIL' RED RIDING HOOD
23. HAWAII FIVE-0

60/20 MISC (NOVELTY, FOLK, FOREIGN & INSTRUMENTALS)-QUIZ # 3

1. A. MR TAMBOURINE MAN
2. C. TURN! TURN! TURN! (TO EVERYTHING THERE IS A SEASON)
3. A. WITCH DOCTOR
4. C. THE LOOK OF LOVE
5. B. THE FOOL ON THE HILL
6. ALLEY-OOP
7. A. MONSTER MASH
8. A. AFTER THE LOVIN'
9. D. GET TOGETHER
10. THE BALLAD OF THE GREEN BERETS
11. C. RINGO
12. C. THE GOOD, THE BAD AND THE UGLY
13. B. THE STRIPPER
14. B. RICHARD HARRIS
15. C. JOHNNY CYMBAL
16. B. THE MARKETTS
17. B. NO MATTER WHAT SHAPE (YOUR STOMACH'S IN)
18. MERCY, MERCY, MERCY
19. D. THE WOODSTOCK FESTIVAL
20. D. GOLDFINGER
21. B. LO MUCHO QUE TE QUIERO (THE MORE I LOVE YOU)
22. D. GREENFIELDS
23. D. DOMINIQUE
24. D. KILLER JOE
25. C. BLACK IS BLACK

MISC (NOVELTY, FOLK, FOREIGN & INSTRUMENTALS)-BONUS

1. D. BARRY MANN
2. B. FLY ME TO THE MOON-BOSSA NOVA
3. C. GUANTANAMERA
4. D. BILL COSBY
5. B. DON'T LET THE RAIN COME DOWN (CROOKED LITTLE MAN)
6. C. SOCIETY'S CHILD (BABY I'VE BEEN THINKING)
7. B. THE GIRL FROM IPANEMA
8. A. OH HOW HAPPY

60/21 MATCH THE WOODSTOCK FESTIVAL ARTIST WITH THEIR SONG

1. E. FREEDOM
2. B. I-FEEL-LIKE-I'M-FIXIN'-TO-DIE
3. G. ROCK AND SOUL MUSIC
4. H. YOUNGER GENERATION
5. L. COMING INTO LOS ANGELES
6. K. JOE HILL
7. J. SOUL SACRIFICE
8. F. GOING UP THE COUNTRY
9. I. WORK ME, LORD
10. A. I WANT TO TAKE YOU HIGHER
11. Q. WE'RE NOT GOING TO TAKE IT
12. P. WON'T YOU TRY
13. D. WITH A LITTLE HELP FROM MY FRIENDS
14. O. I'M GOING HOME
15. N. SUITE: JUDY BLUE EYES
16. M. AT THE HOP
17. C. STAR SPANGLED BANNER
18. T. WOODSTOCK
19. R. PURPLE HAZE
20. S. SWING LOW SWEET CHARIOT

60/22 MATCH THE DANCE HIT WITH THE ARTIST IN THE 60'S

1. E. CHUBBY CHECKER
2. F. CHUBBY CHECKER
3. K. CHUBBY CHECKER
4. H. JOEY DEE & THE STARLITERS
5. M. CHUBBY CHECKER
6. B. SAM COOKE
7. A. THE DOVELLS
8. J. THE MIRACLES
9. S. RUFUS THOMAS
10. Q. HANK BALLARD AND THE MIDNIGHTERS
11. P. CHUBBY CHECKER
12. R. CHUBBY CHECKER
13. I. THE VIBRATIONS
14. G. LITTLE EVA
15. C. THE ORLONS
16. D. THE ISLEY BROTHERS
17. T. DEE DEE SHARP
18. O. MAJOR LANCE
19. L. WILSON PICKETT
20. N. CANNIBAL AND THE HEADHUNTERS

60/23 MATCH THE LEAD SINGER WITH THE GROUP PT 1 IN THE 60'S

1. K. THE SUPREMES
2. N. THE ROLLING STONES
3. Q. THE MIRACLES
4. L. THE LOVIN' SPOONFUL
5. F. THE TEMPTATIONS
6. J. THE CRESTS
7. S. THE FOUR TOPS
8. O. THE DOVELLS
9. W. CREEDENCE CLEARWATER REVIVAL
10. B. THE CRYSTALS
11. D. THE DRIFTERS
12. U. THE DOORS
13. C. THE ANIMALS
14. M. BROOKLYN BRIDGE
15. T. HERMAN'S HERMITS
16. A. SLY & THE FAMILY STONE
17. P. THE VANDELLAS
18. Y. BOB B. SOXX AND THE BLUE JEANS
19. E. THE DRIFTERS
20. X. THE DRIFTERS
21. R. THE UNION GAP
22. H. THE AMERICANS
23. G. THE TEMPTATIONS
24. I. BLOOD, SWEAT & TEARS
25. V. THE LIMELITES

60/24 MATCH THE GROUP WITH THEIR SONG PT 1 IN THE 60'S

1. DD. EVERYDAY PEOPLE
2. HH. HE'S A REBEL
3. SS. THE HOUSE OF THE RISING SUN
4. II. UNDER THE BOARDWALK
5. MM. SAVE THE LAST DANCE FOR ME
6. FF. I CAN'T GET NEXT TO YOU
7. JJ. MY GIRL
8. UU. SHE CRIED
9. VV. YOU MADE ME SO VERY HAPPY
10. LL. STEP BY STEP
11. OO. WHERE DID OUR LOVE GO?
12. XX. SUMMER IN THE CITY
13. RR. WORST THAT COULD HAPPEN
14. YY. (I CAN'T GET NO) SATISFACTION
15. QQ. BRISTOL STOMP
16. TT. JIMMY MACK
17. KK. SHOP AROUND
18. EE. YOUNG GIRL
19. NN. I CAN'T HELP MYSELF
20. WW. MRS BROWN YOU'VE GOT A LOVELY DAUGHTER
21. GG. HELLO, I LOVE YOU
22. AA. DADDY'S HOME
23. CC. PROUD MARY
24. PP. SOME KIND OF WONDERFUL
25. BB. ZIP-A-DEE-D0-DAH

60/25 MATCH THE LEAD SINGER WITH THE GROUP PT II IN THE 60'S

1. P. THE IMPERIALS
2. U. THE CHANTELS
3. H. THE DRELLS
4. Q. BRASIL '66
5. S. THE IMPRESSIONS
6. T. THE RONETTES
7. W. THE SHONDELLS
8. X. THE ENCHANTERS
9. R. THE MINDBENDERS
10. V. THE SHIRELLES
11. M. THE RAIDERS
12. E. THE CHECKMATES LTD.
13. Y. THE ZODIACS
14. A. THE EARLS
15. N. THE ALL STARS
16. B. THE COASTERS
17. C. THE NEW CHRISTY MINSTRELS
18. D. SPENCER DAVIS GROUP
19. O. THE INNOCENTS
20. K. THE JIVE FIVE
21. G. THE FIREBALLS
22. J. THE PIPS
23. F. THE SKYLINERS
24. I. THE PLAYBOYS
25. L. BIG BROTHER & THE HOLDING COMPANY

60/26 MATCH THE GROUP WITH THEIR SONG PT II IN THE 60'S

1. Y. REMEMBER THEN
2. G. CHARLIE BROWN
3. T. GREEN, GREEN
4. I. GIMME SOME LOVIN'
5. W. BLACK PEARL
6. M. PENNIES FROM HEAVEN
7. C. SUGAR SHACK
8. S. TIGHTEN UP
9. Q. THIS DIAMOND RING
10. O. EVERY BEAT OF MY HEART
11. H. MY TRUE STORY
12. L. PIECE OF MY HEART
13. B. KICKS
14. U. SHOTGUN
15. P. A THOUSAND STARS
16. R. GOIN' OUT OF MY HEAD
17. F. THE LOOK OF LOVE
18. V. THE GAME OF LOVE
19. N. IT'S ALRIGHT
20. K. BE MY BABY
21. E. LOOK IN MY EYES
22. A. SOLDIER BOY
23. J. HANKY PANKY
24. D. CRY BABY
25. X. STAY

60/27 MATCH THE LEAD SINGER WITH THE GROUP PT III IN THE 60'S

1. H. THE CHIMES
2. L. THE FOUR SEASONS
3. O. THREE DOG NIGHT
4. R. THE FIRST EDITION
5. I. THE TIJUANA BRASS
6. S. THE DETROIT WHEELS
7. Q. THE MIDNIGHTERS
8. D. THE ROMANTICS
9. E. STONE PONEYS
10. M. THE TECHNIQUES
11. C. THE BLUE BELLES
12. N. THE GENTRYS
13. F. THE RAINBOWS
14. P. THE PLATTERS
15. J. THE DREAMERS
16. K. THE WHO
17. B. THE PHAROAHS
18. A. PLAYBOY BAND
19. G. THE HI-LITES
20. T. JEFFERSON AIRPLANE

60/28 MATCH THE GROUP WITH THEIR SONG PT III IN THE 60'S

1. J. JUDY IN DISGUISE (WITH GLASSES)
2. S. WOOLY BULLY
3. Q. I SOLD MY HEART TO THE JUNKMAN
4. K. OUR DAY WILL COME
5. N. DIFFERENT DRUM
6. C. DENISE
7. B. I WISH THAT WE WERE MARRIED
8. L. ONCE IN AWHILE
9. I. THE LONELY BULL
10. O. I'M TELLING YOU NOW
11. A. PINBALL WIZARD
12. M. SHERRY
13. P. APPLES, PEACHES, PUMPKIN PIE
14. D. KEEP ON DANCING
15. H. ELI'S COMING
16. E. WITH THIS RING
17. F. FINGER POPPIN' TIME
18. G. JUST DROPPED IN (TO SEE WHAT CONDITION MY CONDITION WAS IN)
19. T. DEVIL WITH A BLUE DRESS ON & GOOD GOLLY MISS MOLLY
20. R. WHITE RABBIT

60/29 MATCH THE DUOS AND THEIR HIT SONG IN THE 60'S

1. I,HH. DINAH WASHINGTON, BABY YOU'VE GOT WHAT IT TAKES
2. M,KK. ART GARFUNKEL, MRS ROBINSON
3. L,JJ. BOBBY HATFIELD, YOU'VE LOST THAT LOVIN' FEELIN'
4. Y,PP. BILLY PRESTON, GET BACK
5. N,SS. CHARLIE FOX, MOCKINGBIRD
6. B,OO. EVANS, IN THE YEAR 2525
7. G,NN. CHER, I GOT YOU BABE
8. Q,GG. TAMMI TERRELL, YOUR PRECIOUS LOVE
9. T,QQ. BETTY EVERETT, LET IT BE ME
10. R,CC. APRIL STEVENS, DEEP PURPLE

11. V,RR. FRANK SINATRA, SOMETHIN' STUPID
12. C,BB. PAULA, HEY PAULA
13. D,AA. PHIL EVERLY, CATHY'S CLOWN
14. W,DD. DEAN, SURF CITY
15. U,FF. GRACE, I'M LEAVING IT UP TO YOU
16. E,UU. GORDON, A WORLD WITHOUT LOVE
17. X,MM. THE TEMPTATIONS, I'M GONNA MAKE YOU LOVE ME
18. A,II. DEEDEE, THE MOUNTAIN'S HIGH
19. K,EE. BOBBY PURIFY, I'M YOUR PUPPET
20. H,LL. HERB, CLOSE YOUR EYES
21. P,TT. TEICHER, EXODUS
22. F,YY. JUAN, WHAT'S YOUR NAME
23. S,VV. DAVE, SOUL MAN
24. J,WW. TINA, RIVER DEEP, MOUNTAIN HIGH
25. O,XX. OTIS REDDING, TRAMP

60/30 MATCH THE ARTIST WITH MOVIE/TV SHOW SONG PT 1 IN THE 60'S

1. F. TO SIR WITH LOVE
2. I. MRS ROBINSON
3. G. HELP!
4. K. A HARD DAY'S NIGHT
5. A. HELLO, DOLLY!
6. H. THE HAPPENING
7. E. NORTH TO ALASKA
8. J. SINK THE BISMARCK
9. B. RETURN TO SENDER
10. D. CAN'T HELP FALLING IN LOVE
11. Q. FLAMING STAR
12. S. VIVA LAS VEGAS
13. W. FOLLOW THAT DREAM
14. N. TOWN WITHOUT PITY
15. C. WHERE THE BOYS ARE
16. P. THE MAGNIFICENT SEVEN
17. L. THE THEME FROM 'A SUMMER PLACE'
18. M. OVER THE RAINBOW
19. R. THEME FROM 'EXODUS'
20. X. ZIP-A-DEE-DOO-DAH
21. Y. THE MAN WHO SHOT LIBERTY VALANCE
22. O. MOON RIVER
23. T. DAYS OF WINE AND ROSES
24. U. THEME FROM 'VALLEY OF THE DOLLS'
25. V. THEME FROM 'THE PINK PANTHER'

60/31 MATCH THE SONG WITH MOVIE/TV SHOW PT 1 IN THE 60'S

1. F. HELLO, DOLLY!
2. G. GIRLS, GIRLS, GIRLS
3. I. WHERE THE BOYS ARE
4. C. BLUE HAWAII
5. D. NORTH TO ALASKA
6. E. TO SIR WITH LOVE
7. A. HELP!
8. B. THE HAPPENING
9. K. THE GRADUATE
10. H. SINK THE BISMARCK
11. J. A HARD DAY'S NIGHT
12. N. A SUMMER PLACE

13. O. WIZARD OF OZ
14. T. TOWN WITHOUT PITY
15. S. BREAKFAST AT TIFFANY'S
16. M. THE MAGNIFICENT SEVEN
17. V. FLAMING STAR
18. L. EXODUS
19. Q. VIVA LAS VEGAS
20. W. DAYS OF WINE AND ROSES
21. Y. VALLEY OF THE DOLLS
22. X. THE PINK PANTHER
23. P. FOLLOW THAT DREAM
24. U. SONG OF THE SOUTH
25. R. THE MAN WHO SHOT LIBERTY VALANCE

60/32 MATCH THE ARTIST WITH MOVIE/TV SHOW SONG PT II IN THE 60'S

1. H. BONANZA
2. J. THUNDERBALL
3. N. GOLDFINGER
4. I. YOU ONLY LIVE TWICE
5. P. MIDNIGHT COWBOY
6. G. BABY THE RAIN MUST FALL
7. Q. SKI PARTY
8. F. NEVER ON SUNDAY
9. K. FUNNY GIRL
10. O. BREAKFAST AT TIFFANY'S
11. B. GEORGY GIRL
12. D. YELLOW SUBMARINE
13. A. TRUE GRIT
14. M. HELP!
15. C. THE PRIDE OF MISS JEAN BRODIE
16. R. HANG 'EM HIGH
17. L. ZORBA THE GREEK
18. E. CASINO ROYALE
19. S. BORN FREE
20. T. DR. ZHIVAGO

60/33 MATCH THE SONG WITH MOVIE/TV SHOW PT II IN THE 60'S

1. L. TRUE GRIT
2. M. GEORGY GIRL
3. G. THE PRIDE OF MISS JEAN BRODIE
4. K. YELLOW SUBMARINE
5. J. CASINO ROYALE
6. N. NEVER ON SUNDAY
7. I. BABY THE RAIN MUST FALL
8. E. BONANZA
9. Q. YOU ONLY LIVE TWICE
10. A. THUNDERBALL
11. F. FUNNY GIRL
12. C. ZORBA THE GREEK
13. D. HELP!
14. R. GOLDFINGER
15. P. BREAKFAST AT TIFFANY'S
16. H. MIDNIGHT COWBOY
17. O. SKI PARTY
18. B. HANG 'EM HIGH
19. S. BORN FREE

20. T. DR. ZHIVAGO

60/34 MATCH THE INSTRUMENTAL HIT WITH THE ARTIST PT 1 IN THE 60'S

1. S. HUGH MASEKELA
2. K. RAMSEY LEWIS TRIO
3. O. DAVID ROSE AND HIS ORCHESTRA
4. N. HERB ALPERT & THE TIJUANA BRASS
5. J. MONGO SANTAMARIA
6. R. BOOKER T. & THE MG'S
7. D. THE MARKETTS
8. L. NELSON RIDDLE AND HIS ORCHESTRA
9. F. THE VENTURES
10. A. PERCY FAITH AND HIS ORCHESTRA
11. M. YOUNG-HOLT UNLIMITED
12. B. THE T-BONES
13. H. FERRANTE & TEICHER
14. C. THE SURFARIS
15. Q. BOB CREW GENERATION
16. G. JOE HARNELL AND HIS ORCHESTRA
17. T. HENRY MANCINI AND HIS ORCHESTRA
18. P. HUGO MONTENEGRO, HIS ORCHESTRA AND CHORUS
19. I. MR ACKER BILK
20. E. PAUL MAURIAT AND HIS ORCHESTRA

60/35 MATCH THE INSTRUMENTAL HIT WITH THE ARTIST PT II IN THE 60'S

1. E. MASON WILLIAMS
2. F. HERB ALPERT & THE TIJUANA BRASS
3. T. FLOYD CRAMER
4. C. DON COSTA AND HIS ORCHESTRA AND CHORUS
5. A. AL CAIOLA AND HIS ORCHESTRA
6. I. CANNONBALL ADDERLY
7. B. MAR-KEYS
8. D. RAY CONIFF AND THE SINGERS
9. J. BOOKER T. & THE MG'S
10. G. HERB ALPERT & THE TIJUANA BRASS
11. N. THE TORNADOES
12. P. ROGER WILLIAMS
13. Q. FERRANTE & TEICHER
14. H. THE VENTURES
15. R. LONNIE MACK
16. S. CLIFF NOBLES
17. K. HENRY MANCINI AND HIS ORCHESTRA
18. M. THE CHANTAYS
19. O. KING CURTIS & HIS BAND
20. L. THE MARKETTS

THE SEVENTIES

THE DECADE OF THE 70'S BROUGHT US THE BREAKUP OF THE GREATEST BAND OF ALL TIME, THE BEATLES. YET IT SPAWNED FOUR NEW ACTS, THE OKO ONO BAND, PAUL MCCARTNEY'S WINGS, AND THE SOLO ACTS OF GEORGE HARRISON AND THAT OF RINGO STARR. MOST OF THE BIG MOTOWN ACTS WERE GONE WITH THE EXCEPTION OF THE TEMPTATIONS, STEVIE WONDER, THE FOUR TOPS, THE NEW LINEUP OF THE SUPREMES AND THAT OF THE MIRACLES. NEW GROUPS EMERGED IN THE GORDY STAPLES THAT INCLUDED THE JACKSON FIVE, COMMODORES AND THE SOLO ACT OF DIANA ROSS AFTER HER DEPARTURE FROM THE SUPREMES. INTERNATIONALLY ABBA, OLIVIA NEWTON-JOHN AND A NEW WAVE OF BRITISH ACTS WHICH INCLUDED ELTON JOHN CROSSED OVER TO OUR SHORES. POLITICALLY THE VIETNAM WAR ENDED AND THE WATERGATE SCANDAL BROUGHT DOWN NIXON'S PRESIDENTIAL REIGN. ON AUGUST 16, 1977, A DAY A LOT OF US WILL NEVER FORGET, THE DAY THE MUSIC DIED, AS IT DID ONCE BEFORE IN THE LATE 50'S WHEN BUDDY HOLLY PERISHED, ELVIS WOULD PASS AWAY AFTER RULING THE AIRWAVES AND THE CINEMA SCREEN FOR NEARLY THREE DECADES OF ROCK 'N ROLL. A NEW FAD, KNOWN AS DISCO WAS BORN LED BY THE THREE CROWN PRINCES, THE BEE GEES, AND THE DISCO QUEEN HERSELF, DONNA SUMMER. 'SATURDAY NIGHT FEVER' STARRING JOHN TRAVOLTA AND A BIG MUSICAL CAST THAT INCLUDED THE BEE GEES, BECAME ONE OF THE BIGGEST ROCK CLASSICS THAT EPITOMIZED THE CURRENT ROCK ERA. BARRY WHITE WITH HIS SEXY VOICE ENTERTAINED US ALL. CURTIS MAYFIELD'S 'SUPERFLY' AND ISSAC HAYES' 'SHAFT' BROUGHT US MOVIE SOUNDTRACKS THAT REMINDED US OF OUR SOCIETYS ILLS. THUS THE MUSIC WENT ON AND ROCK AND ROLL SURVIVED YET ANOTHER DECADE. THE FOLLOWING WILL HOPEFULLY BRING BACK SOME OF THOSE FOND BUT NOT FORGOTTEN MEMORIES.

THE 70'S - QUIZZES IN THIS SECTION

70/1	ELVIS		(10 QUESTIONS = 100)
70/2	THE FAB FOUR		(25 QUESTIONS = 100)
70/3	THE REST OF THE BRITISH INVASION	QUIZ # 1	(50 QUESTIONS = 100)
70/4	THE REST OF THE BRITISH INVASION	2	(50 QUESTIONS = 100)
70/5	THE REST OF THE BRITISH INVASION	3	(10 QUESTIONS = 100)
	THE REST OF THE BRITISH INVASION	BONUS	1
70/6	MOTOWN ROCKERS	QUIZ # 1	(50 QUESTIONS = 100)
70/7	MOTOWN ROCKERS	2	(20 QUESTIONS = 100)
70/8	MOTOWN ROCKERS	3	(10 QUESTIONS = 100)
70/9	R&B ROCKERS	QUIZ # 1	(100 QUESTIONS = 100)
70/10	R&B ROCKERS	2	(100 QUESTIONS = 100)
70/11	R&B ROCKERS	3	(10 QUESTIONS = 100)
70/12	POP ROCKERS	QUIZ # 1	(100 QUESTIONS = 100)
70/13	POP ROCKERS	2	(100 QUESTIONS = 100)
70/14	POP ROCKERS	3	(50 QUESTIONS = 100)
70/15	POP ROCKERS	4	(10 QUESTIONS = 100)
	POP ROCKERS	BONUS	3
70/16	COUNTRY ROCKERS	QUIZ # 1	(25 QUESTIONS = 100)
70/17	COUNTRY ROCKERS	QUIZ # 2	(25 QUESTIONS = 100)
70/18	ROCKERS	QUIZ # 1	(100 QUESTIONS = 100)
70/19	ROCKERS	2	(50 QUESTIONS = 100)
70/20	MISC (NOVELTY, FOLK, FOREIGN & INSTRMTLS)	# 1	(25 QUESTIONS = 100)
70/21	MISC (NOVELTY, FOLK, FOREIGN & INSTRMTLS)	2	(10 QUESTIONS = 100)
70/22	MISC (NOVELTY, FOLK, FOREIGN & INSTRMTLS)	3	(50 QUESTIONS = 100)
	MISC (NOVELTY, FOLK, FOREIGN & INSTRMTLS)	BONUS	4
70/23	MATCH THE LEAD SINGER WITH THE GROUP PT 1		(25 QUESTIONS = 100)
70/24	MATCH THE GROUP WITH THEIR SONG PT 1		(25 QUESTIONS = 100)
70/25	MATCH THE LEAD SINGER WITH THE GROUP PT II		(10 QUESTIONS = 100)
70/26	MATCH THE GROUP WITH THEIR SONG PT II		(10 QUESTIONS = 100)
70/27	MATCH THE DUOS AND ALSO THEIR HIT SONG PT 1		(50 QUESTIONS = 100)
70/28	MATCH THE DUOS AND ALSO THEIR HIT SONG PT II		(20 QUESTIONS = 100)
70/29	MATCH THE MOVIE/TV SHOW SONG WITH ARTIST PT 1		(25 QUESTIONS = 100)
70/30	MATCH THE MOVIE/TV SHOW SONG WITH ARTIST PT II		(10 QUESTIONS = 100)
70/31	MATCH THE DISCO HIT WITH ARTIST PT 1		(25 QUESTIONS = 100)
70/32	MATCH THE DISCO HIT WITH ARTIST PT II		(25 QUESTIONS = 100)
70/33	MATCH THE DISCO HIT WITH ARTIST PT III		(10 QUESTIONS = 100)
70/34	MATCH THE INSTRUMENTAL HIT WITH THE ARTIST		(20 QUESTIONS = 100)

34 TOTAL QUIZZES

ELVIS

1. **6 x 10**

NAME THESE SIX POPULAR HITS BY *ELVIS* DURING THE 70'S.
ONE, ABOUT BURNING PASSION.
TWO, WHAT HE ASKED HIS DADDY NOT TO DO.
THREE, ABOUT THOSE RAINDROPS IN A CERTAIN STATE.
FOUR, HIS BIG WONDER HIT SONG, THAT WAS ORIGINALLY RECORDED BY *RAY PETERSON* IN THE LATE 50'S.
FIVE, HIS RENDITION OF A *PAUL ANKA* COMPOSITION ORIGINALLY RECORDED BY *FRANK SINATRA* ABOUT SELF CONTROL.
SIX, HIS LAST RECORDED CHARTED HIT JUST PRIOR TO HIS DEATH ABOUT GOING DOWN.

1) ______________
2) ______________
3) ______________
4) ______________
5) ______________
6) ______________

2. **1 x 10**

IN JUNE OF 1982 THIS RESIDENCE OFFICIALLY OPENED IT'S DOORS AS A MUSEUM. NAME THAT BUILDING WHICH IS THE SECOND MOST VISITED HOUSE IN THE UNITED STATES, THE WHITE HOUSE BEING THE FIRST.
A) GRACIE MANSION
B) MONTICELLO
C) GRACELAND
D) THE FEDERAL RESERVE BUILDING

3. **1 x 10**

NAME THIS SONG THAT SHOULD HAVE BEEN A TOP TEN HIT FOR *ELVIS* THAT WAS ORIGINALLY RECORDED BY *BRENDA LEE* AND EVEN LATER BY *WILLIE NELSON* IN THE 80'S ABOUT SOMEONE WHO WAS IN THEIR THOUGHTS CONSTANTLY.
A) ONCE IN AWHILE
B) TOO BUSY THINKING ABOUT MY BABY
C) ALWAYS AND FOREVER
D) YOU WERE ALWAYS ON MY MIND

4. **1 x 10**

ACCORDING TO *ELVIS*' 'THE ESSENTIAL 70'S MASTERS, WALK A MILE IN MY SHOES', HE COMPLETED AT LEAST 120 RECORDINGS JUST IN THE 70'S ALONE. SOME WERE OLD STANDARDS AND OTHERS NEW. WHICH ONE BELOW WAS **NOT** ONE OF THEM?
A) BRIDGE OVER TROUBLED WATERS
B) I JUST CAN'T HELP BELIEVIN'
C) MAKE THE WORLD GO AWAY
D) I'M SO LONESOME I COULD CRY
E) DON'T IT MAKE MY BROWN EYES BLUE
F) POLK SALAD ANNIE

5. **1 x 10**

WHAT TYPE OF MUSIC WAS *ELVIS* KNOWN FOR RECORDING?
A) R&B
B) COUNTRY
C) GOSPEL
D) POP
E) ALL OF THE ABOVE

70'S **TOTAL POINTS.** **10 x 10 = 100**

THE FAB FOUR

1. **4 x 4**

RINGO STARR RECORDED NUMEROUS HITS AFTER THE BREAK-UP OF *THE BEATLES* INCLUDING THESE FOUR BELOW. NAME THEM.
ONE, HIS VERSION OF AN ORIGINAL *JOHNNY BURNETTE* HIT BACK IN THE 60'S ABOUT SOMEONE GORGEOUS AND ONLY SIXTEEN.
TWO, A NOVELTY SONG ABOUT THOSE VICES HE NO LONGER INDULGES IN THAT INCLUDE MARIJUANA, COCAINE AND WHISKEY, BECAUSE THEY MAKE HIM SNEEZE AND NOT ABLE TO FIND THE DOOR.
THREE, ABOUT WHAT HE HAS OF YOU THAT BRINGS BACK MEMORIES OF PLACES THEY HAVE TRAVELED AND THE REALIZATION THAT YOU WON'T BE BACK LEAVING HIM IN A WORLD OF HURT AND TEARS.
FOUR, HIS RENDITION OF A *PLATTER* HIT SONG OF THE 50'S THAT YOU ARE HIS DESTINY, THE ONE AND ONLY.

1) ________________
2) ________________
3) ________________
4) ________________

2. **11 x 4**

NAME THESE ELEVEN POPULAR HITS BY *PAUL MCCARTNEY & WINGS*.
ONE, ABOUT THAT UNCLE WHO THEY INFLICTED WITH PAIN.
TWO, A JAMES BOND THEME SONG ABOUT LIVING AND DYING.
THREE, ABOUT THE PEOPLE SEARCHING FOR THE BAND ON THE GO.
FOUR, ABOUT SOMEONE'S FARM.
FIVE, ABOUT LISTENING TO WHAT HE HAD TO SAY.
SIX, ABOUT CERTAIN TYPES OF LOVE SONGS, QUITE FOOLISH AT THAT.
SEVEN, ABOUT OPENING THE DOOR SHOULD YOU HEAR A KNOCK.
EIGHT, ABOUT A CERTAIN AMOUNT OF LUCK, TO MAKE IT HAPPEN.
NINE, ABOUT SOMETHING HE DIDN'T WANT YOU TO SAY TONIGHT.
TEN, ABOUT AN AMAZING FEELING.
ELEVEN, ABOUT HIS LOVE, WHO DOES IT WELL.

1) ________________
2) ________________
3) ________________
4) ________________
5) ________________
6) ________________
7) ________________
8) ________________
9) ________________
10) ________________
11) ________________

3. **1 x 4**

JOHN LENNON WITH *THE PLASTIC ONO BAND* CHARTED WHAT SONG BELOW ABOUT THE POSSIBILITY OF THERE BEING NO HEAVEN?
A) NOWHERE MAN
B) HEAVEN ON EARTH
C) IMAGINE
D) HEAVEN MUST BE MISSING AN ANGEL

4. **1 x 4**

THE BEATLES RECORDED A TOP OF THE CHARTS SONG ABOUT THE WISDOM THEY RECEIVED FROM THEIR MOTHER MARY. WHAT WAS THAT CHART TOPPER?
A) MAMA DIDN'T LIE
B) LET IT BE
C) MAMA SAID
D) TAKE TIME TO KNOW HER

5. **1 x 4**

"ANOTHER DAY" WAS A BIG HIT FOR WHAT FORMER *BEATLE* AND WIFE WHICH BECAME THEIR PERSONAL FIRST AFTER THE BREAKUP OF THE FAB FOUR?
A) PAUL MCCARTNEY & LINDA EASTMAN
B) JOHN LENNON & OKO ONO
C) GEORGE HARRISON & PATTIE ANN BOYD
D) RINGO STARR & MAUREEN COX

6. **1 x 4**

THE BEATLES RECORDED A SONG ABOUT MAKING YOU A PART OF THEIR LIFE WHICH ALSO BECAME A BIG HIT FOR *EARTH WIND & FIRE,* BOTH IN THE 70'S.
A) IT'S MY LIFE
B) MY WAY
C) GOT TO GET YOU INTO MY LIFE
D) COME AND GET YOUR LOVE

7. **1 x 4**

THE BEATLES FORMED THEIR OWN RECORD LABEL COMPANY. CHOOSE IT BELOW.
A) REPRISE RECORDS
B) ARISTA RECORDS
C) APPLE RECORDS
D) CAPITOL RECORDS

8. **1 x 4**

GEORGE HARRISON HAD WHAT BIG HIT ABOUT HIS LORD THAT WOULD BECOME HIS FIRST SOLO VENTURE AFTER THE BREAKUP OF *THE BEATLES* AND ALSO REACH THE TOP OF THE CHARTS?
A) WORK ME, LORD
B) THE LORDS PRAYER
C) MY SWEET LORD
D) I THANK THE LORD FOR THE NIGHT TIME

9. **1 x 4**

GEORGE HARRISON RECORDED ANOTHER NUMBER ONE, TOP OF THE CHARTS HIT SONG, ABOUT PEACE AND LOVE. WHAT WAS THAT ONE CALLED?
A) GIVE PEACE A CHANCE
B) GIVE ME LOVE (GIVE ME PEACE ON EARTH)
C) WAR
D) WHAT THE WORLD NEEDS NOW

10. **1 x 4**

"I WANT TO HOLD YOUR HAND" WAS *THE BEATLES'* FIRST TOP OF THE CHARTS HIT SONG BACK IN 1964. WHAT WAS THEIR LAST TOP OF THE CHARTS HIT SONG AS A BAND TOGETHER IN 1970 ABOUT A CERTAIN TYPE OF ROAD?
A) GOODBYE YELLOW BRICK ROAD
B) YOU TAKE THE HIGH ROAD, I TAKE THE LOW ROAD
C) THE LONG AND WINDING ROAD
D) MUST OF GOT LOST

11. **1 x 4**

WHAT FORMER *BEATLE* WOULD GO INTO THE ACTING FIELD AND IN THE PROCESS MEET AND MARRY BARBARA BACH HIS CO-STAR FROM THE MOVIE 'CAVE MAN'.

____

12. **1 x 4**

WHAT WAS GEORGE MARTIN TO *THE BEATLES*?
A) ROADIE
B) RECORD PRODUCER
C) MANAGER
D) ACCOUNTANT

TOTAL POINTS. **25 x 4 = 100**

THE REST OF THE BRITISH INVASION-QUIZ # 1

1. **1 x 2**

ENGELBERT HUMPERDINCK CHARTED WHAT LOVE SONG HE WROTE TO HIS LADYLOVE FOR THE ROMANTIC EVENING JUST SHARED AND TO FURTHER EXPRESS HIS UNDYING LOVE?
A) TOGETHER
B) HAPPY TOGETHER
C) AFTER THE LOVIN'
D) WHEN WILL I SEE YOU AGAIN

2. **1 x 2**

ENGELBERT RECORDED ANOTHER ABOUT A CERTAIN COLD SEASON WHERE THE NIGHTS GROW LONGER YET WARMER FOR PASSION.
A) TIME OF THE SEASON
B) WINTER WORLD OF LOVE
C) SUMMERTIME
D) SEALED WITH A KISS

3. **15 x 2**

NAME THESE FIFTEEN BIG CHARTED HITS BY *ELTON JOHN* DURING THE 70'S.
ONE, A CROCODILE TITLED SONG ABOUT HOPPING AND BOPPING.
TWO, ABOUT A GUY WHOSE A STAR.
THREE, BIDDING FAREWELL TO A CERTAIN COLORED BRICK ROAD.
FOUR, ABOUT A GUY NAMED BENNY AND HIS COMPANIONS.
FIVE, ABOUT NOT WANTING A SUNDOWN.
SIX, ABOUT THAT WICKED PERSON WHO CAME BACK.
SEVEN, HIS RENDITION OF A *LENNON* & *MCCARTNEY* SONG ABOUT LUCY.
EIGHT, ABOUT AN ISLAND PERSON, WHO WORKS THE STREETS AND TALL AND DARK AS COAL.
NINE, ABOUT BEING SAVED TONIGHT.
TEN, ABOUT A CERTAIN FREEDOM THAT HE LOVES AND FOLLOWS IT'S IDEALS.
ELEVEN, ABOUT A ROCKET PERSON WHO DEARLY MISSES HIS FAMILY.
TWELVE, WHAT MAMA CAN'T DO FOR YOU.
THIRTEEN, ABOUT WHAT'S OK FOR SATURDAY NIGHTS.
FOURTEEN, A CERTAIN WORD THAT'S EXTREMELY HARD TO SAY.
FIFTEEN, A DUET WITH *KIKI DEE* ABOUT NOT WANTING A HEARTBREAK.

1) ____________________
2) ____________________
3) ____________________
4) ____________________
5) ____________________
6) ____________________
7) ____________________
8) ____________________
9) ____________________
10) ____________________
11) ____________________
12) ____________________
13) ____________________
14) ____________________
15) ____________________

4. **1 x 2**

VANITY FARE IS BEST REMEMBERED FOR CHARTING WHAT SONG ABOUT A GUY WITH NO CAR FARE WHO TRIED THUMBING A RIDE HOME TO HIS BABE?
A) HITCHIN' A RIDE
B) HELP ME, RHONDA
C) GET ON UP
D) LAST TRAIN TO CLARKSVILLE

5. **1 x 2**

"NIGHTS IN WHITE SATIN", A TOP NUMBER TWO HIT SONG, WAS RECORDED BY WHICH GROUP BELOW WHO HAD A BIG HIT IN THE 60'S WITH "GO NOW!"?
A) THE MOODY BLUES
B) CULTURE CLUB
C) FOREIGNER
D) JEFFERSON STARSHIP

6. **4 x 2**

NAME THESE FOUR GIANT HITS BY *OLIVIA NEWTON-JOHN* IN THE 70'S.
ONE, ABOUT HER NEVER ENDING DEVOTION THAT WAS FEATURED IN HER MOVIE SOUNDTRACK 'GREASE' OPPOSITE JOHN TRAVOLTA AND CO-STARRING STOCKARD CHANNING AND A HUGE CAST OF OTHERS.
TWO, HOW SHE HONESTLY FEELS ABOUT YOU.
THREE, HER BIG MELLOW HIT SONG QUESTIONING IF YOU HAVE EVER BEEN IN A STRESS FREE ENVIRONMENT.
FOUR, QUESTIONING IF SOME MORE PASSION WOULD MAKE THEIR RELATIONSHIP JUST RIGHT.
1) ______________________________
2) ________________________
3) ______________________________
4) ______________________

7. **2 x 2**

OLIVIA NEWTON-JOHN CHARTED TWO DUETS WITH *JOHN TRAVOLTA* THAT WERE FEATURED IN THAT *BLOCKBUSTER* SOUNDTRACK MOVIE 'GREASE'.
ONE, ABOUT SHAPING UP BECAUSE YOU'RE WHAT THEY NEED AND DESIRE IN A SOUL-MATE.
TWO, A BIG HIT WITH THAT HUGE CAST OF TEENAGERS ABOUT THAT CERTAIN SEASON WHEN THEY FELL IN LOVE AND THE KIDS WANTING TO KNOW THEIR EVERY ROMANTIC DETAILS.
NAME THEM.
1) __________________________
2) ______________________

8. **4 x 2**

ROD STEWART CURRENTLY IN HIS FIFTH DECADE OF PERFORMING WAS ONCE A MEMBER OF THE GROUP *FACES*. NAME FOUR OF HIS BIG HITS BELOW.
ONE, ABOUT A GIRL NAMED MAGGIE WHO STOLE MORE THAN JUST HIS HEART.
TWO, ABOUT ANOTHER GIRL THAT LEFT A MARK IN HIS HEART AND HE CAN'T LET GO OF BECAUSE SHE'S ALL THAT AND MUCH MORE THAN JUST A FRIEND.
THREE, QUESTIONING IF HE'S SEXY, LET HIM KNOW.
FOUR, CONFIDENT THAT TONIGHT'S GONNA BE SPECIAL AND JUST RIGHT AND WANTING NO VISITORS OR CALLS TO DISRUPT THEIR PASSIONATE MOMENTS.
1) ______________________
2) ____
3) _________________________**?**
4) ____

9. **1 x 2**

ROD STEWART ALSO RECORDED TWO OTHER HITS BELOW. WHICH ONE WAS **NOT** HIS?
A) HOT LEGS
B) THE FIRST CUT IS THE DEEPEST
C) FEELINGS

10. **12 x 2**

NAME THESE TWELVE GIANT HITS BY THE '*BEE GEES*'.
ONE, A SONG THAT *AL GREEN* WOULD ALSO RECORD ABOUT MENDING SOMETHING THAT WAS BROKEN.
TWO, QUESTIONING WHAT'S HE GONNA DO WITHOUT HER?
THREE, ABOUT A CERTAIN WAY OF TALKING.
FOUR, THEIR BIG BROADWAY TITLED SONG.
FIVE, WHAT THEY ASKED FANNY TO DO.
SIX, WHAT YOU SHOULD BE DOING.
SEVEN, SOMETHING SO POSITIVE COME OUT SO NEGATIVE.
EIGHT, QUESTIONING THE DEPTH OF YOUR LOVE THAT WAS FEATURED IN THE BLOCKBUSTER MOVIE 'SATURDAY NIGHT FEVER' IN THE LATE 70'S.
NINE, STAYING WHAT, THAT WAS FEATURED IN THAT SAME MOVIE ABOVE?
TEN, ABOUT A CERTAIN ILLNESS THAT ONLY OCCURS DURING THE NIGHT AND ALSO FEATURED IN THAT MOVIE STARRING JOHN TRAVOLTA.
ELEVEN, THEIR BIG HEAVEN HIT SONG THAT WAS JUST TOO MUCH.
TWELVE, ABOUT A TRAGIC INCIDENT.

1) ______________________________
2) ______________
3) ______________
4) ___________________
5) __________________________
6) _____________________
7) _______________
8) _____________________
9) _______________
10) ______________
11) _________________
12) ________

11. **4 x 2**

ANDY GIBB, THE YOUNGEST BROTHER OF THE *BEE GEES,* CHARTED THESE FOUR HITS BELOW. NAME THEM.
ONE, ABOUT WHAT HE WANTED TO BE TO YOU.
TWO, WHAT'S THICKER THAN WATER THAT COMES FROM THE HEART?
THREE, A SHADOW SONG WHERE HE COULD ONLY IMAGINE YOU AND HIM ACROSS THE FLOOR IN HIS ARMS EVEN IF JUST FOR A BRIEF MOMENT.
FOUR, ABOUT SOMETHING PRECIOUS OF OURS THAT YOU JUST DON'T DISCARD.

1) ________________________________
2) ____________________________
3) _______________
4) _________________________________

12. **2 x 2**

NAME THESE TWO HITS BY THE GROUP *QUEEN* WITH *FREDDIE MERCURY* IN LEAD.
ONE, A SPORTS CHANT SONG ABOUT WHAT WE ARE WHO HAD TO FIGHT TO EARN IT.
TWO, ANOTHER SPORTS CHANT ABOUT ROCKING YOU.

1) _______________________
2) __________________

13. **1 x 2**

QUEEN ALSO HAD THIS OTHER ABOUT A RHAPSODY. CHOOSE THAT ONE BELOW.
A) RHAPSODY IN THE RAIN
B) BOHEMIAN RHAPSODY
C) RHAPSODY IN BLUE
D) DO WAH DIDDY DIDDY

14. **1 x 2**

ROBERT PALMER RECORDED THIS SONG IN THE LATE 70'S ABOUT WHAT HE TOLD THE DOCTOR OF THE PROBLEM THAT WAS AILING HIM THAT NO PILL COULD CURE. WHAT WAS THAT SONG?

A) GOOD LOVIN'
B) DOCTOR MY EYES
C) DR FEELGOOD
D) BAD CASE OF LOVING YOU (DOCTOR, DOCTOR)

TOTAL POINTS. **50 x 2 = 100**

THE REST OF THE BRITISH INVASION-QUIZ # 2

1. **3 x 2**

JOE COCKER, WHO GAINED HIS PREMIER STARDOM FROM 'THE WOODSTOCK FESTIVAL' BACK IN 1969 HAD THESE THREE HITS IN THE 70'S.
ONE, HIS VERSION OF AN ORIGINAL *BOX TOPS* RECORDING ABOUT A GIRL WHO WROTE SHE COULDN'T GO ON WITHOUT HIM. ALSO CHARTED BY *THE ARBORS.*
TWO, ABOUT A GIRL SO LOVELY AND EVERYTHING HE WISHED FOR.
THREE, HIS RENDITION OF A *LOVIN' SPOONFUL* SONG ABOUT WHAT HE TOLD HIS DARLING.
NAME THEM.

1) ______________
2) __________________________
3) __________________________

2. **1 x 2**

ERIC BURDON, THE FORMER LEAD SINGER OF *THE ANIMALS* IN THE 60'S, WENT ON TO RECORD A SONG WITH THE GROUP *WAR*. NAME THEIR ONLY ONE HIT AS A BAND TOGETHER ABOUT A DREAM HE HAD WHERE HE WAS THE LEAD IN A PORNO FLICK AND TREATED TO WINE.

____

3. **1 x 2**

ACE IS BEST REMEMBERED FOR WHAT BIG HIT THAT QUESTIONED THE LENGTH OF TIME SOMETHING HAD BEEN OCCURRING BECAUSE HE COULDN'T BE FOOLED?
A) HOW LONG
B) SOONER OR LATER
C) ONE SUMMER NIGHT
D) IT ONLY TAKES A MINUTE

4. **5 x 2**

LEO SAYER, THE TALENTED SINGER/SONGWRITER, RECORDED THESE FIVE BIG HITS BELOW.
ONE, ABOUT WHAT YOU MAKE HIM WANT TO DO AND ALL NIGHT AT THAT.
TWO, A NOVELTY SONG ABOUT HIS ABILITY TO DANCE LIKE *ASTAIRE* IF NEED BE IN ORDER TO EAT.
THREE, QUESTIONING THE AMOUNT OF LOVE IT WOULD TAKE TO GAIN YOUR HEART. SHOULD HE WAIT OR FORCE HIMSELF RIGHT IN?
FOUR, THAT WHEN HE'S IN NEED OF YOUR LOVE, ALL HE HAS TO DO IS FANTASIZE AND YOU'RE JUST A BEAT AWAY.
FIVE, A SONG THAT *THREE DOG NIGHT* WOULD GO ON TO RECORD AS WELL AND GAIN RECOGNITION FOR BUT GENERATE A LOT OF ROYALTY FOR *SAYER,* ABOUT THE SHOW AT HAND.
NAME THEM.

1) ___________________________________
2) ___________________________________
3) _________________
4) ____________________
5) ________________________

5. **1 x 2**

DEEP PURPLE HAD A BIG HIT IN 1973 WITH WHAT SONG ABOUT A BURNED DOWN GAMBLING HOUSE THAT LEFT A NASTY RESIDUE CLOUD AS A RESULT OF THAT INFERNO IN THE SKY?
A) SMOKE ON THE WATER
B) FIRE
C) SMOKIN' IN THE BOYS ROOM
D) GET OFF OF MY CLOUD

6. **1 x 2**

NAME THIS MOTION PICTURE STARRING A HUGE CAST OF ARTISTS AND ACTORS THAT INCLUDED: THE *'BEE GEES', PETER FRAMPTON, AEROSMITH, ALICE COOPER, EARTH, WIND & FIRE, BILLY PRESTON,* GEORGE BURNS, STEVE MARTIN, ETC IN 1978 THAT FEATURED MANY OF *THE BEATLES* SONGS.

A) YELLOW SUBMARINE
B) GIVE MY REGARDS TO BROAD ST
C) SGT. PEPPER'S LONELY HEARTS CLUB BAND
D) THE LAST WALTZ

7. **1 x 2**

ONE OF THE ARTISTS ABOVE HAD A BUNCH OF HITS IN THE MID TO LATE 70'S INCLUDING "SHOW ME THE WAY", "I'M IN YOU", AND "BABY, I LOVE YOUR WAY". WHO IS HE?

A) BILLY PRESTON
B) ALICE COOPER
C) PETER FRAMPTON
D) AEROSMITH

8. **1 x 2**

MANFRED MANN'S EARTH BAND DID A RE-MAKE OF WHAT *BRUCE SPRINGSTEEN* SONG ABOUT THE LIGHT?

A) BLINDED BY THE LIGHT
B) LIGHT MY FIRE
C) THE NIGHT THE LIGHTS WENT OUT IN GEORGIA
D) YOU LIGHT UP MY LIFE

9. **2 x 2**

NAME THESE TWO BIG HITS BY *ELECTRIC LIGHT ORCHESTRA*, AKA E.L.O.
ONE, ABOUT A CRUEL LADY WHO DID HIM WRONG.
TWO, ABOUT THEIR REQUEST TO THE OPERATOR TO LET THE PHONE RING A LITTLE LONGER.

1) ______________
2) ________________

10. **1 x 2**

AL STEWART RECORDED TWO SONGS BELOW. WHICH ONE UNFORTUNATELY WAS **NOT** HIS?

A) TIME PASSAGES
B) YEAR OF THE CAT
C) CAT'S IN THE CRADLE

11. **1 x 2**

HOT CHOCOLATE, AN ALL MALE BAND, CHARTED THIS BIG MIRACLE SONG THAT WOULD BE FEATURED IN THE TV SERIES 'TALES OF THE CITY' ABOUT WHAT HE BELIEVED, PRAYED FOR, AND WOULD DIE FOR. CHOOSE THAT SEXY HIT BELOW.

A) SEXY EYES
B) A WALKIN' MIRACLE
C) PILLOW TALK
D) YOU SEXY THING

12. **1 x 2**

THE BUGGLES HAD THE DISTINCTION OF BEING THE FIRST GROUP TO HAVE A SONG FEATURED ON MTV. CHOOSE THAT SONG FIRST CHARTED IN THE LATE 70'S AND RE-RELEASED IN THE EARLY 80'S ON MTV.

A) PRIVATE EYES
B) I CAN'T GO FOR THAT (NO CAN DO)
C) BILLIE JEAN
D) VIDEO KILLED THE RADIO STAR

13. **1 x 2**

LULU, THE POPULAR SINGER/TURN ACTRESS OF THE 60'S, SCORED ONCE AGAIN WITH A SONG ABOUT HER BEING A FOOL. ONE THAT *ARETHA FRANKLIN* WOULD ALSO GO ON TO RECORD. WHAT WAS THAT DOUBLE HITTER?
A) FOOLISH LITTLE GIRL
B) OH ME OH MY (I'M A FOOL FOR YOU BABY)
C) I NEVER LOVED A MAN (THE WAY I LOVE YOU)
D) TO SIR WITH LOVE

14. **1 x 2**

WHAT SINGER TURNED ACTOR CHARTED "FAME" AND "SPACE ODDITY" DURING THE 70'S AND WOULD END UP MARRYING IMAN, THE WELL KNOWN CELEBRITY COVER MODEL?
A) BILLY PRESTON
B) DAVID BOWIE
C) LOBO
D) HUGH GRANT

15. **1 x 2**

MUNGO JERRY, THE ONE HIT WONDER GROUP, HAD THIS BIG SUMMER HIT ABOUT THE FUN ACTIVITIES THAT THEY COULD ENJOY, SUCH AS FISHING, SWIMMING, AND SOCIALIZING WITH WOMEN. WHAT WAS THAT JOYFUL HIT CALLED?
A) SUMMERTIME
B) IN THE SUMMERTIME
C) HERE COMES SUMMER
D) SUMMERTIME BLUES

16. **1 x 2**

THE POLICE, A TRIO BAND OF MEN LED BY *GORDON SUMNER* ALSO KNOWN AS *STING*, CHARTED THIS SONG ABOUT A CERTAIN GIRL WHO WORE A RED DRESS AND WANTED TO ROAM THE STREETS. IT WOULD BE THEIR FIRST OF MANY YET TO COME IN THE 80'S.
A) SHERRY
B) DAWN
C) ROXANNE
D) DONNA

17. **1 x 2**

CHOOSE THE POPULAR HIT SONG BY *THE HOLLIES* ABOUT WHAT HE CONSUMES.
A) SWEET CHERRY WINE
B) APPLES, PEACHES, PUMPKIN PIE
C) THE AIR THAT I BREATHE
D) BREAD AND BUTTER

18. **2 x 2**

NAME BELOW THESE TWO OTHER HITS BY *THE HOLLIES*.
ONE ABOUT A FAMILY MEMBER THAT HE HAD TO CARRY WHO WAS NOT A BURDEN.
TWO, ABOUT A CERTAIN WOMAN IN A CERTAIN COLORED DRESS, THAT WOULD CLIMB TO THE NUMBER TWO SPOT ON THE CHARTS, THEIR BIGGEST EVER.
1) ______________________________
2) ______________________________

19. **2 x 2**

THE ROCK BAND, *LED ZEPPELIN*, CHARTED THESE TWO HITS.
ONE, ABOUT THAT PASSAGE WAY TO HEAVEN.
TWO, WHAT HE WAS GONNA GIVE HIS BABY, EVERY BIT OF IT.
NAME THEM.
1) ____________________
2) ____________________

20. **1 x 2**

10CC RECORDED THIS SONG BELOW ABOUT WHAT HE PERSONALLY CLAIMED ABOUT LOVE, WHICH REACHED THE NUMBER TWO SPOT UP ON THE CHARTS.

A) I'M NOT IN LOVE
B) LOVE IS A HURTIN' THING
C) LOVE AND MARRIAGE
D) (IF LOVIN' YOU IS WRONG) I DON'T WANT TO BE RIGHT

21. **1 x 2**

10CC HAD ANOTHER ABOUT WHAT WE ALSO DO FOR LOVE THAT SOMETIMES REQUIRES A COMPROMISE AND A WHOLE LOT OF COMMUNICATION TO MAKE IT WORK.

A) GAMES PEOPLE PLAY
B) BREAK UP TO MAKE UP
C) THE THINGS WE DO FOR LOVE
D) JUMP (FOR MY LOVE)

22. **1 x 2**

THE FORTUNES ARE MOSTLY REMEMBERED FOR CHARTING A SONG ABOUT WHAT THEY FELT WAS APPROACHING UPON THEM.

A) HERE COMES SUMMER
B) HERE COMES THAT RAINY DAY FEELING AGAIN
C) RAINDROPS
D) ANOTHER DAY

23. **4 x 2**

NAME THESE FOUR POPULAR HITS BY *ERIC CLAPTON* DURING THE 70'S.
ONE, A SONG ABOUT WHO HE CLAIMED HE REALLY SHOT, WRITTEN AND ALSO RECORDED BY *BOB MARLEY*.
TWO, ABOUT THAT GIRL SALLY WHO HE WANTED TO CONVERSE WITH AND HOPEFULLY BED DOWN AND NEVER LEAVE.
THREE, ABOUT THAT FANTASTIC NIGHT.
FOUR, ABOUT A VOW TO KEEP THEIR FRIENDSHIP GOING SINCE THEY COULDN'T LOVE ONE ANOTHER THOUGH HE TRIED.

1) ______________________________
2) ______________________
3) __________________________
4) _______________

24. **1 x 2**

THE GROUP *BAD COMPANY* RECORDED WHAT SONG ABOUT THE SATISFACTION THEY JUST COULDN'T GET?

A) I CAN'T GET NEXT TO YOU
B) CAN'T GET ENOUGH OF YOUR LOVE, BABE
C) CAN'T GET ENOUGH
D) (I CAN'T GET NO) SATISFACTION

25. **1 x 2**

WHAT GROUP CHARTED "SEE ME, FEEL ME" THAT WAS FEATURED IN THEIR ROCK OPERA 'TOMMY'?

A) TEN YEARS AFTER
B) THE WHO
C) THE GUESS WHO
D) QUEEN

26. **1 x 2**

THE ROLLING STONES RECORDED WHAT ROCK 'N ROLL TITLED SONG BELOW?

A) IT'S ONLY ROCK 'N ROLL (BUT I LIKE IT)
B) ROCK AND ROLL HEAVEN
C) ROCK AND ROLL MUSIC
 D) ROCK ME GENTLY

27. **1 x 2**

THE ROLLING STONES ALSO HAD FOUR OTHER HITS BELOW. WHICH ONE WAS **NOT** THEIRS?
A) TUMBLING DICE
B) ANGIE
C) MISS YOU
D) BROWN SUGAR
E) LET IT BE

28. **1 x 2**

CLIFF RICHARD CHARTED A SONG ABOUT THAT EVIL WOMAN WHO YOU BETTER STAY CLEAR AWAY FROM OR SHE'LL SNEAK UP RIGHT BEHIND YOU. CHOOSE THAT HIT BELOW.
A) BLACK MAGIC WOMAN
B) GYPSY WOMAN
C) EVIL WAYS
D) DEVIL WOMAN

29. **1 x 2**

THE SONG "EVERY TIME I THINK OF YOU" WAS CHARTED BY WHAT GROUP BELOW LED BY *JOHN WAITE*?
A) THE MANHATTANS
B) THE FOUNDATIONS
C) THE BABYS
D) THE MINDBENDERS

30. **1 x 2**

THE GROUP *FIRST CLASS* RECORDED WHICH SONG BELOW ABOUT A BEACH GOER BABE? IT WOULD BE THEIR ONLY MAJOR HIT UNDER THIS GROUP NAME.
A) CONEY ISLAND BABY
B) BEACH BABY
C) SURFER GIRL
D) TALLAHASSEE LASSIE

31. **1 x 2**

THIS MALE ARTIST WAS ONCE A MEMBER OF *THE YARDBIRDS* DURING THE 60'S AND THEN WITH *LED ZEPPELLIN* IN THE 70'S. WHO IS HE?
A) JIMMY PAGE
B) ERIC BURDON
C) ROD STEWART
D) RON WOOD

32. **1 x 2**

WHO ARE 'THE BAD BOYS OF ROCK' THAT ARE STILL PERFORMING TO SELL OUT CROWDS HERE IN THE 21ST CENTURY?
A) THE EVERLY BROTHERS
B) THE MONKEES
C) THE ROLLING STONES
D) THREE DOG NIGHT

33. **1 x 2**

PAPER LACE, A ONE HIT WONDER GROUP, RECORDED A SONG ABOUT THAT INFAMOUS NIGHT IN EAST CHICAGO WITH THE COPS AND AL CAPONE'S GANG SHOOTING IT OUT.
A) DEAD END STREET
B) THE NIGHT THEY DROVE OLD DIXIE DOWN
C) THE NIGHT CHICAGO DIED
D) SHOTGUN

34. **4 x 2**

NAME THESE FOUR POPULAR HITS BY *CAT STEVENS* BELOW.
ONE, HIS RECORDING OF A *SAM COOKE* TUNE ABOUT SATURDAY AND NEEDING SOMEONE TO CONVERSE WITH.
TWO, ABOUT A CERTAIN TRAIN ON THE EDGE OF DARKNESS TRYING TO END THE HATRED IN THIS WORLD.
THREE, ABOUT A MEAN WORLD THAT JUST A SMILE WON'T GET YOU BY.
FOUR, ABOUT THE MORNING WHEN IT SIGNIFYS THE CREATION OF ANOTHER DAY.

1) ____________________________
2) __________________
3) __________________
4) _______________________

35. **1 x 2**

FREE, A GROUP OF GUYS, HAD A HIT SONG ABOUT WHAT HE TOLD HER WHEN SHE ARRIVED AT HIS PLACE QUESTIONING HIS INTENTIONS.
A) DON'T LET ME BE MISUNDERSTOOD
B) DON'T GO BREAKING MY HEART
C) ALL RIGHT NOW
D) DON'T THINK TWICE, IT'S ALL RIGHT

TOTAL POINTS. **50 x 2 = 100**

THE REST OF THE BRITISH INVASION-QUIZ # 3

1. **1 x 10**

ALBERT HAMMOND IS BEST REMEMBERED FOR RECORDING THIS SONG BELOW ABOUT WHAT NEVER HAPPENS IN A CERTAIN PART OF CALIFORNIA.

A) RAINDROPS
B) IT NEVER RAINS IN SOUTHERN CALIFORNIA
C) CALIFORNIA SUN
D) LITTLE GREEN APPLES

2. **1 x 10**

WHITE PLAINS, A ONE HIT WONDER GROUP, CHARTED THIS SONG BELOW ABOUT WHAT THEIR BABY CRAVES BECAUSE SHE'S GOT IT ALL AND DOES IT WELL. CHOOSE THAT CRAVING HIT.

A) APPLES, PEACHES, PUMPKIN PIE
B) MY BABY LOVES LOVIN'
C) LITTLE GREEN APPLES
D) SUGAR, SUGAR

3. **1 x 10**

EDISON LIGHTHOUSE, ANOTHER ONE HIT WONDER GROUP, RECORDED WHAT SONG BELOW ABOUT A GIRL NAMED ROSEMARY AND WHAT HAPPENS WHEREVER SHE GOES?

A) EVERYBODY PLAYS THE FOOL
B) LOVE GROWS (WHERE MY ROSEMARY GOES)
C) EVERYBODY'S TALKIN'
D) IT'S GROWING

4. **1 x 10**

IN 1979 THE ARTIST *'M'*, TRUE NAME *ROBIN SCOTT,* CHARTED A SONG THAT WOULD CLIMB TO THE TOP OF THE CHARTS THAT HAD EVERYBODY TALKING, INCLUDING THE COUNTDOWNS, IN THE SUBWAYS, FROM LONDON TO NEW YORK, EVERYWHERE. IT WOULD BE HIS ONE HIT WONDER SONG.

A) POP MUZIK
B) EVERYBODY'S TALKIN'
C) YOU TALK TOO MUCH
D) MR BIG STUFF

5. **1 x 10**

DAVID ESSEX RECORDED THIS ROCK TITLED SONG BELOW THAT MENTIONS JIMMY DEAN IN THE LYRIC LINE AND WOULD BE HIS ONE AND ONLY CLAIM TO FAME SONG. WHAT WAS THAT HIT?

A) ROCK ON
B) AMERICAN PIE (PTS 1 & 2)
C) THAT'LL BE THE DAY
D) OH, BOY!

6. **1 x 10**

DEREK AND THE DOMINOS RECORDED THE SONG "LAYLA" IN THE EARLY 70'S. WHO WAS THE LEAD SINGER WELL KNOWN FOR SINGING THE BLUES AND AS A MEMBER OF VARIOUS GROUPS AT ONE TIME OR ANOTHER, CURRENTLY AS WE SPEAK ON HIS OWN?

A) ROD STEWART
B) GUY MITCHELL
C) ERIC CLAPTON
D) ERIC BURDON

7. **1 x 10**

THE GROUP *JIGSAW* CHARTED A SONG ABOUT THE RESULT OF THE LIE SHE TOLD HIM FOR NO VALID REASON, AFTER HE GAVE HER ALL HIS LOVE. CHOOSE IT BELOW.

A) YOU CHEATED
B) LIAR LIAR
C) SKY HIGH
D) LYIN' EYES

8. **1 x 10**

THE KIKI DEE BAND RECORDED WHAT SONG BELOW ABOUT WHAT SHE POSSESSED THAT HAD RHYTHM?

A) I GOT RHYTHM
B) THE BEAT GOES ON
C) LONG TALL GLASSES (I CAN DANCE)
D) I'VE GOT THE MUSIC IN ME

9. **1 x 10**

GARY GLITTER RECORDED A TUNE THAT WOULD BECOME A POPULAR CHANT SONG DURING SPORTING EVENTS. IT WOULD BE FEATURED IN THE MOVIE 'THE REPLACEMENTS' STARRING GENE HACKMAN AND KEANU REEVES. WHAT WAS THAT SPORTING CHANT SONG?

A) BANG THE DRUM ALL DAY
B) WE ARE THE CHAMPIONS
C) ROCK AND ROLL PART II
D) ANOTHER ONE BITES THE DUST

10. **1 x 10**

CHRISTINE MCVIE, OF *FLEETWOOD MAC*, CHARTED THIS SOLO HIT IN THE MID 80'S ABOUT A LOVER SHE'S FINALLY FOUND WHO'S GOT A GRIP ON HER.

A) HOLD WHAT YOU'VE GOT
B) GOT A HOLD ON ME
C) HOLD ME 'TIL THE MORNING COMES
D) DON'T LET GO

TOTAL POINTS. **10 x 10 = 100**

THE REST OF THE BRITISH INVASION-BONUS

1.

CHRIS REA RECORDED THIS SONG BELOW IN RESPONSE TO WHEN SHE SAID GOODBYE BECAUSE TO HIM IT WAS JUST THE BEGINNING. WHAT WAS THAT SONG?

A) FOOLISH LITTLE GIRL
B) THE FOOL ON THE HILL
C) NEVER CAN SAY GOODBYE
D) FOOL (IF YOU THINK IT'S OVER)

MOTOWN ROCKERS-QUIZ # 1

1. **5 x 2**

THIS POPULAR MOTOWN GROUP HAD A BUNCH OF HITS INCLUDING "EASY", "SWEET LOVE", "MACHINE GUN", AND "JUST TO BE CLOSE TO YOU". NAME THE GROUP AND FOUR OF THEIR OTHER HITS BELOW, NUMBERS TWO THROUGH FIVE.
ONE, THEIR NAME.
TWO, ABOUT A CERTAIN WOMAN BUILT LIKE A ROCK.
THREE, A TRIPLE LADY TITLED SONG WHO HE LOVES SO DEARLY AND NOTHING COULD KEEP THEM APART.
FOUR, ABOUT A MARRIAGE GONE WRONG AND THAT THEY MUST CONTINUE TO GLIDE ON THROUGH CHOPPY WATERS.
FIVE, MORE THE REASON WHY HE LOVES HER DESPITE OF IT ALL.

1) ______________
2) ______________
3) ____________________
4) ____________
5) ____________

2. **1 x 2**

THE SPINNERS CHARTED THEIR ONLY MAJOR HIT FOR THE MOTOWN LABEL IN 1970 DURING THEIR BRIEF STAY AND PRIOR TO THEIR SIGNING UP WITH ATLANTIC RECORDS, ABOUT WHAT IT IS AND DISGRACEFUL AT THAT.

A) SHAME
B) IT'S A SHAME
C) IT'S TOO LATE TO TURN BACK NOW
D) SHAME, SHAME, SHAME

3. **2 x 2**

THIS SONG BY A FORMER MEMBER OF *THE TEMPTATIONS* HAD THE SOUND OF A TRUCK ADDED IN THE BACKGROUND. NAME THAT TUNE (PART 1) AND THAT FORMER *TEMPTATION* MEMBER.

1) ____________________**(PART 1)**
2) ____________________

4. **1 x 2**

THE ARTIST ABOVE ALSO HAD WHAT BOOGIE TITLED SONG BELOW, A TOP NUMBER TWO ON THE CHARTS?

A) BOOGIE DOWN
B) BOOGIE OOGIE OOGIE
C) BOOGIE SHOES
D) BOOGIE FEVER

5. **2 x 2**

SMOKEY ROBINSON & THE MIRACLES CHARTED TWO SONGS WITH THE WORD 'TEARS' IN THE TITLE. ONE WAS RECORDED BACK IN THE 60'S AND BY OTHER ARTISTS INCLUDING *JOHNNY RIVERS* AND YEARS LATER BY *LINDA RONSTADT*, AND THE OTHER SONG IN THE 70'S ABOUT A CLOWN. NAME THEM BOTH.

1) ________________________
2) ________________________

6. **1 x 2**

DURING THE VIETNAM WAR, *EDWIN STARR* CHARTED A SONG ABOUT WHAT FIGHTING DOES AND WHAT GOOD IT SERVES. IT WOULD BE FEATURED IN THE JACKIE CHAN AND CHRIS TUCKER MOVIE 'RUSH HOUR 1' IN 1998. CHOOSE THAT SONG BELOW.

A) WHAT'S GOING ON
B) THE BALLAD OF THE GREEN BERETS
C) WAR
D) BRING THE BOYS HOME

7. **4 x 2**

NAME THESE FOUR POPULAR HITS BY *THE TEMPTATIONS* DURING THE 70'S.
ONE, ABOUT THE CONDITION THE WORLD IS IN TODAY, A GIANT BALL AT THAT.
TWO, THEIR IMAGINATION HIT SONG WITH *EDDIE KENDRICKS* IN LEAD ABOUT THOUGHTS THAT RAN WILD IN HIS MIND.
THREE, ABOUT THEIR PAPA WHO WAS A SCOUNDREL, ALWAYS ON THE GO.
FOUR, ABOUT THAT SHACK WITH THE FLUORESCENT COLORS.

1) ______________________________
2) ______________________
3) ______________
4) __________

8. **1 x 2**

DAVID RUFFIN CHARTED A HEARTBREAKER ABOUT HIS DEPARTING FROM HIS LOVER, NOT FOR SOME OTHER NOR BECAUSE HE DIDN'T LOVE HER ANY MORE. WHAT WAS THAT HEARTBREAKER HIT CALLED?

A) WALK RIGHT BACK
B) WALK AWAY FROM LOVE
C) WALK AWAY RENEE
D) RUN TO HIM

9. **9 x 2**

NAME THESE NINE BIG HITS BY *THE JACKSON FIVE* DURING THE 70'S.
ONE, ABOUT WANTING YOU AGAIN.
TWO, THEIR BIG ALPHABET HIT SONG.
THREE, THEIR ORIGINAL SONG THAT *MARIAH CAREY* WOULD RECORD IN THE MID 90'S FOR HER UNPLUGGED ALBUM ABOUT BEING THERE FOR YOU.
FOUR, ABOUT WHAT THEY CAN'T SAY WHICH WAS ALSO A *GLORIA GAYNOR* HIT.
FIVE, ABOUT A PEARL THAT BELONGED TO THEIR MAMA.
SIX, ABOUT THE TYPE OF DADDY HE WOULD BE TO HIS HONEY, THAT HE WOULD GIVE HER ALL HIS MONEY AND SWEET KISSES.
SEVEN, ABOUT A CERTAIN MACHINE WITH ALL THE FOOT WORKS INCLUDED.
EIGHT, THEIR VERSION OF A *THURSTON HARRIS* TUNE ABOUT SOMEONE LITTLE AND PRETTY.
NINE, ABOUT A WARNING TO HIS DARLING IF SHE WANTED TO BE SAVED.

1) __________
2) ____
3) __________
4) ______________
5) ________
6) ________
7) __________
8) ______________
9) __________

10. **3 x 2**

THIS POPULAR ARTIST FROM MOTOWN HIT IT BIG WITH "GOT TO GIVE IT UP (PT 1)" AND "INNER CITY BLUES (MAKE ME WANNA HOLLER)". NAME HIM AND THESE TWO OTHER HITS BELOW, NUMBERS TWO AND THREE.
ONE, HIS NAME.
TWO, HIS WAR PROTEST SONG ABOUT THE EVENTS CURRENTLY TAKING PLACE.
THREE, ABOUT A FEELING HE COULDN'T HOLD BACK AND TIME TO LET IT FLOW SINCE HIS LOVE WAS SO TRUE.

1) ________
2) __________
 3) __________

11. **1 x 2**

THE ORIGINALS HAD A SONG ABOUT THOSE RINGING SOUNDS THEY HEARD WHENEVER THEY KISSED. JUST THE THOUGHT OF HER LEAVING HIM WOULD MEAN THE END OF THOSE SOUNDS AND OF THEIR RELATIONSHIP. CHOOSE THAT SONG BELOW.

A) RING MY BELL
B) THE BELLS
C) DIFFERENT DRUM
D) WHISPERING BELLS

12. **1 x 2**

THELMA HOUSTON CHARTED A BIG DISCO HIT IN 1977 ABOUT HOW SHE DIDN'T WANT TO END UP WITHOUT YOU OR YOUR LOVE. IT WOULD BE HER FIRST MAJOR HIT AND REACH THE TOP OF THE CHARTS. WHAT WAS THAT BIG DISCO HIT?

A) LOST IN LOVE
B) HELP ME MAKE IT THROUGH THE NIGHT
C) DON'T LEAVE ME THIS WAY
D) LOVE HANGOVER

13. **7 x 2**

DIANA ROSS, NOW AS A SOLOIST, HAD THESE SEVEN POPULAR HITS BELOW.
ONE, HER RECORDING OF A *MARVIN GAYE* AND *TAMMI TERRELL* SONG ABOUT NO OBSTACLE BEING TOO HIGH OR TOO DEEP TO KEEP HER AWAY.
TWO, HER THEME SONG FROM THE MOVIE 'MAHOGANY' IN WHICH SHE CO-STARRED WITH BILLY DEE WILLIAMS, ASKING WHERE YOU'RE BOUND.
THREE, A DISCO HANGOVER HIT SONG THAT SHE DIDN'T WANT A CURE FOR.
FOUR, ABOUT REACHING OUT TO TRY TO IMPROVE THE WORLD.
FIVE, HER HEARTACHE HIT SONG THAT WAS FEATURED IN THE 'LADY SINGS THE BLUES' IN WHICH SHE CO-STARRED WITH BILLY DEE WILLIAMS AGAIN AND RICHARD PRYOR.
SIX, ABOUT WHEN SHE SAW HER HONEY LAST.
SEVEN, HER BIG TOUCHING MORNING HIT SONG.
NAME THEM.

1) ____________________________________
2) _______________________________________
3) _________________
4) ____
5) __________________________
6) __________________________
7) __________________________

14. **4 x 2**

STEVIE WONDER, NO LONGER LITTLE, HAD BUNCHES OF HITS IN THE 70'S INCLUDING: "HIGHER GROUND", "I WISH", "SEND ONE YOUR LOVE", "LIVING FOR THE CITY", AND "SUPERSTITION" JUST TO NAME A FEW. NAME THESE FOUR OTHER HITS BELOW.
ONE, HIS BIG SUNSHINE HIT SONG.
TWO, WITH A TRIBUTE SONG TO *DUKE ELLINGTON*.
THREE, ABOUT A LOVELY CHILD, THAT ONE CAN HEAR AT THE END OF THE SONG.
FOUR, ABOUT BEING YOURS NO QUESTIONS ASKED.

1) _____________________________
2) _____________
3) ____________________
4) ____

15. **1 x 2**

WHO WOULD REPLACE *SMOKEY ROBINSON* AS THE LEAD SINGER OF *THE MIRACLES* IN 1972?

A) JUNIOR WALKER
B) LEVI STUBBS
C) LIONEL RICHIE
D) BILLY GRIFFIN

16. **5 x 2**

COMPLETE THE NAMES OF *THE JACKSON FIVE* FROM THE INITIALS PROVIDED BELOW.

1. J J - 1) ________________
2. J J - 2) ________________
3. T J - 3) ________________
4. M J - 4) ________________
5. M J - 5) ________________

17. **1 x 2**

RARE EARTH KNOWN FOR RECORDING SUCCESSFULL HITS WITH THESE MOTOWN RE-MAKES, "GET READY" AND "(I KNOW) I'M LOSING YOU" HAD ANOTHER BIG HIT, THIS TIME WITH AN ORIGINAL SONG ABOUT WHAT THEY WANTED TO DO THAT WAS SO JOYFUL.

A) CELEBRATE
B) JOY TO THE WORLD
C) LOVELY DAY
D) I JUST WANT TO CELEBRATE

18. **1 x 2**

JERMAINE JACKSON OF THE *JACKSON FIVE* RECORDED A ROMANTIC RE-MAKE OF A *SHEP & THE LIMELITES* HIT SONG ABOUT COMING HOME TO HIS ANGEL FOR GOOD. NAME THAT ROMANTIC DOUBLE HITTER.

____

TOTAL POINTS. **50 x 2 = 100**

70/7

MOTOWN ROCKERS-QUIZ # 2

MATCH THE MOTOWN SONG WITH THE ORIGINAL MOTOWN ARTIST AND THE NEW RE-MAKE ARTIST.

	MOTOWN SONG		ORIGINAL ARTIST		RE-MAKE ARTIST		
1	GET READY	A	THE JACKSON FIVE	AA	THE CARPENTERS	**1**	,
2	YOU KEEP ME HANGIN' ON	B	THE TEMPTATIONS	BB	RARE EARTH	**2**	,
3	OOH BABY BABY	C	THE MIRACLES	CC	RARE EARTH	**3**	,
4	SHOP AROUND	D	THE SUPREMES	DD	LINDA RONSTADT	**4**	,
5	HOW SWEET IT IS TO BE LOVED BY YOU	E	THE MARVELETTES	EE	LINDA RONSTADT	**5**	,
6	PLEASE MR POSTMAN	F	THE MIRACLES	FF	GLORIA GAYNOR	**6**	,
7	HEAT WAVE	G	MARVIN GAYE	GG	JAMES TAYLOR	**7**	,
8	NEVER CAN SAY GOODBYE	H	THE MIRACLES	HH	LINDA RONSTADT	**8**	,
9	(I KNOW) I'M LOSING YOU	I	THE TEMPTATIONS	II	VANILLA FUDGE	**9**	,
10	THE TRACKS OF MY TEARS	J	MARTHA REEVES & THE VANDELLAS	JJ	CAPTAIN & TENNILLE	**10**	,

TOTAL POINTS. **20 x 5 = 100**

MOTOWN ROCKERS-QUIZ # 3

1. **1 x 10**

THE MIRACLES AFTER THE DEPARTURE OF *SMOKEY ROBINSON* CHARTED THIS BIG DISCO SONG THAT WOULD REACH THE TOP OF THE CHARTS FOR GOOD MEASURE.
A) BEST OF MY LOVE
B) ROCK YOUR BABY
C) UPSIDE DOWN
D) LOVE MACHINE (PART 1)

2. **1 x 10**

IN 1971 *THE UNDISPUTED TRUTH,* A MOTOWN TRIO GROUP CONSISTING OF A GIRL AND TWO GUYS, HAD THEIR ONE BIG CLAIM TO FAME SONG ABOUT BEING CAUTIOUS OF THOSE PEOPLE WHO PRETEND TO LIKE YOU, OFFER A HAND SHAKE AND ALL THE WHILE ARE JUST BACKSTABBERS AND A BUNCH OF LIARS THAT NEVER TELL THE TRUTH. WHAT WAS THAT ONE HIT WONDER CALLED?
A) TWO FACES HAVE I
B) SMILING FACES SOMETIMES
C) YOU GOT WHAT IT TAKES
D) THE MOST BEAUTIFUL GIRL

3. **4 x 10**

NAME THESE FOUR BIG SOLO HITS BY *MICHAEL JACKSON* DURING THE 70'S.
ONE, A MOVIE THEME SONG ABOUT A SICK YOUNGSTER AND HIS RODENT FRIEND.
TWO, ABOUT NOT STOPPING UNTIL YOU'RE COMPLETELY SATISFIED.
THREE, ABOUT BEING SOMEWHERE.
FOUR, HIS VERSION OF A *BOBBY DAY* TUNE ABOUT A BIRD UP IN THE TREE.
1) ______
2) ______________________________
3) ________________
4) ________________

4. **1 x 10**

CHOOSE THIS 1970 HIT SONG BY *THE SUPREMES* WITH *JEAN TERRELL* IN LEAD ABOUT CLIMBING UP TO THE TOP.
A) KNOCKIN' ON HEAVEN'S DOOR
B) UP THE LADDER TO THE ROOF
C) UP ON THE ROOF
D) STAIRWAY TO HEAVEN

5. **3 x 10**

NAME THESE THREE POPULAR CHARTED HITS BY *GLADYS KNIGHT & THE PIPS* FOR MOTOWN IN THE EARLY 70'S BEFORE THEIR DEPARTURE FROM THE LABEL.
ONE, A DEPARTING HIT SONG THAT NEITHER WANTED TO BE FIRST.
TWO, ABOUT THE POSSIBILITY OF BEING YOUR LADY.
THREE, THEIR VERSION OF A *SAMMI SMITH* SONG ABOUT NEEDING HELP TO ENDURE ANOTHER NIGHT, EQUALLY HEART WRENCHING.
1) ____
2) _____________________
3) ________________________________

TOTAL POINTS. **10 x 10 = 100**

R&B ROCKERS-QUIZ # 1

1. **1 x 1**

GENE CHANDLER, "THE DUKE OF EARL" MAN OF THE 60'S, CHARTED THIS ONE GROOVY HIT IN THE 70'S ABOUT A CERTAIN SITUATION HOPING TO MAKE THIS GIRL HIS OWN BECAUSE THEY SEEMED TO BE A PERFECT COMBINATION. WHAT WAS THAT SO CALLED GROOVY HIT CALLED?

A) GROOVY KIND OF LOVE
B) BABY IT'S YOU
C) GROOVY SITUATION
D) HEY THERE LONELY GIRL

2. **7 x 1**

BARRY WHITE, THE ROMANTIC SOUL SINGER, HAD THESE SEVEN BIG HITS. NAME THEM BY COMPLETEING THE INITIALS PROVIDED BELOW.

1) I'M G---A L--E Y-- J--T A L----E M--E B--Y

2) C--'T G-T E----H O- Y--R L--E, B--E

3) Y--'-E T-E F---T, T-E L--T, M- E--------G

4) W--T A- I G---A D- W--H Y-U

5) N---R, N---R G---A G--E Y- U-

6) I'-E F---D S-----E

7) I'-E G-T S- M--H T- G--E

3. **1 x 1**

BARRY WHITE ALSO RECORDED THREE OTHER HITS BELOW. WHICH ONE UNFORTUNATELY WAS **NOT** HIS?

A) HONEY PLEASE, CAN'T YA SEE
B) LOVE SERENADE
C) COULD IT BE I'M FALLING IN LOVE
D) IT'S ECTASY WHEN YOU LAY DOWN NEXT TO ME

4. **1 x 1**

LUTHER INGRAM HAD A HIT SONG THAT IF BEING WITH YOU WAS IMMORAL THEN HE WOULDN'T CARE NOR HAVE IT ANY OTHER WAY.

A) (IF LOVING YOU IS WRONG) I DON'T WANT TO BE RIGHT
B) ME AND MRS JONES
C) THE LOVE I LOST (PART 1)
D) BY THE TIME I GET TO PHOENIX

5. **1 x 1**

THE THREE DEGREES CHARTED THIS TOP NUMBER TWO HIT SONG THAT HAD THEM WONDERING ABOUT THEIR NEXT REUNION.

A) MAYBE
B) WHEN WILL I SEE YOU AGAIN
C) REUNITED
D) I'M WONDERING

6. **1 x 1**

"OBLIGATIONS AND TIES" ARE WHAT DROVE THIS COUPLE APART IN A KISS SONG. CHOOSE BELOW THIS ROMANTIC HEARTBREAK HIT BY *THE MANHATTANS.*

A) WHEN WILL I SEE YOU AGAIN
B) KISS AND SAY GOODBYE
C) RELEASE ME (AND LET ME LOVE AGAIN)
D) TOO MUCH, TOO LITTLE, TOO LATE

7. **1 x 1**

THE MANHATTANS CHARTED ONCE MORE, HOW HE COULD NEVER REPLACE YOU WITH ANOTHER.

A) I'LL NEVER FIND ANOTHER (FIND ANOTHER LIKE YOU)
B) FOR ONCE IN MY LIFE
C) YOU'RE THE ONE
D) NEVER BE THE SAME

8. **1 x 1**

CHOOSE THIS SONG BELOW BY *THE MAIN INGREDIENT* ABOUT WHAT EVERYBODY ENDS UP DOING IN THEIR LIFETIME WITH NO EXCEPTIONS. IT'S A SONG *AARON NEVILLE* WOULD GO ON TO RECORD IN THE 90'S.

A) EVERYBODY PLAYS THE FOOL
B) GAMES PEOPLE PLAY
C) DANCE TO THE MUSIC
D) BREAKUP TO MAKE UP

9. **1 x 1**

THE MAIN INGREDIENT CHARTED ANOTHER ABOUT WHAT HE DIDN'T WANT TO BE, IN FACT HE SIMPLY WANTED TO BE LOVED AND DEPENDED ON.

A) SIMPLY BEAUTIFUL
B) WHEN I NEEDED YOU
C) JUST DON'T WANT TO BE LONELY
D) ALL I EVER NEED IS YOU

10. **1 x 1**

THE MOMENTS RECORDED THIS SONG BELOW ABOUT FINDING SOMETHING ON THE STREET AND THEN LOSING IT DOWN THE ROAD. A TUNE *STACY LATTISAW* WOULD ALSO GO ON TO RECORD IN THE 80'S. IN 1980 THEY WOULD BECOME A NEW GROUP WITH THE SAME LINEUP AT ANOTHER RECORD LABEL AS *RAY, GOODMAN AND BROWN*. NAME THEIR STREET SONG.

____

11. **1 x 1**

IN THE EARLY 70'S *FREDA PAYNE* HAD WHAT BIG HIT BELOW ABOUT HER PLEA IN REFERENCE TO THE BOYS AT WAR IN VIETNAM?

A) WAR
B) COMING HOME SOLDIER
C) SOLDIER BOY
D) BRING THE BOYS HOME

12. **1 x 1**

FREDA PAYNE CHARTED ANOTHER ABOUT WHAT REMAINED FROM A BROKEN VOW AND THOUGHTS THAT COULD'VE BEEN.

A) SINCE YOU'RE GONE
B) BAND OF GOLD
C) MEMORIES
D) WITH THIS RING

13. **1 x 1**

CARL DOUGLAS CHARTED A NUMBER ONE HIT SONG ABOUT A MARTIAL ARTS RUMBLE WHERE ALL THE PARTICIPANTS WERE SUPER FAST AND SO MENACING. WHAT WAS THAT NUMBER ONE HIT SONG?

A) WAR
B) WE WILL ROCK YOU
C) KUNG FU FIGHTING
D) RIGHT PLACE WRONG TIME

14. **4 x 1**

NAME THESE FOUR POPULAR HITS BY *HAROLD MELVIN AND THE BLUE NOTES* WITH *TEDDY PENDERGRASS* AT THE HELM.
ONE, ABOUT NOT KNOWING HIM IF YOU CAN'T SEE HIM EYE TO EYE.
TWO, ABOUT LOST LOVE AND LIFE SO MEANINGLESS WITHOUT YOU (PT 1).
THREE, ABOUT THE TERRIBLE LUCK THAT HE POSSESSES WITH NOTHING GOING RIGHT (PT 1).
FOUR, THEIR WAKE UP CALL TO END ALL THE ILLS AND SUFFERING IN THE WORLD BY TEACHING A BETTER WAY ALSO (PT 1).

1) ______________________________
2) ____________________ **(PART 1)**
3) ______________ **(PART 1)**
4) ____________________ **(PART 1)**

15. **1 x 1**

THE TITLE OF THIS SONG CONJURES UP THE IMAGE OF SOMEONE LOOKING FOR THEIR SOULMATE IN THE PERSONAL WANT COLUMNS. CHOOSE THIS SONG BELOW RECORDED BY *THE HONEY CONE*.
A) WANT ADS
B) GET A JOB
C) LOOKS LIKE WE MADE IT
D) LOOKIN' FOR LOVE

16. **1 x 1**

THE HONEY CONE HAD TWO OTHER HITS BELOW. WHICH ONE WAS **NOT** THEIRS?
A) BAND OF GOLD
B) STICK UP
C) ONE MONKEY DON'T STOP NO SHOW (PART 1)

17. **1 x 1**

IN 1979 *PEACHES & HERB* CHARTED THIS ROMANTIC DUET ABOUT A RECONCILIATION AND THE REGRET OF THAT FOOLISH QUARREL THAT LED TO THEIR BREAK UP. IT WOULD BECOME THEIR BIGGEST AND RACE UP TO THE TOP OF THE CHARTS.
A) UNITED WE STAND
B) LET'S STAY TOGETHER
C) TOGETHER
D) REUNITED

18. **1 x 1**

PEACHES & HERB CHARTED ONCE MORE WITH AN UPTEMPO GROOVY DANCE HIT THAT HAD YOU SHAKING. CHOOSE THAT ONE.
A) SHAKE, SHAKE, SHAKE (SHAKE YOUR BOOTY)
B) IT'S YOUR THING
C) SHAKE YOUR GROOVE THING
D) I'M YOUR BOOGIE MAN

19. **1 x 1**

PATTI LABELLE WITH HER GROUP *LABELLE* RECORDED A HUGE MONSTER OF A HIT ABOUT A FRENCH-SPEAKING LADY FROM NEW ORLEANS. THE SONG WOULD BE FEATURED IN THE NICOLE KIDMAN MOVIE 'MOULIN ROUGE' IN THE YEAR 2001 WHICH CO-STARRED EWAN MCGREGOR AND JOHN LEGUIZAMO. WHAT WAS THAT NUMBER ONE HIT CALLED?
A) MY CHERIE AMOUR
B) THE BATTLE OF NEW ORLEANS
C) LADY MARMALADE
D) WITCH DOCTOR

20. **2 x 1**

NAME THESE TWO BIG CHARTED HITS BY *BILLY PRESTON*, THE TALENTED SINGER/MUSICIAN CONSIDERED BY SOME AS 'THE FIFTH BEATLE'.
ONE, ABOUT WHAT YOU CAN GET FROM ZERO.
TWO, QUESTIONING IF IT'LL TURN AROUND CONTINUOUSLY.
1) ______________________
2) ______________________________

21. **1 x 1**

TEDDY PENDERGRASS WENT ON TO A SOLO CAREER AND HAD A HIT WITH WHAT SONG BELOW?
A) CLOSE THE DOOR
B) WHAT AM I GONNA DO WITH YOU
C) IF YOU DON'T KNOW ME BY NOW
D) LADIES NIGHT

22. **1 x 1**

SILVER CONVENTION RECORDED A DISCO HIT IN 1975 THAT WOULD RACE UP TO THE TOP OF THE CHARTS. WHAT WAS THE NAME OF THAT AIRBORNE HIT?
A) I WILL SURVIVE
B) FLY, ROBIN, FLY
C) DON'T LEAVE ME THIS WAY
D) MACHO MAN

23. **6 x 1**

NAME THESE SIX BIG CHARTED HITS BY *ROBERTA FLACK* DURING THE 70'S.
ONE, ABOUT HER FIRST ENCOUNTER WITH YOU THAT WOULD BE FEATURED IN THE CLINT EASTWOOD MOVIE 'PLAY MISTY FOR ME' CO-STARRING JESSICA WALTER AND DONNA MILLS.
TWO, WHAT HIS SONG WAS DOING TO HER THAT ALSO REVEALED MUCH OF HER LIFE'S STORY.
THREE, ABOUT A ROMANTIC FEELING THAT WOULD COME UPON HER EACH TIME THEY MADE CONTACT.
FOUR, A DUET WITH *DONNY HATHAWAY* ABOUT THE PASSION CREATED AS THEY GOT NEARER TO ONE ANOTHER.
FIVE, ABOUT A LOVE THAT WAS NEVER THERE, NOR MEANT TO BE, FULL OF LIES.
SIX, ANOTHER DUET WITH *DONNY HATHAWAY* ABOUT WHO YOU CAN CALL WHEN YOU'RE DOWN, A SONG *JAMES TAYLOR* WOULD ALSO RECORD IN THE 70'S.
1) ______________________________
2) ____________________________
3) ____________________
4) ______________________
5) ____________________?
6) ______________________

24. **4 x 1**

BILL WITHERS RECORDED THESE FOUR POPULAR HITS BELOW. NAME THEM.
ONE, ABOUT THE LACK OF SUNSHINE WHENEVER SHE'S NOT AROUND.
TWO, TO SEEK HIM OUT IN TIME OF SORROW WHEN YOU NEED A FAVOR.
THREE, ABOUT WANTING TO BE MANIPULATED, A TOP NUMBER TWO HIT SONG.
FOUR, ABOUT A CHARMING DAY BROUGHT ON BY YOU. THE RAP GROUP, *THE S.O.U.L S.Y.S.T.E.M* WOULD DO THEIR VERSION OF THIS SONG FOR THE *WHITNEY HOUSTON* AND KEVIN KOSTNER SOUNDTRACK MOVIE 'THE BODYGUARD', TITLE EXTENDED.
1) ____________________
2) ______________
3) ____________
4) ______________

25. **1 x 1**

SYLVIA, FORMERLY OF *MICKEY AND SYLVIA* FAME BACK IN THE 50'S WITH "LOVE IS STRANGE", HAD THIS SEXY HIT BELOW ABOUT THE THINGS SHE WAS GONNA TEACH HIM THAT SCHOOL NEVER DID, WHICH HAD EVERYONE TALKING.

A) EVERYBODY'S TALKIN'
B) DON'T SAY NOTHIN' BAD (ABOUT MY BABY)
C) JUNGLE FEVER
D) PILLOW TALK

26. **1 x 1**

CHUCK BERRY HAD A NOVELTY SONG IN 1972 ABOUT A CERTAIN TOY HIS GRANDMA HAD PURCHASED THAT REQUIRED HOLDING ON TO FROM TIME TO TIME. IT WOULD BE HIS ONLY TOP OF THE CHARTS HIT SONG EVER DURING HIS FABULOUS CAREER. WHAT WAS THAT NOVELTY HIT BELOW?

A) YO-YO
B) BRAND NEW KEY
C) IT'S YOUR THING
D) MY DING-A-LING

27. **1 x 1**

THE BEGINNING OF THE END WAS A ONE HIT WONDER GROUP WHO RECORDED WHAT BIG FUNKY HIT IN THE EARLY 70'S ABOUT THAT ISLAND WITH THE SOULFUL BEAT?

A) KOKOMO
B) FUNKY BROADWAY
C) FUNKYTOWN
D) FUNKY NASSAU (PARTS 1 & 2)

28. **10 x 1**

NAME THESE TEN BIG CHARTED HITS BY *AL GREEN,* THE ROMANTIC BALLAD SINGER.
ONE, A TOGETHER SONG OF HOW YOU BRING OUT THE GOOD AND MAKE HIM WANT TO BE AROUND YOU.
TWO, HIS RENDITION OF A *ROY ORBISON* TUNE ABOUT A GORGEOUS GIRL. IT WOULD BE MADE INTO A MOVIE FEATURING *ROY'S* VERSION STARRING JULIA ROBERTS AND RICHARD GERE IN THE EARLY 90'S.
THREE, ABOUT HIS UNDYING LOVE FOR YOU.
FOUR, HIS VERSION OF A *BEE GEE* RECORDING ABOUT A BROKEN HEART NEEDING REPAIR.
FIVE, HIS RENDITION OF A *RAY PRICE* TUNE ABOUT THE GOOD TIMES.
SIX, ANOTHER RE-MAKE SONG THIS TIME OF A *TEMPTATION* SONG ABOUT NOT BEING ABLE TO COME NEAR YOU.
SEVEN, ABOUT THE BEAUTIFUL FEELING YOU STIR IN HIM WHENEVER YOU SHOWER HIM WITH AFFECTION.
EIGHT, ABOUT WHAT HAPPENS WHEN YOU'RE IN LOVE.
NINE, ABOUT WHAT HE WAS TIRED OF DOING.
TEN, WHAT MADE HIM SO GLAD.

1) ____________________
2) ____________________
3) ____________________________
4) ________________________________
5) ____________________
6) ________________________
7) ____________________
8) ____________________
9) ______________________
 10) ______________________

29. **1 x 1**

AL GREEN HAD FOUR OTHER HITS BELOW. WHICH ONE WAS **NOT** HIS?
A) YOU OUGHT TO BE WITH ME
B) HERE I AM (COME AND TAKE ME)
C) ALWAYS AND FOREVER
D) CALL ME (COME BACK HOME)
E) LOOK WHAT YOU DONE FOR ME

30. **1 x 1**

CHOOSE BELOW THIS SONG BY *CLARENCE CARTER* ABOUT SOMEONE SO RAGGED WHO WAS THE CHOSEN ONE TO CARRY THE FAMILY ON.
A) POOR LITTLE FOOL
B) PATCHES
C) RAG DOLL
D) TRAMP

31. **1 x 1**

MINNIE RIPERTON CHARTED HER ONE AND ONLY CLAIM TO FAME SONG THAT WOULD REACH THE TOP OF THE CHARTS ABOUT SOMETHING SHE LOVED DOING BECAUSE YOU WERE SO BREATHTAKING AND ALL SHE EVER WANTED.
A) EVERYTHING IS BEAUTIFUL
B) LOVIN' YOU
C) ISN'T SHE LOVELY
D) ALL I EVER NEED

32. **4 x 1**

NAME THESE FOUR FUNKY HITS BY *SLY & THE FAMILY STONE* IN THE 70'S.
ONE, THEIR GRATITUDE HIT SONG FOR ALLOWING HIM TO BE HIMSELF.
TWO, ABOUT AN INTERNAL AFFAIR.
THREE, ABOUT WANTING TO TAKE YOU TO A MUCH HIGHER LEVEL WHICH WAS A RE-MAKE OF A PREVIOUS HIT, ALSO FEATURED IN 'THE WOODSTOCK FESTIVAL'
FOUR, WHO THEY THOUGHT WAS A STAR.
1) ______________________________
2) ______________
3) ________________________
4) ___________________

33. **1 x 1**

IN 1974 *THE RIGHTEOUS BROTHERS* RECORDED A TRIBUTE SONG TO SOME OF THE GREAT ROCK AND ROLL ARTISTS WHO PASSED AWAY AND GIVING ONE HECK OF A SHOW, UP ABOVE. IT INCLUDED THE LIKES OF *JIMI HENDRIX, JANIS JOPLIN, OTIS REDDING, JIM MORRISON, JIMMY CROCE* AND *BOBBY DARIN.*
A) ROCK & ROLL MUSIC
B) ROCK AND ROLL HEAVEN
C) REELIN' AND ROCKIN'
D) IT'S STILL ROCK AND ROLL TO ME

34. **2 x 1**

THE STAPLE SINGERS, THE FAMILY GROUP CONSISTING OF THREE DAUGHTERS AND THEIR FATHER WHO STARTED OUT IN GOSPEL, CHARTED "LET'S DO IT AGAIN" AND "TOUCH A HAND, MAKE A FRIEND". NAME THEIR TWO OTHER PREVIOUS HITS BELOW.
ONE, WHERE THEY WERE GOING TO TAKE YOU TO THAT SHOWCASED THEIR GOSPEL ROOTS.
TWO, A RESPECTFUL HIT SONG THAT *BRUCE WILLIS* WOULD ALSO RECORD IN THE 90'S AS BRUNO ABOUT WHAT YOU SHOULD DO IF YOU WANT IT IN RETURN.
1) _____________________
2) __________________

35. **1 x 1**

TIMMY THOMAS RECORDED WHAT SONG BELOW PLEADING TO STOP THE WARS AND TRY LIVING TOGETHER AS BROTHERS THAT WE ARE, REGARDLESS OF THE COLOR OF YOUR SKIN?
A) LET'S LIVE FOR TODAY
B) WHY CAN'T WE LIVE TOGETHER
C) JUST YOU 'N' ME
D) WHY CAN'T WE BE FRIENDS

36. **1 x 1**

CHIC, A GROUP CONSISTING OF THREE GUYS AND TWO GIRLS, HAD THESE THREE MAJOR HITS BELOW. WHICH ONE WAS **NOT** THEIRS?
A) LE FREAK
B) GOOD TIMES
C) HE'S THE GREATEST DANCER
D) DANCE, DANCE, DANCE (YOWSAH, YOWSAH, YOWSAH)

37. **1 x 1**

THE TRAMMPS CHARTED WHAT FLAMING DISCO SONG THAT WAS FEATURED IN THE MOVIE SOUNDTRACK OF 'SATURDAY NIGHT FEVER'?
A) BURNING LOVE
B) DISCO INFERNO
C) BOOGIE SHOES
D) HOT HOT HOT

38. **6 x 1**

NAME THESE SIX BIG HITS BY *DONNA SUMMER* 'THE QUEEN OF DISCO'.
ONE, SOMETHING HOT THAT SHE'S GOTTA HAVE THAT KEEPS HER WAITING FOR A LOVER TONIGHT.
TWO, ABOUT THOSE NAUGHTY GIRLS WALKING THE STREETS AT NIGHT.
THREE, ABOUT WHAT SHE LOVES TO DO TO HER BABY.
FOUR, ABOUT THE FINAL OPPORTUNITY FOR ROMANCE TONIGHT BECAUSE SHE NEEDS YOU BY HER SIDE FOR GUIDANCE AND SUPPORT, FEATURED IN THE MOVIE SOUNDTRACK MUSICAL "THANK GOD, IT'S FRIDAY" IN THE LATE 70'S IN WHICH SHE CO-STARRED.
FIVE, A REMAKE SONG ABOUT A CERTAIN PARK, ORIGINALLY A HIT FOR *RICHARD HARRIS* THE ACTOR, IN THE LATE 60'S.
SIX, ABOUT DOING SOMETHING TO THE LIGHTS.
1) ______________
2) ______________
3) ________________________________
4) ________________
5) __________________________
6) __________________________

39. **2 x 1**

THE CHI-LITES CHARTED THESE TWO BIG HITS BELOW IN THE EARLY 70'S.
ONE, A GIRL TITLED SONG PLEADING THAT HE COULDN'T FIND LOVE IF SHE LEFT HIM. ALSO RECORDED BY *PAUL YOUNG*, THE POPULAR ENGLISHMAN, IN THE EARLY 90'S.
TWO, A SONG ABOUT A GIRL AND WONDERING WHY SHE HAD TO GO, LEAVING HIM ALL ALONE AND HOPING SHE WOULD COME BACK OR AT LEAST WRITE. ALSO RECORDED BY *MC HAMMER* IN THE EARLY 90'S.
NAME THEM.
1) ________________
2) _______________________

40. **4 x 1**

NAME THESE FOUR SMASH HITS FROM THAT BLOCKBUSTER SOUNDTRACK MOVIE BY *CURTIS MAYFIELD* ABOUT THE DRUG WORLD, STARRING RON O'NEAL IN 1972.
ONE, ABOUT THAT GUY NAMED FREDDIE AND HIS FINAL OUTCOME.
TWO, A DRUG DEALER IS ALSO KNOWN AS WHAT?
THREE, THE MOVIE TITLED SONG ABOUT A GUY WHO WAS SUPER BAD.
FOUR, ABOUT A GUY NAMED EDDIE WHO TURNED OUT BAD EVEN THOUGH HE KNEW RIGHT FROM WRONG.

1) ________________

2) ____________

3) ____________

4) ________________________

41. **1 x 1**

THE SMASH HIT ALBUM ABOVE ALSO INCLUDED THREE OTHER SONGS BELOW. WHICH ONE WAS **NOT** FROM IT?
A) NO THING ON ME
B) GIVE ME YOUR LOVE
C) GYPSY WOMAN
D) LITTLE CHILD RUNNING WILD

42. **1 x 1**

THE BAND, *ROSE ROYCE,* RECORDED A NUMBER ONE HIT SONG FEATURED IN A MOVIE OF THE SAME NAME ABOUT THE BUSINESS THAT THEY WERE IN, CARS, STARRING RICHARD PRYOR, GEORGE CARLIN AND THE *'POINTER SISTERS'.* WHAT WAS THAT NUMBER ONE HIT SONG?
A) ROCKET 88
B) CAR WASH
C) HOT ROD LINCOLN
D) VEHICLE

43. **1 x 1**

ROSE ROYCE CHARTED ANOTHER ABOUT WHAT HE WANTED TO DO BECAUSE YOU WERE HIS WISH COME TRUE FOR A LIFETIME AND NEVER DO WRONG. CHOOSE THAT OTHER HIT BELOW.
A) I JUST WANT TO CELEBRATE
B) I WANNA GET NEXT TO YOU
C) I JUST WANT TO BE YOUR EVERYTHING
D) VEHICLE

44. **1 x 1**

CHOOSE THIS POPULAR SONG BY *SISTER SLEDGE*, A FAMILY GROUP CONSISTING OF FOUR SISTERS, THAT WOULD REACH THE NUMBER TWO SPOT HIGH UP ON THE CHARTS ABOUT A UNITED FAMILY OF SISTERS WHO DID EVERYTHING TOGETHER AND HAD LOTS OF FUN DOING IT. DANCING, SINGING AND SO FORTH.
A) REUNITED
B) UNITED WE STAND
C) OUR HOUSE
D) WE ARE FAMILY

45. **1 x 1**

SISTER SLEDGE CHARTED ONCE MORE, ABOUT A MALE DANCER THAT SHE MET AT A DISCO WITH A GORGEOUS BODY, FANCY MOVES AND THE FINEST CLOTHING TO MATCH, THAT SHE HOPED WOULD TAKE HER HOME.
A) DANCING IN THE MOONLIGHT
B) HE'S THE GREATEST DANCER
C) YOU MAKE ME FEEL LIKE DANCING
D) DANCING MACHINE

46. **7 x 1**

NAME THESE SEVEN GIANT HITS BY *ARETHA FRANKLIN*, AKA, 'LADY SOUL'.
ONE, WITH A RE-MAKE OF A *BEN E KING* TUNE ABOUT A ROSE IN A CERTAIN ETHNIC PART OF HARLEM.
TWO, ANOTHER *BEN E KING* TUNE ABOUT NOT PLAYING A SONG OF MEMORIES THEY'RE TRYING TO FORGET.
THREE, ABOUT A FUNKY DANCE THAT YOU ROCK FROM SIDE TO SIDE ON THE FLOOR, OR EVEN IN YOUR CAR.
FOUR, ABOUT CALLING ON HER.
FIVE, HER VERSION OF A *SIMON & GARFUNKEL* SONG ABOUT A BRIDGE.
SIX, ABOUT HER DAYTIME ADVENTURES THINKING OF YOU, AND THAT SHE WOULD BE WHATEVER YOU DESIRED OF HER.
SEVEN, HER RENDITION OF A *MARVIN GAYE* AND *TAMMI TERRELL* SONG ABOUT YOU BEING THE REASON FOR CARRYING ON.

1) ____________________
2) ___________________________
3) ________________
4) _____________
5) ___________________________________
6) ________________
7) ___________________________________

47. **4 x 1**

TAVARES, A FAMILY GROUP THAT CONSISTED OF FIVE BROTHERS CHARTED THESE FOUR BIG HITS BELOW.
ONE, ABOUT WHAT HEAVEN MUST BE LACKING, PART 1, BECAUSE SHE'S HERE WITH HIM AT THIS MOMENT.
TWO, WHAT THEY CLAIMED COULD OCCUR IN SIXTY SECONDS.
THREE, THEIR VERSION OF A *HALL & OATES* TUNE ABOUT A GIRL THAT LEFT.
FOUR, A SONG FEATURED IN THE 'SATURDAY NIGHT FEVER' SOUNDTRACK MOVIE STARRING JOHN TRAVOLTA ABOUT WHAT SHE WAS TO HIM AND EVER MORE.
NAME THEM.

1) ____ **(PART 1)**
2) _____________________________
3) _______________
4) __________________________

48. **3 x 1**

THIS FUNKY GROUP HAD A NUMBER OF HITS IN THE 70'S INCLUDING, "FUNKY WORM" AND "LOVE ROLLERCOASTER", MUST I SAY MORE. NAME THEM AND THEIR TWO OTHER HITS BELOW, NUMBERS TWO AND THREE.
ONE, THEIR NAME.
TWO, ABOUT THE THINGS YOU DO THAT DRIVES HIM HOT LIKE A FLAME WITH YOUR SEXY MOVES AND SWEET TALKING TRASH.
THREE, ABOUT SOMETHING TIGHT TO THE BONE.

1) __________________________
2) ________
3) __________________

49. **1 x 1**

GLORIA GAYNOR HAD A TOP NUMBER ONE HIT SONG IN 1979 ABOUT WHAT SHE WAS GOING TO DO WITH HER LOVE, AND IN TURN, HER LIFE, THAT DIDN'T INCLUDE HIM ANY MORE.

A) WANT ADS
B) I AM WOMAN
C) FEEL LIKE MAKIN' LOVE
D) I WILL SURVIVE

TOTAL POINTS. **100 x 1 = 100**

R&B ROCKERS-QUIZ # 2

1. **4 x 1**

NAME THESE FOUR CHARTED HITS BY *THE O'JAYS*, THE TRIO GROUP OF GUYS. ONE, ABOUT A CERTAIN TRAIN THAT THEY WANTED EVERYONE TO BOARD.
TWO, WHAT THEY LOVED THAT IS SO SOOTHING AND MAKES THE WORLD GO ROUND, PART 1.
THREE, ABOUT A GIRL WITH CHARM, LOOKS AND PLENTY OF LOVING WHO WAS ONCE HIS AND HAVE BACK ONLY IF HE COULD.
FOUR, ABOUT WATCHING YOUR BACK OR THEY'LL TAKE WHAT YOU'VE GOT. A SONG FEATURED IN THE MOVIE 'LOOKING FOR MR GOODBAR', STARRING DIANE KEATON AND RICHARD GERE IN THE LATE 70'S.

1) ______________
2) __________________ **(PART 1)**
3) ____________________
4) ____________________

2. **4 x 1**

EARTH, WIND & FIRE RECORDED THESE FOUR FUNKY HITS BELOW. NAME THEM.
ONE, ABOUT A CERTAIN BRIGHT STAR THAT YOU COULD BE.
TWO, ABOUT BELTING OUT A TUNE.
THREE, ABOUT THE AFTERMATH ONCE THE ROMANCE HAS GONE, A TOP NUMBER TWO HIT SONG.
FOUR, A REMAKE OF A *BEATLES* SONG ABOUT WANTING YOU IN THEIR LIVES.

1) ______________
2) ______________
3) __________________________
4) ________________________________

3. **1 x 1**

AL WILSON HAD WHAT SONG BELOW ABOUT A GAME HE PLAYS WHEN HE WANTS TO REVEAL HIS PASSION AND DEVOTION?
A) GAME OF LOVE
B) SHOW AND TELL
C) SHOW ME
D) GAMES PEOPLE PLAY

4. **1 x 1**

GEORGE MCCRAE CHARTED A BIG HIT WITH WHAT ROCK TITLED SONG BELOW THAT WOULD REACH THE TOP OF THE CHARTS IN 1974?
A) ROCK STEADY
B) ROCK THE BOAT
C) ROCK YOUR BABY
D) ROCK ME GENTLY

5. **1 x 1**

THE GROUP *MFSB*, WHICH STANDS FOR MOTHER, FATHER, SISTER, BROTHER, TEAMED UP WITH *THE THREE DEGREES* TO CHART A SONG CALLED TSOP THAT WAS THE THEME SONG FOR DON CORNELIUS 'SOUL TRAIN' WEEKLY MUSIC SHOW. WHAT DOES TSOP STAND FOR?

____

6. **1 x 1**

THE SYLVERS, A FAMILY GROUP, HAD WHAT CHART TOPPER ABOUT A BOOGIE ILLNESS THAT HIS BABE HAD AND WAS SPREADING ALL OVER TOWN?
A) BOOGIE FEVER
B) BOOGIE DOWN
C) JUNGLE FEVER
D) SATURDAY NIGHT FEVER

7. **1 x 1**

JEAN KNIGHT CHARTED WHAT BIG NUMBER TWO HIT SONG ABOUT SOMEONE WHO THOUGHT HE WAS BEYOND ALL? BIG TIME WITH HIS FANCY THREADS, BUT WAS JUST A LOW DOWN USER AND HEARTBREAKER THAT SHE WANTED NO PART OF.

A) MR BIG STUFF
B) BIG MAN IN TOWN
C) COOL JERK
D) HE'S THE GREATEST DANCER

8. **1 x 1**

THE PRESIDENTS, A GROUP OF GUYS FROM DC, NON POLITICAL OFFICERS, HAD A HIT THAT NUMBERED THE YEARS THAT YOU'VE BEEN GIVING THEM AFFECTION AND SO GRATEFUL FOR IT. WHAT WAS THAT HIT BELOW?

A) 1,2,3
B) 5-10-15-20 (25-30 YEARS OF LOVE)
C) ABC
D) 25 OR 6 TO 4

9. **1 x 1**

JOHNNIE TAYLOR CHARTED THIS DISCO SONG ABOUT A CERTAIN LADY WHO HAD THOSE SEXY MOVES, LIKE IN AND OUT AND ALL AROUND. WHAT WAS THAT DISCO HIT THAT WOULD CLIMB TO THE TOP OF THE CHARTS?

A) DISCO INFERNO
B) DISCO DUCK
C) DISCO LADY
D) DANCING QUEEN

10. **1 x 1**

RONNIE DYSON HAD THIS SONG ABOUT THE PHYSICAL LOVE MAKING THEY HAD, BUT QUESTIONING WHY COULDN'T SHE REACH OUT TO GET TO KNOW HIM BETTER? COMPLETE THE SONG NAME FROM THE INITIALS PROVIDED BELOW.

(IF Y-U L-T M- M--E L--E TO Y-U T--N) W-Y C--'T I T---H Y-U?

11. **1 x 1**

THE *FOUR TOPS* CLAIMED IN THIS SONG THAT THERE WAS NO OTHER LIKE HIS, SENT DOWN FROM HEAVEN, AND SO EASY TO PLEASE.

A) AIN'T NO WOMAN (LIKE THE ONE I'VE GOT)
B) THERE'S NO OTHER (LIKE MY BABY)
C) MY BEST FRIEND'S GIRL
D) USE TA BE MY GIRL

12. **1 x 1**

HURRICANE SMITH HAD THIS SONG BELOW ABOUT WHAT SHE MIGHT SAY.

A) BABE
B) I GOT YOU BABE
C) OH, BABE, WHAT WOULD YOU SAY?
D) BABY COME BACK

13. **1 x 1**

HEATWAVE RECORDED A ROMANTIC BALLAD ABOUT A DREAM COME TRUE THAT SHOULD HAVE REACHED THE TOP OF THE CHARTS. WHAT WAS THAT BALLAD THAT HAS BECOME A POPULAR WEDDING SONG?

A) PLEASE LOVE ME FOREVER
B) I LOVE HOW YOU LOVE ME
C) ALL I HAVE TO DO IS DREAM
 D) ALWAYS AND FOREVER

14. **1 x 1**

HEATWAVE ALSO CHARTED WHAT DISCO PARTY SONG BELOW ABOUT DANCING ALL NIGHT THAT WOULD LAND AT THE NUMBER TWO SPOT HIGH ON THE CHARTS?

A) BOOGIE DOWN
B) BOOGIE NIGHTS
C) BOOGIE, OOGIE, OOGIE
D) BOOGIE SHOES

15. **1 x 1**

CHAIRMEN OF THE BOARD HAD THE BIGGEST HIT OF THEIR CAREER WITH WHAT SONG BELOW THAT HAD HIM PLEADING FOR MORE AMPLE TIME?

A) HELP ME MAKE IT THROUGH THE NIGHT
B) GIVE ME JUST A LITTLE MORE TIME
C) TIME WON'T LET ME
D) TIME IS ON MY SIDE

16. **1 x 1**

THE ISLEY BROTHERS CHARTED THIS SONG BELOW ABOUT A GORGEOUS LADY WITH SEX APPEAL WHOM THEY WANTED TO KNOW AND DO ANYTHING SHE DESIRED IF SHE WERE ONLY HIS.

A) DISCO LADY
B) THAT LADY (PARTS 1 & 2)
C) THE MOST BEAUTIFUL GIRL
D) SEXY EYES

17. **1 x 1**

DOBIE GRAY, "THE IN CROWD" HIT MAN OF THE 60'S, HAD THIS BIG ROCK AND ROLL SONG THAT *MICHAEL BOLTON* WOULD ALSO RECORD IN THE 90'S ABOUT GETTING LOST IN THE MUSIC.

A) REELIN' AND ROCKIN'
B) HAVING A PARTY
C) DRIFT AWAY
D) LET THE MUSIC PLAY

18. **2 x 1**

THIS FAMED JAZZ GUITARIST WOULD GO ON TO CHART THE FOLLOWING TWO SONGS, "THIS MASQUERADE" AND "THE GREATEST LOVE OF ALL". ONE, NAME HIM AND ANOTHER OF HIS BIG HITS BELOW.
ONE, HIS NAME.
TWO, HIS JAZZY VERSION OF A *DRIFTERS* SONG ABOUT THE GLITTER LIFE WHERE THE NEON LIGHTS SHINE. IT WAS FEATURED IN 'ALL THAT JAZZ', DEPICTING THE LIFE OF BOB FOSSE THE FAMED CHOREOGRAPHER STARRING ROY SCHEIDER.

1) ______________________
2) ________________

19. **1 x 1**

THE EMOTIONS, A TRIO OF GIRLS, RECORDED A TOP OF THE CHARTS HIT SONG IN 1977 ABOUT WHAT YOU GOT OUT OF HER THAT INVOLVED LOVE AND AFFECTION?

A) YOU GOT WHAT IT TAKES
B) YOU GOT TO ME
C) BEST OF MY LOVE
D) LOVE IS IN THE AIR

20. **1 x 1**

THE BROTHERS JOHNSON, A BROTHER DUO, HAD TWO OF THE THREE BIG HITS BELOW. WHICH ONE UNFORTUNATELY WAS **NOT** THEIRS?

A) I'LL BE GOOD TO YOU
B) MAGGIE MAY
C) STRAWBERRY LETTER 23

21. **4 x 1**

THE SPINNERS CHARTED NUMEROUS HITS IN THE 70'S INCLUDING: "I'LL BE AROUND", "COULD IT BE I'M FALLING IN LOVE", AND "THEY JUST CAN'T STOP IT (THE GAMES PEOPLE PLAY)". NAME THESE FOUR OTHER HITS BELOW.
ONE, ABOUT A CERTAIN LOVE AFFAIR THAT WAS RARE.
TWO, MIGHTY WHAT, PART 1, THAT CAN TURN THE UNIVERSE AROUND AND ALL OF IT'S INHABITANTS.
THREE, ABOUT THAT ELASTIC MAN WHO LIKES TO JAM AND SO FAR OUT.
FOUR, THEIR DUET HIT WITH *DIONNE WARWICK* ABOUT NOT KNOWING LOVE TIL YOU CAME AROUND.

1) ____________________________________
2) __________________ **(PART 1)**
3) _________________________
4) _______________________

22. **1 x 1**

WILLIAM BELL HAD THIS SONG ABOUT A TRIANGLE LOVE AFFAIR THAT STARTED OUT AS FUN, BUT NOW IT'S GOT HIM ON THE RUN, TRYING TO BE AT THREE PLACES AT ONCE. WHAT WAS THAT SONG?

A) TRYIN' TO LOVE TWO
B) LITTLE DARLIN'
C) TWO LOVERS
D) TWO LITTLE KIDS

23. **1 x 1**

NEW YORK CITY, A ONE HIT WONDER GROUP, CHARTED WHAT SONG BELOW ABOUT A GUY WHO WAS HEARTBROKEN WHEN HIS GIRL LEFT HIM, AND SINCE THEN HAS MET ANOTHER WHO HAS PUT HIM ON THE STRAIGHT AND NARROW AND FREE OF THAT VICIOUS GIRL?

A) ONE FINE DAY
B) I'M DOIN' FINE NOW
C) WITH OR WITHOUT
D) BUT IT'S ALRIGHT

24. **1 x 1**

KING FLOYD RECORDED THIS GROOVING HIT SONG ABOUT A GIRL HE WANTED AS HIS SPOUSE AND TO MAKE PASSIONATE LOVE TO HIM. CHOOSE IT BELOW.

A) GROOVY KIND OF LOVE
B) GROOVIN'
C) SHAKE YOUR GROOVE THING
D) GROOVE ME

25. **1 x 1**

EVELYN CHAMPAGNE KING RECORDED WHAT SONG BELOW ABOUT DISGRACE?

A) IT'S A SHAME
B) SHAME, SHAME, SHAME
C) SHAME
D) CRYING

26. **1 x 1**

JOHNNY NASH RECORDED THIS POPULAR SONG BELOW ABOUT HIS ABILITY TO SEE BECAUSE THE RAIN HAD STOPPED AND THE SKIES LOOKED CRYSTAL CLEAR. A SONG *JIMMY CLIFF* WOULD ALSO RECORD IN THE 90'S AND BE FEATURED IN THE JOHN CANDY MOVIE 'COOL RUNNINGS' IN 1993.

A) SUNNY
B) MY GIRL
C) I CAN SEE CLEARLY NOW
D) A BEAUTIFUL MORNING

27. **1 x 1**

JOHNNY NASH HAD ANOTHER ABOUT A GIRL HE WANTED TO MIX IT UP WITH SO AS TO LIGHT THE FIRE IN THEIR PASSION.

A) SHAKE
B) STIR IT UP
C) SHAKE IT UP
D) LIGHT MY FIRE

28. **1 x 1**

NATALIE COLE, DAUGHTER OF THE LATE GREAT *NAT 'KING' COLE*, HAD THESE THREE BIG HITS BELOW. WHICH ONE WAS **NOT** HERS?

A) I'VE GOT LOVE ON MY MIND
B) THIS WILL BE
C) SHADOW DANCING
D) OUR LOVE

29. **1 x 1**

THE GROUP *RUFUS*, WITH *CHAKA KHAN* IN LEAD, CHARTED WHAT FUNKY SONG BELOW ABOUT SOME GOOD NEWS THEY WANTED TO HEAR?

A) GOOD LOVIN'
B) TELL ME SOMETHING GOOD
C) GOOD TIMIN'
D) TELL HIM

30. **1 x 1**

ANITA WARD HAD HER ONE AND ONLY MAJOR HIT THAT WOULD CLIMB TO THE TOP OF THE CHARTS ABOUT WHAT SHE WANTED DONE WITH HER BELL. WHAT WAS THAT ONE HIT WONDER SONG CALLED?

A) WHISPERING BELLS
B) IF I HAD A HAMMER (THE HAMMER SONG)
C) RING MY BELL
D) THE BELLS

31. **1 x 1**

BETTY WRIGHT CHARTED A SONG BELOW ABOUT HOW SHE LOST A MAN TO THAT CERTAIN KIND OF WOMAN WHO PROWLS ON THESE TYPE OF NEGLECTED MEN AND JUST SWOOP THEM UP.

A) SHE WORKS HARD FOR THE MONEY
B) CLEAN UP WOMAN
C) WORKIN' FOR THE MAN
D) I AM WOMAN

32. **1 x 1**

KOOL & THE GANG, THE VERY POPULAR GROUP, HAD TWO OF THE THREE HITS BELOW. WHICH ONE WAS **NOT** THEIRS?

A) YOU MAKE ME FEEL LIKE DANCING
B) HOLLYWOOD SWINGING
C) JUNGLE BOOGIE

33. **1 x 1**

THE HUES CORPORATION, A TRIO GROUP OF TWO GIRLS AND ONE GUY, RECORDED A BIG HIT WITH WHAT ROCK TITLED SONG THAT WOULD REACH THE TOP OF THE CHARTS ABOUT NOT TIPPING OVER THEIR LOVE AND DEVOTION.

A) ROCK ON
B) ROCK YOUR BABY
C) ROCK ME GENTLY
D) ROCK THE BOAT

34. **1 x 1**

LOU RAWLS RECORDED THE BIGGEST HIT OF HIS CAREER, A TOP NUMBER TWO SONG, ABOUT HOW YOUR SEARCH COULD NEVER LEAD YOU TO A BETTER CARING AND BETTER LOVING PERSON THAN HIM. CHOOSE IT BELOW.

A) MY LOVE
B) YOU'LL NEVER FIND ANOTHER LOVE LIKE MINE
C) RUN TO HIM
D) BEST OF MY LOVE

35. **1 x 1**

LOU RAWLS CHARTED WITH ANOTHER ABOUT A LADY OF PASSION. CHOOSE THAT ONE AS WELL.

A) LADY LOVE
B) LADY
C) THAT LADY (PART 1)
D) LADY MARMALADE

36. **1 x 1**

THE TYMES, THE POPULAR R&B GROUP OF THE 60'S HAD A HIT WITH WHAT SONG BELOW CLAIMING THAT YOU WEREN'T BREAKING ANYONES' HEART BUT ON THE CONTRARY, BROUGHT HIM JOY AND THE DESIRE TO HAVE YOU FOREVER?

A) YOU LITTLE TRUSTMAKER
B) ALWAYS AND FOREVER
C) MAKE ME SMILE
D) HERE AND NOW

37. **1 x 1**

THE SONGS "I'LL NEVER LOVE THIS WAY AGAIN" AND "I'LL NEVER FALL IN LOVE AGAIN" WERE CHARTED BY WHAT POPULAR FEMALE R&B SINGER BELOW WHO HAD BEEN AROUND SINCE THE EARLY 60'S?

A) DENIECE WILLIAMS
B) MARY WELLS
C) GLORIA ESTEFAN
D) DIONNE WARWICK

38. **2 x 1**

THIS SOULFUL SINGER/SONGWRITER TURNED ACTOR AND CURRENTLY A DEEJAY, CHARTED A THEME SONG FOR A MOVIE OF THE SAME NAME STARRING RICHARD ROUNDTREE ABOUT A BLACK PRIVATE EYE WHO WOULD TAKE RISKS TO HELP OUT HIS FELLOW MAN. NAME HIM AND THAT THEME SONG.

1) ________________

2) ______________________

39. **1 x 1**

WHAT WAS THE NICKNAME GIVEN TO THAT SOULFUL ARTIST ABOVE?

A) MR PERSONALITY
B) BLACK MOSES
C) BOOM BOOM
D) MAN IN BLACK

40. **1 x 1**

LOVE UNLIMITED, A TRIO GIRL GROUP MANAGED BY *BARRY WHITE*, RECORDED THIS SONG ABOUT WALKING WITH SOMEONE THAT THEY LOVED. IT WOULD FEATURE *BARRY* ON A PHONE CONVERSATION DURING THE SONG. CHOOSE IT BELOW.

A) YOU TALK TOO MUCH
B) IN THE RAIN
C) WALKIN' IN THE RAIN WITH THE ONE I LOVE
D) JUST WALKING IN THE RAIN

41. **2 x 1**

THIS BALLAD ABOUT A RENDEZVOUS WITH A MARRIED WOMAN, MRS JONES, EARNED THIS ARTIST A TOP OF THE CHARTS HIT SONG AND BIG TIME RECOGNITION. NAME BOTH THE SONG AND ARTIST.

1) ______________________
2) ________________

42. **1 x 1**

RICHIE HAVENS, THE FIRST PERFORMER AT 'THE WOODSTOCK FESTIVAL' IN 1969, CHARTED A HIT WITH WHAT TUNE OF *THE BEATLES* ABOUT THE SUN?

A) HERE COMES THE SUN
B) GOOD MORNING STARSHINE
C) YELLOW SUBMARINE
D) WE'LL SING IN THE SUNSHINE

43. **1 x 1**

WHAT ARTIST BELOW WAS KNOWN AS 'THE RAGGAE MASTER'?

A) ERIC CLAPTON
B) JOHNNY NASH
C) BOB MARLEY
D) JIMMY CLIFF

44. **1 x 1**

CORNELIUS BROTHERS & SISTER ROSE, A FAMILY GROUP AS WELL, HAD THIS BIG HIT ABOUT THE WAY A LADY SHOULD BE TREATED.

A) TREAT HER RIGHT
B) SHE'S A LADY
C) LADY
D) TREAT HER LIKE A LADY

45. **1 x 1**

CORNELIUS BROTHERS & SISTER ROSE HAD ANOTHER, THIS TIME WITH A TOP NUMBER TWO SONG ABOUT IT BEING AWFULLY LATE TO GO BACK AT THIS POINT IN TIME.

A) RIGHT BACK WHERE WE STARTED FROM
B) IT'S TOO LATE
C) NO TIME
D) TOO LATE TO TURN BACK NOW

46. **1 x 1**

MAXINE NIGHTINGALE RECORDED THIS TOP NUMBER TWO HIT SONG ABOUT GETTING BACK TO THE STARTING POINT IN ORDER TO MAKE THEIR LOVE STRONGER. WHAT WAS THAT TOP NUMBER TWO HIT SONG?

A) GET BACK
B) LET'S DO IT AGAIN
C) DO IT ('TIL YOU'RE SATISFIED)
D) RIGHT BACK WHERE WE STARTED FROM

47. **1 x 1**

MAXINE NIGHTINGALE HAD ANOTHER, THIS TIME WITH A LOVE SONG, ABOUT WANTING TO BE TEASED AND STIRRED UP FOR AN ALL NIGHT SESSION WITH THE ONE SHE VOWED TO LOVE AND NEVER LEAVE. WHAT WAS THAT OTHER HIT?
A) LEAD ME ON
B) STIR IT UP
C) GIMME SOME LOVIN'
D) GET READY

48. **1 x 1**

BEN E KING CHARTED WHAT SONG ABOUT YOUR LOVE BEING EXTRAORDINARY, WHICH MADE HIM HOT AND PUT HIM INTO A SPELL, WANTING YOU MORE AND MORE?
A) SUPER FREAK
B) SUPERSTAR
C) SUPERNATURAL THING (PART 1)
D) SUPERSTITION

49. **1 x 1**

THE RITCHE FAMILY, A FEMALE TRIO, CHARTED A SONG ABOUT A CERTAIN DANCE HALL SECOND TO NONE, THAT FEATURED MOTOWN, SALSA AND THE O'JAYS AND MAYBE A SOUL MATE TO BOOT. CHOOSE IT BELOW.
A) AT THE HOP
B) BEST DISCO IN TOWN
C) BOOGIE DOWN
D) DISCO INFERNO

50. **1 x 1**

EDDIE HOLMAN CHARTED THIS POPULAR SONG BELOW ABOUT A LONELY GIRL WHO WAS HEART BROKEN AND HE WANTED SO DESPERATELY TO BE HER LOVING MAN AND REPAIR HER BROKEN HEART. IT TOO WOULD CLIMB TO THE NUMBER TWO SPOT UP ON THE CHARTS.
A) SAD GIRL
B) HEY, GIRL
C) LONELY DAYS
D) HEY THERE LONELY GIRL

51. **1 x 1**

THE FRIENDS OF DISTINCTION HAD THIS BIG HIT ABOUT LOVE AND LONELINESS AND ASKING SOMEONE TO DECIDE ON ONE OR THE OTHER.
A) DON'T LET ME BE LONELY TONIGHT
B) LOVE OR LET ME BE LONELY
C) (LONELINESS MADE ME REALIZE) IT'S YOU THAT I NEED
D) DON'T LEAVE ME THIS WAY

52. **3 x 1**

NAME THESE THREE BIG CHARTED HITS BY *THE 5TH DIMENSION* DURING THE 70'S.
ONE, ABOUT A BELL THAT THEY WOULDN'T HAVE TO RESPOND TO.
TWO, ABOUT HOW SHE COULDN'T CATCH A WINK THINKING OF YOU ALL NIGHT.
THREE, THEIR RE-MAKE OF *THE ASSOCIATION'S* SONG ABOUT SOMETHING THAT WOULD NEVER HAPPEN, BECAUSE THEY WOULD NEVER TIRE OF YOU.

1) ______________________________
2) ____
3) ____________________

53. **1 x 1**

AMII STEWART CHARTED A SONG THAT WAS ORIGINALLY A HIT FOR *EDDIE FLOYD* BACK IN THE 60'S ABOUT A CERTAIN SUPERSTITIOUS KNOCK SO AS NOT TO END UP LOSING YOU. ALSO RECORDED BY *CARLA THOMAS* AS A DUET WITH *OTIS REDDING*. WHAT WAS THAT TRIPLE HITTER CALLED?

A) KNOCKIN' ON HEAVEN'S DOOR
B) KNOCK ON WOOD
C) KNOCK THREE TIMES
D) WHO'S THAT KNOCKIN'

54. **1 x 1**

THE FIVE STAIRSTEPS, A GROUP OF KIDS AND FAMILY MEMBERS, HAD A POPULAR SONG TELLING A CHILD THAT ONE DAY LIFE WOULD BECOME MUCH BETTER AND MOST DEFINITELY, HAPPIER. IT WOULD BE THEIR ONE AND ONLY CLAIM TO FAME SONG. WHAT WAS IT CALLED?

A) EASIER SAID THAN DONE
B) O-O-H CHILD
C) MAYBE TOMORROW
D) GOOD MORNING STARSHINE

55. **1 x 1**

THE PERSUADERS, THE GROUP OUT OF NY, HAD A SONG ABOUT THE CLOSE RELATIONSHIP BETWEEN THE EMOTIONS OF LOVE AND HATE. WHAT WAS IT CALLED?

A) ONLY LOVE CAN BREAK A HEART
B) LOVE WON'T LET ME WAIT
C) RING OF FIRE
D) THIN LINE BETWEEN LOVE AND HATE

56. **7 x 1**

THIS GROUP OF GUYS ARE WELL KNOWN FOR THEIR ROMANTIC HITS INCLUDING "BETCHA BY GOLLY, WOW". WHO ARE THEY AND ALSO NAME THESE SIX OTHER HITS BELOW, NUMBERS TWO THROUGH SEVEN?
ONE, THEIR NAME.
TWO, ABOUT THE CONSTANT BREAK UP THAT THEY GO THROUGH THAT HE'S TIRED OF, HAPPY ONE MOMENT, THEN SAD THE NEXT.
THREE, ABOUT A BRAND NEW FEELING THAT YOU CREATE IN HIM.
FOUR, ABOUT BEING STONED AND GIVING YOU THE WORLD.
FIVE, A TOGETHER HIT SONG WITH US LOVING EACH OTHER.
SIX, ABOUT WHAT YOU ARE THAT NOTHING ELSE MATTERS TO ME.
SEVEN, THE CONSEQUENCES YOU'LL FACE IF YOU TEAR MY HEART APART.

1) ____________________
2) __________________________
3) ________________________________
4) ________________________________
5) ________________________________
6) __________________________
7) ____

57. **1 x 1**

GWEN McCRAE, HAD A HIT SONG ABOUT WANTING TO BE YOUR WHAT, LETTING YOU ROCK HER GENTLY AND ALL NIGHT AT THAT TIL THE SUNRISE. CHOOSE IT BELOW.

A) ROCK THE BOAT
B) ROCK ME GENTLY
C) ROCKIN' CHAIR
D) ROCK AND ROLL HEAVEN

58. **1 x 1**

A TASTE OF HONEY IS BEST REMEMBERED WITH WHAT BOOGIE RHYMING SONG BELOW ABOUT DANCING TIL YOU CAN'T NO MORE?
A) BOOGIE SHOES
B) JUNGLE BOOGIE
C) BOOGIE OOGIE OOGIE
D) BOOGIE ON REGGAE WOMAN

59. **1 x 1**

SHIRLEY AND COMPANY RECORDED WHAT SHAMEFUL HIT SONG BELOW? THE SAME *SHIRLEY* WHO WITH *LEE* CHARTED A BIG HIT IN THE 50'S WITH "LET THE GOOD TIMES ROLL".
A) CLEAN UP WOMAN
B) SHAME, SHAME, SHAME
C) IT'S A SHAME
D) SHAME

60. **1 x 1**

MAJOR HARRIS IS MOSTLY REMEMBERED FOR WHAT PASSIONATE SONG BELOW ABOUT WHAT LOVE WOULDN'T LET HIM DO, NOT EVEN FOR A MINUTE?
A) JUST DON'T WANT TO BE LONELY
B) LOVE ON THE ROCKS
C) THE LOVE I LOST (PART 1)
D) LOVE WON'T LET ME WAIT

61. **1 x 1**

MICHAEL JOHNSON RECORDED A SONG ABOUT WHAT WOULDN'T LAST FOREVER BECAUSE THE SUN HAD TO SHINE SOMETIME.
A) I LOVE THE NIGHTLIFE
B) SOMEWHERE OUT THERE
C) BANANA BOAT (DAY-O)
D) THE NIGHT WON'T LAST FOREVER

62. **1 x 1**

MICHAEL JOHNSON CHARTED STILL ANOTHER ABOUT HOW LIFE WOULD BE WITHOUT HER, VERY SAD, COLD, AND SO BLUE, BECAUSE SHE BROUGHT LIFE INTO HIS WORLD.
A) LOVE IS ALL AROUND
B) BLUE ON BLUE
C) BLUER THAN BLUE
D) I JUST DON'T WANT TO BE LONELY

63. **1 x 1**

THIS GIRL GROUP, *HOT*, CHARTED WHAT SONG BELOW ABOUT A GIRL WHO KNEW HER MAN FOOLED AROUND AND TO GET EVEN SHE WOULD PLAY AN ANGEL AND THEN A DEVIL AT THE OPPORTUNE TIME?
A) BLACK MAGIC WOMAN
B) DEVIL OR ANGEL
C) ANGEL IN YOUR ARMS
D) SHOULD'VE KNOWN BETTER

64. **1 x 1**

SHIRLEY BROWN RECORDED A SONG ABOUT A CONVERSATION ONE WOMAN HAD WITH ANOTHER ADVISING HER TO STEP AWAY FROM HER MAN BECAUSE HE BELONGED TO HER.
A) DON'T MESS WITH BILL
B) MY GUY
C) WOMAN TO WOMAN
 D) I AM WOMAN

65. **1 x 1**

CHERYL LYNN CHARTED THIS DISCO SONG ABOUT SOMETHING THAT HAD TO BE BECAUSE OUR LOVE IS THAT AND SO MUCH MORE.

A) GOT TO BE REAL
B) TRUE
C) HE'S THE GREATEST DANCER
D) MORE, MORE, MORE (PART 1)

66. **2 x 1**

THIS HUSBAND AND WIFE DUO, WHO WERE ORIGINALLY PART OF *THE 5TH DIMENSION*, CHARTED "YOU DON'T HAVE TO BE A STAR (TO BE IN MY SHOW)". NAME THAT HUSBAND AND WIFE DUO.

1) ____________________________
2) ____________________

67. **1 x 1**

THE DELLS CHARTED A SONG ABOUT THOSE FOND PASSIONATE MEMORIES THAT HE NEVER WANTED TO FORGET.

A) REMEMBER THEN
B) THE LOVE WE HAD (STAYS ON MY MIND)
C) STAY
D) ALWAYS ON MY MIND

68. **1 x 1**

IKE & TINA TURNER RECORDED THEIR VERSION OF A *CREEDENCE CLEARWATER RIVIVAL* SONG ABOUT A RIVERBOAT QUEEN. IT WOULD BE THEIR BIGGEST CHARTED HIT. WHAT WAS IT CALLED?

A) PT 109
B) SUZIE Q (PART 1)
C) HAVE YOU EVER SEEN THE RAIN
D) PROUD MARY

69. **2 x 1**

"NEVER CAN SAY GOODBYE" WAS A HIT FOR *ISAAC HAYES* BUT A BIGGER HIT FOR TWO OTHER ARTISTS IN THE 70'S. ONE, BY A FAMILY QUINTET GROUP OF BOYS FROM MOTOWN, AND THE OTHER A BLACK FEMALE ARTIST WHO ALSO CHARTED "I WILL SURVIVE". NAME THOSE TWO ARTISTS.

1) __________________
2) __________________

70. **1 x 1**

THE DRAMATICS ARE MOSTLY REMEMBERED FOR CHARTING THIS SONG BELOW ABOUT WHERE HE WANTED TO BE DURING POURING INCLEMENT WEATHER THAT SOUNDED QUITE STRANGE, CRAZY TO BE EXACT.

A) RAINDROPS
B) IN THE RAIN
C) HERE COMES THAT RAINY DAY FEELING AGAIN
D) UP ON CRIPPLE CREEK

71. **1 x 1**

THE DRAMATICS ALSO RECORDED ANOTHER ABOUT THE ONLY CHOICE YOU HAVE THAT IS SO OBVIOUS TO SEE.

A) SOONER OR LATER
B) JUST ONE LOOK
C) WHATCHA SEE IS WHATCHA GET
D) COME AND GET YOUR LOVE

72. **1 x 1**

CHOOSE BELOW THIS POPULAR DISCO HIT BY *VAN MCCOY AND THE SOUL CITY SYMPHONY ORCHESTRA* THAT NOT ONLY MAKES YOU WANT TO DANCE TO THAT NUMBER BUT ALSO WHISTLE TO IT AS WELL.
A) SHAKE YOUR GROOVE THING
B) THE HUSTLE
C) DISCO INFERNO
D) LOVE MACHINE (PART 1)

73. **1 x 1**

BROOK BENTON CHARTED A SONG ABOUT THAT SOUTHERN CITY THAT WAS UNDERGOING STORMY WEATHER.
A) STORMY WEATHER
B) RAINY NIGHT IN GEORGIA
C) GEORGIA
D) RAINY DAYS AND MONDAYS

74. **1 x 1**

DOROTHY MOORE RECORDED THIS SONG BELOW ABOUT WHAT BECOMES OF HER WORLD WHEN SHE THINKS OF YOU AND THE TIMES SPENT TOGETHER, ALSO RECORDED BY *MONICA* IN THE LATE 90'S? CHOOSE THAT DOUBLE HITTER.
A) MY WHOLE WORLD ENDED (THE MOMENT YOU LEFT ME)
B) MISTY BLUE
C) TOGETHER
D) BLUE ON BLUE

75. **1 x 1**

BLOODSTONE ARE BEST REMEMBERED FOR CHARTING THIS ONE SONG BELOW ABOUT THAT CERTAIN UPLIFTING DRUG FREE SENSATION THAT THEY GET.
A) FEELS SO GOOD
B) FEELS LIKE THE FIRST TIME
C) NATURAL HIGH
D) (YOUR LOVE KEEPS LIFTING ME) HIGHER AND HIGHER

76. **1 x 1**

RAYDIO, THE GROUP PUT TOGETHER BY *RAY PARKER JR*, CHARTED A SONG ABOUT THE VARIOUS CHANGES YOU CAN MAKE, LIKE MAYBE THE COLOR OF YOUR HAIR, YOUR PLACE OF RESIDENCE, OR EVEN YOUR PHONE NUMBER, ETC, BUT NOT THE WAY HE FEELS ABOUT YOU. CHOOSE THAT HIT BELOW.
A) YOU CAN'T CHANGE THAT
B) THE WAY IT IS
C) MY LOVE WILL NEVER DIE
D) FEELS LIKE THE FIRST TIME

77. **1 x 1**

WHAT GROUP DID *TEDDY PENDERGRASS* LEAD WITH, ALTHOUGH IT DID NOT BEAR HIS NAME?
A) THE STYLISTICS
B) THE SPINNERS
C) BILLY WARD AND HIS DOMINOES
D) HAROLD MELVIN AND THE BLUE NOTES

78. **1 x 1**

"HANG ON IN THERE BABY" WAS CHARTED BY THIS MALE ARTIST BELOW, A SONGWRITER BY TRADE, WHO WORKED FOR MOTOWN RECORDS BEFORE SWITCHING OVER TO THE MGM LABEL PRIMARILY AGAIN AS A SONGWRITER.
A) JOHNNY NASH
B) JOHNNY MATHIS
C) JOHNNY BRISTOL
D) JOHNNY MAESTRO

 TOTAL POINTS. **100 x 1 = 100**

R&B ROCKERS-QUIZ # 3

1. **1 x 10**

BOBBY CALDWELL RECORDED HIS ONLY CLAIM TO FAME SONG IN 1979 ABOUT WHAT HE DID FOR LOVE. WHAT WAS THAT CLAIM TO FAME SONG CALLED?
A) TWO OUT OF THREE AIN'T BAD
B) LOVE WON'T LET ME WAIT
C) WHAT YOU WON'T DO FOR LOVE
D) I AIN'T GONNA EAT OUT MY HEART ANYMORE

2. **1 x 10**

GQ, THE BAND, CHARTED WHAT LOVE SONG THAT WAS A RE-MAKE OF A *BILLY STEWART* ORIGINAL HIT BACK IN 1965 ABOUT PROFESSING HIS LOVE FOR YOU?
A) SITTING IN THE PARK
B) FOR YOUR LOVE
C) I DO LOVE YOU
D) SUMMERTIME

3. **3 x 10**

THIS GROUP CHARTED: "TRY TO REMEMBER (THE WAY WE WERE)", "ON AND ON", AND "I'VE GOT TO USE MY IMAGINATION". NAME THEM AND THESE TWO OTHER HITS BELOW, NUMBERS TWO AND THREE, FOR THEIR NEW RECORD LABEL COMPANY, BUDDAH, AFTER THEIR DEPARTURE FROM THE MOTOWN LABEL.
ONE, GROUP NAME.
TWO, ABOUT THAT TRAIN RIDE THEY'LL BE TAKING, HEADING FOR GEORGIA, TO A BETTER LIFE.
THREE, ABOUT YOU BEING THE MOST PRECIOUS THING THAT EVER WALKED INTO HER LIFE DURING THE GOOD AND BAD SHE'S BEEN THROUGH.
1) ____________________________
2) ________________________________
3) ______________________________________

4. **1 x 10**

TYRONE DAVIS RECORDED THIS SONG THAT IF HE HAD THE POWER TO UNDO TIME HE WOULD REMOVE THE PAIN AND LONELINESS HE CAUSED AND BE BACK IN YOUR LOVING ARMS AND NEVER LEAVE YOU THIS WAY AGAIN. WHAT WAS THAT HEARTBREAKER HIT CALLED?
A) TIME WON'T LET ME
B) TURN BACK THE HANDS OF TIME
C) TIME IS ON MY SIDE
D) LOVE IS A HURTIN' THING

5. **1 x 10**

THE BLACKBYRDS CHARTED THE BIGGEST HIT OF THEIR CAREER IN 1975 WITH THIS SONG BELOW ABOUT WHAT THEY WERE DOING WHILE TRYING TO GET HOME, SINGING AND HUMMING AND THINKING OF HER?
A) WALKIN' IN THE RAIN
B) I'M GOING HOME
C) HOMEWARD BOUND
D) WALKING IN RHYTHM

6. **1 x 10**

B.T. EXPRESS CHARTED THIS DISCO HIT SONG ABOUT WHAT YOU HAD TO DO TO GAIN TOTAL SATISFACTION, IT INCLUDED MOANING SOUNDS AND A FINE INSTRUMENTAL PIECE. WHAT WAS THAT DISCO HIT CALLED?
A) DO IT ('TIL YOU'RE SATISFIED)
B) DON'T STOP 'TIL YOU GET ENOUGH
C) DON'T STOP
D) STIR IT UP

7. **1 x 10**

ODYSSEY, A FAMILY TRIO GROUP CONSISTING OF TWO GIRLS AND ONE GUY, RECORDED WHAT DISCO HIT BELOW ABOUT WHAT YOU ARE FROM THE BIG APPLE. LIKE A STAR IN A SHOW OR DANCING TO THE MUSIC EVERYWHERE FROM HARLEM TO BROADWAY.

A) THEME FROM 'NEW YORK, NEW YORK'
B) YOU ARE
C) NATIVE NEW YORKER
D) YOU DON'T HAVE TO BE A STAR (TO BE IN MY SHOW)

8. **1 x 10**

THE FREE MOVEMENT, A GROUP OF SIX, CHARTED A SONG ABOUT WHAT SHE FOUND TO REPLACE YOU?

A) MR BIG STUFF
B) SUGAR DADDY
C) HE'S THE GREATEST DANCER
D) I'VE FOUND SOMEONE OF MY OWN

TOTAL POINTS. **10 x 10 = 100**

POP ROCKERS-QUIZ # 1

1. 2 x 1

YVONNE ELLIMAN CHARTED THESE TWO BIG HITS IN THE 70'S.
ONE, A SONG FEATURED IN THAT BIG BLOCKBUSTER MOVIE 'SATURDAY NIGHT FEVER', STARRING JOHN TRAVOLTA, DONNA PESCOW, AND KAREN LYNN GORNEY, THAT IF SHE COULDN'T HAVE YOU TO HERSELF THEN SHE DIDN'T WANT ANY OTHER.
TWO, WHAT SHE WANTED YOU TO DO AWHILE LONGER AND A LITTLE HARDER BECAUSE SHE WAS CONFIDENT THEY COULD MAKE IT TOGETHER.
NAME THEM.

1) ____________________

2) ________

2. 1 x 1

YVONNE ELLIMAN ALSO HAD ANOTHER WITH HER FINE RENDITION OF A *BARBARA LEWIS* TUNE ORIGINALLY RECORDED BACK IN THE 60'S ABOUT GREETING A STRANGER SHE HASN'T SEEN IN A LONG TIME.

A) HELLO, I LOVE YOU
B) HELLO STRANGER
C) WHERE OR WHEN
D) STRANGERS IN THE NIGHT

3. 1 x 1

JOHNNY MATHIS PAIRED WITH THIS FEMALE SINGER TO RECORD A HEARTBREAK HIT SONG ABOUT A MARRIAGE THAT THEY KNEW HAD TO END. SIMPLY, IT WAS OVER.

A) OVER
B) DON'T LOOK BACK
C) THE LOVE I SAW IN YOU WAS JUST A MIRAGE
D) TOO MUCH, TOO LITTLE, TOO LATE

4. 1 x 1

CHOOSE HIS FEMALE CO-SINGER ON THAT BIG HIT ABOVE.

A) DIANA ROSS
B) DENIECE WILLIAMS
C) PATTI LABELLE
D) ODIA COATES

5. 6 x 1

NAME THESE SIX BIG HITS BY *DAWN*, FEATURING *TONY ORLANDO*.
ONE, ABOUT A GIRL THAT HE FELT THEY COULD MAKE IT AS ONE AND THEIR FUTURE LOOKED PROMISING.
TWO, ABOUT A GIRL DANCING ONE FLOOR BELOW.
THREE, ABOUT A CERTAIN COLORED RIBBON IF YOU WANTED HIM.
FOUR, A *JERRY BUTLER* RE-TITLED SONG ABOUT A TRIANGLE LOVE AFFAIR THAT HE KNEW THE OTHER FELLA WOULD BREAK HER HEART.
FIVE, THEIR VERSION OF A *SAM COOKE* TUNE ABOUT SHOOTING AN ARROW INTO HIS LOVER'S HEART.
SIX, QUESTIONING THE WHEREABOUTS OF HIS GYPSY ROSE.

1) __________

2) ______________

3) ________________________________

4) ___________________________

5) __________

6) ________________________________

6. 1 x 1

DAWN ALSO CHARTED THREE OTHER HITS BELOW. WHICH ONE WAS **NOT** THEIRS?

A) LOOK IN MY EYES PRETTY WOMAN
B) MORNIN' BEAUTIFUL
C) STEPPIN' OUT (GONNA BOOGIE TONIGHT)
D) ONLY THE STRONG SURVIVE

7. **1 x 1**

JANE OLIVER HAD A HIT WITH HER RENDITION OF *A CHIFFONS'* SONG ABOUT SOMEONE EXTREMELY FINE, RECORDED AT A SLOWER AND MORE ROMANTIC PACE.
A) SO FINE
B) YOU'RE SO FINE
C) HE'S SO FINE
D) ONE FINE DAY

8. **1 x 1**

MARY MACGREGOR CHARTED A SONG ABOUT THE BREAKUP OF HER MARRIAGE DUE TO ABSENCES FROM HOME AND NOT FOR LOVING SOMEONE ELSE THAT MADE HER FEEL SO FOOLISH AND SO GUILTY.
A) TORN BETWEEN TWO LOVERS
B) TOO MUCH, TOO LITTLE, TOO LATE
C) MY WHOLE WORLD ENDED (THE MOMENT YOU LEFT ME)
D) BREAKING UP IS HARD TO DO

9. **1 x 1**

IN DECEMBER OF 1976, AT CAESAR'S PALACE, *ELVIS* INTRODUCED THIS MALE PERFORMER AS THE GREATEST SINGER IN THE WORLD. WHO WAS THIS ARTIST? HE WAS KNOWN AS 'THE PAVAROTTI ON A MOTORCYCLE' WHO CHARTED BIG IN THE 60'S WITH "ONLY THE LONELY" AND COUNTLESS OTHERS.

____

10. **7 x 1**

NAME THESE SEVEN BIG HITS BY *CARLY SIMON* DURING THE 70'S.
ONE, A DUET WITH *JAMES TAYLOR* WITH A SONG OF *CHARLIE & INEZ FOXX* ABOUT A BIRD.
TWO, A VAIN HIT SONG ABOUT A GUY WHO'S ONLY INTO HIMSELF.
THREE, A SONG FEATURED IN THE JAMES BOND MOVIE 'THE SPY WHO LOVED ME', ABOUT NO ONE BEING ABLE TO DO IT ANY BETTER, STARRING ROGER MOORE, CURT JURGENS AND BARBARA BACH IN THE LATE 70'S.
FOUR, ABOUT WHO HE BELONGS TO.
FIVE, ABOUT THE WAY IT WAS SUPPOSE TO BE, MOVE IN, RAISE A FAMILY AND GET MARRIED.
SIX, HER BIG NO TIME FOR PAIN SONG.
SEVEN, ABOUT THE EXPECTATION OF HOW THE NIGHT MAY END THAT'S GOT HER WAITING AND HOPING FOR MORE GOOD DAYS TO COME.

1) ________________
2) ________________________
3) _______________________________
4) ________________________
5) ____
6) ______________________________________
7) ____________________

11. **1 x 1**

THE OSMONDS, A QUINTET BROTHER ACT, HAD A SONG ABOUT A FRUIT THAT ONE ALONE CAN'T SPOIL THE REST.
A) LITTLE GREEN APPLES
B) APPLES, PEACHES, PUMPKIN PIE
C) ONE BAD APPLE
D) BANANA BOAT (DAY-O)

12. **1 x 1**

THE OSMONDS HAD TWO OTHER HITS BELOW. WHICH ONE WAS **NOT** THEIRS?
A) YO-YO
B) DOWN BY THE LAZY RIVER
C) KISS YOU ALL OVER

13. **1 x 1**

WAYNE NEWTON, THE POPULAR VEGAS ENTERTAINER, CHARTED WHAT SONG BELOW ABOUT THE WORDS HIS DAUGHTER TOLD HIM WHICH HE COULDN'T STAND TO HEAR THAT CHANGED HIS MIND ABOUT LEAVING HOME?

A) DADDY'S HOME
B) DADDY DON'T YOU WALK SO FAST
C) SUGAR DADDY
D) DON'T CRY DADDY

14. **1 x 1**

THIS CIVIL WAR SONG BY *BO DONALDSON AND THE HEYWOODS* WAS A BIG HIT ABOUT A GUY NAMED BILLY WHO WAS WARNED BY HIS FIANCEE NOT TO BE SO HEROIC. WHAT WAS THAT BIG HIT?

A) WHICH WAY YOU GOING BILLY?
B) BILLY, DON'T BE A HERO
C) DON'T MESS WITH BILL
D) WON'T YOU COME HOME BILL BAILEY

15. **8 x 1**

NAME THESE EIGHT CHARTED HITS BY *BARRY MANILOW*, THE POPULAR SINGER/SONGWRITER DURING THE 70'S.
ONE, EVEN AS WE SPEAK HE THINKS OF YOU AND WHAT THEY HAD.
TWO, WRITING MUSIC BY PUTTING WORDS AND MELODY TOGETHER IN A SONG.
THREE, IT APPEARS WE DID IT.
FOUR, ABOUT A TOAST FOR YOU.
FIVE, A MIRACLE COME TRUE THAT YOU'RE HERE.
SIX, SOMETHING HE COULDN'T DO WITHOUT YOU, LEAVING HIM SAD AND BLUE.
SEVEN, A SONG FEATURED IN THE MOVIE 'FOUL PLAY' STARRING CHEVY CHASE, GOLDIE HAWN AND DUDLEY MOORE ABOUT THE COPA.
EIGHT, ANOTHER SONG FROM THE MOVIE 'FOUL PLAY' ABOUT BEING ABLE TO TAKE ANOTHER CHANCE WITH YOU.

1) ____________
2) _____________________
3) __________________________
4) _____________________
5) _________________
6) _____________________________
7) _____________________________
8) ___________________________________

16. **1 x 1**

BARRY MANILOW HAD FOUR OTHER HITS BELOW. WHICH ONE WAS **NOT** HIS?

A) SOMEWHERE IN THE NIGHT
B) MANDY
C) WEEKEND IN NEW ENGLAND
D) PIANO MAN

17. **3 x 1**

THE GROUP *AMERICA* CHARTED THESE THREE POPULAR SONGS BELOW.
ONE, ABOUT A NAMELESS HORSE IN THE DESERT.
TWO, ABOUT A CERTAIN MAN WITH NO RELATION TO THAT FELLA FROM 'THE WIZARD OF OZ'.
THREE, ABOUT A CERTAIN HIGHWAY IN CALIFORNIA.
NAME THEM.

1) ________________________
2) ____________
3) ___________________

18. **1 x 1**

AMERICA ALSO RECORDED TWO OF THE THREE HITS BELOW. WHICH ONE WAS **NOT** THEIRS?
A) LONELY PEOPLE
B) SISTER GOLDEN HAIR
C) NEW KID IN TOWN

19. **4 x 1**

NAME THESE FOUR BIG SOLO HITS BY *FRANKIE VALLI.*
ONE, AN ADORING EYE SONG.
TWO, HIS RENDITION OF A *RUBY & THE ROMANTICS* SONG, ABOUT EVENTUALLY HAVING A DAY OF THEIR OWN.
THREE, ON GOD THERE'S NO OTHER HE WOULD RATHER BE, SINCE HE'S GOT YOU.
FOUR, A MOVIE TITLED THEME SONG OF THAT BIG SLICK MOTION PICTURE STARRING *OLIVIA NEWTON-JOHN* AND *JOHN TRAVOLTA*.
1) ______________________
2) ____________________
3) __________________
4) _________

20. **1 x 1**

LOBO, TRUE NAME *ROLAND KENT LAVOIE*, CHARTED: "ME AND YOU AND A DOG NAMED BOO", "I'D LOVE YOU TO WANT ME", AND "WHERE WERE YOU WHEN I WAS FALLING IN LOVE". NAME THIS OTHER ABOUT WHAT HE DIDN'T WANT TO BE BECAUSE HIS FEELINGS WERE TOO STRONG THAT FRIENDSHIP WOULD BE OUT OF THE QUESTION.
A) DON'T EXPECT ME TO BE YOUR FRIEND
B) WHY CAN'T WE BE FRIENDS
C) FEELINGS
D) ONLY THE STRONG SURVIVE

21. **11 x 1**

NAME THESE ELEVEN POPULAR HITS BY THE GROUP *CHICAGO*.
ONE, ABOUT BEING IN THE PARK ON A CERTAIN DAY OF THE WEEK.
TWO, YOU AND HIM TOGETHER IN LOVE FOREVER, WHAT HE HOPED FOR.
THREE, DAYS COME AND GONE, WITH OLD MEMORIES OF YEARS GONE BY.
FOUR, IF YOU WENT AWAY YOU'D TAKE A PIECE OF HIM AS WELL.
FIVE, WHAT HE WISHED ABOUT YOUR PRESENCE.
SIX, MAKE HIM DO WHAT, IF SHE STAYS?
SEVEN, HIS QUESTIONING WHAT TIME IT WAS.
EIGHT, ABOUT A BIG SURPRISE.
NINE, ABOUT A CERTAIN LOVER.
TEN, FEELING WHAT DAY BY DAY?
ELEVEN, HIS COLORFUL WORLD FULL OF HOPE AND LOVE.
1) _______________________
2) ___________________
3) ____________
4) ______________________
5) ______________________
6) __________________
7) ____?
8) ___________________________
9) ________________
10) __________________________
11) __________________

22. 1 x 1

CHICAGO CHARTED TWO OTHER HITS BELOW. WHICH ONE WAS **NOT** THEIRS?
A) JOY TO THE WORLD
B) I'VE BEEN SEARCHING SO LONG
C) 25 OR 6 TO 4

23. 1 x 1

THE DEFRANCO FAMILY RECORDED A SONG ABOUT THAT GOOD VIBRATION CAUSED BY A WONDERFULL SENSATION WITHIN YOUR SOUL, AND WITH THE BODY TEMPERATURE RISING. WHAT WAS THAT SONG CALLED?
A) HEART OF STONE
B) HEART AND SOUL
C) HEART BEAT-IT'S A LOVEBEAT
D) HEARTACHE TONIGHT

24. 1 x 1

HAMILTON, JOE FRANK & REYNOLDS CHARTED A SONG ABOUT THE THINGS YOU CAN TAKE, WHICH INCLUDED HIS MONEY, BUT DON'T TAKE YOUR LOVE AWAY BECAUSE IT COULD ONLY LEAVE HIM BROKENHEARTED AND IN A POOL OF TEARS IF YOU DID.
A) PLEASE STAY
B) DON'T GO BREAKING MY HEART
C) OUR LOVE (DON'T THROW IT ALL AWAY)
D) DON'T PULL YOUR LOVE

25. 1 x 1

HAMILTON, JOE FRANK & REYNOLDS RECORDED ANOTHER ABOUT WHAT HE WAS DOING ONCE AGAIN.
A) CAN'T HELP FALLING IN LOVE
B) FALLIN' IN LOVE
C) DREAMIN'
D) CRYING IN THE RAIN

26. 1 x 1

RICKY NELSON CHARTED A MADISON SQUARE GARDEN EVENT SONG THAT HAD YOKO, MARY LOU, AND JOHNNY B. GOODE IN THE HOUSE. WHAT WAS THAT PARTY HIT THAT TAUGHT HIM A LESSON IN LIFE?
A) HAVING A PARTY
B) SPLISH SPLASH
C) GARDEN PARTY
D) CELEBRATION

27. 3 x 1

NAME THESE HITS BY *PAUL ANKA* WHICH INCLUDED TWO WITH *ODIA COATES*.
ONE, WHAT HE BELIEVES ABOUT THEIR RELATIONSHIP BECAUSE THEY'RE SO IN LOVE AND ALWAYS MAKING EACH OTHER FEEL SO GOOD.
TWO, WHAT YOU WERE HAVING THAT WAS OBVIOUS TO SEE AND PUT A GLOW IN YOUR FACE WHICH ONLY PROVED YOUR LOVE FOR HIM.
THREE, ABOUT THE DIFFERENT STAGES IN YOUR LIFE WITH ALL THE MEMORIES FROM GOOD TO BAD THAT YOU COULDN'T FORGET.
1) ____
2) _____________________
3) __________________

28. 1 x 1

PAUL ANKA ALSO CHARTED TWO OTHER HITS BELOW. WHICH ONE WAS **NOT** HIS?
A) JUBILATION
B) I GO CRAZY
C) ONE MAN WOMAN/ONE WOMAN MAN

29. **1 x 1**

WHAT DIDN'T *MAC DAVIS* WANT HIS BABY TO DO?
A) BABY DON'T GET HOOKED ON ME
B) LISTEN TO WHAT THE MAN SAID
C) DON'T LET GO
D) BABY DON'T GO

30. **7 x 1**

NAME THESE SEVEN POPULAR HITS BY *PAUL SIMON*, AFTER HIS BREAK-UP FROM *ART GARFUNKEL*.
ONE, ABOUT A REUNION OF TWO FAMILY MEMBERS.
TWO, ABOUT THE FIFTY WAYS TO DO SOMETHING, BUT DON'T ASK ROY OR THAT GUY STAN FOR ANY CLUES.
THREE, ABOUT TWO FRIENDS DOWN AT THE SCHOOLYARD.
FOUR, ABOUT THE FEAR OF DOING HARM DUE TO HIS CURRENT WACKY FRAME OF MIND EVEN WITH THE LAPSE OF YEARS GONE BY.
FIVE, ABOUT HOW MOMMA THREATENS TO TAKE AWAY HIS FAVORITE CAMERA.
SIX, ABOUT HIS MOTHER'S LOVE REGARDLESS OF HIS SINS.
SEVEN, ABOUT THE CLOSER HE GETS TO HIS DESTINATION, THE MORE HE SLIPS AND SLIDES.

1) ______________________________
2) ______________________________
3) ____
4) ____________________________________
5) ________________
6) _________________________
7) ______________________

31. **1 x 1**

THE TRIO OF *PAUL SIMON, ART GARFUNKEL* AND *JAMES TAYLOR* RECORDED A SONG OF *SAM COOKE'*S ABOUT WHAT HE DIDN'T CLAIM AND WHAT HE DEFINITELY KNEW, TITLE SLIGHTLY CHANGED.
A) THINK
B) BUT YOU KNOW I LOVE YOU
C) (WHAT A) WONDERFUL WORLD
D) I DON'T KNOW WHY (BUT I DO)

32. **2 x 1**

THIS THEME SONG ABOUT A TEACHER AND HIS MISCHIEVOUS STUDENTS FROM A TV SITCOM STARRING GABE KAPLAN AND JOHN TRAVOLTA, WAS A BIG HIT FOR THIS FORMER LEAD SINGER OF *THE LOVIN' SPOONFUL*. NAME THE SONG AND THAT FORMER LEAD SINGER.

1) _______________
2) ____________________

33. **1 x 1**

ANDY KIM HAD A MAJOR HIT ASKING HIS BABE TO DO SOMETHING TO HIM AND SO TENDERLY AT THAT, AND NEVER LET HIM GO.
A) GENTLE ON MY MIND
B) ROCK ON
C) ROCK ME GENTLY
D) LOVE ME TENDER

34. **1 x 1**

NAME THIS SONG BY *ROBERT JOHN* IN 1972 THAT WAS ORIGINALLY A TOP OF THE CHARTS HIT SONG FOR *THE TOKEN*S IN THE EARLY 60'S ABOUT A LION IN THE MIGHTY JUNGLE.

 ____

35. **1 x 1**

ROBERT JOHN ALSO CHARTED A BIG HEARTBREAKER ABOUT CERTAIN EYES, CAUSED BY A BROKEN ROMANCE THAT WAS BOUND TO END. CHOOSE IT BELOW.
A) DON'T IT MAKE MY BROWN EYES BLUE
B) SAD EYES
C) LOOK IN MY EYES
D) LYIN' EYES

36. **8 x 1**

NAME THESE EIGHT BIG CHARTED HITS BY *LINDA RONSTADT*.
ONE, HER VERSION OF A *BETTY EVERETT* SONG ABOUT THAT NO GOOD PERSON SHE'S OVER WITH.
TWO, ANOTHER RE-MAKE, THIS TIME WITH AN *EVERLY BROTHERS* TUNE, ABOUT WHEN WILL SHE FIND TRUE LOVE CAUSE SHE'S TIRED OF BEING CHEATED ON.
THREE, WITH A *VANDELLAS* HIT TUNE ABOUT A BURNING SENSATION SHE GETS WHEN SHE'S WITH HIM.
FOUR, A RE-MAKE OF A *ROY ORBISON* SONG ABOUT A BAYOU AND HAVING LEFT IT AND HER BABE, HOPING SOMEDAY TO GO BACK TO THEM BOTH.
FIVE, A RE-MAKE OF A *BUDDY HOLLY* TUNE ABOUT SOMETHING EASY.
SIX, A *MIRACLES* SONG ABOUT THEIR BABY WHO SHE WRONGED WITH ANOTHER AND NOW MUST LIVE WITH THE CONSEQUENCES IN PAIN, TEARS AND SORROW.
SEVEN, ANOTHER *MIRACLES'* TUNE ABOUT TEARS, A TRACKFUL AT THAT.
EIGHT, ANOTHER *HOLLY* RE-MAKE ABOUT THE DAY YOU'LL BE SAYING GOODBYE.

1) ____________________
2) ________________________________
3) _____________
4) _______________
5) ___________________
6) _____________________
7) _________________________
8) _________________________

37. **1 x 1**

VICKI LAWRENCE, WHO CO-STARRED IN 'THE CAROL BURNETTE SHOW', WENT ON TO RECORD WHAT SONG ABOUT THAT NIGHT IN GEORGIA?
A) THE DEVIL WENT DOWN TO GEORGIA
B) THE NIGHT THE LIGHTS WENT OUT IN GEORGIA
C) GEORGIA ON MY MIND
D) A RAINY NIGHT IN GEORGIA

38. **3 x 1**

NAME THESE THREE HITS BY *BARBRA STREISAND* WHICH INCLUDES TWO DUETS.
ONE, A FLOWER SONG WITH *NEIL DIAMOND*.
TWO, ABOUT NO MORE WHAT, WITH *DONNA SUMMER,* THAT IT HAD TO END BECAUSE THEY HAD THEIR FILL AND WANT HIM OUT EVEN BY FORCE IF NEED BE?
THREE, A THEME SONG FROM A ROBERT REDFORD MOVIE IN THE 70'S THAT SHE CO-STARRED ABOUT MEMORIES, SOME PAINFUL, AND SOME BEAUTIFUL.

1) ________________________________
2) ______________________________________
3) ________________________

39. **1 x 1**

STREISAND CHARTED THREE OTHER HITS BELOW. WHICH ONE WAS **NOT** HERS?
A) HELP ME MAKE IT THROUGH THE NIGHT
B) THE MAIN EVENT/FIGHT
C) LOVE THEME FROM 'A STAR IS BORN (EVERGREEN)'
D) STONEY END

40. **1 x 1**

THIS MALE SINGER/SONGWRITER BELOW HAD A BIG HIT WITH "LOWDOWN" AND ANOTHER CALLED "LIDO SHUFFLE". HE ALSO WROTE AND RECORDED THE SONG "WE'RE ALL ALONE" THAT *RITA COOLIDGE* WOULD ALSO CHART. WHO WAS THAT TALENTED MALE ARTIST?

A) ERIC CLAPTON
B) DON HENLEY
C) GLENN FREY
D) BOZ SCAGGS

41. **1 x 1**

BRIAN HYLAND CHARTED THIS SONG BELOW THAT WAS ORIGINALLY A MAJOR HIT FOR *THE IMPRESSIONS* IN THE 60'S ABOUT A CERTAIN LOVELY WOMAN THAT TRAVELED IN A CARAVAN FROM TOWN TO TOWN WHO PUT HIM IN A TRANCE.

A) BLACK MAGIC WOMAN
B) THE GYPSY CRIED
C) GYPSY WOMAN
D) WOMAN'S GOT SOUL

42. **1 x 1**

THIS SON OF *SHIRLEY JONES* AND JACK CASSIDY RECORDED A REMAKE SONG OF *THE CRYSTALS* CALLED "DA DOO RON RON" THAT WOULD CLIMB TO THE TOP OF THE CHARTS ABOUT THAT GIRL NAMED JILL. WHO WAS HE?

A) SHAWN CASSIDY
B) JACK JONES
C) DAVID CASSIDY
D) DAVY JONES

43. **1 x 1**

THE FOUR SEASONS WITH *GERRI POLCI,* THEIR DRUMMER IN LEAD, CHARTED THIS SONG BELOW ABOUT A NIGHT IN A PARTICULAR MONTH BACK IN THE 60'S. IT WOULD RESURFACE IN THE 90'S WITH AN UPTEMPO CLUB MIX ADDITION AND TITLE SLIGHTLY CHANGED.

A) MY GIRL
B) DECEMBER, 1963 (OH, WHAT A NIGHT)
C) BE MY BABY
D) SHERRY

44. **3 x 1**

NAME THESE THREE BIG HITS BY *CAPTAIN & TENNILLE*, THE HUSBAND AND WIFE DUO.
ONE, ABOUT WHAT SHE HOPED THAT WOULD BIND THEM.
TWO, WHAT SHE WANTED TO DO TO YOU.
THREE, THEIR VERSION OF A *MIRACLES'* HIT SONG ABOUT WHAT THEIR MOTHER TOLD THEM TO DO.

1) ______________________________
2) ___________________________________
3) ______________

45. **1 x 1**

MAUREEN MCGOVERN CHARTED A SONG FOR THE MOVIE 'THE POSEIDON ADVENTURE', STARRING GENE HACKMAN, SHELLY WINTERS AND ERNEST BORGNINE ABOUT A DISASTROUS BOAT CRUISE AND HOLDING ON THROUGH THE STORM.

A) SLOOP JOHN B
B) SINK THE BISMARCK
C) THE MORNING AFTER
 D) 26 MILES (SANTA CATALINA)

46. **1 x 1**

MAUREEN MCGOVERN ALSO RECORDED A SONG FOR 'THE TOWERING INFERNO' MOVIE STARRING PAUL NEWMAN, STEVE MCQUEEN, WILLIAM HOLDEN, O J SIMPSON AND RICHARD CHAMBERLAIN ABOUT A TALL BUILDING ON FIRE, AND US REACHING OUT TO HOLD ONE ANOTHER BEFORE IT'S TOO LATE.

A) FIRE
B) BURNING LOVE
C) WE MAY NEVER LOVE THIS WAY AGAIN
D) TOWER OF STRENGTH

TOTAL POINTS. **100 x 1 = 100**

POP ROCKERS-QUIZ # 2

1. **1 x 1**

HARRY NILSSON CHARTED THIS ONE BIG HIT ABOUT NOT BEING ABLE TO LIVE IF IT'S NOT WITH YOU. CHOOSE IT BELOW.
A) SINCE I DON'T HAVE YOU
B) WITHOUT YOU
C) KISS AND SAY GOODBYE
D) IF I CAN'T HAVE YOU

2. **1 x 1**

MELANIE, ONE OF THE WOODSTOCK PERFORMERS, RECORDED WHAT SONG BELOW THAT WOULD RACE TO THE TOP OF THE CHARTS ABOUT TRYING TO GET TOGETHER WITH THAT FELLA WHO SEEMS TO BE AVOIDING HER AND THOSE NEW SKATES?
A) BREAKIN' IN A BRAND NEW BROKEN HEART
B) NEW KID IN TOWN
C) BRAND NEW KEY
D) YOU MAKE ME FEEL BRAND NEW

3. **1 x 1**

MELANIE CHARTED TWO OTHER HITS BELOW, INCLUDING ONE WITH THE BACKING OF THE *EDWIN HAWKINS SINGERS*. WHICH ONE WAS **NOT** HERS?
A) LAY DOWN (CANDLES IN THE RAIN)
B) WHAT HAVE THEY DONE TO MY SONG MA
C) FREEDOM

4. **1 x 1**

PHOEBE SNOW RECORDED THE FIRST AND BIGGEST MAJOR HIT OF HER CAREER IN 1975 ABOUT A CULTURED MAN WHO MAKES THINGS RIGHT. WHAT WAS THAT BIG MAJOR HIT?
A) HANDY MAN
B) POETRY MAN
C) MUSIC BOX DANCER
D) POETRY IN MOTION

5. **7 x 1**

NAME THESE SEVEN BIG CHARTED HITS BY *BILLY JOEL*, THE POPULAR LONG ISLANDER OUT OF NEW YORK.
ONE, ABOUT A CERTAIN PIANO ENTERTAINER WHO PERFORMS REQUESTS FOR TIPS IN A JAR.
TWO, PLEADING WITH HER NOT TO CHANGE.
THREE, ABOUT WHAT ANTHONY WAS PLANNING TO DO.
FOUR, ABOUT THE KIND OF PEOPLE THAT SEEM TO DIE AT AN EARLY AGE.
FIVE, ABOUT A GENUINE LADY IN HIS PRESENCE.
SIX, HIS BIG LIFE TITLED SONG THAT WOULD BE USED AS THE THEME SONG FOR THE TOM HANKS TV SITCOM COMEDY 'BOSOM BUDDIES'.
SEVEN, ABOUT A BIG SHOW OFF PERSON, SO THEY THINK.
1) ______________
2) __________________________
3) ___________________________________
4) _______________________________
5) __________________________
6) _____________
7) _____________

6. **1 x 1**

THE '*POPPY FAMILY*' CHARTED A TOP NUMBER TWO SONG ABOUT A GUY NAMED BILLY BEING QUESTIONED ABOUT HIS DESTINATION. NAME THAT BILLY SONG.
________________________________?

7. **1 x 1**

THE GRASS ROOTS RECORDED WHAT SONG BELOW ABOUT THOSE ALLURING EYES LOOKING THROUGH HIS SOUL?

A) SAD EYES
B) MY EYES ADORED YOU
C) TEMPTATION EYES
D) LOOK IN MY EYES

8. **1 x 1**

THE GRASS ROOTS CHARTED ANOTHER ABOUT HOW WITHIN TIME SOMETHING'S GONNA GET YOU THAT YOU WON'T BE ABLE TO DENY ANY LONGER. CHOOSE IT.

A) IT'S NOW OR NEVER
B) SOONER OR LATER
C) WHERE OR WHEN
D) TONIGHT'S THE NIGHT (GONNA BE ALRIGHT)

9. **1 x 1**

ALAN O'DAY, A SONGWRITER BY TRADE, HAD WHAT NUMBER ONE HIT SONG IN 1977 ABOUT A DISGUISED ANGEL SENT FROM ABOVE IN RESPONSE TO HIS PRAYERS? IT WOULD BE HIS ONE AND ONLY RECORDING AS A SINGER.

A) SECRET AGENT MAN
B) (YOU'RE THE) DEVIL IN DISGUISE
C) UNDERCOVER ANGEL
D) ANGEL IN YOUR ARMS

10. **1 x 1**

CHOOSE THE SONG BELOW BY *ERIC CARMEN* ABOUT HIS DESIRE NOT TO WANT TO LIVE ALONE ANY MORE, A TOP NUMBER TWO. A SONG *CELINE DION* WOULD ALSO GO ON TO RECORD IN THE LATE 90'S.

A) ONE
B) ME AND YOU AND A DOG NAMED BOO
C) ALL BY MYSELF
D) ALL ALONE AM I

11. **1 x 1**

MICHAEL PARKS, THE ACTOR, WHO STARRED IN THE TV SERIES 'THEN CAME BRONSON' IN THE LATE 60'S ABOUT A GUY WHO DROVE A MOTORCYCLE AND ROAMED THE U.S.A., CHARTED THIS HIGHWAY HIT SONG BELOW.

A) VENTURA HIGHWAY
B) LONG LONESOME HIGHWAY
C) ROUTE 66 THEME
D) LIFE IN THE FAST LANE

12. **6 x 1**

DONNY OSMOND RECORDED AT LEAST SIX RE-MAKE SONGS OF OTHER ARTISTS. MATCH THE SONGS HE RECORDED WITH THE ORIGINAL ARTISTS.

	SONG		**ARTIST**		
1.	LONELY BOY	A)	JIMMY CHARLES	**1.**	
2.	THE TWELFTH OF NEVER	B)	PAUL ANKA	**2.**	
3.	PUPPY LOVE	C)	FREDDIE SCOTT	**3.**	
4.	HEY, GIRL	D)	JOHNNY MATHIS	**4.**	
5.	GO AWAY LITTLE GIRL	E)	STEVE LAWRENCE	**5.**	
6.	A MILLION TO ONE	F)	PAUL ANKA	**6.**	

13. **4 x 1**

NAME THESE FOUR BIG HITS BY *CAROLE KING*, THE TALENTED SONGWRITER WHO TURNED TO SINGING IN THE 70'S WITH HER 'TAPESTRY' ALBUM.
ONE, ABOUT HOW THEIR RELATIONSHIP IS BREAKING UP WITH NO CHANCE OF RECONCILIATION THOUGH THEY HAVE AND IT'S TOO FAR GONE.
TWO, ABOUT HOW YOU STIR UP HER EMOTIONS WHENEVER YOU'RE AROUND THAT SHE CAN'T SEEM TO CONTROL NOR THINK AND WANT YOU EVER MORE THAT IS SIMPLY EARTH SHATTERING.
THREE, ABOUT BEING AWAY FROM YOU IS SUCH A PAINFUL AND LONELY FEELING THAT SHE CAN ONLY THINK OF HOLDING YOU IN HER ARMS. IT'S A SONG THAT *ROD STEWART* WOULD GO ON TO RECORD IN THE 90'S AS PART OF A TRIBUTE ALBUM BY MANY TO HER.
FOUR, ABOUT THAT MAN WHO COULD TAKE HER BLUES AWAY, LIFT HER UP AND PUT HER DOWN TO HER KNEES WITH HIS MUSIC.

1) ________________
2) ________________________
3) ________________
4) ____________

14. **1 x 1**

RANDY VANWARMER CHARTED A BIG HEARTBREAKER HIT IN 1979 THAT WOULD BECOME HIS ONE AND ONLY CLAIM TO FAME SONG ABOUT THAT GIRL WHO LEFT HIM AT THE WRONG TIME IN HIS LIFE. CHOOSE IT BELOW.

A) JUST WHEN I NEEDED YOU MOST
B) WHEN I NEED YOU
C) SHE AND I
D) RIGHT PLACE WRONG TIME

15. **1 x 1**

TODD RUNDGREN RECORDED WHAT SONG BELOW ABOUT NOT WANTING TO WORK BUT JUST PLAY HIS INSTRUMENT CONTINUOUSLY. SOMETHING THAT HE'S BEEN DOING SINCE HIS CHILDHOOD DAYS.

A) PLAYGROUND IN MY MIND
B) SIMON SAYS
C) PLAY THAT FUNKY MUSIC
D) BANG THE DRUM ALL DAY

16. **2 x 1**

TODD RUNDGREN ALSO HAD THESE TWO OTHER HITS BELOW.
ONE, REALIZING HE HAD FEELINGS FOR THIS GIRL WHEN HE SAW WHAT IN HER EYES?
TWO, ABOUT A GIRL HE CONSTANTLY CALLS AND THINKS ABOUT AND WOULDN'T CHANGE HER IN ANY WAY.
NAME THEM.

1) _____________________
2) ________________

17. **1 x 1**

KENNY NOLAN CHARTED A SONG ABOUT WHAT HE LIKED DOING NIGHTLY BECAUSE HE COULD PRETEND HE WAS IN PARADISE HOLDING YOU IN HIS ARMS AND LOVING YOU.

A) DREAMIN'
B) I WISH THAT WE WERE MARRIED
C) MY PRAYER
D) I LIKE DREAMIN'

18. **1 x 1**

DAN HILL RECORDED A SONG, HIS FIRST MAJOR HIT, ABOUT WHAT HAPPENS FROM TIME TO TIME THAT ISN'T NECESSARILY PHYSICAL. CHOOSE THAT TOUCHING HIT SONG BELOW.
A) TOUCH ME IN THE MORNING
B) SOMETIMES WHEN WE TOUCH
C) OUT OF TOUCH
D) TOUCH ME

19. **4 x 1**

NAME THESE FOUR HITS BY *JAMES TAYLOR,* THE SINGER/SONGWRITER.
ONE, WITH A *CAROLE KING* COMPOSITION WHEN THINGS ARE GOING WRONG ALL YOU HAVE TO DO IS CALL DURING ANY SEASON YEAR ROUND.
TWO, A *MARVIN GAYE* TUNE ABOUT SOMETHING SWEET, ALSO RECORDED BY *JUNIOR WALKER & THE ALL STARS* IN THE 60'S.
THREE, HIS VERSION OF A *JIMMY JONES* SONG ABOUT A HELPFUL PERSON STRICTLY FOR THE LADIES. ALSO RECORDED BY *DEL SHANNON.*
FOUR, HIS BIG RAIN SONG ABOUT WHAT HE HAS SEEN AND EXPERIENCED BUT ALSO HOPING TO SEE YOU ONCE MORE.
1) ____________________
2) ____
3) _____________
4) __________________

20. **1 x 1**

JAMES TAYLOR CHARTED THESE THREE OTHER HITS BELOW. WHICH ONE WAS **NOT** HIS?
A) DON'T LET ME BE LONELY TONIGHT
B) YOUR SMILING FACE
C) PEACE TRAIN
D) SHOWER THE PEOPLE

21. **1 x 1**

A SONG ABOUT A TROUBLED CHILD IN TOWN BECAME A BIG NUMBER ONE HIT FOR *NICK GILDNER* IN 1978. IT WOULD ALSO BE HIS ONE AND ONLY CLAIM TO FAME SONG.
A) O-O-H CHILD
B) HONEY CHILE
C) MY ANGEL BABY
D) HOT CHILD IN THE CITY

22. **1 x 1**

WHAT DIVA/ACTRESS CHARTED THE "LOVE THEME FROM A STAR IS BORN (EVERGREEN)" FROM HER MOVIE THAT CO-STARRED *KRIS KRISTOFFERSON*?
A) JUDY GARLAND
B) DIANA ROSS
C) BARBARA EDEN
D) BARBRA STREISAND

23. **1 x 1**

GORDON LIGHTFOOT RECORDED A BUNCH OF HITS IN THE 70'S INCLUDING WHAT SONG BELOW THAT QUESTIONED IF YOU HAD ANY IDEA WHAT HE WAS THINKING OF? IT WAS HIS FIRST AND GAINED HIM HIS PREMIER STARDOM.
A) GOIN' OUT OF MY HEAD
B) IF YOU COULD READ MY MIND
C) ALL IN MY MIND
D) THINK

24. **1 x 1**

SKYLARK, A ONE HIT WONDER GROUP, CHARTED WHAT SONG ABOUT A CERTAIN GENTLE FLOWER THAT HE HOPES TO MAKE HIS? GROWING FREE AND LIKE A CHILD ABLE TO DREAM.

A) YOU DON'T BRING ME FLOWERS
B) WILDFLOWER
C) FLOWERS ON THE WALL
D) YOU LIGHT UP MY LIFE

25. **1 x 1**

IN 1974 *TERRY JACKS* HAD WHAT TOP OF THE CHARTS HIT SONG THAT WOULD BE HIS ONLY MAJOR HIT AND CLAIM TO FAME SONG ABOUT THE SUN?

A) THE SUN AIN'T GONNA SHINE (ANYMORE)
B) SEASONS IN THE SUN
C) I CAN SEE CLEARLY NOW
D) HERE COMES THE SUN

26. **1 x 1**

ENGLAND DAN & JOHN FORD COLEY HAD A BIG ROMANTIC BALLAD ABOUT HIS STRONG DESIRE TO SEE YOU AT ANY COST AND WITH NO PARTICULAR PLACE TO GO. WHAT WAS THAT BIG ROMANTIC BALLAD CALLED THAT WOULD CLIMB TO THE NUMBER TWO SPOT ON THE CHARTS?

A) I'D LOVE YOU TO WANT ME
B) SHERRY
C) I'D REALLY LOVE TO SEE YOU TONIGHT
D) WHY CAN'T WE BE FRIENDS?

27. **1 x 1**

ENGLAND DAN & JOHN FORD COLEY RECORDED ANOTHER ABOUT WHAT HE GOES THROUGH AT NIGHT THAT SEEMS TO NEVER END. WHERE HE CAN'T SLEEP JUST THINKING OF YOU. CHOOSE THAT HIT BELOW.

A) NEVER, NEVER GONNA GIVE YA UP
B) ENDLESS LOVE
C) ENDLESS SLEEP
D) NIGHTS ARE FOREVER WITHOUT YOU

28. **1 x 1**

NEIL SEDAKA WOULD CHART A SONG ABOUT STROLLING WITH HIS LADY IN THE RAIN SHARING LOVE AND LAUGHTER. WHAT WAS THAT SONG CALLED?

A) IN THE RAIN
B) WALKIN' IN THE RAIN WITH THE ONE I LOVE
C) JUST WALKING IN THE RAIN
D) LAUGHTER IN THE RAIN

29. **1 x 1**

NEIL SEDAKA HAD THESE TWO OTHER HITS BELOW IN THE 70'S WHICH INCLUDED A RE-MAKE OF ONE OF HIS EARLIER HITS OF THE 60'S. WHICH ONE WAS **NOT** HIS?

A) BAD BLOOD
B) BREAKING UP IS HARD TO DO
C) LOVE WILL KEEP US TOGETHER

30. **1 x 1**

DAN HARTMAN RECORDED AN INSTANT HIT SONG ABOUT WHAT YOU GOT HIM DOING THAT HE WANTS MORE OF YOUR LOVE, AGAIN AND AGAIN. NAME THAT INSTANT HIT SONG.

A) MORE LOVE
B) MORE, MORE, MORE (PART 1)
C) INSTANT REPLAY
D) LET'S DO IT AGAIN

31. **1 x 1**

"I THINK I LOVE YOU", A TOP NUMBER ONE HIT SONG, WAS CHARTED BY *SHIRLEY JONES* WITH HER STEPSON *DAVID CASSIDY* AND THEIR GROUP. WHAT WAS THE GROUP'S NAME?

A) PAUL REVERE AND THE RAIDERS
B) THE PARTRIDGE FAMILY
C) THE RASCALS
D) THE COWSILLS

32. **2 x 1**

THESE TWO SONGS "HE WILL BREAK YOUR HEART" AND "HE DON'T LOVE YOU (LIKE I LOVE YOU)" ARE THE SAME SONG EXCEPT SUNG BY TWO DIFFERENT ARTISTS USING DIFFERENT SONG TITLES. THE FIRST WAS RECORDED BY A SOLOIST IN THE 60'S WHO EVOLVED OUT OF *THE IMPRESSIONS,* AND THE SECOND IN THE 70'S BY A TRIO GROUP CONSISTING OF ONE MALE LEAD SINGER AND TWO BACKUP GIRL SINGERS. NAME BOTH ARTISTS.

1) ______________
2) _________________ **&** ________

33. **2 x 1**

PAT BOONE, THE BIG ROCK 'N' ROLLER OF THE LATE 50'S AND EARLY 60'S, HAS A DAUGHTER WHO WOULD GO ON TO RECORD HER OWN BIG POP HIT. NAME HER AND THAT BIG HIT ABOUT BRIGHTENING UP HER LIFE. THE SONG WAS FEATURED IN A MOVIE OF THE SAME NAME RECORDED BY STUDIO PERFORMERS.

1) ________________
2) ___________________________

34. **1 x 1**

JOHNNY RIVERS CHARTED THIS SONG BELOW ABOUT WHAT HE AND HIS GIRL WERE DOING TO THE MUSIC ON THE RADIO THAT WAS SO ROMANTIC. CHOOSE THAT ONE.

A) SWAYIN' TO THE MUSIC (SLOW DANCING)
B) DANCE TO THE MUSIC
C) DANCE WITH ME
D) ON THE RADIO

35. **1 x 1**

MARIA MULDAUR CHARTED A SONG ABOUT HER RENDEZVOUS WITH HER SHEIK AT MIDNIGHT FOR ROMANCE AT THE DESERT'S RETREAT WHERE YOUR CAMEL WOULDN'T BE NEEDED. NAME THAT SONG.

____

36. **1 x 1**

MORRIS ALBERT RECORDED WHAT SONG BELOW ABOUT CERTAIN INNER EMOTIONS THAT HE WAS TRYING TO ERASE, CAUSED BY LOST LOVE THAT HE WOULD NEVER REGAIN?

A) FEELINGS
B) TOUCH ME
C) SEE ME, FEEL ME
D) CAN'T YOU HEAR MY HEARTBEAT

37. **1 x 1**

THE BAND '*OZARK MOUNTAIN DAREDEVILS*' RECORDED WHAT SONG ABOUT A GIRL NAMED JACKIE WHO'S ALWAYS SAD AND NEVER SATISFIED?

A) HIT THE ROAD JACK
B) JACK & DIANE
C) JACKIE BLUE
D) SAD GIRL

38. **1 x 1**

THE GROUP *AMBROSIA* CHARTED THIS SONG BELOW ABOUT A GIRL HE USED TO BE WITH AND CAN STILL SEE IN HIS DREAMS OR WHEN HE'S WITH ANOTHER, WHICH ONLY PROVES HE STILL HAS STRONG FEELINGS FOR HER.

A) HOW LONG
B) LOVIN' YOU
C) HOW MUCH I FEEL
D) YOU MAKE LOVING FUN

39. **1 x 1**

FIREFALL HAD THIS BIG HIT ABOUT A WOMAN THAT HE'S ALWAYS FANTASIZING ABOUT AND NOT JUST BECAUSE OF HER GOOD LOOKS OR WHAT SHE SAYS OR DOES, BUT HOW HE FEELS WHEN SHE'S NEXT TO HIM.

A) AIN'T NO WOMAN (LIKE THE ONE I'VE GOT)
B) YOU ARE THE WOMAN
C) BABE
D) WHEN I NEED YOU

40. **1 x 1**

FIREFALL RECORDED ANOTHER ABOUT WHAT HE TOLD HER NOT TO FORGET.

A) REMEMBER THEN
B) JUST REMEMBER I LOVE YOU
C) I DO LOVE YOU
D) BABY IT'S YOU

41. **1 x 1**

BETTE MIDLER, THE TALENTED SINGER TURNED ACTRESS, RECORDED A BOOGIE WOOGIE HIT SONG THAT WAS AN ORIGINAL *ANDREW SISTERS'* TUNE DONE BACK IN THE 40'S ABOUT A BUGLE BOY. WHAT WAS THE FULL NAME OF THAT SONG?

A) JUNGLE BOOGIE
B) BOOGIE WOOGIE BUGLE BOY
C) BOOGIE FEVER
D) BOOGIE OOGIE OOGIE

42. **1 x 1**

WHAT WAS THE NAME OF THAT POPULAR SONG BY *BETTE MIDLER* ABOUT WANTING TO DANCE, WHICH WAS A ROMANTIC VERSION OF A *BOBBY FREEMAN* R&B SONG HE ORIGINALLY CHARTED BACK IN THE LATE 50'S?

A) DO YOU LOVE ME
B) DANCE WITH ME
C) DANCING IN THE MOONLIGHT
D) DO YOU WANT TO DANCE?

43. **1 x 1**

THE BAND, *LOOKING GLASS,* RECORDED THIS SONG BELOW ABOUT A GIRL WHO TENDED BAR IN THE HARBOR AND WHAT SHE WAS TOLD BY A SAILOR.

A) BRANDY (YOU'RE A FINE GIRL)
B) ONE FINE DAY
C) COME SAIL AWAY
D) COME ON DOWN TO MY BOAT

44. **1 x 1**

JENNIFER WARNES CHARTED THIS SONG ABOUT THAT PROPER TIME OF THE DAY FOR LOVING. WHAT WAS IT CALLED?

A) JUST ANOTHER DAY
B) AFTERNOON DELIGHT
C) RIGHT TIME OF THE NIGHT
D) SOMETIMES WHEN WE TOUCH

45. **1 x 1**

MELISSA MANCHESTER RECORDED THIS MIDNIGHT TITLED SONG BELOW ABOUT TRYING TO MAKE IT ONE MORE TIME IF THEY WOULD ONLY GIVE IT THEIR FINAL BEST.

A) MIDNIGHT BLUE
B) MIDNIGHT AT THE OASIS
C) MIDNIGHT TRAIN TO GEORGIA
D) WALKIN' AFTER MIDNIGHT

46. **1 x 1**

MELISSA MANCHESTER ALSO HAD ANOTHER ABOUT SOMETHING SHE DIDN'T WANT YOU TO DO, AND NOT LOUD.

A) SHOUT (PARTS 1 AND 2)
B) DON'T CRY OUT LOUD
C) WHISPERING BELLS
D) DON'T CRY FOR ME ARGENTINA

47. **4 x 1**

NAME THESE THREE BIG CHARTED HITS BY *HELEN REDDY*.
ONE, A SONG ALL WOMEN WOULD BE PROUD OF BECAUSE OF HER POLITICAL STAND AND HER PRIDE FOR WHAT SHE IS AND FOR BEING INVINCIBLE.
TWO, ABOUT A DELTA PERSON WHO MANY THOUGHT WAS CRAZY AND LIVING IN THE PAST. ALSO RECORDED BY *TANYA TUCKER*, THE COUNTRY SINGER.
THREE, ABOUT HER ANGIE.
FOUR, ABOUT THE WAY A LADY SHOULDN'T BE TREATED.

1) ______________
2) ______________
3) ______________
4) ____________________________

48. **1 x 1**

HELEN REDDY RECORDED TWO OTHER SONGS BELOW. WHICH ONE WAS **NOT** HERS?

B) LEAVE ME ALONE (RUBY RED DRESS)
C) SHE'S A LADY
D) YOU AND ME AGAINST THE WORLD

49. **7 x 1**

NEIL DIAMOND THE SINGER/SONGWRITER HAD BUNCHES OF HITS IN THE 70'S INCLUDING: "STONES", "DESIREE'", AND "IF YOU KNOW WHAT I MEAN". NAME SEVEN OF HIS OTHER HITS BELOW.
ONE, ABOUT HIS ROSIE CHILD, WHO MAKES HIM SING, SMILE, AND HAPPY.
TWO, HIS BIG BLUE TITLED HIT SONG.
THREE, HIS BIG FLOWER HIT AS PART OF A DUET WITH *BARBRA STREISAND*.
FOUR, ABOUT WHAT SHE WAS ALWAYS IN, WEARING THAT IS.
FIVE, ABOUT THE TWO CITIES HE'S TORN ABOUT, ONE WHERE HE WAS RAISED AND THE OTHER WHERE HE CURRENTLY RESIDES.
SIX, ABOUT A TYPE OF MAN THAT HE WOULD BE UNTIL HE FINDS THAT GIRL WHO WON'T PLAY AROUND AND STAY BY HIM.
SEVEN, WHAT HE WANTED YOU TO DO WITH YOUR WORDS AND HIS TUNE?

1) ____________________
2) ____________________
3) ____________________________
4) _________________________
5) _______________
6) _______________
7) ____________

50. **1 x 1**

BOB WELCH WOULD CHART A SONG ABOUT A GIRL WITH CERTAIN EYES THAT'S GOT HIM EXCITED, DREAMING, AND HOPING SHE'D BE HIS TONIGHT.
A) BETTE DAVIS EYES
B) EBONY EYES
C) BROWN EYED GIRL
D) BROWN EYED WOMAN

51. **1 x 1**

DON MCLEAN, THE SINGER/SONGWRITER, HAD WHAT POPULAR TRIBUTE SONG TO *BUDDY HOLLY,* A TOP NUMBER ONE ABOUT THAT DAY WHEN THE MUSIC STOPPED?
A) OH, BOY!
B) AMERICAN PIE (PTS 1 & 2)
C) THE CAT'S IN THE CRADLE
D) THAT'LL BE THE DAY

52. **1 x 1**

YVONNE ELLIMAN AND THEN *HELEN REDDY* WOULD CHART A SONG FEATURED IN THE ROCK OPERA 'JESUS CHRIST, SUPERSTAR'. SELECT THAT SONG BELOW.
A) TIME IN A BOTTLE
B) I DON'T KNOW HOW TO LOVE HIM
C) PROMISES, PROMISES
D) EASY

53. **2 x 1**

DONNY AND HIS SISTER, *MARIE,* HAD A STRING OF RE-MAKE DUET HITS OF OTHER ARTISTS INCLUDING THESE TWO BELOW.
ONE, THEIR VERSION OF A *DALE & GRACE* SONG ABOUT LEAVING THE DECISION MAKING UP TO YOU.
TWO, THEIR RENDITION THIS TIME OF A *MARVIN GAYE* AND *TAMMI TERRELL SONG* ABOUT NOT BEING NEARLY AS GOOD AS THE ORIGINAL THING.
NAME THEM.
1) ________________________________
2) ______________________________________

54. **7 x 1**

THIS GROUP HAD A BIG HIT WITH "RHIANNON (WILL YOU EVER WIN)". NAME THEM AND SIX OF THEIR OTHER HITS BELOW, NUMBERS TWO THROUGH SEVEN.
ONE, THEIR NAME.
TWO, WITH *STEVIE NICKS* IN LEAD, ABOUT VISIONS AND MEMORIES.
THREE, ABOUT GOING OR STAYING BECAUSE LOVING YOU MAY NOT BE THE RIGHTEOUS THING.
FOUR, ABOUT NOT GIVING UP, BECAUSE THE FUTURE WILL BE HERE AND A WHOLE LOT BETTER.
FIVE, WITH *CHRISTINE MCVIE* IN LEAD ABOUT THE JOY YOU BROUGHT WITH THAT MAGIC SPELL YOU WORKED ON HER AND THE SWEET LOVING THAT WAS FUN
SIX, WITH *CHRISTINE MCVIE* IN LEAD ABOUT WHAT YOU'RE GONNA SAY TO HER THAT'S GOT HER FALLING WEAKER AND WEAKER WITH YOUR PASSIONATE MOVES.
SEVEN, *CHRISTINE MCVIE* IN LEAD AGAIN, ABOUT WHAT SHE WAS, WAY OVER, BECAUSE OF THE FEELING THAT SHE WAS WASTING HER EFFORTS.
1) ___________________
2) ________
3) ___________________
4) ______________
5) ___________________________
6) ___________________
 7) ______________

55. **1 x 1**

THIS JAZZY INSTRUMENTAL SINGING GROUP WAS ONCE KNOWN AS *CHICAGO TRANSIT AUTHORITY* AND LATER CHANGED THEIR NAME. WHAT WAS THEIR NEW NAME?

____

56. **1 x 1**

MARK LINDSAY CHARTED THE SONG "ARIZONA" ABOUT THAT INDIAN MAIDEN WITH THE BRAIDS IN THE EARLY 70'S. WHAT GROUP DID HE FRONT WITH AS THE LEAD SINGER DURING MOST OF THE 60'S AND EARLY 70'S?
A) PAUL REVERE AND THE RAIDERS
B) THE ANIMALS
C) THE MONKEES
D) DAVE CLARK FIVE

57. **1 x 1**

"VINCENT" WAS A TRIBUTE SONG TO THE ARTIST VAN GOGH WHO WAS A TROUBLED MAN MENTALLY WHO WOULD DIE BY HIS OWN HANDS, BUT WHAT A LASTING LEGACY HE LEFT BEHIND, SKETCHES AND PAINTINGS. WHO SANG IT?
A) CHER
B) PAUL ANKA
C) DON MCLEAN
D) NEIL DIAMOND

58. **1 x 1**

JOHN STEWART, A ONE TIME MEMBER OF *THE KINGSTON TRIO*, RECORDED A SONG ABOUT THE REWARD YOU CAN GET IN THE MUSIC BUSINESS FOR SELLING ENORMOUS AMOUNTS OF SONGS.
A) GOLD
B) THE COVER OF 'ROLLING STONE'
C) TONY AWARD
D) GRAMMY

59. **1 x 1**

JOE WALSH CHARTED WHAT SONG ABOUT BEING BLESSED WITH ALL THE FORTUNE AND FAME HE'S ACCUMULATED AND THE THINGS HE'S SEEN AND DONE?
A) LIFE IN THE FAST LANE
B) LIFE'S BEEN GOOD
C) I JUST WANT TO CELEBRATE
D) SUPERSTAR

60. **1 x 1**

GALLERY CHARTED A SONG ABOUT WANTING TO BE BY YOUR SIDE BECAUSE YOU LIFTED HIM UP WHEN HE WAS DOWN AND HE LOVES EVERYTHING ABOUT YOU.
A) GLAD ALL OVER
B) GLAD YOU'RE MINE
C) HAPPY TOGETHER
D) IT'S SO NICE TO BE WITH YOU

61. **1 x 1**

DANIEL BOONE RECORDED WHAT SONG ABOUT A GORGEOUS WEEKEND DAY, WITH THE SUN AND NATURE, AND LOVE ALL AROUND?
A) BEAUTIFUL SUNDAY
B) LOVE IS ALL AROUND
C) SATURDAY IN THE PARK
D) PLEASANT VALLEY SUNDAY

62. **1 x 1**

THE THEME SONG FOR THE 'LAVERNE AND SHIRLEY' TV SITCOM BY *CYNDI GRECCO* WAS ABOUT ACHIEVING THEIR GOALS AND INSPIRATIONS AND THAT NOTHING COULD STOP THEM. CHOOSE IT BELOW.

A) WE'RE A WINNER
B) OH HOW HAPPY
C) MAKING OUR DREAMS COME TRUE
D) DREAMS

63. **1 x 1**

ALICIA BRIDGES RECORDED WHAT BIG DISCO HIT ABOUT WHAT SHE LOVES ABOUT THE NIGHTTIME WHERE SHE COULD GET SOME ACTION AND BOOGIE ON THE DANCE FLOOR?

A) ON BROADWAY
B) NIGHTS IN WHITE SATIN
C) I LOVE THE NIGHTLIFE
D) BOOGIE NIGHTS

64. **1 x 1**

THE GROUP *STARBUCK* ARE MOSTLY REMEMBERED FOR WHAT BIG HIT BELOW ABOUT THE MOONLIGHT AND THE JOY IT CAN BRING?

A) SHADOWS IN THE MOONLIGHT
B) ONE SUMMER NIGHT
C) MOONLIGHT FEELS RIGHT
D) MOON RIVER

TOTAL POINTS. **100 x 1 = 100**

POP ROCKERS-QUIZ # 3

1. **1 x 2**

WALTER EGAN CHARTED WHAT SONG ABOUT A GIRL WHO GREW SO CLOSE TO HIM THAT HE COULDN'T LET HER GO, AS IF HE THEY WERE BONDED SIDE BY SIDE LIKE TWO PIECES OF METAL?

A) REUNITED
B) MAGNET AND STEEL
C) GET CLOSER
D) DON'T LET GO

2. **1 x 2**

CHOOSE THE *PERRY COMO* SONG ABOUT SOMETHING THAT COULDN'T BE.

A) JUST MY IMAGINATION
B) I JUST CAN'T HELP BELIEVING
C) IT'S IMPOSSIBLE
D) THE IMPOSSIBLE DREAM (THE QUEST)

3. **1 x 2**

PERRY COMO RECORDED ANOTHER ABOUT EXPRESSING HIS LOVE FOR YOU THAT WAS WRITTEN AND RECORDED BY *DON MCLEAN.* CHOOSE IT BELOW.

A) PAPA LOVES MAMBO
B) I THINK I LOVE YOU
C) AND I LOVE YOU SO
D) STILL THE ONE

4. **5 x 2**

CHER THE VERY POPULAR FEMALE SINGER/TURNED ACTRESS AND QUITE THE FASHION LEADER CHARTED NUMEROUS HITS. NAME THESE FIVE BELOW.
ONE, ABOUT A CERTAIN BREED.
TWO, ABOUT THOSE UNDESIRABLE GYPSYS AND THEIR COHORTS.
THREE, ABOUT A CERTAIN SHADED LADY.
FOUR, ASKING TO BE ESCORTED SOMEWHERE.
FIVE, ABOUT THE PATH OF PASSION.

1) ________________
2) __________________ **&** ____________
3) ________________
4) ________________
5) ______________________

5. **1 x 2**

EDDIE MONEY HAD THIS HIT TELLING HIS BABE TO STICK WITH HIM THROUGH GOOD TIMES AND BAD, BUT JUST HANG ON.

A) BABY HOLD ON
B) BE MY BABY
C) FOR THE GOOD TIMES
D) DON'T LET GO

6. **1 x 2**

CLINT HOLMES CHARTED WHAT SONG BELOW ABOUT LITTLE MICHAEL AND THAT IMAGINARY PLACE WITH CHILDREN LAUGHING AND PLAYING THAT WOULD CLIMB TO THE NUMBER TWO SPOT ON THE CHARTS?

A) THE LETTER
B) ALL IN MY MIND
C) PLAYGROUND IN MY MIND
D) I THINK I LOVE YOU

7. **3 x 2**

NAME THESE THREE BIG HITS BY THE DUO, *SEALS & CROFTS*.
ONE, ABOUT A GIRL WHO'S LIKE A GEM, A PRECIOUS STONE, THAT HE COULD NEVER FIND ANOTHER.
TWO, THAT IF YOU WANT HIS LOVE AND TO BE BY YOUR SIDE THEN YOU MUST RECIPROCATE AND DO ONLY FOR HIM.
THREE, ABOUT A CERTAIN BREEZE DURING A CERTAIN SEASON THAT MAKES HIM FEEL SO GOOD.

1) ________________
2) ______________
3) ________________

8. **1 x 2**

REX SMITH RECORDED A SONG ABOUT SOMEONE THAT TOOK HIS BREATH AWAY. WHAT WAS IT CALLED?

A) DON'T LEAVE ME THIS WAY
B) BREATHLESS
C) YOU TAKE MY BREATH AWAY
D) CAN'T YOU HEAR MY HEARTBEAT

9. **1 x 2**

NICOLETTE LARSON CHARTED A SONG ABOUT WHAT IT WOULD TAKE TO MAKE THINGS RIGHT AND RESOLVE THEIR DIFFERENCES. IT WOULD BE HER FIRST MAJOR HIT AND GAIN HER STARDOM.

A) WHOLE LOT OF SHAKIN' GOING ON
B) TOO MUCH, TOO LITTLE, TOO LATE
C) TOO MANY FISH IN THE SEA
D) LOTTA LOVE

10. **1 x 2**

TOBY BEAU THE POP BAND, HAD THIS ONE CLAIM TO FAME SONG, A HEARTBREAKER ABOUT HIS ANGEL WHO HE FELT WAS LEAVING HIM FOR SOME OTHER GUY.

A) DEVIL OR ANGEL
B) ANGEL OF THE MORNING
C) MY ANGEL BABY
D) THE ANGELS LISTENED IN

11. **1 x 2**

THE GROUP *EDWARD BEAR* HAD THIS HIT ABOUT WHAT HE WAS GOING TO DO FOR THE VERY LAST TIME. CHOOSE IT BELOW.

A) SAVE THE LAST DANCE FOR ME
B) PLAY THAT FUNKY MUSIC
C) LAST SONG
D) SONG SUNG BLUE

12. **1 x 2**

THE *'STARLAND VOCAL BAND'*, CONSISTING OF TWO GUYS AND TWO GIRLS, CHARTED A SONG THAT WOULD REACH TO THE TOP OF THE CHARTS ABOUT WHAT THEY ENJOYED IN THE MID DAY THAT DIDN'T HAVE TO WAIT TIL NIGHT.

A) ESCAPE (PINA COLADA SONG)
B) DAYDREAM
C) TAKIN' CARE OF BUSINESS
D) AFTERNOON DELIGHT

13. **1 x 2**

R. DEAN TAYLOR HAD A BIG INDIANA TITLED SONG ABOUT BEING WANTED BY THE AUTHORITIES AND THE REASON HE COULDN'T GO BACK HOME. NAME IT.

____

14. **2 x 2**

CHER RECORDED THESE TWO DUET HITS BELOW WITH *SONNY BONO*.
ONE, ABOUT COWBOY'S CHORES THAT JUST NEVER SEEM TO END.
TWO, WHO THEY ONLY NEEDED.
NAME THEM.
1) ______________________________
2) ______________________________

15. **1 x 2**

RITA COOLIDGE HAD WHAT TOP NUMBER TWO HIT SONG THAT WAS A RE-MAKE OF A *JACKIE WILSON* TUNE ABOUT WHAT YOUR LOVE WAS DOING TO HER, TITLE SLIGHTLY CHANGED?
A) DON'T GO BREAKING MY HEART
B) (YOUR LOVE HAS LIFTED ME) HIGHER AND HIGHER
C) BREAKING UP IS HARD TO DO
D) IT HURTS TO BE IN LOVE

16. **1 x 2**

CLIMAX, ANOTHER ALL MALE BAND WITH *SONNY GERACI* IN LEAD*,* CHARTED A BIG ROMANTIC HIT ABOUT THAT VALUABLE TIME SPENT WITH YOU. IT WOULD BE THEIR ONLY MAJOR HIT, BUT WHAT A CLASSIC IT WOULD TURN OUT TO BE.
A) DIAMOND GIRL
B) FOR YOUR LOVE
C) PRECIOUS AND FEW
D) FOR YOUR PRECIOUS LOVE

17. **1 x 2**

BOBBY SHERMAN THE POPULAR TV PERSONALITY WHO STARRED IN 'HERE COME THE BRIDES' RECORDED THE SONG "EASY COME, EASY GO". WHAT WAS THIS OTHER QUESTIONING IF SHE WOULD STILL BE HIS CAUSE THE THOUGHT OF HER WAS DRIVING HIM INSANE DUE TO HIS BRIEF DEPARTURE?
A) HELP ME, RHONDA
B) JULIE, DO YA LOVE ME
C) MY MARIA
D) P.S. I LOVE YOU

18. **1 x 2**

GINO VANNELLI CHARTED A SONG ABOUT WHAT HE WANTED TO DO.
A) I JUST WANT TO CELEBRATE
B) I JUST WANNA STOP
C) I WANT TO HOLD YOUR HAND
D) I JUST WANT TO BE YOUR EVERYTHING

19. **1 x 2**

THE SONG "LOVE THE ONE YOU'RE WITH" WAS A POPULAR HIT BY THIS ONE TIME MEMBER OF *BUFFALO SPRINGFIELD* AND THEN WITH *CROSBY, STILLS, NASH & YOUNG*. WHO WAS THAT ARTIST?
A) GRACE SLICK
B) NEIL YOUNG
C) ERIC CLAPTON
D) STEVEN STILLS

20. **1 x 2**

DAVE LOGGINS HAD A POPULAR SONG PLEADING TO HIS GIRL TO COME JOIN HIM AS HE DRIFTED FROM TOWN TO TOWN, BOSTON, DENVER AND FINALLY L.A. SHE REFUSED, ASKING HIM TO COME BACK HOME. WHAT WAS THAT SONG?

A) DRIFT AWAY
B) PLEASE COME TO BOSTON
C) RUNAWAY
D) BABY COME BACK

21. **1 x 2**

SIMON & GARFUNKEL CHARTED THESE THREE BIG HITS BEFORE THEIR BREAKUP IN THE 70'S. WHICH SONG BELOW WAS **NOT** THEIRS?

A) BRIDGE OVER TROUBLED WATER
B) CECILIA
C) IN THE YEAR 2525
D) EL CONDOR PASA

22. **1 x 2**

THE GROUP *KANSAS* RECORDED A SONG ABOUT SOMETHING IN THE WIND, AND HOW WE CAN ALL END UP.

A) BLOWIN' IN THE WIND
B) FLY LIKE THE WIND
C) DUST IN THE WIND
D) THE WAYWARD WIND

23. **1 x 2**

NORMAN GREENBAUM HAD A BIG HIT ABOUT AN IMAGE HIGH UP ABOVE WHICH BECAME HIS CLAIM TO FAME SONG.

A) SPIRIT IN THE SKY
B) IMAGE OF A GIRL
C) THERE'S A MOON OUT TONIGHT
D) A THOUSAND STARS

24. **8 x 2**

THE CARPENTERS, A SISTER AND BROTHER ACT, WERE VERY SUCCESSFUL IN THE 70'S. NAME THESE EIGHT GIANT HITS BELOW.
ONE, ABOUT THEIR DESIRE TO BE NEXT TO YOU.
TWO, ABOUT BEING ON TOP EVER SINCE YOU'VE BEEN AROUND.
THREE, THEIR RENDITION OF A *MARVELETTES* HIT TUNE, ASKING HER POSTMAN IF THERE'S ANY MAIL FOR HER.
FOUR, ABOUT THOSE STORMY DAYS AND MONDAYS.
FIVE, ABOUT SINGING A SONG OF GOOD THINGS FOR YOU AND ME.
SIX, YESTERDAY'S MEMORIES BROUGHT ON BY OLD SONGS.
SEVEN, THEIR VERSION OF A *HERMAN'S HERMITS* HIT SONG ABOUT A HUSH.
EIGHT, JUST THE BEGINNING, WITH SO MUCH AHEAD.

1) ____________________________________
2) _____________________
3) ____________________________
4) ____________________________
5) _______
6) _______________________
7) ______________________________________
8) _____________________________

25. **1 x 2**

GARY WRIGHT RECORDED WHAT TOP NUMBER TWO HIT SONG ABOUT WHO HE THOUGHT COULD HELP HIM MAKE IT THROUGH THE PAINFUL AND STRESSFUL NIGHT AND TAKE HIM ON A JOURNEY HIGH ABOVE?

A) HELP ME MAKE IT THROUGH THE NIGHT
B) DREAM WEAVER
C) I LIKE DREAMIN'
D) MAGIC CARPET RIDE

26. **1 x 2**

STEPHEN BISHOP CHARTED WITH A HIT ABOUT SOMETHING THAT WAS GOING ON CONTINUOUSLY.

A) ALONE AGAIN (NATURALLY)
B) GOING IN CIRCLES
C) ON AND ON
D) OVER AND OVER

27. **1 x 2**

WHO WAS **NOT** A MEMBER OF THE GROUP, *DAWN*?

A) TONY ORLANDO
B) THELMA HOPKINS
C) MEL CARTER
D) JOYCE VINCENT

28. **1 x 2**

THE *'CARPENTERS'* ALSO RECORDED ANOTHER THAT WAS FEATURED IN THE MOVIE 'LOVERS AND OTHER STRANGERS' ABOUT WHAT THEY PROBABLY KNEW OR FELT, STARRING GIG YOUNG, BEA ARTHUR AND RICHARD CASTELLANO.

A) (I KNOW) I'M LOSING YOU
B) YOU'RE NO GOOD
C) FOR ALL WE KNOW
D) ALWAYS ON MY MIND

29. **1 x 2**

SAMMY JOHNS CHARTED A SONG ABOUT MAKING LOVE TO HIS ANGEL IN HIS GENERAL MOTORS VEHICLE. CHOOSE IT BELOW.

A) KEEPING THE FAITH
B) CHEVY VAN
C) PINK CADILLAC
D) TAKIN' CARE OF BUSINESS

30. **1 x 2**

PLAYER, A MALE GROUP, HAD WHAT TOP NUMBER ONE HIT SONG PLEADING TO THEIR LOVED ONE TO RETURN BECAUSE HE HAS REALIZED THE WRONG HE COMMITTED AND WANTING A SECOND CHANCE TO MAKE IT RIGHT?

A) BABY COME BACK
B) PLEASE COME TO BOSTON
C) COME BACK WHEN YOU GROW UP
D) GET BACK

31. **1 x 2**

DAVID SOUL OF 'STARSKY & HUTCH' TV FAME CHARTED WHAT SONG BELOW PLEADING TO HIS BABY ON WHAT NOT TO DO? THEY MADE IT HERE SO FAR, AND THERE'S STILL SOME PASSION LEFT, SO GIVE IT ANOTHER TRY.

A) CAN'T WE TRY
B) DON'T GIVE UP ON US
C) ONE MORE TRY
D) BABY HOLD ON

32. **1 x 2**

THIS POPULAR SONG BY *PAUL DAVIS* WAS ABOUT HIS REACTION WHEN HE LOOKED INTO HER EYES BECAUSE HE JUST COULDN'T HIDE THE FEELING INSIDE.

A) CRAZY
B) I GO CRAZY
C) LOOK IN MY EYES PRETTY WOMAN
D) WITCHCRAFT

33. **1 x 2**

PAUL DAVIS CHARTED ANOTHER THAT WAS A TRIBUTE SONG TO *STEVIE WONDER, LINDA RONSTADT, ELTON JOHN* AND *JONI MITCHELL*. WHAT WAS THAT ONE CALLED?

A) ROCK AND ROLL HEAVEN
B) SUPERSTAR
C) GIVE PEACE A CHANCE
D) AMERICAN PIE (PTS 1 & 2)

34. **1 x 2**

THE DISCO SINGER, *ANDREA TRUE CONNECTION*, RECORDED A SONG ASKING IF YOU WERE SATISFIED WITH THE ACTION AND THE REPLY WAS WHAT BELOW? IT WOULD FEATURE A LOT OF INSTRUMENTAL DISCO MUSIC AND A LIMITED AMOUNT OF RHYMING REPETITIOUS PHRASES.

A) CAN'T GET ENOUGH OF YOUR LOVE, BABE
B) TOO MUCH HEAVEN
C) I LOVE THE NIGHTLIFE
D) MORE, MORE, MORE (PART 1)

35. **1 x 2**

JD SOUTHER CHARTED WHAT SONG BELOW ABOUT IT NOT BEING A CRIME TO NEED SOMEBODY? THAT ALL YOU HAD TO DO WAS CALL ON HIM FOR COMFORT BECAUSE HE'S BEEN THERE AND KNOWS THE FEELING SO WELL.

A) YOU WERE ON MY MIND
B) I GOTTA BE ME
C) YOU'RE ONLY LONELY
D) WHEN I NEED YOU

36. **1 x 2**

MAC DAVIS, THE SINGER/SONGWRITER TURNED ACTOR, HAD A SONG THAT ALLUDED TO HIS NOT BEING READY FOR FAMILY TIES.

A) HOOKED ON A FEELING
B) BABY DON'T GET HOOKED ON ME
C) KISS AND SAY GOODBYE
D) FAMILY AFFAIR

TOTAL POINTS. **50 x 2 = 100**

POP ROCKERS-QUIZ # 4

1. 1 x 10

ANDREW GOLD CHARTED WHAT SONG BELOW THAT HAD A SIMILAR TITLE PREVIOUSLY RECORDED BY *PAUL ANKA* IN THE LATE 50'S WITH DIFFERENT LYRICS ABOUT A BOY WHO WAS SAD AND NEGLECTED? HE WOULD ALSO RECORD ANOTHER CALLED "THANK YOU FOR BEING A FRIEND" THAT WOULD EVENTUALLY BE THE THEME SONG FOR THE TV COMEDY SITCOM 'THE GOLDEN GIRLS'.

A) WHERE OR WHEN
B) LONELY BOY
C) MR LONELY
D) SAD EYES

2. 1 x 10

THIS GROUP WITH A FEMALE LEAD SINGER AND A THREE GUY BACKUP BAND HAD A HIT WITH THE MOVIE TITLED SONG "ONE TIN SOLDIER (THE LEGEND OF BILLY JACK)" STARRING TOM LAUGHLIN. WHAT WAS THAT GROUP?

A) BLONDIE
B) PAT BENATAR
C) STONE PONEYS
D) COVEN

3. 1 x 10

THE SANDFORD/TOWNSEND BAND CHARTED WHAT SONG BELOW ABOUT THAT GIRL WITH THE MIST IN HER EYES THAT HE KNEW WAS DOING HIM WRONG AND DIDN'T CARE IF SHE LEFT?

A) LYIN' EYES
B) SMOKE ON THE WATER
C) SMOKE FROM A DISTANT FIRE
D) DIFFERENT DRUM

4. 1 x 10

THIS TALENTED FEMALE ARTIST COULD SING IN ANY MUSIC CATEGORY SHE WISHED, INCLUDING POP, ROCK, COUNTRY, R&B, OR EVEN LATIN. SHE WAS ONCE PART OF A GROUP, THEN WENT SOLO, THEN IN A TRIO GROUP, PART OF A DUO AND IN FRONT OF A BIG BAND. WHO IS THIS VERSATILE PERFORMER?

A) GLADYS KNIGHT
B) DOLLY PARTON
C) DIANA ROSS
D) LINDA RONSTADT

5. 1 x 10

LEIF GARRETT, THE CHILD ACTOR/TURNED SINGER, CHARTED A RE-MAKE OF A *DION* HIT SONG ABOUT THAT UNFAITHFUL GIRL WHO RAN ALL OVER TOWN ON HIM. WHAT WAS THAT DOUBLE HITTER?

A) RUBY BABY
B) RUNAROUND SUE
C) PEGGY SUE
D) MUSTANG SALLY

6. 1 x 10

JONATHAN EDWARDS RECORDED THIS SONG BELOW THAT HAD HIM SPEAKING TO THE SUN TO GO AWAY AND THEN LATER ASKING IT TO COME BACK. WHAT WAS THAT SONG?

A) SUNSHINE
B) DON'T LET THE SUN GO DOWN ON ME
C) SUNSHINE ON MY SHOULDERS
D) DON'T LET THE SUNSHINE CATCH YOU CRYING

7.

1 x 10

ELVIN BISHOP CHARTED A SONG ABOUT WHAT HE WAS DOING WITH THAT GIRL WHEN CUPID'S ARROW STRUCK HIM HARD AND PUT A MAJOR HOLD ON HIM.
A) HOLD ME TIGHT
B) HYPNOTIZED
C) STUCK IN THE MIDDLE WITH YOU
D) FOOLED AROUND AND FELL IN LOVE

8.

1 x 10

THE SONG "MY MARIA" AN UPLIFTING LIVELY TUNE WAS THIS TEXAN'S ONLY MAJOR CLAIM TO FAME SONG. WHO WAS HE?
A) ROD STEWART
B) B.W. STEVENSON
C) ERIC CLAPTON
D) CONWAY TWITTY

9.

1 x 10

BOBBY BLOOM HAD WHAT BIG HIT BELOW ABOUT A CERTAIN BAY IN THE ISLAND OF JAMAICA?
A) KOKOMO
B) KEY LARGO
C) MONTEGO BAY
D) FUNKY NASSAU (PARTS 1 & 2)

10.

1 x 10

JEFFERSON STARSHIP HAD THIS SONG ABOUT HOW THEY WOULD GET BY IF YOU BELIEVED IN WHAT?
A) (I BELIEVE) THERE'S NOTHING STRONGER THAN OUR LOVE
B) YOU SEXY THING
C) MIRACLES
D) I JUST CAN'T HELP BELIEVING

TOTAL POINTS. **10 x 10 = 100**

POP ROCKERS-BONUS

1.

THIS MALE ARTIST, A SUCCESSFUL SONGWRITER, CHARTED "DO YOU WANNA MAKE LOVE" THAT QUESTIONED YOUR DESIRES TO MAKE PASSIONATE LOVE OR SIMPLY PLAY AROUND. WHO WAS THAT ONE HIT WONDER ARTIST BELOW?
A) LEO SAYER
B) PETER GABRIEL
C) ENGLAND DAN
D) PETER MCCANN

2.

"FOR THE LOVE OF HIM" WAS A SONG CHARTED BY WHAT FEMALE ARTIST IN 1970 WHICH WAS HER SECOND MAJOR HIT AND THE BIGGEST OF HER CAREER?
A) BRENDA LEE
B) BOBBI MARTIN
C) EYDIE GORME
D) BOBBIE GENTRY

3.

MARIE OSMOND, ALL FOURTEEN YEARS OF HER, RECORDED A RE-MAKE OF AN *ANITA BRYANT* SONG ABOUT THOSE IMITATION FLOWERS WHICH WERE NO DIFFERENT THAN THE LOVE YOU HAD FOR HER. WHAT WAS THAT DOUBLE HITTER?
A) ARTIFICIAL FLOWERS
B) PAPER ROSES
C) WILDFLOWER
 D) IT'S ONLY MAKE BELIEVE

COUNTRY ROCKERS-QUIZ # 1

1. **7 x 4**

NAME THESE SEVEN BIG HITS BY *ANNE MURRAY,* THE CANADIAN DIVA DURING THE 70'S.
ONE, ABOUT A BIRD THAT SHE WOULD FLY AWAY WITH.
TWO, ABOUT DANNY, HER HONEY, WHO SHE'S IN LOVE WITH.
THREE, ABOUT NEEDING YOU BECAUSE OF THE STRENGTH AND HOPE YOU PROVIDE FOR HIM.
FOUR, ABOUT BROKEN WHAT, THAT TIME WILL NOT HEAL.
FIVE, ABOUT FALLING FOR YOU ONCE MORE.
SIX, ABOUT A TYPE OF SONG SHE WANTS TO SING AND ROCK TO ALL NIGHT.
SEVEN, ABOUT THOSE SILHOUETTES IN THE NIGHT LIGHT.

1) ____________
2) __________________
3) __________________
4) ________________________
5) ______________________________
6) ____________
7) ______________________________

2. **4 x 4**

NAME THESE FOUR HITS BY *KENNY ROGERS* IN THE 70'S.
ONE, A GIRL *LITTLE RICHARD* ORIGINALLY SANG ABOUT IN THE 50'S.
TWO, ABOUT A GIRL WHO WAITS FOR HER MAN NIGHTLY AND HAS FAITH IN.
THREE, ABOUT SOMEONE WHO DECORATED HIM.
FOUR, ABOUT A CHARACTER HE WOULD PORTRAY IN THE MOVIES, WHERE YOU DON'T COUNT YOUR LOOT TIL THE GAME IS OVER.

1) ____________
2) ____________________
3) ___________________________
4) ________________

3. **1 x 4**

KENNY ROGERS ALSO HAD A HIT WITH HIS FORMER GROUP 'THE FIRST EDITION' ABOUT A FIRE OF LOVE THAT WILL BURN FOREVER.
A) SOMETHING'S BURNING
B) FIRE
C) FIRE AND RAIN
D) HOT HOT HOT

4. **1 x 4**

KEITH CARRADINE, THE ACTOR, RECORDED A SONG ABOUT BEING GULLIBLE WHEN IT CAME TO ROMANCE, THAT HE WOULD BE THERE IN A FLASH IF THE OPPORTUNITY AROSE. IT WAS FEATURED IN THE MOVIE 'NASHVILLE' WHICH HE CO-STARRED WITH HENRY GIBSON, KAREN BLACK AND LILY TOMLIN IN THE MID 70'S.
A) EASY
B) ABC
C) I'M EASY
D) 1-2-3

5. **1 x 4**

CHARLIE DANIELS BAND CHARTED BELOW THIS GEORGIA TITLED SONG THAT WOULD BE FEATURED IN THE 'URBAN COWBOY' SOUNDTRACK MOVIE STARRING JOHN TRAVOLTA AND DEBRA WINGER. WHAT WAS THAT GEORGIA HIT?
A) GEORGIA ON MY MIND
B) THE DEVIL WENT DOWN TO GEORGIA
C) MIDNIGHT TRAIN TO GEORGIA
D) THE NIGHT THE LIGHTS WENT OUT IN GEORGIA

6. **1 x 4**

SAMMI SMITH, A FEMALE SINGER, HAD A POPULAR HIT ABOUT NEEDING HELP TO GET THROUGH THE LATTER PART OF THE DAY. A SONG THAT *GLADYS KNIGHT & THE PIPS* WOULD ALSO RECORD AND EQUALLY EMOTIONAL.
A) WEDDING BELL BLUES
B) HELP ME MAKE IT THROUGH THE NIGHT
C) WHATEVER GETS YOU THROUGH THE NIGHT
D) MIDNIGHT TRAIN TO GEORGIA

7. **1 x 4**

"THE KING IS GONE" WAS A TRIBUTE SONG TO *ELVIS PRESLEY.* CHOOSE THE ARTIST BELOW TO CHART THAT SONG.
A) CARL PERKINS
B) TERRY STAFFORD
C) COLONEL TOM PARKER
D) RONNIE MCDOWELL

8. **1 x 4**

DOLLY PARTON THE POPULAR COUNTRY SINGER/SONGWRITER TURNED ACTRESS HAD WHAT BIG HIT IN 1977 ABOUT A GUY WHO KEEPS MESSING UP HER HEAD THATS GOT A STRANGLEHOLD ON HER THAT SHE BREAKS EVERYTIME HE WALTZES IN WITH THAT SMILING FACE?
A) YOU'VE REALLY GOT A HOLD ON ME
B) HERE YOU COME AGAIN
C) WHAT AM I GONNA DO WITH YOU
D) ROCK AND ROLL WALTZ

9. **1 x 4**

LARRY GATLIN RECORDED THIS SONG REFERRING TO A PRECIOUS METAL.
A) PRECIOUS AND FEW
B) GOLD
C) DIAMONDS AND PEARLS
D) ALL THE GOLD IN CALIFORNIA

10. **1 x 4**

MICKEY GILLEY CHARTED THIS SONG FOR THE 'URBAN COWBOY' SOUNDTRACK MOVIE STARRING JOHN TRAVOLTA AND DEBRA WINGER. IT WAS ORIGINALLY A BIG HIT FOR A FORMER *DRIFTER, BEN E KING,* BACK IN THE 60'S.
A) LOOKIN' FOR LOVE
B) SPANISH HARLEM
C) STAND BY ME
D) I (WHO HAVE NOTHING)

11. **5 x 4**

NAME BELOW THESE FIVE BIG HITS BY *JOHN DENVER,* THE SINGER/SONGWRITER TURNED ACTOR.
ONE, ABOUT SOMETHING ON HIS SHOULDERS.
TWO, ABOUT HIS SWEETHEART ANNIE.
THREE, ABOUT THANKING GOD FOR WHAT HE IS.
FOUR, ABOUT A PLACE BACK HOME IN VIRGINIA THAT HE LONGED FOR.
FIVE, ABOUT THE HIGH COLORADO ROCKY MOUNTAINS.
1) ____________________
2) ____________
3) ______________________
4) ______________________
5) ________________

12. **1 x 4**

MICHAEL MURPHEY RECORDED THIS SONG BELOW ABOUT A PONY AND WHAT SHE NAMED IT. CHOOSE IT BELOW.

A) A HORSE WITH NO NAME
B) WILDFIRE
C) DUST IN THE WIND
D) BERNARDINE

TOTAL POINTS. **25 x 4 = 100**

COUNTRY ROCKERS-QUIZ # 2

1. **1 x 4**

RAY PRICE CHARTED A HEARTBREAKER ABOUT A ROMANCE COMING TO AN END BUT HE WANTED TO PRETEND YOU STILL LOVED HIM JUST ONCE MORE. IT WAS ALSO RECORDED BY *AL GREEN*.

A) FOR THE GOOD TIMES
B) IT'S ONLY MAKE BELIEVE
C) HE'LL HAVE TO GO
D) HOW CAN YOU MEND A BROKEN HEART

2. **1 x 4**

CRYSTAL GAYLE, THE LONG-HAIRED COUNTRY BEAUTY AND SISTER OF *LORETTA LYNN*, HAD A BIG POPULAR SONG ABOUT HER BROWN EYES TURNING A DIFFERENT COLOR WHENEVER SHE'S SAD. WHAT WAS THAT BIG POPULAR SONG THAT WOULD REACH THE NUMBER TWO SPOT ON THE CHARTS?

A) BROWN EYED WOMAN
B) BROWN EYED GIRL
C) DON'T IT MAKE MY BROWN EYES BLUE
D) PRETTY BLUE EYES

3. **1 x 4**

CRYSTAL GAYLE HAD ANOTHER ABOUT WHAT HE DID IN HIS SLEEP THAT CAUSED HER TO WORRY.

A) TOSSIN' AND TURNIN'
B) TALKING IN YOUR SLEEP
C) CRYING
D) YOU TALK TOO MUCH

4. **3 x 4**

NAME THESE THREE BIG HITS BY *GLEN CAMPBELL*.
ONE, A COWBOY SONG, WHICH WAS THE TITLE OF A MOVIE STARRING *DOLLY PARTON* AND SYLVESTER STALLONE.
TWO, ABOUT THOSE NIGHTS IN THE LOWER SECTION OF THE COUNTRY WITH ITS BEAUTY AND GOOD FEELING IT GIVES OFF.
THREE, WHAT HE WANTED HIS HONEY TO DO.

1) ______________________
2) ____________________
3) ____________________

5. **3 x 4**

NAME BELOW THESE THREE POPULAR HITS BY *CHARLIE RICH*.
ONE, BEHIND WHAT WHEN SHE REARRANGES HER HAIR DOWN?
TWO, ABOUT THAT BEAUTIFUL GIRL WHO LEFT HIM.
THREE, WHAT BECOMES OF HIM EACH TIME YOU TOUCH HIM.

1) ______________________
2) ___________________________
3) ________________________________

6. **1 x 4**

JERRY REED, THE SINGER/SONGWRITER TURNED ACTOR, CHARTED TWO OF THE THREE HITS BELOW IN THE 70'S. WHICH ONE WAS **NOT** HIS?

A) A COWBOYS WORK IS NEVER DONE
B) AMOS MOSES
C) WHEN YOU'RE HOT, YOU'RE HOT

7. **1 x 4**

BILLY SWAN RECORDED THIS SONG BELOW ABOUT WANTING TO BE HELPFUL TO HIS BABE WITH ANY PROBLEM, JUST CALL.

A) HELP!
B) I CAN HELP
C) HELP ME MAKE IT THROUGH THE NIGHT
D) HELP YOURSELF

8. **1 x 4**

WHO IS KNOWN AS 'THE SILVER FOX'?

A) KENNY ROGERS
B) CHARLIE RICH
C) JOHNNY CASH
D) WILLIE NELSON

9. **1 x 4**

EDDIE RABBITT, THE SINGER/SONGWRITER, HAD A POPULAR HIT THAT DEALT WITH JEALOUSY AND DOUBTS. WHAT WAS IT CALLED?

A) DEVIL OR ANGEL
B) SUSPICIONS
C) TELL HER NO
D) YOU CAN HAVE HER

10. **1 x 4**

THE NITTY GRITTY DIRT BAND RECORDED A SONG ABOUT A RAGGEDY LOOKING MAN WHO COULD DANCE AND LEAP LIKE NO OTHER. A SONG *SAMMY DAVIS JR.* WOULD ALSO PERFORM IN HIS ACT. WHAT WAS THAT DOUBLE HITTER CALLED?

A) MR BIG STUFF
B) MR BOJANGLES
C) MR LEE
D) MR TAMBOURINE MAN

11. **3 x 4**

NAME THESE THREE POPULAR CHARTED HITS BY *FREDDY FENDER*.
ONE, ABOUT COMING TO YOUR AID BEFORE WHAT FALLS?
TWO, ABOUT TIME SPENT FOOLISHLY SINCE SHE LEFT HIM WITH THE BLUES AND SO LONELY.
THREE, WHAT SHE'LL END UP LOSING WHICH WAS ORIGINALLY A *BARBARA LYNN* RECORDING BACK IN THE 60'S.

1) ______________________________
2) ______________________________
3) __________________________

12. **1 x 4**

LYNN ANDERSON CHARTED A SONG ABOUT SOMETHING SHE DIDN'T PROMISE YOU. IT WOULD BE HER CLAIM TO FAME SONG. WHAT WAS THAT SONG?

A) PROMISES, PROMISES
B) MY LOVE
C) ROSE GARDEN
D) MAKE IT WITH YOU

13. **1 x 4**

TOM T HALL RECORDED A SONG ABOUT THE MANY THINGS HE LOVED, WHICH INCLUDING BABY DUCKS, SQUIRRELS, LIFE AND YOU TOO. WHAT WAS THAT SONG BELOW?

A) LOVE ON THE ROCKS
B) I LOVE THE NIGHTLIFE
C) I LOVE MUSIC
D) I LOVE

14. **1 x 4**

JOE SOUTH CHARTED A SONG ABOUT BEFORE CRITICIZING AND MAKING ACCUSATIONS DO WHAT TO GET A TRUE HONEST PERSPECTIVE VIEW? A SONG THAT *ELVIS* WOULD ALSO RECORD IN THE 70'S.

A) WALK A MILE IN MY SHOES
B) BOOGIE SHOES
C) I WANT TO WALK YOU HOME
D) I'M WALKIN'

15. **1 x 4**

DAVE MASON RECORDED THIS SONG BELOW ABOUT A BROKEN ROMANCE WHERE HE AND HIS PARTNER COULD NO LONGER AGREE TO ANYTHING, WITH NO ONE PERSON TO BLAME.

A) BREAKING UP IS HARD TO DO
B) WE JUST DISAGREE
C) GO YOUR OWN WAY
D) RELEASE ME (AND LET ME LOVE AGAIN)

16. **1 x 4**

"BLUE EYES CRYING IN THE RAIN" WAS A SONG CHARTED BY THIS BIG TIME COUNTRY SINGER/SONGWRITER TURNED ACTOR AND FARM AID HUMANITARIAN. WHO IS HE?

A) DON GIBSON
B) JOHNNY CASH
C) WILLIE NELSON
D) KRIS KRISTOFFERSON

17. **1 x 4**

"CONVOY" WAS A SONG ABOUT A SLEW OF TRUCKS DRIVING TOGETHER IN FORMATION AND COMMUNICATING THROUGH CB RADIOS. WHICH ARTIST BELOW WAS RESPONSIBLE FOR THAT SONG THAT REACHED THE TOP OF THE CHARTS?

A) BROOKLYN BRIDGE
B) THREE DOG NIGHT
C) C.W. MCCALL
D) EDDIE KENDRICKS

18. **1 x 4**

RAY STEVENS, THE NOVELTY SINGER, CHARTED A BEAUTIFUL HIT SONG ABOUT NOT JUDGING OTHERS BY THEIR OUTER SHELL BUT FROM WITHIN. WHAT WAS THAT BEAUTIFUL HIT SONG?

A) ISN'T SHE LOVELY
B) IT'S A BEAUTIFUL MORNING
C) YOU'RE SIXTEEN
D) EVERYTHING IS BEAUTIFUL

19. **1 x 4**

THE '*BELLAMY BROTHERS*', A BROTHER DUO ACT, CHARTED WHAT SONG BELOW PLEADING TO RELEASE YOUR LOVE, LET IT SHOW AND SHINE LIKE A BIRD OR A STREAM. NOW CHOOSE IT.

A) BABY, I LOVE YOUR WAY
B) LET'S GET IT ON
C) LET IT BE
D) LET YOUR LOVE FLOW

TOTAL POINTS. **25 x 4 = 100**

ROCKERS-QUIZ # 1

1. **1 x 1**

THE MALE ROCK BAND, *BLUES IMAGE,* RECORDED A SONG IN THE EARLY 70'S ABOUT A JOURNEY THAT SIX DOZEN AND ONE GUYS TOOK BY SAILING TO SOME PLACE ON THEIR MYSTERIOUS BOAT. WHAT WAS THAT SONG?
A) RIDE CAPTAIN RIDE
B) UP ON CRIPPLE CREEK
C) MUST HAVE GOT LOST
D) XANADU

2. **2 x 1**

NAME BELOW THESE TWO RECORDED HITS BY *ORLEANS,* ANOTHER MALE BAND. ONE, ABOUT YOU BEING THE ONLY ONE, WITH FEELINGS THAT COULD NEVER CHANGE.
TWO, REQUESTING YOUR HAND AS HIS PARTNER ON THE DANCE FLOOR.
1) ____________________
2) ____________________

3. **1 x 1**

THE GROUP *REDBONE,* HAD A BIG HIT ABOUT THEIR LOVE. THAT IF YOU WANTED IT THEN GO FOR IT, IT'S THERE FOR THE TAKING. A SONG *REAL MCCOY,* THE R&B TRIO GROUP, WOULD ALSO RECORD IN THE 90'S TO AN UPTEMPO CLUB SOUND.
A) COME AND GET YOUR LOVE
B) GET CLOSER
C) LOVE ME DO
D) IT'S NOW OR NEVER

4. **3 x 1**

GRAND FUNK, FORMERLY KNOWN AS *GRAND FUNK RAILROAD* CHARTED A BUNCH OF HITS IN THE 70'S INCLUDING THESE THREE BELOW.
ONE, ABOUT THAT CERTAIN BAND FROM THE USA.
TWO, THEIR VERSION OF A SONG ORIGINALLY RECORDED IN THE 60'S BY *LITTLE EVA* ABOUT A CERTAIN NEW DANCE OR MOTION THAT'S EASY TO DO, A SONG *KYLIE MINOGUE* WOULD ALSO RECORD IN THE 80'S.
THREE, WHAT THAT SWEET LITTLE MAMA IS THAT SENDS THOSE CHILLS UP THROUGH HIS BODY AND THE FIRE IN HIS HEART WHEN HE HOLDS HER.
1) ______________________________
2) ________________________
3) ______________________________

5. **2 x 1**

DR. HOOK AND THE MEDICINE SHOW HAD THESE TWO VERY POPULAR HITS BELOW.
ONE, ABOUT SOMEONE'S MOTHER AND THAT OPERATOR WHO KEPT INTERRUPTING.
TWO, WANTING THEIR PORTRAIT ON THE COVER OF A FAMOUS MAGAZINE. FOR THE RECORD, IT DID OCCUR ON THE MARCH 29, 1973 ISSUE NUMBER 131. NAME THEM.
1) _________________________
2) ____

6. **1 x 1**

"LOVE HER MADLY" AND "RIDERS ON THE STORM" WERE CHARTED BY WHAT ROCK BAND BELOW?
A) THE ROLLING STONES
B) THE DOORS
C) LED ZEPELLIN
D) THE MAMAS AND THE PAPAS

7. **3 x 1**

NAME THESE THREE OTHER HITS BY *DR. HOOK*.
ONE, HIS RENDITION OF A *SAM COOKE* TUNE ABOUT A SIXTEEN YEAR OLD.
TWO, ABOUT SHARING WHAT THIS EVENING TO END THEIR LONELINESS?
THREE, ABOUT HOW BEING IN LOVE WITH A GORGEOUS WOMAN MAY BE DIFFICULT BECAUSE EVERYBODY DESIRES HER.

1) ________________
2) ________________________________
3) ____

8. **8 x 1**

THREE DOG NIGHT HAD NUMEROUS HITS DURING THE 70'S INCLUDING "SHAMBALA", "ONE MAN BAND", AND "SURE AS I'M SITTIN' HERE". NAME THESE EIGHT OTHER HITS BELOW.
ONE, WHAT HIS MAMA TOLD HIM.
TWO, A SONG FEATURED IN THE MOVIE SOUNDTRACK OF 'THE BIG CHILL', STARRING GLENN CLOSE AND JEFF GOLDBLUM AND COUNTLESS OTHERS IN THE 80'S ABOUT A JOY TO US ALL.
THREE, WHERE HE'S NEVER TRAVELED THAT INCLUDES SPAIN AND ENGLAND.
FOUR, ABOUT TWO OPPOSITE COLORS, TOGETHER THEY SEE THE LIGHT.
FIVE, A SONG WRITTEN AND ALSO ORIGINALLY RECORDED BY *LEO SAYER* ABOUT PUTTING ON A SHOW NO MATTER WHAT.
SIX, ABOUT WANTING TO COURT YOU WITH A LOVE SONG.
SEVEN, ABOUT A SPECIAL OCCASION WHEN YOU'RE DANCING WITH THE MUSIC.
EIGHT, ABOUT THAT OLD SONG THAT WAS MOST LIKEY WRITTEN FOR US.

1) _______________________________
2) ___________________
3) _______________________
4) ___________________
5) _______________________
6) _______________________
7) _______________
8) ________________________________

9. **1 x 1**

BURTON CUMMINGS, THE FORMER LEAD SINGER OF *THE GUESS WHO*, RECORDED A SONG ABOUT LOST LOVE, WITH THE ADVISE NOT TO DO ANYTHING FOOLISH, TO BE STRONG AND BE FIRM. WHAT WAS THAT HIT?

A) ONLY THE STRONG SURVIVE
B) STAND BY ME
C) STAND TALL
D) FOOLISH LITTLE GIRL

10. **1 x 1**

BLOOD, SWEAT & TEARS CHARTED WITH WHAT RHYMING HIT SONG BELOW?

A) ALLEY-OOP
B) HI-DE-HO
C) CHICK-A-BOOM (DON'T YA JES' LOVE IT)
D) LIL' RED RIDING HOOD

11. **1 x 1**

TOMMY JAMES, LESS *THE SHONDELLS*, HAD A HIT SONG ABOUT DRAGGING WHAT?

A) DRAGGIN' THE LINE
B) STOP DRAGGIN' MY HEART AROUND
C) DON'T STOP
D) TIRED OF TOEIN' THE LINE

12. **1 x 1**

THE BAND *EXILE* HAD THIS ROMANTIC SONG ABOUT THEIR DESIRE TO KISS EVERY PART OF YOU. LATER THEY WOULD BECOME A SUCCESSFUL COUNTRY GROUP.
A) KISS YOU ALL OVER
B) ('TIL) I KISSED YOU
C) KISS AND SAY GOODBYE
D) HEAD TO TOE

13. **1 x 1**

CHOOSE BELOW THE LEAD SINGER OF THE *DOORS* WHO WOULD DIE OF DRUG AND ALCOHOL ABUSE AT AN EARLY AGE IN THE EARLY 70'S.
A) JIMMY DEAN
B) JIMI HENDRIX
C) JIM MORRISON
D) JIM CROCE

14. **1 x 1**

KENNY LOGGINS RECORDED A DUET WITH *JIM MESSINA* ABOUT WHAT YOUR MAMA DIDN'T DO.
A) MAMA DIDN'T LIE
B) MAMA SAID
C) YOUR MAMA DON'T DANCE
D) MAMA CAN'T BUY YOU LOVE

15. **1 x 1**

KENNY LOGGINS ALSO RECORDED ANOTHER DUET, THIS TIME WITH *STEVIE NICKS* OF *FLEETWOOD MAC*, ABOUT SOMETHING HE CALLS YOU.
A) YOU'VE GOT A FRIEND
B) WHENEVER I CALL YOU FRIEND
C) YOU'RE THE ONE
D) EARTH ANGEL

16. **6 x 1**

NAME THESE SIX POPULAR HITS BY THE GROUP, *K C AND THE SUNSHINE BAND.*
ONE, WHAT THEY LIKE WHEN YOU TAKE THEIR HAND OR WHISPER SWEET NOTHIN'S AND START THEM UP.
TWO, ABOUT THEIR GETTING DOWN TO DANCE AND MAKE ROMANCE.
THREE, THEIR BIG BOOTY HIT SONG THAT HE WANTS YOU TO SHAKE CONTINUOUSLY.
FOUR, ABOUT A BOOGIE MAN THAT HE CLAIMED TO BE THAT YOU COULD MANIPULATE ANY WHICH WAY YOU WANTED.
FIVE, ABOUT WHAT HE WANTED HIS LOVE TO DO CONTINUOUSLY THAT WOULD REACH THE NUMBER TWO SPOT ON THE CHARTS.
SIX, ABOUT CERTAIN SHOES THAT I PUT ON TO PLAY WITH YOU.
1) ________________________________
2) ____________________
3) ____
4) ______________________
5) ______________________
6) ________________

17. **1 x 1**

"INDIAN RESERVATION (THE LAMENT OF THE CHEROKEE RESERVATION INDIAN)" ABOUT A RED MAN'S TRIBE WHO ONE DAY MAY RETURN TO ITS GLORY DAYS WAS RECORDED BY A GROUP OF *RAIDERS* WHO WORE REVOLUTIONARY WAR ATTIRE AND LED BY A COLONIAL HERO. NAME THE GROUP.

____

18. **5 x 1**

NAME THESE FIVE POPULAR HITS BY *THE DOOBIE BROTHERS.*
ONE, WITH *MICHAEL MCDONALD* IN LEAD, ABOUT THE OPINIONS OF A FOOL.
TWO, ABOUT THE COLOR OF THE MISSISSIPPI RIVER WATER AT NIGHT AND THAT FUNKY MUSIC THEY LONGED TO HEAR ALL NIGHT.
THREE, ABOUT LISTENING TO WHAT, THAT MAKES THE WORLD GO ROUND.
FOUR, ABOUT A CERTAIN TRAIN ON THE MOVE.
FIVE, ABOUT DOING WHAT ON THE STREETS BECAUSE YOUR PROMISES MEAN VERY LITTLE?

1) ____________________
2) ____________
3) ____________________
4) _________________
5) ____________________

19. **1 x 1**

THE GROUP *BOSTON* CHARTED A SONG ABOUT WHAT THEY FELT AFTER DREAMING THAT WAS SO TRUE.
A) MORE THAN A FEELING
B) FEELINGS
C) FEELS LIKE THE FIRST TIME
D) ONLY IN MY DREAMS

20. **1 x 1**

NEIL YOUNG HAD A POPULAR SONG ABOUT A MINER IN SEARCH OF THAT MOTHERLOAD. WHAT WAS IT CALLED?
A) HEART OF GLASS
B) HEART OF GOLD
C) THE HEART OF ROCK & ROLL
D) HEART AND SOUL

21. **1 x 1**

ALIVE AND KICKING, ANOTHER ONE HIT WONDER GROUP, CHARTED THIS SONG ABOUT A CERTAIN TIGHT HOLD AND A BEAUTIFUL FEELING AT THAT. CHOOSE IT BELOW.
A) TIGHTER, TIGHTER
B) HOLD ME TIGHT
C) FEELS SO GOOD
D) FEELS LIKE THE FIRST TIME

22. **1 x 1**

WILD CHERRY, A WHITE MALE GROUP, HAD THIS BIG HIT IN 1976 THAT WOULD CLIMB TO THE TOP OF THE CHARTS ABOUT THAT BOY WITH THE FUNKY SOUND. A SONG *VANILLA ICE* WOULD ALSO RECORD IN THE EARLY 90'S. WHAT WAS THAT DOUBLE HITTER CALLED?
A) FUNKYTOWN
B) FUNKY BROADWAY
C) PLAY THAT FUNKY MUSIC
D) FUNKY WORM

23. **1 x 1**

"GREEN-EYED LADY" ABOUT THAT LADY OF PASSION AND DAUGHTER OF NATURE WAS CHARTED BY WHICH GROUP BELOW?
A) COMMODORES
B) RAY, GOODMAN & BROWN
C) SUGARLOAF
D) LITTLE RIVER BAND

24. **4 x 1**

NAME THIS ALL MALE GROUP THAT CONSISTED OF A POLICEMAN, A COWBOY, AN INDIAN, A CONSTRUCTION WORKER, A MOTORCYCLE GUY AND AN ARMY MAN, AND THREE OF THEIR BIG HITS BELOW, NUMBERS TWO THROUGH FOUR.
ONE, THEIR NAME.
TWO, ABOUT A LOCAL ASSOCIATION WHERE YOUNG MEN CAN GO WHEN THEY'RE DOWN ON THEIR LUCK OR JUST WANT TO HANG OUT.
THREE, THEIR BIG NAVY HIT SONG WHERE THEY CAN SAIL THE SEAS AND DEFEND THEIR HOMELAND.
FOUR, ABOUT A RUGGED KIND OF GUY AND NO WE'RE NOT REFERRING TO RANDY SAVAGE, THE POPULAR WRESTLER.

1) ________________________
2) __.__.__.__.
3) _________________
4) ______________

25. **1 x 1**

STORIES RECORDED THIS SONG BELOW ABOUT AN INTERRACIAL RELATIONSHIP BETWEEN A BLACK GIRL AND HER WHITE BOYFRIEND AND THE FIGHT THAT ERUPTED WHEN HE TOOK HER HOME TO MEET HIS PARENTS. WHAT WAS THAT SONG?

A) HE AIN'T HEAVY, HE'S MY BROTHER
B) BROTHER LOUIE
C) BROTHER LOVE'S TRAVELLING SALVATION SHOW
D) LOUIE LOUIE

26. **1 x 1**

THIS HARD DRINKING, BLUES SINGING, WHITE FEMALE ARTIST WHO DIED OF A DRUG OVERDOSE, CHARTED A POSTHUMOUS HIT SONG CALLED "ME AND BOBBY MCGEE". SHE WAS FEATURED IN 'THE WOODSTOCK FESTIVAL' BACK IN 1969. WHO WAS THAT ARTIST?

A) JANIS JOPLIN
B) JOAN BAEZ
C) GRACE SLICK
D) MELANIE

27. **5 x 1**

NAME THESE FIVE POPULAR HITS BY THE LATE GREAT *JIM CROCE*.
ONE, ABOUT A GUY YOU DON'T DARE MESS WITH.
TWO, ABOUT A DOUBLE BAD CAT NAMED LEROY.
THREE, ABOUT HIS CONVERSATION WITH THE OPERATOR.
FOUR, A BOTTLE HIT SONG FEATURED IN THE MOVIE 'SHE LIVES', STARRING DESI ARNAZ JR.
FIVE, WHAT HE'S GONNA TELL YOU THROUGH A SONG.

1) ____________________________________
2) ________________________
3) ____
4) _____________________
5) ____

28. **1 x 1**

THE ALLMAN BROTHERS BAND, ONE OF THE POPULAR SOUTHERN BANDS, RECORDED A SONG BELOW ABOUT HOW HE WAS BORN A CERTAIN MAN. CHOOSE THIS TOP NUMBER TWO HIT SONG BELOW.

A) DUKE OF EARL
B) RAMBLIN' MAN
C) BORN TO RUN
D) BORN TO BE WILD

29. **3 x 1**

CROSBY, STILLS, NASH & YOUNG CHARTED THESE THREE HITS BELOW.
ONE, A *JONI MITCHELL* SONG ABOUT THAT FAMOUS FESTIVAL BACK IN 1969.
TWO, ABOUT TUTORING YOUR KIDS AND THEY'LL LOVE YOU FOR IT.
THREE, ABOUT A PLEASANT HOUSE WITH PETS.
NAME THEM.

1) ______________
2) ________________________
3) ______________

30. **3 x 1**

NAME THESE THREE BIG HITS BY *STEVE MILLER BAND.*
ONE, ABOUT THE GUY SOME FOLKS CALLED MAURICE.
TWO, HIS KEEP ROCKING HIT SONG ALL ACROSS AMERICA, INCLUDING PHOENIX AND ATLANTA, WHERE PAYBACK WILL EVENTUALLY TURN OUT SO SWEET.
THREE, ABOUT AN EAGLE, A TOP NUMBER TWO SONG, THAT *SEAL* WOULD ALSO RECORD IN THE 90'S FOR THE MICHAEL JORDAN ANIMATION MOVIE 'SPACE JAMS'.

1) _____________
2) ________________
3) ______________________

31. **1 x 1**

STEVE MILLER BAND CHARTED TWO OTHER HITS BELOW. WHICH ONE WAS **NOT** THEIR SONG?

A) JET AIRLINER
B) SWINGTOWN
C) PROUD MARY

32. **5 x 1**

NAME THESE FIVE CHARTED HITS BY *BOB SEGER & THE SILVER BULLET BAND.*
ONE, ABOUT CERTAIN MOVES IN HIS '60 CHEVY.
TWO, ABOUT WHAT HE CLAIMED BECAUSE NOTHING'S CHANGED.
THREE, ABOUT HAVING TONITE WHICH WAS ALSO RECORDED AS A DUET BY *KENNY ROGERS* AND *SHEENA EASTON* IN THE 80'S.
FOUR, A ROCK AND ROLL HIT SONG THAT WAS FEATURED IN THE MOVIE 'RISKY BUSINESS', STARRING TOM CRUISE AND REBECCA DEMORNAY AND ALSO USED IN CHEVY TRUCK COMMERCIALS.
FIVE, ABOUT THOSE NIGHTS IN TINSELTOWN.

1) _______________
2) _________________
3) ____________________
4) _________________________
5) ____________________

33. **1 x 1**

BLONDIE, THE GROUP WITH *DEBBIE HARRY* IN LEAD, RECORDED A HIT WITH THIS HEART TITLED SONG BELOW.

A) HEART OF STONE
B) HEARTACHE TONIGHT
C) HEART OF GOLD
D) HEART OF GLASS

34. **1 x 1**

THE GROUP HEART RECORDED TWO HITS BELOW. WHICH SONG WAS **NOT** THEIRS?

A) GO YOUR OWN WAY
B) BARRACUDA
C) MAGIC MAN

35. **1 x 1**

AEROSMITH CHARTED A SONG THAT THE RAP GROUP *RUN-DMC* WOULD ALSO CHART IN THE 80'S ABOUT WHAT SHE TOLD HIM TO DO.

A) WALK AWAY RENEE
B) WALK THIS WAY
C) WALK LIKE A MAN
D) WALK ON THE WILD SIDE

36. **1 x 1**

BRUCE SPRINGSTEEN, THE POPULAR SINGER/SONGWRITER OUT OF NEW JERSEY, HAD A SONG ABOUT WHAT HE WAS BORN TO DO.

A) BORN TO BE WILD
B) BORN FREE
C) BORN TO RUN
D) RAMBLIN' MAN

37. **1 x 1**

JAY & THE AMERICANS CHARTED A RE-MAKE OF *THE RONETTES* HIT SONG ABOUT THE RAIN. WHAT WAS THAT DOUBLE HITTER CALLED?

A) I WISH IT WOULD RAIN
B) BE MY BABY
C) IN THE RAIN
D) WALKIN' IN THE RAIN

38. **1 x 1**

THE BEACH BOYS CHARTED A HIT WITH A TUNE OF *CHUCK BERRY'*S ABOUT A CERTAIN TYPE OF MUSIC IF YOU CARED TO DANCE.

A) DO YOU WANT TO DANCE
B) SWEET LITTLE SIXTEEN
C) ROCK AND ROLL MUSIC
D) BARBARA ANN

39. **1 x 1**

DOCTOR JOHN RECORDED THIS SONG BELOW ABOUT BEING SOMEWHERE AT THE WRONG POINT IN TIME.

A) RIGHT PLACE WRONG TIME
B) IT AIN'T ME BABE
C) RIGHT TIME OF THE NIGHT
D) (IF LOVING YOU IS WRONG) I DON'T WANT TO BE RIGHT

40. **1 x 1**

CHOOSE THIS HARD ROCK GROUP THAT WERE PAINTED UP, WORE COLORFUL SPANDEX CLOTHING TO MATCH, PLATFORM SHOES, AND CHARTED THE SONG "BETH" ABOUT NOT COMING HOME BECAUSE HE AND THE BOYS WERE STILL PLAYING WHICH ALWAYS LEFT HER SO EMPTY AND ALL ALONE.

A) KISS
B) EXTREME
C) GUNS N' ROSES
D) AEROSMITH

41. **1 x 1**

FRIJID PINK, THE ROCK GROUP, CHARTED WITH A HIT SONG OF *THE ANIMALS* ORIGINALLY RECORDED BACK IN THE 60'S ABOUT A CERTAIN HOUSE.

A) BRICK HOUSE
B) THE HOUSE THAT JACK BUILT
C) THE HOUSE OF THE RISING SUN
D) I'M GONNA TEAR DOWN YOUR PLAYHOUSE

42. **1 x 1**

RICKI LEE JONES, A FEMALE ARTIST, RECORDED A HIT SONG ABOUT A GUY NAMED CHUCK E. AND WHAT HE WAS IN. NAME IT.

____

43. **1 x 1**

MEAT LOAF WOULD RECORD A HEARTBREAKER ABOUT A ROMANCE WHERE ONE PARTICIPANT WANTED AND NEEDED THE OTHER WHO COULDN'T COMMIT TO A PERMANENT LOVE RELATION. WHAT WAS THAT HIT CALLED?

A) TWO OUT OF THREE AIN'T BAD
B) I CAN HELP
C) TELL HER NO
D) WE'LL SING IN THE SUNSHINE

44. **1 x 1**

THE CARS, THE ALL MALE BAND OUT OF BOSTON, CHARTED THIS SONG BELOW ABOUT A GIRL THAT USED TO BE HIS BUT NO LONGER SO.

A) YOU WERE MINE
B) USE TA BE MY GIRL
C) MY BEST FRIEND'S GIRL
D) TELL HER NO

45. **1 x 1**

THE BAND CHARTED A SONG ABOUT A CERTAIN CREEK. WHAT WAS THAT HIT?

A) BLACK WATER
B) DIRTY WATER
C) THE WEIGHT
D) UP ON CRIPPLE CREEK

46. **1 x 1**

THE HARD ROCK BAND *KISS* CHARTED WHAT POPULAR ROCK TITLED SONG ABOUT WANTING TO PARTY EVERY DAY AND ROCK EVERY NIGHT?

A) ROCK AND ROLL ALL NITE
B) ROCK AND ROLL HEAVEN
C) ROCKIN' PNEUMONIA AND THE BOOGIE WOOGIE FLU
D) I LOVE ROCK 'N ROLL

47. **1 x 1**

PACIFIC GAS & ELECTRIC, A ONE HIT WONDER GROUP WITH THE SOULFUL SOUND, HAD WHAT SONG THAT QUESTIONED YOUR READINESS TO BE CARRIED, SO AS NOT TO BE ALONE?

A) COME AND GET YOUR LOVE
B) ARE YOU READY?
C) HIT ME WITH YOUR BEST SHOT
D) PEOPLE GET READY

48. **1 x 1**

THIS MALE ARTIST, NAMED ALICE, WORE MAKEUP AND SPANDEX AND CHARTED A HIT WITH "YOU AND ME" ABOUT THE SIMPLE LIFE AND WRAPPING HIMSELF AROUND YOU TO BRING ECSTACY IN THE PROCESS. WHAT WAS HIS FULL NAME?

____

49. **1 x 1**

JACKSON BROWNE HAD THIS HIT ABOUT WHAT HE WAS RUNNING ON BECAUSE OF THE FEAR THAT HE COULD NOT KEEP HIS ROMANCE GOING.

A) RUN TO HIM
B) RUNAWAY
C) RUNNING ON EMPTY
D) JUST MY IMAGINATION (RUNNING AWAY WITH ME)

50. **1 x 1**

BOZ SCAGGS RECORDED THIS SONG THAT WAS FEATURED IN THE MOVIE SOUNDTRACK 'LOOKING FOR MR. GOODBAR', STARRING DIANE KEATON AND RICHARD GERE ABOUT SOMETHING THAT WAS DIRTY.

A) BACK STABBERS
B) LOVE HANGOVER
C) LOWDOWN
D) LOW RIDER

51. **5 x 1**

NAME THESE FOUR BIG HITS BY *B J THOMAS*.
ONE, A DONE WRONG HIT SONG, THAT HAD A VERY LONG TITLE.
TWO, ABOUT SOMETHING HE JUST COULDN'T HELP.
THREE, HIS RAINDROP HIT SONG FEATURED IN THE MOVIE 'BUTCH CASSIDY AND THE SUNDANCE KID', STARRING PAUL NEWMAN AND ROBERT REDFORD.
FOUR, ABOUT WHAT HE CLAIMED THE GIRL WAS GONNA DO THIS TIME AROUND.
FIVE, A LULLABY HIT SONG THAT HIS MOMMA WOULD SING TO SOOTHE HIM.

1) ______________________________
2) ______________________________
3) ______________________________
4) ______________________________
5) ______________________________

52. **1 x 1**

THE JAGGERZ, ANOTHER ALL MALE ONE HIT WONDER GROUP, HAD A TOP NUMBER TWO HIT SONG ABOUT THE KIND OF PERSON WHO LIKES TO FLIRT WITH THE OPPOSITE SEX USING THEIR PICKUP LINES HOPING TO SCORE FOR WHAT THEY'RE AFTER. WHAT WAS THAT ONE HIT WONDER SONG?

A) SMOOTH OPERATOR
B) THE RAPPER
C) SWEET TALKIN' GUY
D) PLAYBOY

53. **3 x 1**

DARYL HALL & JOHN OATES, THE VERY POPULAR ROCK DUO, RECORDED THESE THREE BIG HITS BELOW. NAME THEM.
ONE, ABOUT A GIRL THAT LEFT, ALSO RECORDED BY *TAVARES*.
TWO, ABOUT THAT GIRL SARA WHO TOGETHER WILL GIVE EACH OTHER COMFORT AND WARMTH.
THREE, ABOUT THAT WEALTHY CHICK.

1) ______________
2) ______________
3) ______________

54. **1 x 1**

THE IDES OF MARCH, A ROCK BAND, CHARTED THIS SONG BELOW CLAIMING TO BE YOUR WHAT, IN HIS BLACK SEDAN, WHERE HE WOULD TAKE YOU ANY PLACE YOU WISHED BECAUSE OF HIS STRONG DESIRES TO HAVE YOU AND BE YOUR ALL.

A) LOVERBOY
B) I'LL TAKE YOU THERE
C) YOU'RE ALL I NEED TO GET BY
D) VEHICLE

55. **1 x 1**

WHO BELOW WAS NOT A MEMBER OF THE 'EAGLES'?

A) GLENN FRY
B) DON HENLEY
C) JOE WALSH
D) RUSSELL HITCHCOCK
E) TIMOTHY SCHMIT

56. **2 x 1**

STEELY DAN, ANOTHER ROCK BAND, HAD NUMEROUS HITS IN THE 70'S INCLUDING "DO IT AGAIN, THEIR FIRST, AND "REELING IN THE YEARS. NAME THESE TWO OTHERS BELOW.
ONE, ABOUT A NUMBER THEY DIDN'T WANT RIKKI TO FORGET OR LOSE.
TWO, ABOUT THAT POPULAR COVER GIRL THAT HE WAS CORRESPONDING WITH THAT HE HAD HER PHOTOGRAPH.

1) ______________________________

2) ______

TOTAL POINTS. **100 x 1 = 100**

ROCKERS-QUIZ # 2

1. **1 x 2**

THIS GROUP CHARTED A NUMBER OF HITS INCLUDING: "THE WORLD IS A GHETTO", "THE CISCO KID", AND "WHY CAN'T WE BE FRIENDS". AT ONE TIME THEY BACKED *ERIC BURDON* AND ALSO SHARED A BIG HIT WITH HIS "SPILL THE WINE". WHO WERE THEY?
A) THE ANIMALS
B) EARTH, WIND & FIRE
C) WAR
D) THE SHONDELLS

2. **1 x 2**

THE STAMPEDERS, A TRIO BAND, HAD WHAT SONG BELOW ABOUT A CERTAIN CITY LADY?
A) KANSAS CITY
B) LADY MARMALADE
C) KENTUCKY WOMAN
D) SWEET CITY WOMAN

3. **1 x 2**

TOTO CHARTED A SONG ASKING HIS GIRL TO HOLD ON BECAUSE HE WANTED TO GET OFF HIS CHEST ALL THE BAD THINGS THAT SHE HAD SAID AND DONE TO EVERYONE. CHOOSE THAT SONG BELOW.
A) HOLD ON! I'M COMING
B) HOLD THE LINE
C) HOLD WHAT YOU'VE GOT
D) HOLD ME TIGHT

4. **3 x 2**

CREEDENCE CLEARWATER REVIVAL CONTINUED TO CHART HITS IN THE EARLY 70'S WHICH INCLUDED: "UP AROUND THE BEND" AND "LOOKIN' OUT MY BACK DOOR". NAME THESE THREE OTHERS BELOW.
ONE, WHO THEY PLAYED WITH BY USING THEIR INSTRUMENTS AND WHO WERE ALWAYS ON THE GO?
TWO, WONDERING IF THE POURING RAIN COULD BE STOPPED.
THREE, WHAT THEY ALSO WANTED TO KNOW ABOUT THE SIGHT OF THE RAIN.
1) ____________________
2) _________________________
3) _______________________________

5. **1 x 2**

THE GROUP, *PABLO CRUISE*, CHARTED THESE TWO HITS "COOL LOVE", AND "WHATCHA GONNA DO". WHAT WAS THE NAME OF THIS OTHER ABOUT NOT BEING AFRAID OF FINDING A NEW START, THAT THE MINUTE THE PAIN PASSES LOVE WILL COME NATURALLY?
A) LETS DO IT AGAIN
B) ABC
C) SHOW ME THE WAY
D) LOVE WILL FIND A WAY

6. **1 x 2**

THE SONG "MY SHARONA" ABOUT THAT GIRL SHARONA WAS CHARTED BY WHICH MALE GROUP BELOW THAT TOOK IT TO THE TOP OF THE CHARTS IN 1979?
A) FOREIGNER
B) DURAN DURAN
C) THE KNACK
D) THE FOUR SEASONS

7. **1 x 2**

POCO, A MALE ROCK BAND, RECORDED THIS HEARTBREAK HIT SONG BELOW ABOUT A DEPARTED RELATION THAT WHENEVER HE HEARS HER NAME HE BREAKS DOWN CRYING, REALIZING THAT SHE'S STILL WRAPPED AROUND HIS HEART AND LOVES HER IN HIS OWN CRAZY WAY.

A) CRAZY
B) CRAZY LOVE
C) CRAZY LITTLE THING CALLED LOVE
D) I GO CRAZY

8. **1 x 2**

LYNYRD SKYNYRD, THE ALL MALE SOUTHERN ROCK BAND, CHARTED WHAT SONG ABOUT THEIR HOME STATE WHICH WOULD BE FEATURED IN THE MOVIE 'CON AIR' IN THE LATE 90'S, STARRING NICOLAS CAGE, JOHN MALKOVICH AND JOHN CUSACK?

A) GEORGIA ON MY MIND
B) KENTUCKY RAIN
C) INDIANA WANTS ME
D) SWEET HOME ALABAMA

9. **1 x 2**

LOU REED RECORDED A SONG ABOUT THE HUSTLING WORLD OF PROSTITUTION AND WHERE THEY WERE TOLD TO GO IN THAT MEAN PART OF TOWN. WHAT WAS THAT SONG?

A) THE NIGHT CHICAGO DIED
B) WALK ON THE WILD SIDE
C) SOUTH STREET
D) DOWN IN THE BOONDOCKS

10. **1 x 2**

THIS GROUP LED BY *ERIC CARMEN* CHARTED THE SONG "GO ALL THE WAY" ABOUT GETTING TOTAL SATISFACTION BY HOLDING ON AND NOT LETTING GO. WHAT WAS THE GROUP HE FRONTED WITH ON THAT SONG?

A) LOBO
B) RASPBERRIES
C) PETER FRAMPTON
D) THE RASCALS

11. **1 x 2**

J. GEILS BAND, OUT OF BOSTON, RECORDED A SONG ABOUT WHAT PROBABLY HAPPENED TO HIM BECAUSE HE FOOLISHLY LET HER GET AWAY.

A) STUCK IN THE MIDDLE WITH YOU
B) HIT THE ROAD JACK
C) MUST OF GOT LOST
D) LOVE ON A TWO WAY STREET

12. **1 x 2**

BROWNSVILLE STATION HAD A BIG HIT ABOUT SOMETHING THAT WAS PROHIBITED IN THE BOY'S ROOM AT SCHOOL. NAME IT.

____

13. **1 x 2**

PATTI SMITH GROUP CHARTED A SONG ABOUT WHO THE NIGHT BELONGED TO.

A) PROMISES IN THE DARK
B) I LOVE THE NIGHTLIFE
C) BECAUSE THE NIGHT
D) TONIGHT'S THE NIGHT

14. **6 x 2**

NAME THESE SIX CHARTED HITS BY *FOREIGNER.*
ONE, ABOUT A SENSATION FOR THE VERY FIRST TIME AND NEVER LIKE BEFORE
TWO, ABOUT SOMETHING HOT AND FEELING SO GOOD.
THREE, ABOUT THE WAY YOU ARE, SO FRIGID, AND YOU'RE GONNA PAY.
FOUR, ABOUT A DIRTY BOY.
FIVE, ABOUT THE MIND GAMES THAT YOU PLAY, INSTEAD OF GIVING YOUR LOVE.
SIX, THE VISION HE HAS THE MINUTE HE GETS INTOXICATED.

1) ______________________________
2) ______________
3) ______________
4) ______________________
5) ______________
6) ________________

15. **2 x 2**

THIS GROUP HAD A NUMBER OF HITS DURING THEIR CAREER. "LADY" AND "COME SAIL AWAY" WERE TWO SUCH HITS. NAME THEM AND THIS OTHER SONG WHICH CLIMBED TO THE TOP OF THE CHARTS IN 1979 ABOUT HIS WOMAN THAT HE'S GONNA MISS BADLY WHILE ON HIS SHORT TRIP AWAY BECAUSE SHE'S THE ONE THAT GIVES HIM THE COURAGE AND ENDURANCE TO CARRY ON, AND LOVES DEARLY.

1) ________
2) ________

16. **1 x 2**

ATLANTA RHYTHM SECTION, A SOUTHERN ROCK BAND, RECORDED A SONG ABOUT WHAT HE WAS IN, BECAUSE SHE HYPNOTIZED HIM TO THE POINT THAT NOTHING ELSE MATTERED BUT HER.

A) SO IN TO YOU
B) LIFE IN THE FAST LANE
C) I GO CRAZY
D) GYPSY WOMAN

17. **1 x 2**

THIS ROCK GROUP, *WET WILLIE*, CHARTED A SONG THAT WHEN THINGS GO WRONG, AND YOU'VE GOT THE BLUES, JUST DO WHAT AND IT'LL HELP YOU CARRY ON IN LIFE?

A) CRYING
B) CELEBRATE
C) JUMP
D) KEEP ON SMILIN'

18. **1 x 2**

THE SONG "DREAM ON" WAS RECORDED BY THIS POPULAR ROCK BAND BELOW LED BY *STEVE TYLER*. WHAT WAS THE GROUP HE FRONTED WITH?

A) JOURNEY
B) RUN-D.M.C.
C) AEROSMITH
D) FLEETWOOD MAC

19. **1 x 2**

KING HARVEST, A ROCK GROUP, HAD A SONG ABOUT EVERYONE DANCING UNDER THE LIGHT OF THE MOON. CHOOSE IT BELOW.

A) TONIGHT'S THE NIGHT
B) DANCING IN THE MOONLIGHT
C) WALKIN' AFTER MIDNIGHT
D) ONE SUMMER NIGHT

20. **1 x 2**

LEE MICHAELS CHARTED THIS SONG BELOW WANTING TO KNOW IF HE MADE HIMSELF CLEAR.
A) DO YOU KNOW WHAT I MEAN
B) WHAT I'D SAY (PT 1)
C) TWO OUT OF THREE AIN'T BAD
D) HAVE YOU HEARD

21. **1 x 2**

IN THE 70'S *THE GUESS WHO* FROM CANADA CHARTED A SONG ABOUT A CERTAIN TYPE OF WOMAN THEY WANTED NO PART OF, A SONG *LENNY KRAVITZ* WOULD GO ON TO RECORD IN THE LATE 90'S. WHAT WAS THAT DOUBLE HITTER CALLED?
A) BROWN EYED WOMAN
B) YOU'RE NO GOOD
C) AMERICAN WOMAN
D) EVIL WOMAN

22. **3 x 2**

THE GUESS WHO CHARTED THESE THREE OTHER HITS BELOW.
ONE, ABOUT GIVING AN OVATION TO A FAMOUS DEEJAY, THE SAME ONE WHO WAS FEATURED IN THE 'AMERICAN GRAFFITI' MOVIE IN THE 70'S AS A DJ.
TWO, ABOUT WHAT HE DOESN'T HAVE, NOT EVEN FOR BETTER DAYS OR EVEN FOR A FRIEND.
THREE, WHAT THEY WOULD SHARE AS A RESULT OF LIVING AS ONE AND DOING THINGS TOGETHER.
NAME THEM.
1) ____________________________
2) ______________
3) ____________________

23. **11 x 2**

NAME THESE ELEVEN POPULAR HITS BY *THE EAGLES*.
ONE, THE BEST THAT COMES FROM HIS HEART.
TWO, SOONER OR LATER ONE EVENING, HE'LL FIND WHAT HE'S BEEN LOOKING FOR, A WOMAN FULL OF WICKED PASSION.
THREE, ABOUT A CITY WOMAN WHO CAN'T HIDE HER EYES, HEADING FOR TOWN TO COMMIT ADULTERY.
FOUR, ABOUT TAKING IT TO THE EXTREME ONCE AGAIN.
FIVE, A NEW KID ON THE BLOCK THAT EVERYBODY'S TALKING ABOUT.
SIX, ABOUT A LOVELY HOTEL.
SEVEN, ABOUT LIVING ON THE EDGE.
EIGHT, ABOUT A HEARTACHE APPROACHING THIS EVENING.
NINE, ABOUT LIGHTENING UP THE LOAD AND TAKING IT SLOW.
TEN, ABOUT A SCARY DEVIL WOMAN FULL OF WITCHCRAFT.
ELEVEN, ABOUT A TRANQUIL RELAXED FEELING.
1) _____________________
2) ____________________________
3) ________________
4) ____________________________
5) _____________________
6) ________________________
7) ____________________________
8) ________________________
9) ____________________
10) ________________
11) __________________________________

24. **5 x 2**

NAME THESE FIVE BIG HITS BY *BREAD*, THE MALE TRIO BAND, LED BY *DAVID GATES.*
ONE, PLEADING WITH HIS BABY THAT HE WANTS HER AND NEEDS HER.
TWO, ABOUT ALL HE WOULD GIVE ONLY TO HAVE HER BACK.
THREE, ABOUT WANTING TO START A RELATIONSHIP WITH YOU THAT HE WAS CONFIDENT WOULD WORK OUT WELL.
FOUR, ABOUT BEING LOST AND HELPLESS IF HE COULDN'T HAVE YOU BY HIS SIDE.
FIVE, ABOUT THAT JOURNAL BOOK WITH LOCK AND KEY THAT HE HAD FOUND, THAT STATED YOU TOO HAD FOUND WHAT YOU'VE BEEN LOOKING FOR IN HIM.

1) ________________________
2) _____________________
3) _____________________
4) _____________________________
5) __________

25. **1 x 2**

BREAD HAD THESE FOUR OTHER HITS BELOW. WHICH ONE WAS **NOT** THEIRS?
A) IT DON'T MATTER TO ME
B) HERE COMES THE SUN
C) THE GUITAR MAN
D) IF
E) AUBREY

26. **1 x 2**

FIVE MAN ELECTRICAL BAND RECORDED A HIT ABOUT THE NOTICES THAT WERE DISPLAYED EVERYWHERE YOU GO, GIVING COUNTLESS INFORMATION WHETHER YOU WANTED IT OR NOT THAT INCLUDED: DO THIS, DON'T DO THIS, NEED A CARD TO GET IN, ETC. WHAT WAS THAT HIT?
A) WALK DON'T RUN
B) WANT ADS
C) THINK
D) SIGNS

TOTAL POINTS. **50 x 2 = 100**

MISC (NOVELTY, FOLK, FOREIGN & INSTRUMENTALS)-QUIZ # 1

1. **1 x 4**

BADFINGER, THE WELCH GROUP, OUT OF *THE BEATLES* APPLE RECORDS LABEL, CHARTED "DAY AFTER DAY" AND "NO MATTER WHAT". NAME THIS OTHER ABOUT WHAT YOU HAD TO DO AND QUICKLY BEFORE IT DISAPPEARS.
A) I DO
B) AFTERNOON DELIGHT
C) COME AND GET IT
D) LET'S GET IT ON

2. **1 x 4**

JOAN BAEZ, THE ANTI-WAR AND CIVIL RIGHTS ACTIVIST, RECORDED A SONG ALSO CHARTED BY THE GROUP, 'THE BAND', ABOUT OLD DIXIE. NAME IT.

____

3. **1 x 4**

BACHMAN TURNER OVERDRIVE RECORDED THE SONG "TAKIN' CARE OF BUSINESS". THEY CHARTED ANOTHER THAT WOULD REACH THE TOP OF THE CHARTS ABOUT WHAT THIS BABE TOLD THAT HOME BOY CONCERNING THE LOVE THEY JUST HAD, YET TO EXPERIENCE, AND THAT HE WOULD NEVER FORGET.
A) TWO OUT OF THREE AIN'T BAD
B) YOU AIN'T SEEN NOTHING YET
C) AIN'T NOTHING LIKE THE REAL THING
D) I CAN'T GET NEXT TO YOU

4. **1 x 4**

WALTER ZEVON RECORDED A SONG ABOUT WHO HE CLAIMED HE SAW IN SOHO WHO LOOKED A LOT LIKE LON CHANEY JR IN DISGUISE AND COULD HOWL LIKE THE REAL THING. CHOOSE THAT ONE.
A) CLAP FOR THE WOLFMAN
B) FRANKENSTEIN
C) WEREWOLVES OF LONDON
D) MONSTER MASH

5. **1 x 4**

THIN LIZZY, THE IRISH GROUP, HAD THIS HIT SONG CONCERNING THE WHEREABOUTS OF THE BOYS. CHOOSE IT BELOW.
A) THE BOYS ARE BACK IN TOWN
D) BRING THE BOYS HOME
C) WHERE THE BOYS ARE
D) FOLLOW THE BOYS

6. **1 x 4**

JONI MITCHELL CHARTED A SONG ABOUT NEEDING HELP BECAUSE SHE'S GETTING THAT CRAZY FEELING AGAIN.
A) HELP ME
B) HELP!
C) FEELINGS
C) CRAZY

7. **1 x 4**

RICK DEES, THE FORMER HOST OF 'SOLID GOLD' AND CURRENTLY THE WEEKLY TOP 40 RADIO DJ, CHARTED WHAT DISCO SONG WITH HIS CAST OF IDIOTS, A TOP NUMBER ONE, THAT WOULD BE HIS ONE AND ONLY ABOUT BEING ON THE DANCE FLOOR ACTING STRANGE?
A) DISCO INFERNO
B) DISCO LADY
C) FLY, ROBIN, FLY
 D) DISCO DUCK (PART 1)

8. **1 x 4**

AVERAGE WHITE BAND, ALSO KNOWN AS *AWB,* CHARTED WHAT INSTRUMENTAL HIT THAT ONLY VOCALLY REPEATED THE SONG TITLE ABOUT GATHERING UP ALL THE PARTS?

A) BITS AND PIECES
B) LET'S PUT IT ALL TOGETHER
C) PICK UP THE PIECES
D) TEQUILA

9. **1 x 4**

THE BLUES BROTHERS, CONSISTING OF *JOHN BELUSHI* AND *DAN AYKROYD* AS THE TWO FRONT MEN, CHARTED WHAT POPULAR *SAM AND DAVE* HIT SONG BELOW?

A) RAW-HIDE
B) SOUL MAN
C) GO NOW!
D) SWEET SOUL MUSIC

10. **1 x 4**

PAUL STOOKEY OF *PETER, PAUL & MARY* FAME, HAD THIS WEDDING TITLED SONG BELOW. WHAT WAS THAT WEDDING SONG?

A) WEDDING SONG (THERE IS LOVE)
B) WEDDING BELL BLUES
C) DOWN THE AISLE (WEDDING SONG)
D) THE HAWAIIAN WEDDING SONG (KE KALI NEI AU)

11. **3 x 4**

NAME THESE THREE BIG POPULAR HITS BY *TOM JONES* DURING THE 70'S.
ONE, A RE-MAKE OF A *CLYDE MCPHATTER* SONG THAT WITHOUT AFFECTION THERE WOULD BE NOTHING.
TWO, ABOUT A LADY THAT HE CLAIMED WAS HIS.
THREE, HIS VERSION OF A *BEN E KING* SONG ABOUT NOT HAVING ANYTHING BUT NEVERTHELESS STILL ADORES YOU.

1) ______________________________
2) __________________
3) ________________________

12. **1 x 4**

MOUTH & MACNEIL, A MALE AND FEMALE DUO, CHARTED WHAT SONG BELOW THAT WAS QUITE LOUD AT TIMES AND WOULD PUT THEM IN THE ONE HIT WONDER CATEGORY AS WELL?

A) SHOUT
B) TWIST AND SHOUT
C) FIRE
D) HOW DO YOU DO?

13. **1 x 4**

'THE LAST WALTZ' WAS BOTH A FINAL ALBUM AND A MOVIE DOCUMENTARY PUT TOGETHER IN 1976 AS A TRIBUTE TO A BAND WHO WAS DISBANDING. IT FEATURED *BOB DYLAN, VAN MORRISON, NEIL YOUNG, JONI MITCHELL, NEIL DIAMOND, DR JOHN, RINGO STARR* AND A FEW OTHERS. WHAT WAS THE BAND BEING HONORED?

A) THE BEATLES
B) THREE DOG NIGHT
C) THE BAND
D) THE MIRACLES

14. **1 x 4**

RANDY NEWMAN, THE SINGER/SONGWRITER, CHARTED THIS BIG NOVELTY SONG BELOW THAT MIGHT HAVE OFFENDED MANY A SMALL PERSON. IT WOULD CLIMB TO THE NUMBER TWO SPOT WAY UP ON THE CHARTS. WHAT WAS THAT BIG NOVELTY HIT CALLED?

A) HIGH HOPES
B) SHORT PEOPLE
C) YOU MUST HAVE BEEN A BEAUTIFUL BABY
D) BABY TALK

15. **1 x 4**

GERRY RAFFERTY ALSO HAD A TOP NUMBER TWO HIT SONG WHICH WAS HIS FIRST MAJOR HIT THAT WOULD GAIN HIM HIS INITIAL STARDOM WITH WHAT SONG BELOW ABOUT A CERTAIN STREET?

A) DOWN ON THE CORNER
B) BAKER STREET
C) DEAD END STREET
D) LOVE ON A TWO WAY STREET

16. **1 x 4**

WALTER MURPHY & THE BIG APPLE BAND RECORDED THIS BIG CLASSICAL INSTRUMENTAL HIT NAMED AFTER A VERY FAMOUS COMPOSER ABOUT A FIFTH. IT WAS FEATURED IN THE MOVIE SOUNDTRACK OF 'SATURDAY NIGHT FEVER' THAT PROBABLY *CHUCK BERRY* & *LINDA RONSTADT* WOULD HAVE APPROVED OF.

A) CLASSICAL GAS
B) A FIFTH OF BEETHOVEN
C) (JUST LIKE) ROMEO & JULIET
D) ROLL OVER BEETHOVEN

17. **1 x 4**

BONNIE TYLER, THE WELCH SINGER, HAD A MAJOR HIT ABOUT A BROKEN HEARTACHE ROMANCE. WHAT WAS IT CALLED?

A) HEARTACHE TONIGHT
B) IT'S A HEARTACHE
C) HEART OF STONE
D) ONE LESS BELL TO ANSWER

18. **1 x 4**

CHUCK MANGIONE RECORDED THIS BIG INSTRUMENTAL NUMBER BELOW ABOUT A SENSATION THAT FELT AWFULLY GOOD.

A) YOU MAKE ME FEEL LIKE DANCING
B) FEELS SO GOOD
C) FEEL LIKE MAKIN' LOVE
D) FEELS LIKE THE FIRST TIME

19. **1 x 4**

HERB ALPERT WOULD RECORD WHAT LIVELY INSTRUMENTAL HIT WITH PEOPLE CLAPPING AND HIS HORN RISING IN LEAD?

A) ZORBA THE GREEK
B) THE ENTERTAINER
C) RISE
D) ON BROADWAY

20. **1 x 4**

THIS THEME SONG FROM THE MOVIE 'ROCKY' BY *BILL CONTI* IN THE MID 70'S STARRING SYLVESTER STALLONE, TALIA SHIRE AND CARL WEATHERS WAS A BIG HIT ABOUT SOMETHING THAT WAS GONNA OCCUR IMMEDIATELY IF NOT SOONER. IT WAS ALSO A INSTRUMENTAL HIT FOR *MAYNARD FERGUSON* AROUND THE SAME PERIOD OF TIME.

A) SOMETHING
B) GO NOW
C) GONNA FLY NOW
D) RIGHT TIME OF THE NIGHT

21. **1 x 4**

JOHN PAUL YOUNG HAD A ROMANTIC SONG ABOUT SOMETHING THAT WAS IN THE ATMOSPHERE AND SPREADING GOOD VIBES.

A) LOVE IS IN THE AIR
B) LOVE IS ALL AROUND
C) RIGHT TIME OF THE NIGHT
D) WALKIN' IN THE RAIN WITH THE ONE I LOVE

22. **1 x 4**

THE GROUP, *STEALERS WHEEL*, RECORDED A SONG ABOUT BEING STUCK WITH YOU, CIRCUS ACTS ON ONE SIDE AND COMEDIANS ON THE OTHER. CHOOSE IT.

A) GOODBYE CRUEL WORLD
B) HOOKED ON A FEELING
C) STUCK IN THE MIDDLE WITH YOU
D) EVERYBODY LOVES A CLOWN

23. **1 x 4**

BYRON MACGREGOR CHARTED A READING OF A GORDON SINCLAIR NEWSPAPER EDITORIAL TRIBUTE COMMENDING THE UNSELFISHNESS OF THE AMERICAN PEOPLE. FROM THE MARSHALL PLAN, TO THE ASSISTANCE IN EARTHQUAKES, IN THE REBUILDING OF FAILING RAILROADS, BOOSTING FOREIGN MONETARY TO AVOID COLLAPSE AND THE FUNDING OF THE AMERICAN RED CROSS THAT HAS GONE BANKRUPT SEVERAL TIMES. WHAT OTHER NATION CAN SEND A MAN TO THE MOON AND BACK OR BUILD A QUALITY AIRPLANE, ETC. WHAT WAS THAT TRIBUTE READING BELOW.

A) THE OSCARS
B) AMERICA THE BEAUTIFUL
C) THE AMERICANS (A CANADIAN'S OPINION)
D) YANKEE DOODLE DANDY

TOTAL POINTS. **25 x 4 = 100**

MISC (NOVELTY, FOLK, FOREIGN & INSTRUMENTALS)-QUIZ # 2

1. **1 x 10**

THE LATIN GROUP, *MOCEDADES*, CHARTED WHAT HIT SONG THAT WAS SUNG TOTALLY IN SPANISH ABOUT YOU BEING THE ONE? CHOOSE THAT HIT BELOW.

A) BANG BANG
B) EL WATUSI
C) ERES TU
D) WATERMELON MAN

2. **1 x 10**

JOHNNY COLON, THE LATIN SINGER, HAD A HIT WITH THIS BLUES TITLED SONG BELOW ABOUT THAT L.S.D. (LOVE, STRONG, DYNAMIC) HOLD ON HIM. WHAT WAS THAT LATIN HIT?

A) SINGING THE BLUES
B) BLUE MONDAY
C) BOOGALOO BLUES
D) BLUE BAYOU

3. **1 x 10**

REUNION, A GROUP OF STUDIO SINGERS, CHARTED THIS NOVELTY SONG THAT PAYS TRIBUTE TO AN ENORMOUS STRING OF ARTISTS, SONGS, RECORD LABELS AND DJ'S. INCLUDING *JOHNNY RIVERS, STEELY DAN, WILSON PICKETT, BB KING, ERIC CLAPTON, CARLY SIMON, ROLLING STONES, PETER, PAUL & MARY, BOBBY VEE*, "SUGAR SUGAR", "YUMMY YUMMY", CBS, WARNER BROTHERS, AND ALAN FREED TO NAME <u>ONLY JUST A FEW</u>. CHOOSE THAT TRIBUTE SONG BELOW.

A) STAND BY ME
B) LIFE IS A ROCK (BUT THE RADIO ROLLED ME)
C) ROCK 'N ME
D) VIDEO KILLED THE RADIO STAR

4. **1 x 10**

RUPERT HOLMES HAD A NOVELTY HIT CONCERNING AN AD HE REPLIED ABOUT WHAT HE LIKED TO DO THAT INCLUDED GETTING DRENCHED IN THE RAIN, DRINKING CHAMPAGNE, FRUITY ALCOHOL DRINKS, THE OCEAN, AND NOT INTO HEALTH FOODS NOR EXERCISING. WHAT WAS THAT NOVELTY HIT, BUT DON'T GO ASKING HIS OLD LADY?

A) SPILL THE WINE
B) ESCAPE (THE PINA COLADA SONG)
C) WALKING IN THE RAIN
D) SPIDERS & SNAKES

5. **1 x 10**

DAVE EDMUNDS DID A RE-MAKE OF A *GALE STORM* HIT SHE CHARTED BACK IN THE MID 50'S ABOUT WHAT HE HEARD THAT DIDN'T MATTER CAUSE SHE WASN'T COMING IN, AND TO GO BACK WHERE SHE CAME FROM.

A) I HEAR YOU KNOCKING
B) I HEARD IT THROUGH THE GRAPEVINE
C) CAN'T YOU HEAR MY HEARTBEAT
D) KEEP A KNOCKIN'

6. **1 x 10**

THE DISCO GROUP *SANTA ESMERALDA* WITH *LEROY GOMEZ* IN LEAD HAD A HIT WITH A RE-MAKE OF *THE ANIMALS* HIT SONG, THAT HAD A LATIN BEAT AND A LOT OF CLAPPING MIXED IN, ABOUT WHAT HE APPEARED TO BE DUE TO HIS EDGINESS. WHAT WAS THAT RE-MAKE HIT?

A) SPILL THE WINE
B) DON'T LET ME BE MISUNDERSTOOD
C) WE GOTTA GET OUT OF THIS PLACE
D) COME A LITTLE BIT CLOSER

7. **1 x 10**

DADDY DEWDROP, TRUE NAME RICHARD MONDA, CHARTED A NOVELTY SONG ABOUT THAT CHICK WITH THE BLACK BIKINI AND WHAT THEY TOLD HIM ABOUT HER THAT HE COULDN'T UNDERSTAND.

A) CHANTILLY LACE
B) ITSY BITSY TEENIE WEENIE YELLOW POLKADOT BIKINI
C) CHICK-A-BOOM (DON'T YA JES' LOVE IT)
D) AT MY FRONT DOOR (CRAZY LITTLE MAMA)

8. **1 x 10**

"LOVE'S THEME" WAS A BIG INSTRUMENTAL HIT PUT TOGETHER BY THIS TALENTED ARTIST WHO UTILIZED HIS *LOVE UNLIMITED ORCHESTRA*. WHO WAS THAT TALENTED ARTIST?

A) MASON WILLIAMS
B) BARRY WHITE
C) PAUL ANKA
D) HERB ALPERT

9. **1 x 10**

MIKE POST, THE ORCHESTRA LEADER, HAD WHAT INSTRUMENTAL HIT WITH A THEME FOR A TV SITCOM STARRING JAMES GARDNER AS A PRIVATE EYE?

A) THE ROCKFORD FILES
B) BO DIDDLEY
C) PETER GUNN THEME
D) THEME FROM SHAFT

10. **1 x 10**

SAMANTHA SANG, THE AUSTRALIAN LASSIE, HAD A BIG HIT WITH A TUNE THAT HAD *BARRY GIBB* DOING THE BACKING THAT SOUNDED MORE OF A *BEE GEE* TYPICAL SONG IF ANYTHING, ABOUT WHAT SHE WAS GOING THROUGH THAT WAS STRESSFUL. WITH TEARS AND WORRIES IF HE WOULD EVER COME BACK TO HER. WHAT WAS THAT BIG HIT AND HER ONLY CLAIM TO FAME SONG?

A) EMOTION
B) JUST DON'T WANT TO BE LONELY
C) HELP ME MAKE IT THROUGH THE NIGHT
D) DON'T LEAVE ME THIS WAY

TOTAL POINTS. **10 x 10 = 100**

MISC (NOVELTY, FOLK, FOREIGN & INSTRUMENTALS)-QUIZ # 3

1. **2 x 2**

BAY CITY ROLLERS, THE BAND OUT OF SCOTLAND, RECORDED THESE TWO SONGS BELOW. NAME THEM.
ONE, ABOUT A CERTAIN NIGHT OF THE WEEKEND WHERE THEY DANCE TO ROCK AND ROLL MUSIC.
TWO, THEIR VERSION OF A *DUSTY SPRINGFIELD* SONG ABOUT WANTING TO BE WITH SOMEONE WHO HAS A HOLD ON HIM.
1) ____________________
2) ____________________________

2. **2 x 2**

NAME THESE TWO BIG HITS BELOW BY *ABBA,* THE INTERNATIONALLY KNOWN GROUP FROM SWEDEN.
ONE, ABOUT THAT SEVENTEEN YEAR OLD GIRL WHO LOVED TO DANCE WHEN THE MOOD WAS RIGHT BUT NOT NECESSARILY OF ROYALTY EVEN THOUGH SHE HAD THE TITLE.
TWO, SOMEONE WHO WAS FIGHTING FOR FREEDOM ACROSS THE RIO GRANDE, AND WITH NO RELATION TO ONE MR LAMAS.
1) _______________
2) __________

3. **1 x 2**

ABBA ALSO RECORDED THREE OF THE FOUR HITS BELOW. WHICH ONE UNFORTUNATELY WAS **NOT** THEIRS?
A) KNOWING ME, KNOWING YOU
B) TAKE A CHANCE ON ME
C) THE NAME OF THE GAME
D) SILLY LOVE SONGS

4. **1 x 2**

MECO MONARDO WITH *THE CANTINA BAND* HAD THIS INSTRUMENTAL MOVIE THEME HIT STARRING MARK HAMILL, CARRIE FISHER AND HARRISON FORD THAT FEATURED SPACE TRAVELS AND OTHER GALAXIES. NAME IT.

____

5. **1 x 2**

GILBERT O'SULLIVAN, THE IRISH LAD, RECORDED A TOP OF THE CHARTS HIT SONG ABOUT BEING ALONE ONCE MORE.
A) ALL ALONE AM I
B) ALONE AGAIN (NATURALLY)
C) MR LONELY
D) ALL BY MYSELF

6. **1 x 2**

GILBERT O'SULLIVAN HAD ANOTHER ABOUT WHAT HE TOLD HIS DOG OVER AND OVER AND THOUGH IT WAS BAD HE HAD NO INTENTIONS OF PUTTING IT OUT FOR GOOD. WHAT WAS THAT OTHER HIT?
A) ME AND YOU AND A DOG NAMED BOO
B) YAKETY YAK
C) GET DOWN
D) OVER AND OVER

7. **1 x 2**

'*SHOCKING BLUE*', THE DUTCH SINGERS, CHARTED A SONG THAT HAD THE SAME TITLE TO ONE RECORDED BY *FRANKIE AVALON* IN THE 50'S BUT WITH DIFFERENT LYRICS. ALSO CHARTED BY *BANANARAMA* IN THE LATE 80'S. NAME THIS PLANET TITLED SONG.

 ____

8. **1 x 2**

THE TEE SET, A ONE HIT WONDER BAND, RECORDED WHAT FRENCH TITLED SONG BELOW ABOUT THAT CHILD OF NATURE WHO HE ADORES AND THE ANSWER OF HIS PRAYERS?

A) LADY MARMALADE
B) BON APETITE
C) MA BELLE AMIE
D) MY CHERIE AMOUR

9. **1 x 2**

THE CHAKACHAS, ALSO A ONE HIT WONDER STUDIO GROUP, RECORDED THIS PROVOCATIVE SONG BELOW ABOUT A CERTAIN FEVER. IN THE SONG YOU CAN HEAR PEOPLE MOANING. WHAT WAS THAT PROVOCATIVE SONG?

A) FEVER
B) JUNGLE FEVER
C) PILLOW TALK
D) LAST NIGHT

10. **1 x 2**

LITTLE RIVER BAND, THE AUSTRALIAN GROUP, RECORDED A SONG ABOUT LOSING TO THE QUEEN OF HEARTS BECAUSE HE'S GOT NO LUCK WHEN IT COMES TO LOVE. LONELINESS DRIVES HIM INSANE BUT HE FIGHTS ON TO OVERCOME HIS SADNESS.

A) THE LOVE I LOST (PART 1)
B) LONESOME LOSER
C) LOST WITHOUT YOUR LOVE
D) LONELY BOY

11. **2 x 2**

LITTLE RIVER BAND HAD TWO OTHER BIG HITS BELOW. NAME THEM
ONE, BY LISTENING TO OUR FAVORITE SONGS IT WILL HELP BRING BACK MEMORIES GONE BY.
TWO, ABOUT HOW SPECIAL SHE IS TO HIM, AND BEING THERE WHEN HE NEEDED SOMEONE.

1) ____________________
2) ________

12. **1 x 2**

HARRY CHAPIN, THE SINGER/SONGWRITER AND HUMANITARIAN GAINED HIS INITIAL STARDOM IN 1972 WITH THE SONG "TAXI". NAME THE OTHER, A TOP OF THE CHARTS HIT SONG TWO YEARS LATER ABOUT WHAT WAS IN THE CRADLE.

____

13. **1 x 2**

BOB DYLAN SCORED ONCE AGAIN WITH THIS BIG HEAVEN HIT SONG BELOW ABOUT WHAT HE FELT AND THE REASON FOR WANTING THAT BADGE OFF.

A) HEAVEN MUST BE MISSING AN ANGEL
B) HEAVEN ON EARTH
C) KNOCKIN' ON HEAVEN'S DOOR
D) HEAVEN IS A PLACE ON EARTH

14. **1 x 2**

HOT BUTTER, TRUE NAME STAN FREE, WAS A ONE HIT WONDER STUDIO MUSICIAN WHO CHARTED THIS INSTRUMENTAL NUMBER BELOW FEATURING POPPING SOUNDS?

A) BREAD AND BUTTER
B) ICICLES AND POPSICLES
C) POPCORN
D) PATA PATA

15. **1 x 2**

FERRANTE & TEICHER, THE TWO PIANISTS, HAD A POPULAR THEME SONG FOR A MOVIE OF THE SAME NAME STARRING DUSTIN HOFFMAN AND JON VOIGHT. WHAT WAS THAT POPULAR THEME SONG CALLED?

A) RHINESTONE COWBOY
B) MIDNIGHT COWBOY
C) URBAN COWBOY
D) A COWBOY'S WORK IS NEVER DONE

16. **1 x 2**

PRATT & MCCLAIN CHARTED A SONG THAT BECAME THE NEW THEME FOR A TV SITCOM THAT ORIGINALLY FEATURED *BILL HALEY*'S "(WE'RE GONNA) ROCK AROUND THE CLOCK" AS IT'S THEME. CHOOSE THE NEW SONG FOR THAT HAPPY SHOW BELOW.

A) THE WONDER YEARS
B) THE ROCKFORD FILES
C) THEME FROM S.W.A.T.
D) HAPPY DAYS

17. **1 x 2**

MARVIN HAMLISCH HAD WHAT INSTRUMENTAL HIT THAT WAS FEATURED IN THE MOVIE 'THE STING' IN THE EARLY 70'S ABOUT A PERFORMER STARRING PAUL NEWMAN AND ROBERT REDFORD?

A) RAINDROPS KEEP FALLIN' ON MY HEAD
B) MY BABY MUST BE A MAGICIAN
C) THE ENTERTAINER
D) MR BOJANGLES

18. **1 x 2**

"THE STREAK" WAS A NOVELTY SONG ABOUT A UNIQUE MAN WHO WORE NO CLOTHING AND WOULD RUN BY GIVING ALL A FREE SHOW, THAT WOULD HAVE ETHEL JOINING HIM ON THE CHASE. WHO CHARTED THIS NOVELTY SONG?

A) JIM STAFFORD
B) TOM SMOTHERS
C) RAY STEVENS
D) RICK DEES AND HIS CAST OF IDIOTS

19. **3 x 2**

NAME THESE THREE SONGS BY *SANTANA*, THE POPULAR LATIN AMERICAN BAND LED BY *CARLOS SANTANA*.
ONE, ABOUT A CERTAIN MAGIC LADY.
TWO, ABOUT SOMETHING EVIL THAT SHE HAD TO CORRECT.
THREE, A SONG SUNG TOTALLY IN SPANISH WITH A POPULAR BEAT Y TAN RICO, ASKING HOW IT GOES IN SPANISH.

1) ______________________
2) ____________
3) ______________

20. **1 x 2**

JIM STAFFORD CHARTED THIS NOVELTY SONG ABOUT WHAT MARY LOU TOLD THAT BOY BY THE SWIMMING HOLE IN ORDER TO LOVE HER, ABOUT THE THINGS THAT SHE DIDN'T LIKE.

A) SPIDERS & SNAKES
B) SMOKIN' IN THE BOY'S ROOM
C) CATCH A FALLING STAR
D) UP ON THE ROOF

21. **1 x 2**

THE NEW SEEKERS RECORDED A SONG ABOUT THEIR DESIRE AND TO DO IT IN PROPER HARMONY. THIS SONG WAS ALSO A HIT FOR THE *HILLSIDE SINGERS*. NAME IT BY COMPLETING THE INITIALS PROVIDED BELOW.
I'D L--E T- T---H T-E W---D T- S--G (I- P-----T H-----Y)

22. **1 x 2**

VAN MORRISON, THE POPULAR IRISH LAD, CHARTED A SONG BELOW THAT WAS NOT REFERRING TO A GAME YOU PLAY.
A) SIMON SAYS
B) RED RUBBER BALL
C) DOMINO
D) LOVE THEME FROM 'ROMEO & JULIET'

23. **12 x 2**

MATCH THESE TWELVE POPULAR SONGS WITH THE WORD 'ROCK', ROCKIN' OR 'ROCK 'N' ROLL' WITH THE ARTIST WHO RECORDED IT IN THE 70'S.

	'ROCK' TITLED SONG		**ARTIST**		
1.	ROCK AND ROLL HEAVEN	**A)**	ARETHA FRANKLIN	1.	
2.	ROCKIN' ROBIN	**B)**	THE HUES CORPORATION	2.	
3.	ROCK STEADY	**C)**	KISS	3.	
4.	ROCK AND ROLL LULLABY	**D)**	MICHAEL JACKSON	4.	
5.	ROCK AND ROLL MUSIC	**E)**	DAVID ESSEX	5.	
6.	ROCK ME GENTLY	**F)**	JOHNNY RIVERS	6.	
7.	ROCK ON	**G)**	GEORGE MCCRAE	7.	
8.	ROCK THE BOAT	**H)**	THE RIGHTEOUS BROTHERS	8.	
9.	ROCK YOUR BABY	**I)**	B J THOMAS	9.	
10.	ROCK 'N ME	**J)**	THE BEACH BOYS	10.	
11.	ROCK AND ROLL ALL NITE	**K)**	STEVE MILLER BAND	11.	
12.	ROCKIN' PNEUMONIA AND THE BOOGIE WOOGIE FLU	**L)**	ANDY KIM	12.	

24. **1 x 2**

MARMALADE, A ONE HIT WONDER GROUP OUT OF SCOTLAND, HAD THIS BIG REFLECTIONS HIT SONG BELOW.
A) REFLECTIONS
B) REFLECTIONS OF MY LIFE
C) DOUBLE VISION
D) I CAN SEE CLEARLY NOW

25. **1 x 2**

JUDY COLLINS, THE SINGER/SONGWRITER, CHARTED A HURT SONG ABOUT A BROKEN RELATION WITH ONE PARTNER DOWN ON THE GROUND AND THE OTHER IN MID AIR. SHE DIDN'T THINK IT WAS AMUSING SO WHERE WERE THE CLOWNS? A SONG *FRANK SINATRA* WOULD ALSO RECORD. WHAT WAS THAT HURT SONG?
A) BOTH SIDES NOW
B) STUCK IN THE MIDDLE WITH YOU
C) SEND IN THE CLOWNS
D) SOMETHIN' STUPID

26. **1 x 2**

STEVE MARTIN AND THE TOOT UNCOMMONS HAD A NOVELTY ONE HIT WONDER SONG THAT HE WOULD PERFORM DRESSED UP AS AN EGYPTIAN ON THE 'SATURDAY NIGHT LIVE' TV COMEDY SHOW ABOUT THE BOY KING WITH HIS DONKEY WHO WERE UNEARTHED THAT HAD PEOPLE FLOCKING ON LONG LINES JUST TO SEE. NAME IT

____

27. **1 x 2**

CHEECH & CHONG, THE COMEDY DUO, RECORDED A NOVELTY SPORTS SONG THAT THEY WOULD SHOWCASE ON DON KERSHNER'S 'MIDNIGHT SPECIAL' WEEKLY TV CONCERT TO PROMOTE THE SONG. WHAT WAS THAT SPORTS TITLED SONG?
A) BASKETBALL JONES
B) ROCK AND ROLL PART 2
C) WE WILL ROCK YOU
D) WE ARE THE CHAMPIONS

28. **1 x 2**

OCEAN, ANOTHER ONE HIT WONDER GROUP, CHARTED THIS BIG POPULAR SONG BELOW ABOUT THE MAN FROM GALILEE WHO PERFORMED MIRACLES WITH WATER AND THE SEA. IT WOULD REACH THE NUMBER TWO SPOT ON THE CHARTS. WHAT WAS THAT RUNNERUP CALLED?
A) OH HAPPY DAY
B) AMEN
C) PUT YOUR HAND IN THE HAND
D) AVE MARIA

29. **1 x 2**

THIS OPENING CHANT "OOGA CHAGA" COMES FROM WHAT SONG BY *BLUE SWEDE,* THE GROUP FROM SWEDEN? THE SONG ITSELF, NOT THE CHANT, WAS ORIGINALLY A HIT FOR *B J THOMAS* ABOUT WHAT HE WAS HOOKED ON BECAUSE SHE'S ALL THAT AND MUCH MORE.
A) BABY DON'T GET HOOKED ON ME
B) HOOKED ON A FEELING
C) I JUST CAN'T HELP BELIEVING
D) BOTTLE OF WINE

30. **1 x 2**

THIS POPULAR OLDIES GROUP ACHIEVED A LOT OF FAME FROM THEIR APPEARANCE AT THE 1969 WOODSTOCK FESTIVAL AND IN THE MOVIE SOUNDTRACK OF 'GREASE'. THEY SANG COUNTLESS SONGS OF OTHER ARTISTS OF THE 50'S AND 60'S WITH A TOUCH OF COMEDY. WHO WERE THOSE BOYS?
A) THE COASTERS
B) THE ROBINS
C) THE WONDER WHO
D) SHA NA NA

31. **2 x 2**

THIS MALE ENTERTAINER, SINGER, DANCER, COMEDIAN TURN ACTOR, HAD A HIT IN 1972 FROM THE MOVIE 'WILLY WONKA AND THE CHOCOLATE FACTORY' STARRING GENE WILDER AND JACK ALBERTSON ABOUT THAT MAN WITH THE TREATS. NAME BOTH THE ARTIST AND THAT HIT.
1) __________________
2) _______________

32. **1 x 2**

ERIC WEISSBERG & *STEVE MANDELL,* BANJO PLAYERS, HAD AN INSTRUMENTAL HIT FEATURED IN THE SOUNDTRACK OF 'DELIVERANCE', STARRING BURT REYNOLDS, JON VOIGHT AND NED BEATTY. NAME THIS DUELING HIT.

____

33. **1 x 2**

THE *'EDGAR WINTER GROUP'* RECORDED A POPULAR HIT ABOUT A MONSTER BORIS KARLOFF WOULD OFTEN PLAY.

A) WEREWOLVES IN LONDON
B) PURPLE PEOPLE EATER
C) MONSTER MASH
D) FRANKENSTEIN

TOTAL POINTS. **50 x 2 = 100**

MISC (NOVELTY, FOLK, FOREIGN & INSTRUMENTALS)-BONUS

1.

JOE TEX CHARTED THIS NOVELTY SONG BELOW ABOUT WHO HE CAUGHT SNEAKING AROUND THAT PROMISED HE'D BE NEXT IF SHE EVER BROKE UP WITH HER BOYFRIEND. SHE MADE THE PROMISE SO IT'S TIME THEY START KISSING AND DOING OTHER THINGS LOVERS DO, SO GIVE IT TO HIM NOW.

A) PROMISES, PROMISES
B) WE BELONG TOGETHER
C) I GOTCHA
D) YES, I'M READY

2.

JOE TEX RECORDED ANOTHER ABOUT A GIRL WHO ALMOST BROKE HIS HIP WHILE AT A DISCO WHO HE WAS TRYING TO AVOID. CHOOSE THAT ONE.

A) DISCO INFERNO
B) WE GOTTA GET OUT OF THIS PLACE
C) BOOGIE ON REGGAE WOMAN
D) AIN'T GONNA BUMP NO MORE (WITH NO BIG FAT WOMAN)

3.

FOXY, A LATIN GROUP, CHARTED A DISCO SONG ABOUT WHAT SHE WANTED FROM A GUY THAT WAS EQUALLY WILD AND CRAZY. ONE OF ITS MEMBERS SOUNDED LIKE *RICK JAMES* WITH HIS "SUPER FREAK PT 1" HIT SONG. CHOOSE IT BELOW.

A) LE FREAK
B) GET OFF
C) PLAY THAT FUNKY MUSIC
D) BEST DISCO IN TOWN

4.

"ONE TOKE OVER THE LINE" WAS A HIT SONG FOR WHAT DUO BELOW WHO WERE AT THE RAILROAD STATION WAITING FOR THAT TRAIN RIDE HOME AND ABOUT BEING ONE TOO MANY OVER THE NORM, AS IN ONE TOO MANY DRINKS, ONE TOO MANY ANYTHING?

A) ENGLAND DAN & JOHN FORD COLEY
B) LOGGINS & MESSINA
C) BREWER & SHIPLEY
D) THE RIGHTEOUS BRIOTHERS

MATCH THE LEAD SINGER WITH THE GROUP PT 1 IN THE 70'S

	LEAD SINGER		GROUP	
1	PAUL REVERE	A	THE JACKSON FIVE	1
2	ADAM CLAYTON THOMAS	B	THE TEMPTATIONS	2
3	MICK JAGGER	C	HAROLD MELVIN AND THE BLUE NOTES	3
4	KENNY ROGERS	D	THE FOUR SEASONS	4
5	JAY BLACK	E	BLONDIE	5
6	LEVI STUBBS	F	CHICAGO	6
7	LIONEL RICHIE	G	THE SUNSHINE BAND	7
8	DAVID GATES	H	THE RAIDERS	8
9	TEDDY PENDERGRASS	I	THE MEDICINE SHOW	9
10	STEVE TYLER	J	THE PIPS	10
11	JIM MORRISON	K	WINGS	11
12	DENNIS EDWARDS	L	THE FIRST EDITION	12
13	STING (GORDON SUMNER)	M	THE FAMILY STONE	13
14	MICHAEL JACKSON	N	THE ROLLING STONES	14
15	FRANKIE VALLI	O	BLOOD, SWEAT & TEARS	15
16	PATTI LABELLE	P	LABELLE	16
17	FREDDY MERCURY	Q	COMMODORES	17
18	DEBRAH HARRY	R	THE AMERICANS	18
19	KC	S	THE PARTRIDGE FAMILY	19
20	SYLVESTER (SLY) STEWART	T	BREAD	20
21	GLADYS KNIGHT	U	THE DOORS	21
22	DR HOOK	V	AEROSMITH	22
23	DAVID CASSIDY	W	THE FOUR TOPS	23
24	PETER CETERA	X	QUEEN	24
25	PAUL MCCARTNEY	Y	THE POLICE	25

TOTAL POINTS. 25 x 4 = 100

MATCH THE GROUP WITH THEIR SONG PT 1 IN THE 70'S

	GROUP		SONG	
1	THE JACKSON FIVE	A	AIN'T NO WOMAN (LIKE THE ONE I'VE GOT)	1
2	THE TEMPTATIONS	B	ROXANNE	2
3	HAROLD MELVIN AND THE BLUE NOTES	C	BROWN SUGAR	3
4	THE FOUR SEASONS	D	I THINK I LOVE YOU	4
5	BLONDIE	E	EASY	5
6	CHICAGO	F	WE WILL ROCK YOU	6
7	THE SUNSHINE BAND	G	SUGAR DADDY	7
8	THE RAIDERS	H	LADY MARMALADE	8
9	THE MEDICINE SHOW	I	LOVE HER MADLY	9
10	THE PIPS	J	HEART OF GLASS	10
11	WINGS	K	WALKIN' IN THE RAIN	11
12	THE FIRST EDITION	L	HI-DE-HO	12
13	THE FAMILY STONE	M	WALK THIS WAY	13
14	THE ROLLING STONES	N	INDIAN RESERVATION	14
15	BLOOD, SWEAT & TEARS	O	PAPA WAS A ROLLIN' STONE	15
16	LABELLE	P	MAKE IT WITH YOU	16
17	COMMODORES	Q	THE COVER OF 'ROLLING STONE'	17
18	THE AMERICANS	R	THE LOVE I LOST (PART 1)	18
19	THE PARTRIDGE FAMILY	S	DECEMBER, 1963 (OH, WHAT A NIGHT)	19
20	BREAD	T	BOOGIE SHOES	20
21	THE DOORS	U	FAMILY AFFAIR	21
22	AEROSMITH	V	SILLY LOVE SONGS	22
23	THE FOUR TOPS	W	SOMETHING'S BURNING	23
24	QUEEN	X	IF I WERE YOUR WOMAN	24
25	THE POLICE	Y	IF YOU LEAVE ME NOW	25
			TOTAL POINTS.	25 x 4 = 100

MATCH THE LEAD SINGER WITH THE GROUP PT II IN THE 70'S

	LEAD SINGER		GROUP	
1	TONY ORLANDO	A	RADIO	1
2	JAMES (JT) TAYLOR	B	EAGLES	2
3	JOHN LENNON	C	EAGLES	3
4	BURTON CUMMINGS	D	CREEDENCE CLEARWATER REVIVAL	4
5	DON HENLEY	E	FOREIGNER	5
6	GLENN FREY	F	KOOL & THE GANG	6
7	BOB SEGER	G	PLASTIC ONO BAND	7
8	LOU GRAMM	H	THE SILVER BULLET BAND	8
9	JOHN FOGERTY	I	THE GUESS WHO	9
10	RAY PARKER JR	J	DAWN	10

TOTAL POINTS. 10 x 10 = 100

70/26

MATCH THE GROUP WITH THEIR SONG PT II IN THE 70'S

	GROUP		SONG	
1	RAYDIO	A	AMERICAN WOMAN	1
2	EAGLES	B	FEELS LIKE THE FIRST TIME	2
3	EAGLES	C	JUNGLE BOOGIE	3
4	CREEDENCE CLEARWATER REVIVAL	D	OLD TIME ROCK & ROLL	4
5	FOREIGNER	E	KNOCK THREE TIMES	5
6	KOOL & THE GANG	F	ONE OF THESE NIGHTS	6
7	PLASTIC ONO BAND	G	IMAGINE	7
8	THE SILVER BULLET BAND	H	LYIN' EYES	8
9	THE GUESS WHO	I	YOU CAN'T CHANGE THAT	9
10	DAWN	J	TRAVELIN' BAND	10

TOTAL POINTS. 10 x 10 = 100

MATCH THE DUO'S AND ALSO THEIR HIT SONG PT 1 IN THE 70'S

	1ST DUO		2ND DUO		SONG		
1	OLIVIA NEWTON-JOHN	A	RICHARD CARPENTER	AA	REUNITED	1	,
2	DIONNE WARWICK	B	BILLY DAVIS JR	BB	RICH GIRL	2	,
3	JOHNNY MATHIS	C	JIM MESSINA	CC	(YOU'RE) HAVING MY BABY	3	,
4	PAUL ANKA	D	DIANA ROSS	DD	AIN'T NO STOPPIN' US NOW	4	,
5	NEIL DIAMOND	E	CHER	EE	MOCKINGBIRD	5	,
6	DONNA SUMMER	F	STEVIE NICKS	FF	WHENEVER I CALL YOU FRIEND	6	,
7	ELTON JOHN	G	LINDA MCCARTNEY	GG	A COWBOYS WORK IS NEVER DONE	7	,
8	PEACHES	H	DONNY HATHAWAY	HH	CECILA	8	,
9	DARYL HALL	I	WHITEHEAD	II	NO MORE TEARS (ENOUGH IS ENOUGH)	9	,
10	MARILYN MCCOO	J	WAR	JJ	TOO MUCH, TOO LITTLE, TOO LATE	10	,
11	CAPTAIN	K	BOBBY HATFIELD	KK	WHERE IS THE LOVE	11	,
12	KAREN CARPENTER	L	HERB	LL	MY MISTAKE WAS TO LOVE YOU	12	,
13	PAUL MCCARTNEY	M	ODIA COATES	MM	PLEASE MR POSTMAN	13	,
14	PAUL SIMON	N	CROFTS	NN	YOUR MAMA DON'T DANCE	14	,
15	ROBERTA FLACK	O	ART GARFUNKEL	OO	THEN CAME YOU	15	,
16	MCFADDEN	P	MARIE	PP	SPILL THE WINE	16	,
17	MARVIN GAYE	Q	BARBRA STREISAND	QQ	YOU DON'T HAVE TO BE A STAR (TO BE IN MY SHOW)	17	,
18	KENNY LOGGINS	R	BARBRA STREISAND	RR	YOU DON'T BRING ME FLOWERS	18	,
19	ERIC BURDON	S	DENIECE WILLIAMS	SS	YOU'RE THE ONE THAT I WANT	19	,
20	SONNY BONO	T	SPINNERS	TT	LOVE WILL KEEP US TOGETHER	20	,
21	BILL MEDLEY	U	KIKI DEE	UU	DON'T GO BREAKING MY HEART	21	,
22	JAMES TAYLOR	V	TENNILLE	VV	I'M LEAVING IT ALL UP TO YOU	22	,
23	SEALS	W	JOHN OATES	WW	UNCLE ALBERT	23	,
24	KENNY LOGGINS	X	CARLY SIMON	XX	ROCK AND ROLL HEAVEN	24	,
25	DONNY	Y	JOHN TRAVOLTA	YY	GET CLOSER	25	,

TOTAL POINTS. 50 x 2 = 100

70/28

MATCH THE DUOS AND ALSO THEIR HIT SONG PT II IN THE 70'S

	1ST DUO		2ND DUO		SONG		
1	JOHN OATES	A	TEICHER	AA	MIDNIGHT COWBOY	1	,
2	CROFTS	B	SONNY BONO	BB	SHAKE YOUR GROOVE THING	2	,
3	FERRANTE	C	CAPTAIN	CC	BASKETBALL JONES	3	,
4	CHEECH	D	MCCLAIN	DD	SHE'S GONE	4	,
5	ERIC WEISSBERG	E	JOHN FORD COLEY	EE	ALL I EVER NEED IS YOU	5	.
6	ENGLAND DAN	F	PEACHES	FF	SHOP AROUND	6	,
7	PRATT	G	SEALS	GG	HAPPY DAYS	7	,
8	CHER	H	DARYL HALL	HH	SUMMER BREEZE	8	,
9	TENNILLE	I	CHONG	II	DUELING BANJOS	9	,
10	HERB	J	STEVE MANDELL	JJ	I'D REALLY LOVE TO SEE YOU TONIGHT	10	,

TOTAL POINTS. 20 x 5 = 100

MATCH THE MOVIE/TV SHOW SONG WITH THE ARTIST PT 1 IN THE 70'S

	SONG		ARTIST	
1	GREASE	A	BARBRA STREISAND	1
2	NIGHT FEVER	B	BEE GEES	2
3	CAR WASH	C	YVONNE ELLIMAN	3
4	I AM WOMAN	D	DONNA SUMMER	4
5	BEN	E	ROBERTA FLACK	5
6	THEME FROM SHAFT	F	BARBRA STREISAND	6
7	THE WAY WE WERE	G	CARLY SIMON	7
8	IF I CAN'T HAVE YOU	H	MICHAEL JACKSON	8
9	YOU'RE THE ONE THAT I WANT	I	B J THOMAS	9
10	THE MORNING AFTER	J	RHYTHM HERITAGE	10
11	THEME FROM 'MAHOGANY' (DO THEY KNOW WHERE YOU'RE GOING TO)	K	SHIRLEY BASSEY	11
12	STAYIN' ALIVE	L	BEE GEES	12
13	THE FIRST TIME EVER I SAW YOUR FACE	M	JOHN SEBASTIAN	13
14	NOBODY DOES IT BETTER	N	WINGS	14
15	LOVE THEME FROM 'A STAR IS BORN'	O	THE CARPENTERS	15
16	LAST DANCE	P	HELEN REDDY	16
17	RAINDROPS KEEP FALLIN' ON MY HEAD	Q	ISAAC HAYES	17
18	THE MAIN EVENT/FIGHT	R	FRANKIE VALLI	18
19	HAPPY DAYS	S	MAUREEN MCGOVERN	19
20	LIVE AND LET DIE	T	BARBRA STREISAND	20
21	WELCOME BACK	U	OLIVIA NEWTON-JOHN	21
22	THEME FROM 'S.W.A.T.'	V	ROSE ROYCE	22
23	HOPELESSLY DEVOTED TO YOU	W	DIANA ROSS	23
24	FOR ALL WE KNOW	X	JOHN TRAVOLTA & OLIVIA NEWTON-JOHN	24
25	DIAMONDS ARE FOREVER	Y	PRATT & MCCLAIN	25

TOTAL POINTS. 25 x 4 = 100

70/30

MATCH THE MOVIE/TV SHOW SONG WITH THE ARTIST PT II IN THE 70'S

	SONG		ARTIST	
1	HOW DEEP IS YOUR LOVE	A	DEBBY BOONE	1
2	LET'S DO IT AGAIN	B	KEITH CARRADINE	2
3	STAR WAR'S THEME	C	BEE GEES	3
4	I GOT A NAME	D	CURTIS MAYFIELD	4
5	BARRETTA'S THEME (KEEP YOUR EYE ON THE SPARROW)	E	BARRY MANILOW	5
6	YOU LIGHT UP MY LIFE	F	RHYTHM HERITAGE	6
7	I'M EASY	G	THE STAPLE SINGERS	7
8	READY TO TAKE A CHANCE AGAIN	H	MECO MONARDO/CANTINA BAND	8
9	MAKING OUR DREAMS COME TRUE	I	CYNDI GRECCO	9
10	SUPERFLY	J	JIM CROCE	10

TOTAL POINTS. 10 x 10 = 100

MATCH THE DISCO HIT WITH THE ARTIST PT 1

	SONG		ARTIST	
1	THE HUSTLE	A	DONNA SUMMER	1
2	FLY, ROBIN, FLY	B	DIANA ROSS	2
3	NIGHT FEVER	C	A TASTE OF HONEY	3
4	DANCING MACHINE	D	SILVER CONVENTION	4
5	CAR WASH	E	AMII STEWART	5
6	LADIES NIGHT	F	TAVARES	6
7	I LOVE THE NIGHT LIFE	G	LIPPS, INC	7
8	TURN THE BEAT AROUND	H	WALTER MURPHY & THE BIG APPLE BAND	8
9	LOVE HANGOVER	I	VAN MCCOY & THE SOUL CITY SYMPHONY ORCHESTRA	9
10	DISCO LADY	J	KOOL & THE GANG	10
11	KNOCK ON WOOD	K	K C AND THE SUNSHINE BAND	11
12	FUNKYTOWN	L	BEE GEES	12
13	A FIFTH OF BEETHOVEN	M	THE JACKSON FIVE	13
14	IF I CAN'T HAVE YOU	N	ALICIA BRIDGES	14
15	HEART OF GLASS	O	ROSE ROYCE	15
16	DISCO INFERNO	P	JOHNNIE TAYLOR	16
17	YOU SHOULD BE DANCING	Q	EVELYN CHAMPAYNE KING	17
18	SHAME	R	YVONNE ELLIMAN	18
19	I'M YOUR BOOGIE MAN	S	HEATWAVE	19
20	DISCO DUCK (PART 1)	T	BEE GEES	20
21	MORE THAN A WOMAN	U	THE TRAMMPS	21
22	MORE THAN A WOMAN	V	BLONDIE	22
23	HOT STUFF	W	RICK DEES AND HIS CAST OF IDIOTS	23
24	BOOGIE NIGHTS	X	BEE GEES	24
25	BOOGIE OOGIE OOGIE	Y	VICKI SUE ROBINSON	25

TOTAL POINTS. 25 x 4 = 100

70/32

MATCH THE DISCO HIT WITH THE ARTIST PT II

	SONG		ARTIST	
1	THAT'S THE WAY (I LIKE IT)	A	ANDY GIBB	1
2	BEST OF MY LOVE	B	GEORGE MCCRAE	2
3	GET DOWN TONIGHT	C	SISTER SLEDGE	3
4	ROCK YOUR BABY	D	PEACHES & HERB	4
5	NEVER CAN SAY GOODBYE	E	THE HUES CORPORATION	5
6	WE ARE FAMILY	F	MCFADDEN & WHITEHEAD	6
7	CELEBRATION	G	DONNA SUMMER	7
8	FRESH	H	GLORIA GAYNOR	8
9	UPSIDE DOWN	I	THE EMOTIONS	9
10	TAKE YOUR TIME (DO IT RIGHT)	J	SISTER SLEDGE	10
11	SHADOW DANCING	K	MARVIN GAYE	11
12	ROCK THE BOAT	L	KOOL & THE GANG	12
13	(SHAKE, SHAKE, SHAKE) SHAKE YOUR BOOTY	M	VILLAGE PEOPLE	13
14	GOT TO GIVE IT UP (PART 1)	N	NU SHOOZ	14
15	I WILL SURVIVE	O	VILLAGE PEOPLE	15
16	AIN'T NO STOPPIN' US NOW	P	K C AND THE SUNSHINE BAND	16
17	LOVE MACHINE (PART 1)	Q	DIANA ROSS	17
18	MORE, MORE, MORE (PART 1)	R	K C AND THE SUNSHINE BAND	18
19	I CAN'T WAIT	S	THELMA HOUSTON	19
20	HE'S THE GREATEST DANCER	T	THE MIRACLES	20
21	SHAKE YOUR GROOVE THING	U	ANDREA TRUE CONNECTION	21
22	MACHO MAN	V	K C AND THE SUNSHINE BAND	22
23	BAD GIRLS	W	KOOL & THE GANG	23
24	Y.M.C.A.	X	GLORIA GAYNOR	24
25	DON'T LEAVE ME THIS WAY	Y	THE S.O.S. BAND	25

TOTAL POINTS. 25 x 4 = 100

70/33

MATCH THE DISCO HIT WITH THE ARTIST PT III

	SONG		ARTIST	
1	SHAME, SHAME, SHAME	A	CHIC	1
2	I FEEL LOVE	B	ABBA	2
3	PLEASE DON'T GO	C	BARRY WHITE	3
4	IT ONLY TAKES A MINUTE	D	SHIRLEY AND COMPANY	4
5	BOOGIE SHOES	E	TAVARES	5
6	HEAVEN MUST BE MISSING AN ANGEL (PART 1)	F	K C AND THE SUNSHINE BAND	6
7	LE FREAK	G	TAVARES	7
8	DANCING QUEEN	H	DONNA SUMMER	8
9	THE BEST DISCO IN TOWN	I	THE RITCHIE FAMILY	9
10	YOU'RE THE FIRST, THE LAST, MY EVERYTHING	J	K C AND THE SUNSHINE BAND	10

TOTAL POINTS. 10 x 10 = 100

MATCH THE INSTRUMENTAL HIT WITH THE ARTIST IN THE 70'S

	INSTRUMENTAL		ARTIST	
1	GONNA FLY NOW (THEME FROM ROCKY)	A	AVERAGE WHITE BAND	1
2	THEME FROM 'S.W.A.T.'	B	HOT BUTTER	2
3	STAR WARS THEME	C	DEODATO	3
4	LOVE'S THEME	D	BILLY PRESTON	4
5	A FIFTH OF BEETHOVEN	E	MARVIN HAMLISCH	5
6	FRANKENSTEIN	F	MECO MONARDO/CANTINA BAND	6
7	FEELS SO GOOD	G	BILLY PRESTON	7
8	PICK UP THE PIECES	H	LOVE UNLIMITED ORCHESTRA	8
9	THE ENTERTAINER	I	B.T. EXPRESS	9
10	DUELING BANJOS	J	EDGAR WINTER GROUP	10
11	MIDNIGHT COWBOY	K	HERB ALPERT	11
12	POPCORN	L	CHUCK MANGIONE	12
13	THEME FROM 'THE ROCKFORD FILES'	M	RHYTHM HERITAGE	13
14	JUNGLE FEVER	N	ERIC WEISSBERG & STEVE MANDELL	14
15	SPACE RACE	O	WALTER MURPHY & THE BIG APPLE BAND	15
16	ALSO SPRACH ZARATHUSTRA (2001)	P	BILL CONTI	16
17	RISE	Q	FRANK MILLS	17
18	OUTA-SPACE	R	FERRANTE & TEICHER	18
19	EXPRESS	S	MIKE POST & HIS ORCHESTRA	19
20	MUSIC BOX DANCER	T	THE CHAKACHAS	20
			TOTAL POINTS.	20 x 5 = 100

(70'S ANSWER SHEETS)

70/1 ELVIS

1. 1) BURNING LOVE
   2) DON'T CRY DADDY
   3) KENTUCKY RAIN
   4) THE WONDER OF YOU
   5) MY WAY
   6) WAY DOWN
2. C. GRACELAND
3. D. YOU WERE ALWAYS ON MY MIND
4. E. DON'T IT MAKE MY BROWN EYES BLUE
5. E. ALL OF THE ABOVE

70/2 THE FAB FOUR

1. 1. YOU'RE SIXTEEN
   2. NO NO SONG
   3. PHOTOGRAPH
   4. ONLY YOU
2. 1) UNCLE ALBERT
   2) LIVE AND LET DIE
   3) BAND ON THE RUN
   4) JUNIOR'S FARM
   5) LISTEN TO WHAT THE MAN SAID
   6) SILLY LOVE SONGS
   7) LET 'EM IN
   8) WITH A LITTLE LUCK
   9) GOODNIGHT TONIGHT
   10) MAYBE I'M AMAZED
   11) MY LOVE
3. C. IMAGINE
4. B. LET IT BE
5. A. PAUL MCCARTNEY & LINDA EASTMAN
6. C. GOT TO GET YOU INTO MY LIFE
7. C. APPLE RECORDS
8. C. MY SWEET LORD
9. B. GIVE ME LOVE (GIVE ME PEACE ON EARTH)
10. C. THE LONG AND WINDING ROAD
11. RINGO STARR
12. B. RECORD PRODUCER

70/3 THE REST OF THE BRITISH INVASION-QUIZ # 1

1. C. AFTER THE LOVIN'
2. B. WINTER WORLD OF LOVE
3. 1) CROCODILE ROCK
   2) DANIEL
   3) GOODBYE YELLOW BRICK ROAD
   4) BENNY AND THE JETS
   5) DON'T LET THE SUN GO DOWN ON ME
   6) THE BITCH IS BACK
   7) LUCY IN THE SKY WITH DIAMONDS
   8) ISLAND GIRL
   9) SOMEONE SAVED MY LIFE TONIGHT
   10) PHILADELPHIA FREEDOM
   11) ROCKET MAN
   12) MAMA CAN'T BUY YOU LOVE

13) SATURDAY NIGHT'S ALRIGHT FOR FIGHTING
14) SORRY SEEMS TO BE THE HARDEST WORD
15) DON'T GO BREAKING MY HEART

4. A. HITCHIN' A RIDE
5. A. THE MOODY BLUES
6. 1) HOPELESSLY DEVOTED TO YOU
   2) I HONESTLY LOVE YOU
   3) HAVE YOU NEVER BEEN MELLOW
   4) A LITTLE MORE LOVE
7. 1) YOU'RE THE ONE THAT I WANT
   2) SUMMER NIGHTS
8. 1) MAGGIE MAY
   2) YOU'RE IN MY HEART (THE FINAL ACCLAIM)
   3) DA YA THINK I'M SEXY?
   4) TONIGHT'S THE NIGHT (GONNA BE ALRIGHT)
9. C. FEELINGS
10. 1) HOW CAN YOU MEND A BROKEN HEART
    2) LONELY DAYS
    3) JIVE TALKING
    4) NIGHTS ON BROADWAY
    5) FANNY (BE TENDER WITH MY LOVE)
    6) YOU SHOULD BE DANCING
    7) LOVE SO RIGHT
    8) HOW DEEP IS YOUR LOVE
    9) STAYING ALIVE
    10) NIGHT FEVER
    11) TOO MUCH HEAVEN
    12) TRAGEDY
11. 1) I JUST WANT TO BE YOUR EVERYTHING
    2) (LOVE IS) THICKER THAN WATER
    3) SHADOW DANCING
    4) (OUR LOVE) DON'T THROW IT ALL AWAY
12. 1) WE ARE THE CHAMPIONS
    2) WE WILL ROCK YOU
13. B. BOHEMIAN RHAPSODY
14. D. BAD CASE OF LOVING YOU (DOCTOR, DOCTOR)

70/4 THE REST OF THE BRITISH INVASION-QUIZ # 2

1. 1) THE LETTER
   2) YOU ARE SO BEAUTIFUL
   3) DARLING BE HOME SOON
2. SPILL THE WINE
3. A. HOW LONG
4. 1) YOU MAKE ME FEEL LIKE DANCING
   2) LONG TALL GLASSES (I CAN DANCE)
   3) HOW MUCH LOVE
   4) WHEN I NEED YOU
   5) THE SHOW MUST GO ON
5. A. SMOKE ON THE WATER
6. C. SGT. PEPPER'S LONELY HEARTS CLUB BAND
7. C. PETER FRAMPTON
8. A. BLINDED BY THE LIGHT
9. 1) EVIL WOMAN
   2) TELEPHONE LINE
10. C. CAT'S IN THE CRADLE
11. D. YOU SEXY THING
12. D. VIDEO KILLED THE RADIO STAR

13. B. OH ME OH MY (I'M A FOOL FOR YOU BABY)
14. B. DAVID BOWIE
15. B. IN THE SUMMERTIME
16. C. ROXANNE
17. C. THE AIR THAT I BREATHE
18. 1) HE AIN'T HEAVY, HE'S MY BROTHER
    2) LONG COOL WOMAN (IN A BLACK DRESS)
19. 1) STAIRWAY TO HEAVEN
    2) WHOLE LOTTA LOVE
20. A. I'M NOT IN LOVE
21. C. THE THINGS WE DO FOR LOVE
22. B. HERE COMES THAT RAINY DAY FEELING AGAIN
23. 1) I SHOT THE SHERIFF
    2) LAY DOWN SALLY
    3) WONDERFUL TONIGHT
    4) PROMISES
24. C. CAN'T GET ENOUGH
25. B. THE WHO
26. A. IT'S ONLY ROCK 'N ROLL (BUT I LIKE IT)
27. E. LET IT BE
28. D. DEVIL WOMAN
29. C. THE BABYS
30. B. BEACH BABY
31. A. JIMMY PAGE
32. C. THE ROLLING STONES
33. C. THE NIGHT CHICAGO DIED
34. 1) ANOTHER SATURDAY NIGHT
    2) PEACE TRAIN
    3) WILD WORLD
    4) MORNING HAS BROKEN
35. C. ALL RIGHT NOW

70/5 THE REST OF THE BRITISH INVASION-QUIZ # 3

1. B. IT NEVER RAINS IN SOUTHERN CALIFORNIA
2. B. MY BABY LOVES LOVIN'
3. B. LOVE GROWS (WHERE MY ROSEMARY GOES)
4. A. POP MUZIK
5. A. ROCK ON
6. C. ERIC CLAPTON
7. C. SKY HIGH
8. D. I'VE GOT THE MUSIC IN ME
9. C. ROCK AND ROLL PART II
10. B. GOT A HOLD ON ME

THE REST OF THE BRITISH INVASION-BONUS

1. D. FOOL (IF YOU THINK IT'S OVER)

70/6 MOTOWN ROCKERS-QUIZ # 1

1. 1) COMMODORES
   2) BRICK HOUSE
   3) THREE TIMES A LADY
   4) SAIL ON
   5) STILL
2. B. IT'S A SHAME
3. 1) KEEP ON TRUCKIN' (PART 1)

2) EDDIE KENDRICKS
4. A. BOOGIE DOWN
5. 1) THE TRACKS OF MY TEARS
2) THE TEARS OF A CLOWN
6. C. WAR
7. 1) BALL OF CONFUSION (THAT'S WHAT THE WORLD IS TODAY)
2) JUST MY IMAGINATION (RUNNING AWAY WITH ME)
3) PAPA WAS A ROLLIN' STONE
4) PSYCHEDELIC SHACK
8. B. WALK AWAY FROM LOVE
9. 1) I WANT YOU BACK
2) ABC
3) I'LL BE THERE
4) NEVER CAN SAY GOODBYE
5) MAMA'S PEARL
6) SUGAR DADDY
7) DANCING MACHINE
8) LITTLE BITTY PRETTY ONE
9) THE LOVE YOU SAVE
10. 1) MARVIN GAYE
2) WHAT'S GOING ON
3) LET'S GET IT ON
11. B. THE BELLS
12. C. DON'T LEAVE ME THIS WAY
13. 1) AIN'T NO MOUNTAIN HIGH ENOUGH
2) DO YOU KNOW WHERE YOU'RE GOING TO
3) LOVE HANGOVER
4) REACH OUT AND TOUCH (SOMEBODY'S HAND)
5) GOOD MORNING HEARTACHE
6) LAST TIME I SAW HIM
7) TOUCH ME IN THE MORNING
14. 1) YOU ARE THE SUNSHINE OF MY LIFE
2) SIR DUKE
3) ISN'T SHE LOVELY
4) SIGNED, SEALED, DELIVERED, I'M YOURS
15. D. BILLY GRIFFIN
16. 1) JACKIE JACKSON
2) JERMAINE JACKSON
3) TITO JACKSON
4) MARLON JACKSON
5) MICHAEL JACKSON
17. D. I JUST WANT TO CELEBRATE
18. DADDY'S HOME

70/7 MOTOWN ROCKERS-QUIZ # 2

1. B,BB. THE TEMPTATIONS, RARE EARTH
2. D,II. THE SUPREMES, VANILLA FUDGE
3. C,DD. THE MIRACLES, LINDA RONSTADT
4. F,JJ. THE MIRACLES, CAPTAIN & TENNILLE
5. G,GG. MARVIN GAYE, JAMES TAYLOR
6. E,AA. THE MARVELETTES, THE CARPENTERS
7. J,EE. MARTHA REEVES & THE VANDELLAS, LINDA RONSTADT
8. A,FF. THE JACKSON FIVE, GLORIA GAYNOR
9. I,CC. THE TEMPTATIONS, RARE EARTH
10. H,HH. THE MIRACLES, LINDA RONSTADT

70/8 MOTOWN ROCKERS-QUIZ # 3

1. D. LOVE MACHINE (PART 1)
2. B. SMILING FACES SOMETIMES
3. 1) BEN
   2) DON'T STOP 'TIL YOU GET ENOUGH
   3) GOT TO BE THERE
   4) ROCKIN' ROBIN
4. B. UP THE LADDER TO THE ROOF
5. 1) NEITHER ONE OF US (WANTS TO BE THE FIRST TO SAY GOODBYE)
   2) IF I WERE YOUR WOMAN
   3) HELP ME MAKE IT THROUGH THE NIGHT

70/9 R&B ROCKERS-QUIZ # 1

1. C. GROOVY SITUATION
2. 1) I'M GONNA LOVE YOU JUST A LITTLE MORE BABY
   2) CAN'T GET ENOUGH OF YOUR LOVE, BABE
   3) YOU'RE THE FIRST, THE LAST, MY EVERYTHING
   4) WHAT AM I GONNA DO WITH YOU
   5) NEVER, NEVER GONNA GIVE YA UP
   6) I'VE FOUND SOMEONE
   7) I'VE GOT SO MUCH TO GIVE
3. C. COULD IT BE I'M FALLING IN LOVE
4. A. (IF LOVING YOU IS WRONG) I DON'T WANT TO BE RIGHT
5. B. WHEN WILL I SEE YOU AGAIN
6. B. KISS AND SAY GOODBYE
7. A. I'LL NEVER FIND ANOTHER (FIND ANOTHER LIKE YOU)
8. A. EVERYBODY PLAYS THE FOOL
9. C. JUST DON'T WANT TO BE LONELY
10. LOVE ON A TWO WAY STREET
11. D. BRING THE BOYS HOME
12. B. BAND OF GOLD
13. C. KUNG FU FIGHTING
14. 1) IF YOU DON'T KNOW ME BY NOW
    2) THE LOVE I LOST (PART 1)
    3) BAD LUCK (PART 1)
    4) WAKE UP EVERYBODY (PART 1)
15. A. WANT ADS
16. A. BAND OF GOLD
17. D. REUNITED
18. C. SHAKE YOUR GROOVE THING
19. C. LADY MARMALADE
20. 1) NOTHING FROM NOTHING
    2) WILL IT GO ROUND IN CIRCLES
21. A. CLOSE THE DOOR
22. B. FLY, ROBIN, FLY
23. 1) THE FIRST TIME EVER I SAW YOUR FACE
    2) KILLING ME SOFTLY WITH HIS SONG
    3) FEEL LIKE MAKIN' LOVE
    4) THE CLOSER I GET TO YOU
    5) WHERE IS THE LOVE?
    6) YOU'VE GOT A FRIEND
24. 1) AIN'T NO SUNSHINE
    2) LEAN ON ME
    3) USE ME
    4) LOVELY DAY
25. D. PILLOW TALK

26. D. MY DING-A-LING
27. D. FUNKY NASSAU (PARTS 1 & 2)
28. 1) LET'S STAY TOGETHER
    2) OH, PRETTY WOMAN
    3) I'M STILL IN LOVE WITH YOU
    4) HOW DO YOU MEND A BROKEN HEART
    5) FOR THE GOOD TIMES
    6) I CAN'T GET NEXT TO YOU
    7) SIMPLY BEAUTIFUL
    8) LOVE AND HAPPINESS
    9) TIRED OF BEING ALONE
    10) I'M GLAD YOU'RE MINE
29. C. ALWAYS AND FOREVER
30. B. PATCHES
31. B. LOVIN' YOU
32. 1) THANK YOU (FALETTINME BE MICE ELF AGIN)
    2) FAMILY AFFAIR
    3) I WANT TO TAKE YOU HIGHER
    4) EVERYBODY IS A STAR
33. B. ROCK AND ROLL HEAVEN
34. 1) I'LL TAKE YOU THERE
    2) RESPECT YOURSELF
35. B. WHY CAN'T WE LIVE TOGETHER
36. C. HE'S THE GREATEST DANCER
37. B. DISCO INFERNO
38. 1) HOT STUFF
    2) BAD GIRLS
    3) LOVE TO LOVE YOU BABY
    4) LAST DANCE
    5) MACARTHUR PARK
    6) DIM ALL THE LIGHTS
39. 1) OH GIRL
    2) HAVE YOU SEEN HER
40. 1) FREDDY'S DEAD
    2) PUSHERMAN
    3) SUPERFLY
    4) EDDIE YOU SHOULD KNOW BETTER
41. C. GYPSY WOMAN
42. B. CAR WASH
43. B. I WANNA GET NEXT TO YOU
44. D. WE ARE FAMILY
45. B. HE'S THE GREATEST DANCER
46. 1) SPANISH HARLEM
    2) DON'T PLAY THAT SONG
    3) ROCK STEADY
    4) CALL ME
    5) BRIDGE OVER TROUBLED WATERS
    6) DAY DREAMING
    7) YOU'RE ALL I NEED TO GET BY
47. 1) HEAVEN MUST BE MISSING AN ANGEL (PART 1)
    2) IT ONLY TAKES A MINUTE
    3) SHE'S GONE
    4) MORE THAN A WOMAN
48. 1) THE OHIO PLAYERS
    2) FIRE
    3) SKIN TIGHT
49. D. I WILL SURVIVE

70/10 R&B ROCKERS-QUIZ # 2

1. 1) LOVE TRAIN
   2) I LOVE MUSIC (PART 1)
   3) USE TA BE MY GIRL
   4) BACK STABBERS
2. 1) SHINING STAR
   2) SING A SONG
   3) AFTER THE LOVE HAS GONE
   4) GOT TO GET YOU INTO MY LIFE
3. B. SHOW AND TELL
4. C. ROCK YOUR BABY
5. THE SOUND OF PHILADELPHIA
6. A. BOOGIE FEVER
7. A. MR BIG STUFF
8. B. 5-10-15-20 (25-30 YEARS OF LOVE)
9. C. DISCO LADY
10. (IF YOU LET ME MAKE LOVE TO YOU THEN) WHY CAN'T I TOUCH YOU?
11. A. AIN'T NO WOMAN (LIKE THE ONE I'VE GOT)
12. C. OH, BABE, WHAT WOULD YOU SAY?
13. D. ALWAYS AND FOREVER
14. B. BOOGIE NIGHTS
15. B. GIVE ME JUST A LITTLE MORE TIME
16. B. THAT LADY (PARTS 1 & 2)
17. C. DRIFT AWAY
18. 1) GEORGE BENSON
    2) ON BROADWAY
19. C. BEST OF MY LOVE
20. B. MAGGIE MAY
21. 1) ONE OF A KIND (LOVE AFFAIR)
    2) MIGHTY LOVE (PART 1)
    3) THE RUBBERBAND MAN
    4) THEN CAME YOU
22. A. TRYIN' TO LOVE TWO
23. B. I'M DOIN' FINE NOW
24. D. GROOVE ME
25. C. SHAME
26. C. I CAN SEE CLEARLY NOW
27. B. STIR IT UP
28. C. SHADOW DANCING
29. B. TELL ME SOMETHING GOOD
30. C. RING MY BELL
31. B. CLEAN UP WOMAN
32. A. YOU MAKE ME FEEL LIKE DANCING
33. D. ROCK THE BOAT
34. B. YOU'LL NEVER FIND ANOTHER LOVE LIKE MINE
35. A. LADY LOVE
36. A. YOU LITTLE TRUSTMAKER
37. D. DIONNE WARWICK
38. 1) ISAAC HAYES
    2) THEME FROM SHAFT
39. B. BLACK MOSES
40. C. WALKIN' IN THE RAIN WITH THE ONE I LOVE
41. 1) ME AND MRS JONES
    2) BILLY PAUL
42. A. HERE COMES THE SUN
43. C. BOB MARLEY
44. D. TREAT HER LIKE A LADY

45. D. TOO LATE TO TURN BACK NOW
46. D. RIGHT BACK WHERE WE STARTED FROM
47. A. LEAD ME ON
48. C. SUPERNATURAL THING (PART 1)
49. B. BEST DISCO IN TOWN
50. D. HEY THERE LONELY GIRL
51. B. LOVE OR LET ME BE LONELY
52. 1) ONE LESS BELL TO ANSWER
    2) (LAST NIGHT) I DIDN'T GET TO SLEEP AT ALL
    3) NEVER MY LOVE
53. B. KNOCK ON WOOD
54. B. O-O-H CHILD
55. D. THIN LINE BETWEEN LOVE AND HATE
56. 1) THE STYLISTICS
    2) BREAK UP TO MAKE UP
    3) YOU MAKE ME FEEL BRAND NEW
    4) I'M STONE IN LOVE WITH YOU
    5) LET'S PUT IT ALL TOGETHER
    6) YOU ARE EVERYTHING
    7) YOU'LL NEVER GET TO HEAVEN (IF YOU BREAK MY HEART)
57. C. ROCKIN' CHAIR
58. C. BOOGIE OOGIE OOGIE
59. B. SHAME, SHAME, SHAME
60. D. LOVE WON'T LET ME WAIT
61. D. THE NIGHT WON'T LAST FOREVER
62. C. BLUER THAN BLUE
63. C. ANGEL IN YOUR ARMS
64. C. WOMAN TO WOMAN
65. A. GOT TO BE REAL
66. 1) BILLY DAVIS, JR.
    2) MARILYN MCCOO
67. B. THE LOVE WE HAD (STAYS ON MY MIND)
68. D. PROUD MARY
69. 1) THE JACKSON 5
    2) GLORIA GAYNOR
70. B. IN THE RAIN
71. C. WHATCHA SEE IS WHATCHA GET
72. B. THE HUSTLE
73. B. RAINY NIGHT IN GEORGIA
74. B. MISTY BLUE
75. C. NATURAL HIGH
76. A. YOU CAN'T CHANGE THAT
77. D. HAROLD MELVIN AND THE BLUE NOTES
78. C. JOHNNY BRISTOL

70/11 R&B ROCKERS-QUIZ # 3

1. C. WHAT YOU WON'T DO FOR LOVE
2. C. I DO LOVE YOU
3. 1) GLADYS KNIGHT & THE PIPS
   2) MIDNIGHT TRAIN TO GEORGIA
   3) BEST THING THAT EVER HAPPENED TO ME
4. B. TURN BACK THE HANDS OF TIME
5. D. WALKING IN RHYTHM
6. A. DO IT ('TIL YOU'RE SATISFIED)
7. C. NATIVE NEW YORKER
8. D. I'VE FOUND SOMEONE OF MY OWN

70/12 POP ROCKERS-QUIZ # 1

1. 1) IF I CAN'T HAVE YOU
   2) LOVE ME
2. B. HELLO STRANGER
3. D. TOO MUCH, TOO LITTLE, TOO LATE
4. B. DENIECE WILLIAMS
5. 1) CANDIDA
   2) KNOCK THREE TIMES
   3) TIE A YELLOW RIBBON ROUND THE OLE OAK TREE
   4) HE DON'T LOVE YOU (LIKE I LOVE YOU)
   5) CUPID
   6) SAY, HAS ANYBODY SEEN MY SWEET GYPSY ROSE
6. D. ONLY THE STRONG SURVIVE
7. C. HE'S SO FINE
8. A. TORN BETWEEN TWO LOVERS
9. ROY ORBISON
10. 1) MOCKINGBIRD
    2) YOU'RE SO VAIN
    3) NOBODY DOES IT BETTER
    4) YOU BELONG TO ME
    5) THAT'S THE WAY I'VE ALWAYS HEARD IT SHOULD BE
    6) HAVEN'T GOT TIME FOR THE PAIN
    7) ANTICIPATION
11. C. ONE BAD APPLE
12. C. KISS YOU ALL OVER
13. B. DADDY DON'T YOU WALK SO FAST
14. B. BILLY, DON'T BE A HERO
15. 1) EVEN NOW
    2) I WRITE THE SONGS
    3) LOOKS LIKE WE MADE IT
    4) THIS ONE'S FOR YOU
    5) IT'S A MIRACLE
    6) CAN'T SMILE WITHOUT YOU
    7) COPACABANA (AT THE COPA)
    8) READY TO TAKE A CHANCE AGAIN
16. D. PIANO MAN
17. 1) A HORSE WITH NO NAME
    2) TIN MAN
    3) VENTURA HIGHWAY
18. C. NEW KID IN TOWN
19. 1) MY EYES ADORED YOU
    2) OUR DAY WILL COME
    3) SWEARIN' TO GOD
    4) GREASE
20. A. DON'T EXPECT ME TO BE YOUR FRIEND
21. 1) SATURDAY IN THE PARK
    2) JUST YOU 'N' ME
    3) OLD DAYS
    4) IF YOU LEAVE ME NOW
    5) WISHING YOU WERE HERE
    6) MAKE ME SMILE
    7) DOES ANYBODY REALLY KNOW WHAT TIME IT IS?
    8) BABY, WHAT A BIG SURPRISE
    9) NO TELL LOVER
    10) FEELIN' STRONGER EVERY DAY
    11) COLOUR MY WORLD
22. A. JOY TO THE WORLD

23. C. HEART BEAT-IT'S A LOVEBEAT
24. D. DON'T PULL YOUR LOVE
25. B. FALLIN' IN LOVE
26. C. GARDEN PARTY
27. 1) (I BELIEVE) THERE'S NOTHING STRONGER THAN OUR LOVE
    2) (YOU'RE) HAVING MY BABY
    3) TIMES OF YOUR LIFE
28. B. I GO CRAZY
29. B. BABY DON'T GET HOOKED ON ME
30. 1) MOTHER AND CHILD REUNION
    2) 50 WAYS TO LEAVE YOUR LOVER
    3) ME AND JULIO DOWN BY THE SCHOOLYARD
    4) STILL CRAZY AFTER ALL THESE YEARS
    5) KODACHROME
    6) LOVES ME LIKE A ROCK
    7) SLIP SLIDIN' AWAY
31. C. (WHAT A) WONDERFUL WORLD
32. 1) WELCOME BACK
    2) JOHN SEBASTIAN
33. C. ROCK ME GENTLY
34. THE LION SLEEPS TONIGHT
35. B. SAD EYES
36. 1) YOU'RE NO GOOD
    2) WHEN WILL I BE LOVED
    3) HEATWAVE
    4) BLUE BAYOU
    5) IT'S SO EASY
    6) OOH BABY BABY
    7) TRACKS OF MY TEARS
    8) THAT'LL BE THE DAY
37. B. THE NIGHT THE LIGHTS WENT OUT IN GEORGIA
38. 1) YOU DON'T BRING ME FLOWERS
    2) NO MORE TEARS (ENOUGH IS ENOUGH)
    3) THE WAY WE WERE
39. A. HELP ME MAKE IT THROUGH THE NIGHT
40. D. BOZ SCAGGS
41. C. GYPSY WOMAN
42. A. SHAWN CASSIDY
43. B. DECEMBER, 1963 (OH, WHAT A NIGHT)
44. 1) LOVE WILL KEEP US TOGETHER
    2) THE WAY I WANT TO TOUCH YOU
    3) SHOP AROUND
45. C. THE MORNING AFTER
46. C. WE MAY NEVER LOVE THIS WAY AGAIN

70/13 POP ROCKERS-QUIZ # 2

1. B. WITHOUT YOU
1. C. BRAND NEW KEY
3. C. FREEDOM
4. B. POETRY MAN
5. 1) PIANO MAN
    2) JUST THE WAY YOU ARE
    3) MOVIN' OUT (ANTHONY'S SONG)
    4) ONLY THE GOOD DIE YOUNG
    5) SHE'S ALWAYS A WOMAN
    6) MY LIFE
    7) BIG SHOT

6. WHICH WAY YOU GOIN' BILLY?
7. C. TEMPTATION EYES
8. B. SOONER OR LATER
9. C. UNDERCOVER ANGEL
10. C. ALL BY MYSELF
11. B. LONG LONESOME HIGHWAY
12. 1) B. PAUL ANKA
    2) D. JOHNNY MATHIS
    3) F. PAUL ANKA
    4) C. FREDDIE SCOTT
    5) E. STEVE LAWRENCE
    6) A. JIMMY CHARLES
13. 1) IT'S TOO LATE
    2) I FEEL THE EARTH MOVE
    3) SO FAR AWAY
    4) JAZZMAN
14. A. JUST WHEN I NEEDED YOU THE MOST
15. D. BANG THE DRUM ALL DAY
16. 1) I SAW THE LIGHT
    2) HELLO IT'S ME
17. D. I LIKE DREAMIN'
18. B. SOMETIMES WHEN WE TOUCH
19. 1) YOU'VE GOT A FRIEND
    2) HOW SWEET IT IS (TO BE LOVED BY YOU)
    3) HANDY MAN
    4) FIRE ABD RAIN
20. C. PEACE TRAIN
21. D. HOT CHILD IN THE CITY
22. D. BARBRA STREISAND
23. B. IF YOU COULD READ MY MIND
24. B. WILDFLOWER
25. B. SEASONS IN THE SUN
26. C. I'D REALLY LOVE TO SEE YOU TONIGHT
27. D. NIGHTS ARE FOREVER WITHOUT YOU
28. D. LAUGHTER IN THE RAIN
29. C. LOVE WILL KEEP US TOGETHER
30. C. INSTANT REPLAY
31. B. THE PARTRIDGE FAMILY
32. 1) JERRY BUTLER
    2) TONY ORLANDO & DAWN
33. 1) DEBBY BOONE
    2) YOU LIGHT UP MY LIFE
34. A. SWAYIN' TO THE MUSIC (SLOW DANCING)
35. MIDNIGHT AT THE OASIS
36. A. FEELINGS
37. C. JACKIE BLUE
38. C. HOW MUCH I FEEL
39. B. YOU ARE THE WOMAN
40. B. JUST REMEMBER I LOVE YOU
41. B. BOOGIE WOOGIE BUGLE BOY
42. D. DO YOU WANT TO DANCE?
43. A. BRANDY (YOU'RE A FINE GIRL)
44. C. RIGHT TIME OF THE NIGHT
45. A. MIDNIGHT BLUE
46. B. DON'T CRY OUT LOUD
47. 1) I AM WOMAN
    2) DELTA DAWN
    3) ANGIE BABY

4) AIN'T NO WAY TO TREAT A LADY
48. C. SHE'S A LADY
49. 1) CRACKLIN' ROSIE
2) SONG SUNG BLUE
3) YOU DON'T BRING ME FLOWERS
4) FOREVER IN BLUE JEANS
5) I AM…I SAID
6) SOLITARY MAN
7) PLAY ME
50. B. EBONY EYES
51. B. AMERICAN PIE (PTS 1 & 2)
52. B. I DON'T KNOW HOW TO LOVE HIM
53. 1) I'M LEAVING IT ALL UP TO YOU
2) AIN'T NOTHING LIKE THE REAL THING
54. 1) FLEETWOOD MAC
2) DREAMS
3) GO YOUR OWN WAY
4) DON'T STOP
5) YOU MAKE LOVING FUN
6) SAY YOU LOVE ME
7) OVER MY HEAD
55. CHICAGO
56. A. PAUL REVERE AND THE RAIDERS
57. C. DON MCLEAN
58. A. GOLD
59. B. LIFE'S BEEN GOOD
60. D. IT'S SO NICE TO BE WITH YOU
61. A. BEAUTIFUL SUNDAY
62. C. MAKING OUR DREAMS COME TRUE
63. C. I LOVE THE NIGHTLIFE
64. C. MOONLIGHT FEELS RIGHT

70/14 POP ROCKERS-QUIZ # 3

1. B. MAGNET AND STEEL
2. C. IT'S IMPOSSIBLE
3. C. AND I LOVE YOU SO
4. 1) HALF BREED
2) GYPSYS, TRAMPS & THIEVES
3) DARK LADY
4) TAKE ME HOME
5) THE WAY OF LOVE
5. A. BABY HOLD ON
6. C. PLAYGROUND IN MY MIND
7. 1) DIAMOND GIRL
2) GET CLOSER
3) SUMMER BREEZE
8. C. YOU TAKE MY BREATH AWAY
9. D. LOTTA LOVE
10. C. MY ANGEL BABY
11. C. LAST SONG
12. D. AFTERNOON DELIGHT
13. INDIANA WANTS ME
14. 1) A COWBOYS WORK IS NEVER DONE
2) ALL I EVER NEED IS YOU
15. B. (YOUR LOVE HAS LIFTED ME) HIGHER AND HIGHER
16. C. PRECIOUS AND FEW
17. B. JULIE, DO YA LOVE ME

18. B. I JUST WANNA STOP
19. D. STEVEN STILLS
20. B. PLEASE COME TO BOSTON
21. C. IN THE YEAR 2525
22. C. DUST IN THE WIND
23. A. SPIRIT IN THE SKY
24. 1) (THEY LONG TO BE) CLOSE TO YOU
    2) TOP OF THE WORLD
    3) PLEASE MR POSTMAN
    4) RAINY DAYS AND MONDAYS
    5) SING
    6) YESTERDAY ONCE MORE
    7) THERE'S A KIND OF HUSH (ALL OVER THE WORLD)
    8) WE'VE ONLY JUST BEGUN
25. B. DREAM WEAVER
26. C. ON AND ON
27. C. MEL CARTER
28. C. FOR ALL WE KNOW
29. B. CHEVY VAN
30. A. BABY COME BACK
31. B. DON'T GIVE UP ON US
32. B. I GO CRAZY
33. B. SUPERSTAR
34. D. MORE, MORE, MORE (PART 1)
35. C. YOU'RE ONLY LONELY
36. B. BABY DON'T GET HOOKED ON ME

70/15 POP ROCKERS-QUIZ # 4

1. B. LONELY BOY
2. D. COVEN
3. C. SMOKE FROM A DISTANT FIRE
4. D. LINDA RONSTADT
5. B. RUNAROUND SUE
6. A. SUNSHINE
7. D. FOOLED AROUND AND FELL IN LOVE
8. B. B.W. STEVENSON
9. C. MONTEGO BAY
10. C. MIRACLES

POP ROCKERS-BONUS

1. D. PETER MCCANN
2. B. BOBBI MARTIN
3. B. PAPER ROSES

70/16 COUNTRY ROCKERS-QUIZ # 1

1. 1) SONGBIRD
   2) DANNY'S SONG
   3) YOU NEEDED ME
   4) BROKEN HEARTED ME
   5) I JUST FALL IN LOVE AGAIN
   6) LOVE SONG
   7) SHADOWS IN THE MOONLIGHT
2. 1) LUCILLE
   2) SHE BELIEVES IN ME
   3) YOU DECORATED MY LIFE

4) THE GAMBLER
3. A. SOMETHING'S BURNING
4. C. I'M EASY
5. B. THE DEVIL WENT DOWN TO GEORGIA
6. B. HELP ME MAKE IT THROUGH THE NIGHT
7. D. RONNIE MCDOWELL
8. B. HERE YOU COME AGAIN
9. D. ALL THE GOLD IN CALIFORNIA
10. C. STAND BY ME
11. 1) SUNSHINE ON MY SHOULDERS
2) ANNIE'S SONG
3) THANK GOD I'M A COUNTRY BOY
4) TAKE ME HOME COUNTRY ROADS
5) ROCKY MOUNTAIN HIGH
12. B. WILDFIRE

70/17 COUNTRY ROCKERS-QUIZ # 2

1. A. FOR THE GOOD TIMES
2. C. DON'T IT MAKE MY BROWN EYES BLUE
3. B. TALKING IN YOUR SLEEP
4. 1) RHINESTONE COWBOY
2) SOUTHERN NIGHTS
3) HONEY COME BACK
5. 1) BEHIND CLOSED DOORS
2) THE MOST BEAUTIFUL GIRL
3) EVERYTIME YOU TOUCH ME (I GET HIGH)
6. A. A COWBOYS WORK IS NEVER DONE
7. B. I CAN HELP
8. B. CHARLIE RICH
9. B. SUSPICIONS
10. B. MR BOJANGLES
11. 1) BEFORE THE NEXT TEARDROP FALLS
2) WASTED DAYS AND WASTED NIGHTS
3) YOU'LL LOSE A GOOD THING
12. C. ROSE GARDEN
13. D. I LOVE
14. A. WALK A MILE IN MY SHOES
15. B. WE JUST DISAGREE
16. C. WILLIE NELSON
17. C. C.W. MCCALL
18. D. EVERYTHING IS BEAUTIFUL
19. D. LET YOUR LOVE FLOW

70/18 ROCKERS-QUIZ # 1

1. A. RIDE CAPTAIN RIDE
2. 1) STILL THE ONE
2) DANCE WITH ME
3. A. COME AND GET YOUR LOVE
4. 1) WE'RE AN AMERICAN BAND
2) THE LOCO-MOTION
3) SOME KIND OF WONDERFUL
5. 1) SYLVIA'S MOTHER
2) THE COVER OF 'ROLLING STONE'
6. B. THE DOORS
7. 1) ONLY SIXTEEN
2) SHARING THE NIGHT TOGETHER

3) WHEN YOU'RE IN LOVE WITH A BEAUTIFUL WOMAN
8. 1) MAMA TOLD ME (NOT TO COME)
2) JOY TO THE WORLD
3) NEVER BEEN TO SPAIN
4) BLACK AND WHITE
5) THE SHOW MUST GO ON
6) LET ME SERENADE YOU
7) CELEBRATE
8) AN OLD FASHIONED LOVE SONG
9. C. STAND TALL
10. B. HI-DE-HO
11. A. DRAGGIN' THE LINE
12. A. KISS YOU ALL OVER
13. C. JIM MORRISON
14. C. YOUR MAMA DON'T DANCE
15. B. WHENEVER I CALL YOU FRIEND
16. 1) THAT'S THE WAY (I LIKE IT)
2) GET DOWN TONIGHT
3) (SHAKE, SHAKE, SHAKE) SHAKE YOUR BOOTY
4) I'M YOUR BOOGIE MAN
5) KEEP IT COMIN' LOVE
6) BOOGIE SHOES
17. PAUL REVERE AND THE RAIDERS
18. 1) WHAT A FOOL BELIEVES
2) BLACK WATER
3) LISTEN TO THE MUSIC
4) LONG TRAIN RUNNIN'
5) TAKIN' IT TO THE STREETS
19. A. MORE THAN A FEELING
20. B. HEART OF GOLD
21. A. TIGHTER, TIGHTER
22. C. PLAY THAT FUNKY MUSIC
23. C. SUGARLOAF
24. 1) THE VILLAGE PEOPLE
2) Y.M.C.A.
3) IN THE NAVY
4) MACHO MAN
25. B. BROTHER LOUIE
26. A. JANIS JOPLIN
27. 1) YOU DON'T MESS AROUND WITH JIM
2) BAD, BAD LEROY BROWN
3) OPERATOR (THAT'S NOT THE WAY IT FEELS)
4) TIME IN A BOTTLE
5) I'LL HAVE TO SAY I LOVE YOU IN A SONG
28. B. RAMBLIN' MAN
29. 1) WOODSTOCK
2) TEACH YOUR CHILDREN
3) OUR HOUSE
30. 1) THE JOKER
2) ROCK 'N ME
3) FLY LIKE AN EAGLE
31. C. PROUD MARY
32. 1) NIGHT MOVES
2) STILL THE SAME
3) WE'VE GOT TONITE
4) OLD TIME ROCK & ROLL
5) HOLLYWOOD NIGHTS
33. D. HEART OF GLASS

34. A. GO YOUR OWN WAY
35. B. WALK THIS WAY
36. C. BORN TO RUN
37. D. WALKIN' IN THE RAIN
38. C. ROCK AND ROLL MUSIC
39. A. RIGHT PLACE WRONG TIME
40. A. KISS
41. C. THE HOUSE OF THE RISING SUN
42. CHUCK E.'S IN LOVE
43. A. TWO OUT OF THREE AIN'T BAD
44. C. MY BEST FRIEND'S GIRL
45. D. UP ON CRIPPLE CREEK
46. A. ROCK AND ROLL ALL NITE
47. B. ARE YOU READY?
48. ALICE COOPER
49. C. RUNNING ON EMPTY
50. C. LOWDOWN
51. 1) (HEY WON'T YOU PLAY) ANOTHER SOMEBODY DONE SOMEBODY WRONG SONG
    2) I JUST CAN'T HELP BELIEVING
    3) RAINDROPS KEEP FALLIN' ON MY HEAD
    4) THIS TIME THE GIRL IS GONNA STAY
    5) ROCK AND ROLL LULLABY
52. B. THE RAPPER
53. 1) SHE'S GONE
    2) SARA SMILE
    3) RICH GIRL
54. D. VEHICLE
55. D. RUSSELL HITCHCOCK
56. 1) RIKKI DON'T LOSE THAT NUMBER
    2) PEG

70/19 ROCKERS-QUIZ # 2

1. C. WAR
2. D. SWEET CITY WOMAN
3. B. HOLD THE LINE
4. 1. TRAVELIN' BAND
   2. WHO'LL STOP THE RAIN
   3. HAVE YOU EVER SEEN THE RAIN
5. D. LOVE WILL FIND A WAY
6. C. THE KNACK
7. B. CRAZY LOVE
8. D. SWEET HOME ALABAMA
9. B. WALK ON THE WILD SIDE
10. B. RASPBERRIES
11. C. MUST OF GOT LOST
12. SMOKIN' IN THE BOY'S ROOM
13. C. BECAUSE THE NIGHT
14. 1) FEELS LIKE THE FIRST TIME
    2) HOT BLOODED
    3) COLD AS ICE
    4) DIRTY WHITE BOY
    5) HEAD GAMES
    6) DOUBLE VISION
15. 1) STYX
    2) BABE
16. A. SO IN TO YOU
17. D. KEEP ON SMILIN'

18. C. AEROSMITH
19. B. DANCING IN THE MOONLIGHT
20. A. DO YOU KNOW WHAT I MEAN
21. C. AMERICAN WOMAN
22. 1) CLAP FOR THE WOLFMAN
    2) NO TIME
    3) SHARE THE LAND
23. 1) BEST OF MY LOVE
    2) ONE OF THESE NIGHTS
    3) LYIN' EYES
    4) TAKE IT TO THE LIMIT
    5) NEW KID IN TOWN
    6) HOTEL CALIFORNIA
    7) LIFE IN THE FAST LANE
    8) HEARTACHE TONIGHT
    9) TAKE IT EASY
    10) WITCHY WOMAN
    11) PEACEFUL, EASY FEELING
24. 1) BABY I'M A WANT YOU
    2) EVERYTHING I OWN
    3) MAKE IT WITH YOU
    4) LOST WITHOUT YOUR LOVE
    5) DIARY
25. B. HERE COMES THE SUN
26. D. SIGNS

70/20 MISC (NOVELTY, FOLK, FOREIGN & INSTRUMENTALS)-QUIZ # 1

1. C. COME AND GET IT
2. THE NIGHT THEY DROVE OLD DIXIE DOWN
3. B. YOU AIN'T SEEN NOTHING YET
4. C. WEREWOLVES OF LONDON
5. A. THE BOYS ARE BACK IN TOWN
6. A. HELP ME
7. D. DISCO DUCK (PART 1)
8. C. PICK UP THE PIECES
9. B. SOUL MAN
10. A. WEDDING SONG (THERE IS LOVE)
11. 1) WITHOUT LOVE (THERE IS NOTHING)
    2) SHE'S A LADY
    3) I (WHO HAVE NOTHING)
12. D. HOW DO YOU DO?
13. C. THE BAND
14. B. SHORT PEOPLE
15. B. BAKER STREET
16. B. A FIFTH OF BEETHOVEN
17. B. IT'S A HEARTACHE
18. B. FEELS SO GOOD
19. C. RISE
20. C. GONNA FLY NOW
21. A. LOVE IS IN THE AIR
22. C. STUCK IN THE MIDDLE WITH YOU
23. C. THE AMERICANS (A CANADIAN'S OPINION)

70/21 MISC (NOVELTY, FOLK, FOREIGN & INSTRUMENTALS)-QUIZ # 2

1. C. ERES TU
2. C. BOOGALOO BLUES

3. B. LIFE IS A ROCK (BUT THE RADIO ROLLED ME)
4. B. ESCAPE (THE PINA COLADA SONG)
5. A. I HEAR YOU KNOCKING
6. B. DON'T LET ME BE MISUNDERSTOOD
7. C. CHICK-A-BOOM (DON'T YA JES' LOVE IT)
8. B. BARRY WHITE
9. A. THE ROCKFORD FILES
10. A. EMOTION

70/22 MISC (NOVELTY, FOLK, FOREIGN & INSTRUMENTALS)-QUIZ # 3

1. 1) SATURDAY NIGHT
   2) I ONLY WANT TO BE WITH YOU
2. 1) DANCING QUEEN
   2) FERNANDO
3. D. SILLY LOVE SONGS
4. STAR WARS THEME
5. B. ALONE AGAIN (NATURALLY)
6. C. GET DOWN
7. VENUS
8. C. MA BELLE AMIE
9. B. JUNGLE FEVER
10. B. LONESOME LOSER
11. 1) REMINISCING
    2) LADY
12. CAT'S IN THE CRADLE
13. C. KNOCKIN' ON HEAVEN'S DOOR
14. C. POPCORN
15. B. MIDNIGHT COWBOY
16. D. HAPPY DAYS
17. C. THE ENTERTAINER
18. C. RAY STEVENS
19. 1) BLACK MAGIC WOMAN
    2) EVIL WAYS
    3) OYE COMO VA
20. A. SPIDERS & SNAKES
21. I'D LIKE TO TEACH THE WORLD TO SING (IN PERFECT HARMONY)
22. C. DOMINO
23. 1) H. THE RIGHTEOUS BROTHERS
    2) D. MICHAEL JACKSON
    3) A. ARETHA FRANKLIN
    4) I. B J THOMAS
    5) J. THE BEACH BOYS
    6) L. ANDY KIM
    7) E. DAVID ESSEX
    8) B. THE HUES CORPORATION
    9) G. GEORGE MCCRAE
    10) K. STEVE MILLER BAND
    11) C. KISS
    12) F. JOHNNY RIVERS
24. B. REFLECTIONS OF MY LIFE
25. C. SEND IN THE CLOWNS
26. KING TUT
27. A. BASKETBALL JONES
28. C. PUT YOUR HAND IN THE HAND
29. B. HOOKED ON A FEELING
30. D. SHA NA NA
31. 1) SAMMY DAVIS JR

2) THE CANDY MAN
32. DUELING BANJOS
33. D. FRANKENSTEIN

MISC (NOVELTY, FOLK, FOREIGN & INSTRUMENTALS)-BONUS

1. C. I GOTCHA
2. D. AIN'T GONNA BUMP NO MORE (WITH NO BIG FAT WOMAN)
3. B. GET OFF
4. C. BREWER & SHIPLEY

70/23 MATCH THE LEAD SINGER WITH THE GROUP PT 1 IN THE 70'S

1. H. THE RAIDERS
2. O. BLOOD, SWEAT & TEARS
3. N. THE ROLLING STONES
4. L. THE FIRST EDITION
5. R. THE AMERICANS
6. W. THE FOUR TOPS
7. Q. COMMODORES
8. T. BREAD
9. C. HAROLD MELVIN AND THE BLUE NOTES
10. V. AEROSMITH
11. U. THE DOORS
12. B. THE TEMPTATIONS
13. Y. THE POLICE
14. A. THE JACKSON FIVE
15. D. THE FOUR SEASONS
16. P. LABELLE
17. X. QUEEN
18. E. BLONDIE
19. G. THE SUNSHINE BAND
20. M. THE FAMILY STONE
21. J. THE PIPS
22. I. THE MEDICINE SHOW
23. S. THE PARTRIDGE FAMILY
24. F. CHICAGO
25. K. WINGS

70/24 MATCH THE GROUP WITH THEIR SONG PT 1 IN THE 70'S

1. G. SUGAR DADDY
2. O. PAPA WAS A ROLLIN' STONE
3. R. THE LOVE I LOST (PART 1)
4. S. DECEMBER, 1963 (OH, WHAT A NIGHT)
5. J. HEART OF GLASS
6. Y. IF YOU LEAVE ME NOW
7. T. BOOGIE SHOES
8. N. INDIAN RESERVATION
9. Q. THE COVER OF 'ROLLING STONE'
10. X. IF I WERE YOUR WOMAN
11. V. SILLY LOVE SONGS
12. W. SOMETHING'S BURNING
13. U. FAMILY AFFAIR
14. C. BROWN SUGAR
15. L. HI-DE-HO
16. H. LADY MARMALADE
17. E. EASY

18. K. WALKIN' IN THE RAIN
19. D. I THINK I LOVE YOU
20. P. MAKE IT WITH YOU
21. I. LOVE HER MADLY
22. M. WALK THIS WAY
23. A. AIN'T NO WOMAN (LIKE THE ONE I'VE GOT)
24. F. WE WILL ROCK YOU
25. B. ROXANNE

70/25 MATCH THE LEAD SINGER WITH THE GROUP PT II IN THE 70'S

1. J. DAWN
2. F. KOOL & THE GANG
3. G. PLASTIC ONO BAND
4. I. THE GUESS WHO
5. B. EAGLES
6. C. EAGLES
7. H. THE SILVER BULLET BAND
8. E. FOREIGNER
9. D. CREEDENCE CLEARWATER REVIVAL
10. A. RAYDIO

70/26 MATCH THE GROUP WITH THEIR SONG PT II IN THE 70'S

1. I. YOU CAN'T CHANGE THAT
2. F. ONE OF THESE NIGHTS
3. H. LYIN' EYES
4. J. TRAVELIN' BAND
5. B. FEELS LIKE THE FIRST TIME
6. C. JUNGLE BOOGIE
7. G. IMAGINE
8. D. OLD TIME ROCK & ROLL
9. A. AMERICAN WOMAN
10. E. KNOCK THREE TIMES

70/27 MATCH THE DUOS AND ALSO THEIR HIT SONG PT 1 IN THE 70'S

1. Y,SS. JOHN TRAVOLTA, YOU'RE THE ONE THAT I WANT
2. T,OO. SPINNERS, THEN CAME YOU
3. S,JJ. DENIECE WILLIAMS/ TOO MUCH, TOO LITTLE, TOO LATE
4. M,CC. ODIA COATES, (YOU'RE) HAVING MY BABY
5. Q,RR. BARBRA STREISAND, YOU DON'T BRING ME FLOWERS
6. R,II. BARBRA STREISAND, NO MORE TEARS (ENOUGH IS ENOUGH)
7. U,UU. KIKI DEE, DON'T GO BREAKING MY HEART
8. L,AA. HERB, REUNITED
9. W,BB. JOHN OATES, RICH GIRL
10. B,QQ. BILLY DAVIS JR, YOU DON'T HAVE TO BE A STAR (TO BE IN MY SHOW)
11. V,TT. TENNILLE, LOVE WILL KEEP US TOGETHER
12. A,MM. RICHARD CARPENTER, PLEASE MR POSTMAN
13. G,WW. LINDA MCCARTNEY, UNCLE ALBERT
14. O,HH. ART GARFUNKEL, CECILIA
15. H,KK. DONNY HATHAWAY, WHERE IS THE LOVE
16. I,DD. WHITEHEAD, AIN'T NO STOPPIN' US NOW
17. D,LL. DIANA ROSS, MY MISTAKE WAS TO LOVE YOU
18. C,NN. JIM MESINA, YOUR MAMA DON'T DANCE
19. J,PP. WAR, SPILL THE WINE
20. E,GG. CHER, A COWBOYS WORK IS NEVER DONE
21. K,XX. BOBBY HATFIELD, ROCK AND ROLL HEAVEN

22. X,EE. CARLY SIMON, MOCKINGBIRD
23. N,YY. CROFTS, GET CLOSER
24. F,FF. STEVIE NICKS, WHENEVER I CALL YOU FRIEND
25. P,VV. MARIE, I'M LEAVING IT ALL UP TO YOU

70/28 MATCH THE DUOS AND ALSO THEIR HIT SONG PT II IN THE 70'S

1. H,DD. DARYL HALL, SHE'S GONE
2. G,HH. SEALS, SUMMER BREEZE
3. A,AA. TEICHER, MIDNIGHT COWBOY
4. I,CC. CHONG, BASKETBALL JONES
5. J,II. STEVE MANDELL, DUELING BANJOS
6. E,JJ. JOHN FORD COLEY, I'D REALLY LOVE TO SEE YOU TONIGHT
7. D,GG. MCCLAIN, HAPPY DAYS
8. B,EE. SONNY BONO, ALL I EVER NEED IS YOU
9. C,FF. CAPTAIN, SHOP AROUND
10. F,BB. PEACHES, SHAKE YOUR GROOVE THING

70/29 MATCH THE MOVIE/TV SHOW SONG WITH THE ARTIST PT 1 IN THE 70'S

1. R. FRANKIE VALLI
2. B. BEE GEES
3. V. ROSE ROYCE
4. P. HELEN REDDY
5. H. MICHAEL JACKSON
6. Q. ISAAC HAYES
7. A. BARBRA STREISAND
8. C. YVONNE ELLIMAN
9. X. JOHN TRAVOLTA & OLIVIA NEWTON-JOHN
10. S. MAUREEN MCGOVERN
11. W. DIANA ROSS
12. L. BEE GEES
13. E. ROBERTA FLACK
14. G. CARLY SIMON
15. F. BARBRA STREISAND
16. D. DONNA SUMMER
17. I. B J THOMAS
18. T. BARBRA STREISAND
19. Y. PRATT & MCCLAIN
20. N. WINGS
21. M. JOHN SEBASTIAN
22. J. RHYTHM HERITAGE
23. U. OLIVIA NEWTON-JOHN
24. O. THE CARPENTERS
25. K. SHIRLEY BASSEY

70/30 MATCH THE MOVIE/TV SHOW SONG WITH THE ARTIST PT II IN THE 70'S

1. C. BEE GEES
2. G. THE STAPLE SINGERS
3. H. MECO MONARDO/CANTINA BAND
4. J. JIM CROCE
5. F. RHYTHM HERITAGE
6. A. DEBBY BOONE
7. B. KEITH CARRADINE
8. E. BARRY MANILOW
9. I. CYNDI GRECCO
10. D. CURTIS MAYFIELD

70/31 MATCH THE DISCO HIT WITH THE ARTIST PT 1 IN THE 70'S

1. I. VAN MCCOY & THE SOUL CITY SYMPHONY ORCHESTRA
2. D. SILVER CONVENTION
3. L. BEE GEES
4. M. THE JACKSON FIVE
5. O. ROSE ROYCE
6. J. KOOL & THE GANG
7. N. ALICIA BRIDGES
8. Y. VICKI SUE ROBINSON
9. B. DIANA ROSS
10. P. JOHNNIE TAYLOR
11. E. AMII STEWART
12. G. LIPPS, INC
13. H. WALTER MURPHY & THE BIG APPLE BAND
14. R. YVONNE ELLIMAN
15. V. BLONDIE
16. U. THE TRAMMPS
17. T. BEE GEES
18. Q. EVELYN CHAMPAYNE KING
19. K. K C AND THE SUNSHINE BAND
20. W. RICK DEES AND HIS CAST OF IDIOTS
21. F. TAVARES
22. X. BEE GEES
23. A. DONNA SUMMER
24. S. HEATWAVE
25. C. A TASTE OF HONEY

70/32 MATCH THE DISCO HIT WITH THE ARTIST PT II IN THE 70'S

1. P. K C AND THE SUNSHINE BAND
2. I. THE EMOTIONS
3. R. K C AND THE SUNSHINE BAND
4. B. GEORGE MCCRAE
5. H. GLORIA GAYNOR
6. C. SISTER SLEDGE
7. L. KOOL & THE GANG
8. W. KOOL & THE GANG
9. Q. DIANA ROSS
10. Y. THE S.O.S. BAND
11. A. ANDY GIBB
12. E. THE HUES CORPORATION
13. V. K C AND THE SUNSHINE BAND
14. K. MARVIN GAYE
15. X. GLORIA GAYNOR
16. F. MCFADDEN & WHITEHEAD
17. T. THE MIRACLES
18. U. ANDREA TRUE CONNECTION
19. N. NU SHOOZ
20. J. SISTER SLEDGE
21. D. PEACHES & HERB
22. M. VILLAGE PEOPLE
23. G. DONNA SUMMER
24. O. VILLAGE PEOPLE
25. S. THELMA HOUSTON

70/33 MATCH THE DISCO HIT WITH THE ARTIST PT III IN THE 70'S

1. D. SHIRLEY AND COMPANY
2. H. DONNA SUMMER
3. J. KC AND THE SUNSHINE BAND
4. E. TAVARES
5. F. KC AND THE SUNSHINE BAND
6. G. TAVARES
7. A. CHIC
8. B. ABBA
9. I. THE RITCHIE FAMILY
10. C BARRY WHITE

70/34 MATCH THE INSTRUMENTAL HIT WITH THE ARTIST IN THE 70'S

1. P. BILL CONTI
2. M. RHYTHM HERITAGE
3. F. MECO MONARDO/CANTINA BAND
4. H. LOVE UNLIMITED ORCHESTRA
5. O. WALTER MURPHY & THE BIG APPLE BAND
6. J. EDGAR WINTER GROUP
7. L. CHUCK MANGIONE
8. A. AVERAGE WHITE BAND
9. E. MARVIN HAMLISCH
10. N. ERIC WEISSBERG & STEVE MANDELL
11. R. FERRANTE & TEICHER
12. B. HOT BUTTER
13. S. MIKE POST & HIS ORCHESTRA
14. T. THE CHAKACHAS
15. D. BILLY PRESTON
16. C. DEODATO
17. K. HERB ALPERT
18. G. BILLY PRESTON
19. I. B.T. EXPRESS
20. Q. FRANK MILLS

BACK COVER ANSWER SHEET

1. SUGAR SHACK
2. SHERRY
3. CHUCK E'S IN LOVE
4. CHANTILLY LACE
5. 1) OTIS WILLIAMS
   2) PAUL WILLIAMS
   3) MELVIN FRANKLIN
   4) EDDIE KENDRICKS
   5) DAVID RUFFIN
6. FOR YOUR LOVE
7. GET A JOB
8. 16 TONS
9. BREAD AND BUTTER
10. DON'T GET HOOKED ON ME
11. DON & PHIL
12. PARTY DOLL
13. WE BELONG TOGETHER
14. TELL LAURA I LOVE HER
15. DO WAH DIDDY DIDDY
16. DENISE
17. PROUD MARY
18. HAROLD MELVIN AND THE BLUE NOTES